Readers all applaud *Thy Kingdom Come!*

"With the release of his fourth book, ***Thy Kingdom Come,*** Mr. Israel has accomplished *something rare*—a credible work of science fiction, written for an audience of believers, that compares in style to the works of Asimov, Heinlein, and Clarke, but with none of the philosophies propounded by those gentlemen. *Thy Kingdom Come* does for the realm of science fiction what Peretti's *This Present Darkness*...and Burkett's *The Illuminati* did for the general fiction genre... Don't be intimidated by the length of this novel, for it moves quickly and dramatically toward its climax in such a way as to seem almost effortless. *A great read! You won't regret for a moment picking it up—except when you have a difficult time putting it down!"*

"*Mr. Israel has achieved a unique accomplishment*—a perfect synthesis of traditional 1950s and '60s science fiction and scripturally sound prophecy. All the conventional characters are here: a mad scientist, his stunning but innocent daughter, a robot with personality, a computer with staggering intelligence and unlimited powers, and a villain embodying the deepest evil in the universe. How they interact, in a context of beyond-the-bounds technology, makes *a rousing good tale*, which, into the bargain, explores the principles and eternal possibilities of biblical faith and personal relationship with the Creator of the cosmos. A*mazing!* I hope Mr. Israel writes lots more books—*and that I get to read them all!*"

"I'll readily admit to having fairly demanding criteria for what makes good reading: timely subject-matter, well researched, with characters that spring to life in front of me...real people with virtues and hang-ups, who have to figure things out like I do—one step at a time. Sometimes their decisions—their adventures—take them to far-away places, and take me with them. *Thy Kingdom Come* is just such a book. It's *bold and creative...*combining sci-fi with biblical prophecy; featuring great heroes, disgustingly real villains, stooges, and pawns, and a 'curve ball'...*This is a book I just couldn't put down*! If you love a good story, *Thy Kingdom Come* is for you. *Just make sure you buckle up—it's a wild, wonderful ride you won't soon forget!*"

"*Thy Kingdom Come is as instructive spiritually as it is outrageously enjoyable to read!* The author subtly and deliciously weaves the Gospel into an imaginative world laced with real possibilities. The reader is too busy having fun to be aware he's learning about Messiah."

“Mr. Israel has created in this *splendid volume* a most masterful blend of quantum mechanics, cybernetics, exobiology, the latest Voyager discoveries from our solar system, and end-time prophecies no scientist or layman should miss reading…*a serious but fun-filled adventure loaded with humor and cybernetic fantasy!* His vast understanding of these fields makes even science fiction seem real…*I just simply enjoyed reading it!* [He's] boldly gone where no science fiction writer has gone before! *I can't wait to read more…*”

“*Thy Kingdom Come* was a first for me in many ways…but, because I'd read *The Storm*, I knew I'd love this book. *And so I did!* After having it on my shelf for awhile, I finally sat down and “dove in”. Six days later, reluctantly, I finished the adventure.”

“*Thy Kingdom Come* kept me spellbound during a three-day reading adventure created by Isaac Israel. Extremely well written and intriguing, this book *did* create one problem for me: *I couldn't turn the pages fast enough—although I wanted to savor each fascinating moment in the story!* Upon finishing this book, I distinctly remember thanking G-d for such a man who'll no doubt steer millions of readers to an uncompromising look ahead—beyond the stars and beyond our imaginations—to carry forth the message of our Creator!"

The above comments were given voluntarily and without remuneration.

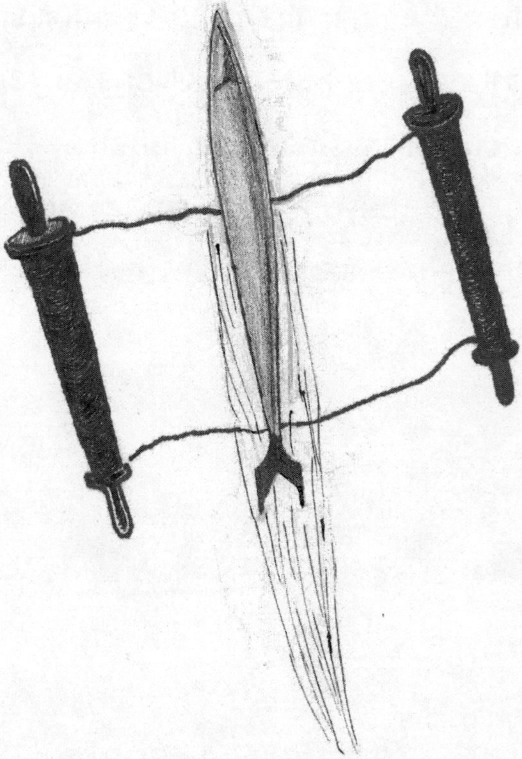

Thy Kingdom Come

Volume Four of the Late Earth Chronicles

Thy Kingdom Come

Library of Congress Catalog # 92-80078

ISBN# 978-1-893734-18-0

(All Scripture quotations from the Authorized King James Version)

To my beloved wife, Henaynei

This book is lovingly dedicated to my wife, who became involved in its creation as if it was her own, and who read each page as soon as it came off the typewriter. (Yes, kids! The first draft was written on a *typewriter,* back in 1988.) I cannot express the love and gratitude I have for Henaynei, or my appreciation for the patient cross she bears as the wife of a science fiction writer. If every poor fabulist was blessed with such a helpmeet, millions of novels lying fallow in the minds of factory-workers and waitresses, cabbies and cops, pilots and pastors, might all have a chance to be read. And every writer needs at least to be read.

It's as simple as this: There are "wives of writers", and there are "writers' wives", the former being something of an unfortunate accident (in the wives' opinion, at any rate), the latter being a ministry of loving devotion, a *calling*. My wife (*Baruch HaShem:* Praise the L-rd), is numbered among the latter. She provided me with twelve years of uninterrupted full-time writing and study, years I used to improve my technique and acquire a college education through private study. (I tend to be an autodidact; school-desks give me hives.) I pray I'll prove worthy of her hard work and constant devotion.

I conceived this novel as a retro science fiction space-opera in fond memory of Robert Anson Heinlein and Isaac Asimov, two of the "Big Three" who passed away while the first draft was being written. May it serve as a humble tribute to all the literary heroes of my youth—writers such as A.E. van Vogt and Clifford Simak—whose opinions on religion I may disdain, but whose brilliance and imagination I shall always admire.

Special acknowledgements to Thomas F. Coleman, friend of my youth, who turned me on to astronomy and science fiction; and to John Blumenthal, who recently completed his *own* first novel. G-d bless you both.

The author in Monument Valley (1973) Photo by R. Mistler

PREFACE TO THE SECOND EDITION

There's nothing more odious than an author's preface to a work of fiction. I beg the reader to believe that I approach the task with distaste, that I would never burden him (her or it) with such a monstrosity if I did not believe it to be absolutely necessary.

The thought occurred to me as I was formatting the first edition of *Kingdom* (back in 1991) that a word or two might be proffered in explanation. So I included them in the least abhorrent place I could find—the end of the book. But it soon became apparent that, at least for this particular experiment, my afterword wasn't doing the trick. Some readers were putting the book down before getting to the afterword, totally missing what I'd hoped would be their greatest pleasure in reading the novel. In short, they were making snap judgments, mistaking parody for ineptitude, tongue-in-cheek for clumsiness.

Not everyone wants a tyro writer to succeed. So it's hardly surprising that when old friends from back home receive a copy of his self-published effort, their initial assumption will likely be that if the book were any good it would have been accepted by a "legitimate" publishing house. They remain blissfully unaware that literally hundreds of famous authors—many of whom they themselves revere—began their careers by publishing their own works. L. Frank Baum was informed by a "legitimate" publishing house that his children's book, *The Wonderful Wizard of Oz*, was a stinkeroo. He was forced to publish it at his own expense. All three Brontë sisters self-published their first joint project, a poetry anthology that sold two copies. Henry David Thoreau paid Ticknor & Co. $450.00 to publish a thousand copies of *A Week on the Concord and Merrimack Rivers*. Over seven hundred were returned to him unsold, causing him to remark, somewhat drolly: "I now have a library of nearly nine hundred volumes, over seven hundred of which I wrote myself." (Thoreau wrote consistently for almost his entire lifetime before selling a book to a "legitimate" publisher.) Mary Shelley's famous poet husband helped her produce the first edition of *Frankenstein: The Modern Prometheus*. Other self-published writers include Mark Twain and Upton Sinclair; a more comprehensive listing would extend for pages.

Unaware of this, old friends from back home will approach a self-published novel dubiously, expecting it to be a stinkeroo. (Oscar Wilde wasn't wrong when he observed that "Anyone can sympathize with the sufferings of a friend, but it requires a fine nature to sympathize with a friend's success.") With this presupposition firmly in mind—born of the secret hope that their friend will fail—they're quick to find fault. They suddenly become proofreaders, picking up on every error in spelling or punctuation. (They've no idea that great writers like Hemingway and Fitzgerald were wretched spellers.) And should the book contain subtle levels of parody—well, they're simply not going to get it. They'll decide that the writer is trying to impress them with devices that went out of style with the jitterbug. They'll toss the novel aside, never reaching the afterword in which the writer reveals his intent.

One of my readers—thankfully not an old friend from back home—realized my intent for this book *before* reaching the afterword. She articulated it over ten years ago, calling the novel "**...a perfect synthesis of 1950s and 60s science fiction** [40s and 50s, actually] **and scripturally sound prophecy. All the conventional characters are here: the mad scientist, his stunning but innocent daughter, a robot with personality, a computer with staggering intelligence and unlimited powers, and a villain embodying the deepest evil in the universe!**"

But I don't want the reader to think of this novel as parody. It contains *elements* of parody, to be certain, but not to the extent, I hope, of distracting one from the story. In my misspent youth I read many book-length parodies. They were fine for a few laughs, even if I revered the authors being lampooned. But the laughs grew stale, usually by the fourth or fifth chapter, and I don't believe I finished a single one. The reason was clear to me even then: Parody is a delightful art form as long as the author restricts it to short pieces honed like daggers. Stretching it to novel length dulls the satirical edge. Parody fits the short story (or short-short) formula well, but the novel format will simply not accommodate its relentless slapstick, its lack of plot, profluence, climax, or resolution.

It wasn't parody I wanted to write when I started *Kingdom.* I was writing it to entertain my new bride, Henaynei, who was suffering from a severe spinal problem and confined to bed. She'd enjoyed Isaac Asimov in her teens—the robot stories in particular—and many other tales by the Golden Age science fiction writers—writers who'd served their apprenticeships in pulp magazines such as *Amazing Stories* and *Astounding Science Fiction.* So I began to incorporate this pulp style, and was gratified to find her hungrily devouring each chapter as it rolled off my typewriter. (Interestingly, I was experiencing another dimension of futurism as I worked on the story. I began it on a manual Royal portable, composed the middle of it on a Smith Corona electric, completed it on a Brother electric, and revised it on a Sony word processor—an entire computer devoted to nothing but word processing. I'm beginning this second revision on a Dell PC, using Microsoft Word 2003. So it might be said that a science fiction novel ushered me into the computer age.)

As I began to compose this light entertainment for my beloved, illustrating it with little cartoons so my ten-year-old stepson could also enjoy it (see the end of this preface), I began to notice that it was "gelling", that my "light entertainment" was turning into a vehicle that might carry me across the finish line of every writer's first major marathon—the full-length novel. I began to take it more seriously. I attempted to avoid cliché plots by asking my wife where she thought the story would go next, then deliberately veering off in another direction. The daunting idea of a *first novel* wasn't intimidating to the point of writers' block, since I was designing the story more like a puzzle or a game, chapter-by-chapter, unconcerned, at least initially, with what was developing. My sole concern was that my new bride would be entertained, that she might forget her pain for a while.

The term "retro" was unfamiliar to me when I wrote *Kingdom* in 1988. The *Star Wars* films were obviously retro, yet I don't recall anyone referring to them as such. It wasn't until the mid-'90s that I encountered the term in reference to a made-for-television film called *The Rocketeer.* By then the first edition of *Kingdom* had already been published, and it was too late to include the brief subtitle, "a retro space-opera", which might have explained everything.

Retro is not parody, nor is it strictly imitation. Consider a popular automobile at the time of this writing, the PT Cruiser. It instantly reminds one of a 1940s coupe. But it's not an *imitation* of a 1940s coup—purchasing a kit and assembling a reproduction would accomplish that result. Its resemblance is not at all meticulous; it's the consequence of a few cleverly chosen lines that conjure up the *feel* of the original. Nor is the PT Cruiser a *parody* of a 1940's coupe. The designers at Chrysler had the serious intent of putting a functional vehicle on the road, with features distinctive enough to make it the success it appears to be.

Similarly, retro fiction (or film) is an attempt to create a *valid story* that readers (or viewers) can enjoy, while adding a few carefully chosen strokes to conjure up the feeling of the original genre, to create a second level of appreciation—a feeling of *nostalgia.* From the moment, back in 1977, when I saw those columns under the title "Episode IV" scrolling up the screen in *Star Wars*—recapping the events of an imaginary (until 2005) previous episode—I knew I was about to experience an old-timey science fiction serialization reminiscent of the Flash Gordon serials of the '30s and '40s, enhanced by modern film technology. I wasn't disappointed. This second level of appreciation increased the impact of *Star Wars,* as viewers who'd never imagined they could enjoy science fiction fell instantly in love with one of its most archaic forms—the space-opera—a form invented in the 1920s by E.E. ("Doc") Smith. They thrilled to the story unfolding on the screen, to its awesome futuristic settings, while, on a higher level, appreciating its nostalgic feel.

But it's important to note that *Star Wars* has been treasured by millions of young people who've been utterly unaware of the history of science fiction, or of the genre of space-opera being reproduced on the screen—just as we must assume that there are drivers who enjoy the PT Cruiser without recognizing, or even caring about, its nostalgic look. *Retro fiction must provide sufficient entertainment at the story level.* I'm pleased to report that *Kingdom* has delighted numerous readers, young and old, for its story-line alone. In fact, teenage believers who've known nothing about pulp science fiction or space-opera were its most ardent fans.

I should mention at this juncture that many narratives contain what can only be described by an oxymoron: *retro futures.* These are depictions of future environments that deliberately conjure up the visual (or fictive) art of earlier science fiction eras. For example: many of the youthful writers whose fertile imaginations informed the Golden Age of pulp science fiction were city-dwellers. For them, man's adventurous spirit was epitomized by skyscrapers thrusting up toward heaven. The Chrysler Building and the Empire State Building resembled rockets about to launch into space. When these young city-dwellers reached into their imaginations to invent future worlds, they quite reasonably found themselves depicting great sprawling burgs. Reshaping what existed around them—the 1940s metropolis—they "futurized" it simply by making it bigger and more automated. Van Vogt, for instance, created his wonderful "City of The Machine" in *The World of Null-A*, while Isaac Asimov trumped all the young urban SF writers by creating Trantor, an entire planetary surface covered by wall-to-wall city!

If a *contemporary* science fiction filmmaker created a future world consisting, say, of a gargantuan city with the unmistakable lines of a 1940's metropolis—including flying machines that follow the contours of '40s automobile design and soldiers who dress like Nazis—the result would be *Sky Captain and the World of Tomorrow*, or 1940's retro. A *retro future.* (In a similar way, one might create 1930s retro, or 1950s retro.)

But we're discussing, primarily, the retro science fiction novel. My first encounter with retro science fiction in the written form was Robert A. Heinlein's *The Number of the Beast.* (This is not to suggest that there weren't earlier examples of the form, and better ones, but simply that I was unaware of them.) *The Number of the Beast* was a disappointment, not because of its retro style but in spite of it. Heinlein, the "Dotty Dean of Science Fiction," was in the midst of his solipsistic period, when all his characters, male and female, spoke in his own voice and seemed obsessed with the bedroom. (Not for the joy of sex—Heinlein's sex dialogues were weirdly devoid of eroticism—but in order to reproduce endless versions of themselves.) It was a novel of interminable Heinlein banter, apparently stressing one of the author's pet theories about established authority. It had its fun moments, but it left me flat.

What drew me into the book was its very first line: "'He's a Mad Scientist and I'm his Beautiful Daughter.'" That line, with its capitalizations, was a road sign signaling a fascinating turnoff, a nostalgic romp through pulp-era science fiction. Not parody, mind you—although it had its tongue-in-cheek elements—but retro.

Another retro SF novel of that period (which conjured up the Golden Age with somewhat more success) was written by pulp writer turned religionist, creator of Dianetics (a.k.a. Scientology) L. Ron Hubbard. I refer to his sprawling epic, *Battlefield Earth.* I can think of nothing else by Hubbard worth reading, but for a study of retro science fiction in the epic novel form, *Battlefield Earth,* along with the author's forward to the book, should prove worthwhile.

In a novel, when this secondary level of appreciation—this nostalgic element—also contains a note of parody or other commentary on the genre being reproduced, it becomes *metafiction*—fiction commenting on fiction. If the writer's purpose is to make the reader so conscious of the genre he's recreating that he deliberately jerks him out of the story and makes the commentary more important than the narrative—with the usual result of making *himself* the focal point rather than the characters—we have a form of metafiction known as *deconstructive* fiction. But deconstruction was not Heinlein's intent. Nor was it Hubbard's. Nor was it mine in writing *Kingdom.*

So what *was* my intent? Not evangelism, certainly. Having seen (or rather heard) the depths to which contemporary Christian music has fallen—due to its faulty premise that one must reach the nonbeliever by regurgitating the music he enjoys, modifying only the lyric content—I shun the idea of tailoring my fiction to appeal to the lost. If some lost soul should encounter a copy of one of my novels and turn to Yeshua while reading it, I'll rejoice. But to decide that reaching him is worth pandering to his tastes—well, I might as well include pornography as a *sure* way of getting his attention. (Like the stripper with John 3:16 tattooed on her stomach.) When the tribal pounding of gagsta-rap or the deafening power chords of "heavy metal" are employed as evangelistic tools, we find ourselves jumping into the mosh pit with the lost, rather than reaching in to pull them out. This does *not* mean that religious music must forever be played on pump-organs by skinny old biddies with tortoiseshell glasses. *Religious art should grow!* It should explore and develop higher forms. But it should be aimed at the believer, not the lost. The only tool mentioned in Scripture for reaching the lost is the preaching of the Word (Romans 10:14). Spiritual music prepares the soul to receive the Word.

Anyway, why metafiction? When I was in my teens I had a precocious friend who held television in contempt. I, on the other hand, was a TV addict; I was mesmerized by the thing. I sat in front of the "boob tube", as my generation later dubbed it, with mouth and mind wide open, in uncritical awe of its black-and-white wonderland. When I watched TV with my friend, however, he'd toss acerbic comments at the screen, particularly during commercials, but also during the shows themselves. He wouldn't interrupt to the extent of distracting me from the illusion, however. His jibes made me laugh; they added *an additional dimension* of enjoyment to television. I enjoyed watching TV with him. It was like having my own personal sixties version of *Mystery Science Theatre.* But it had another effect: it taught me to engage a degree of cynicism in my viewing. No longer would I watch TV uncritically, sopping up everything I saw without involving those higher dimensions of reason that prevent us from becoming merely a herd of pigs at an electronic trough. Decades later, when I began watching TV with my stepson, I performed the same function for him. It made our TV viewing more interactive and fun, and it offered him the same opportunity to think outside the "box," as it were.

So I believe that adding a subtle dimension of parody to written fiction allows *a secondary level of appreciation,* engaging higher levels of reasoning while educating young readers to develop that degree of cynicism necessary to survive in a world dominated by electronic media. While outright parody fails to perform this function—since engaging the reader's *own* critical faculties is vital—the retro model seems made for the task. (This is not to say that a writer can't dial the level of parody up or down depending on his requirements. My novel *Machines of Loving Grace,* for example, contains a more perceptible measure of parody than *The Storm,* while my short story, *People of the Plain,* is pure parody.)

Why science fiction? I write science fiction because I love it, and because I want to interest young Messianic Jews and Christians in the possibilities of space. I believe space holds the answer to many of man's material dilemmas—overpopulation, pollution, limited fossil fuel reserves, and the imminent glacial ice-flow (dubbed "global warming" by dupes who blame humans for it). Mankind must expand outward to the other worlds of our magnificent solar system—worlds G-d created for us. We'll enjoy longer, healthier lives in the semi-weightless environments of space habitats. We'll find cleaner sources of nuclear fuel, like Helium-3, which can be mined from the Lunar regolith. Earth's population burden will be significantly reduced—Its gravity alone will deter recolonization!—and the use of clean nuclear fuel will restore Earth to the pristine planet it was intended to be when *HaShem* "took man, and put him into the Garden of Eden to dress it and to keep it." (This is not a postmillennial view, by the way. Only Messiah, upon His return, can make the Earth the paradise He originally created it to be. But wouldn't it bless Him if we demonstrated some good stewardship of the planet He made for us, some care and devotion for *all* His creatures?)

I want to inspire young believers to join in the great adventure of space exploration. As for those who claim that the Second Advent makes such an endeavor moot, I'd remind them of the old adage: While we must *act* as if Messiah were returning at any moment, we must *plan* as if He were not. (Messianic expectations reached a remarkable pitch during the mid 19th century, but aren't we glad Americans didn't stop planning for the future?) I also want to point young believers toward more wholesome sources of science fiction than those available today—the tales of the Golden Age. If they can ignore their militant atheism, they'll find the stories of that era free of prurient content and extremely positive in their attitude toward technological achievement, viewing mankind as a unique species destined to conquer the stars. By the late 1950s and '60s, as all art tends to do, the more "literary" forms of SF gradually turned dark, pessimistic, even paranoid. (With all due respect to their remarkable talents as writers, who'd want to live in a future crated by Phillip K. Dick, Alfred Bester, or William Gibson?)

But there was a downside to the Golden Age. The stories of that era were written by adolescent boys just learning the craft; they bristled with flaws, with those peculiar errors of technique common to the untrained. One such example is characterization by "tags"—for instance, whenever Perry White of TV's *Superman* hollered "Great Caesar's Ghost!" I wanted to poke fun at this technique by employing character tags in *Kingdom*. In the chapter entitled "The Trap" (page 518), when my unseen shuttle pilot uses the antiquated expression "ten-four," the reader should instantly recognize the crafty Brother Wallace. Another character tag is in use whenever Paul Moscowitz sweeps his robes aside, which he does frequently. It was *not* my intent, however, to employ these tags—in the way the pulp writers did—to avoid the grueling task of characterization. I wanted my "tagged" characters to come to life the way well-drawn characters should, while wearing their tags for all to see. One reader commented that *Kingdom* contained "**characters that spring to life in front of me...real people with virtues and hang-ups, who have to figure things out like I do—one step at a time**." Story characters with tagged personality traits cannot "spring to life," which is one of the subconscious frustrations adults often encounter while reading pulp fiction.

Another huge flaw in Golden Age science fiction was its treatment of women. As it turns out, those pimple-faced geeks with coke-bottle glasses who forged the genre—Sorry, guys, but I've seen the pictures!—were not yet interested in girls. Girls just got in the way. If they appeared in pulp science fiction at all, it was merely to serve as "love-interests"—a necessary function begrudgingly employed. Adolescent writers tend to draw females idealistically: innocent and beautiful and submissive, the kind who'd never reject the attentions of, say, a pimple-faced geek with coke-bottle glasses. The results are not real women. For my purposes in *Kingdom*—including my determination to keep sexual tension away from center stage—it was extremely difficult to make Robin Denton "spring to life" while providing her with this pulpish occupation. All I could do in her case was offer a solid, credible justification for her sexual innocence and naïveté—a childhood spent with an exceptional but inhuman companion.

In an effort to mitigate the parody and make this novel more tribute than satire, I incorporated most of the grand motifs of the Golden Age, brainchildren of the following giants: Isaac Asimov (for the ubiquitous robots and, of course, the odd spelling of *Jeri* Kline—as in *Hari* Seldon); Robert Heinlein (for the friendly, conspiratorial supercomputer); Clifford Simak (for the pastoral scenes); A. E. van Vogt (for the dizzying time-jumping and place-jumping); and Ray Bradbury (for the wallscreens). There's no need to inform the savvy reader that this is in no way plagiarism. If the above authors owned copyrights to such ideas there'd be no more science fiction being written. Historians of the genre are in general agreement that most of its (technological) concepts were mined completely dry by 1950. (Some say as early as 1940!) With the exception of those rare trail-blazers that come along every decade or so—William Gibson's "cyberspace" (*Neuromancer*), for example, or Greg Bear's "nanites" (*Blood Music*)—most science fiction consists of individualistic treatments of very old themes by new writers.

The only technological notion I believed might have been unique to *Kingdom*—the "simuchamber"—was trumped by ol' Gene Roddenberry. While I was deep into my first draft, developing the idea of a chamber in which computer-generated images deceived the senses—an idea I'd toyed with unsuccessfully in 1982—*Star Trek: TNG* introduced the "holodeck". (I recall weeping openly.)

In another unhappy coincidence, I named one of my major characters in *Kingdom* John Sheridan. Years later a TV show came on the air called *Babylon 5*. Its main character was a man named John Sheridan. (Needless to say, I've changed that name.)

On a subtler level, aficionados should note some stylistic imitation—that light touch of parody I spoke of earlier—Asimov, Van Vogt, Heinlein, etc.

Having nobly defended the first edition of *Kingdom,* I don't wish to imply that I'm at all satisfied with it—which is why I'm approaching the task of a final revision. Beyond the numerous inexcusable spelling errors—What can I say? The Sony had no spellchecker!—and the overabundance of draggy commas, other elements cried out for change. More effort might have been devoted to my characters, to streamlining the narrative, tightening the dialogue, updating the science. (A parody, or imitation, of the Golden Age would have Venus covered with muggy swamps and inhabited by dinosaurs. Mars would be a dying world of shrinking canals and advanced civilizations in decline. Retro science fiction, on the other hand, seeks to present valid contemporary science—with the obligatory "shlock science" of ray guns and tachyon beams—in a style evocative of earlier forms.)

But I'll try to accomplish such alterations surgically, without removing those elements that evoke the old masters of pulp science fiction, that make this novel a retro science fiction space-opera.

Chesed v'shalom b'Shem Yeshua haMashiach. (Grace and peace in the Name of Jesus Christ.)

Keep your pressure suit tight, and walk in the light!

Isaac Israel - July 4th, 2005

Sarasota, FL.

Jeeves

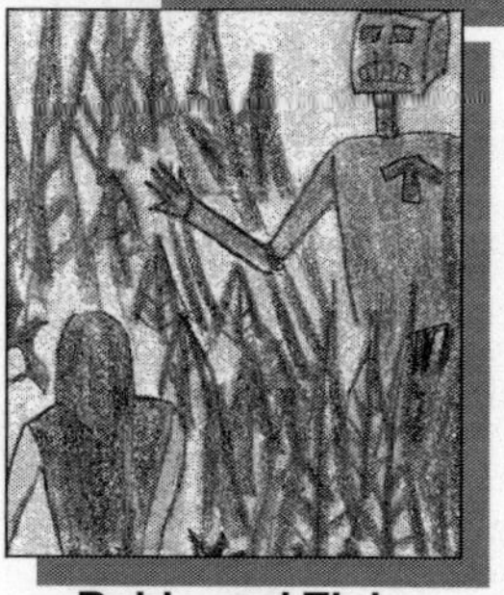

Robin and Tink

Prologue

There was life out there.

This dusky corner of the universe simply swarmed with living things of every variety.

What no one could have anticipated was that all of it would be confined to our Local Group of galaxies, and that very little of it would prove sapient. Only one out of every billion life-forms was capable of abstract thought, that is, the ability to communicate with others of its kind, whether by means of chemical triggers, physical gyrations, or by some form of speech. Of this fraction, fewer still were possessed of written communication; a mere handful fashioned artifacts that could, by the loosest definition, be called art; and only six races other than mankind had developed atomic energy and, hence, spaceflight. Scientists of the previous two centuries would have blushed at this intellectual deficiency among the stars, at the vindication of the *anthropic principle* of cosmology—that humanity was indeed the "crown of creation", the paragon of all sentient life.

Mankind was virtually G-dlike when compared with every other self-aware entity. And there existed only a thousand living species in the entire universe with whom men were able to communicate with any degree of success…

Royal Galactic Historical Society
© 9977 A.E

M. Grinder © StarCovenant Productions

Book One

"Longknife"

***"Through me you pass into the city of woe…
All hope abandon, ye who enter here."***

-Dante Alighieri

The Divine Comedy

-From a speech by Israeli Prime Minister Moshe Bierman, before the Knesset, on April 1st, 2088:

"Incrementalism was the key to the New World Order under President Charles Coffey—or *Maitreya*, as he is known to billions of souls across this benighted planet. First came the European Union, then the Pan-American Union. (When U.S. citizens discovered that their porous border with Mexico was not the result of neglectful political management, but the first step in a century-old conspiracy to alter the sociological complexion of the United States and render it the equal of such countries as Uruguay—the Trans-Texas corridor was already humming with traffic and the Pan-American Union was a reality.) Then came the Mid-East Union, which required the gradual subjection of the state of Israel to global policy. Were it not for the destruction of the Dome of the Rock—the unofficial act of a rogue Israeli group called *Nakam* (Revenge) and the subsequent attack upon Israel by all the Islamic nations—we would not have been forced into the grim necessity of all-out war with the Arab world—which had been the plan of *Nakam* in the first place. The Temple Mount Wars, as the conflict is now called, ended with Israel in control of most of the Middle East. Relinquishing that control at the insistence of the Party for World Peace, Israel cautiously entered into a peace-pact with the Global Confederacy led by U.S. President Charles Coffey and the Pan-American Union. After three-and-a-half short years, it seems, that pact is being shattered by *Maitreya* himself. What will happen next is anyone's guess, but, whatever it may be, it will not be good for Israel."

The Temple

Jerusalem Dome.

A palpable silence falls over the ancient city as the sinking sun splashes its bricks with gold. In the Knesset, members of Likud have ceased battling for control of the now-disenchanted coalition led by P.M. Moshe Bierman. The heart of this coalition, the ultra-orthodox Agudat Yisrael party, has been striving for primacy, filibustering over a point of *halachic* law. No non-Jews, it argues (joined enthusiastically by the Shas party), should be allowed to pass from the Court of the Gentiles into the inner court of the Temple. “Blasphemy!” declares one MK, “Defilement! Desecration of the sacred precincts clearly forbidden by Torah! And yet people are still being allowed entry within its walls. Thousands of tourists file through it every year on the heels of yammering tour-guides, flashbulbs glinting off the arms of the great *menorah*. Only physical restraint on the part of the Temple guards keeps them from the Innermost Place, lest they defile the *Kodesh haKodeshim* and render the entire Temple void!"

But even these impassioned pleas have been interrupted this morning. The Prime Minister has called a special session to deal with information just obtained from Mossad that the U.S. is about to launch nuclear missiles at Israel.

α

A tall man stands on a high balcony of the King David Hotel, overlooking the deserted David Hamelech Street. A rather unexceptional man, save for something in his eyes that occasionally seems to pierce right to the soul. At the moment, however, these eyes appear slightly unfocused, as if watching some inner dream unfold, a dream unrelated to the events in the city below. Otherwise the expression is one of acute boredom.

The man's apparel seems at first glance quite ordinary: a plain gray double-breasted suit and gray-striped tie. Closer inspection reveals the expensive taste of the wearer. The suit is cut of the finest cloth, tailored to disguise his wealth, to make the tall man appear unimpressive to the casual observer, to hide the sinuous muscles beneath, to distract attention from the enigmatic eyes the way a snake-charmer's decorative basket conceals the deadly cobra within.

As the tall man surveys the silent streets of Jerusalem, the slightest smile turns up the corners of his mouth. He draws back a shirt-cuff and glances at his gold Rolex watch.

"Six twenty-nine," says the watch politely.

His smile broadens to a grin. "This is it!" he whispers.

Behind him, a man in a white robe steps out onto the balcony. His feet are silent as a cat's.

"Maitreya."

The tall man turns to look at him. His face betrays no surprise at the approach of the cat feet; he's been awaiting their soft tread.

"Yes, Raj."

"The *Kohen haGadol* has arrived, my lord."

"The High Priest himself? I thought he'd be busy in the Knesset. He's taking a chance coming here. He must be hungrier than we thought."

"He awaits you in the sitting room."

"Alone?"

"Two Levites are with him, for protection."

"Are they armed?"

"I do not believe so, lord, though they are wearing loose robes. I can employ the metal detector if you wish."

Maitreya shakes his head. "No need for that. If they plan to assassinate me, we'll know it soon enough."

Raj bows deeply. "Yes, my lord."

"Pour some wine for our guests. Serve them food. Prepare our sacrifice. This is my moment, Raj. The stars have foretold it."

"Yes, lord. And I am honored to have been chosen."

"Your family's been loyal to me for thirty years."

"Yes, Maitreya."

"You've earned the honor through your devotion."

Raj bows again without answering.

"Go fatten up the High Priest. Fill his belly with exotic delights. Be obsequious. Lull his body with oils and his mind with *prana*. Meanwhile I'll make a call to Washington."

"Yes, lord."

Following his robed assistant into the suite, Maitreya turns right into a small office and closes the door behind him. It only takes a minute for his high-priority call to go through.

General Neely, head of the Joint Chiefs, appears on the screen.

"Mr. President!" he says with obvious surprise.

"General. Things in Jerusalem are going precisely as planned. I should be back in Washington around three o'clock tomorrow morning."

"Very good, Mr. President."

"I have a holoconference scheduled with all the Arab PWP members—four A.M. our time, later for all of them. I'm sure I'll have some serious space-lag to contend with, but I want to meet with you and Admiral Forrester in the Oval Office as soon as the conference is over."

"Yes, sir."

"Bill—I'm afraid our new science adviser, Carl DePalma, just had a total nervous breakdown."

"What?"

"He was a good man, a very good man. But now he just keeps babbling about something on that atavist island…never mind. I'll give you the details when I see you. Just make sure Quinton shows up. I'm depending on you, Bill. Keep things together until I return."

"Everything's just fine, Mr. President—discounting the usual problems with the Vice Admiral on Luna, that is."

"What's the old windbag up to now?"

"Nothing important, nothing we don't have a tight grip on. Don't let your concerns about Washington interfere with what you must do."

"I won't, Bill. And thank you."

"I'm happy to serve."

"Good. Give my regards to your wife; I'll see you in the morning."

"Thank you, sir."

Maitreya snaps off the connection and crosses the room. Taking a moment to straighten his tie and catch his breath, he opens the door and moves with deliberate calmness to greet his esteemed guest, Levi Aaron, *Kohen Gadol* of all Israel.

Raj should have rendered the High Priest fairly tractable by this time, he muses. *Everything's working out exactly as I planned. Victory will be mine, there's no doubt about it.*

After all, it's written in the stars...

The Apostle

An old man took a leisurely stroll along the shore.

He wore a toga-like robe draped with a *tallit*—a Jewish prayer shawl with sky blue stripes and white fringes. A matching blue *kepah*, or skullcap, sat on his balding head. He had a full, gray beard, streaked with white, and went barefoot on the cool sand. He paused just beyond the reach of the surf, filling his nostrils with the tang of the sea, exulting in the cry of the gulls and the thundering of the waves.

The beach wasn't real. It was entirely simulated by an advanced computer aboard the spaceliner *Empress*, returning from her farthest port of call—the icy moons of Saturn. For recreation her passengers could spend a few hours in the simuchambers, enjoying computer-simulated Earthlike environments that looked, smelled, even felt like the real thing. It was an expensive diversion, but the old man was traveling in style. Every morning at a certain time—the clocks aboard ship were synchronized with Greenwich Mean—he'd take his walk along the beach, white toga flapping in the breeze, gulls wheeling above the crashing surf, night's deep blackness fading into metallic gray, then blue-gray, and finally a deep rosy-red as the tip of the sun's crimson sphere peeked over the boundary of sea and sky. The illusion of wet sand—even including the sting of tiny shells on the soles of his feet—was perfect.

Were the simulators to be suddenly turned off, he knew, there'd be nothing around him but bare metal walls—above and below and on every side. But the chambers were never shut off while someone was inside. The operator had casually informed him that a sudden transition from the sensory images to the silent reality of the empty chamber might result in a "negative psychological effect", whatever *that* meant! There was even a disclaimer-notice above the entry portal reminding passengers that they entered at their own risk.

However convincing and tactile the simulations appeared, they were being somehow "projected" into the portion of his brain called the thalamus—or so the operator had explained—interfering with "proper" signals surging through his nervous system from the environment. "Like a dream," the operator had offered with an oily grin, as if to a child. Indeed, inside the simuchamber these mental images seemed far more vivid to his ageing body, his failing senses, than what he perceived outside of one. It was profoundly nostalgic, he realized. Like being a child again, all his senses sharp and clear. If he wasn't careful these chambers could easily become addictive.

He continued on his morning stroll by the imaginary sea, unconcerned for the moment with its addictive properties, happy for the brief respite from the demands of life. *A costly respite, indeed*, he reminded himself. *Two hours in this chamber cost more than the average asteroid miner earns in a month of grueling toil!* Had these morning constitutionals not been included in his fare (paid for by the young Church on Mars), he would never have been so frivolous with the believers' money.

The total sum he'd collected from the new Polis Marineris colony was enough to make one giddy. It was enough, at least, for a one-way ticket to a pioneer colony among the moons of Saturn, and the assurance of a comfortable retirement in one's autumn years. A certain robust independence reigned in the orbits of the gas giants;

their settlements were too remote to take the Terran bit in their mouths without bucking.

Even Wilbur Denton, the famous inventor who'd designed and built this very spaceliner and its ingenious simuchambers, had his headquarters on Mimas. All of Saturn's moons affected some display of throwing off the colonial yoke. As the popular saying went, "No one asks questions on Saturn."

With a shake of his head, the old man repented of such whimsical musings, tempting as they were. What would an old codger like himself do with ten million credits? It wasn't the prospect of material riches that tempted him, but the hope it offered for the fugitive Christians on Earth. *And for myself?* he thought. *For there are people who want to kill me—who'll stop at nothing to silence me.*

α

A young man dressed in wrinkled black clothing—shoulders and arms powerful, hair dark and curly, expression grim—paused at the intersection of two steel corridors. A group of armed guards passed by, the sound their boots fading away down the hallway. He moved swiftly to the portal of Paul's simuchamber. Its high arch glowed red to indicate it was occupied.

He looked both ways to be certain no one was watching and quickly tapped a series of numbers into a keypad on the right-hand arch. The arch buzzed. *Calm down!* he told himself. *You're making mistakes!* He tried again, fingering the keys more carefully.

The portal whooshed open before him, revealing a room of huge dimensions. The distant figure of a man in a toga moved across the metal floor, footfalls echoing around the walls.

He slipped through the open portal and it hissed shut behind him.

The Transaction

Maitreya lifts his wine glass to the High Priest and takes a sip, watching the man cautiously as he drinks.

"*Lechayim*," says the High Priest. "To life."

Glasses drained, the two men lean back in their chairs and eye each other like cats, each waiting for the other to speak, each keeping his own dark counsel.

"Have the arrangements been made," Maitreya inquires at last, "for my tour of the inner Temple?"

"All will be as you requested," says the *Kohen haGadol* with an oily grin.

"The Holy of Holies as well?"

"You realize, of course, Mr. President—" A deadly glare from Raj causes him to stammer, "I mean, lord Maitreya! I was about to say that there are important men in the Knesset who would deem such a tour—er, highly improper. In fact, they've been debating the issue of whether or not to bar all non-Jews from the inner courts, confining them to the Court of the Gentiles."

"Yes, I'm well aware of those men and their opinions."

"My own Shas party would demand both our lives if they knew you'd set foot in the *Kodesh haKodeshim*. Or, for that matter, that I myself had entered it, since it's not Yom Kippur and I've not been ritually bathed and secluded for the requisite period of time. The Law is quite dogmatic about such things, Mister—er, *lord* Maitreya."

"Are you afraid your G-d will strike you dead, High Priest? Or are you just pressing me for more of your grossly inflated Israeli shekels?"

"*Chas vachalelah!*" cries Levi Aaron. "G-d forbid! But… since it is you who brings up the subject of shekels—"

"Yes, yes, of course! The price of your precious tour has gone up. I anticipated that. I've already instructed Raj to offer you an additional two million. But I warn you, priest, I'll go no higher. It's extortion as it is."

"Hmmm," says the High Priest, almost rolling his eyes with delight. "Perhaps *three* million?"

This fool barters like an Arab! "Don't be absurd! You know I could probably find my own way inside the Temple for nothing. Raj hasn't been idle these past weeks, High Priest. He's an efficient spy. Rather good with disguises."

But he apparently hasn't noticed, reflects the High Priest, *that practically the entire Israeli Army is hidden in those tunnels! I'll have to be extremely careful choosing the route we take.* "If that were true," he says, "we would not be having this conversation. My dear lord Maitreya, please try to understand my position. I know you are revered in America and around the world as a guru, as a kind of god, in fact. You live in that splendid American White House. Why shouldn't the One True G-d, the G-d of Israel, have such a magnificent House—a House restored to its original splendor, as in the days of Herod?"

"Herod was despised by your people, wasn't he?"

"True, but he was a gifted architect. We must give credit where it's due. Flavius Josephus recorded that Herod constructed the *Kadosh haKadoshim* of solid gold shingles. He placed a golden mirror within, to reflect the rays of the rising sun into the chamber. How incredibly beautiful it must have been! How worthy of the G-d of Avraham, Yitzhak, and Ya'acov! And yet look at it now. Consider for a moment this rebuilt Sanctuary of ours. It is *nothing* by comparison! Israel is a poor nation in these times, lord Maitreya. We cannot afford the sort of lavish accouterments Herod possessed. A *shonda!* A scandal it is! Ten million shekels will do little to remedy the situation. To ask for only three more millions…" The High Priest shrugs and sighs.

"I don't suppose you plan to divert any of these millions for, let's say, your personal expenses?"

"What? And rob *HaShem? Chas vachalelah!*"

"As you say, High Priest. But I didn't invite you here to question your integrity, merely to discover how much it will cost to compromise it."

"You're an amusing man, Maitreya. But you'll pardon me if your brand of humor leaves me flat. I have heard your threats in the media—threats of making war on my country with nuclear missiles. And you talk of integrity! But, to answer you, I plan to invest your money in the enrichment of the Sanctuary."

"And of your reputation, as a result?"

"Have it your own way."

"High Priest, are you trying to tell me you actually believe in this—this impotent, invisible Jehovah? Come now! Let's be frank with one another. Your interest in the Temple and its adornment is purely self-serving, as is my desire to enter the Holy of Holies. I simply desire to gaze upon it, as I've gazed upon every other sacred precinct on Earth. So I may tell my followers that I've partaken of its power. I could lie about it, I suppose. Those mindless sycophants of mine would believe whatever I tell them. I suppose it's just that I've never been denied access to any relic before. And I deem it a sort of—challenge? It's worth twenty-two million shekels to satisfy my curiosity—but no more. To you it's another million; to me it's a matter of principle. Don't play me for a fool, priest. Your motives and mine are identical."

"Truly?" The High Priest holds out his wine glass for Raj to refill. "Please enlighten me on that point."

"As the man who'll return the Temple to its former glory, you'll be the most beloved High Priest since—whoever first laid its cornerstone."

"Solomon," says the priest.

"Okay, Solomon. Your name will go down in history along with those of the Rambam, Rashi, Akiva..."

"Delightful."

"Be reasonable, priest. You have your *own* disciples, your *own* sycophants. You deceive them just as I deceive mine. I came prepared to offer you a huge sum to make that prestige possible—including an additional two million in anticipation of your last-minute extortion. But please, don't tell me you're honestly doing it for the glory of G-d! Save it for your Sanhedrin, your contemptible Shas party, and your ignorant masses. I despise being taken for a fool, especially by a man who makes his living in the same racket."

"Racket?" gasps the High Priest, feigning incredulity. "You claim to be *Moshiach!* Most of the world's population worships you. This you call a racket?"

"Come now, priest. You're rather ill-suited to play the role of Pollyanna with me. Are you going to waste more of my time with this drivel? Will you make me withdraw my offer?"

"Hardly! Hardly, lord Maitreya! I was only seeking to inform you of the difference between us."

"There *is* none."

"Respectfully, lord, there is. I claim to be a mere *servant* of G-d. You, on the other hand, claim to be G-d *Himself.* This does not constitute a major distinction in your mind? How can you perpetrate such an outright blasphemy and then say we're in the same racket?"

"Spare me, priest! I make no claim to be your Jehovah, nor do I preach a single jot or tittle of your Torah. Therefore, from your point of view, I'm committing no blasphemy."

"Not altogether true, lord Maitreya. You are called the New Age *Christ*, the Anglicized Greek term for *Moshiach*. By claiming to be the Messiah you are indeed treading rather heavily on the precepts of Judaism."

"I didn't summon you here for a lesson in Judaism, priest, not did I expect to be lectured by you! I must insist that you conduct me to the Temple at once, as you've agreed to do. My servant Raj will show you the money before we depart; you may count it right here. Then, according to our agreement, you may verify that Raj is indeed taking that same briefcase along with us, that no switch has been made. Raj will hold it until we're inside the Holy of Holies. He'll hand it over and our business will be concluded. Are these terms acceptable to you? Or shall I terminate our interview and explore other options? Make up your mind at once."

"My dear lord Maitreya! Those *are* the terms agreed upon, and I shall abide by them. But you understand that the Ark in the chamber is not the original one, only a copy?"

"That doesn't matter, it's the locality that's significant."

"This is true. Once again I insist that it be only yourself and not your manservant who passes through the *parakhet* into the chamber."

"Both Raj and his briefcase will remain outside—within my sight, of course—until I'm satisfied that I am indeed within the Holy of Holies. I want to be certain you won't harm him while I'm inside the curtain and make off with the money before I'm satisfied. Raj is a valuable servant and a devoted disciple. I can't risk letting him come to harm. In fact, I'd prefer it if you entered the sanctuary with me. Your guards can watch Raj and the money, and I can have *you.* For insurance."

The High Priest shakes his head, causing the flesh of his double chin to jiggle. His eyes widen.

"No! I will not go in!"

"Then our conversation is at an end."

"But—please understand, lord Maitreya! I *cannot* go inside. It would mean my life!"

"I see! *We* can be slain by your jealous G-d! It won't bother your conscience one iota when you order your guards to remove the briefcase from my dead servant's hands. I can hardly believe my ears! Do you truly believe you'll be killed in there?" Maitreya cannot tell the priest that it'll never happen, that it's not only written in the stars, but also in the Scriptures, that the Son of Satan will stand in the Holy Place and defile it. Nor can he tell the fool how he *plans* to defile it—not with the blood of a pig, but with human blood, the blood of the High Priest himself! *How can this ridiculous priest know that his superstitious aversion is creating a major complication? It isn't fear of what I may do to him that's causing his reluctance, but fear of what his G-d may do to him! If he only knew that I also believe in the existence of his G-d. I had that Tyrant in my face for eons, and I despise Him with every atom of my being! It's this fat Jew's G-d I've come here to usurp, to supplant, to destroy! This complication presents a problem, certainly, but I'll cross that bridge when I come to it. If the priest won't accompany me beyond the curtain, even under our subtle hypnosis, it might be necessary to force poor Raj to serve as the sacrifice.* The thought of plunging a knife into his servant's faithful heart gives Maitreya only the slightest twinge of remorse. He feels no loyalty toward Raj; he only hates to lose a good servant. *Raj has been carefully trained in Chandrapur; he has talents few men possess. He'll be difficult to replace.*

No matter! I must fulfill the mission that's been mine from the moment of my birth. I must become the vessel of Lucifer's power! Only I, of all men on the Earth, can receive the infilling from below. And only in the Holiest Place on Earth can I receive it. Yes, I'd planned to repay the priest for his effrontery by driving the ceremonial dagger into his fat scheming breast! He thinks of the knife resting in its case in his office, the blade a razor-sharp fragment of the Spear of Destiny—an artifact once in the possession of Napoleon Bonaparte and Adolf Hitler. *But any human victim will do. If not the priest then Raj or one of the Levites. Any human sacrifice—something G-d despises—performed in the Holy Place, will constitute the ultimate defilement of the Temple, the abomination that will make it desolate. The Holy Tyrant will scream from his Heaven as the power of Lucifer surges into my body. And that power will make me master of the world!*

"Would you like Raj to show you the money?" he offers

"Certainly!" says the High Priest. "There's nothing I'd rather gaze upon than the sight of a hundred million shekels."

"A hundred and two."

"Yes, of course. And, after we drink another toast with this delightful wine, I shall escort you to the entrance of our secret passageway. You'll find it a fascinating tour, my dear lord Maitreya. It's the very labyrinth through which the Ark was taken during the Babylonian invasion of 616 BCE, and in which it was hidden from the Babylonians and, later, from the Romans. It is the best way to sneak a non-Jew past the guards."

He's lying, Maitreya muses. *If they knew where those tunnels were, they'd know where the Ark is hidden. They wouldn't have needed to construct a substitute. What's he up to? What are the Israelis hiding under the Temple? What don't they want me to see?*

"I told you, priest, I'm of Jewish descent. A Levite like yourself."

Levi Aaron raises a chubby hand to his lips, suppressing a smile. "You're last name is Coffey."

"My father was Anglican, it's true. But my mother was Jewish—Janet Levinthal. Her ancestors were Lithuanian Jews. They moved to Germany at the turn of the 20th century. A hundred and fifty years ago—during the Nazi persecutions, when Jews were still allowed to leave Germany—they emigrated to the United States and settled in Boston."

"No one knows of this?"

"No, priest, no one knows. And I'll slit your throat if you repeat it."

"Never in a million years! But even granting that, where you intend to go no man on earth is allowed, including a Levite. Only the High Priest, and only on *Yom Kippur*. Levite or no, you must still enter by way of the tunnels. It is quite safe, I assure you."

Maitreya glances at the two Levite guards standing stiffly at attention behind the priest.

"Will they talk?" he asks. "Aren't you afraid they might covet a share of your newfound wealth? In return for their silence?"

"Don't be absurd! These men are absolutely loyal. I cannot vouch for the rest of the Temple guard, but as for these two you needn't worry. Besides, they know that if they were to betray me I'd cut out their tongues."

"You're beginning to sound more like an Arab sheik than a Jewish priest."

"Arabs and Jews," chuckles the *Kohen haGadol*, "despite our frequent—er, disagreements?—are cousins, after all."

"And you, my dear High Priest, are the greatest rogue in all of Israel!"

Levi Aaron raises his glass into the air, vibrating with laughter. "As you Americans like to say, 'I'll drink to that.'"

Maitreya lifts his own glass. "*Lechayim!*"

The Threat

Something dark and brooding insinuated itself into the old man's morning ritual, the cold breath of the Reaper over the hairs of his neck.

"'Cast me not out in the time of my old age!'" he whispered, his voice lost beneath the pounding surf. "'For mine enemies speak against me. They that lay wait for my soul take counsel together, saying, G-d hath forsaken him. Persecute and take him, for there's none to deliver him.'"

Were his persecutors back on Earth any more real than these clever simulations? Could they reach him out here, millions of miles away in space? Wasn't fear, after all, a bit like the transient visions of a simuchamber—*HaSatan,* the Adversary, plucking that repetitive death-song on the strings of his soul—just as the slick young chamber operator brought him sensations of sand and sea from a panel of potentiometers and switches? Even with rumors of an assassination plot swirling around him—*what of them*? Were his weapons carnal, like theirs? Or were they mighty to the pulling down of strongholds? And yet—his prayer just now *had* seemed rather small and ineffectual under the roar of the tide…

Illusions nonetheless! he decided with his usual obstinacy.

Just there, he knew, beyond that jutting finger of rock, breakers spilling aprons of foam along its jagged length—stood a cold metal wall. He had merely to walk over and feel of it. But why? Such a beautiful illusion was far too pleasant—and expensive!—to expose. *Isn't it the same with our fears? Don't our hearts cling to them, even when our minds know better*? This sort of weakness would never do. Like his namesake, the Apostle Paul, he must run the bitter race to the end. "To live is Messiah," Rabban Sha'ul had declared, "to die is gain." When the death angel came to take him, he'd be ready. *But it's not time yet. Not yet…*

The gold bracelet on his wrist—another gift from the Martian Church—produced a faint chime. He depressed a diamond-sized button on one of its links and raised it to his lips.

"Yes?" he said. "What is it?"

"Brother Paul!" came a thin, urgent voice from within the ornament. "Someone's broken into your chamber!"

"Are you certain?" he asked, immediately realizing what a stupid question it was.

"Yes, quite certain, Reverend. He's approaching you from behind. If you turn around, sir, you'll see him."

Turning, Paul noticed a youthful male figure, all in black, moving with purposeful strides across the sand. His blood froze. "So," he said under his breath. "You've come for me already, Mr. Death Angel! I was just thinking of you. Tell me, is this how it will end for the poor brethren on Earth? And for myself, the last apostle to the solar system? Killed by a lone assassin on a beach that doesn't exist?"

"Sir?" said the bracelet.

"Thank you kindly," he told it. He tried to suppress the bitter edge in his voice. "I've just now determined, Brother Wallace, that I'm not ready to die. Thousands of souls are relying on me, and I refuse to be assassinated!"

"Very good, sir," said Brother Wallace. "In that case, might I suggest that you run?"

"Run?"

"Yes, sir. Just head for the opposite exit. I'll meet you there. Ship's guards have been alerted; they're on their way. And—if I may be so bold, sir—you might want to shake a tailfeather."

"I'll shake no such thing! The last evangelist in the solar system will not go scurrying from danger like a startled rat! I'll confront this assassin where I stand!"

"That's fine, Reverend." The bracelet sounded pained.

"Tell me…"

"Sir?"

"Is the gentleman—armed?"

"Detectors indicate no weapons, sir."

"Well, that's reassuring. Bring him on, then, the villain!"

"But he's still pretty big."

"Yes, Brother Wallace, I can see that." Paul's bravado deflated like a punctured balloon. "He *is* a rather burly fellow, now you mention it."

"Yes, sir. 'Burly' describes him perfectly."

The intruder was much closer now, his strides more rapid, more determined. He had the wild look of a man who'd gambled everything on one last, desperate act. *How did he get in*? *Shouldn't there be sentries at the portal*? Paul was rapidly becoming the most wanted man in the solar system—and for someone to be allowed to just stroll into his chamber uninvited was the grossest negligence! Suppressing his rising fear with bluster, as was his habit, he resolved to give Brother Wallace a stern talking-to. And Captain Mills, too, for that matter. After all, he'd been given Mill's assurance of safe conduct on this voyage.

A sudden sensation of *déjà vu* passed over him, an eerie feeling that he'd experienced this before, that he was locked into a crazy Ferris-wheel of events that kept repeating themselves endlessly throughout time. And then something stranger still. A faint flickering past his inner eye, an absurd picture of himself standing in the depths of space, like a Greek god astride the stars, a cosmic Moses shouting, "Let my people go!" Then the vision was gone, and with it the sensation of *déjà vu*. He was left with the beach and the black-clad stranger.

Raising the bracelet to his lips, he said, "Thank you, Brother Wallace; I'll consider your sage advice," He snapped off the connection. *Security chief indeed!*

Regarding the approaching figure under bushy gray brows, he threw back his shoulders and steadied himself to meet his angel of death…

The Chamber

Five shadows glide through the ancient passage with no light to assist them. The High Priest has cautioned Maitreya about using flashlights; the slightest beam may be detected through cracks in the masonry. What he's neglected to tell him is what lies in the labyrinthine tunnels on the other side of the wall: Half the IDF lurks in underground habitats prepared in the event of a nuclear attack by the United States—by the very American President he's now leading to the *Kodesh haKodeshim!* He can't betray his own country! His own people! *Do Americans think everyone can be bought?* Besides, he's familiar with every square inch of his secret passageway and has no need of flashlights.

But Maitreya is still wary. They've traveled in darkness for well over a mile, snaking tunnels leading them in circles for all he knows. Suddenly the Levites stop in their tracks. The darkness is palpable. He hears the sound of shuffling feet. One of their escorts slips behind him. A knife-blade touches his throat, raising goose-flesh. There's a dull thud and a painful grunt from Raj. The shallowness of the breathing in his ear, the odor of wine and garlic, tells him it's the priest who holds the knife. *That makes sense*, he decides. *The Levites recognize that the servant is more dangerous than the master. They're making certain he's out of the way.*

Another grunt from Raj, followed by the sound of beefy fists striking flesh—*smack...smack...smack.* He hears Raj's brief-case hit the floor with a loud rattle, the echo pattering down the tunnel like the retreating footsteps. He can picture what's happening: One of the Levites is gripping Raj from behind, probably around the neck, choking him, while the other beats him repeatedly about the face. Raj is making all the appropriate noises, groaning and sobbing for all he's worth. Maitreya pictures blood spattering from smashed lips, yet he knows that Raj feels nothing. He's seen the manservant wrap his fingers around the tip of a glowing poker and grin. No—each amateurish blow will only serve to strengthen Raj. He'll appear to hold out for a long time, so as not to make it too easy for them.

The smacking and scuffling cease.

The High Priest whispers harshly in his ear.

"What a fool you are! Surely you didn't expect me to lead you to the Holy of Holies—a filthy, anti-Semitic dog like you?" His voice turns as cold, as hard-edged as the blade he's pressing against Maitreya's throat. "Blasphemer! Idolater! You call yourself *Moshiach?* How long I've waited to avenge the name of *Elohim!* I'm doing the world a great favor. But rest assured, your money will be put to good use. As for yourself—well, I'm afraid you will disappear, Mr. President of the United States. Your body will be laid to rest behind one of these stones, and no one will ever find you. In time you'll be utterly forgotten. Just another of the world's many false Messiahs."

Maitreya sighs. He calmly speaks his servant's name into the darkness.

"Yes, lord?" Raj replies.

"Our moment has finally come."

"Your moment to *die*, blasphemer!" cries the High Priest.

The blade cuts deeper; warm blood trickles down Maitreya's neck. *Now!* his brain screams. *Fill yourself with hate! Hate, hate, hate, hate, hate!*

"Now, Raj!"

Two throats gasp simultaneously, filling the tunnel with muffled groans.

Turning, Maitreya directs every ounce of his strength, all the power of *prana* within him, at the High Priest. He reaches out with the speed of a striking serpent and snatches one fleshy wrist, twisting it. There's a shriek of pain. The knife clatters on stone. Sucking air into his lungs, Maitreya lets loose a piercing animal wail filled with all the rage he's drawn from the priest's body. He uses *prana* to shape the emotion into a hammer, striking the priest with its full force, slamming him back against the wall with a sickening smack and a painful expulsion of breath.

"Raj!" he shouts. "The flare!"

The tunnel bursts alight as Raj ignites the torch he's been concealing. Crimson fire dances on stone, illuminating Raj's horribly battered and bloody face as he holds the torch aloft. Black fissures of blood run down his cheek and neck. His eyes are crimson, mask-like, inhuman. Wide with murderous triumph. Revealed by the flickering torch, the dead Levites lay crumpled at his feet, staring up at their killer with empty eyes, their lives extinguished by a power they couldn't possibly comprehend, puppets with severed strings.

Maitreya turns back to the High Priest and works on keeping him pinned to the stones with telekinetic power. Arms akimbo, eyes bulging, Levi Aaron stares into the face of his executioner. He knows he will die any moment now…yet death does not come. He hangs for long, torturous minutes in the flickering torchlight, ribs slowly cracking, tongue unable to cry out, unable to plead for mercy. Maitreya speaks to him in a soft, almost tender, voice:

"According to your vile history, High Priest, a king by the name of Antiochus once sacrificed a pig in the Temple of your impotent God—upon the very *kapporet* of the Ark! He was seeking power from his gods, the spirits tell me, not just the humiliation of the so-called 'chosen people.' I shall do likewise, priest. I shall also sacrifice a pig on your precious, holy altar, your *Aaron ha-Brit!* The blood of this pig will desecrate it forever!

"Do you think this is power, High Priest? This force that, by a mere thought, can crush the life out of you? It's nothing! When the blood of my sacrifice flows over the altar, I shall receive power that will make this seem feeble. Lucifer himself will fill my body and soul! I shall be Lucifer incarnate!

"You had the effrontery to call me a fool, but it's *you* who are the fool, High Priest. That weakling Yeshua came to your people centuries ago, and they failed to recognize Him. Their priests—men like you—gave Him over to the Romans for crucifixion. You think yourself righteous and holy—and so very *superior!* Yet you're Satan's delight. You crucify your Messiah afresh with every greedy day of your life!"

So he's not *a Jew, the filthy liar! I knew it, G-d help me*!

"I can see your thoughts, High Priest. Don't call upon your G-d now. It's far too late for you. And besides, He's already defeated. Lucifer needs only one man to destroy every last Jew on this planet, just as he used one frustrated Austrian artist to wipe out six million of them over a century ago. Where was your G-d then? You may ask yourself that. And where is He now? The Dragon holds all the governments of Earth in his hands. Another Holocaust has begun. And I swear an oath to you, High Priest, that not a single Jew, or Jew-loving Christian, will remain alive when I'm finished. When I've sacrificed my pig on the altar, I shall be the most powerful being on this planet! By a mere thought I will call up beasts from the depths of the earth, creatures that will lay waste to every abode of man! Then every last human being will be my slave!"

Maitreya turns to his servant and grins. "Come, Raj. Let us bring our pig to the altar. The special ceremonial knife is in the briefcase, on top of the money he'll never see. It must be a proper sacrifice, after all."

"Yes, lord."

Raj hands the torch to Maitreya and takes hold of the terror-stricken High Priest, slinging the huge trembling body over his shoulder with less effort than it takes to hoist a sack of grain. Maitreya moves off, flickering torchlight fading away down the stone passageway. Raj hurries after him.

Levi Aaron tries to scream. He's totally paralyzed, unable

to produce more than a faint, idiotic jibbering. To be lifted helplessly and carried at a run through the torch lit tunnel is frightening enough. Having no control over his body is terrifying! How is it possible for human beings to wield such awesome power? Or *are* they human at all?

Raj catches up with Maitreya and they continue in silence. Finally, he whispers his master's name.

"Yes, Raj?"

"Could it be that the priest tricked us? That he's led us in a false direction?"

"No, Raj. He was planning that ambush. He never expected us to arrive at our destination. These tunnels have many dark niches where two bodies might be safely interred, and none the wiser. Rest assured, this is the right passageway. I saw it in the priest's thoughts. I was expecting his attack; didn't you hear the warning I sent you with my mind?"

"Yes, lord. But I was only able to block out the pain of my beating. Your warning did not come in time for me to prepare for more than that. I simulated the sounds of pain in order to gain that time, but I'm afraid my body sustained some serious injuries in the process. Eventually I shall have to release my mental control, lord, and I am afraid I will be of little use to you then."

"For that I'm sorry, Raj, but all three of our escorts were taking precautions against their thoughts being perceived. It was the weak priest who gave it away, and then only at the last minute. Look, Raj! Do you see that faint glow?"

"Yes, lord, I see it."

"Stay here."

Maitreya lowers the torch to the floor, where it slowly sputters out. He moves cautiously toward a dim golden light penetrating through an opening in the stones. As he advances to only a few meters from its source, he stops short and lets out a string of rather eloquent curses.

"What is it, lord?"

"By the horns of Lucifer! The foul priest *has* tricked us, after all!"

The priest lets out a strangled cry—a shout of victory forced between useless lips. Raj leaps forward, the stout body balanced across his shoulders, and gazes toward the terminus of the passage.

Flickering light splashes the stonework from what appear to

be candle-flames reflecting off golden surface-es. *The menorah!* Raj exults. *This is the Holy Sanctuary! And not nearly as impoverished as the High Priest led us to believe! It is not the Holy of Holies itself, but only the breadth of two ceiling-high curtains separates us from that sacred chamber!* Yet the entrance is securely barred. In the unsteady light he can see where the spiked ends of iron rods have been driven deep into the stones, above and below.

"Raj," whispers Maitreya in his ear. "Can you do it?"

Raj is doubtful. As long as it's necessary to concentrate so much psychic energy on blocking out the pain of his injuries, he may not be able to muster up the reserve power the job requires. Yet he won't express these doubts. Instead, he lowers the priest's body to the floor, moves quickly to the barred entrance and crouches, listening. For a full minute he remains alert for any sound coming from inside the Sanctuary, a cough or an inhalation of breath, anything that might indicate a trap. There's nothing.

Satisfied, he takes hold of the iron bars with both hands, draws in a lungful of air, places his feet wide apart, knees bent, and pulls. His biceps bulge. Perspiration soaks through the thin cloth of his garment, exposing rippling muscles across his back. He expels harsh puffs of air between clenched teeth, then gulps in more air and pulls again. His body bends like a bow. He strains harder, drops of sweat raining from his uplifted face.

Slowly, the bars begin to bend outward.

Maitreya helps by concentrating his psychic power upon the iron, picturing it in his mind as plastic, malleable—trying to alter its atomic structure, to melt it with the *prana*-force in the surrounding air.

Raj groans, straining at the metal, his copious perspiration dampening the stones at his feet. He begins to slip but refuses to release his grip upon the bars. Little by little, millimeter-by-millimeter, the bars give way.

"Good, Raj!" Maitreya shouts. "We're almost there! Just a few inches more! A few inches!"

But Raj has reached the limit of his reserve power. He releases his mental control over the pain of his injuries, allowing some of it to leak through to his mind. He draws back. It's too intense! And yet…

Before Maitreya realizes what he's doing, Raj gives a final

inhuman tug at the bars, opening the gates of his brain to allow the full intensity of the anguish to flood through to his senses. The pain is like fire! He shrieks. His body convulses. He concentrates that involuntary reflex into one final burst of power, parting the bars with an almost human groan.

"No, Raj! No!"

But it's too late. With a bloodcurdling scream, Raj forces the bars open another full inch, then drops sideways onto the wet stones with a gush of breath. His heart bursts from the strain. He dies, staring blankly upward.

"No!" Maitreya cries. He leaps over the body of his dead servant and grasps the partially-bent bars. Projecting every ounce of power he possesses on the weakest point in the metal, he lets out an anguished shriek of frustration. He tugs wildly at the metal, screaming like a tortured animal, screaming and moaning, feet slipping in the dead man's bloody sweat, eyes bugging out of their sockets.

And the bars finally obey.

They part like rubber in his hands, and he drops, sobbing, gulping air into his lungs, willing the pain in his ribs to cease.

"We've done it, Raj," he pants. "Nothing can defeat us now."

But Raj is silent, terribly still and frail in the arms of death. It is no grin of triumph Maitreya sees etched forever upon the purplish lips, but a grimace of horror. In those empty eyes Maitreya sees the first glimmer of comprehension, of the terror every servant of the Dark Prince experiences when he stands at last upon the threshold of *Gehenom*—when the eyes of his soul suddenly open upon a flaming eternity.

But Maitreya does not comprehend it. He interprets it as an expression of physical pain, for he fully expects Raj's spirit to be rejoicing in paradise. Lucifer has promised him rewards. He's assured him over and over, until he believes it without question, until he's agreed to sacrifice his soul for the castles he's glimpsed floating in the air, castles defended by brilliantly scaled flying dragons of every hue, wings outspread, nostrils flaring—a universe where nymphs offer heartbreaking hymns to the setting sun, where bloated gas worlds hang, just dimly seen, in the azure sky. "*No, my son,*" Lucifer's voice has assured him in these vivid dreams, "*There is no need to fear. Passing from this life is merely crossing a gateway into a realm of perpetual splendor. You shall not surely die…"*

α

Strong hands grip Levi Aaron by the wrists and slowly drag him across the cold stone floor. His robe snags as he's yanked through an opening in the bars. Metal scrapes his skin; jagged fingernails cut his wrists; his arms are nearly stretched out of joint by the fierce, relentless tugging. He's certain they'll break before Maitreya can force his body through the aperture.

Then everything turns black…

As he regains consciousness he sees familiar crimson tapestries moving past him on either side. Cool cedar floor-planks run along his naked back where his robe has been torn almost completely away. He's being dragged through the *teradzis*, between the veils! With a mighty effort he tries to cry out for help. Nothing emerges from his lips but that pitiful jibbering.

They reach an opening in the thick curtain to the left, the very threshold of the *Kadosh haKadoshim*. Staring wildly, he sees the acacia-wood Ark, but he's unable to raise his head to see its golden lid, the *kapporet* flanked by two golden *k'ruvim*. It terrifies him! His heart pounds in his chest; his skin turns cold and slimy with foul-smelling sweat. *The Holy Ark of the Lord!* his brain screams. *The dwelling place of HaShem! But why haven't I been struck dead? Why have I been allowed to penetrate into the forbidden place? Where's the Shekhina? Where's the flesh destroying wrath of Elohim?*

His thoughts are shattered by the voice of Maitreya. That child of Hades is intoning some unholy dirge in an unknown tongue. It turns his blood cold. *How can the fiend be doing this*? *Where's the Shekhina if not here, defending the Ark? The angels above the kapporet—are they deaf and blind? Where is the Ruach Elohim? Where is the cleansing fire from heaven? Has this monster been telling the truth? Can he be more powerful than HaShem? No, that's impossible!*

His body is lifted into the air by an unseen force, the same force that pinned him to the wall of the tunnel. As the golden *kapporet* presses against the raw skin of his back, his eyes bulge with horror, his tongue escapes from his lips, hanging limply, flapping against his chin.

The tall figure of Maitreya looms over him, still chanting his unholy requiem. He raises a bejeweled ceremonial dagger high into the air, clasping the haft in his fists, eyes glaring, triumphant. Candlelight glints from the curved blade. *Such a strange blade*! The steel glows brightly as if burning with a flame all its own. As the priest watches, mesmerized, the blade drifts left and right like the head of a serpent.

Maitreya stops singing. His eyes gleam as he holds the knife above his head, shining with an unwholesome, drug-like ecstasy.

"Fill me, O Prince of Darkness!" he shouts, his voice echoing around the Chamber. "Take your place in this temple of my body! Fill it with your power!"

With a sudden, brutish wail, he plunges in the blade.

The priest sees it arc downward. He doesn't feel it enter his body, only the thud of Maitreya's fists against his chest. A warm stickiness oozes over his belly. *It can't be blood, can it? It can't be my own death I'm watching!*

Up goes the blade and down again. Dark blood spatters the demon's clothes, his face, his hair. The priest feels oddly disconnected from the scene, not comprehending. There's something unreal about it. Something dreamlike. *A nightmare! That's what it is! Wake up!* But the devil-man shrieks again and he suddenly knows it's no dream. *I'm being stabbed to death on the Ark of the Covenant! I'm being offered as a sacrifice to Satan!*

The blood-splattered face above him begins to morph into something utterly grotesque. With the sight of his own blood splashing over the face of a demon, Levi Aaron plunges backward into a gaping pit of blackness. Backward, still trying to scream, into the sulfurous heart of *Gehenom*.

The Admiral

As the rotorwing plunged from its flightway at an all-clear from the commuter matrix, Admiral Quinton Forrester glanced down at the presidential mansion. The dawning sun lent it a virginal, shell-like pinkness. It always thrilled him to see its colonial frame rising above the tropical lawns and gardens, the stately rows of royal palms. There was a bracing sense of majesty about it. Over three hundred years of American nationhood were represented by this structure, although Forrester knew it wasn't the same edifice as the one erected in 1792. He grinned as he recalled his American history, wondering what its first occupant, John Adams, would have thought if he had known that the White House would be standing one day on this grassy knoll, surrounded by tropical rainforest, far from its original site. That site, along with the rest of America's former eastern seaboard, was now submerged beneath the rising tides of the Atlantic.

The environmentalists of the early twenty-first century had been right about global warming, he reflected, but greatly mistaken about its cause. They'd blamed human-generated pollutants when the culprit was planet Earth itself!

Forrester had learned all about it in his classes at Annapolis: What most people called the Ice Age had been but the most recent of *numerous* glaciations (or ice-flows), all of them comprising a *greater* Ice Age. Geologists had been teaching for almost two centuries that during this greater Ice Age, which they called the Pleistocene Epoch, there had been at least *twenty* glaciations—ice flowing and receding over the planet like pseudopods of a monstrous, white amoeba. The most recent glaciation they had dubbed Würm.

It was during Würm that people had dwelt in caves, seeking shelter from the bleak, frigid world of descending ice, chipping knives out of flint, painting scenes of the animals they hunted on fire-lit cavern walls. Advancing glaciers created an ice-bridge from Europe to Canada. And as ice conquered the North, Earth's equatorial regions experienced periods of drenching rain, called "pluvials".

The climate enjoyed on much of Earth's surface during the rapid ascent of man—rapid by geologic reckoning, they claimed—was only a brief "interglacial" or "temperate" period between ice flows. "Little ice ages" had appeared during this interglacial period, one in particular extending from the 11th to the 17th centuries. (It was said that in the 1600s one could skate on solid ice from Manhattan Island to the mainland.) And they all began with long periods of global warming.

The glaciers would flow again. Temperatures would rise worldwide; tropical storms would increase in strength and in number; winters would be shorter, summers hotter; glaciers would crumble and melt; polar ice caps would shrink, causing the oceans to rise. The coastlines of all the continents on Earth would be inundated. The

Florida Keys would disappear, and the Antilles, greater and lesser, would shrink dramatically.

And then, slowly, the ice would descend.

Just as they'd predicted, Forrester mused darkly, the process had begun in the late twentieth century, increasing apace through the beginning of the twenty-first. They called it the Alderson Glaciation, and it had nothing whatever to do with human pollution.

Forrester snapped himself out of his senseless reverie. He'd be landing soon. Who could say what would greet him at the White House? The President had just returned from a secret trip to Israel—what he was up to there nobody at the White House would say. But, whatever it was, he'd immediately summoned Forrester and General Neely to a meeting in the Oval Office.

The President's recent behavior was troubling to Forrester, but he didn't dare say anything about it. Sometimes he even thought the man was reading his thoughts.

The Greeting

Palm fronds and tripinnate leaves of the blooming acacias rustled in the blast of rotor blades as the craft hovered over the landing-pad known, jokingly, as "the lawn". It landed with a sudden jolt. Forrester was pressed about by helmeted Secret Service agents and nearly thrust out of the rotorwing onto the grass. Over the roar of the blades and the rustle of leaves he heard the chatter of a huge troop of capuchin monkeys as they made an indignant retreat through the branches above. *Filthy things!* he thought. *They always sound like they're laughing at you. Can't they keep them away from the White House at least?* They chattered in his ears as he ran with his two bodyguards for the rear entrance of the building. "*There he goes!*" they seemed to mock from the safety of the high branches. "*There goes Admiral Quinton Forrester! President Coffey's trained poodle!*"

They were incapable of speech, of course. Forrester knew that. As tenuous as it might be at times, he still had a grip on his sanity. But it was rather disconcerting to be greeted at the White House by a sound so similar to derisive laughter.

Even worse than the monkeys were the large cats. Rich people purchased them illegally—for pets!—then abandoned them when they grew dangerous. The cats would meet, mate—and there went the neighborhood! Just last night in Miami there'd been a case in the news of a large animal, probably a cat, mauling a pilot to death in the cabin of his antique Cessna.

"Can't you gas those foolish things?" he shouted to the Secret Service agent at his right, trying to be heard over the noise. Both agents were dressed in tight black suits with blue unicorn armbands on their left arms, gray flackjacket vests, and sleek gray helmets on their heads, visors pulled down.

"What foolish things, sir?"

"The monkeys!" he yelled. "The blasted monkeys! Can't you find a way to keep them away from here?"

The agent muttered something and then pressed close against him as they crossed an open area, shielding the Admiral against the possibility of a sniper and guiding him safely through the portal and to the elevator. The second agent tapped the "up" button, but Forrester saw that the elevator was already on its way down. It hummed to a stop, made a pinging sound, and the door slid open from floor to ceiling with a hiss. Inside stood an elderly black man in a crisp Army uniform. He held out his hand as the guards practically shoved Forrester inside. Forrester took the hand and shook it firmly.

"Welcome back, Admiral," said General William Neely. "The President's been waiting for you. And not very patiently, I might add."

"Blast it all, Bill!" grumbled Forrester as the door hissed shut and he felt the sudden queasy sensation of the two-story leap in the pit of his stomach. "I came as soon as I could."

"Of course," said Neely sympathetically. "But he's rather beside himself this morning. You know how he gets. He's just completed an important holoconference with the Arab PWP leaders, and that certainly did not improve his mood."

"What does he need the Arabs for? We've been independent of fossil fuel for half a century. Without a demand for crude oil they're nothing."

"That's true. But they're members of the PWP. And they have an old saying: 'The enemy of my enemy is my friend.' You have to admit, Quinton, they all hate Israel as much as the President does."

"I'll bet he wants another update on the Luna situation. He knows more about it than we do, but he's always demanding updates. They're only excuses to get us on the hot seat. Me especially."

"Well, you *are* the Master's number one boy."

Forrester caught the note of sarcasm and shook his head. "Don't make me laugh," he said. "The White House chef has more influence than I do. I look like an admiral, I talk like an admiral, and I photograph well in a uniform. But we both know what I am."

The word "traitor," left unspoken, echoed between them as if it he'd screamed it at the top of his lungs. Neely gave a cheerless grin.

"What we *both* are, Quinton."

The elevator hissed open. As they stepped out onto the polished hardwood floor, Forrester glanced around at the decorative foliage and flowering vines clinging to the walls all around. *It cost a fortune*, he thought angrily, *for the White House to arrange and care for all this lousy vegetation!* Everyone had plants in their homes these days, growing over their bland, adobe-textured walls. They were a pleasant change from the old paint-and-wallpaper interiors of former times, and they required practically no care at all. The machines took care of everything. So why did the White House need to employ those blasted decorator robots, mincing about the opulent rooms and bickering about the furniture? Who needed them? *The Master should boot those androids out on their effeminate metal ears!*

He turned to Neely in exasperation. "We're dealing with humans on Luna, after all," he complained. "Not robots. Can't he see that it's a delicate operation up there? If that capitalist revolution gets out of control, we'll find ourselves back in the days of the robber barons. The New World Order will be in shambles, and Luna will have a knife at our throats. It's a delicate game, and a deadly one."

"Which is why I insisted on keeping your overstuffed Vice Admiral Bowlen out of the assassination plot."

"Listen, Bill, I was suffering under the delusion that *I'm* in charge of naval operations in the solar system. Including the covert operations of Naval Intelligence."

"You *are*, Quinton; you *are*. Don't get defensive."

They turned into a long corridor, their footsteps muffled by plush carpeting.

"Bowlen has clout nobody else has," Forrester said. "He

can get things done. By the way, I set up a meeting between him and that Air Force Lieutenant, Matt Baker. Baker's head of Agitprop, fancies himself a key player. I put him in charge of hiring our hit man. We'll see if he can keep Bowlen in line."

"I have to be honest with you, Quinton. I don't trust your Vice Admiral as far as I can throw him. And it'd take an Olympic weightlifter just to budge him."

Forrester chuckled. He shared Neely's sentiments about the Vice Admiral on Luna. In fact, it was Forrester who'd banished the fool to Luna in the first place. Now he was regretting it. "I was trying to say that the Master forgets he's dealing with humans on Luna. Mortal behavior can be somewhat perplexing to the gods."

"The gods my foot! Just between you and me," Neely said, stopping suddenly and drawing the Admiral's ear to his mouth. "I channeled again last night."

"We have to keep moving, Bill. And, besides, you know he can hear everything. Our whispers. Maybe even our thoughts!"

"What do *I* care if he hears? I'll be on a shuttle to Titan in seven days. Listen to me. I contacted my spirit guide in the hotel room and—"

"The President's strictly forbidden that!"

"I know. And I think I know why, too. *He* appeared instead. It's the third time he's come to me."

"Your old pal? Attalose?"

"Attal*us*. Attalus the Third. *Pontifex Maximus*, the Chief Bridge Builder. The supreme head of the Babylonian cult in Pergamus—the one who assassinated the Jew-loving Church leaders and turned the headship of Christendom over to the mystery cults of Rome in 133 C.E."

"I know my history, Bill. Attalus had his followers infiltrate the Church under the banner of Nicolatianism. They substituted Babylonian cultism for Christianity's original Hebraic religion. A brilliant coup."

Seeing Neely glance at him with renewed respect, Forrester sighed. "I haven't maintained my rank of Admiral by forgetting the catechism I learned at Annapolis: 'The plan," he recited, "'was carried out in various stages, throughout the first five centuries of the Common Era. The first was the expulsion of Jews and Judaism from the Christian faith. They effectively utilized the Sabbath-day dispute for that purpose'—always a sore spot. 'The second was the fusing of Catholicism with the Greek and Babylonian mystery-cults. The first stage began at Pergamus under the influence of your Attalus III. The Nicolatian infiltrators, under his authority, eliminated all of the Jew-lovers in the Gentile Church.' *Nico laity*, of course, means power over the laity or uninitiated. 'Their coup actually began with the ten-year campaign at Smyrna, when the Messianic Jews were imprisoned and Nicolatian rule was solidified under Attalus, who maintained the ancient Babylonian title of *pontiff*. Smyrna became the "Synagogue of Satan," ruled and dominated by the mystery-cults of antiquity.' The New Testament makes mention of these activities, I believe, in Revelation chapter two, verses five through eleven. I'll refrain from quoting this passage, if you don't mind, Bill. It was part of the Rites, but the Master recently outlawed any recitation of Scripture. By the way, the term 'synagogue' in the passage was deliberately mistranslated by Christian scholars. 'Synagogue' in Greek means simply a gathering; neither a Jewish gathering nor a Christian one. It should simply read 'Congregation of Satan', but 'synagogue' makes it sound like the Jews were the perpetrators of the coup, rather than its victims."

"I'm impressed! Go on."

"Don't you think we ought to make haste for the Oval Office?"

"In a moment. Please continue."

"Bill, is this some kind of loyalty test?"

"No, of course not! I'm impressed by your knowledge of the Rites, Quinton, that's all. I don't come across too many officers who take them seriously enough to remember them."

"Well, I did—at the time, anyway." Forrester's pride had been appealed to. There'd be no stopping him now. "'When the Babylonian revolution spread to the Pergamus church, the question arose whether it might not be prudent to sever Christianity from Judaism altogether, to simply tie it in to the mystery-cults rather than the Hebrew *T'nach*. But Pergamus wasn't known as 'Satan's Seat' for nothing. The subtlety of Lucifer saved the day. Catholicism overtly maintained its roots in Hebraic Messianism by holding onto the Old Testament. But, covertly, it was pure mystery cult.

"'Clement of Alexandria waged an unsuccessful battle against this masterful perversion of Christendom, but he failed.

The worship of Dionysus was transformed into the worship of Mary. The Medieval depiction of Mary's ascension into heaven—and her supposed coronation by Christ—were merely transpositions of the Diana/Zeus cult of Greece, which was a transformation of the Isis/Osirus cult of Egypt, which in turn was a transformation of the Semiramis/Nimrod cult of Babylon. So the mystery cults of antiquity survive today in Christian disguise. Mystery Babylon.'"

"The original Christians were wiped out?" Neely prodded. "Those who, like the Apostles, continued to observe Mosaic Law?"

Forrester realized, with an inward groan, that the general wanted more.

"Yes. 'It was obvious that any close ties or associations with Judaism would expose the conspiracy to attack by rabbinic scholars, who'd certainly see it for what it was. It became necessary to remove both the Jews and their sympathizers from Christendom entirely, to demonize them if possible. Not an easy job, considering the fact that all the Apostles had been Jews, that the whole New Testament—with the possible exception of Luke and Acts—was written by Jews.

"'The Jerusalem brethren, who'd always maintained a strong Jewish tradition, were forced to capitulate during the reign of Hadrian. They were seduced into electing the Gentile bishop, Marcus, to rule over them. He demanded that they relinquish the Law of Moses in order to appease the Nicolatians. Many did. Those who persisted in the Jewish customs were marked by the epithet "Ebionites"—poor ones—and eventually banished from the Church, a remarkable and swift denial of Christianity's Hebraic roots. Even among mainstream Protestants of today, the term 'Ebionites' is used against Messianic Jews whose Hebrew orthodoxy would have been applauded by the Apostles, Paul included.

"'Once the first century Christians were cut off from the Hebrew roots of their religion, it was an easy matter to subvert all of Christendom to the mystery cults. All that remained, really, was to create the anti-Semitic propaganda that kept European Jewry in perpetual misery. Although Christ himself was a Jew, if the Jews could be characterized as Christ-killers and enemies of the Church, their knowledge of the perversion of Christian doctrine would never come to light.'

"The original form of Christianity still hasn't returned, even after more than five hundred years of Protestantism. Messianic Judaism exists, yes, but only in Israel, among the Jews who've escaped the Master's little Holocaust. The Protestants have continued many of the rites of Catholicism; they celebrate Christ's resurrection with obvious fertility symbols—rabbits and eggs—and they call it Easter, after the pagan goddess Ishtar. Constantine outlawed the Christian version of Passover, once called the *paskah*, in a declaration at the Council of Nicea dripping with anti-Semitic rhetoric. He called the Jews an 'odious rabble!'"

"Yes, I've read it. Go on."

"Okay, another example: Christians persist in celebrating Christ's birthday on December 25th, the actual birthdate of the pagan god Mithras. As a body, they've accepted these feasts as their own without hesitation."

"That's where I get confused, Quinton."

"How so?"

"Well, if a particular Christian celebrates Easter and Christmas in honor of Christ, rather than the pagan deities—and if such rites only serve to solidify his faith in Christ—how can we consider him compromised?"

"That's the ingenious part, Bill. From the very start, Israel's G-d has stubbornly judged the nations by their treatment of His chosen people. By substituting pagan feasts for Jewish ones, we've convinced our Christian friends that Judaism is a foreign faith, rather than the very fountainhead of Christianity. Or, at best, a primitive throwback to grace-killing legalism. The Catholic crusaders and the Spanish inquisitors displayed their anti-Jewishness for all to see. The masses were encouraged to eat a wafer for salvation, bowing down to it as it was carried through the streets in a silver monstrance, worshipping it as the actual body of Christ—while hacking Jews to pieces left and right and burning them to death in their synagogues. The world's first 'Big Lie.'

"Protestantism fared much worse. Catholicism had its anti-Jewish outbursts and a millennium of murder, but the Protestants have anti-Semitism—which is much better. Back in 1543, Martin Luther, the father of Protestantism, wrote a tract entitled 'On the Jews and their Lies.' He advised his followers to treat Jews like dogs. The Holocaust in Luther's own Protestant Germany saw his advice being followed quite literally. Actually, German dogs were treated far better than Jews.

"The only exceptions are the evangelical Christians, Bible-believing or born-again Christians. Many of them have come to recognize the validity of orthodox Messianic Judaism, and many support Israel. Christian Zionists are even helping Jews escape the President's recent 'detainment' edict. But we're taking care of *them* as well. Shipping them off with their Jew friends to Malheur Relocation Center in Oregon. And good riddance! Their ashes will help the forests grow. Now let's get going, Bill, before we're both in deep trouble."

"Of course. The President convened that holoconference with the Arabs as soon as he returned from Jerusalem. He was shut up with the Arabs from four A.M. until an hour or so ago."

"All the more reason to stop dawdling and see what he wants."

"I'm sorry for delaying you, Quinton. Please don't mention this little talk to anyone."

"These are troubling times, Bill. We all need reassurance now and then."

They began moving toward the Oval Office.

"But—I can't help feeling," whispered General Neely, "that something's about to go dreadfully wrong."

The Beast

The President stood up to greet them, his rangy figure silhouetted by a great curved window overlooking the tropical gardens. The view was framed by two flags: the blue-and-white unicorn flag of the Party for World Peace, and the Stars and Stripes. As the two men drew nearer they noticed the dark, brooding features. Forrester saw what looked like a knife-wound across Coffey's throat, just above the Adam's apple. Had someone tried to assassinate the President?

"Thank you for coming, Gentlemen. We have a dire emergency on our hands, and I must request—no, demand—that nothing said in this room be repeated."

"Sir," said Forrester, reddening, "you can trust us implicitly."

"Of course, of course. Forgive me, but I'm beside myself with worry. Marla Steinman, my bride to be—was on her way back from this ill-conceived Caribbean vacation arranged by Carl DePalma. The man's gone quite insane; I don't know why I trusted him."

Forrester was stunned. *With everything going on in the world, can this "dire emergency" concern one of the President's gopi girls?*

"All that aside," the President continued, "she was visiting her brother, Benjamin, the dolphin researcher. Apparently something went terribly wrong. She cut her vacation short and was hurrying back to Washington, when—well, I don't know exactly *what* happened. According to her own statement she killed the pilot of the shuttle-plane the moment they landed in New Miami."

"She—*killed* him?"

"Yes. And quite brutally, I understand. She claimed he was an Israeli spy; that he was trying to gain access to the White House. But it gets worse! While she was searching for a vidphone booth to make contact with Washington, she was waylaid by another Mossad agent who took her to his hotel room and attempted to interrogate her about the fate of his compatriot. She apparently killed him, too."

Forrester and Neely opened their mouths simultaneously, but nothing came out. The President continued: "She used the phone in his hotel room to contact me. The call was routed to one of our Secret Service agents, Sibley Dannon. Marla told Agent Dannon that she'd killed two Israeli spies and that she had information about a mole on the White House staff. Agent Dannon selected a cleanup crew to dispose of the body and took off immediately to bring Marla home. She hasn't returned. A half-hour ago the cleanup-crew reported in. They said Marla went berserk, grabbed Agent Dannon's gun, locked them up in the bathroom, kidnapped Dannon and made off in her hovercar. Where they may have gone we've no idea. But I want you both here with me for the next few hours. If we can get a fix on that car, we may need to scramble some raptors and go after them. Order them down."

"What if Marla refuses to land when they order her to?" Forrester asked.

"Then they'll have to shoot her down, won't they?" said the President.

Forrester shook his head. "Did you just say 'shoot her

down'?"

"General Neely," said the President. "You're dismissed. Quinton, stay awhile, would you?"

"Of course, Mr. President."

Forrester heard Neely beating a grateful retreat behind him.

"There are other problems, Quinton," Coffey continued when they were alone. "Problems in space—on Luna in particular."

"Mr. President," said Forrester, launching into his rehearsed defense. "We're dealing with humans on Luna—"

"We're dealing with a conspiracy of shameless capitalists! They study Ayn Rand as if her books dropped down from heaven! We should have destroyed them all!"

"We tried, sir," said Neely.

"And then there's the Christian-Zionist problem."

"The most troublesome are being dealt with, sir."

"Yes, Quinton, thanks to my extermination camps. But we both know that not all of them have given up their loyalty to Israel. The Jew-lovers among them follow an evangelist by the name of Paul Jason Moscowitz, a despicable Russian Jew and an old friend of the Israeli Prime Minister. They call him 'Brother Paul." I want his head on a charger, Quinton. I want to mount it on a spike on top of the Wailing Wall for everyone to see. Are you aware of his popularity?"

"That appeal is dwindling, sir. His telecast was taken off the air and he's fled into space."

"Listen to me, Quinton. We must show the Jews how to find peace. We must help them level the terrible *karma* hanging over them. They've always been hated, driven from place to place. But we must assist them into the peace of oblivion. All of them. Once and for all."

"We've been assisting them all we can, sir."

"Then why, may I ask, have you allowed that turncoat Jew radio broadcaster, Jeri Kline, to escape? We were keeping him alive to discredit the Christian Bible, to spread his atheism. He was of more use to us suffering under his miserable Jewish *karma* than in the arms of peace. But then something happened, didn't it? He suddenly embraced Jesus Christ and disappeared! You let him slip away!"

"I was just informed of this last week, Mr. President—that Jeri Kline joined a Christian cell and is now working against us.

But I couldn't possibly have predicted it. He despised the Christians, especially Moscowitz. He considered him a traitor to Judaism."

"He must be found, this Jeri Kline," said the President of the United States. "And he must be gassed, along with Paul Moscowitz. Is all of this clear to you?"

"Quite clear, sir."

"Then don't disappoint me, Quinton, or I'll have you gassed as well."

The Peace Guard

In keeping with the punctuality that ruled his life, Giles Hadley entered his apartment at precisely six P.M., stepping across the lush carpeting to the food alcove. His wife, Lisa, no less predictable than Giles himself, was engrossed in her nightly meditation seminar on the holovision—which accounted for his hushed entrance every evening—her face lit by the flickering glow of the wallscreen. Rather than using vocal instructions to activate the food-unit, he tapped them in manually so as not to disturb Lisa. He sat wearily in his chair and watched the kitchen table unfold like a lotus blossom before him, waiting for the unit to prepare his frozen meal. He'd grown to despise the tranquil voice that greeted his arrival every night from the holoscreen. He'd always tried to ignore it while dinner was preparing, but, as usual, he didn't succeed.

"As you know," said the instructor in a voice suited to telling fairytales to children, "Lord Maitreya, our President and beloved world leader, has issued a warning regarding inner-channeling this month. Certain cosmic disturbances require us to forgo our regular visit from Doctor Lurian. And I would remind you that any attempt to contact your spirit-guide during this astrological period, *Lisa*, will surely result in disruption of mental control. I don't have to add that it would also be displeasing to our beloved Ascendant Master."

Hadley, though himself a tenured professor of biotec and computer science, still couldn't resist a childlike sense of astonishment at the way each holoscreen personalized the programs for its user. Not so much by including the viewer's first name, as it had just done—no magic to that, it was simply a matter of reading it off her bluecard—but by incorporating the viewer's behavioral traits into its presentation.

Bluecards were temporary substitutes for the mark of the new regime that was placed either on the wrist or the forehead. The mark was an indelible tattoo indicating the location of a powerful identity chip, a chip with a fifty-gigabyte memory. On it was recorded far more than mere names and birthdates. A homing device revealed the citizen's location at all times. Up-to-the-minute bank balances and credit ratings enabled him to purchase everything he needed by simply placing his wrist, or forehead, against a scanner plate.

Since there were some who, for one reason or another, were not ready to take the mark, the government had provided an interim solution, one that would enable them to buy and sell—at least temporarily. The bluecard.

Unlike the chip, the bluecard contained holograms and voiceprints of the bearer, making it impossible for unauthorized persons to use it. It also contained a personality profile. When read by the wallscreen it enabled the story-characters to involve each viewer in a program in a uniquely personal way. In Lisa's case, the card had informed her wallscreen of a tendency toward unrealistic expectations and immaturity. Lisa, the card revealed, required frequent explanations whenever she was confronted by change. And the pleasant face on the screen was now providing them.

"I know you're obedient, *Lisa*," the holoscreen intimated, "and that you don't need this warning." (*Fiddlesticks!* thought Hadley. *If she didn't need it, you wouldn't be giving it!*) "But please believe me when I tell you that we've had cases of severe mental breakdowns resulting from reckless behavior in this area. The psychic resonances are in a state of profound disturbance. I can't emphasize enough the dangers of channeling at this time, and the need for restraint on your part, *Lisa*. Do you understand this injunction?"

"Yes," said Lisa. "Of course I understand."

"Good," said the holoscreen. "I wouldn't want you to be frightened, *Lisa*, or hurt in any way. We've become such good friends, you and I."

"Yes," said Lisa, "we have."

"There are those, I know, who've become psychologically dependant on their spirit guides. That's a natural and very understandable thing. The best way to avoid the discomfort of sudden weaning from our guides' companionship is to enter into basic instruction once again—to start with our *chakra* exercises, like we did as children. No one is so advanced in meditation techniques that they can't do with a review of the basics. And these elementary exercises will, eventually, result in our reunion with our guides. So cheer up, put a smile on your face, and breathe deeply. It will please the Master to know you're happy. You *are* happy, *Lisa*, aren't you?"

"Yes," said Lisa. "Very happy."

"Fine." There was a pause as the screen shifted its mental gears. "The Master thanks you for the secret you shared with us tonight, *Lisa*. It must have been difficult for you to hold it back for so long. And I promise you that once the initial pain of loss is over, you'll be at peace about it. Do you believe me?"

"I hope so. I mean, yes."

Hadley wondered what Lisa's secret had been, but dismissed it as more inner-healing nonsense. The food-unit chimed. He crossed the alcove and slid open the plastic shield in the face of the unit, withdrawing a steaming tray of TVP-loaf and carrying it back to the table. The soothing voice was drawing the seminar to a close.

"Until tomorrow night, *Lisa*, I leave you in the Heart of Lord Maitreya, who loves us all so very, very much. Don't forget his great words: 'We live for the vision of World Peace in our Global Village. We gladly sacrifice our minds and our collective will for our beloved Mother Gaia, who gave us birth.' May you live always, *Lisa*, in peace and safety. Goodnight."

Hadley imagined the image of the instructor extending both hands toward the screen, wrists crossed, palms held forward in the international sign for peace and brotherhood. And he imagined Lisa returning the gesture. He heard his wife whisper "Good night", almost lovingly, to the holoscreen. The music of sitar and tabla faded as she appeared in the doorway of the alcove.

"Hello," she said.

"Hello, darling." Hadley speared a forkfull of TVP and stuck it between his teeth, chewing slowly, thoughtfully. Glancing up at his wife, he noticed that she wasn't seating herself across the table, as was her usual habit, but remained standing in the alcove's arch, watching him.

Their relationship had been seriously strained for some time, ever since she'd discovered that he was a member of a Christian cell-group. Returning early from a shopping trip one afternoon, she'd found Hadley and two others: the mayor of Phoenix-Mesa, Sam Browne; and the famous radio broadcaster, Jeri Kline—*praying!* She couldn't believe her eyes! Wasn't Kline an atheist? And the mayor! The three of them had Bibles in their laps. They appeared to be concluding what had obviously been a prayer meeting. The volume was turned low on the wallscreen, but the familiar face of "Brother Paul" floated before them in three-dimensional realism, eyes closed in prayer.

That was back in the days when his weekly program, *New Heaven, New Earth*, was still being broadcast from the high-tech Zion Temple in Flagstaff—before the peace guards burned it to the ground. Hadley was inclined to admit, however, that Lisa had taken the shock in stride. She hadn't badgered him about it. But she *had* insisted that he stop watching Paul's program—which he did—and that he toss his Bible down the disposal chute—which he did *not.* He'd merely hidden it. It was her hope that without Paul's program to feed on, Hadley would eventually be released from its spell. But after six months of waiting, she'd finally given up. And with good reason.

A friend who worked on Hadley's staff at the Multiversity of Phoenix-Mesa inadvertently revealed that the professor always left his office promptly at four o'clock. Lisa knew how tediously punctual and regular he was, so she'd worked it out: It only took ten minutes by monorail to get home, which left two whole hours unaccounted for. Further investigation proved that Hadley was still attending illegal daily Bible studies. A Christian cell group, with her husband as a member! And the mayor too! And Jeri Kline! It was more than she could bear. She considered turning him in to the authorities, but suddenly the Zion Temple was gone, the pirate stations that had beamed Paul's broadcasts were raided and closed down, and the cell-groups were disbanded. All would be well, now, she reassured herself. Her wayward husband would come to his senses.

Then came the mysterious disappearance of the Christians.

Holovision newscasts reported that they were evacuating all the major American cities and converging on Phoenix Mesa, under the protection of Mayor Browne. A later report said that they'd departed Phoenix Mesa and were crossing the unprotected desert wastelands on some fanatic mission no one understood. But, wherever they'd gone and for whatever twisted purpose, Giles had not chosen to join them. He'd remained in Phoenix-Mesa with Lisa. She interpreted this as the salvation of their marriage and became suddenly affectionate.

Until recently, that is—until Giles reverted again to his late arrivals. That, she realized with horror, could mean only one thing.

Her interest in any and all information regarding Brother Paul's teachings had made her something of an expert. She knew that the cells had been disbanded, and that the entire congregation had embarked on a dangerous exodus across the Arizona wastelands. She was even aware that military bombing raids were being planned against the fugitives, but that the government had been given false information about their location. (The "pilgrims", as they called themselves, wore black and traveled only at night.) But they'd be found, eventually. Either by infrared imaging, or when they ran out of provisions and had to purchase them in one of the unprotected city-states dotting the northern Arizona desert.

Yet none of this concerned her nearly as much as the information she'd received that a few of the Phoenix-Mesa Christians had *not* been called out of the city when the cells were disbanded—*the pastors!* Giles had not merely been a *member* of the illegal cell, he'd been its *leader!* Brother Paul had requested that the pastors remain behind, that they sacrifice their lives if need be, to assist latecomers to the faith. So her husband was not only an outlawed Christian, but a remarkably fanatical one—so dedicated to his perverted cause that he willingly risked death for it.

In short, he was a very dangerous man.

And yet she still loved him. She confronted him with her knowledge, begged him to abandon his uncivilized, extremist beliefs. In response to her tearful pleas, he'd taken her trembling shoulders in his hands, smiled warmly, and promised to pray for her soul. She'd hated that most of all!

Thinking back on these events, Hadley decided that things had leveled off, that they'd achieved a state of mutual acceptance. (*Shalom ba'bayit*, Brother Paul called it—peace in the house.) Hadley knew she loved him, and that she'd resisted turning him in to the Peace Guard as long as he kept quiet about his faith, as long as he didn't watch Paul's broadcast or read his Bible in front of her, as long as there was hope that he'd eventually acknowledge the error of his ways.

Meanwhile he continued to accept more and more dangerous assignments, all of them vital to the persecuted Church. He began making contact with a young courier sent from Brother Paul. They called him the "newsboy." The lad, Jimmy Sanders, carried a copy of the Phoenix-Mesa Sun to Paul's hideaway every day, along with the televangelist's secret communications. Likewise, if Hadley had anything to communicate to Paul, he sent it via the boy. Young Sanders wouldn't reveal Paul's whereabouts, of course, but Giles assumed he must be hiding somewhere close to the city—since the boy had no transportation. He delivered his news on foot.

All the boy required of Hadley was a fresh copy of the *Phoenix Mesa Sun*. That was before the exodus into the wastelands, during the period when Charles Coffey was consolidating his power base and preparing for his military takeover of the United States government. Hadley found himself wishing he'd delivered one particular edition himself, however. He wondered what Paul's reaction had been to the headline that read:

CHARLES COFFEY IN CONTROL OF U.S. GOVERNMENT—DECLARES MARTIAL LAW.

Shortly after he'd handed that edition to Paul's newsboy the secret cells were suddenly disbanded and the exodus began.

Obviously Brother Paul was taking no chances with the PWP.

There'd been many more assignments since then, increasingly more dangerous: bringing the Gospel to those whose hearts were still open to the Truth, providing shelter and food for those who'd received Christ, risking detection with every passing day. The sad news reached him that the last Messianic rabbi in America, Isaac Kellerman, along with his devoted wife, Sarah, had been arrested and shipped off to Malheur Relocation Center in Oregon. Time was growing short; evangelistic efforts were stepped up. Meanwhile, Hadley continued to bank on Lisa's devotion—and on her silence.

But now, watching her standing stiffly in the archway, her features working with some repressed fear or guilt, he realized with a shock that he had dangerously miscalculated. He now knew the "painful secret" she'd revealed to the wallscreen just before he'd come home.

Lisa had turned her husband in to the Peace Guard.

Hadley lifted his tray and stood, carrying it into the living room and taking a seat by the UV screen overlooking the city skyline. He dropped the tray onto his lap, no 1onger hungry. Beneath him plunged the canyons of skyscraper apartment buildings lit by the firefly-flickering of hovercars darting in and out of above-ground parking hives. Farther below he could see the lush, tropical vegetation at ground level, almost lost to view in the gathering dusk. He'd been born in Phoenix Mesa; he'd never known any other way of life but this. As a plum-colored dusk fell over the city he watched the glittering stars appear one by one. He loved this place. He would never leave it; that much he'd always known. Even when it was about to destroy him he couldn't run from it. He wouldn't even protest. And for this he must repent. Before he breathed his last he must repent of his love for this technological Babylon, pray that G-d would forgive him. He thought of his students at the Multiversity, of the lectures on biotech he'd never deliver.

"G-d forgive me!" he whispered. "Forgive me for loving it all."

He heard Lisa cross the room to stand behind him, smelled her sweet perfume in the air, the fragrance he'd always associated with love and acceptance. It turned bitter in his nostrils. She didn't speak. What for? They both knew what she'd done. Besides, even if she changed her mind now, it wouldn't matter. It was out of her hands. No, this wasn't the time for wasted recriminations. Lisa had done what she believed to be right. It was time to be silent, to rest together in the last few minutes of their union—to remember how it had been. He heard a stifled sob, felt a hot teardrop touch the back of his neck. He couldn't hate the woman who'd killed him. What good would hatred do him now? He felt only pity for her. "And forgive Lisa, too," he prayed.

The peace guards burst into the apartment some time later—how much later, he couldn't tell—using a master entry-card in the door slot. He heard them cross the living room, felt Lisa draw away. The dinner tray still rested in his lap, its contents cold, forgotten. Judging by the sounds there were three of them standing behind his chair. He straightened his shoulders and kept his eyes fixed on the city skyline. The city he loved.

"Yes?" he said. "What can I do for you?"

"Professor Giles Hadley?" said a female voice. With a twist in his gut he recognized it as the voice from the holovision, the voice of Lisa's instructor. He detected no hint of its usual soothing manner. It was a bureaucrat's monotone, cold, emotionless, dead.

"That's correct," he replied. "I am he."

"Professor—you've been accused of treasonous crimes against the government of the United States."

"The dictatorship of Charles Coffey, you mean?"

"Against the government of the United States," the voice repeated calmly. "That accusation having been duly investigated, we find you guilty and sentence you to death. It will be painless. Do you understand?"

"Yes," he told the voice, repeating what he'd heard Lisa tell it so many times before. "I understand."

"You have a right to the identity of your accuser before the sentence is carried out."

"That won't be necessary," he said. "I know the identity of my accuser. Please carry out your sentence, and may G-d forgive you for it."

"Very well."

There came a sharp hiss, like the lunge of a serpent, followed by Lisa's moaning cry and the soft smack of a poison dart as it tore through his shirt and lodged in his spine. He felt the numbing effect of its paralytic venom. The woman was right; it *was* painless.

Hadley lurched forward, the contents of the tray spilling over the carpet. He gripped the arms of the chair in an effort to remain erect, but the world was slipping away. His hands refused to obey. His flesh turned cold.

But what was this? Warm hands taking his? Lisa? No…a tall figure…a gentle voice… As he fell forward into the abyss of darkness, the warm hands drew him up…away.

The empty corpse of Professor Giles Hadley struck the floor with a soft thud. He didn't feel it hit the floor, nor did he hear Lisa's pitiful sobs as she gazed down at his remains, a broken doll splayed out over the uneaten remnants of his frozen dinner. He knew nothing else of the world he'd departed: of the phony obituary announcing his death; of the funeral attended only by Lisa and her instructor; or of Lisa's quiet suicide, a few months later, an event that received only a brief comment in the Phoenix-Mesa Sun.

He knew nothing of any of it.

And that was good.

Very good...

The Calling

Paul Jason Moscowitz sat back in his contour chair, adjusted the folds of his *tallit*, and looked over what he'd written in his palm-com:

א

We see, by combining the predictions of Rabban Sha'ul (the Apostle Paul) and Yeshua (Jesus)—Romans 11:25 and Luke 21:24—that there was indeed reason to believe that 1967, the year Jerusalem returned to Israeli hands, was also the year the "Times of the Gentiles" came to an end. According to Sha'ul the Jews' partial blindness to Yeshua's Messiahship would then be lifted from their eyes.

Although Yeshua did refer to Jerusalem in his prophecy, the "treading down" of that city was only significant as it related to the Temple, *HaShem's* earthly dwelling-place. But since the Temple Mount was still being "trodden down by the Gentiles"—until 2065, when the Dome of the Rock was obliterated and the Third Temple was moved to its proper place—the Times of the Gentiles could not be said to have fully ended.

1967 was, as it were, the *beginning* of the end. And there is certainly compelling evidence that it was indeed the year when the blindness began to be lifted.

This was the year of the "Summer of Love", when hippies (thousands of them Jewish) were being reached in unprecedented numbers by what they called "Jesus Freaks" in Haight Ashbury. The newly born-again Jewish believers eventually formed an organization (under the auspices of the Christian Church) known as Jews For Jesus. Its founder was a man by the name of Moshe Rosen.

From these primitive beginnings in Haight Ashbury, Jewish revival spread with astonishing speed. Christians were pointing to these young people of Jewish birth and upbringing, rejoicing that *Hashem* was keeping His promise to His people. They were *not* pointing to each other and saying, "Look at *us!* We're the lost tribes of Israel coming back to G-d!" They were pointing to the *Jews.*

This was a *Jewish* revival. Why did so many non-Jews want to steal it from the chosen people and keep it for themselves? How could they possibly believe that, if they *did* steal it away from those for whom G-d intended it, anything good would remain when they were done? Did they think they could steal a revival intended for others and be blessed by it?

ב

Let us begin in this chapter to trace the development of the Messianic synagogual movement from that "lifting of the blindness" in 1967, to 2020, when the synagogues suddenly disintegrated into thousands of scattered home fellowships called *havurot*—the rise of the *K'hillat HaDerech* (the Community of "The Way").

In Philadelphia, very early on, a couple who'd accepted Yeshua in the sixties and had maintained their vibrant Jewish lifestyle—Joe and Debbie Finkelstein—founded a seminal home Bible study that became a magnet for Jewish hippies, earning it the sobriquet "Fink's Zoo" for the wild-looking longhaired youths who frequently attended it. The "Zoo" represented a desire on the part of young Jewish believers to move away from the "churchiness" of Jews For Jesus and closer to traditional Judaism. (One of the major voices of what came to be called TEMJP—the emerging Messianic Jewish paradigm—was Dr. Stuart Dauermann, former composer and arranger for Liberated Wailing Wall, the music ministry of Jews For Jesus.)

Among the teenage members of the Hebrew Christian Alliance of America's youth organization (the YHCA) there was a discernable move toward a deeper Jewish experience. A man named Martin Chernoff was the inspiration for this move. His three children, Hope, David and Joel (singer-songwriter of a duo called Lamb), were drawn into the heart of his vision.

A powerful impetus of the Spirit suddenly descended upon the youth of the HCAA in the year 1970, during their youth conference. A new style of praise and worship was spontaneously taken up by the young Hebrew Christian longhairs gathered there. Typical of the sixties generation, these youths eschewed the old manner of worship. They rejected Christian hymns and began creating a folk-style Messianic "hymnal" of their own, composed primarily for guitars and vocals. This was not music the older generation could appreciate, and a rift was created between the generations. G-d had his fan in His hand; He was separating the wheat from the chaff. Those who were not prepared to be carried forward would become increasingly irrelevant as the Alliance approached the 21st century.

Backed by Martin Chernoff, the YHCA took up the banner. These youngsters, along with alumni of "Fink's Zoo" and Jews for Jesus, eventually formed the intellectual and spiritual nucleus of the synagogual movement

In 1973, the Biennial Conference of the Hebrew Christian Alliance of America would hear a controversial proposal by Martin Chernoff to change its name (and hence its direction) to the Messianic Jewish Alliance of America. The election of Chernoff that year to president of the HCCA paved the way for change. (In 1970, while praying, Martin claimed to have seen a vision of the words "Messianic Judaism" written across the sky. But this new name would not be accepted by the Alliance until 1975.)

Messianic Judaism was moving into a *new* phase—that of Torah observance. Sadly, as often happens in spiritual awakenings, the innovators of previous decades—who, in this case, were primarily Charismatic—lagged behind. The entire idea of organized liturgy, of praying from *siddurim* (prayer books), ran against the grain of the "uninhibited" worship that had characterized the Charismatic renewal of the '60s and '70s.

Some who rejected this Torah-positive direction became propagandists against it. One of their most common objections was that the Messianic synagogues were becoming "so sensitive about offending Jews that they were forgetting their primary purpose—to preach the Gospel." (This allegation was, of course, absurd. The drive to make Messianic synagogues more comfortable for Jews was, in fact, making them *more effective* in reaching Jews with the Gospel. Statistically, over the centuries, the Church had proven a miserable failure in this regard. Persecutions, crusades, ghettoization, inquisitions, and finally the Holocaust in Protestant Germany had turned Jewish hearts away from the Yeshua by the millions.) Those who desired a more "churchy" form of Messianism were unwittingly helping the Enemy prevent the synagogual movement from creating a Jewish-friendly environment for the preaching of the Gospel.

It should be noted at this point that, while a Jewish-friendly environment was a positive side effect of the Torah revival, it was not the primary motivation of its core membership. These Messianic Jews were not keeping Torah to reach other Jews with *haB'sorah*, but because it is biblically correct—"New Testament" correct—for Jewish believers in Yeshua to do so. Messianic hermeneutics emerging every year in those decades of growth were demonstrating, beyond a doubt, that the Apostles—Rabban Sha'ul, Shimon Kefa (Peter), Ya'acov (James), and the others—had maintained strict Jewish observance *after* accepting Yeshua the Messiah. (See Appendix II for articles).

Eventually—in an effort to capitalize on the popularity of Messianic Judaism, and to muddy the terminology—every Hebrew-oriented congregation was calling itself "Messianic". Within a single decade the term had pejorated to where, in most people's minds, a Messianic Jew was any Jewish person who believed in "Jesus", whether he attended a church and never wore a *yarmelkeh* or opened a *siddur*, or whether he was Orthodox in his worship. Meanwhile, Charismatic Christians were joining the movement in droves, arguing vociferously against such issues as *kashrut* (kosher laws) and especially *Hilchot Niddah* (ritual purity laws). They wanted to keep the movement a *church*, where speaking in tongues and being "slain in the spirit" were more common than *t'fillin* (phylacteries.)

But at the turn of the 21st century Messianic Judaism could ill afford to remain "uninhibited" in its worship, to be open to every spiritual wind. Demonic deceptions such as the Toronto Vineyard "blessing"—which had infiltrated Charismatic churches through their laxity toward Scripture, their emphasis on experience over instruction—were now, thanks to its large Charismatic membership, infiltrating Messianic Judaism as well.

For many Jews, the Torah revival in Messianic Judaism became an island of sanity in a hurricane of false doctrinal winds blowing through the Body of Messiah. It was through obedience to Torah that Messianic Jews were wearing *tzitziot* so that "ten Gentiles" might take hold of them and say, "We will go with you, for we hear that G-d is with you." (Zech. 8:23: the word translated "skirt" in the King James Version is *kanaf,* the corner of a garment from which the *tzitziot* or fringes descended; Numbers 15:38. Grasping hold of a rabbi's *tzitziot* for a blessing was common in Israel. See Matt. 14:36.) According to this prophecy Messianic Jews must be dynamic enough to attract Gentiles to follow them to G-d. (In other words, they must be believers in Yeshua who demonstrate the power of the *Ruach* in their daily lives.) But they *also* need to be Torah observant—otherwise why would they be wearing *tzitziot*? And, thirdly, they must be **Jews**—not Gentiles pretending to be Jews, not Christians playing "Jewish dress-up." (After all, it's the Gentiles in this prophecy who are seeking them out.)

Ultimately, these Charismatic Christian members would succeed in destroying the Messianic synagogual movement and scattering believing Jews to the winds.

That is, until the emergence of Rabbi Isaac Kellerman, America's last Messianic rabbi, who regathered the scattered Jewish believers under an effective *Bet Din*, codifying the various halachic determinations of that *Bet Din* in his famous book *Messianic Doctrines.* Rabbi Kellerman was arrested by the PWP, and it is believed that he perished in the Malheur Relocation Center in Oregon. At the time of this writing, however, there has been no confirmation of the rumors of gas-chambers and crematoria in use at Malheur, though history will write the final word on that.

It was just a few days before Paul's encounter with the intruder in the simuchamber, and he'd been using the quiet weeks between planets to complete the final chapters of what he privately considered to be his *magnum opus*: a five-volume history of Messianic Judaism covering two centuries, from 1888 to 2020. This final volume documented the rise of Messianism to a worldwide movement of considerable influence at the turn of the 21st century, followed by the "Two House" apostasy brought in by its Gentile members, and the consequent submergence of the movement. Jewish members were scattered, either to local churches or Hassidic congregations. Some of them renounced Yeshua. Others began meeting from house to house, as in Bible times, continuing to study Torah in the light of Yeshua's teachings. There'd be a brief revival of Messianic Judaism under the great Rabbi Isaac Kellerman—founder of the IMJBD (the International Messianic Jewish *Bet Din*) and author of *Messianic Doctrines*—but his sudden arrest would signal the end of that revival in the United States.

Brother Paul had been born in 2031. His childhood years had seen the GR (the Great Reconstruction), when the advent of hovercars made ground-cars obsolete. City populations were lifted upward into skyscraping habitats, instead of outward into urban sprawl. Asphalt streets were ripped up, to be replaced by sylvan parks, public gardens, and quiet walkways. It was a time of noise, dust, and confusion.

As a teenager Paul witnessed the New Age movement beginning its "peaceful" ascent to power. He was caught between two equally senseless forms of racism: the anti-Semitism of the New Agers, and the loathing of Gentiles it inspired in his own people. At the age of ten he'd seen a mysterious vision of *HaShem* while playing in an abandoned building. But that vision was almost forgotten as he grew to young adulthood. Only the acts of nihilism he waged against society were capable of moving him. But when he was moved, he was eloquent. He possessed an extraordinary gift of speech, an ability to sway huge crowds with words and gestures. A fire burned within him. And whenever he rose to speak, that fire consumed all who listened.

As a raging young Zionist, constantly inebriated with whisky, brilliant, articulate to the point of being finicky about his grammar, possessed of a peculiar magnetism, Paul alienated most of his friends, lost a pretty wife named Rachel in an ugly divorce, and finally found himself surrounded by a small band of sycophants, Jewish thugs drawn to his violence and nihilism.

It was during this time in his life that he staggered into a New Trenton tent revival, inebriated and brimming with vitriol. He left, hours later, sober and full of the wine of the Spirit.

He'd been drawn to the tent by the raucous, off-key singing of the faithful, thinking they'd make good sport for him. But when he lurched into the canvas-and-sawdust chapel, the hymns had concluded and the sermon begun. All was quiet and reverent within. He'd hoped to be able to join the chorus in songs like "Onward Christian Soldiers"—was that song about the European crusaders who burned Jewish synagogues (with the Jews inside, whenever possible), looted Jewish homes, raped Jewish women and slaughtered their husbands and fathers? He'd wanted to raise his voice in loud denigration of that song, interspersing obscenities with the lyrics, until they asked him to leave. (They never fought, these Christians.) He might be able to get in one or two solid punches at their insipid faces, and that would be reward enough. But the singing had stopped. No "Onward Christian Soldiers" to mock.

Well, what difference did it make? He'd mock it anyway.

And he did.

Clinging to one of the broad tent poles, he shouted at the top of his lungs, cursing congregation and preacher alike. He railed at them in his drunkenness, his speech too slurred to be understood. Then he broke into an obscene rendition of "Onward Christian Soldiers". That got a rise from the ushers, who came to escort him out. He offered them his middle finger in a gesture even Christians could interpret, and was surprised when one of them, a colossal black deacon, lifted a balled fist in reply. The deacon was winding up to send Paul Moscowitz to meet the Devil when the evangelist, A. R. Williams, intervened.

At a word from Williams the ushers returned to their seats, leaving Paul to continue his abuse. Paul should have been delighted, but he was frustrated instead. He began to lash at the preacher with his tongue, pouring out all the obscenity in his heart, rising above the whiskey fog to deliver the most eloquent, verbal assassination of his young life. One particular remark brought the entire congregation to its feet, groaning like a wounded beast. Nobody spoke that way to Brother Williams! Nobody ever had; nobody ever would! But Williams held out his arms for silence, and the flock obediently, albeit reluctantly, sat down.

As for Williams himself, he weathered Paul's storm of blasphemy with his feet firmly planted on the makeshift podium. He was unperturbed, steady, compassionate. Paul hated him all the more for this, and wore his voice hoarse with insults. Still the preacher did not speak. He did not move. He did not allow his congregation to evict Paul, nor did his face display the slightest anger at the raging youth. He absorbed every insult, every blasphemy, as he imagined Christ having done—because this young demon-ravaged soul was one of G-d's chosen people. A

Jew. And it happened that A. R. Williams had a deep abiding compassion for the Jews. Paul Jason Moscowitz had come to the right place at the right time, and Williams was determined not to miss the opportunity. He recognized Paul's long sidecurls, called *payis*, as the style of the young Zionists. The sight filled him with pity. He understood thc rage Paul felt at the persecution of his people, both historic and contemporary. He felt somewhat responsible himself. After all, he reflected, had the Church loved the Jews as much as Christ had, this poor creature wouldn't be filled with revulsion for His followers.

Williams wanted very badly to bring this young man to his Messiah.

Give me this soul tonight, Father! he prayed. *I want to see this young man in Your Kingdom, if You must bend heaven and Earth to accomplish it!*

Begging his congregation's indulgence, Williams fetched a battered leather-bound Bible from his podium, held it aloft, and began to preach a new message. It dripped with blood, billions of gallons of sacrificial blood that the Jewish priests had dashed upon the sacred altar from the days of Moses until 70 C.E., when the armies of Titus destroyed the Second Temple and left not one stone upon another.

Paul was riveted. The tent swirled about him in a seasick mist. He clutched the tent pole with both hands, attending to every word.

"And now," Williams cried, striding across the pulpit with his Bible tucked under his arm, gazing directly at Paul as if the young Zionist were alone with him in the tent. "And now, young man, the Jews have destroyed the Dome of The Rock, that foul shrine of Islam! And they've met the resulting fury of all thirteen Arab Nations with tanks and guns and military might. The Temple Mount Wars, as you called them. Israel has achieved total victory at last—over all Islam! Her borders encompass every inch of the land G-d promised to his servant Abraham."

"Alright!" Paul slurred. "I finally heard something I can say 'amen' to! Total victory!" He cupped his hand around an imaginary wine glass and lifted a cynical toast to the assembly. "And no thanks to you good Christian Soldiers, I might add. Total victory, preacher! What do you think of that?"

"Israel's victory was G-d's will, young man. It's nothing

less than the fulfillment of Divine prophecy—*that's* what I think of it. But to what end did your people wage their war against Islam?"

"Palestine attacked Israel, backed by the rest of the Arab nations. We fought back and we won. That's all there is to it. It's an old, old story."

"Yes, of course Palestine attacked. Because the Israelis demolished their Dome of the Rock."

"Please!" said Paul. "You're breaking my heart! Even in their defeat, the sons of Ishmael still vow to drive every Jew into the sea!"

"Why," Williams went on, ignoring Paul's response, "did the Israelis destroy that mosque? I'll tell you. So they can unearth the treasures of Herod's Temple and perform the sacrificial rites on the *true* Ark of the Covenant, not on that imitation ark they're using now. Isn't that right? So they can raise the Ark from the dust of the ages?"

"I don't know the minds of the *kohenim*."

"Then tell me what they do every Yom Kippur."

"They atone for our sins," he said.

"They once fasted for atonement, didn't they? Before the Third Temple was constructed? Why don't they fast now?"

"The animal sacrifices have resumed, of course."

Williams strode back to the pulpit and slammed his Bible down upon it with a resounding snack. "And animal sacrifices obliterate sins?"

"Yes."

"No! Leviticus 17:11 declares: *key nefesh habasar ba-dahm*. The life of the flesh is in the blood. And G-d gave you the blood on the altar *l'kapar al-nafstakhem*, as a *kapar*, a covering for your souls."

Paul was so astonished at this Christian preacher's knowledge—not only of the *lashon ha kodesh*, the holy tongue, but of Torah Law as well—that he couldn't reply.

"Animal blood *atones*, my young Jewish friend. It *covers*, but it does not *obliterate*. Why do you think G-d required blood? Why did He say 'the life of *ha-basar* is *ba'dahm*, and I have given it to you upon *ha-mizbakh* to make atonement for your souls: for it is the blood that maketh an atonement for the soul?' For centuries the Jews fasted on Yom Kippur, depriving themselves of food for a day, when the Mosaic Covenant *expressly* states that 'without the blood there is no atonement.' Did your rabbis consider it a primitive, distasteful rite, this slaughter of animals, this spilling of blood? Apparently not, for they gladly returned to the practice as soon as the Temple was rebuilt. They fool no one, my friend. Your rabbis have always believed in the efficacy of the blood; they only lacked a Temple in which to offer it. And yet that blood only *covers*; it does not obliterate!"

Brother Williams bowed his head and drew a breath, speaking softly now: "Rabbis from all over the world, suffering under great persecution, in need of a symbol to unite their people, to inspire young men like yourself, began to pressure the Knesset to destroy that Muslim abomination, so they might unearth Herod's Temple. This presented some difficulty. They'd been carefully excavating beneath the Temple, developing a sense of the dimensions and the floor plan of the previous one, hoping to find where the *hekdesh*, the Temple articles, were located. Suddenly they realized that everything was wrong. Their new Temple was in the wrong place! It *was* the Dome of the Rock that sat squarely upon the site of Herod's Temple. And then one dark night a mysterious group calling itself *Nakam,* "Revenge" in Hebrew, set their explosives and eradicated the mosque. The Temple Mount Wars flared up, and quickly ended. Now the search for the true Ark can begin. It can become a rallying cry for Jews everywhere.

"But, my friend—until it's found, what of the sacrifices performed on the *false* Ark. At best they can only *cover*, not obliterate. At worst…"

Williams stepped to the edge of the wooden podium and gazed down at Paul, sweat pouring from his brow in rivers, soaking his shirt.

"At worst," he said, "they might incur the wrath of Almighty G-d!"

Paul met his gaze in silence. For the first time in his life he had no ready reply.

"As *HaShem* promised through the prophet Malachi," Williams went on, "He sent a man with the spirit of Elijah to herald the coming of Messiah. *Yochanan ha Matbeil*, or John the Baptist, as we call him. He lived in the wilderness of Jordan, as had Elijah. He was filled with *haRuach haKodesh* from his mother's womb. And when he saw the Rabbi called *Yeshua*—"Salvation" in Hebrew—walking on the banks of the Jordan, this prophet Yochanan, sent by G-d to herald the Messiah—pointed to Yeshua and cried out, *'Heenay seh haElohim*! Behold the Lamb of G-d, which taketh away the sin of the world!' Why did he call this young Hebrew carpenter the *Seh haElohim*? And why a lamb? Do you know the answer, son? Of course you understand the meaning of the *Pesach* lamb, and of the blood on the doorposts that caused the Angel of Death to pass over the Jewish houses in Goshen. So can you tell me who this young carpenter really was?"

Paul knew. His hands were clammy with sweat. He clung desperately to the tent pole, feeling his entire world, his entire vain philosophy of life, being swept away by the wind of Truth. Something within him bore witness to the veracity of the preacher's words. Yeshua was the only one who made sense of Torah. Without this *Seh haElohim* what was the purpose of the sacrifices? And where was the atonement for his ancestors when Rome caused them to cease for almost two thousand years? He knew, yet he still felt compelled to resist, to fight the preacher with all the strength in his body.

"Just tell me one thing, preacher," he said. "If you can!"

"I'll surely try."

"Tell me this one thing and I swear before the G-d of Israel, *Eli Avraham, Yitzchak, v'Ya'acov*—G-d of Abraham, Isaac, and Jacob—that I'll fall on my face right here and accept Yeshua—your 'Jesus.' Truly, and for the rest of my life."

A palpable silence filled the tent.

"I swear before G-d!"

"Go on, son. What is your question?"

"Show me where *HaShem* said *anything* about a 'New Testament.' We Jews have the Mosaic Covenant, the Avrahamic, and the Davidic. What do we need with a *new* covenant, a new testament? Surely if G-d were going to make a new covenant with us, He would have spoken it through one of His prophets. Show me, preacher, where G-d said *anything*—and I mean clearly, unambiguously, without you interpreting it for me—about establishing some new covenant. Show me that, and I'll believe."

Smiling warmly, Williams flipped the pages of his Bible. "If I show you what you ask, son, in clear, unambiguous language, not in symbolic allegory or anything like that—can we hold you to your word?"

"Show me," said Paul. "Just show me."

"Very well," said Brother Williams. "Though I would have enjoyed a more difficult challenge. I'm reading from the book of the prophet Jeremiah. Jeremiah was a prophet of Israel during the reign of King Zedekiah, as you know. The words of this book are considered part of the Jewish canon. Do you dispute the place of Jeremiah in the Jewish canon, young man?"

"Of course not," said Paul. "The prophetic books are not part of Torah, necessarily, but they *are* part of the *T'nach*, the Jewish Bible. I don't recall limiting you to the Pentateuch, so read on. I'll listen to old Yermeyahu."

"So you agree that G-d spoke through Yermeyahu."

"Absolutely."

"Good. In the thirty-first chapter and the thirtieth verse in your *T'nach*—the thirty-first verse in Christian Bibles—*HaShem* says to the nation Israel through Yermeyahu: 'Behold, the days come, sayeth *Adonai*, that I will make a *Brit Chadashah*—a New Covenant—with the house of Israel and with the house of Judah: Not according to the Covenant that I made with their fathers'—the Mosaic Covenant—'in the day that I took them by the hand to bring them out of the land of Egypt; which covenant they brake, although I was an husband unto them, sayeth *Adonai*…'"

Before Williams had finished quoting the Scripture Paul was on his knees, crying out to G-d. The man who'd one day be known as "Apostle to the Solar System"—*Sheliach* (Messenger) to the last remaining Church under the sun—was that night born into the *Malchut haShamayim*, the Kingdom of Heaven.

But his earthly trials were not over.

He wisely kept his newfound faith from his Orthodox parents, so that he might continue his discipleship under A. R. Williams. He read his new King James Bible—along with dozens of research books—under his blanket at night, in the fading beam of an old glolight. But the day finally came when he was to be ordained, and, out of respect for his father, he confessed his belief.

His father responded as he'd predicted he would. Jason Moscowitz ripped his shirt from his body and evicted Paul from the house, severing him from the family and from Israel for all time, proclaiming him dead. As Paul wept bitterly in the alley beneath the kitchen window, the light of his own *yahrtzeit* candle threw a grotesque dancing shadow of his huddled figure against the brick walls.

Then his father's tear-choked voice began chanting: "*Yiskadal v'yiskadash, sh'mai rabboh…*" *Kaddish* for his dead son.

Paul never returned.

α

A.R. Williams increased his evangelistic efforts as the New Age vigilantes, the Peace Guard, began roaming the streets, splashing crude accusations on the walls in red paint. One of these accusations required no words, just a sign—a six-pointed star.

None of this came as a surprise to Brother Williams, who increased his evangelistic efforts during the construction years—until his assassination by the peace guards in 2058—and who gladly supplied the young student with a number of priceless old volumes. The most inspirational of these, Paul thought, was *The Imitation of Christ* by Thomas à Kempis.

He also studied the writings of Helena Petrovna Blavatski, founder of the New Age movement, and Alice Bailey, her most prominent disciple. From these books Paul was able to uncover the history and purpose of the network rising to power in the late twenty-first century. Now he knew the reason for the growing persecution of the Jews, and, trembling beneath his blanket, he realized with alarm the direction it would ultimately take. On every page of Alice Bailey's books was her belief in Aryanism, a belief similar to that once held by Adolf Hitler. Bailey's philosophy was fundamental to the organizations that were now rebuilding all the major cities of the world.

While Christianity slept the New Age movement had been spreading its poison. The average New Ager was never informed of the anti-Semitism inherent in his movement. Instead, he believed himself to be working for a new and better world, a millennium of peace and prosperity for all, the end of global warming and world hunger, the evolution of a higher consciousness. This higher consciousness was to be achieved through meditation, particularly those techniques which had evolved from a blending of Hinduism and shlock-science over a century ago. TM, EST, and biofeedback were introduced into the mainstream of Western culture until, by the year 2020, Europeans and Americans were turning out for seminars of mass hypnosis, placing themselves under the control of a handful of New Age gurus. During these seminars, they were gradually indoctrinated into the esoteric knowledge of the "Masters", who claimed they'd been sent to usher in the Aquarian Age, to prepare mankind for the coming of Christ.

This "Christ" who was to come and set the world to rights differed significantly from the Biblical Messiah, although the New Agers didn't seem to notice or care. He was a Messiah who would give them what they wanted—hedonistic pleasures of every variety, without condemnation, and a final end to war. He was called *Maitreya*. Originally he was slated to appear in 1982, but the man who'd made that prediction, a popular lecturer named Benjamin Creme, had been mistaken. In the 1990s some thought the Reverend Sum Yung Moon was the Maitreya. Even Moon thought so. But the movement quickly covered up such embarrassments and continued to prepare for the advent of the New Age Messiah.

They used many of the same tactics, Paul noted, that Hitler had employed in the 1930s: indoctrination of the young; the outlawing of public depictions of Christianity; its replacement by ancient Eastern cults; the teaching that a post-Atlantian "super race", the Aryans, would emerge to rule the world; and the clever deployment of an elite force, ostensibly organized to protect the citizenry in a time of rising urban crime. Hitler had called his crack troops the Brown Shirts. Mao had called the brutal soldiers of the Cultural Revolution the Red Guard. The New Age conspiracy called their elite troops the Peace Guard. Deployed throughout the major cities of Earth by the year 2077, the Peace Guard appeared at first to be a benevolent breed. Their blue berets and unicorn armbands were a comforting sight to subway commuters and pedestrians walking deserted streets at night. They were not merely tolerated; they were welcomed.

But shortly after the urban relocation and restructuring there were suddenly a lot more peace guards about the streets. People looked the other way as they began to harass Jewish businessmen and smash their shop windows. Fundamentalist and Evangelical churches that spoke out against such treatment of G-d's chosen people were also singled out for persecution. Their New Testament revealed a Messiah who differed radically from the one awaited by the New Agers. And neither He nor they would be tolerated for very long.

When Paul's beloved teacher, Brother Williams, was gunned down in the street by the Peace Guard, Paul went into hiding with the remaining members of his congregation. He'd wanted to join the Messianic K'hillah, to assist his fellow Jews in their flight to Israel. But who would watch over Williams' flock?

The choice had been made for him.

His closest advisers, the core of whom eventually became his evangelistic team, urged him to change his name. It was dangerous enough to be a Christian evangelist in those times; to be *Jewish* as well was a death sentence. There was, in fact, only one Jew they were aware of who'd managed to stay alive while speaking out publicly against the government. That was the sensationalist radio broadcaster, Jeri Kline.

A young man with a gift for stirring up controversy, a syndicated program, and an inexplicable hatred for Paul Moscowitz, Jeri Kline advocated a strident new Zionism. He condemned the anti-Semitic government policies. He called for a revolution of Jews around the world. He even called the Peace Guard a pack of hoodlums. And yet he remained alive. It was his outspoken atheism that saved him. Whatever else he was saying, Jeri Kline was undermining people's faith in Scripture—and that was a quality worth investing in. When criticized for its open persecution of the Jews, the government would point to Kline as an example not only of its religious toleration, but its toleration of criticism as well. Unwittingly, Kline was working for the system he loathed.

Paul Jason Moscowitz was a different story. While his Christianity was still somewhat tolerated, his Jewishness was not. And so he agreed to change his last name, if only he could think of another. He was too busy with matters of life and death to waste time selecting aliases for himself. For so many years his friends had referred to him as "Brother Paul." And so, owing to his procrastination in selecting a suitable *nome de guerre*, he became known throughout the planets as Brother Paul.

He made an attempt to establish a church with the funds his followers contributed. He purchased a piece of property in the heart of Flagstaff, Arizona and built the great Zion Temple, a project that eventually put him in debt. Throughout a six-month media campaign, the last evangelistic fundraiser in history, the Zion Temple paid off its debts and began operating in the black.

Thousands of believers flocked to the Temple to see Paul preach. He had a flamboyant style, gliding across the stage in a long, toga-like robe—a flair for the dramatic he claimed to have inherited from Aimee Semple McPherson. He continued to wear a prayer shawl, to pray in the *lashon kodesh* (the holy tongue) three times a day, and to lay *t'fillin* (phylacteries). The Hebrew prayer and *t'fillin* were *mitzvot* he observed in privacy, only his staff was aware of them. He thought such observances might confuse his Christian flock, who did not observe Judaism and who might not understand that he still perceived himself as a Jew.

G-d honored his faithfulness. Testimonies of miraculous healings brought his name into public awareness. An attempt was made on his life during a crusade in New Trenton—the city where President Charles Coffey had emerged into public view. Paul received thousands of threatening letters every week. But the power of G-d was with him, and he continued unruffled by the danger.

"I am," he stated in a famous interview for the Washington Post Clarion, "the last evangelist on Earth. I am willing to lay down my life for the Gospel of Jesus Christ, and that's all there is to say."

"But, haven't you been accused of everything from tax fraud to conspiracy against the government?" protested the reporter. "Polls say that over ninety-per-cent of the people in this country consider you a charlatan, bilking little old ladies for their grocery money, preying on the ignorance of the masses. What do you say in the face of such universal criticism?"

"The Devil is the prince of this world," Paul replied. "If the world loved me, I would question my own ministry. I'm happy to be mistrusted and despised by those who worship idols. The Bible says that an idolater is nothing more than a devil worshiper. And devil worshipers, it's only 1ogical to assume, would love me were I a devil. Perhaps they'd proclaim me their leader. But I'm *not* a devil; I'm a disciple of Jesus Christ—a servant of the Most High G-d.

"But I'll tell you something that'll certainly brand me as a lunatic among your readers. I watched my dearest friend, the man of G-d who led me to Christ and poured himself out to me—the man who taught me the precious truths of G-d's word—I watched as he was ruthlessly gunned down by two so-called Peace Guards.

It was a dreadful sight; I've never forgotten it. But, as much as I loved that old man, and as much as I'm certain he's now resting in the bosom of Abraham—he made one fatal mistake. It's a mistake I shall not repeat. Reverend Williams often spoke of the possibility that he'd be martyred for the cause of Christ. I can't say whether or not he feared it, necessarily, but it was something he often said.

"The thing I want to tell your readers is this: I shall never confess that I might be martyred for the cause of Christ! Let every devil do what he will! I shall not go home to be with the L-rd until He calls me! I shall not be killed until the work he has given me is accomplished! And I shall continue this confession even in the face of Satan himself!"

Shortly after this interview appeared there was a "spontaneous" demonstration in Flagstaff and Paul's Zion Temple was burned to the ground. His staff moved quickly to protect him. Against his stubborn protests, they flew him via hovercar to a remote cabin in the Superstition Mountains, where they kept him cloistered for months. As the weeks dragged by, he grew increasingly irritable. He demanded to be supplied with a daily newspaper, and stubbornly insisted on the old fashioned newsprint-on-woodpulp variety, not disks. When he realized that the situation in the cities was growing more dangerous for Christians, he decided he needed a swift courier who could carry more than newspapers. Jimmy Sanders, the young lad who braved the trip each day—who Paul fondly referred to as his "newsboy"—was risking life and limb to carry information back and forth from Paul to his contact in Phoenix-Mesa, a multiversity professor by the name of Giles Hadley.

When the report came of Hadley's execution, Paul was enraged. He demanded to be set at liberty. His staff resisted. The Church could not survive, they argued, without his leadership. He must remain in hiding.

α

"We'll have to show it to him," remarked Phillipe Esteban one afternoon. He tossed a copy of the *Sun* across the table with a frown. Phil had been a close friend of the evangelist's since Brother Williams was killed, and a trusted member of the staff. He knew how Paul would react and dreaded it.

Paul's attorney, John Cowan, took another sip of coffee and

lifted a corner of the paper. Running his eyes down the columns—an ability he'd developed from his profession—he took in the entire story at a glance.

"It's inevitable, isn't it?" he said. "How long did we think we could keep him shut away out here, with no one to preach to but kangaroo rats and coyotes? He's an exhorter, after all."

"I don't know," Esteban replied, running a sweaty palm over his balding scalp. "Just until it blows over, I guess. Until the threats stop."

Cowan, a huge African-American built like a pro basketball player, rose to his full seven feet and tucked the newspaper under his arm.

"You know as well as I do, Phil, that the threats will never stop. It's been six months since *New Heaven, New Earth* went off the air. He's heartsick about that. Besides, who are we to keep the last evangelist on Earth from preaching the Gospel?"

Esteban dismissed the comment with a wave of his hand.

"We're trying to save his life, Little John, and you know it! In fact, as I recall, this self-imposed exile of ours was *your* idea."

"Yes," Cowan agreed, advancing a few steps to place a hand on Esteban's shoulder. "Yes, it was. And it was a good idea. But lately I've felt the Holy Spirit convicting me that it's time. You can't tell me you haven't felt it too."

Esteban avoided the attorney's gaze, lowering his head into his hands and massaging the temples with his fingers.

"I've got a throbbing headache, Little John. Hades itself can't be a degree hotter than this place. And I'm tired. Bone tired. Go ahead. Show him the paper."

Cowan wanted to reply, but thought better of it. Esteban was getting old. He was exhausted from the effort to protect Paul's life. To add to his difficulties, no one had ever seen the evangelist so tempermental. It was unlike Paul, and it was wearing them down. Six months in the heart of an unrelenting furnace had finally done them in. *It's just as well*, Cowan thought ruefully. *I couldn't bear to play one more game of chess.*

Turning stiffly, he opened the door and stepped out into the blazing sunlight.

The Superstitions

As the Alderson Glaciation began its reshaping of the world, global warming increased to an astonishing degree. The plants and animals of the American Southwest, having been furnished by their Creator with mechanisms designed to protect them from the desiccating affects of the sun, were the last to die. The sun was gradually killing off everything.

The largest percentage of desert life, both predator and prey, was strictly nocturnal, while cold-blooded reptiles, which fed on insects and required the warmth of the sun to wake them from their sluggish rest, spent only brief periods in its rays. Rattlesnakes lay in scaly coils under cholla cacti during the noontime hours when the solar radiation was the most deadly. There they slept, stirring only at dusk to hunt small nocturnal rodents, the packrats and field mice that made up their diet. Elf owls and the great horned owl also experienced little interruption of their habits, for they had always prowled the night. And their tiny prey was abundant.

It was the smaller insect-eating reptiles, the myriad species of lizards, especially, that first began to go extinct—right after the insects upon which they fed. This decline in the insect population would seriously disrupt the ecology of the world, but the end was still decades away.

For the many species of desert flora, the key to survival was water. Tough and hardy, covered from top to bottom with sticky spines, the cacti promised to remain after the animals had disappeared. Few new ones would propagate, but the oldsters were a long-lived breed with no plans to retire. The secret of their survival was in their basic design, in the thousands of spines covering them. While offering little protection from the woodpeckers and other creatures dependent on cacti, these spines were essential as shading devices. The elaborate crosshatched shadows they cast on plant surfaces offered an effective umbrella against the dehydrating effects of the sun.

Desert life lingered on because it had been created with adaptations to protect it from aridity. The sun had always been an enemy of the desert, making it what it was, sucking the few drops of moisture from everything that fought to hoard it, turning it into a juiceless zone where only specialized creatures could eke out a bare subsistence in the dust. And thus, even with its increased destructive power, the sun would have a hard time destroying those plants and animals that had marked it as an enemy since creation. They would prove the toughest to kill.

Paul felt oppressed in this dried out corner of the earth. But, like the rugged life surrounding him, he knew himself to be a survivor. His hide was as tough as a snake's. As the sun began to slide below Weaver's Needle to the west, painting the sky with lovely pastel hues, he'd don his wide-brimmed hat and black clothing for camouflage, hang a pair of binoculars around his neck, and leave the claustrophobic darkness of his cabin to stroll beneath the stars. He knew the constellations well enough, but out here there were millions of stars he'd never seen. The sky was brimming with them.

Recalling Moses, who was driven from *Mitzrayim* to spend much of his life in the Sinai, awaiting his call from G-d, Paul wondered if the old patriarch had gazed up at the same bright stars, praying to his G-d and wondering if his time of exile would ever end. For, like Moses, Paul knew that G-d's people were suffering under intense persecution while he hid away in the wilderness, waiting for the L-rd to awaken him to his mission. He tried to find solace in the symbols around him: the frogs, for example, whose eggs now lay dormant in the dust of rocky crevices. The eggs might lie there for years, silent, lifeless, until a few drops of rain awakened them. Then a desert miracle would occur! The night air would fill with the chirping of thousands of tiny frogs—frogs appearing as if from nowhere!

"To everything," King Solomon had said, "there is a season; and a time to every purpose under heaven."

But when would Paul's time come?

The Exodus

Paul knelt in the dry arroyo, a pair of field glasses pressed against his eyes. *There it is!* he thought with a sense of triumph. *The nest of the great homed owl!* He'd awakened in the dark last night to a doleful hooting, and had watched from his window, eyes growing slowly accustomed to the moonlight. He was rewarded with a glimpse of the owl swooping down from its perch on a tall saguaro, snatching up its prey—probably *dipodomis,* the little kangaroo rat that foraged after dark—and disappearing in a flutter of wings. Finding its nest by day, however, had proven to be quite a task. It was not in the saguaro, where he'd first spotted the owl, but perched atop a barrel cactus by the dry riverbed. It looked a bit ridiculous, like a fur hat on a Hassid. Here, where patches of thick brush awaited the next gush of spring rain, Paul crouched. He became as silent and invisible as his surroundings, waiting for the horned owl to return to its nest. He occupied himself with this vigil for over half-an-hour, until other equally fascinating creatures crossed the lenses of his binoculars. For instance, the male tarantula scuttling along the sand a few meters away.

Adjusting his optics to pull the creature into sharper focus, Paul was surprised to see that he'd caught one in search of a mate. It bore an odd, oversized bundle on its back as it ran. It's progeny.

"Farewell, Mr. Tarantula," said Paul. "I'm afraid it'll be a short honeymoon for you."

But the spider didn't need to be reminded. It was the male's grim task to find a female of his species and pass his bundle to her as quickly as possible, then beat a fast retreat. For the female had genetic instructions to kill her mate as soon as he'd delivered the goods. *Nature's analogue of the strange woman?* Paul mused. *An arachnid Mata Hari? Perhaps, had human sexuality been designed like the tarantula's, AIDS wouldn't have wiped out a third of the world's population by 2030.* He laughed to himself, dismissing it as the conjecture of a man who'd never known a woman. New Age environmentalists had taken a rather gruesome view of AIDS, explaining it as Gaia's way of reducing the population to less dangerous levels. But the plague hadn't seemed to interfere with human sexuality to any noticeable degree. Not, at any rate, once the antidote had been found. The fear of casual sex that had dominated the first few decades of the 21st century was gone by the time Paul reached adulthood. Humanity, like the tarantula, was back to business as usual.

Once again, his attention was diverted by the appearance of another desert creature. He swung his binoculars to the right, shifting the focus as he turned, until he had in his sights the beautiful, lumbering reptile he'd longed to observe for all these months. Long tail curling around the base of an ocotillo, a garishly striped Gila monster hove into view, basking in the rays of the sun. M*agnificent!* Paul thought. *Much larger than I'd expected!*

The snap of a twig brought him to his feet, heart pounding. John Cowan stood at the lip of the arroyo, looking down with a broad grin. He held a newspaper in his hand.

Paul was panting from the start the attorney had given him. *Sneaking up behind me like an Apache! Well, two can play at that game!*

"Little John!" he said. "I didn't see you."

"Spy anything interesting, sir?"

"Yes, as a matter of fact. That huge Gila monster."

Cowan froze. "Where?"

"Don't move!" Paul said. "It's just a few meters behind you, by that prickly pear. No! Don't turn around, whatever you do! That's it. Stay right there and don't move a muscle." Paul watched the creature slip away in search of food. At the rate Gila monsters moved, Cowan would have ample time to write out his will and enjoy a leisurely last meal before it struck—if "struck" was the proper term. They didn't strike in the way snakes did, but ground their venom slowly through the skin. So misunderstood was the Gila monster that it had to be protected from human beings. Cowan was in no danger.

"Where is it now?" the attorney pleaded.

"I wouldn't move just yet if I were you. They're very unpredictable. Why, you could just move your head the slightest bit and—" Paul snapped his fingers to demonstrate the suddenness of its attack. The sound made Cowan stiffen.

"Can't you get rid of it?"

"I'm afraid not, Little John," Paul sighed. "We'll just have to pray it moves on." Another baldfaced lie; the lizard had already disappeared into the chaparral.

"V-very g-good, sir," Cowan stammered.

"But—as long as I have your undivided attention, there *are* a few things we should discuss."

Cowan blinked. "Certainly not *now*, Reverend!" Maybe you should run for help. Brother Esteban has a hunting rifle—"

"Oh, I dare not," said the evangelist. "One sudden move may alert the creature and…" he made a face. "We simply can't risk it. At any rate, I wish to inform you that I'm quite prepared to depart our homely little hideaway, right at this moment, in fact. You may give me the keys to your hovercar. In return, I give you my solemn word that I'll tell you the moment you're out of danger."

"Brother Paul!" cried Cowan. "I can't believe you'd stoop to such—such malicious extortion! Sir, it's the heat. The heat's affected your mind."

"Undoubtedly!" Paul agreed. "Six months of baking like a piece of crockery in this furnace has unquestionably affected my mind. I'm a raving lunatic, I assure you. I'm desperate and quite dangerous. Now, do I get the keys?"

"Please, sir!"

"I can no longer allow my own staff to hold me prisoner in these desolate mountains. The entire Church is without leadership. The brethren need me."

Cowan sighed. "I have the keys right here in my pocket, Reverend. But I insist that you take me along with you."

"Nothing doing. Now throw me the keys."

Cowan remained stock still. "I can't believe this! You're acting like a thug in a B-rated holovid."

"I've been driven to it! Toss me those keys, Little John. But be careful. Move very slowly."

"Think of what you're doing, sir!"

"I promise I'll repent. Just as soon as I leave these horrid mountains behind."

Cowan grinned. He slid his left hand toward his pocket.

"You.know something, sir?" he said. "I don't believe you."

"Eh?"

"I don't believe there's a Gila monster behind me. I think you're bluffing, sir."

A sly grin spread across Paul's face.

"Now *there's* a deadly wager," he said. "Are you willing to call my bluff?"

"Sir," said Cowan, "you wouldn't hurt a fly." He stepped forward, glancing only briefly behind him to confirm his suspicions.

"Well, there *was* a Gila monster!" Paul said petulantly. "And I would have let it bite you."

"Right, sir." Cowan stepped down into the arroyo, holding out the copy of the Phoenix-Mesa Sun. "There's some bad news in today's paper. I thought you should see it."

Paul snatched it from his hand. His eyes took in the headline: **CHARLES COFFEY IN CONTROL OF U.S. GOVERN-**

MENT—DECLARES MARTIAL LAW.

"So," he said. "They've done it."

"Yes, sir. At one o'clock this morning, President Blair was physically removed from office and publicly denounced. The Party for World Peace is in power."

"Charles Coffey! The President!"

"More like the Fuhrer, sir."

Paul crumpled the newspaper with his fists and tossed it aside.

"Little John, I can no longer remain in hiding! Lives are at stake! Thousands of our brethren may be slaughtered by this—this Nazi!"

Cowan nodded. "Yes, sir."

"I must get in touch with the Israeli Prime Minister at once. Moshe Bierman is an old friend. He assured me he'd send rescue planes for our people if the situation warranted such a course of action. I believe it's come to that. Little John, you must act as my liaison with the various cells, and with Mayor Browne. We have to begin rounding up the brethren—"

"Sir," Cowan interrupted, "we're ready. Brother Esteban's relented. He has some good ideas. Let's go back to the cabin and work out the details in some degree of comfort, shall we?"

"A charming idea. Thank you, Little John."

"Sir," said Cowan as they weaved through the creosote, "you've often spoken of the need for an evangelistic tour of the planets, particularly Mars and Luna? It occurs to me that this would be the perfect time for just such a mission. We need the funds, desperately."

"Nonsense! You're treating me like a senile old fool. Does my staff mean to send me off into space at this crucial hour? Is that it? Retire the old man? And who's planning to take my place at the helm? You? Ridiculous! You're a fine attorney, Little John, but you're no preacher. You still have trouble finding the book of Philippians."

Cowan laughed. "Not any more, Reverend. Not since you showed me the formula."

"Go eat peach cake."

"Exactly. G-E-P-C: Galatians, Ephesians, Philippians, Colossians."

"Remind me to stick a gold star on your forehead, Little

John. But ‘Go Eat Peach Cake’ won’t make an evangelist out of a sow’s ear, if I may be blunt. I suppose Phil Esteban plans to take over while I’m being choked to death by Martian dust on the Elysian Plain, preaching to a congregation of rust-covered miners.”

“Reverend, please! No one’s forcing your retirement, and you know it. We’re only thinking of your safety.”

“Fiddlesticks! Are you mad, Little John? You want me to leave the brethren a time like this?”

“No, sir, of course not! Hear me out. The spaceliner *Empress* will complete its return run from Saturn orbit in three weeks. It’ll dock at Luna for another week before heading out again. That’ll give us four weeks to organize the exodus. To be honest, if it takes us any longer than four weeks we’ll all be dead, anyway. Brother Madden and I can take over from there. We won’t need you tramping across the wastelands. We have plenty of qualified leaders in the cells. And think of the opportunity it would be for you to visit the offworld brethren. They’ll need encouragement, too. Encouragement only you can give them.”

“No. It’s impossible.”

“Frankly, sir, it’s the elders’ will that you remove yourself from danger. You’re simply too important to be risking your life.”

“I’ve been risking my life for twenty years! Don’t be absurd!”

“We’re not being absurd; we’re being realistic. Now, Elder Rice has agreed to lead the exodus—once you’ve set everything in motion, of course. There may not be another chance for you to tour the planets; we don’t have any idea what the new government will do. If you wait for the next flight, sir, it’s possible that they’ll refuse to allow you to board. Or perhaps try to ‘detain’ you—if you catch my meaning. The way the political situation looks right now, they’ll need time to consolidate their forces, to tighten their grip. Meanwhile, Mars and Luna need you to bring them the Gospel in person. I urge you to consider it, sir. It’s what we all want.”

Paul nodded. “I’ll consider it, Little John.”

“Something else of interest, sir.”

“Yes?”

“Jim Sanders, your ‘newsboy’, brought in a radio last week. I’ve been listening to nightly. With all that’s been going on—”

“While you’ve kept *me* in the dark!”

Cowan nervously cleared his throat. “Uh—yes, sir. But, at

any rate, I heard something that might cheer you up."

"What could possibly cheer me up at this juncture?"

"Jeri Kline, sir. The atheist. The one who's been denounceing you so stridently since you became a believer."

"Yes? What about him?"

"Well—it's very strange sir. His program has gone off the air. All at once, without any warning."

"Hmmm," said Paul. "I certainly don't mourn the loss of that vulgar broadcast. But, somehow, the news doesn't please me."

Cowan was surprised. "Why not, sir?"

"When my enemies suddenly disappear, Little John, it tends to make me nervous. I like to know precisely where they are at all times."

"Kline may have served his purpose for Charles Coffey. It's very likely he was paid for his years of service with a poison dart in the back. I wouldn't put it past the new President."

"True, Little John, he might have been killed. But I have a strange feeling he's still alive—and that we've not yet heard the last from our iconoclastic Mr. Kline."

"Well. I hope your feeling is wrong."

"So do I. Although we both know my feelings rarely are."

The Exhortation

And so it was that Brother Paul became a passenger on the *Empress,* the first and only interplanetary ship of its class in the solar system. But he made sure his staff came along with him.

All the plans for the exodus having been made, he contacted the Israeli Prime Minister and arranged to have the pilgrims journey across the wastelands, following the Verde River from Phoenix-Mesa up the Mogollon Plateau, then across the high desert to the Navajo reservation called Monument Valley. From there they'd be secretly airlifted out of the country to Israel. John Cowan was sent to Phoenix-Mesa to discuss with Mayor Browne the possibility of suspending the city's security measures—just long enough to allow fugitive Christians to enter unchallenged. Elder Rice and his assistant, Brother Bernard, would organize them into teams. Mayor Browne agreed. He gave the pilgrims permission to roam the dumps outside the city, mounds of non-recycled metal and outmoded machinery from the Great Reconstruction. There they found materials for building makeshift wagons. He also donated most of the provisions for their journey. This was much appreciated, since most of the pilgrims' bluecards had been confiscated. (The few who retained them were impoverished.) It also served to free up the remainder of the Church's funds to pay for horses.

The horses presented the biggest problem. Purchased from private ranchers throughout the country, they were shipped via superconductor-rail to Kansas, then transferred to freight cars and sent in one shipment to Phoenix-Mesa. This shipment was delayed until the last minute, and here the Mayor's cooperation was desperately needed. For it was a tense few hours as over five hundred horses were led around the outskirts of the city by paid sympathizers. The pilgrims massed outside to meet them, and when the last animal was hitched to its wagon the exodus was ready to begin.

Paul was flown out by hovercar to make his final speech before the throng. As he stood before the disposessed, black-garbed saints, faces shadowed under wide-brimmed hats, it occurred to him that they resembled Mormons setting off in search of Zion. But it was camouflage that made these garments necessary, not religious fashion. They'd have to do all their journeying by night, beneath the moon. No one could travel the desert by day and live.

He lifted his voice, standing upon a hastily erected platform outside the glittering lights of Phoenix-Mesa:

"*Chesed v'shalom*—grace and peace my dear brothers and sisters. As you know, I have a mission to the planets that cannot be delayed. The new Martian colony, Polis Marineris, and its infant Church have received no broadcasts of *New Heaven, New Earth*, nor any word of the situation here on Earth for seven months now. Yet, when my advisors first suggested that I undertake this voyage, I was reluctant to go.

"If you only knew how much I love you all! I long to be with you in this great exodus to the Holy Land. But the L-rd has sheep that are not of this flock, and they also need to be fed and encouraged. I pray that the situation in Israel will be such that our broadcasts to Mars and Luna may be resumed from there, and that our contact with the brethren in the far-flung colonies can continue unabated. But, as you are all aware, these are the Latter Days spoken of by the prophet Joel. Soon we shall see the signs of the L-rd's return: 'blood and fire and vapor of smoke. The sun will be turned to darkness, and the moon to blood, before that notable day arrives.' We hear rumors of a revolution on Luna, a revolution against the current evil administration. Perhaps we shall soon see nuclear flares blazing across the lunar surface, turning it the color of blood." He paused for effect, pointing at the thin, silver crescent hovering over the city. A thousand pairs of eyes blinked whitely back at him.

"*Chaverim*—brethren! I was called to be an evangelist. The job of pastor is not one I have ever coveted, since it requires a peculiar temperament I fear I do not possess. I have stated publicly that I'm the last evangelist, but now that America's churches are scattered—now that the churches in a once free and G-d-fearing nation have been reduced to but a thousand souls about to leave their homes and families behind to seek sanctuary in Israel—I have, by default it seems, become the last Apostle as well. I am old, my friends. I've fought the good fight. And my soul longs to journey with you to *Eretz Yisrael*, where it might rejoice with yours, where it might find rest and delight in the shadow of the Holy Temple. But the solar system looks to me for hope. And, as Brother Cowan reminds me, I may not live to make another such voyage into space. And so I'm leaving you in the competent hands of Elder Rice and Brother Bernard. They shall judge among you. Trust them. Follow them as you would me. Obey them in everything, for I have set them in authority over you as faithful servants of Almighty.

"I pray the anointing of the *Ruach haKodesh* shall be upon them, to guide them in this awesome task. The journey ahead will be long and hard. Therefore I admonish you to remember the need for order and discipline. It was murmuring and rebellion that caused the children of Israel to wander in the wilderness for forty years. This shall be *your* wilderness testing. Do not fail me. Take a lesson from the children of Israel. Obey your leaders. Do not murmur against them or rebel against G-dly discipline. Acquit yourselves as befits the children of *HaShem*, the King of the Universe. I'm not abandoning you in this hour of severe testing! I'm setting out to encourage the thousands of your brethren on Luna and Mars. I shall greet them in your name, and tell them of your brave expedition to the Holy Land. They shall take heart in the knowledge that you've triumphed over every obstacle—and all the planets will rejoice when you plant your feet upon *Eretz Yisrael*. G-dspeed, my beloved!"

A tremendous cheer went up from the throng as Paul was

whisked away by hovercar to the penthouse Brother Esteban had reserved for him and his staff. There they waited out the final few days before their departure into space; and there Paul fought the oppressive weight of guilt hanging over him—guilt for having abandoned the brethren in their greatest time of trial.

The Ship

The spaceliner *Empress* was a colossal flying city.

Along the inner hull of her spherical midsection thousands of crewmembers, ship's guards, and the employees of various enterprises lived and worked. There were high-rise office buildings and hotels; hydroponic gardens, miniature farms for the production of both food and oxygen; sylvan parks; and twisting above-"ground" thoroughfares bustling with human traffic. People traveled from place to place on foot, on bicycles, or—if they were truly adventurous—on hang-gliders. The *Empress* was at full capacity for her maiden voyage, carrying six thousand passengers and crew. And for those embarked on their first flight out to Saturn orbit, the trip was anything but dull.

Her colossal thrusters were fueled by Helium-3 (found in abundance in the lunar regolith). It produced a clean nuclear reaction, making thick lead shielding unnecessary. The *Empress* functioned on the simple premise that "slow and steady wins the race," or, more accurately, that "slow and steady" can become incredibly swift if the thrust is applied in small but steady increments over vast distances. The globular hub of the vessel encompassed a self-contained, Earth-like environment, divided into sections or habitats. While it was far too small to allow for such dramatic atmospheric phenomena as rainstorms, it did allow for a mild cycle of evaporation and condensation that produced such agreeable effects as morning dew and sweet, unpolluted air. (Actually, it could have been argued that the shipboard environment was far healthier than that of Earth.) Gravity was maintained at slightly less than Earth-normal by a controlled rotation of the hub.

Simple but elegant.

The engines driving the ship were standard: Liquid hydrogen—in the small amounts needed to create its periodic, steady boosts-forward—was forced into a reactor, where nuclear fission raised its temperature to a superheated state. Superheated hydrogen rushed out through a linear array of titanic aerospike nozzles at the stern, allowing it, theoretically, to attain speeds in excess of 650 million mph, the speed of light. Sustained thrusts of massive power were possible with this system, which could compete admirably with Navy warships for sheer speed. But the economy of the steady-thrust method was preferred over the old style of leap-and-fall that had characterized the early days of spaceflight.

Rockets and shuttles of the old NASA days had spectacular liftoffs, but they were also spectacularly wasteful. The *Empress* wasted not a quark. Remarkably, it worked its wonders with technology that had been on the drawing boards before the Mercury program of the early 1960s, before a man named Glenn was tossed through the upper atmosphere in the sardine can called "Friendship Seven". It had been there in theory, not in fact, because the eggheads of Mercury had insisted upon the heavy booster design over the steady-thrust. Those were the days of ridiculously tall firecracker ships triumphing over Earth's gravity-well by wasting millions of tons of fuel on the launching pad—just to get of the ground! Once beyond the pull of Earth, they floated to their destinations, expending only tiny retro-rocket thrusts to correct variations in pitch and yaw. But their return trips required even more wasteful bursts of fuel. As archaic, and even silly, as the old Tin Lizzie appeared from the perspective of the 1960's, so did the leap-and-fall rockets of the NASA-era appear from the perspective of the late 21st century. All modern ships were constructed in orbit, utilizing the advantages of freefall. Gigantic hull-sections could be swung into place by a relatively robust infant, provided, of course, that the infant was fitted out with an EVA jetpack. The completed vessel could then be sent on its way by an even smaller nudge from its thrusters, without Earth's 5.9742×10^{24} kg mass to overcome.

By the standards of 2088, the early NASA space shuttles were as wasteful as they were hilarious to watch on old two-D vids.

Like the 19th century ocean liners that were first to carry Marconi's "Wireless Telegraph", the *Empress* was the first to carry TBC (Tachyon Beam Communication), a system employing faster-than-light particles to overcome that bane of interplanetary travel—time lag. A message to Mars, even on a laser-beam, took over five minutes under the best conditions to reach its receiver.

Then there'd be another five minutes for the reply to beam back—at *least* ten minutes from the time a question was asked to the time the answer was received. The Jupiter-lag was ridiculous, the Saturn-lag insufferable—until the harnessing of the quixotic tachyon. Now spacers could chatter between planets like teenagers on vidphones.

This solved one problem—dangerous lags in responses—but it created another: It was difficult if not impossible for two spacers to argue over the old system; the lag between message and response helped to cool hot heads. But with instant communication came raw nerves, bad tempers, and, even worse, trivial banter about the hottest date on Ganymede or the best accommodations on Titan. Spacers simply shrugged all this off as the price one paid for progress, then switched to an empty channel for peace and quiet.

The passengers aboard the *Empress* were the only spacefarers with no complaints. They chose from a long list of technological delights, receiving prompt service from spider-shaped robots closeted in the walls. There were rooms with games so realistic that some passengers were known to spend every waking hour in digital realms of adventure. It was reputed that Captain Roy Mills, when his schedule allowed, routinely won a fortune (or lost it) in the plush gambling casinos of the Las Vegas Deck. Thousands of gallons of alcoholic beverages were consumed on one voyage to Saturn, and it was necessary to replenish the ship's stores from the hydroponic distilleries on Enceladus.

The *Empress* was well worth her exorbitant fare. No one seemed overly concerned with the lack of lower-class elements on board. In fact, comparing the *Empress* with earlier space vehicles was less apt than comparing it with seafaring luxury liners of old. A delightfully slow voyage with every conceivable comfort provided.

For the "last evangelist," however, such hedonistic accouterments held little charm.

The Benefactor

One event of interest had occurred as Paul boarded the

Martian shuttle on his way back to Luna. He'd spent months touring the pioneer outposts of that frozen desert world while the *Empress* completed its outbound voyage. When she finally returned to Mars orbit, he gave a hasty farewell speech to the Martians of *Polis Marineris* colony and boarded a shuttle. It took a few minutes to achieve escape velocity, rising slowly upward through the salmon-colored sky. He chose a window seat in order to obtain a clear view of the cratered surface shrinking below him. He'd forgotten that even the gradual-thrust system created an increase in gees toward the upper atmosphere, but remembered it when he felt his back being pressed into the material of his chair. Held there by an invisible hand, he was no longer able to view the planet until the thrusters shut down. When they did, and he found himself bobbing against his harness in zero-g, he pressed his face against the porthole for one last breathtaking view. Anyone could tell that spaceflight was a new experience for him, but he didn't mind.

Suddenly the craft let loose another sustained thrust and the shuttle's steward announced that normal gravity would be maintained for the next five minutes. Passengers could unbuckle their harnesses and stretch their legs for a while. Paul had just completed the task of unfastening when a voice startled him.

"First time off Earth?"

He looked into the grinning face of the man seated next to him, a man in his late forties. The face sported a neatly trimmed goatee, and the head—save for a few tufts of hair around the ears—was as bald as an egg. The face seemed to leap out at him from a magazine cover, as if it belonged to someone famous, someone he should recognize.

The man solved the mystery for him, taking Paul's hand and pumping it enthusiastically.

"I heard you were making a tour of Mars and Luna, Brother Paul, so I came all the way out from Saturn for the crusades. My name's Denton, by the way. Wilbur Denton. It's simply glorious what the L-rd's doing in the new Martian colony!"

As soon as the stranger's name had left his lips, Paul's breath caught in his throat. All the scattered scraps of newsprint in his memory came together with a thunderous crash. This was the man whose company, Saturn Enterprises, had designed and built the *Empress*. Wilbur Denton—of course! Number one on the Fortune Five Hundred for twenty years; eccentric and recluse in his own fabulous city on Mimas, built inside Herschel crater; the richest human being alive; and an unquestioned genius in the realm of supercomputer technology. The man who'd been beaming huge sums of money to Paul's ministry.

That Wilbur Denton!

"Yes," Paul replied, trying not to betray his surprise. "You say you've come all the way from Saturn—to attend my crusades?"

"Well, Mimas, actually," Denton joked. In the case of the gas giants, which were uninhabitable, it was common parlance to refer to the planet rather than its moons. When the *Empress* advertised Saturn as its farthest port of call, for example, it meant the Saturnian *system*—with stops at all the inhabited moons.

"Yes, of course. Mimas. I'm humbled, sir. It's an honor to have someone of your reputation—"

"Nonsense, Reverend! To be present at such an historic event, sir, is an honor for *me*."

"Well," said Paul, searching for an appropriately humble response. "I'm glad to know you appreciate the work of the L-rd. With all the persecution back on Earth, it's rare to find someone of your status in the world community taking a stand for Christ."

Denton's face lit up like a child's. He'd not as yet released Paul's hand, and the evangelist began to fear that he might never do so. He pumped it up and down once again, his countenance radiating boyish enthusiasm.

"Yes!" he exclaimed. "That *is* what I'm doing, isn't it? Taking a stand for Christ!"

It crossed Paul's mind that the rumors of Denton's madness might have been accurate, after all. "I should like to take this opportunity to thank you, Mr. Denton, for the generous gifts you've bestowed upon the Church in recent months. If only you knew how desperately they're needed." *And.* he added silently: *if only you knew how much of it went to purchase horses!* He wasn't sure Denton would have approved of his money being put to such a use.

"You're quite welcome, of course. And you can count on more assistance from me. Much more."

"How very generous of you. sir. May the L-rd reward you richly."

"He already has!" said Denton, finally releasing his grip on Paul's hand. "Brother Paul, you and I must meet again before we arrive on Luna. There's something of vital importance that I must discuss with you. *Vital* importance!" The boyish grin was gone, as if wiped from his features. In its place was the look of a man on a desperate errand—a very sane and solemn man. "In fact," Denton lowered his voice conspiratorially and leaned closer. "I know what's happened on Earth, sir. The Party has taken control of the United States, just as it did with the European Union. And there are rumors of a revolution on the moon."

"I've heard those rumors."

"I know many of the instigators. Good capitalists like myself, every one of them dedicated to individual freedom and private ownership. A new generation of Paul Reveres and John Hancocks. They want their piece of the Lunar pie—and by Heaven they deserve it! They've slaved for years down in those airless mineshafts. And there are certainly enough of them. They outnumber their bosses a hundred to one. They could easily take control."

"What if they *do* take control? What if the PWP loses the moon?"

"The outer colonies will follow the Lunies in open rebellion. If they succeed, they'll turn Luna's nuclear arsenal on the Earth. Earth will respond, and there's your Armageddon, Reverend."

"The Party seeks to control the entire solar system?"

"Of course! Socialism is a cancer. It either spreads or it dies."

"Impossible!"

"Not so impossible. We once thought the New Agers were a bunch of crackpot theosophists, remember? Now they practically control the Earth. One last little prize—Luna—and they'll rule all of humankind. The Earth-Luna system is the heart of the solar system, Reverend. Any planet cut off from their resources will wither and die. Believe me, they can do it."

Paul leaned back in his seat and turned his face to the porthole. He watched as the gargantuan hull of the *Empress*—Denton's own creation—floated nearer. Its docking-bay dilated like the mouth of a whale to engulf them. He suddenly felt like old Jonah falling helplessly into the belly of a "great fish". A panic not unlike claustrophobia gripped him. He fought it back.

"Mr. Denton," he said at last. "You've taken me by surprise with all this talk of political intrigue. Frankly, I'm not quite sure how to respond."

"That's why I insist we must talk, Reverend. And it's

important that we do so before we arrive on Luna. It's a matter of life and death—yours."

He stood up and took Paul's hand again. The boyish grin was back on his face as he resumed his annoying pulping action.

"Well, goodbye, then, Reverend," he said. "You're the one man in the solar system I admire. I can't tell you what a pleasure it's been to meet you!"

"The pleasure was all mine," Paul murmured, but Denton had broken away and was disappearing among the debarking passengers. It occurred to him only after the man was out of sight that Denton could have made his acquaintance at any time during the long Martian crusade. Why had he waited until they were leaving the planet?

And then it hit him.

Denton hadn't been on Mars at all!

The man hadn't lied about it, exactly—he'd merely implied it. But he'd certainly lied about wanting to see the Martian crusades.

Paul considered it possible, even likely, that Denton had flown down on this very shuttle for the express purpose of delivering his enigmatic warning. Now that he thought about it, he didn't recall seeing Denton among the passengers awaiting the shuttle down on the surface. No—he was certain of it. Denton had *not* been among them. He must have just arrived on the *Empress* from Saturn—on the mighty space-liner he himself had built!

α

The weeks passed slowly on his return trip to Luna, and yet there was no word from Denton. Paul went so far as to check the passenger list to be certain his name appeared, that the man who'd accosted him on the shuttle had not been an impostor. (It was Denton, all right.) He debated whether or not to mention the extraordinary encounter to his staff, but decided against it. They'd just say the man was crazy; they'd reiterate the stories of his infamous eccentricities. Having met the man, Paul wasn't sure he could disagree with that premise. After all, Denton had warned him about some "matter of life and death" and then suddenly vanished without a trace, save for the blinking letters of his name on the passenger list. Where *was* he?

It occurred to Paul that an entry on the list didn't prove the man was Denton, only that he'd somehow acquired—or perhaps falsified—Denton's I.D. (No bluecards off world.) It would be an easy task for someone with the proper connections—a government agent, perhaps? Was he sent to spy on them, to gain their confidence in the guise of an eccentric multimillionaire lavishing funds on their ministry? Plastic surgery was as simple as having a tooth filled. He might even be the assassin Phil Esteban had been so concerned about on the trip out to Mars. But Paul's instincts rejected that idea. Somehow he was sure that Denton was who he claimed to be.

But why hadn't he contacted Paul as he'd promised? Still, Paul felt no inclination to discuss the matter with his staff. Nor would he take any steps to contact Denton himself. It might not do to appear too eager. If there *was* a government agent posing as Wilbur Denton, he might be trying to trap Paul into conspiring against the PWP. (A CD of Paul's voice in treasonous conversation would be sufficient evidence to hang him.) And yet the feeling arose within him once again that Denton was no spy for the government, but precisely what he appeared to be. Well—if he wanted to contact Paul badly enough, nothing would stop him.

After a time, Paul's curiosity about Denton and his "something of vital importance" faded away in the midst of chapel services, Bible studies with his staff, the writing of his Messianic Jewish history, and detailed plans for the Lunar crusade.

α

On the trip out to Mars he'd spent much of his time in leisurely conferences with his team, planning the now-completed and unexpectedly fruitful Martian tour. To Paul's delight, hundreds of pioneers flocked to Polis Marineris, the new colony on the southern rim of Mariner Canyon, from as far afield as Argyre Crater in the Nereidum and Charitum Ranges. The warm reception to his messages, the souls pouring down the isles to give their hearts to the L-rd, were fond memories for the evangelist whose broadcasts of *New Heaven, New Earth* had so suddenly left the air after being faithfully beamed to Mars for the past twelve years. None of them blamed Paul. Martian explorers reported having picked up his signal on everything from the most advanced holoscreens in the settlement to jury-rigged receivers of the poorest quality. Many spoke of the comfort those broadcasts had been to them. They missed their sense of contact with the Church on Earth, but there was nothing they could do but offer their hard-earned credits to assist the pilgrims in their flight. And this they had done. In greater abundance than Paul had dared hope for!

Phil Esteban, senior member of the staff, was awestruck by the success of the Martian tour. He talked of little else on the way back. Although rumors of an attempt on Paul's life suddenly abounded, tempering the enthusiasm of the rest of the team, Esteban's exuberance was infectious. It was hard to believe that, on the trip out, he'd been urging Paul to cancel the Lunar crusades scheduled for the return voyage to Earth.

"Mars' atmosphere is thin," Esteban had warned, "but at least it *has* one. You have to be careful, Paul. Pace yourself when you speak outdoors. Don't get winded in your suit. Keep the fans on high and stay cool. The temperature this time of year at the equator is about fifty degrees Fahrenheit. It'd be cool without the pressure suit. And a simple oxygen mask would probably keep you breathing comfortably—if not for the low atmospheric pressure. That's the killer. You have to remember that it's a hostile environment."

"I understand, Phil," said Paul. "I'll be careful."

"But compared to Luna, Mars is a paradise. The moon's an airless vacuum. No outdoor meetings are possible there, unless you intend to bounce around in one-sixth gee, thumping Lunies on their helmets with your Bible."

The image made Paul laugh.

"What about Tranquility Arena? We could draw capacity crowds every night. It holds thousands under a huge geodesic dome. And I understand it has real grass, as well. It sounds like the perfect place for a rally."

"Sure, Reverend, just perfect. But you know the political situation on Luna. The miners are battling the provisional government now. They hate being under Party control. There's a revolutionary group in every mineshaft from Tranquility to Mare Imbrium. Frankly, the moon's a hornets' nest of insurrection—"

"Phil!" Paul cut in, placing a hand on his friend's shoulder. "I know all this. What's your point?"

"My point, sir, is that everyone on Luna *expects* us to use Tranquility Arena. You've heard the rumors about an assassination attempt. Where there's smoke, as they say, there's usually fire. Remember that lunatic who took a shot at you in New Trenton?"

"Of course, Phil. That's not an event one easily forgets."

"There's no way I can lct you speak at Tranquility. In fact, I recommend we beam Luna and cancel the crusades altogether."

"Cancel? Cancel the potential salvation of a thousand souls?" Paul shook his head emphatically. "No! I certainly didn't leave the brethren on Earth to cancel crusades on the moon. The tension there is all the more reason for me to preach, Phil, not to run from my commission like—like Jonah! I'll hear no more about cancellations."

Phil Esteban's features took on the look of carved stone. "Yes, Reverend," he said, and abruptly stalked away.

Paul had never seen the man so sullen, so deeply distraught, as he'd been on the remainder of the voyage to Mars.

But the success of the Martian crusades had changed all that. Esteban suddenly became the most confident member of the team. He began calling Paul by his first name once again. He'd even beamed Luna, telling them of Paul's intention to preach to as many people as wanted to hear the Word. Still wary of approving the Tranquility Arena facility, he was absorbed in the task of selecting alternative sites.

The fear of impending assassination had lifted at last.

The Interloper

Now Paul was facing that fear again.

Across the sandy beach of an imaginary seashore, a young man in black was approaching with determined strides. Two guards, fully armed, emerged from the entrance-portal behind the intruder. They called to him, their voices lost to Paul's ears in the crashing of the surf—but not, he knew, to the intruder's.

For the interloper—and for the guards advancing on him at a full sprint—there was no illusion of sea and sand. To their perceptions they were advancing across a bare metal floor. Every footstep, every command to halt, echoed loudly around the curved walls of the chamber, a thunderous reverberation in the intruder's ears. Why wasn't he stopping, then? Why did he continue on his desperate errand, as if driven?

Paul could now see his features with clarity. He placed his

age at twenty-five or so, a handsome fellow wearing a curiously wrinkled suit of black clothing and at least a three-day growth of stubble across his broad chin. Dark curls, damp with sweat, fell over his brow.

His eyes were large, dark, determined. His shoulders were unusually broad, slightly out of proportion to the rest of his body, as if he'd been developing his biceps at the expense of the rest of his body. As he drew closer, Paul's fear changed to a feeling of—what was it?—sympathy? Protectiveness? Something in the man's appearance, something familiar. Yes, of course! The protectiveness was an old instinct from decades of persecution, a *kindredness*—if there *was* such a word—that went beyond one's political convictions. The intruder's prominent aquiline nose and thick, dark eyebrows, were an unusual sight on American territory these days. But they were features Paul himself shared.

Lundsman!

He began to move forward—*toward* the intruder.

Had he stayed put, the guards would have easily caught up with his assailant before the man could reach him. But Paul was helping to shorten the distance between them, placing himself in imminent danger. His bracelet began to chime—Brother Wallace trying to warn him away. He ignored it and pressed on, moving even faster, the shouts of the approaching guards going unheeded by the intruder. One of them dropped to his knees, raising a rifle to his shoulder and sighting carefully along the barrel at the young man's back. This would be no warning shot.

"Stop!" Paul cried, waving his arms in the air, palms forward, momentarily forgetting that their hearing wasn't muted by the surf. But of course they could hear him.

"Stop!" he called again.

The intruder was only meters away. Paul saw brute fear in his eyes. Yes, the man was certainly a Jew. And, whatever his errand, Paul couldn't let him fall into the hands of the guards without knowing his mission. If his mission was to kill, then so be it. Paul's survival instinct strove against an urge to trust and protect his own kind, to risk his life, if necessary. Besides, Brother Wallace had detected no weapon. Did he intend to strangle Paul with his bare hands? Unlikely. Yet the crouching guard had not lowered his rifle in response to Paul's cry. He was taking careful aim. The second guard was still running, a pistol in his hand…

"Don't fire!" he shouted. "I *know* this man!"

It was a lie. The guard lowered the rifle, rose to his feet, and slid his arm through the shoulder strap, letting the weapon dangle harmlessly at his side. His companion slowed to a panting walk. Paul made a mental note to repent of his sin at some later time—if lying to save a life was indeed a sin. (What of the Christians who'd lied to the Gestapo about sheltering Jews in their homes? Were they sinning? The rabbis said no; their words affirmed life. By protecting innocent souls from the Nazi wolves, they'd actually been bearing witness to a higher Truth.)

He'd have to pray about that.

Suddenly the young man was upon him, facing him boldly. A cold fear gripped him, but he stood his ground, looking the intruder over with experienced eyes. *He's a stowaway*, Paul thought. *What else could account for his disheveled appearance?* His black outfit looked as if he'd been sleeping in it for weeks. And the stubble on his chin gave the impression of a man for whom bathing had become a rare luxury. Dark circles rimmed his eyes, yet he had a certain indefinable bearing—even in his wrinkled black outfit—a bearing that spoke of notoriety, success. The top buttons of his shirt were open, revealing the same dark, curly hair that adorned his head. An expensive bracelet circled his left wrist. The disproportionate mass of his arms and shoulders heaved as he struggled to catch his breath, as he tried to frame his words. It was time, Paul decided, for a convincing display of bravado. He hoped he could pull it off.

"How did you get in here, young man?" he demanded.

The intruder grinned in a friendly way. The effect, Paul thought, was rather pleasant.

"I bribed a guard," he admitted.

"Impossible!" Paul said with a wave of his hand; his eyebrows drew together like gathering storm-clouds. "They're too highly paid. Now, either you tell me the truth, young man, or I'll turn you over to those two." He indicated the approaching guards. "They take a dim view of stowaways."

The fellow seemed impressed by Paul's observation. He lowered his eyes. Paul felt a surge of compassion for him, and softened his tone as much as he dared.

"Are you Jewish?" he inquired.

"Yes," said the intruder. "My name's Jeri Kline."

"Jeri Kline!" Paul said, stunned. "The radio broadcaster?"

The young man looked up and grinned again.

"Talk show host, yes. I'm sure you've heard of me."

Relieved, Paul moved forward and embraced him. Kline stiffened, taken aback by such an unwarranted display of affection.

"Don't say a word!" Paul whispered in his ear. "Let me do the talking."

"Okay," Kline nodded.

"Jeri! How good it is to see you!" Paul cried, loud enough for the guards to overhear. "Where have you been keeping yourself? You look simply *dreadful!*"

Kline's body relaxed as the guards stepped up behind him, returning the embrace with an enthusiasm that surprised even Paul. Breaking away, Paul addressed the guards with the calm assurance of a man suddenly reprieved from a death sentence. He reminded himself not to lie this time—yet weren't there sins of omission as well?

"This young man," he said, "is Jeri Kline, the American radio personality. We know each other well." He shot an ironic glance at Kline. Kline winked back. It was certainly no lie, but the guards were not as gullible as he'd assumed.

"Yeah, bitter enemies from way back," one of them chuckled.

"Officer!" Paul replied with a look of genuine surprise. "The religious opinions expressed by Mr. Kline on his radio program are an exercise of free speech. We disagree, of course. But that hasn't influenced the warm friendship that's always existed between us."

He was lying again, but there was no helping it. Kline cocked an eyebrow at this growing string of falsehoods. Keeping the professional grin pasted on his unshaven face, he drew a friendly arm around Paul's shoulders.

"That's right, gentlemen," he chimed in, taking the burden of equivocation from the evangelist to himself. "Brother Paul and I have been friends for many years."

The guards looked from one to the other, calculating. The outspoken one gave Paul a wry grin.

"Then perhaps you can explain, sir," he said, "why your friend's name doesn't appear on the passenger list."

"An oversight, of course. Another typical computer malfunction, I should think. You youngsters rely far too much on those imbecilic machines."

"Come now, Reverend—"

"A man of Mr. Kline's economic station," Paul interrupted, "does not need to stow away on a spaceliner. Your ship's computer has made a grievous error. And your captain can expect to be hearing from Mr. Kline's attorney."

The second guard took in Kline's disheveled appearance with obvious suspicion. "Yes, but—"

"That'll be all, gentlemen. If you'd take the time to double check the passenger list, you'll find that Mr. Kline's fare has been paid in full. Round trip to—where was it?"

"Saturn," Kline supplied.

"Round trip to Saturn. He travels first class, of course."

"Of course," said the first guard, giving in. His expression revealed that he would do precisely as Paul had suggested—as soon as possible.

"Thank you," Paul said, "for your timely response to what you perceived to be a dangerous situation. I shall commend you both to your superiors."

The guards nodded and withdrew. When they were a safe distance away, Paul pressed the button on his bracelet. A contrite voice responded.

"Sorry, Reverend! I don't know how he could have gotten in!"

"Yes," Paul replied, mindful of the acoustic properties of the chamber and keeping his voice low. "As you told me once before, Brother Wallace. Now, listen to me carefully."

"Sir?"

"The name of our interloper is Jeri Kline."

"The radio nut?"

Paul shot a glance at Kline. The young man's grin broadened at this familiar assessment of his vocation.

"Indeed," Paul confirmed. "The radio nut."

"The atheist?"

"The same. Now I want you to contact Captain Mills and arrange for round-trip fare to be paid in Mr. Kline's name."

"Round-trip, sir? To where?"

"Pardon me, Brother Wallace. To Saturn."

"Saturn? That's seven thousand credits!"

"*Ten* thousand. Mr. Kline travels first class."

"Yes, sir." Wallace's voice sounded pained. "Uh—anything else, Reverend?"

"Now that you mention it, see if you can procure one of the empty suites on our own deck for our young guest."

Wallace sighed. "Very unusual procedure, sir. I'm not sure the Captain will be amenable—"

"If he refuses, ask it as a personal favor to me."

"I'm sure that'll change his mind!" said Wallace. "And what if he still refuses?"

"Then double the fare, of course."

The reception's bad, sir. I thought you said 'double the fare.'" The words seemed to lodge in Wallace's throat like syntho-chicken bones.

"The reception is perfect and you're wasting precious time. Brother Madden is in charge of accounting, is he not?"

"He is, sir."

"Then I'll take the matter up with him." Paul snapped off the connection, remembered something, and pressed the button again.

"Brother Wallace?"

"Yes, Reverend."

"As reluctant as I am to squander the Martian Church's donations…"

"Of course."

"I believe it would be a good idea to pay for another hour in the simulator."

"Certainly, sir."

"And would you arrange to include Mr. Kline in the simulation?"

"Done."

"I thank you, again, Brother Wallace."

"Yes, sir. Anything else?"

"No, that'll be all."

Paul watched the expression on Kline's face as the young man's share of the simulation kicked in, suddenly transforming his surroundings from curving gray walls to what Paul himself was experiencing—the sound of thundering surf, the scent of brisk, clean air, the salty breeze against his skin. Paul's simulation cleverly included the sight of Kline's hair and garments fluttering in the wind, just as Kline himself was experiencing it. Paul smiled when the young man nearly lost his balance as the solid floor beneath his feet turned to pliant sand. Kline gazed, enraptured, as the dizzying, disorienting moment whisked him to the virgin shore of a terrestrial ocean. Turning the simulation on, apparently, did not have the same "negative psychological effect" as turning it off without warning. It was not usually done, but Paul noted that it *could* be done, filing it for future reference. Kline looked around and let out a sigh.

"I've never seen the ocean!"

"Nor are you seeing it now," Paul reminded him. "It's all produced by the ship's mainframe computer.'

"I'd sure like to have *that* computer!"

"Don't be silly. It's probably just another mindless tangle of silicon and wires."

"No," said Kline. His voice carried a note of certainty. "No, I don't think so."

He drew in a deep breath, letting it out in another sigh of awe. "This computer is special, Brother Paul—*very* special. Did you ever think that in the wrong hands such a machine could be dangerous?"

"Hmmm." Paul considered the implications and shivered in the cool breeze. Then he shrugged it off. "No, there must be strict regulations governing the proper use of such technology."

"I hope so."

"Shall we walk?" he offered.

"Sure," said Kline. "Lead the way."

They ambled some distance in silence before Paul spoke.

"So, to what do I owe the honor of this—unannounced visit, Mr. Kline?"

Kline looked up, still somewhat awestruck, at the seagulls spinning overhead.

"First of all, Reverend," he began, "I think you should know that your friend, Brother Wallace, was wrong about me."

"In what way?"

"In every way, sir. About my being a nut, for instance."

"Please, Mr. Kline. Accept my apologies for Brother Wallace's thoughtless remark."

"It wasn't thoughtless, Reverend. Just wrong. I'm really quite sane."

"I don't doubt it for a moment."

"I'm not a nut, sir, and I'm not an atheist."

Paul laughed aloud. "Come now, Mr. Kline. On your radio program you characterized my ministry as—how did you put it? 'Brother Paul's Circus for the Senile'? That was one epithet I recall with distaste. And then there was my favorite: 'The Opiate of the Asses'!"

"I guess you *have* heard of me."

"More of you," said Paul, "than it might have been prudent for me to hear. My staff, you'll be gratified to know, never missed a broadcast. I've been blessed with a very zealous group of advisors who make it their business to keep me informed about my detractors—of whom there are legion. G-d has granted me the wisdom, however, to attribute such vulgar remarks to the enemy of our souls, Mr. Kline, rather than to the unfortunate individuals he uses as mouthpieces."

"I expressed a lot of—uncharitable sentiments on my program, Reverend."

"I detect a gift for understatement that has hitherto eluded me, Mr. Kline. 'Uncharitable sentiments' you say? But they're *your* sentiments. And you're entitled to your opinion."

"My opinion has changed, sir."

"Changed?" Paul stopped in his tracks. "I don't understand. In what way?"

"There's something you never knew about me, Reverend. Very few people knew, in fact, except for family and friends and a select group of coworkers. I appreciate your telling the guards that you recognized me, but you obviously didn't. You've never seen a photograph of me."

"No, that's true. I haven't."

"If you'd seen some of my publicity photos, you'd have noticed that they were all taken from the waist up, every one of them. It was done at my insistence. I included some detailed stipulations in my contracts concerning interviews, photos, holovision appearances—anything having to do with my personal life. I even used an assumed name while traveling."

As they began walking again, Paul tried to understand this young man. None of what Kline was saying seemed to have anything to do with his stowing away aboard the *Empress*. Or risking his life for this meeting with a man he openly despised.

"By the way—thank you, Brother Paul," Kline said. "I was so keyed up that I neglected to thank you for saving my life. And paying all that money for my fare."

"Never mind," said Paul. "You were a fellow Jew in danger. We're kinsmen, aren't we? No matter what our beliefs? The Sages teach that once a Jew, always a Jew. Who can unchoose what G-d has chosen?"

"Yes. I suppose so. But thank you anyway. I hope I can make it up to you and the members of your church. The money, I mean."

"Put the money out of your mind, Mr. Kline. Please continue."

"Well—you see, Reverend, I had a secret I was trying to keep hidden from the world."

"What secret?"

"I was a paraplegic, sir—completely paralyzed below the waist. I lived my life in a wheelchair."

Paul tried to conceal his shock. Was Kline telling him the truth? The husky young man was walking beside him, undeniably well and whole! And yet he recalled being surprised by Kline's top-heavy build, attributing it to a lifestyle of exercising only the top half of his body. Precisely what being confined to a wheelchair would do.

"I didn't know," Paul murmured, unsure of what he should say in response to this revelation.

"Few did. When I was six years old, I contracted polio. And for as long as I can remember—clearly, anyway—I was in a wheelchair. I didn't let it stop me. I learned to play basketball in it. I…I dated girls in it. And I did all of my radio shows in it. I wanted to accomplish so much, Brother Paul, despite my handicap—perhaps *because* of it. I was determined to be accepted by the world as a normal man, a *whole* man. Radio broadcasting seemed perfect for me. Popularity. Fame. And an audience that would never know my secret. Until *you* came along."

"Me? I'm not sure I follow you."

"As your fame as a Hebrew Christian evangelist grew, my hatred for you grew in direct proportion."

"But why?"

Kline turned to face him. He was clearly agitated, recalling his pain and humiliation. "Can't you understand? There you were—a Jew, which was hard enough for me to accept—claiming that G-d is gracious and merciful. But I'd been a cripple all my life, chained to that ridiculous wheelchair. Only half a man—"

"Unadulterated self pity!" Paul interrupted. "You had accomplished more than most men accomplish on two good legs. From what you've told me, you lived an active, fulfilling life."

"Active, yes. And you're right about the self pity, too. But you've never been handicapped, Brother Paul, and you can't know what it's like. It was that very feeling of inadequacy that drove me to achieve so much. But no matter what I achieved it was never enough. I was driven, Reverend, by this absurd belief that I wasn't a whole man. I don't know. Perhaps if I'd let myself fall in love… let myself try. A good wife...well, all that's just twenty-twenty hindsight. I was *afraid* to try, afraid to fail! In other areas that wasn't true, perhaps. But with women…you understand. And so I was alone, alone with my anger and my feelings of inadequacy. And I hated. Oh, yes, I hated many things, Reverend. Many people. But *you* most of all."

"That makes no sense! You didn't know me; we'd never met."

"It was what you represented, Reverend. That, and my own belief that I'd never walk again. You see—if *HaShem* was truly compassionate, why had He allowed me to become crippled in the first place? I blamed Him for my polio, not the real enemy, not the one who 'comes to steal, kill, and destroy.' I blamed *HaShem*. He might heal others, but He wouldn't heal *me*. As I saw it, there were only three logical possibilities—" Kline began to relax as he spoke. "One: that G-d *does* perform miracles today, but that He refused mine. I was too wicked and depraved to receive one of His precious miracles, which, in your ministry, seemed to fall like rain. Or two: that as a Jew I'd believed all my life in an impotent G-d who couldn't heal. And yet, the Christ of the Christians—bitter enemies and persecutors of our people for centuries—was the true Messiah."

"They're one and the same, Mr. Kline. '*Shema Yisrael, Adonai Elohaynu, Adonai echod.*' Hear O Israel, the L-rd our G-d, the L-rd is One.'"

"Yes, I know that now. But, as a Jew yourself, surely you can understand the dilemma it created for me. Surely you went through something similar."

Paul recalled his experience in the Gospel tent, those many years ago—an angry young Jew screaming obscenities at the preacher—hating him, hating everyone. Irrationally, violently, utterly.

"Yes. Of course."

"And, thirdly: I could reject both possibilities, because they were unacceptable on every level. I could reject G-d. So I became an atheist. More than that, I began a campaign, a personal vendetta, against you and your ministry. Against everything you stood for. Against your Messiah who willingly healed everyone but me. I was directing all the frustration, the loneliness, and the bitterness of my youth into a dreary hate campaign."

"'And Saul,'" Paul quoted, "'yet breathing out threatening and slaughter against the disciples of the L-rd…'"

"Yes, sir. Exactly. Just like that fellow Saul in the Bible, my hatred of G-d's people became, for a while at least, my ticket to success. My fame just seemed to skyrocket. I was expressing the rage of a G-dless generation. As you said yourself, I was the Devil's mouthpiece. And I'm ashamed of that."

"Go on. Tell me the rest."

"Well, the time came for me to put my money where my mouth was, so to speak. You were planning a crusade in Sparks, Nevada, and my listeners expected me to lash out more bitterly against you as the time drew nearer. I didn't disappoint them. Oddly, one of my callers became an unwitting vessel of G-d's mercy. She suggested that that someone should go to your crusade with a team of electronics experts and get to the bottom of all those phony miracles. The idea galvanized me. The following day I announced that I would be the one to expose you. I'd attend the Sparks crusade and bring back proof—proof that Paul Moscowitz was a snake-oil salesman, a defrauder and a cheat, a pious swindler." A sneer came to Kline's face as he remembered, hating himself.

"I wonder why my staff didn't tell me about that broadcast, just to let me know what you were up to."

"Maybe they thought it might distract you."

"Maybe."

"Anyway, the response was exactly as I'd predicted. Emails poured into the station, congratulating me on carrying the banner of rationalism, on having the courage to resist the last bastion of the religious right. The station manager gave me another raise. The newslinks took up the story and ran with it. I became a worldwide celebrity overnight."

"How nice for you."

"I was at the peak of my popularity and fame. The hatred that had fueled my success seemed justified. I drew strength from all the angry, frustrated callers. I knew in my heart that I would finally bring you down."

"Demon spirits," said Paul in a comforting tone, "seek out the hurting and hopeless ones."

"That was me, all right—hurting and hopeless. But how could I see that? I was on top of the world. I was wealthy. My name was a household word. How could I admit to being frustrated, unfulfilled, hopeless? That vendetta of mine even helped me forget my handicap. I was obsessed with the thought of ruining you."

Paul felt his heart going out to this young Jew, so confused, and yet so terribly driven by forces beyond his comprehension. So like himself as a young Zionist.

"It was G-d you were trying to destroy, son, not me."

"I know that now."

"So what happened?"

"I went to the Sparks crusade. I dyed my hair gray and wore a fake moustache and glasses. I selected a team of experts, made up mostly of personal friends and coworkers from the station who were aware of my handicap. As I waited for you to mount the podium my hatred just seemed to explode until it filled every cell in my body. I can't explain it exactly. I had a feeling, a sensation of—catharsis. Am I making sense?"

"Yes," Paul said, once again recalling his experience in the revival tent. "More than you realize."

"I was seated up front with the other folks in wheelchairs. They seemed so hopeful. How could they fall for such an obvious sham? And how could anyone be so evil, so depraved, as to foist this hoax on them? To give them hope when there *was* no hope? And then I wondered how many of them were themselves fakes, hired to play the part of cripples, to leap out of their wheelchairs at a touch from your hand, leaving the rest of us to wonder why G-d hadn't done the same for us. Wasn't our faith perfected? Was there some evil in us, unrevealed, that caused G-d to pass over us? How

I despised your con game! The greater my proximity to you, it seemed, the greater my rage. Can you ever forgive me?"

"If Messiah has forgiven you," said Paul affectionately, "How can I do any less? That hatred consuming you—it was not your own. It belonged to the demons oppresssing your spirit. Demons grow rather uncomfortable when in proximity to the *Ruach haKodesh*."

"Yes. I see that now. But, then, as you began to speak, even the sound of your voice repulsed me. I wanted to spit in your face."

"What *did* you do?"

"I listened."

"Good."

"And, as I listened, I....well, I just can't explain *what* happened."

Kline stopped in his tracks. His voice faltered and he fell silent, staring down at the sand.

"Yes?" Paul prompted.

"It seemed that your voice was like—like the blade of a sword cutting into the core of my being. With every word that blade swung back and forth, cutting deeper and deeper. And then....I began to weep. For the first time since I can remember I was weeping!"

As Kline described the event, vivid memories of the Sparks crusade come flooding into Paul's mind. There was something *HaShem* wanted him to remember about that night....something he'd been instructed to do in the Spirit. And there'd been a promise...."

"When you finished your sermon," Kline continued, "you stepped down from the podium and began walking directly toward me...."

That's it! Paul thought. *A gray-haired man in a wheelchair, the promise G-d gave me...* "I remember," he said. "There was an elderly man with glasses in the front row. The Lord spoke to me as I was closing the message. He said: '*Do you see the man in the wheelchair? Command him to walk in My Name, and I will perform a mighty miracle. That man is not what he appears to be. He has come here as your enemy. But tonight he will become your friend. In days to come he will be a comfort to you, because I have ordained it from his birth.*'"

Paul glanced at Jeri Kline, who looked back at him with an odd expression. It was an experience Paul had always referred to by the Greek word *rhema*, that moment when the plans of mortal man and the plans of his Maker seemed to collide with a crash of revelation—when Paul would look up from his petty circumstances, as if popping his head through a cloud, to see the bigger picture. The sensation only lasted a moment, but it was obvious that Kline had felt it too.

"Please continue," Paul said.

"You were walking toward me and I thought: 'He recognizes me! He knows who I am! He's going to expose me!' I was afraid of you, although there was no reason for it. As you came closer I gripped the arms of my chair until my knuckles turned white. Then you were looking down at me. Your eyes were filled with a power—a *knowledge*—I can't find the words! You looked right into me, as if you not only recognized me, but knew me intimately. You knew what I'd come to do! Suddenly all the fear drained from my heart. I sat exposed, naked. Your eyes seemed to take in all the anger and bitterness I'd held for you, to understand and forgive it all. There was no need to fear you. You weren't going to reveal my identity, the fact that I was a cripple. You weren't going to expose my sin, to bring vengeance on me for wanting to destroy you. But then I thought: 'It's not this man's eyes I'm looking into. Not the man I came here to harm. *Not a man at all!* These are the eyes of—*Messiah!*' I knew something was going to happen. A strange sensation came over me, as if I were about to be hurled from that wheelchair—straight into the air. And then you spoke. You used Hebrew, knowing I was Jewish. You said, '*B'Shem Yeshua haMashiach, ha-gatz'ri koom heet-halech!'* In the name of Jesus Christ, rise up and walk!"

Kline spun around, grasping Paul's shoulders with both hands. "And I did! I walked! And I've been walking ever since! You raised me out of that wheelchair, Brother Paul!"

"I did no such thing, young man. I couldn't cure an ant of an earache. It was Almighty G-d who raised you up, and you must give Him alone the glory for it."

"But He used *you* to do it. A man I despised. A man I swore to destroy."

"I am nothing. He made use of me in your case because I was the focus of your demonic hatred. G-d has His own reasons for using such puny vessels as you and I. What did you do then?"

"I knelt and gave my heart to the L-rd. I poured out my soul to Him and asked forgiveness for the wicked things I'd done. And I promised to be a *ba'al t'shuvah*, a master of repentance. I was under heavy conviction from the Holy Spirit. The words of my atheistic broadcasts came back to me in a new light. How many people had I harmed with my blind hatred? How much faith—how many souls—had I personally destroyed? That night I wept gallons of tears. Cleansing tears, because I knew I was forgiven, despite what I'd done. I had made G-d my enemy, yet He was welcoming me home as a son! I felt His hands on my shoulders through the whole thing, forgiving me, reassuring me, filling my heart with a peace I hadn't known since before the polio struck me down. I wanted to make everything right. I wasn't the least bit ashamed to go on the radio and tell the world what Messiah had done for me, the great miracle He'd performed for one who'd despised Him. Not just in my body, in my heart as well. But I made one mistake."

"Yes?"

"I was so excited—so naïve, so certain my miracle would change everything—I came walking—more like bouncing—into the studio the next day. No wheelchair. I never wanted to sit in that thing again, for any reason. The station manager saw me, and, well—I had to tell him everything. I couldn't very well deny what G-d had done, and I thought it would open his eyes. You see, I'd always thought he liked me, Reverend. He treated me special, always gave me whatever I asked for, always smiling at me. I didn't realize he was getting grants from New Age organizations to keep my program on the air. That he was only patronizing me. That all along I'd been nothing more than a commodity to him. If only I'd spent one more day in that wheelchair! If only I'd come to work in it, like every other day, I might have made it to that microphone! And I would have told the world that your ministry was no fraud—that you'd healed me and made a believer out of me!"

Paul placed a hand on Kline's arm and continued walking. Kline followed.

"And so your station manager fired you," Paul said.

"On the spot. 'You're not getting near that microphone,' he said. I tried to convince him that the news of my healing was even more sensational than my attacks on your ministry. It would create controversy, more listeners. But he was having none of it. He explained that his station had a reputation for objectivity. *Objectivity!* Can you believe it? My healed body was just about the most objective fact one could find! But I realized, Reverend, that for most people, scientific or journalistic objectivity is nothing more than a synonym for unbelief. Claim that G-d doesn't exist and, by definition, you're *objective.* Claim that He exists and you've *lost* objectivity. It's insidious! Being invisible to the eye, G-d can never be an objective fact. Even if you provided material proof, it wouldn't matter. The media believes what it wants to believe and calls itself objective. And I learned something else, too. Love of money is definitely the root of all evil. My boss told me he wasn't about to turn his station into a freak show." Kline gave a bitter laugh. "As if it wasn't a freak show to begin with—with me as the main attraction!"

"Don't allow bitterness to take root again. It was more than stubborn unbelief on your station manager's part, more than the lure of filthy lucre. It was fear. He feared the consequences—and with good reason. The people sponsoring your broadcasts are now in control of the government. And the government executes believers these days."

"I suppose I shouldn't be so hard on him."

"Judge his actions, not his soul. Leave that final judgment to G-d. So, your source of income suddenly dried up, which is why you had to stow away on this flight. There are no credits on your bluecard, Mr. Kline, is that correct?"

"That about sums it up, Reverend. I'm flat broke. But please call me Jeri."

"Alright, Jeri. We have no need of bluecards here, you know. There's no PWP. Interplanetary space is a free country, as it were."

"I'm glad of that."

"But it also explains why you risked your life to find me. Now that you're a believer, without employment, without money, perhaps about to have your card revoked, you wanted to apply for work on my staff—in broadcasting, perhaps?"

"Not at all! I don't mean to appear ungrateful, but the thought never occurred to me. After the libelous things I said about you, I never imagined you'd *consider* hiring me. The truth is

I'm finished with broadcasting for good."

"Nonsense!" said Paul, dismissing the notion with a wave of his hand. "*HaShem* needs your gift more than ever in these times. After all, He gave it to you. Your testimony will shake the world, Jeri! It will do more irrevocable harm to the minions of Satan than a hundred of my own crusades. Surely you can see that."

"Perhaps, Reverend. I don't know. I'm just not ready to go back to it right now. Without all that hatred churning up inside me, I might not have the old fire."

"You'll have the fire of the Holy Ghost. What you had before was 'strange fire.' But, Jeri, if you don't need my assistance, why did you run that deadly race with those guards just now? What is it you want?"

"I want to warn you."

"Warn me? About what?"

"About the moon, sir."

"What about the moon?"

"I've learned certain things, Reverend. From very reliable sources. Things you need to know."

Paul directed a piercing gaze into Kline's dark eyes. "What things, precisely?"

"There's a plot to assassinate you, sir. If you set foot on the moon—anywhere on the moon—you'll be killed."

The Conspiracy

Lieutenant Matthew Baker, USAF, showed up an hour early for his rendezvous with the man called "Smith". He found the domed cafe in Sinus Iridum, their prearranged meeting place, and sat near a ceiling-high bubble in the back. Baker spent a few moments gazing out across the Bay of Rainbows, a lifeless slab of sun-scorched rock and silver-gray dust enclosed within jagged mountain ridges. He marveled at the disparity between the lunar features and their romantic names. If those venerable old stargazers who'd given them such promising designations had only been able to gaze upon their "oceans" and "bays" from the perspective enjoyed by the average "Lunie," how surprised they would have been!

Over the eastern ridge of Sinus Iridum, the glittering curve of the Mare Imbrium Dome could be seen. It housed an immense mining complex over thirty kilometers across and two deep. A hundred thousand miners lived and worked in those shafts.

He drew a palm-com out of his shirt pocket, opened it up, and resumed reading. It was Ayn Rand's outlawed novella, *Anthem.* Written a century and a half ago, in 1937, it depicted a socialist dystopia where men were identified by numbers, where the word "I' was nonexistent, and where a person spoke of himself as "we". All greatness, all nobility, all achievement had been lost in the mists of the past, until a lone man came upon an ancient electric light.

Rubbish!

Baker had been deleting every copy of *Anthem* he could find on the moon, but they kept popping up like weeds—along with Rand's other two contraband novels, *The Fountainhead* and *Atlas Shrugged.* Anti-socialist fantasies by other authors were turning up as well—Orwell's *1984* and *Animal Farm*, for instance, and Zamyatin's *We*. It was a thankless, frustrating job, but Baker's soul blazed with an all-consuming hatred for counter-revolutionary propaganda. Unrestrained capitalism had had its day, and all that had come of it was the brutal exploitation of the workers.

Oh, certainly the moon's first miners had received exorbitant hazard pay—commensurate with the risks they were taking—and were all sumptuously housed, at least by Lunie standards. But all that eventually changed. Work hours were increased, pay-levels lowered, and accommodations reduced. True enough, there were no documented cases of exploitation or abuse before the PWP took over Lunar affairs, but it was only a matter of time. All the other inhabited moons in the solar system were still operating on individualistic principles of private property and personal gain. Even unionized capitalism, tending as it did toward greed and abuse, was certainly alluring. So the workers needed to be vigilant in order to prevent it from returning, for greed was a powerful motivator.

Baker's mission had been to prevent the return of the old order. The PWP had formed covert three-man cells on Luna, based on the old communist undercover networks of the early 20th century—(according to this cell principle, a conspirator under interrogation could expose only two others)—to spy on the miners, confiscate contraband materials, and, if necessary, eliminate the more dangerous elements by assassination.

The assassination branch had no name; it did not exist.

Some might think this a great deal of trouble to go to, Baker mused, *particularly in the case of a book like* Anthem. *Could a tiny novella push hundreds of thousands of miners over the edge? But it had happened before. One book,* The Communist Manifesto, *had totally altered human events, proving that words could be dangerous weapons. And dangerous weapons, along with dangerous people, had to be eliminated for the good of the masses.*

This turned his thoughts to Paul Jason Moscowitz, the so-called "Last Apostle to the Solar System." Religion was another category of counterrevolutionary thought that could not be tolerated. "*Pie-in-the-sky—Suffer through this life and rewards await you in the next.* Moonpellets! Religion put the masses to sleep, opiated them as Marx had put it, prevented them from rising up and changing their circumstances by force. Now Paul Jason Moscowitz was coming to bring his evangelistic opiates to Luna. But the Party had deemed otherwise. Luna was going to be the last stop on Brother Paul's crusade. It was Baker's job to see to that.

He spotted a man matching Smith's description: tall; wiry; swarthy; close-cropped hair; long, thin nose. He lingered in the entranceway until he spotted Baker, then walked slowly and deliberately toward the back table, spun a chair around, and sat on it backwards. He glared at Baker with contempt.

"Lieutenant Baker," he drawled. "Right?"

"That's right."

"I wasn't expecting someone like *you.*" He emphasized the word "you" with distaste.

"I'm sorry to be such a disappointment. What were you expecting?"

"Someone," Smith shot back, "who looks like he has the stomach for this sort of thing."

"Oh, I assure you, Mr. Smith—not a very imaginative code-name, is it?" He waved his hand for a server. "I assure you I have the stomach for it. Now, shall we order our drinks and get down to business?"

Smith ordered a double shot of bourbon—pricey Earthside stuff, not the usual poison from Enceladus. *Twenty credits' worth,* Baker calculated. *And on my tab*! *Well, no matter. Let this microcephalic rat have his moment of glory. As long as he serves his purpose, he can throw his weight around—within limits, of course.*

Baker noted Smith's contemptuous snort as he ordered his usual plum wine, something the rat apparently wouldn't be caught dead ordering. He allowed himself the private hope that Smith's slug of bourbon would burn a gaping ulcer in his stomach-lining. As long as he survived to complete his contract, he could expire in any number of unappetizing ways—and most likely would. *Perhaps*, Baker thought, *I'll have a hand in it myself. I'd like that very much.* When their drinks arrived, served on black napkins decorated with crescent Earths in the corners, Smith began:

"I want it understood," he said, "that I'll be using a knife for this job, not a gun. Guns are barbaric, noisy, and obvious. You can't smuggle a gun past the most antiquated surveillance system on Luna. You people know that. This isn't a suicide mission."

"Of course not, Mr. Smith," said Baker in the most sardonic tone he could muster. "We wouldn't want you to take any unnecessary risks; there's far too much at stake." He was telling the truth. This vermin's life was of little concern to him, but Smith was the only man on Luna who could do the job. He'd come highly recommended and, much to his distaste, Baker knew it. "What I fail to understand is why a knife would go undetected, when a pistol wouldn't."

"Wood," said the rat.

"It *would*?"

"No, *wood*—the material. I make my blades out of wood, Lieutenant. Whittle them myself. They're sharp as steel and well balanced, too. And I can throw them with great accuracy."

As he spoke, Smith slid his fingers through his greasy hair, then reached out quickly and snatched Baker's collar in his fist. Baker stiffened as the bony knuckles grazed his neck. A clammy chill ran down his spine.

"Smith!" he protested. His voice was a trifle more shrill than he might have wanted. The rat released his grip.

"Turn around," said the rat.

"What?"

"I said 'turn around'—*Lieutenant* Baker."

Cautiously, Baker turned his head to glance at the white-paneled section of the wall to the right of the window bubble. Imbedded in the wall, a few feet from his head, the handle of a thin stiletto vibrated with the force of Smith's invisible throw. Baker turned to the grinning assassin.

"Impressive," he said. "But hitting a wall is not the same as hitting a man in the heart from fifty feet."

"I use a knife," Smith reiterated.

"Suit yourself. But I warn you never to touch me like that again. Is that clear?"

Smith displayed jagged teeth. "Sure *Lieutenant*," he said. "I was only demonstrating. I could simply reach out to grab someone in the crowd and put a wooden blade in Brother Paul's heart—"

"Quiet!" Baker hissed. "Are you crazy? Never speak that name to me in public! Or in private, for that matter. And from now on you'll perform your—*demonstrations*—on those of your own class."

"Yes, *sir*!"

"You're not impressing me, Mr. Smith."

"Then don't hire me."

Baker ignored the response, as Smith had known he would. "Now listen to me carefully. We have two new problems that will require you to disappear for a few days. The *Empress* is arriving on schedule, but we have no way of knowing which site the target will select to make his appearance. It'll definitely *not* be Tranquility Arena; that much is certain at this point. As you can see, Mr. Smith, our tactics are in need of some quick and drastic revision."

"No prob, Lieutenant. I can be anywhere on Luna within a few hours' notice. Find out where he's going to be; that shouldn't present any difficulties for you. His staff is working out an alternative site?"

"Yes."

"And you know how to contact me."

"Yes. But you must await my word. And be ready to move."

"I'm always ready. What's your other problem?"

"Well—this is embarrassing," Baker admitted, tossing down the remainder of his wine with a grimace. "Trustworthy sources inform me that a certain Jew by the name of Jeri Kline has 'got religion', as they say. It seems that, once a contented atheist, our Mr. Kline has had an encounter with the Man Upstairs." Baker pointed to the ceiling.

"Yeah," said the rat. "A little birdie told me. It's that talk-show host from Earth, right?"

"Right." Baker cleared his throat. "And I also have it on

good authority that he's made contact with the—'target.'"

"Where?"

"On the *Empress*. He' s a passenger on the same flight."

"Hmmm…"

"Exactly. We believe he's informed the 'target' of our little plan."

Smith appeared visibly deflated by the news. He was seeing fifty thousand American credits take wing before his eyes.

"That complicates things," he said.

"It does more than that, I'm afraid. It might eliminate the need for your—*services*—altogether." Baker was hardly certain of this, but he enjoyed deflating the man's hopes.

"Well, what do we do now?"

"I've just finished telling you. We wait. That's all we can do. And if your golden opportunity does arrive, you may have to whittle *two* of those wooden knives."

"One for the 'target'—and one for Jeri Kline."

"Precisely," said Baker. He waved a hand for service. "At twice the agreed-upon price, of course."

"Two hundred thousand credits," the rat murmured reverently.

"That's correct. Now—I'll buy you one more drink, Mr. Smith, so that we may toast a profitable next meeting. We'll not meet again in person, not until the job is completed. And, after you've finished your drink, I'd appreciate it if you'd promptly remove yourself from my sight."

"My pleasure," quoth the rat.

α

Paul called a strategy meeting for one P.M. ship's time in his suite. When his staff arrived, he introduced them one at a time to his guest. They greeted Kline in a variety of ways, the kindest of which was visibly cool. And then, as was their custom, they opened with prayer. Paul lifted up the Lunar crusade to the Lord. "We ask, Heavenly Father, that Your will be done in this endeavor. You know our circumstances, L-rd. I ask, also, that You be with our brother, Jeri, Father, as he relates the things that have come to his knowledge concerning our visit to the moon. We ask that You minister peace to your servants. Let us receive what our brother has to say without fear or anger. We ask for wisdom. Stir up the Word of Wisdom in our spirits, that we may be like Solomon and know Your perfect will in these dire circumstances. As always, we place our fate in Your hands, O L-rd, trusting that all things are in keeping with your Plan. *B'Shem Yeshua haMashiach*—in the precious name of Jesus Christ we pray. Amen."

He waited until everyone was settled, helped himself to a well-stuffed chair, and ran his fingers swiftly over the panel on its arm.

"I'm ordering refreshments," he said. "The usual for everyone, I assume. How about yourself, Mr. Kline?"

"I asked you to call me Jeri, sir. I'll have a Moonpop with ice. A tall one; I'm thirsty."

"One tall Moonpop for our friend—Jeri," Paul said, keying in the order and shaking his head. "It took me a while to get accustomed to these first-class accommodations," he remarked. "I must warn you that my last attempt to order Moonpop was an utter failure. I wound up with a case of beer."

Kline laughed. "I can just picture you polishing *that* off!"

"I was tempted," Paul chuckled, "I don't mind telling you. On the flight out to Mars, tensions were running high, weren't they, Phil?"

Esteban nodded and smiled. Paul noticed the relaxed pose of his old friend on the divan across the room. Esteban's scalp was almost completely bald now, now. Wrinkles had cut deep furrows across his brow, extending across gaunt cheeks. *Phil's getting older*, he thought. *We all are.* He hated to break Kline's news to his trusted companion, especially since his emotional state had improved so markedly on the return trip from Mars. But, of course, there was no choice.

He allowed his affectionate gaze to pass around the room, from face to beloved face. There in the straight-backed chair sat Rob Madden, Paul's financial adviser. Rob came from America's Deep South. Georgia, wasn't it? He'd been an avid churchgoer, albeit an unconscious anti-Semite, when Paul had made his acquaintance over twenty years before. Since then he'd become devoted to the evangelist. He possessed accounting skills which Paul had immediately put to good use in the ministry, plus a jocular, teddy-bear nature that stood in stark contrast to Esteban's periodic brooding spells. Madden wore a full beard, now almost snow-white. A jolly Santa, stout as a keg, he'd amassed a repertoire of jokes, puns, and obscure witticisms that were as dry as they were endless. His cheeks flushed each time he tossed one out, a low rumble beginning deep in his belly and rising in pitch to become infectious laughter—the actual cause of the positive responses he received. When Madden laughed, people laughed with him. Convinced it was his wit that elicited their approval, Madden persisted with his terrible puns. But everyone loved him too much to tell him how dull they really were.

Next to Madden sat a seven-foot African-American named John Cowan. Paul had begun calling him "Little John" years ago, and the nickname stuck. Even seated, Little John towered over everyone else in the room. But it wasn't his size that made Cowan a giant in Paul's eyes. This soft-spoken gentleman with a coiled halo of black hair framing his brow was a legal genius. His knowledge of law and his stunning courtroom presence had won many a battle for the cause of Christ, against those who sought to use the Constitution to outlaw Christianity. Unfortunately, the battle had been lost the moment Charles Coffey took control of the White House, but without Cowan's legal brain and tireless devotion, it might have been lost years before. In short, Little John was an invaluable member of the team.

Finally Paul's gaze drifted to the thin face of J.R. Cavindale, a face known the world over, a face that represented the very best in spiritual music. James had joined the team not long after Paul and Phil Esteban had taken over the ministry from the murdered Reverend Williams. His beautiful, passionate tenor had struck Paul as the most magnificent voice ever lifted in praise. That, combined with his seemingly limitless musical knowledge and genius for arrangement, completed what had for years been a most powerful and dynamic ministry. Not the least of Cavindale's talents was his instinct for holovision broadcasting. He'd produced Paul's holovision program, *New Heaven, New Earth*, from its inception. And the results had always been first class. But Cavindale, like the rest of them, was getting old. The unrelenting pace of the crusades was taking its toll on him. His world famous countenance had lately begun to show discernible signs of stress and fatigue.

James needs an apprentice, Paul decided, *someone he can disciple in the art of broadcasting, someone to take a bit of the load off his shoulders. And this young fellow, Kline, seems to have come along at just the right moment, with all the necessary skills. G-d is good!*

Sighing, he turned his gaze on their young guest.

"Mr. Kline," he informed his staff, "would like us to call him Jeri."

Phil Esteban sniffed. Paul ignored him. "Jeri, would you be kind enough to relate to this collection of antiques the news you brought me this morning?"

"Certainly, Reverend. I've been stowing away on this ship for months, waiting for an opportunity to speak with you. I couldn't take the shuttle down to Mars without being caught, so, while you and your team went dirtside, I was forced to remain aboard. All the way out to Saturn and back. When you re-boarded—well, I knew I had to take the chance, no matter how dangerous it was. I had to warn you, Reverend."

"Warn me of what, Jeri? Please tell these gentlemen precisely what you told me."

Kline looked around the room at the elderly faces staring back at him like the holos he'd seen of Mount Rushmore.

"There's a plot to assassinate Brother Paul, the moment he debarks on Luna."

Paul saw Esteban stiffen. "Go on," he said.

"You simply cannot set foot on the moon, Reverend, under any circumstances."

Esteban drew himself up to the edge of the divan and regarded Kline sternly.

"How do you know this?" he demanded. "Young fellow, there are rumors circulating all over the solar system about alleged attempts on the Reverend's life. I've had my fill of them, to be frank with you. Rumors, that's all. We've all heard them."

"This is no rumor, Brother Esteban."

"How can you be certain?"

"With all due respect, sir—I'm not at liberty to tell you how I know. Just that I *do* know."

"I see," Esteban countered. "You can't tell us how you know, and yet you'd have Brother Paul cancel the most important crusade of this entire tour! Do you have any idea how much planning goes into a crusade, young fellow? Have you the slightest conception of the complex arrangements—*costly* arrangements—that are being undertaken on Luna even as we speak? How many thousands of people are depending on us?"

"Now, wait just one minute, Phil!" Paul broke in. "Wasn't it *you* urging me to cancel the Lunar crusade just three months ago?"

"Yes, but—"

"No 'buts'. It's true that I've never cancelled a crusade before. Nor am I inclined to cancel this one. But I think we should hear Jeri out. Go on, young man."

"Thank you, sir. Gentlemen, I'm sorry I can't give you more information, but I've given my word. A sacred oath. I assure you, however, that I wouldn't have gone to this kind of trouble if I wasn't absolutely certain of my source, if I hadn't spent considerable time and effort checking the story out myself. My source is trustworthy. And he's in a position to hear a lot of things. Not just rumors."

"Continue, son," Madden prompted him. "We're listening."

"It seems that the assassination of Brother Paul—in the opinion of the PWP—would send a message to those plotting to overthrow the Party on Luna that it's not afraid to eliminate anyone who threatens its control. They believe it'll quiet the hot-heads and squelch the insurrection."

"They wouldn't dare!" Cowan said. "It would be more of a provocation than a deterrent."

"They're prepared to take that chance. If there's a revolution on Luna, Earth will respond with nuclear threats. When push comes to shove, they believe Luna will back down and submit."

"And what if it doesn't?"

"We don't want to think about that. We don't *need* to think about that. We just need to cancel the Luna crusade. If Brother Paul sets foot on Luna, he's a dead man. And the Earth-Moon system will be pushed to the brink of nuclear war."

There was silence as the team contemplated his words. Across the room, at floor-level, a circular portion of the wall dilated to admit a six-legged servo shaped like a silver spider. Each stiff motion of its jointed legs produced a whirring sound. Its upper surface was flattened to accommodate a broad silver tray, upon which rode six crystal glasses. As the spider moved about the room, not a single glass shook, not a single ice-cube rattled.

"Well," said Paul. "Our drinks have arrived, and just in

time. Help yourselves, gentlemen." The spider assisted by pausing in front of each of them, having determined their exact locations by light-sensors on the tips of its waving antennae. When everyone had taken a glass, it reversed course and retreated "backwards" into its lens-like lair.

Kline took a long, thirsty gulp of Moonpop and continued.

"Forgive me," he said, "if I appear to be instructing my elders in matters of which you're already aware, but the situation on the moon is critical. These people are fighting for control of Luna; they won't think twice about killing anyone who threatens them. *Anyone*. But I'm repeating myself. There it is gentlemen; do what you will with it."

"I believe," said Paul, "that all mankind's conflicts have spiritual roots. The only thing that can affect this tragic situation for the better is a good old-fashioned revival. More than ever, Jeri, I'm convinced that my place right now is on the moon."

"But, Reverend!" Kline protested. "What good can you do the Lunies when you're buried under six feet of moondust?"

"My life is in G-d's hands."

"Yes, sir; of course." Kline looked thoughtfully at his drink, turning it around in his hands, making ice rattle against the sides of the glass. "Have you considered that my stowing away on the *Empress* might have been G-d's plan? Maybe He sent me here to warn you—to *prevent* you from going to Luna."

"Perhaps," said Paul. "I can't rule out the possibility. It is something that will require prayer. In fact, I suggest we all pray about—"

A high-pitched beeping interrupted. It was a familiar enough sound, and Paul keyed in his personal code.

"Yes?" he said.

"Sorry to disturb you, Reverend." The voice of Captain Mills emanated from a tiny speaker-grid in the arm of his chair. Paul hadn't punched in the code for visual, an omission that indicated his desire for privacy.

"Not at all, Captain," he said. "How may I help you?"

"If you have guests in your suite, Reverend, I think it would be best if we spoke in private. It's urgent, I'm afraid. Can we meet in, say, five minutes? It won't take long."

Kline leaned over to Paul. "Be careful," he whispered.

Paul nodded. "May I bring along a member of my staff?"

"I'd prefer it if you came alone," said Mills. "The nature of my business is—confidential."

Paul thought quickly. "Captain," he said. "I've been rather concerned of late about some rumors that have been circulating—in regard to a possible attempt on my life." He paused to glance over at Kline, who gave him the thumbs-up. "As you can well imagine, I feel less than easy traveling the ship alone. Perhaps we can strike a compromise."

"Certainly," said Mills. "I'll gladly send one of my men to accompany you."

"No. I think it would be best for me to go in the company of my attorney, Brother Cowan." Paul's tone was final. "Where shall we meet, Captain?"

"My quarters." Mills sounded not the least bit pleased, but what else could he do short of abduction?

"In ten minutes?"

"Very good."

"We'll be there," said Paul, closing the connection with a tap of his finger. "So, gentlemen. What do you think?"

"I don't trust him," Kline said.

"I do believe you're beginning to make me paranoid, Jeri."

"I'm just urging caution," Kline replied. "I think you should proceed from this point forward with the understanding that your life's in imminent danger."

"Your point," said Paul, rising from his chair, "is well taken. Little John, would you be so kind as to accompany me to the Captain's quarters?"

Cowan stood.

Kline said, "Let me go with you, sir."

"No Jeri," Paul crossed the room, Cowan following in his wake. "If I'm correct in my evaluation of our captain's urgent tone, *you* are likely to be the subject of our conversation. I want to know what he has to say. With you there, he wouldn't be able to speak freely."

"I thought my fare was paid."

"It was," said Paul, turning at the door. "But either the captain is curious about my motive in protecting you, or there's something else on his mind. In either case, I'm sure your name will come up more than once in our conversation. Gentlemen, wait here for me. I'll be back in a half hour or so. If not, send Brother Wallace after me."

The door hissed open. Paul, with Little John trailing silently behind, stepped out of the suite and down the corridor.

The Captain

They found Captain Mills in his suite pouring over holographic maps and star charts strewn over a transparent glass desk on the far wall. His quarters were sparsely decorated, func-tional, lacking in warmth—although Paul noticed that much of the furniture was imported asteroid-sculpture of immeasurable value. Yet it left one with the distinct impression that its owner was a man who cared little for unessential embellishments, either in his terse surroundings or in conversation. He was a man who wouldn't waste words. Had they known that his suite had been designed as a self-contained escape pod capable of being jettisoned from the *Empress* in case of emergency, they'd have been doubly uncomfortable.

Mills was in his late forties, sported a full black beard, and puffed incessantly on the stem of a yellowish meerschaum pipe. His bearded face was suspended in a cloud of acrid pipe-smoke. As he looked up from his work, gesturing for them to sit, Paul perceived the soul of a man greatly tormented.

Finding themselves seats among the pitted gray asteroid - shapes—which, Paul noted with surprise, turned out to be rather comfortable—they waited for Mills to acknowledge them. He remained absorbed in his calculations, tapping the keys of his computer with grunts of disapproval, then slapping his hands down on the pile of charts and shaking his head.

"With spaceflight as routine as it is today," he grumbled, "you'd think there'd be a reliable set of maps somewhere. A sailor on Earth has it made, gentlemen. Maybe he has a few shifting currents to deal with, but at least the continents are relatively stationary. Out here," he indicated the vastness of the solar system with a wave of his hand, "everything's in motion. You'd expect that the current planetary conjunction would simplify matters. It doesn't. I'm beginning to believe that mathematics is an imprecise art at best. We need a new way of measuring things."

"Captain," Paul replied with a smile. "Would you have us lose confidence in the safety of spaceflight?"

Mills poked his pipe-stem in Paul's direction, stabbing the air as he spoke.

"Why not? Listen, Reverend. I don't have that much confidence in it myself. And I have twenty years flight-time under my belt. I think the longer you spend in space, the less you comprehend it." He placed the pipe-stem between his teeth and produced a few quick rings of blue smoke. They floated up to the ceiling to join a swirling gray cloud on its way to the air-vents. "Take *your* vocation for example," he said, eying Paul. "What could be simpler than quoting a few archaic verses to a mob of uneducated yokels who still think the Earth is flat? And if you need a few extra coins in your coffers, you just go on the tube and whine about an impending economic disaster, and the loot comes jingling in. Now that's the life!"

Paul was aware of Little John's discomfort during this monologue, but maintained a polite smile.

"How ironic, Captain," he said, "since all I heard *you* did was set a heading on your computer and run for the gambling casinos on the Las Vegas Deck. I suppose we both have a lot to learn about each other."

Mills let loose a sudden roar, which Paul interpreted as laughter. He stood up and crossed the room, hand extended. "Put her there, Reverend!" he bellowed. "I admire a man who can take it on the chin and bounce back like that. Tempers get too thin out in space. It's refreshing to meet someone who doesn't let things get under his skin."

Paul reached out to shake the proffered hand. "An occupational necessity, Captain Mills."

"Yes, very good. An occupational necessity. And this," he said, turning to Little John—who did not accept his hand with the same alacrity as had Paul—"is the legendary Christian attorney, John Cowan."

"That's correct," said Paul. "Brother Cowan and I are both curious as to the purpose of this meeting, Captain. We were involved in a rather important conference ourselves. Might I ask you to come directly to the point?"

"Of course, of course!" Mills seated himself on a piece of asteroid and leaned back, sucking thoughtfully on his pipe. Paul noted that his uniform was slightly rumpled as though he'd just arisen from a nap. "It's about that fellow who snuck aboard my ship."

"You're referring to Jeri Kline, the well known radio personality. I won't insult your intelligence by insisting that your computer was in error. It's true. Mr. Kline boarded the *Empress* without paying his passage. But since the matter of his fare has been more than adequately attended to, I can't see that you'd have any objection to his presence. I assure you, Captain, if it were not for circumstances that imperiled his very life, he'd never have chosen such an—unorthodox—means of departure. I remind you once again that his fare *has* been paid; he's traveling first class. That should put an end to the matter. And I should add that he's now a permanent member of my staff. I've taken him on as co-director of my holovision broadcasts, and as such he's due the same respect and consideration—"

"Reverend!" Mills cut in, sounding wounded. "I wouldn't *think* of harassing Mr. Kline, or of interfering in the slightest way with your mission. But try to see it from *my* point of view. There are some pretty important people on Luna who've taken more than a passing interest in Mr. Kline's activities. Military people, Reverend, with whom, happily, I'm longer numbered. I'm a commercial pilot on the payroll of Galaxy Tours, no longer a Navy man. And the officer who contacted me about Mr. Kline was a mere lieutenant—an *Air Force* lieutenant at that." Mills said the words "Air Force" the way one might say "sewer rat".

"But this *Air Force* lieutenant assured me that he was working at the behest of the Naval Admiralty. The Admiralty, Reverend! Think of it, sir. I—a mere spacer, an insignificant spaceliner captain—have little or no interest in naval problems. Or in your Mr. Kline, for that matter. As you say, his fare is paid; all's well from my viewpoint. But if you look closely at my uniform you'll note the dearth of brass adorning it. Commercial space-captains are kind of like bus-drivers, Reverend; we have no brass and no clout. The Admiralty, however—well, sir, that's quite a different story. These people have gold trinkets all *over* their chests. They're bent over from the weight of them. And we former Navy types are downright Pavlovian when it comes to brass. The more brass we see, the more we tend to grovel. A pitiful spectacle, I admit, but there it is. With the Admiralty so interested in Mr. Kline's movements—well, I'm sure you can see how it puts the matter in an entirely different light. Some very powerful people are asking about your guest."

"My *associate*," Paul corrected. "As I've pointed out, Mr. Kline is a member of my staff. Whatever concerns him concerns me. Therefore, I must inquire as to the nature of these messages you've received. What possible interest could such high-ranking military personnel have in Brother Kline's affairs?"

"If only," said Mills between puffs, "I were at liberty to say."

Paul rose abruptly from his seat. Little John followed suit. "In that case, Captain Mills, there's nothing we can accomplish in this interview. If you don't mind, Brother Cowan and I will be on our way. More pressing matters await us in my suite."

"Sit down, Reverend!" It was obvious from the Captain's tone that capitulation was distasteful to him, but he wasn't about to surrender so easily. "Perhaps there *are* a few things I can reveal. But try to understand my position."

"Try to understand *mine*, Captain. There is little I can do to assist you until I know precisely the content of these communications from Luna. At least those that concern Mr. Kline."

"Very well; if you insist. There's reason to believe that your—*associate*—is guilty of treasonous acts. A certain Lieutenant Matthew Baker has begun extradition procedures that may force me to turn Kline over to the authorities on Luna. Mind you, I'm not obliged to follow the suggestions of an *Air Force* lieutenant, *or* the Navy brass, for that matter. But Baker assures me that this accusation originated in places rather—elevated, if you catch my drift. Government places. Now, don't get me wrong! I work in space because I detest the Party and everything it stands for. Wilbur Denton is *my* kind of man. You can take President Coffey and swing him from the rafters, as far as I'm concerned. But the government has a long reach these days, and I'm loath to place my neck in a noose."

"Treasonous acts?" Paul said. He tried to look indignant. "I promise you, my dear Captain Mills, there's no one on my staff who's engaged in treasonous acts!"

Mills sat and puffed his meerschaum, lost in thought. "In regard to your *associate*, Jeri Kline, I have it on good authority that he's long been one of your most vociferous detractors."

"First of all," Paul replied, "Brother Kline's former beliefs do not concern you. Secondly, he's well within his rights to have had a change of heart, and to have offered his services to my ministry. An offer I've accepted."

"Granted, granted, Reverend. But my question is, how much do you really know about *Brother* Kline? Up until recently, the world has known him as an atheist—which is neither here nor there to me, being somewhat of an agnostic myself. But I perceive it as matter of great concern to *you.* As I understand it, he was rather notorious for his views."

"His political views are not known to me."

"Precisely. And he's also a Jew, is he not?"

The muscles in Paul's face tightened; his eyes ignited into twin flames.

"And so, my dear Captain, am I."

Mills appeared thunderstruck. His mouth opened and closed like a ventriloquist's dummy, but no sound emerged, Paul gave him no time to recover.

"You've accused a member of my staff of treason, and now you've maligned my heritage! My attorney is a witness. I can see no further point in this discussion." He rose to his feet. "Come, Brother Cowan. I don't believe the captain has anything of value to add to his gross insults."

Mills recovered as Paul and Little John were crossing the room to the door. The attorney's hand was already on the button when Mill's said: "I do have one thing to add, Reverend."

Paul turned.

"I can promise you," Mills said, "that by the time we arrive on Luna I'll have received direct orders to put Mr. Kline off my ship—to turn him over to the military authorities there. I don't fancy traitors, Brother Paul."

"Or Jews, either," Paul retorted.

"As you wish. But I'm warning you, sir. If the order comes I'll have your associate placed in custody. I'll *personally* turn him over to Naval Command on Luna. If you try to stop me, you'll be facing trial as an accomplice. Then let Attorney Cowan do what he can on your behalf. Do we understand one another?"

"Quite," said Paul. "I shall earnestly pray for your soul, Captain."

"One week, Reverend. We'll arrive at Luna in one week."

α

The door to Paul's suite swished open. Kline rose to greet

them.

"What happened?" he said.

"Sit down, Jeri," Paul ordered.

Kline obeyed, surprised by Paul's abrupt tone. The evangelist gestured for Little John to take a seat, while he himself remained standing. The others, familiar with the look on Paul's face, said nothing.

Paul had suggested that Little John remain silent during their interview with the Captain. In this way he could be certain the attorney wouldn't inadvertently reveal more than he wanted Mills to know. And it would also free Cowan's mind for a careful analysis of the Captain's reactions, in order to determine how much of what Mills said was reliable.

"What do you think, Little John?" Paul now inquired.

"I think," said Cowan, "that our Captain is under intense duress."

"The man is obviously tormented," Paul agreed. "Did you see how aggressive he became when I challenged him? I had to do some fancy footwork to stay in control. Gentlemen, we appear to be in a very grave situation."

"What's happened?" Cavindale inquired.

"It seems the captain of this vessel—in which we are all virtual prisoners for the duration of our voyage—has placed himself in direct opposition to our cause. He's promised us safe passage, and I believe his sense of honor as a former naval officer will prevent him from going back on his word. But he's in a position to make things rather uncomfortable for us."

Cowan said, "I think the authorities on Luna have put a great deal of pressure on him. Stress is written all over his face."

"Yes," Paul said. He crossed the room to his chair and sat down, taking a sip from his now-warm glass of water.

"Pressure about what?" Kline asked.

"About *you*, Jeri," said Paul. "Now, I'm going to ask you a few direct questions, and I want you to answer them. Tell me the truth, son. No subterfuge, no protecting the innocent and all that. Your appearance on this ship has created quite a stir, and I simply must have all the facts if I'm going to shield you."

"Shield me? From what?"

"From being arrested—tossed in the brig, or whatever they call it aboard a spaceliner. From being turned over to the military police on Luna."

Kline leapt to his feet. "On what charge?" he demanded.

"The charge is treason."

"Treason! They must be crazy, Reverend! Stowing away aboard a spaceliner is certainly illegal, but it's hardly treasonous!"

"Oh, I agree," said Paul. "If that's all you've done. Now sit down, Jeri, and answer some questions."

Reluctantly, Kline obeyed.

"So," Paul began, "how did you get aboard this vessel?"

Kline opened his mouth to reply, but Paul silenced him with an upraised hand. "The truth, now, Jeri. 'The truth will set you free.'"

Kline sighed.

"One of the guards," he said.

"Come now. We've been through that before."

"Honestly, Reverend. One of the ship's guards, a petty officer. He helped me sneak past the sentries at the door of your simu-chamber."

"How?"

"He called them aside, so I could slip past them."

"Now don't tell me you bribed him!" The guards aboard the *Empress* were unbribable, not because of their unselfish dedication to duty, but because it was too cushy and well-paid a job to put at risk.

"No, sir," said Kline. "He was also the one who snuck me aboard ship at the ISS. He tampered with the shuttle records. You see, Reverend, he's the officer who informed me of the plot against your life."

"Hold it one moment, son," Cowan cut in. "There is something here that doesn't add up."

"I can think of a couple myself," Paul said. "For instance, why didn't this officer warn me himself? If, as you say, he was the one with the knowledge, why risk his job to smuggle *you* aboard, when he had access to me with no difficulty."

"You underestimate the risk, sir. It wasn't just his job. He might have been able to reach you, sure. But after that, what would happen to him? He couldn't ask for asylum in your church, as I have. I was free to contact you and ask for your protection. You have safe conduct; you could protect me. Defying the law to protect my friend, however, would present difficulties for you. Morally, I mean. Brother Paul, we were both convinced that if my friend contacted you in any overt way, to warn you, he'd be shoved out an airlock. He calls it 'sucking vacuum," a very graphic term. These people are capable of anything, Reverend. But he did work hard to get me to you. You owe him a lot, sir. And I owe him his anonymity. It might mean his life."

"I understand, Jeri," said Paul. "Believe me, I do. But if we're to give you the asylum you require, I'm afraid you must violate that oath. We must know who our allies are. This alleged plot—"

"Not alleged, Reverend. It's a fact."

"For the time being," Paul said, "I'm taking nothing for granted. But there are other problems with your story."

"Yes," said Cowan. "Like how have you been eating on board? And sleeping? Assuming for a moment that you snuck on board at Mars, which you say you did not, that's still a long time without food or sleep. But you boarded from the ISS, correct?"

"Yes," said Kline.

"Which means you've been on board the *Empress* for months. How have you survived so long in hiding?"

"Not easily." Kline said with forced humor. He sat back in his chair, defeated. "Alright, gentlemen. I'll tell you the whole story from the beginning."

"That," said Paul, "would be refreshing. And so would another round of drinks." He tapped his fingers on the console, keying in a new order. Apparently this meeting was going to take longer than anticipated.

The Stowaway

As Paul prepared to retire that "evening" his mind kept playing over the events of the day. And a rather busy day it had been! John Cowan was asleep in the outer room, splayed across the divan like a beached dolphin, snoring loudly. The snoring didn't disturb Paul; he was glad to have the big man keeping an eye on him, albeit a closed one. Little John, he knew, was a light sleeper; the slightest suspicious sound would bring him instantly awake.

Earlier, Cowan had become restless. He'd suddenly arisen, left the suite and headed off down the corridor, returning about fifteen minutes later and dropping right off to sleep. Beyond the walls, brother Wallace's security team worked in shifts, using the most advanced technology to watch over him. But Little John's familiar snoring was more comforting to Paul than all of Wallace's high-tech sleuthing.

Paul concluded his bedtime *shema* and drew back the bedcovers. He climbed in slowly, fluffing up a pillow to prop his head. He was in the habit of reading two chapters in the Bible every night, after *ma'ariv* prayer, but as he adjusted his reading-glasses and opened the Scriptures to his place in Matthew, he realized that his mind was too full of the day's mysteries to fully concentrate on the Word. Resting the Bible on his chest, he gazed up at the ceiling and surrendered to the nagging puzzles buzzing around in his head.

Kline's story, he decided, was reasonable enough, once one navigated through the twists and turns. The officer who'd smuggled Kline aboard the *Empress* was a friend of his, and a believer. When the *Empress* came to the ISS to recruit crew-members for its maiden voyage, he was assigned the rank of Chief Petty Officer. The position gave him access to computer records and a certain degree of authority over the ships guard. As a space-tech who'd worked his way up the ranks by dogged devotion to low-paying, high-risk jobs repairing computer systems in space, Edward Moore had developed a remarkable skill as a hacker, a capability he'd exploited to help Kline board the *Empress* undetected.

A Navy man originally, Moore's Christianity was a well-kept secret. Paul found this quite reasonable, given the current political situation. Christians in the military averaged rather short life-spans in space these days, many of them ending up "sucking vacuum" as Moore would say, their umbilicals mysteriously cut, floating bloated and dead in their own silent orbits alongside the beams they'd been welding.

Paul pushed the gruesome picture out of his mind, returning to Kline's story.

Chief Petty Officer Edward Moore had come to Messiah through the tenacious soul-winning efforts of a lay evangelist on Earth, prior to his being assigned this tour on the *Empress*. His ears became attuned to every scrap of scuttlebutt relating to the deaths of fellow believers out in space; rumors of legislation on Luna limiting the exercise of any but government-approved religions; or evidence that a new recruit might be a brother in the L-rd, in need of support and protection.

At one of Paul's crusades—Kline wasn't sure which—Moore became an avid devotee of his ministry. He tuned in to the *New Heaven, New Earth* broadcasts through the crackling static of homemade receivers tucked away in his quarters or hidden in the recesses of his pressure-suit. Floating high above the curving, wheeling arc of Earth, laboring over some technical problem or other, he listened hungrily to every sermon he was able to pick up.

His experience was mostly on the ISS—where the Earth-Luna shuttle docked on its flights to the moon and back troubleshooting with the electrical crew, replacing or rewiring an occasional solar-cell out on the colossal dish, or just pulling guard duty. It was dull work at times, but Moore was a born spacer. He volunteered for extra EVA when someone took sick, exulting in the sensation of floating at the end of a tether, free-falling in a lazy orbit above the world, as alone and free as any human could be in the crowded, claustrophobic hive of man. On the night-side, when the station's orbit took him beyond the glare of the sun, he watched the cities sparkle like diamonds against the dark breast of Earth.

Edward Moore had found his element, high above creation—"a self-appointed inspector of snowstorms." as Henry Thoreau had once quipped. To the other techs, such outworld views only confirmed the insignificance of a planet lost in an outer arm of the Milky Way galaxy, far from the busy galactic hub, a mere speck of dust, as it seemed to them, overrun by a species of hominid apes called humanity. But not to Moore. Not at all!

Moore was utterly geocentric in his thinking, awestruck by the intricate wonders of his watery world, certain that the probabilities against its having evolved even the most *infinitesimal* life forms were astronomical. The more he studied the theory of evolution, the more absurd it seemed that those theoretical unicel-lular bits of protoplankton could have survived the millions of years of turbulent planetary upheaval that must have existed during the Precambrian epoch, as paleontologists claimed. Earth's atmosphere, they said, had been tenuous, its surface frigid and inhospitable. Volcanic activity in its seething core produced dense clouds of smoke and some greenhouse warming, but not enough to provide a stable environment for the protracted, leisurely course of cellular evolution. The vagaries of the theory had always out-weighed its certainties. It would require a miracle for life to evolve on the third planet from the sun—or any of Sol's rocky children, for that matter—but such a complex miracle as evolution seemed far more likely to most people than the simple miracle of Creation. To Moore, gazing down at the planet of his birth, only the Hand of G-d could explain those sparkling jewel-boxes of intelligent life below. In that, he was serenely confident.

Regrettably, he spent most of his time dirtside. It was the Navy's belief that a man's spacelegs had to be proven by brief stints in orbit. So Moore bided his time, shuttling between Earth and the L-5 stations on a bi-monthly schedule, watching out for "new fish" who might require his assistance. He caught Paul's broadcasts faithfully, though secrecy often made that difficult in space. But he gladly ran the risk. Paul's preaching and Cavindale's ministry in song often moved him to tears. He was stirred by the nagging conviction that he must do his part to bring the Truth to all who would listen, yet the instinct for survival in the cramped quarters of space made him overly cautious. On Earth he tried to compensate for that caution by working in evangelism whenever possible. His dedication and enthusiasm were an inspiration to many.

As his appreciation of Brother Paul increased, his bitterness toward another broadcaster grew apace. Jeri Kline, the atheist talk-show host and detractor of Paul's ministry, turned his blood to ice. How could anyone libel a man so dedicated to the preaching of the Gospel? Moore prayed for release from his growing hatred of Kline, the man's mockery of all that was sacred to him—but the obsession only lodged itself deeper in his soul. During dirtside R-and-R he'd frequently call Kline's program under false names, quoting Scriptures in an attempt to break the man's demonic oppression. But Kline's derisive laughter, and the sneering commentary that followed, convinced him that the man was a true reprobate, a disciple of Satan.

When his stint was up, Moore decided against reenlistment. The skills he'd developed in the Space Navy made him an excellent candidate for a job on the *Empress*, which he'd heard was heading for Earth in search of crewmen. The money was simply too good to resist. So he hung up his spacesuit and shuttled down to Earth, settling in his hometown of Phoenix-Mesa to await the

Empress' arrival at the ISS.

It was not surprising, Paul decided, that when Moore finally encountered Jeri Kline in the flesh—in a Phoenix-Mesa Christian cell meeting—he was horrified that such a demon should defile hallowed ground. It reminded Paul of the situation encountered by his namesake, the Apostle Paul—old Rabban Sha'ul—after his Damascus Road encounter with Yeshua. He imagined how the early Messianic Jews must have feared arrest and torture at the sight of that hated face in their midst, and the Spirit-led eloquence needed by Sha'ul to ease their anxieties.

But Moore chose to be harmless as a dove, as Messiah had admonished, yet wise as a serpent. He waited to assess the situation, to determine what this ravening wolf-in-sheep's-clothing was up to at a clandestine prayer meeting. And it was at that meeting that Moore first heard Jeri Kline's astounding testimony.

Kline was anointed. His testimony was awe-inspiring, edged with the desperation of a lonely life jaded by success, bruised by a crippling disease. But as he neared the end, recounting the events of that wondrous night at the Sparks crusade, his voice began to soar on wings of rapture. Everyone was silent, awestruck. None of them knew that Kline had been a paraplegic, confined to a wheelchair since childhood. They empathized with his rage and rejoiced in his miracle. Tears flowed freely as he concluded his testimony.

Moore's hatred melted away. He rushed forward, tears flowing, and embraced Kline before the assembly. He took the microphone and confessed his own sin—the murderous feelings that had once gripped his heart. "But, praise G-d!" he concluded. "Now I'm free! Thanks to this man—this man I always considered my enemy."

The congregation—which on that auspicious occasion had included Giles Hadley and Sam Browne, the mayor of Phoenix-Mesa—burst into spontaneous praise, applauding the two men as they embraced before a makeshift altar.

α

Moore and Kline became the best of friends. They met as often as Moore's demanding schedule allowed. He'd finally landed the job of Chief Petty Officer aboard the *Empress*, which put him in charge of the ship's guard—all of them former officers of the Space Navy, now private employees of Galaxy Tours.

But there was much work for him to do before the maiden voyage, still months away. A lot of refitting and "battening down" as he called it. With six thousand passengers cruising out to Saturn, the *Empress* had to be in perfect "ship-shape." So Moore was spending a great deal of time on board, attending to his duties, shuttling down every now and then for a week of R and R.

Kline was often depressed in the wake of his healing, though he couldn't pinpoint precisely why. (He'd lost his talk show and was periodically destitute, but that didn't fully account for it.) Moore went out of his way to assist. He brought food to Kline's frequently neglected apartment whenever he was dirtside, and the two would pray together. Kline was out of fellowship, afraid to make the rounds of the underground churches, to share his testimony with strangers. He was becoming increasingly withdrawn. Together they burned the midnight oil. They discussed current events and current dangers. These were times of refreshing for Kline, his only connection with the Church. He was aware that his new friend was desperately trying to compensate for the hatred he'd once cherished, hatred for a radio personality who no longer existed. But he couldn't bring himself to discourage the visits. Whatever the man's motive, Kline desperately needed his friendship. The brief fellowship they shared between Moore's longer and longer tours in space eased the pain over his lost career. Yet, despite all this, he was falling into a deep, almost suicidal, depression. Moore struggled to pull him out of it, but to no avail.

It was around this time, according to Jeri, that Moore first heard of the plot to assassinate Brother Paul on Luna. Cautiously, he worked to verify it, dropping hints here and there—not too many and not too eagerly—then gauging the reactions, relying on spacer-savvy to guide his conclusions. He quickly acquired more evidence than he needed or wanted. Names had been dropped, important names, high ranking names.

His first instinct was to go to Kline with the story. Kline was a trusted friend, and a man whose background made him aware of the need for confidentiality. He knew how to protect his sources, all the way to HUAC trials, if necessary, for Moore was aware that his life was now in danger. Someone who knew what *he* knew could find himself sucking vacuum. This was no game of amateur detective he was playing, and he didn't like the idea of keeping such knowledge to himself. A trusted confidant was a great insurance policy. If certain parties were planning a sudden "accident" for Moore, the existence of a friend who could go public with the story might cause them to reconsider. And who was better able to go public than the controversial loudmouth, Jeri Kline? Besides, he'd feel better just knowing someone else was privy to this dark secret of his.

Of course, Brother Paul had to be warned. Kline assured him that he'd done the right thing by confiding his secret. Together they hatched a daring scheme to get Kline on board the *Empress*, rehearsing every detail until they had it memorized. After a while Moore noticed his friend's depression beginning to lift. Now that Kline had a purpose, a mission to carry out—saving the evangelist who'd saved him—their meetings became charged with exhilaration, the rush of shared danger, the bonding of comrades united on a deadly errand.

Moore knew he couldn't risk being seen talking with Brother Paul. But as an unknown party on the inside he could do a great deal to facilitate Kline's mission. He could hide Kline in his own quarters aboard the *Empress*, feed him, do his laundry along with his own. And he could keep his friend up to date on the evangelist's movements about the ship until a definite pattern revealed itself—a pattern predictable enough to allow for one brief encounter.

Yet Brother Paul's movements had proved to be far from predictable. In fact, on the way out to Mars they'd seemed deliberately erratic. Paul smiled, recalling Brother Wallace's tactics for protecting him.

Debarking on Mars had proven impossible. Kline was forced to remain aboard the *Empress* all the way out to Saturn and back. The situation became desperately difficult. Their plan was failing.

Paul boarded the *Empress* again at Mars, but on the return trip to Luna, when they'd just about given up hope of making contact, the evangelist suddenly added a new routine to his morning schedule—his walks in the simuchamber. After observing this constitutional for a week, satisfying themselves as to its regularity, they decided to make their move.

And now, Paul thought as he drifted off to sleep, *there's a new piece for our puzzle. A certain Chief Petty Officer, Edward Moore.*

Paul knew him only from Jeri's account, and yet, if the story were true, Moore might turn out to be a vital puzzle-piece indeed! He reminded himself to have Little John check on Moore's background—and, for that matter, Kline's as well. The ship's extensive library should contain enough holographs of Kline, and other pertinent information, for the attorney to verify his story.

"The day is sufficient," Paul decided, "unto the evil thereof." He'd sort it all out tomorrow.

Soon he was fast asleep.

The Surface

Lieutenant Matthew Baker, bathed in Earthglow, was out on the surface of the moon. As his rover wended its way along the rim of Laplace Promontory—a sheer cliff dropping thousands of feet to the floor of Mare Imbrium, the "Sea of Rains," where not a drop of rain had ever fallen—he kept an eye on the tread marks before him. Such imprints, once embedded in the dust, left enduring trail-markers for others to follow. It was the surest way to avoid disaster.

Yet trips on the surface bored him. There was very little color on the moon and no variety whatever. Silver-gray cliffs, black rilles and featureless mares—studded here and there with oval solar-collectors embedded in the regolith—stretched in all directions to the horizon. Even the odd effect the closeness of that horizon had on one's perceptions quickly palled. To Baker, the only thing of beauty on the moon was the Earth, hovering like a cat's-eye marble in the pitch-black, star-dusted sky.

He followed the treads down narrow switchbacks, heading for the flat plain of Mere Imbrium. He could see the circular dimple of the Laplace-A crater pocking the geometrically flat plain, half of the crater blue-lit by Earth, half in ebony shadow. A few kilometers to the north, where the "sea" of dust touched the horizon, the Mare Imbrium complex raised its glittering dome against the stars. To the south, Earthglow threw the long stark shadows of Montes Apennines far across the plain.

The only sound in his ears, as he carefully negotiated the steep trail, was his own breathing, hollow and faintly disturbing within his helmet. It sounded like someone else's breathing, not his own. And it always made him feel vulnerable.

As he passed the halfway point of his descent, Baker made out the faintest glint of Earthglow off another rover. It was moving toward him across Mare Imbrium, still a good distance away. Squinting against the reflection of Earth in his visor, he could see it was indeed a vehicle like his own. And he knew it belonged to Vice Admiral Miles Bowlen.

If they both proceeded at their current rate of speed, they'd meet at Laplace-A precisely on time.

α

Vice Admiral Miles Bowlen was a large enough man in ordinary clothes, but in a bulky pressure-suit he was gargantuan. Such corpulence resulted from the same inactivity and hedonism typical of all high-ranking officers on Luna, but in Bowlen's case it was magnified by a factor of ten. He liked the soft life and he intended to remain in its cushy embrace.

Rapidly sizing up the political situation on the moon after his exile to its cold and loveless plains—the result of his own vulgarity and ineptitude, he'd been assured— Bowlen soon realized that one had to adapt to survive. And Bowlen had to do much more than survive; he had to flourish. He had to thrive and grow, not only in political influence—military advancement having been denied him—but apparently in sheer girth as well. His suited form barely fit in the tiny rover that groaned along under his weight in a lumbering roll.

He muttered into his helmet at the sight of the approaching vehicle, wondering what in blazes he was doing out here on this impossible terrain, on the moon he hated with every grain of his being. For a meeting with an Air Force lieutenant? Bowlen detested the Air Force almost as much as he detested the moon. What was this upstart lieutenant after? Everybody was after something.

The message Bowlen had received—and through the proper channels, he'd noted sardonically—bore the terse command: MEET BAKER LT. MATTHEW U.S. A.F. 0800 TOMORROW LAPLACE-A. He'd disposed of it according to procedure.

Air Force personnel are involved in this? Bowlen thought. Well, whatever Baker had to say, it had better be important. No one brought Vice Admiral Miles Bowlen out onto the surface he so thoroughly loathed unless there was a blasted good reason!

In the shadow of the crater's southern wall, Bowlen parked his rover and watched as Baker drew up alongside, then switched on his helmet radio with a grunt of displeasure. This far away from the Imbrium Complex, hidden in the transmission-shadow of the crater's ridge, it would be impossible for anyone to pick up their conversation. Obviously a meeting between the two men in either of their bases had been deemed a security risk. *Well*, Bowlen thought, *let's get this farce over with!*

"I had to cancel a game of Tycho hold-'em to drive out here, Lieutenant," he boomed into Baker's helmet. "What's so blasted important?"

Baker didn't bother to grovel. "Party Central ordered this meeting, sir. There's little either of us can do with such an order but comply."

Bowlen found it hard to disagree. The PWP had been good to him, over all, and he saw no reason to snuff the golden goose. But this trip out to Laplace-A was sacrifice enough. He didn't owe Party Central the additional humiliation of taking orders from an Air Force lieutenant with an attitude. No, Baker would have to work for Bowlen's cooperation.

"Go on, then!" he snapped. "Relay your message and let's head back. These clandestine rendezvous are so much childishness, if you ask me."

"Yes, sir," Baker's voice hissed in Bowlen's helmet. "I've worked out a plan that's been tentatively approved by covert ops. It requires your assistance."

"What plan?" Bowlen said, his impatience growing with every additional minute he was forced to remain on the surface.

"I've not been cleared to relate the details, but—"

"Humph!" said Vice Admiral Miles Bowlen.

"—I can give it to you in its general implications."

"Bah!" said Vice Admiral Miles Bowlen.

"The plan involves the assassination of an interplanetary figure," Baker's voice continued. "All the details have been carefully worked out, and the target is on the way."

"Who's the target?" Bowlen pressed. He resented the fact that an Air Force lieutenant was privy to things he was not. Despite the fact that it was Baker's own plan, he couldn't see why the Party hadn't taken him into its confidence in a matter so vital. And besides, the man's arrogance was exasperating.

"I can't tell you that, sir. I've been instructed to keep the identity secret, pending security clearance from Party Central. Only those directly involved in the mission can be privy."

"What?" the Vice Admiral barked. "How dare you bring me out to this appalling place to play James Bond with me? If you want my assistance, you'd better answer my questions!"

"The *Party* wants your assistance," Baker corrected, his voice cold and hollow. "Which means the *President* wants your assistance. The President always gets what he wants, sir. As you and I both know."

"Humph!" said Bowlen. Baker's reply had been a poorly veiled threat, but what could be done about it? He resented being reduced to such impotent rumblings. Someday, he vowed, he'd fix this impudent lieutenant.

"Unfortunately," said Baker, "we've encountered a slight snag."

"Indeed. How unfortunate for you."

"There was a leak."

"There's always a blasted leak!" Bowlen protested. "While important personnel like myself are denied details—pending security clearance from Party Central—idiots, noncoms, and civilians are joking about those same precious details over drinks! This assignment has all the credibility of a circus sideshow. I'd sooner trust my secrets to the bearded lady!"

Baker's voice continued as soon as Bowlen lifted his finger from the "send" button, cool and unaffected by the tirade. "Someone," he said, "has managed to contact the 'target' and warn him. The Party believes that, while we can't get the 'target' himself to play into our hands, it might be possible to take steps that would—persuade him."

"Him?" Bowlen let the lieutenant's blunder sink in. "Go on."

"This ally of his, the one who warned him of our plan—I've been using some creativity to invent a few treasonous offences with which he might be charged and extradited to Luna."

"You think they'll stand up?"

"They don't have to stand up, Admiral," Baker replied. "They only have to force the target into our sights. He'll never allow his ally to face imprisonment on false charges. He'll step out into the light, and we'll nail him."

"Very nice," Bowlen said, not at all convinced. "So what do you need *me* for?"

"We need you to beam the captain of the *Empress*."

"Roy Mills. I know him."

"Exactly. That's why we want you to contact him and demand that he arrest this troublemaker and turn him over to the proper authorities as soon as they arrive in Lunar orbit."

"May I have the troublemaker's name? Or am I presuming too much?"

Baker ignored the sarcasm. "Jeri Kline," he said.

"Jeri Kline…Jeri Kline. The name sounds familiar."

"I've already beamed Captain Mills and warned him about Kline. But he wants to hear it from Navy brass; he doesn't trust the word of an Air Force lieutenant."

"Smart man."

"And you're the highest ranking naval officer on Luna."

"How convenient for the Party. And for you."

"The Party requests, sir, that you beam Mills as soon as possible. The name again is Jeri Kline and the charge is treason against the United States. I was ordered to make sure you received both those elements clearly. You know how these radios can garble things."

"Jeri Kline—treason against the United States. And what if Mills asks for details? He's no fool either, you know."

"He's a commercial spaceliner pilot. You're Vice Admiral of the Space Navy. You aren't obliged to *give* him any details. Just relay the order. Appeal to his patriotism, to his former naval service. Tell him his President needs him—anything. But you have to do it immediately. The *Empress* is only a week away."

"Anything else?"

"No, sir. That's all."

"Then I'll be getting back to my card game—that is, if Party Central doesn't object."

Bowlen started his rover and began to negotiate a wide turn, heading back in the direction of the Imbrium complex. It would be nice to breathe fresh air from the hydroponics again, he thought, instead of this stale stuff circulating in his helmet.

"Thank you, Admiral," came the hollow, sardonic voice of Matthew Baker.

"Humph!" said Vice Admiral Miles Bowlen.

α

Baker headed back to Sinus Iridum, automatically following his own rover-treads. He allowed his mind to review the conversation with Bowlen. *That fat, pompous egomaniac!* he thought bitterly. The Party had plans for the Vice Admiral, but that was something else they were keeping from the arrogant windbag. Baker was glad. He wondered if they'd eventually order *him* to do it. It would be a real pleasure. He directed his attention to the tricky job of climbing the narrow switchbacks up the side of Laplace Promontory. It was rough out on the surface, and he was aware of how much Bowlen feared it. *With good cause*, he mused. *A man could get killed out here.*

The Pilgrims

The old woman was dying.

Peter Rice knew it, but there was nothing he could do. He passed a hand over the worn leather cover of the Bible in his lap as he watched the woman's bony fingers clutch the corner of her khaki blanket, his own hand moving unconsciously in sympathy with hers.

She was little more than a gaunt skeleton, pale skin stretched over a brittle frame, eyes huge in a shrunken head.

Rice found himself wishing she would die, then cursed himself for a fool. The Devil mocked him from behind those wide, delirious eyes. Hadn't he brought her family together to pray? Why did death cling so tenaciously to her?

He rose to his feet and stretched his aching bones. *You're old!* the mocking serpent hissed in his mind. *As feeble as the old crone before you!*

Exhaustion, bone numbing and oppressive, prevented him from answering. He crossed the dirt floor and threw open a tent-flap, stepping wearily out into the noonday heat. Starvation, he told himself. He knew no prayer for starvation. Why had Brother Paul left him in charge of this—this mess?

Constant human traffic had worn a rutted, dusty rudiment of a road through the encampment. As he headed in the direction of his own tent, Rice adjusted his wide-brimmed hat against the beating sun. He'd heard tales at his mother's knee of a once warm and benevolent yellow star, happy children playing, growing, thriving in its life-giving rays. Rice had never known such a kindly sun. He'd been born during a time of intense global warming and extreme ultraviolet concentration. One had to be careful of exposure. Sunburns were severe, cancerous, often fatal. And out here on the open desert, daytime temperatures often reached 120 degrees Farenheit.

Domestic animals surged in a chaotic mass, the air was rank with the smell of them. Knowing they were being slaughtered at a faster rate now—even some of the dogs, he'd been told—due to the scarcity of food, did not encourage him. The situation was critical. Discontent was as thick in the air around him as the clucking and barking of the animals. And all he had with which to fight it was a regimen of daily discipline. And a plan—a plan to lead a thousand hungry, weary souls into the heart of the Wastelands, to Monument Valley.

They'd actually made it as far as the fortress town of Cameron, farther than he'd dared hope in the beginning. But their resolve—his own included—was being eroded by the duststorms, by the heat and the aridity of the high desert plateau. If all went well, they'd reach the spot where four states converged, where the Israeli planes would find them. If not, they'd perish out here. There was little room for error; so much rested on the cooperation of the Knesset, and upon the funds from the Martian Church winging their way toward Earth.

Rice knew that Paul had a crusade or two to preach on Luna before he could bring the desperately needed money home to the pilgrims. In an emergency, he could send brother Cowan on ahead with the funds, but he needed Cowan at his side. All this had been explained to them before Paul's departure, and they'd agreed that the Lunar crusades were vital enough to justify a week's delay. But, even then, the only places where cash was still honored were the fortified towns scattered across the desert—towns like Cameron, which had taken them an extra night's traveling just to avoid—dangerous places at best. Fear and uncertainty grew. And now, Rice thought bitterly, he was glimpsing the same ugly truth Moses had seen in the wilderness of Sinai: murmuring and rebellion in the camp. Inevitably, some of the more vocal saints had come to question his authority, perhaps to plot an uprising against him. Did they want to return to the cities where the necessities of life were denied them? Where their lives were in constant jeopardy? *Better than to die out here!* the Serpent taunted him. *Like the old woman!*

It was hunger that had eroded their reason. A new flag was flying over America, the emblem of cruel power—a white unicorn on a field of blue. Blue for peace, the banner lied. White for purity.

The Party for World Peace.

And the Party for World Peace was more deadly to a professing Christian than the brutal dust storms tearing across the plateau, or the grinding hunger about to claim its first victim. Surely, had they remained in the cities, they'd all be dead by now, not just Sister Cooke. And she was still hanging on, G-d bless her! Couldn't they see that? Most of them carried bluecards, but their funds were depleted. In the cities, like men dying of thirst on a raft at sea, they'd starve to death in the midst of plenty. Or be executed outright. Turning back was suicide. Out here, at least, they had a chance in a million, which was better than no chance at all.

But there were some who were willing to exchange anything at all for food—even to the extent of bowing down to idols. "We'll keep our faith in our hearts," they reassured one another. But it wouldn't be long, Rice knew, before they'd allow those chips in their bluecards to be injected beneath the skin of their wrists and foreheads. A small black number to indicate its location—**666**—and all who willingly received it would be lost forever. There'd be no hiding their faith in their hearts.

How many of them are willing to die for their belief in G-d? he wondered. He knew only what his own heart was saying. He would continue on to meet the Israeli planes. Not with haughtyness, but with hope. He couldn't live without hope—however slender—or without the L-rd. He'd go alone if he had to. He wouldn't—he *couldn't!*—turn back now. There'd be some who would follow him and some who'd return. That was in G-d's hands, not his.

As he entered his tent, he was struck by the leaden heat and the stench of body odor. A tall, lanky figure was stretched across his cot, thoroughly at home. His hair was matted with dirt; the knees of his denims were torn and mud-stained. A thin coating of dust seemed to have settled on him permanently.

"How's the old woman doing," the man asked.

Rice dropped into a folding chair and reached for his metal

cup. From a steaming kettle on a solar-powered hotplate, he poured himself some stale coffee. Holding the cup in his hand, he sloshed the liquid around absentmindedly before replying.

"I'm afraid she won't make it through the night," he said.

The tall man's grin was inappropriate, but somehow welcome. "All of us may be joining her soon enough," he said.

"How many times," Rice scolded, "have I warned you about speaking death over this enterprise, Bernard? If we *do* meet with an unfortunate end, G-d forbid, let it not be due to a rebellion sewn by your cynical tongue."

Bernard laughed. "It'll be due to drinking hot coffee in this hundred-degree heat."

"All the water must be boiled," Rice said. "And better hot than lukewarm. Besides, why should I listen to *your* complaints? You've spent the last three days in the big city."

"Flagstaff's not what it's cracked up to be, let me tell you."

"Perhaps. But a far sight better than this filthy mobile animal farm I'm dragging across the Wastelands."

"Agreed," said Bernard. "You look exhausted, Peter. Do you want to lie down? I'll gladly surrender my cot."

"*My* cot."

"Yes, *your* cot. Seriously, brother, you look about done in."

Rice took a sip from the metal cup and burned his lips.

"No," he said. "No, thanks. I think I need to talk to someone, just for a few minutes."

"I'm all ears."

Rice searched for a way to begin, for the key to the floodgate of pent-up doubt and heartache. It was no use. "I'm going to have to send you back," he said abruptly, changing the subject.

"Back?"

"Not as far as Flagstaff."

"Where then?"

"Cameron."

"Fortified town. Bad reputation."

"Yes, I know. But it can't be helped. "We need to make further use of your bluecard."

Bernard's face turned grim. "What for this time?"

"To beam a message to the *Empress*, to make Brother Paul aware of our situation."

Bernard reached for the coffee pot. "He won't cancel those

crusades on Luna. We both know that. And, what's more, we wouldn't want him to."

"I know. I know," Rice replied with a shake of his head. "But I must tell him that one of our people is dying, and that Mayor Browne's supplies are running out. Perhaps he'll send brother Cowan with the funds. Or cut the crusade short."

"Or, perhaps," observed Brother Bernard, "we'll all sprout wings and fly away."

Rice was silent.

There was nothing else to say.

α

They buried Sister Cooke in the morning. No flowers, no organ music, no sounds of mourning, just a few ragged pil-grims gathered at the side of a hastily dug grave prepared during the night. No work was ever done in the daylight.

The mourners began to appear in reluctant knots before Sol's first rays limned the flat horizon. In the pre-dawn haze Rice began his eulogy.

Glancing around at the stony-white faces under black, broad-brimmed hats, he opened his Bible to the fourteenth chapter of John's Gospel and began to read:

"'Let not your heart be troubled: ye believe in G-d, believe also in me. In my father's house are many mansions: if it were not so, I would have told you. And if I go to prepare a place for you, I will come again, and receive you unto myself; that where I am, there ye may be also.'" He paused to clear his throat. The only other sound was the doleful moan of the wind as it blew, unhindered, across the cinnamon plain.

Not even the sound of birds accompanied them as they lowered her body into the blood-red dust.

Dust to dust…

α

As the afternoon sun dropped below the horizon, the encampment came alive. Stakes were pulled up, tents hastily folded, and supplies (what little remained of them) packed away in preparation for the next phase of the journey. Discontent lay heavy on the atmosphere as Rice moved about the camp, supervising the hitching of the horses to various bizarre conveyances they called "wagons." From junkyards outside Phoenix-Mesa, heaped high with old, rusted ground-cars, they'd welded together this menagerie now being hitched to teams of fatigued horses. The ingenuity of their construction was endlessly amusing to Rice. Some were made entirely of wood appropriated from abandoned houses, but the lack of skilled wheelwrights in the company made it necessary for even these wooden vehicles to ride on rubber tires.

The merry buzz of laughter, conversation, and song that had accompanied their earlier journeys was conspicuously absent. A pall had fallen over their labors, which Rice perceived as an evil omen.

At dusk the caravan was ready. He mounted his tired old nag and slapped her haunch with an open hand.

"Git," he said.

"Ho!" cried another voice.

With a mournful groaning of metal axles, the long line of "wagons" crept forward.

They always journeyed beneath the light of the moon, dividing their exodus into phases paralleling those of Earth's satellite. As the familiar orb waned through its gibbous phase and into a faint crescent, preparations would be made for another rest-period during the new moon. As Luna began to wax in the black desert night, they'd break camp and move again.

Riding at the head of the line, Rice gazed up at the thin, gaunt fingernail-paring rising over the plain. Had Brother Paul reached it? Was he even now preaching to great throngs somewhere on that barren chunk of rock? Brother Bernard had been gone for over twenty-four hours now, having departed on his mission to Cameron at sunset the previous day. Rice wondered if he'd gotten the message through to Paul. No point worrying about it, he decided. There were more pressing matters to occupy him.

α

Brother Bernard caught up with the caravan on the third night, as they were passing the ruins of Tuba City, following the winding course of the Moenkabi Wash. The moon was brighter than it had been on the first night of travel, and Rice could just make out a slender figure approaching on foot from the southwest. Holding his right hand aloft and drawing back on the reins, he bellowed for the caravan to halt. With a mighty squeal and rumble, the wagons obeyed.

"What is it, Elder?" came a female voice from behind him. Rice pointed in the direction of the approaching figure. "It must be Brother Bernard!" he told her. "I wonder what happened to his mount."

"The poor man! He must be dying of thirst!"

"I'm going out to meet him. Wait for us."

"Can we water our horses in the creek, Elder?"

"No, not before we've tested the water. Just rest up a while."

He set off at a rapid canter. As he drew closer he could see that the man was walking with difficulty, staggering. Distances on the flat desert terrain played tricks with his vision. It seemed he'd ridden quite a distance before he finally drew his mount to a halt. The tall man seemed not to notice him at first, continuing undaunted on his crooked way.

"Brother Bernard," said Rice.

The man stopped, unsteady on his feet. He looked up at Rice and grinned in his old familiar way, teeth glinting in the moonlight. Coated with the dust of miles, dust that had come to be a part of him these last few weeks, he looked to Rice like a pathetic grinning scarecrow wobbling on a broken stake.

"Peter," he croaked. "Nice of you to....to come out..."

"Don't mention it," Rice said. "You know, Bernard, I've never seen anyone collect dust like you do."

"The next time.... you need to make a....phone call? Make it....yourself."

"Rice grinned back. "Is that any way to speak to your elders?"

"Blow it out your ear—Elder," said Bernard, and promptly fell on his face.

α

The water in Moenkabi Wash proved too polluted to drink. Rice found a spot in one of the wagons on which to lay Brother Bernard, then ordered a sister to fetch a canteen and feed some water to him a drop at a time. He waited until his friend was asleep, climbed out of the wagon, and mounted his horse, riding down the line to make sure all was well. Hungry faces glared at him over crusts of bread and precious bits of dried meat. Rice had no desire to know what sort of meat it was. (Except to Brother Paul, who strictly kept the Jewish kosher laws, meat was meat.) But salt was used to preserve those tough slabs of jerky, and salt only increased the thirst.

A few pilgrims smiled or waved in greeting as he cantered by, but Rice knew he was unpopular. Rebellion always began at the gut level. It resulted from misery, and misery was here in abundance. From which quarter would his nemesis arise? He searched each of the dusty faces for a clue. *How about Brother Morrison?* he speculated as his gaze took in the hard-lined features of the septuagenarian. Morrison's small eyes followed him as he passed, his head nodding stiffly. *Yes, it could easily begin with the old man's sharp tongue*. And yet, would an enemy necessarily be someone he mistrusted? All he could be certain of was that he *had* an enemy—somewhere. And if help didn't arrive soon, that enemy would strike.

Rice turned his horse around and slapped her on the side, returning to the head of the line at a furious gallop. When he'd taken his place at the front, he let out a loud "Ho!"

His wagon-train began to rumble across the Arizona desert.

The Priority Beam

"Table pays twenty," said the robot.

Captain Mills slapped his cards down on the green baize blackjack table and watched his last pile of chips being swept away by a deft robotic hand. The blackjack machine began to flip out another hand of cards, face down, to each of the eager gamblers hunched over the table.

Puffing nervously at the stem of his meerschaum, Mills dug around in his pants' pocket for his lucky chip. He'd never lost that magical, plastic disk, nor had he ever cashed it in, not even in moments of desperation. After it had done its job of turning his luck around, he was always careful to return it to his pocket.

The robot finished dealing, scanning the table with stereoscopic lenses, two ogling eye-like sensors shaded by a plastic visor. Mills tossed his lucky chip onto the table. With a nervous flutter in the pit of his stomach, he turned his cards over and glanced at them.

A jack and a queen. Twenty!

He turned the hand face down and placed his lucky chip on top of it. The robot dealt itself one extra card. “Table pays eighteen,” it announced.

Mills’ luck was changing!

Something touched his right shoulder. He spun around to look into the face of a young midshipman, still showing signs of acne.

“What is it?” he grumbled, rubbing his beard.

“Priority-one beam, from Luna. You can take it in your quarters, sir.”

Mills’ indignant scowl softened into a look of concern.

“Here it comes.” he sighed.

“Pardon, sir?”

“Nothing,” Mills said. He pushed himself away from the table, returning the lucky chip to his pocket. Scooping up the few chips the robot slid to him, he made his way across the floor of the crowded casino.

He knew who it was on the other end of that tachyon beam, and he dreaded answering the call.

α

The amazing girth of Vice Admiral Miles Bowlen filled the holoscreen as soon as Mills settled himself in one of the larger asteroid chairs and tapped a button on the arm-panel.

“Roy Mills!” the Vice Admiral bellowed. “You old space-dog!”

Mills suddenly longed for the good-old days before the taming of tachyons, when the lag in communications provided sufficient time to compose one’s reply.

“Admiral Bowlen,” he said, improvising what he hoped would look like a sincere, comradely smile. “It’s been a long time, sir.” *Not long enough!* he thought.

“How’s your luck holding out at the blackjack table?” Bowlen grinned.

“No better than your moongolf, I suspect.” Mills tried his

best to keep the imitation smile pasted on his face. It was already producing a rather uncomfortable sensation in the muscles of his cheeks. Did the "old man" know how much he detested him? Probably. Mills couldn't have cared less.

"What's your handicap these days, sir?" he said. The fake smile became easier to maintain as he recalled the corpulent Miles Bowlen in his bulky pressure-suit, swinging at a ball in one-sixth gee. Bowlen had a wicked slice, which, on the moon, resulted in some pretty comical shots. The face in the holoscreen turned glum.

"Never mind the moongolf," Bowlen said, bulbous lips drawn down at the corners. "This is a priority one beam."

"So the fellow told me." Mills had no intention of relating the grim situation at the blackjack table. No sense giving the man a reason to gloat.

"Well," said Bowlen, "I'll get right to the point."

"Do that, Admiral."

"There's a traitor aboard your ship. A traitor and a spy. He's been found guilty of treasonous crimes against the United States."

"Hmmm. Serious stuff."

"Indeed."

"Jeri Kline?"

"Huh?"

"Jeri Kline is the man's name, is it not?"

"Precisely! I won't ask how you know, but I want him placed behind bars at once, and turned over to me as soon as you arrive in Lunar orbit. Put him in the brig, Roy, under heavy guard. He's dangerous. As a matter of fact, you'd better supervise that part yourself."

"No, sir."

"Pardon?"

"No brig on the *Empress*, sir. We confine prisoners to their cabins, under house arrest."

"Rather unorthodox, isn't it?"

"Not really. We deal mostly with drunks, fist-fights, disturbing the peace, domestic violence, things like that. A prison on board would distress the passengers. The *Empress* is financed by private concerns—Saturn Enterprises and Galaxy Tours. It's a commercial vessel."

"What about your ship's guard? Don't they function as

military troops?"

"They hold naval ranks, sir, but they're private security guards, not military troops."

"Hundreds of them? For jealous drunks and wife beaters?"

"Not primarily—no, sir. They're commissioned to protect the sensitive technology of the *Empress* from commercial espionage, sabotage, and theft. The simuchambers for example, or the computer running the ship. Competitors are still trying to ascertain how they work, and apparently only Saturn Enterprises knows their secrets. One of the company's office buildings is actually located on board. There have been some break ins on Mimas, although our building is extremely secure. More secure than the rest of the ship, actually. But back to the issue at hand: We have no brig on the *Empress*, yet that shouldn't prevent our keeping Mr. Kline in custody for the duration. As long as you understand three things."

"What three things?"

"That this is a *commercial* liner, not a military vessel; that I'm a *commercial* pilot, not an officer in the Space Navy; and that I don't have to take orders from you—sir."

"Of *course* I understand that, Roy! I'm appealing to your loyalty as an American citizen, not issuing orders. If necessary, we *can* commandeer your vessel in the interests of national security, but I see no need for such drastic action in this case."

Mills stroked his beard thoughtfully. Since when did Miles Bowlen give a hoot about issues like loyalty, patriotism, or treasonous crimes against the United States—*any* states, for that matter? Warning bells went off in his head. Something didn't add up. Bowlen was a crass opportunist, with a black mark on his record to boot. Roy Mills smelled an old, familiar rat. He'd heard enough generalities ("treasonous crimes," "traitor," "spy") from that Air Force pain-in-the-neck, Matt Baker. The man had the slimy look of a fanatic; anything he said would sound suspicious. And why all this obscure blather about treasonous crimes? Generalities. No specified charges. Mills knew Bowlen would never be trusted with *truly* sensitive information, so that couldn't be the reason for his dissembling. He decided to press the issue and to carefully watch Bowlen's response.

Concealment had never been the Vice Admiral's strong suit.

"What are the specific charges against Kline?"

For the briefest instant, Bowlen took on the appearance of a pig with an apple in its mouth.

"You know that's classified, Roy."

"Moonpellets, Miles!" (He'd decided to quit calling Bowlen "sir". It was a vestigial reflex conceding authority.) "You know I can't arrest a passenger on suspicion of 'treasonous crimes.' You need to give me a specific charge."

"Are you defending this terrorist, Roy?"

Mills paused. Why would Bowlen jump to *that* conclusion? Demanding clarification hardly implied collusion. Bowlen was losing his cool. *Why?*

Suddenly Mills was pleased with the effects of instantaneous transmission. It was giving him a distinct advantage.

"Of course I'm not defending him!" he said. "Why would you even consider such an accusation, Miles? I'm merely requesting clarification. Hardly an unusual request, is it?"

"No—I suppose not."

"You need to understand that there's a rather formidable attorney on board who *will* defend Jeri Kline. He doesn't need *my* help. Ever hear of John Cowan?"

Bowlen turned green. "What about him?"

"Well, despite the fact that he's fearless, tenacious, and has never lost a single case in his entire career, he has a certain vested interest in Kline's welfare."

"How so?"

"It seems Kline's become a member of Brother Paul's staff. I assume you've heard of the world famous evangelist."

"Who hasn't?"

"Brother Paul is a passenger on my ship, along with his team. I've given them safe conduct."

Bowlen's face seemed to brighten, as though he'd just pieced together some puzzle in his mind.

"Brother Paul, eh?" he said.

"Exactly. And Kline's taken a job on his broadcasting crew. Which means John Cowan automatically becomes Kline's legal champion."

"I see."

"Let me put it this way, Miles. If I arrest Kline on some ambiguous charge like 'treasonous acts,' I'll lay you odds he turns up on Luna with John Cowan stuck to his side like superglue. Not to mention all of Brother Paul's holovision cameras, ready to record the event for an interplanetary audience. For that matter, they can start broadcasting right from this ship. I haven't the authority to prevent it. By the time we reach Luna, we'll have the entire solar system on our backs—particularly the young Martian colony, which is sympathetic toward Brother Paul. We can ill-afford a strike on Mars. So if I'm going to butt heads with the sharpest attorney on Earth, I'd better be armed with the facts."

"Deep space! I don't care if he brings the President with him, Roy; I want that traitor in chains!"

"Fine. Give me a specific charge and I'll tie him up for you with a pretty pink ribbon. But without anything more substantial, I can't guarantee that Cowan won't have him free in ten minutes. Then we'll both end up with egg on our faces. Be reasonable, Miles. All I need is a few details to make the charges stick."

Bowlen's face had been turning a deep shade of crimson as Mills spoke. Now he thundered over the holoscreen: "Captain Mills! This request comes directly from the President! If you do not turn Jeri Kline over to me the *minute* you enter Lunar orbit, I'll inform the White House of your refusal to cooperate. Your ship will be boarded by the Space Navy and your career, and possibly your life, will be terminated. Do I make myself clear?"

"Abundantly," Mills said. "Is that all?"

"That's all."

"Then I'll be signing off. Keep working on that dreadful slice of yours."

He caught a glimpse of Bowlen's bulldog scowl as the holoscreen went black. Pressing another button on the arm of his chair, he heard the voice of his Chief Petty Officer over the communicator. What was his name? Moore! Yes, that was it—Edward Moore.

"Captain?" said Moore.

"A passenger," said Mills, "by the name of Jeri Kline. I want him placed under house arrest immediately. Confine him to his suite under armed guard, with orders to shoot if he tries to escape. No one goes in or out of that suite without my express permission, understand?"

"Uh—yes, sir."

"And have one of your men contact Brother Paul. Ask him

to remain in his quarters—also, at my request."

"Yes, Captain."

Mills broke the connection and stood up, heading for the door.

There was more to this affair than met the eye. And he'd get to the bottom of it, one way or another.

α

Chief Petty Officer Edward Moore snapped off his radio, the Captain's orders still ringing in his ears. Unbuckling his holster, he strode down the corridor to where two guards stood at attention. He knew precisely where Kline was, and he must appear to be carrying out his orders. It was a good thing he'd decided to stash away that little piece of equipment, just in case. If only he'd found the time to teach Kline how to use it....

α

"Reverend."

Paul awakened slowly. No, it couldn't possibly be morning already! Opening his eyes, he winced at bright light streaming in from around Cowan's tall silhouette in the doorway.

"Reverend, wake up!"

"I'm awake; I'm awake. What is it, Little John?"

"A beam from Earth, sir. Brother Bernard."

Paul sat up straight. "Brother Bernard? Put him on immediately!"

"Wouldn't you like to get dressed, first?"

"Never mind that!" Paul said, reaching over and dialing the bedroom light up to full. "If Bernard's expending precious funds on a tachyon beam, it must be urgent. Let's not waste the pilgrims' money on vanity. Put the call on my screen, if you please."

Cowan held out a remote control and aimed it at the wall across from Paul's bed. Light pulsed. The visual was cluttered with "snow"—after all, Brother Bernard was probably calling from one of the poorly maintained stations in the Wastelands. His face on the screen was wan and streaked with dust, distorted into crazy-mirror shapes by the weak, pulsating beam. But his voice was clear.

"Brother Paul!"

"Yes, Bernard. You look exhausted, my friend. Are you well? Where are you beaming from?"

"Cameron, Arizona, sir."

"Wonderful! You must be close to the pickup point, then."

"Yes, sir. My mount was appropriated by same marauders along the way. They had guns…"

"The others?"

"They're all well, sir. Only one death on route. The old woman, Sister Cooke. They buried her this morning."

Paul shook his head and sighed. "If only I'd been there! Were it only possible to be in two places at once!"

"Don't blame yourself, sir. Actually, we've done pretty well, considering. Only one death so far. And we've almost reached Monument Valley."

"Yes, that *is* good. We must praise the L-rd for it. I suppose it was unrealistic of me to expect you to come so far on foot without casualties. But, still, I deeply regret the loss of that staunch woman of G-d."

"We all do, Reverend. Elder Rice is taking it particularly hard. He asked me to make this call."

"To inform me about Sister Cooke?"

"No, sir. We wouldn't want to concern you with such distressing news, if not for—well, sir—this call is rather expensive. All the remaining church funds are on my own bluecard…"

"Say no more, Brother Bernard. I quite understand. Is there a way for you to—reverse the charges?"

"Yes, sir." Paul saw Bernard reach out and tap some buttons. The screen pulsated as he keyed in the digits. "Thank you, sir. But I was instructed to inform you that our resources are at the critical point. Mayor Browne's supplies have all been consumed, and we're having to subsist by slaughtering our animals. Brother Morrison was severely punished for killing one of the horses. But, of course, once the horse *was* killed—well, we couldn't waste it. Some of the dogs are missing, too. The dogs are all pets, as you know, and dearly loved by those who brought them along. Tensions are rising."

"I see."

"Sister Cooke died of starvation, sir. The children and the elderly are particularly susceptible. There've been two childbirths on route—one stillborn, the other struggling. Elder Rice suspects there's some pilfering going on. It's possible that Sister Cooke's provisions found their way into someone else's wagon. Perhaps she didn't wish to complain—to make trouble for the thief. She was like that."

Paul nodded, frowning. "Yes. The situation is far more critical than I'd imagined, Brother Bernard. Please forgive me. We're only a week away from Luna. If you can just hold out for just another week, I shall send Brother Cowan down in a shuttle with some funds for you. It'll take him a day or so to find a fleet of hovercars willing to fly him from the Phoenix-Mesa spaceport to Monument Valley, but he'll be there with plenty of provisions, I promise you."

"Thank you, sir. The news will be encouraging to the pilgrims. It's been a hard journey."

"I understand, Bernard. But I must urge you all to press on to the pickup point. You'll arrive there before Brother Cowan can reach you with the provisions, but that simply cannot be helped. The airlift to Israel is your only hope."

"I know that, sir."

"I'm an old man, Bernard," said Paul. "I'll never have another opportunity to bring a crusade to the moon. All the reports we've been getting indicate that Luna's population is desperately in need of revival. The authorities are facing revolution. The miners need exhortation and encouragement. I can see no possible way to cancel my engagements there."

"We all understand that, sir. Sister Cooke was one of the staunchest supporters of the Lunar crusade. The Church on Earth has no monopoly on persecution."

"I regret to say you're quite correct."

"In my opinion, Reverend. Elder Rice has been an exemplary leader under the circumstances. We can survive another week. We'll make it to the pickup point. It's just that…"

"Go on. You may speak freely." Paul gestured for Cowan to leave the room. The big man disappeared like a shadow as Paul nodded to the face on the screen. Bernard, looking relieved, continued.

"I believe Elder Rice is concerned about the possibility of revolt. There's been same ugly talk…."

"The spirit of Korah! I warned you to be on your guard

against it."

"Yes, sir. Elder Rice has been very vigilant in that regard. But he knows, as I do, that the pilgrims do not hold him in the same esteem as they hold you. The presence of an apostle—you, sir—is desperately needed to restore order. And yet you're millions of kilometers away in space. Even if you *were* inclined to cancel your crusades, you couldn't arrive in time to stem the rebellion."

"Things are that serious!"

"Yes, Reverend. Otherwise Elder Rice wouldn't have asked me to make this call. He couldn't put it into words, but I understood. He's desperate. He's afraid someone might try to—assassinate him."

"I see. Tell me, does your station have a digital record-unit?"

Bernard's face distorted, fish-eye-like, as he leaned closer to the camera-lens to examine the instructions printed on the machine.

"Yes, sir," he said.

"Good. Insert your bluecard."

Bernard obeyed. A series of green digits flashed in the lower right of the wallscreen, displaying the current charges. Paul glanced at them and whistled softly. *Tachyon beams are certainly a luxury for the private citizen,* he thought. He climbed out of bed and crossed the room to the holoscreen panel, keying in the digits listed on the panel for activating the record mode. A circular, red light popped on at the top of the screen, indicating "ready."

"Now," he said. "Start your recording when I give you the word."

"Got it," said Bernard.

Paul fetched his toga from one of the bedposts and donned it. He checked himself in the mirror and then turned to face the screen.

"Begin," he said.

The dot at the top of the screen turned blue. Paul drew back his shoulders.

"Brethren," he said. "*Chesed v'shalom b'Shem Yeshua ha-Mashiach*—Grace and peace to you in the Name of Jesus Christ. I pray the L-rd will strengthen you for this final leg of your journey. He's brought you this far and He will not abandon you—He'll speed you to your destination. Think of that destination, brothers and sisters. *Eretz Yisrael*! Keep the vision of *Yerushalayim* in your hearts and minds. *Eem eshkachaych Yerushalayim, teeshkach y'meeni. Teedbak l'shonee l'chee-kee, eem-lo ezkrachi, eem lo a-a-leh et Yerushalayim al rosh simcha-tee!* 'If I forget thee, O Jerusalem, let my right hand forget her cunning. If I do not remember thee, let my tongue cleave to the roof of my mouth; if I prefer not Jerusalem above my chief joy!' Don't let Satan steal it from you now; you're almost there! I'm sending our dear brother, Little John, to you. He'll bring food, clothing, water—whatever you need. Receive him into your camp with the same love and honor with which you'd receive me. Little John is dearer to me than my own right arm. Treat him accordingly. Let him judge among you, with submission, as befits children of light.

"I'll not mince words, brethren. It has come to my attention that there is murmuring and *lashon harah*—evil-speaking—among you. How can such a thing exist among those who claim to have the indwelling of the Holy Spirit? When I come again to you, shall it be with the rod of correction? Will you break my heart? Will you rend it in two? I cannot be with the brethren on Luna and with you also. That's why I've ordained leaders to serve in my stead. By speaking evil of them, you are speaking evil of me, and thus of Messiah Himself, by Whose Hand I was ordained.

"Or may I expect you to search your souls and repent of the evil you contemplate? For there are some among you who are even plotting murder against the leader G-d has placed over you. I can hardly utter such an accusation! Yet it's true. Their hearts are filled with darkness.

"Need I remind you what our L-rd says of rebellion? It is as the sin of witchcraft! Need I remind you of His warning: 'touch not mine anointed'? Beloved, when Little John comes to you—remember—he comes with my authority..."

α

The portal of Paul's suite chimed softly, announcing a late caller.

Cowan was seated on the divan, listening to Paul's epistle to the pilgrims and wondering what awaited him on Earth.

Paul was granting him total apostolic authority over the expedition! Was he worthy of such honor, such immense responsibility? The chiming of the portal interrupted his thoughts. Pressing a button on the arm of the divan he caused the door of Paul's bedroom to slide shut on silent gears, so their late-night guest wouldn't interrupt the message. The touch of another button slid the portal of the suite upward.

Captain Mills stood on the threshold, eyes narrow above a bushy, black beard.

"Come in, Captain," Cowan offered. "How can I help you?"

Mills strode into the room, hands clasped behind him. His brooding features signaled ill tidings.

"Where's Brother Paul?" he demanded in his usual gruff, overloud voice. Cowan was glad he'd thought to close Paul's door before admitting the Captain. Mills was displaying the arrogance of a man used to getting his way, a man for whom people dropped what they were doing the instant he hove into view. *Not so in this suite!* thought Cowan.

"The Reverend is occupied with an important call from Earth, and cannot be disturbed. If you'll please take a seat, he should be with you in a moment."

Mills dropped sullenly into one of the chairs across from the attorney, tapping his fingers on the table beside it. Cowan ignored this display.

"Drink, Captain? We take wine on sabbaths and festivals, but don't approve of hard spirits. However, we frequently entertain important guests who do not share our convictions."

Mills nodded, frowning. "Scotch and water, thank you."

Cowan played his fingers over the face of a console in the table in front of him. A spider-mech came buzzing from its lair in the wall, carrying the Captain's drink on its back. Reaching for it, Mills nodded his thanks and turned the glass up to his mouth. A small shudder ran through him.

"Excellent."

"Cutty Sark," said Cowan. "I believe it's your preference."

"By Mars, it is! The real thing, too, not that swill they peddle out on Enceladus." He displayed his approval by bending his elbow again.

"You appeared to be in need of a jolt, to use the vernacular.

Tell me, Captain, what is your business with Brother Paul so late in the evening?"

Mills shook his head. "That's for his ears only."

"Pardon me for being forward, Captain, but I'll be privy to any business you have with the Reverend. I'm Brother Paul's legal counsel and he does very little without me at his side. You might try to reconcile yourself to my presence."

Mills grunted his displeasure.

Just then the bedroom door slid open and the evangelist swept into the room with a cordial smile—a false smile, Cowan noted. Something important was up, and Brother Paul was pouring on the official charm for Mills' benefit.

"Hello, my dear Captain," he said, reaching out his hand.

Mills took it, perplexed.

"To what do I owe the pleasure of this unexpected visit?"

Typically, Mills did not waste words. "Your—associate, Kline," he said, careful to use Paul's preferred title for the radio announcer, "is being arrested for treason as we speak. He'll be confined to his suite under armed guard until we reach Luna, where he'll be turned over to the proper authorities. I gave the order myself."

Cowan sat forward in his chair, alert and on the offensive. Paul had requested that he remain silent during their first interview with Mills, but now there was nothing restraining him. "Would you care to repeat the charge, Captain Mills?" he said.

"The charge," Mills replied, looking uncomfortable, "is treason against the United States."

Discerning Mills discomfort, Cowan pressed the issue. "Come now, Captain—treason against the United States? What sort of treason are we talking about? Espionage? Political assassination? Sabotage? What's the specific charge? And what's the evidence against him?"

"The Admiralty was not at liberty to—"

"Not at liberty? Or not cooperative? As you yourself know, sir, a Christian is hardly safe these days on any planet except Mars. Such trumped-up charges have been leveled against the innocent on numerous occasions, and there's a clear legal precedent for demanding specific complaints and evidences before any minister of the Gospel can be taken into custody. State vs. Miller, 2031."

"Minister? See here, Mr. Cowan! This man's no minister of

the Gospel, and we all know it!"

Paul smiled. "I know nothing of the kind, Captain Mills. Every member of my staff is automatically an ordained minister. And, as I pointed out at our last meeting, Brother Kline is now a member of my staff."

"Moonpellets!" snapped Mills.

"Pardon, Captain? There is no need to cuss."

"Look, Reverend. I didn't come down here to be played with. I—I came to help you."

"Help me? How?" Paul shot Cowan a puzzled look. The attorney shrugged, turning to Mills.

"Captain," he said, "please tell us what's on your mind."

"Well—" For a moment, Mills looked like a man desperately struggling with a difficult decision. "Reverend. I don't buy this business about treason any more than you do."

This time it was Cowan's turn to look surprised.

"You don't? Then why have you had him arrested?"

"For his protection." Mills put a hand to his throat and rubbed it gently. "And mine. Listen, gentlemen, ropes irritate my neck. If I disobeyed the President of the United States there'd be a necktie party on Luna—with me as guest of honor. And, as you can imagine, hanging by the neck in one-sixth gee can be a particularly prolonged and painful procedure."

"Well, we certainly wouldn't want you to hang!" exclaimed Paul.

"Nor," added Cowan, "do we want to see Jeri Kline hanged. He's as innocent as you are."

"I'm sure of it," said Mills sadly. "But the fact that I'm even having this conversation with you puts my life in jeopardy. The PWP is a cold-blooded group."

Paul nodded. "We know that. And we appreciate the serious risk you're taking."

"Understand—I'm not doing this for Kline's sake. I don't care one whit for the man. It just so happens there's someone for whom I care even less. The Vice Admiral on Luna. I don't trust him. He's not Navy, if you know what I mean. He's a rank opportunist and a swindler. And I think—yes, I think I'll enjoy being the fly in his ointment. He's up to something unsavory, gentlemen, that's for certain. And it may be that, by disobeying him, I'm doing my country a service. I hope so. I truly hope so."

"What do you plan to do?" Cowan asked.

"I'm placing Kline under house arrest. I have no choice in the matter. He'll be confined to his suite, but, rest assured, he'll be well treated. Wc will not interrogate or harass him in any way. And I'll do my best to see that he's made as comfortable as possible. Messages from both of you will be carried to him freely. He'll not be given access to a holoscreen, however. Prisoners are not allowed such access—for obvious reasons—and my officers would think it unusual if I made an exception in his case. One of them might even report it to the authorities on Luna. I can't risk that. On the other hand, there's nothing in the regulations that says I have to make a prisoner uncomfortable, or refuse him access to spiritual comfort or legal counsel. In fact, I believe I'm under constraint to provide both, should the accused demand them. I assume, Brother Paul, that he *has* made such demands?"

"Oh, yes!" said Paul. "Quite adamantly."

"Very well. Then I shall see to his needs personally."

"Thank you, Captain. May the L-rd reward you for your kindness."

"May he keep me from the rope."

"But, if I may ask—how will you arrange to have Brother Kline released from custody before we arrive on Luna, and they demand you turn him over?"

Mills shifted uneasily in his chair.

"I have no idea, Reverend," he replied. "But I'm working on it."

α

Jeri Kline was strolling on the Vista Deck with Phil Esteban, Paul's senior advisor. The old man was just gaining his spacelegs, and the view of the distant Earth-Moon system—two sparkling dots on a field of ebony—was making him ill. The trip to the Vista Deck, along a moving belt suspended across the middle of the ship's spherical hub, had caused his face to turn an ever-deeper shade of sea-green. His old agoraphobia rose up until he felt the impulse to turn and run, screaming, back to his cabin. And he might have done so had such an ignoble display not required his returning over the same length of beltway he'd have to endure simply by staying put. Brother Paul had asked him to escort Kline to the Vista Deck, to keep the young stowaway out of Mills' sight for a while. Had Paul known of his agoraphobia he'd never have made such a request.

Phil listened to Kline's testimony of miraculous healing at the Sparks, Nevada crusade. As they strolled from one view of space to the next, Esteban wondered why Kline was wearing such a bulky nylon jacket. The jacket was oversized, in the latest style of Earth. But it *was* rather warm on the Vista Deck, and Kline kept it zippered to the neck. He was obviously uncomfortable; perspiration popped out on his forehead, ran down his cheeks. And yet he resisted every suggestion that he remove the jacket. Strange….

Although they'd left Paul's suite in a hurry, Kline had insisted on stopping at his own rooms. Esteban had waited in the corridor for what had seemed an unreasonably long time until Kline reappeared, zipped up in that floppy jacket. He tried to get Kline to remove it, but the young fellow became more irritable at each suggestion. It was obvious the kid was suffering in the thing, but it was equally obvious that he intended to keep it on, and zipped up to the neck.

Kline continued his story, eyes flashing with the memory of deliverance and healing. Esteban, following his every gesture, shrugged off his thoughts about the nylon jacket and listened with deepening interest.

The Dream

Brother Bernard awakened to the rumble and lurch of a moving wagon. His mouth was dry and every muscle ached from his long hike. Someone—Elder Rice, he supposed—had covered him with a blanket. How long had he been unconscious?

He suddenly remembered the holodisk containing Brother Paul's epistle. Reaching down, he felt the outside of his pants' pocket for the inch-round disk. It was still there. *Good!* he thought, and lay back. As he closed his eyes, he imagined himself preaching before the entire community of pilgrims, tall and authoritative, a commanding figure. There wasn't much to that preaching business, he decided; it was all showmanship. He could handle that. *Yes*, he was telling the sea of worshipful faces in his mind. *Rice is dead, poor fellow. And now John Cowan, Paul's trusted emissary, has met with a fatal accident on his way to meet us with the provisions.* Who could lead them now but himself? Hadn't Elder Rice entrusted him with secret knowledge? Hadn't he been close to Rice from the beginning, the valiant elder's staunchest friend? Now it was time to reveal the *true* mission upon which they'd embarked. Paul and Rice had explained that they were crossing the Wastelands to meet Israeli planes, planes that would fly them to the Holy Land. *But it was a lie!* He imagined himself recounting to the faces around him how he'd argued with Rice many times over the expediency of such a deception—of keeping the good pilgrims in ignorance of their *real* mission. But Rice had insisted that it was in the interests of security, for their own good. He could imagine the chorus of groans that would accompany that statement! Now that Rice was dead, he would tell them, it was time for the truth.

They were sent out here to the Wastelands, not to run like cowards from the land of their birth—but to build a great city! A city dedicated to Messiah, where all believers would be safe from persecution. The fortified cities in the Wastelands were free from government interference, and so would their city be. New Jerusalem, it would be called. And they themselves would have a hand in erecting it—the actual home of their returning King! Not in faraway Israel, but here! Right where they were standing! *Listen!* he imagined himself crying out, caught up in his own vision. *Can you hear the angels? Can you hear them? This is the very spot where Christ will set His feet! G-d is finished with Israel and the Jews! Haven't they rejected Him time after time? Didn't they crucify Him? They're even now being judged—in a special facility in Oregon. Judged and condemned to death!* He felt their response washing over him like a tsunami. *Why in the world would Messiah set up His Kingdom in Israel? No, the biblical prophecies about Jerusalem are allegorical, not literal. Israel is finished. The Church is Israel! And the New Jerusalem will be here! It's here that Christ will come! Right here, to America!"*

They'd follow him wherever he led! And they'd build a city—not for Jesus Christ, but for Brother Bernard. And not merely a city, but an empire!

Who could stop him? The PWP had offered him an empire in exchange for his cooperation. All he was required to do was make certain this foolhardy band of rebels submitted to the next government census—when their bluecards would be done away with and replaced by the mark of loyalty. But that census would come, they'd assured him, only after New Jerusalem had set up adequate defenses. Brother Bernard trusted no one, not even the PWP. *And what's the harm in receiving that mark?* He would ask. *You've all possessed bluecards, haven't you? I still have mine. The mark is nothing more than a permanent bluecard grafted into the skin. It can never be stolen or revoked. It isn't the Mark of the Beast, no matter what Brother Paul says. Paul lied to us about this awful exodus, didn't he? How can we trust anything he says?*

Bernard felt no guilt about deceiving them; it was all for their own good. And once everything was made ready, the President of the United States—Maitreya himself!—would at last reveal himself as the Messiah of the Acquarian Age! Then they'd see! He'd put an end to all hunger and war and injustice. Why couldn't these fools understand? Why was it necessary to deceive them in this way? Why couldn't they—with all their supposed piety—simply recognize their Messiah? Why did they flee so desperately from the truth? Well, no matter. They would all understand soon enough.

Hadn't Elder Rice already intimated that Bernard would succeed him as leader of the exodus if tragedy should befall him? Bernard's future leadership was assured. All he needed to do was make certain that tragedy *did* befall Elder Rice. At first his plan had been to let the others take care of Rice in their own way. Rumors of assassination were everywhere, thanks to him. Afterward, filled with remorse, they'd be as easy to lead as sheep to the shearers. And their remorse would serve as a goad to spur them on to building his city.

But the rebellion had taken far too long to foment, despite all his efforts.

If they'd indeed risen against the Elder, the bravest among them would have been exposed. It would have been a simple thing to order their excommunication, to cast them out from the midst of the people as punishment for their deed. Bernard wouldn't have to kill them; the Wastelands would do it for him. Such an action would appear compassionate, yet firm, the act of a G-dly leader, assuring Bernard's place in their affections, leaving him in undisputed command.

But now everything had changed. They were too close to their destination for him to rely on their cooperation. He'd have to get rid of Rice himself.

He'd had no choice but to transmit the message to Brother Paul, just as Rice had given it to him. (He'd added a few details, of course, like Rice's desperation and fear.) There were too many possibilities of discovery if he'd neglected to beam that message. And so he'd ridden to Cameron with every intention of obeying. When the PWP agents had met him on the way, taking his horse in order to explain his delay—*And blast them to the Oort Cloud!*—he'd told them everything. They'd already known the location of the exodus, and had for some time. But there was a better plan than arousing public outcry by nuking the pilgrims into oblivion. It had been their intention from the start, not to kill the rebels, but to turn them against Brother Paul. To put them under the leadership of a proven disciple of Maitreya—someone like Brother Bernard. They'd approved of Bernard's plan to beam the message, to act as if nothing were amiss. And then they sent him on his way—*on foot!*

Miraculously, Paul had recorded that epistle. And no one else on Earth knew of its existence but Bernard. In the absence of Rice and Cowan, it would confer upon Bernard complete apostolic authority. It would also serve to strengthen that apostleship, to root out any rebels who might remain in the camp—rebels who might want to conspire against Bernard. If he timed its showing correctly, he'd have no assassins under *his* leadership.

Nothing to worry about, he decided, caressing the holodisk with his left hand as he drifted off to sleep. No one suspected him. And no one knew that John Cowan was on his way to Earth in a week's time. No one but Bernard. Cowan would find a fleet of hovercars at the spaceport, all right. And drivers who'd be more than willing to fly him out to Monument Valley—drivers who'd also happen to be in the payroll of the PWP. Very convincing accidents had been arranged before.

As he was helped into unconsciousness by the hypnotic swaying of the wagon, Bernard had no way of knowing that Elder Rice had left the wagon train hours before. This wasn't one of Rice's usual reconnaissance trips. As Bernard dreamt of an empire in the desert, Rice was riding toward Cameron at a full gallop.

α

The man called Smith reached out a hand to answer the humming wallscreen. Matt Baker's face appeared.

"Ah! Lieutenant! Good news, I hope."

The 3-D image of Matt Baker grinned sardonically, the grin seeming to take up the entire expanse of the filthy wall. A piece of brown paint dislodged itself from a damp patch to the right of the screen and drifted to the floor.

"One week," said the grinning face. "The word just came down. Seven days, and then we strike."

"I'll be ready," said Smith. "And—oh!" Smith drew one of his wooden knives from behind his neck—where he always kept one secured with tape—and waggled it at the screen for effect. "I'll be needing some credits in advance, Lieutenant. For expenses." He held out his hands to indicate the crumbling interior of his cubicle.

Baker sighed. "How much?"

"How does fifteen-hundred sound?"

"A thousand sounds better."

Their eyes locked for a moment.

"A thousand should be fine," said Smith.

"Apart from financial extortion, is there anything else you require?"

"That's it. For now. Have the credits placed in my account tomorrow morning, no later than ten o'clock. I'm off cubicle-hunting today."

"Delightful," said Baker. "Best of luck to you. So, Mr. Smith, I'll be signing off. No need to prolong this discussion."

"No. I'll hear from you in a week."

Baker's face disappeared from the screen.

The Savant

Seated with Captain Mills and John Cowan in his suite, Paul noticed the tiny diamond on the face of his bracelet glimmering insistently, as it did when the beeper was turned off. He was glad he'd taken that precaution.

"If you gentlemen will excuse me," he said, rising from his chair. "I'll only be a moment."

"Of course," Mills replied.

"If you come up with any ideas in my absence—about how to save Brother Kline, I mean—please fill me in when I return."

"Will do, Reverend," said Cowan, who'd also noticed the flickering of Paul's bracelet.

Paul stepped into the bedroom and closed the door behind him. He tapped the gold button on the side of the bracelet. "Yes, Brother Wallace?"

"Sir," came the tiny voice. "Sorry to interrupt your chat with the Captain, but has he informed you that he's ordered Kline's arrest?"

"Yes, just now."

"Very good…"

"Something else, Brother Wallace?"

"Did you know that Wilbur Denton is aboard the *Empress*, sir?"

"Actually, I was wondering when he'd take his place in this puzzle of ours. Yes, Brother Wallace; I had the pleasure of making his acquaintance on the shuttle up from Mars."

"Why didn't you inform security?"

"That's a good question. I suppose I was waiting to see if he'd contact me again."

"Well, he has."

"Good."

"Did you know Denton's the major stockholder of Saturn Enterprises, the company responsible for building this ship?"

"I'm not altogether ignorant of current affairs. Especially when it comes to someone of Mr. Denton's reputation. You say he's tried to contact me?"

"Yes, sir. He just called your private number a few moments ago. I thought you'd want to be informed right away."

"My *private* number?"

"That's right. The one no one's supposed to know except your staff. All such calls are automatically routed through the security suite."

"Yes, yes," said Paul impatiently. "How did Denton gain access to my private number?"

"My question exactly, sir. But if you don't mind an educated guess, I'd say from the ship's computer."

"Hmmm."

"The only other alternative is a security leak. And I can guarantee that no one on your staff has leaked information."

"I'm trusting you implicitly, Brother Wallace."

"There's no leak, Reverend. I'm positive of it."

Paul was silent for a moment. "I see," he said.

"May I inquire, sir, what Denton said to you on the shuttle?"

"He acted strangely. He spoke of an impending revolt on Luna."

"Very similar to Jeri Kline's story, isn't it?"

"Yes, very."

An odd noise came from the tiny speaker in Paul's bracelet. It was Wallace whistling through his teeth.

"Let's handle this carefully, Brother Wallace. Until we have more information, we should keep it to ourselves."

"Ever think you might have missed your calling, sir? You'd make a fine security officer. You have a truly devious mind."

"*Devious?* Me? *Chas vachalelah!* G-d forbid!"

"Yes, sir."

"It seems to me that the best way to acquire more information is to contact Denton right away."

"Keep it up and you'll put me out of a job, Reverend. I was just about to suggest that myself."

"And we wouldn't want to alert Captain Mills, of course."

"I don't suppose you have some devious plan to get around *that* little problem. Or do you?"

"I certainly do." Paul went to the bedside table and picked up his pen, scribbling a few words on a note pad. "What cabin is Mr. Denton occupying?"

"He has private rooms in the Saturn Enterprises building, sir. It's the tallest building in the commercial sector. Suite nine hundred—nine-zero-zero—on the top floor."

"I'll be sending Little John," Paul said, folding up the note and cupping it in the palm of his hand. "As soon as I break off with you, I want you to call my suite on the holoscreen. Ask for Little John. Call him away on some urgent business. Invent something."

"Will do."

"That's all, then. What's the correct term in undercover jargon? Over and out? Roger Wilco?"

"No, sir," Wallace chuckled. "I don't believe there is one."

"Well—let's say over and out, then."

"Right, sir. Over and out."

Paul pressed the button. Moving quickly to the intercom by the bedroom door, he flipped it on and waited until he heard the buzz of the holoscreen in the other room. He heard Brother Wallace conferring with Cowan; then Cowan's voice speaking apologetically to Captain Mills, begging his pardon for having to rush off so unexpectedly. But such was the legal profession. One could never keep decent hours…

Paul snapped off the intercom and reached for the button to activate the door. As it swished open, he stepped into the suite and feigned surprise at seeing Cowan about to depart.

"Are you leaving, my friend?" he said.

"I'm afraid so, Brother Paul. Some late business with one of my clients—a certain Mr. Wallace.

"An interesting case?"

"Fascinating."

As Paul crossed the room to where Cowan was standing, it occurred to him that Captain Mills would probably be so relieved at the attorney's departure that he'd suspect nothing. Paul was still not sure just how far the Captain could be trusted. Extending his hand to Cowan, he pressed the folded piece of notepaper into the tall man's palm and said, "Why can't you ever take a vacation from your work, counselor? You need a good rest more than another retainer."

"There's no rest," said Cowan, "for the wicked." Paul laughed and opened the portal for him.

"Please come back and join us as soon as you can, Little John."

"I will, Reverend. This shouldn't take long."

"Take as much time as the case requires," Paul told him. As Cowan stepped through the portal and down the corridor, Paul closed it with a sigh of relief.

"Well, Captain," he said, returning to his chair. "What did you and Little John determine about our friend, Brother Kline?"

α

At this time of night, the commercial sector of the *Empress* was dark and quiet. It wasn't the thick darkness of terrestrial night, however. On shipboard, night was suggested by a general dimming of the artificial sunlight and the extinguishing of the garish swirl of neon. Brother Wallace, the staff's security guard, was also a history buff. He'd explained that such elaborate neon displays had been common on Earth in the 1940s and 50s. They became an art form in their own right, until it was decided that they presented a danger to ground-car traffic. Cowan could understand how they could be a distraction back in the days before computerized traffic-control, when people actually steered their vehicles. But even the dramatic displays in the commercial sector, now thankfully extinguished for the night, were only a pale shadow of the Las Vegas Deck's glittering neon kaleidoscope, which continued twenty-four hours a day.

As Cowan ambled across the park toward the massive skyscraper, its broad sign advertising Saturn Enterprises, he was thankful this wasn't Earth. A night-time stroll through such a park in any city on his home planet was unthinkable. Even with the stepped-up presence of the Peace Guards, street gangs roamed the parks virtually unmolested. Here on the *Empress*, where the ratio of ship's guards to citizens was vastly higher, one was more apt to be harassed by an overzealous security officer checking bluecards and wrist-marks than by any criminal element. But, for those without either—or identity papers granting exception—life could be made rather difficult just the same.

As he stepped through the entrance and glanced around for an elevator, he couldn't help wondering what Denton would have to contribute to the mystery. He found an elevator, entered it, and told it to carry him to the 900th floor.

α

Wilbur Denton, bald pate gleaming under a hovering lamp, set down his pocket-sized New Testament and reached for the holoscreen console on his desktop. Excitement kept him from concentrating on his reading. This was the moment when all his years of careful planning, all his costly preparations, would finally be justified. *If only Christine could be here to see it!*

It was with profound disappointment that he received the news from his secretary that John Cowan, not Brother Paul, stood in the waiting room.

"Send him in," Denton ordered, hardly able to keep the frustration out of his voice.

"Yes, Mr. Denton."

"And Becky…"

"Yes, sir."

"You may retire now. I'll be quite all right."

"Are you sure?"

"Quite sure."

"Very well, sir. Goodnight, then."

"Goodnight."

When the office hissed open and Cowan entered, Denton's discouragement partially lifted. This man was extraordinarily tall and muscular, his presence commanding. When the attorney spoke, Denton noticed that his voice was quiet—deceptively quiet. He knew of Cowan's reputation and admired it. Perhaps *this* was the man he should be speaking to, rather than Brother Paul.

"I must apologize," Cowan said, "for the urgent business that detains Brother Paul. He wishes me to tell you that he regrets not being able to come in person. He's long desired to make the acquaintance of such a generous contributor to G-d's work. Please accept his humble apologies, sir. He invites you to meet with him personally, as soon as his schedule allows."

He's lying through his teeth! Denton thought as he rose to shake the attorney's hand. *Paul wouldn't have forgotten our meeting on the shuttle. But he apparently neglected to mention it to his attorney. Why*?

"Never mind, never mind," he insisted, gesturing for his guest to take a seat. "I'll have that pleasure soon enough, I'm sure. It's just that my business with Brother Paul is rather urgent and extremely—sensitive."

"I can assure you that—" Cowan began his stock confidentiality speech, but Denton cut him off sharply.

"I know all about that, counselor. And I also—I hope you don't mind—had you hologrammed and voice-printed before you entered. Standard procedure. If you weren't John Cowan, we'd not be having this discussion. And, since I also know of your reputation for client-attorney confidentiality, there's no reason to proffer the standard assurances."

Cowan appeared to be taken aback.

"Please," Denton said soothingly. "Please don't be offended, counselor. I'm afraid these precautions are so much a part of my daily existence that I sometimes forget their effect on others. You must realize, however, that for a man in my position—with the kind of enemies I seem to attract—such elaborate security measures are necessary."

"Of course," said Cowan, not looking convinced.

"I called Brother Paul," Denton went on, "because I find myself in a position to be of service to him."

"In what way?"

Denton rose and turned his back to Cowan, He gazed out through the ceiling-high window at the dazzling skyline of the commercial sector. He had created this ship, yet its beauty and functionality never ceased to fill him with wonder. A flying city, spinning within the hub of an interplanetary liner! There was no sensation or spinning, of course, just as there was no sensation of the Earth's axial rotation, but the buildings at the sector's foreshortened horizon turned gradually upward into the "sky," following the gentle curve of the hull. Had he been able to lean out the window and glance upward, he'd see the city stretching overhead like a diamond-studded rainbow.

"To be frank with you," he said, "there's little that goes on, either in this vessel or in the solar system, for that matter, of which I can afford to be ignorant. I had hoped to speak with Brother Paul in person because I desired to confess my sins. To be forgiven for a life of greed and selfishness."

Spiritual guidance wasn't strictly Cowan's field, but Denton was pleased to see that the attorney didn't brush his comment aside.

"The L-rd is right here, Mr. Denton. *He's* your mediator. You need only confess your sins to Him."

"And this I have done, many times. But I still feel the need to ask forgiveness from the man of G-d. My contributions to his ministry have been extravagant, yes. But they were offered with improper motives."

"How's that?"

"As a means of expunging my guilt, Mr. Cowan. I was trying to wash away my sins with filthy lucre."

"I'm sure Brother Paul would understand, sir. If you've repented, as you say, then the sin has been forgiven."

α

The bald man turned from the window and fixed his eyes on the attorney. He reminded Cowan of the old photos of Vladimir Lenin he'd seen in encyclopedias: the bald head, the angular features, the dark goatee.

"Paul," said Denton, "may indeed understand. But I'm not sure *you* do. You see—I know what's happening on Luna. I know about your friend, Jeri Kline. And I know about the assassination plot. In short, Mr. Cowan, I can help."

"We're grateful," Cowan replied, "but there's no need. Captain Mills has already offered his assistance."

Denton sat down at his desk, looking thoughtful.

"Soon," he said, "our good Captain will be overwhelmed with his own difficulties. He values his life, and the forces arrayed against him are deadly."

"What forces?"

"Powers that extend all the way to the Oval Office. I have good reason, my dear Mr. Cowan, for wanting to oppose the PWP. I am, after all, the quintessential capitalist—and very comfortable as such. Independence and freedom are the oxygen I breathe. But this Maitreya they're all giving their allegiance to, President Charles Coffey—I believe he's the Antichrist himself."

"Brother Paul would agree."

Denton closed his eyes for a moment, absorbed in thought. When he spoke, it was with utter conviction: "Mr. Cowan. I believe it's time for every Christian to join the battle against this devil Maitreya and his political machine. Soon no one alive will be able to oppose him. He'll aim nuclear weapons at the moon, and no resistance will then be possible."

"What can we do to stop him?"

"I have a great deal of power, Mr. Cowan. My wealth has purchased this power. The building in which you now sit is a gargantuan computer complex, far more intelligent than any yet invented. It dwarfs the mainframe I designed to run the *Empress*, with all of that system's complexity. It is, in fact, the most advanced computer ever devised by man. It thinks like a human being. It reasons. It responds in nanoseconds to every stimulus. And its 'central nervous system', if you will, makes the human brain appear that of an imbecile by comparison. It is also equipped for self-defense, in case any hostile power should attempt to take it over—as many of my competitors already have tried to do, and failed. Years ago I took steps to render all such attempts futile."

"I'm afraid I've missed your point."

"It is my wish to see this building and all of its resources placed at the disposal of Brother Paul."

"But—Mr. Denton, I—"

"That would include Jeeves, of course."

"Jeeves?"

"The supercomputer I was just describing. I named him Jeeves, after a character created by P.G. Wodehouse. Have you ever read Wodehouse, Mr. Cowan?"

"Can't say that I have. My practice leaves me little time for recreational reading."

"A shame. But, never mind. I understand you're grateful, and it's the least I can do."

"But—"

"You see, I've had the most unusual dreams. Seven dreams during seven nights. And in these dreams I've heard the voice of G-d." Denton stood to his feet. "The L-rd has spoken to me, and this is His express will." He reached out a hand, and Cowan rose to take it, remembering too late to close his gaping mouth. Was the man insane? The interview was plainly at an end. As Denton ushered him to the door, Cowan tried to find his voice.

"Tell me," Denton inquired, "what's being done with our most valuable cargo?"

"I—I'm not sure—what you're referring to."

"Jeri Kline," said Denton. "Our favorite fugitive from 'justice.' Before this ordeal is through, Mr. Kline is destined to play a vital role in it."

"I believe he's wandering somewhere about the ship," Cowan said, unwilling to risk too much information. "In plain view."

"Ah!" said Denton, "The best place to hide is always in plain view! Have you ever read 'The Purloined Letter' by Edgar Allan Poe? But, of course—you only just told me you've no time for recreational reading. In that story, you see, the letter in question was sitting right on the mantelpiece, in plain view." He paused for a moment and added: "If Mr. Kline is captured, he must try to escape."

"That's already been arranged."

"Very good."

"But I'm not sure I'll be able to contact him. To tell him to come here to hide, sir, if that's what you were about to suggest."

"It was," said Wilbur Denton, giving him a gentle shove out the door. "But there's nothing to worry about on that score. I'll make certain he knows where to go."

Cowan turned, hand raised to object, and bumped his nose against the cold steel of Denton's office door. He hadn't heard it slide shut behind him.

α

It was midnight before the ship's guards discovered Kline and Esteban on the Vista Deck.

"Maybe we should head back to my suite," Kline had suggested. "I can punch up a soothing cup of herbal tea for you, Brother Esteban; you look like you could use one."

Relief had showed on Esteban's face.

"Wonderful idea, Jeri!" He took Kline's arm and steered him in the direction of the flashing exit sign. "I still have a few questions to ask you. Fascinating story! Simply fascinating…"

The exit-portal dilated and two armed guards entered, weapons at the ready. One of them, Kline noticed with relief, was his friend Eddie Moore.

"What do you want?" Esteban demanded.

"Which of you," Moore inquired, pointing from Kline to Esteban with the barrel of his rifle, "is Jeri Kline?"

"I am he," said Kline.

"The captain has ordered that you be placed under arrest, Mr. Kline. Please don't resist. Innocent people may be hurt."

"That's ridiculous!" Esteban protested. "This man has committed no crime. I demand to speak with Captain Mills."

"That you may," said Moore. "If you wish to accompany your friend, here."

"Mr. Kline's attorney," Esteban pressed, ignoring the rifles, "is John Cowan. You've heard of him, I'm sure."

Moore shrugged, playing his part to the hilt.

"He'll be present before we agree to speak to anyone. Mr. Kline has a right to his attorney being present when any charges are read. And you'd better have some evidence to support them! This is a private vessel, run under civilian law. And Mr. Kline—Reverend Kline, I should say—is an ordained minister of the Gospel. You'd best keep that in mind."

Moore jerked his rifle in the direction of the portal. "You're free to go, sir. *Reverend* Kline, please come with us."

Esteban opened his mouth to protest, but Kline silenced him with an upraised hand. "It's all right, Brother Esteban. I'll go with these men."

Yet, as they strode toward the portal between the two guards, Esteban kept his eyes peeled for the first opportunity to escape.

The Rescue

This was the part Esteban hated.

The *Empress* was designed with a rotating hub that created artificial gravity along its inner hull. Within the hub, all the passengers and crew lived and worked along a broad, longitudinal strip, like a spokeless wheel, spinning about a central region of zero-g. On the inner surface of the sphere, gravity was maintained at an Earthlike 1-g. As one moved away from the surface, toward the center of the sphere, gravity lessened rapidly to zero. Standing on the hub's surface, the world of the *Empress* was very much like Earth, unless one concentrated on the reverse aspect of its curvature. On Earth, one stood on the outside surface of a sphere, which curved gently downward at the horizon. Here, on the *inner* surface of a much *smaller* sphere, the horizon curved abruptly upward and overhead, so that, looking toward the "sky", one had the sensation of hanging from the ceiling, gazing down at the tops of buildings. Traveling in a straight line on the "east-west" axis eventually brought the traveler back to his starting point, which could be disorienting to many passengers on their first flight. But the most difficult part, for Esteban, was negotiating the ramp to and from the Vista Deck. Had he known what the trip entailed, he'd never have agreed to go.

The Vista Deck was positioned amidships, in a transparent dome on the northern surface of the hub's north-south axis. Entering and exiting the dome was accomplished by a moving ramp spanning the ship's inner hull and dividing the sphere in two. As they moved at ten kilometers an hour across the north-south axis, from the Vista Deck to the opposite hull, they were suspended in the midst of a spinning city. Except for a tube-like tunnel through which the ramp passed in the zero-G center of the span, Esteban had a clear view of the upside-down world in every direction. In the center, had the tube not blocked his view, he would suddenly have sensed its wild spinning on its axis, and would have felt like a fly in the middle of a spinning rod. It was a wild sensation even hardened spacers were unaccustomed to, hence the tunnel.

As grateful as he was for that short span of tube, he wished it extended for the entire length of the ramp. Beyond it, while there was no sensation of spinning, there was still the sickening vertigo of crossing a realm in which every direction was down. When Esteban looked up, he was looking down—down at the tall spires of the commercial sector, with its skyscrapers, offices, and shopping malls. Glancing in the opposite direction gave a similar view, little hovercars glimmering like fireflies around jeweled spires. So Esteban kept his eyes fixed on the ramp at his feet. There was no sensation of motion or height when he did so, unless he was foolish enough to peer over the railing. And that he absolutely refused to do.

Preoccupied with fighting his agoraphobia, Esteban had forgotten about Jeri's plight. He raised his eyes slowly, until he was looking directly ahead along the ramp, doing his best to ignore the night glitter of the city above and below. The young fellow seemed quite at ease, considering the circumstances. He stood in the lead, the guards aiming their rifles at his bulky, nylon jacket. Esteban looked back down at his feet. *Just to relax in a normal chair*, he thought, *with nothing overhead but the ceiling!*

A sudden shout caused him to look up. He saw Kline running ahead along the ramp—much faster in the reduced gravity than was possible on the surface—tugging at the nylon jacket. He appeared to be in a hurry to be rid of it. Distant skyscrapers in the background, twinkling with electric lights, made it appear that Kline was running downward, rather than horizontally. One of the guards raised his rifle, taking careful aim at Kline's back. The other dropped back a few steps, crouching…

All of this seemed to Esteban to be happening in slow motion. And none of it made any sense: young Kline running along the ramp as if he could outrun rifle bullets, the only figure moving with speed. The fact that he was moving in the same direction as the ramp's ten-kilometer-per-hour descent did not seem to inhibit his swiftness, to Esteban's perception. And that desperate tugging at his jacket as he seemed to plunge toward the buildings below. Everything else appeared frozen.

Esteban waited for the sound of the rifle, expecting it at any instant. The force of the blast would certainly knock Kline over the side of the ramp like a rag doll. But the guard who'd dropped back did the strangest thing of all. Instead of firing at Kline, he ran forward, tossed his rifle aside, and tackled the other guard at the knees, knocking him flat on his face. Esteban watched, incredulous, as the two men rolled from side to side. He wanted to shout to Kline, but his mouth, already open, would produce no sound. The guard with the rifle, now encumbered by his weapon, was loathe to relinquish his grip on it. The other had managed to roll over on top of him, and was raising his fist to strike a powerful blow. Esteban noticed that it was the guard who had spoken so harshly to him on the Vista Deck.

Meanwhile, Kline had managed to get free of his jacket, tossing it over the side. He was a good distance away now, but Esteban could see an odd piece of equipment strapped to his back. No *wonder* the lad had been wearing that bulky jacket! He'd been concealing—*that! Whatever* it was…

Kline stopped, turned back in Esteban's direction, and waved. Esteban waved back instinctively, not understanding why. Kline placed an open palm against his chest. With a great rush of flame his body soared upward, arms stretched over his head.

Esteban followed with his eyes, gripping the railing against the dizziness, yet unable to look away. Kline dropped like a stone to the city below—or above—Esteban was no longer certain which. Nor, he realized sadly, would it matter to Kline in the least.

He held on with a white-knuckle grip, watching his young friend plunge down …down….down…

And then, amazingly, Kline pulled out of his dive and swooped to the right, performing a graceful loop-de-loop in mid-air. As if catching a gust of wind, he floated like a leaf on a gentle breeze around the spire of the tallest skyscraper, hovered for the briefest instant over a ledge just beneath the spire, then dropped easily onto the ledge and disappeared from view.

By this time Esteban knew what had happened. Brief bursts of flame from Kline's falling body had made it apparent. "A jetpack!" he whispered. "The little fool was concealing a jetpack under his jacket!"

"Hey!" called a voice from off to his left. "Brother Esteban!"

"Huh?" Esteban turned, still a bit stunned by what he'd just witnessed. The guard had succeeded in knocking his companion unconscious and was now picking up one of the two rifles.

"Can you run, sir?" he called.

"Yes," Esteban replied. "I—I think so."

"Well, I think we'd better put some distance between ourselves and my friend here. If we make it off the ramp before he comes to, we might have a chance of getting away. Do you understand, Brother Esteban?"

"Yes, I understand. But—how do you know me? I don't recall giving you my name. And you called me 'brother'—"

"No time to explain. We have to let off this ramp, and fast."

"All right, son," Esteban replied. "Lead the way. Just take it easy, will you?"

"Now! Move!"

Keeping his eyes glued to the ramp at his feet, Esteban ran as if his life depended on it. And, for all he knew, it did.

α

The sensation of falling was disconcerting. Kline tried to change direction as he sped toward the skyscrapers below, the rate of his fall increasing as he was propelled toward the surface of the sphere. But all he accomplished was a sudden jerk to the right, in the direction of the unpopulated section of the hull. Another attempt to control his fall sent him in a crazy loop.

Why had he let himself be talked into using this infernal jetpack in the first place? He must have been mad! As he was caught by the ship's artificial gravity, he felt sudden air resistance, wind rushing past his ears with a deafening roar. The tops of the sky-scrapers in the commercial sector grew as he dropped like a stone.

Trying to still the rising panic in his breast, Kline made another attempt to manipulate the controls of the jetpack. He'd been pressing them too hard! This time he managed to veer more gradually to the left; but realized with a chill that he would never be able to master the harness-control in time to avoid being smashed to a pulp on the streets below.

And the ground was rushing toward him now with breath-less speed!

α

<Mr. Kline.>

He wasn't conscious at first of the voice in his mind. It seemed but another part of the jangling, clamoring mental activity that was his panic. Even when it uttered his name for the second time he didn't recognize that it was a female voice, or that it spoke with unnatural calmness under the circumstances. Later he decided that he must have thought it emanated from a speaker in his jet-pack, because he answered it.

"Yes!" he shouted over the rush of wind. "Help me!"

<Do you see the tall building just below you and to the right?>

Kline looked. Leaping up at him was the spire of the Saturn Enterprises skyscraper, the tallest building in the commercial sector.

"Yes!" he said. It sounded like a squeal carried away by the rushing wind.

<That's where you want to land—on top of it. Do you see the little balcony just below the needle?>

It was then that Kline realized, with increasing panic, that the voice wasn't audible. It was in his head, like a thought.

So this is it! he thought. *This is what happens to the mind when you're falling to your death.* It seemed appropriate that the voice was female and pretty, the most pleasant sound a lonely man could conjure up at the moment of death. He considered the strangeness of the phenomenon in an odd moment of calmness, as he resigned himself to his fate.

<No,> said the voice in his heed. <You're not going to die. I can save you, if you'll do as I say.>

"I'll try!" shouted Kline. (For some reason it helped him to verbalize his thoughts. Perhaps it increased his faith in the reality of the voice.)

<Good. Now, try to flip your body around so that your feet are pointing toward the ground. Use the wind-resistance.>

Kline tried it, consuming precious seconds and at least a hundred meters. The spire of the Saturn Enterprises building was much closer now. *Too close!* But at least he'd succeeded in changing his position; he was now falling—feet first. *What now*?

<Now,> came the voice in answer to his thought, <press the middle button of the three buttons on your harness-control, very lightly. And only once.>

Kline obeyed. He felt a sudden, painful jerk, as if giant hand had caught hold of his collar, arresting his fall. He did a complete summersault that ended up with his feet pointing downward again.

<You pressed it too hard,> the voice calmly explained. <The controls are extremely sensitive. Try it again—lightly.>

He tried it again, feeling another tug at his shoulders. This tug was *more* painful, since the previous one had sprained his shoulder muscles. The harness-straps bit into him, and he groaned. But the effect was smoother. He didn't spin into a back-flip this time, and the rate of his fall had decreased. He also realized that the voice *was* being projected into his mind! How it was being done, he couldn't fathom. But nowhere in his memory or experience was the information now assisting him to work the jetpack. So it *couldn't* be his mind playing tricks on him.

Very carefully, obeying the instructions to the best of his ability. Kline managed to position himself closer to the needle of the skyscraper, which was still rushing toward him at a disconcerting rate of speed. He tapped the middle button a few more times, and his descent began to slow to the point where landing on the slim, circular ledge seemed possible—almost easy. He was filled with a sudden elation.

<Don't get cocky, Jeri,> the pretty voice in his head scolded. <We still have a distance to go yet, and this is the tricky part. Now, press the button on the right. *Your* right.>

Kline obeyed. "Who *are* you?" he asked. "How can you read my thoughts?"

<Too much,> said the voice. <Left button, just a touch.>

In this way, Kline was able to master the harness-controls and swoop down to a smooth landing on the pinnacle of the Saturn Enterprises building. Still trembling from the panic of his deathward plunge, he unstrapped the jetpack and removed it from his shoulders, massaging them with crossed hands. As he rubbed the pain out of them, he moved around the circular balcony—thankful for its metal railing—and searched for some kind of entrance. It seemed that he'd gone completely around the spire before he discovered it. A portal in the shape of an arch.

It slid open before him.

<Welcome to Saturn Enterprises, Mr. Kline,> said the pretty voice in his mind.

α

"According to Brother Kline," Paul was saying to Captain Mills as they lifted their glasses from the back of the spider-mech, "there's a plot to assassinate me the moment I arrive on Luna. I must say that I find the situation extremely—incommodious."

Mills chuckled at the understatement.

"Not that I value this life to any great extent," Paul went on. "'To be absent from the body is to be present with the Lord.' A happy prospect, I can assure you, for a man of my advancing years. But there are some people back on Earth whose survival depends on my continuing health."

"Does Kline have any idea who might be embroiled in this plot?"

"I can't tell you that for certain, but I think not. It involves some people in very high positions; that much he was able to determine."

"Bowlen!" Mills grunted.

"Pardon?"

"Nothing—I was just thinking of a swine on Luna who's probably up to his little pink ears in this scheme. At any rate, Brother Paul, you do realize that I have no choice but to follow orders at this juncture. If there *is* a nest of assassins on the moon it wouldn't do to alarm them before we can catch them at their game. For me to refuse to arrest Kline would result in—well, I'd rather not think about it. Meanwhile the conspirators would have time to scatter into the woodwork. I doubt it would make your situation any safer. Perhaps we can devise some sort of counter plan in the meantime. But I'll have to report to thc Vice Admiral, to tell him I have Jeri Kline safely in custody. That will make them relax for a while. They might even get sloppy, tip their hand. Who knows?"

"Yes, of course," Paul said. He was interrupted by a buzzing from Mills' communicator. Mills unclipped it from his belt and flipped a switch.

"Mills here."

"Captain!" came a shrill voice. "I *had* him, sir, but he got away."

"Tell me you're not talking about Jeri Kline."

"I'm afraid I am, sir."

"How?"

"He stole a jetpack from the supply deck somehow. He was wearing it under a bulky, nylon jacket. When we were bringing him in he just—well, he just flew away…sir."

"And you stood there and let him?"

"No, sir. I tried to stop him, but he had an accomplice. I was struggling with this accomplice while Kline made good his escape."

Mills shot a cold glance at Brother Paul.

"Someone from Brother Paul's staff?" he asked.

"No, sir. One of the guards. An officer."

Mills' jaw dropped.

"Which officer?"

"Chief Petty Officer Moore, sir."

"Moore? Are you nuts?"

"No, sir. He went with me personally, to take Kline into custody. But then he jumped me from behind and knocked me unconscious. Just before he hit me I saw Kline take off from the Vista Deck ramp using the jetpack, but that's *all* I saw. He flew straight up, sir, in the direction of the commercial sector."

Anger twisted Mills' face as he listened. He exploded with rage. "Find them both!" he yelled into the communicator. "I want them both in front of me in one hour! Do you understand?"

"Yes, sir."

"I'll be in my quarters. Bring them there. "

“Right, sir. Out.”

“Out.”

Mills rose to his feet. “So your friend used a jet-pack. Any idea how he got his hands on it?"

“Captain Mills,” Paul protested, “I assure you—”

The portal hummed, announcing a visitor. Glad for the timely distraction, Paul pressed the switch to open the door.

John Cowan strode into the room.

“Little John!” said Paul. “Jeri escaped from custody! Someone apparently gave him a jetpack.”

Cowan looked ill.

“And it seems,” Paul continued, “that one of the ship’s guards assisted him in his—er, flight.”

“Enough!” snapped Mills. “Enough of the innocent act!” He strode past Cowan with a brusque nod of his head. “You can play games all you like, but I’ll get to the bottom of this, Brother Paul. And if there’s been even the slightest action that could be construed as obstruction, even in the broadest sense, heads are going to roll. Lawyers, Evangelists, officers—whomever. Am I making myself clear?”

“Quite.”

Tapping the button on the wall with more force than the operation required, Mills marched off down the hallway.

Paul stroked his chin. “I wonder who *did* give Jeri that jetpack.”

Cowan dropped wearily into the chair Mills had just evacuated. He kicked off his shoes and sighed. “I did, sir.”

Paul sat up straight. “*You?*”

“Yes, sir. I did it last night, while you were in bed reading your Scriptures. I suggested he wear it to the Vista Deck. I thought it would be best to keep it a secret from Brother Esteban, though. It would only have caused the old boy unnecessary stress.”

“But—where did you get such a thing?”

“Brother Moore—Edward Moore, Kline’s friend. He approached me yesterday and asked that I meet him in the corridor in front of Jeri’s suite. Remember I took that brief walk before bed?”

“Yes, now that you mention it. So he approached you after our meeting with Jeri?”

“Yes.”

“You met with him and *he* stole the jetpack. You gave it to

Jeri, then came back here and fell asleep on the divan. Until the beam from brother Bernard woke me."

"Correct, sir. When Moore first approached me, I surmised who he was from Jeri's story, but he introduced himself politely and requested that I meet with him at a specific time. When I met him later we hardly exchanged a word. He took me to the equipment closet and handed me the jetpack. I knew what it was for."

"Well, Little John, it looks as if Jeri has gotten completely away—for the time being, at least. I wonder where he is?"

"I may be able to shed some light on that, also."

Paul looked at Cowan quizzically.

"Go on."

Cowan related the details of his interview with Wilbur Denton. When he was finished, Paul shook his head.

"What do you think? Is Denton an agent of G-d in this situation?"

"It's difficult to say—at this point in time, anyway. He *seemed* sincere, but a little—I don't know. Fanatical."

"We're all fanatics in our ways, Little John. Even atheists are fanatics. Is it his story about having had ecstatic dreams?"

"Not exactly, sir. I believe he's had dreams, and of the sort he described. But there was a look in his eye—as if he were exulting in some elaborate scheme. I'm not sure I can explain it any better than that. He had that 'wait and see' look, if you take my meaning. It made me uncomfortable. And the way he hurried me out of his office…"

"Wilbur Denton," said Paul, "is a very powerful man. He may be the richest man in the solar system."

"Indeed, sir. It took him five years to build this ship. Saturn Enterprises sold it to Galaxy Tours for more money that either of us can imagine. According to Denton, the *Empress* contains some very sophisticated technology."

"That kind of wealth is certain to corrupt a man—the 'absoute power' referred to in the old adage."

"I'd tend to agree, sir. But what if he's serious? What if he plans to do precisely as he says—to place all his wealth and techology at your disposal?"

Paul exhaled in a long, low whistle. "It staggers the imagintion, Little John. It would set the Antichrist's timetable back at least a century. The Church would be wealthier than the United

States of America, or China. But the theological questions it raises are even more unfathomable. What if it's *not* G-d's will for the Antichrist to forestall his appearance—or for the Church to overpower him? After all, it *is* written in prophecy that he'll arise and enslave the Earth, as he's now doing."

"I see what you mean. What if Judas Iscariot was prevented from betraying the L-rd? How would it have affected the eternal destiny of mankind?"

"For the worst, Little John. Where would our salvation be found if Messiah had not been betrayed and crucified? To defeat this evil, at this time, may actually be working at cross purposes to G-d's Divine Plan. And If I've prayed a single prayer from the depths of my soul, it's been: '*Thy kingdom come; thy will be done.*' Not *my* will, Little John, or yours, or the Church's—but the L-rd's. How can we be certain that Denton isn't offering us a Trojan Horse? Accepting his offer will require far more prayer and meditation than time allows, I'm afraid. We're less than a week from Luna, and I simply cannot allow my own desires to interfere with G-d's will in this situation. I must *know* His will!"

"All I can tell you is what Denton told me. He's had some very strange dreams, and in these dreams, apparently, the L-rd commanded him to put the Saturn Enterprises building at your disosal."

"But what use do we have for a skyscraper on a spaceiner?"

"It has some sort of supercomputer built into it, sir. And it may be where Jeri is hiding."

Paul was silent for a long time. Shaking his head, he looked into Cowan's eyes and said, "What can all this mean, Little John?"

Cowan had no reply.

The Challenge

Back in his quarters Roy Mills ordered a call put through to Vice Admiral Bowlen on Luna. It was 1:10 A.M. according to the readout on the holoscreen—rather early to be bothering the old grinch!—and it didn't make Mills happy to have to do it. But if he knew Bowlen, the jerk would want to be kept up to date on everything. It wouldn't do to have lost Kline on shipboard, then wait for a convenient time to report the incident. No—Bowlen would have to give up some of his beauty sleep.

While he waited the long minutes for the beam to bounce from VLA receiver-transmitters on Earth to the L-5 dish, and finally to the moon—an arrangement he never quite understood—he poured himself a Scotch and water from one of the asteroid-shaped cabinets in the kitchen area. Once the beam reached Luna, communication would be instantaneous. But there was always that annoying wait.

Tachyon beams, the most quixotic and unfathomable streams of particle-waves in the universe, knew nothing of time. Time presented no barrier to them, since, theoretically, they existed outside the bounds of relativistic space. Like mirror-images of the electrons in matter, which could not attain to the speed of light, tachyons moved at superluminary velocity, and could not be slowed down to the speed of light. Thus, a message carried by tachyon beam could cross the universe in an instant. *Less* than an instant, in fact, for an instant was a measurement of time, however small. Tachyons could even escape the monstrous gravity-well of a black hole, a well so deep even light became trapped within it. It staggered his mind to conceive of such a possibility, that a distress call from beyond the event-horizon of a black hole could actually be received—albeit from a crew that had been crushed into quarks a moment before the message was sent! Quantum physics had made a mess of the nice Euclidian universe of olden times. Even Einstein had rebelled against its bizarre implications. Schrödinger's cat (the hypothetical feline simultaneously dead and alive), Heisenberg's uncertainty principle, Hilbert space vectors—the entire cosmos functioned with perfect mathematical predictability, yet persisted in defying common sense. It was enough to have to pilot a vessel through such an Alice-in-Wonderland universe. To have to deal with Vice Admiral Bowlen at the same time was intolerable.

Mills was fairly worked up when Bowlen's ugly face filled his holoscreen, eyes heavy-lidded from sleep, a bathrobe draped over his body like a canvas tossed over a hippopotamus.

"What is it Mills?" he snapped. "Most of the civilized plants are in bed at this hour!"

Mills bit his lip. "Something's come up. I thought you'd want to be informed right away."

"What's come up?" said Bowlen, jowls quivering.

"Well, sir. I had Jeri Kline in custody—"

"Had? I don't like the sound of that word."

"He escaped. And I regret to report that it was one of my guards who assisted him."

There came an indistinct flurry of motion and a huge thud from the holoscreen. Bowlen had thumped a hammy fist on his desktop. "Do you expect me to swallow a yarn like that? One of your guards helped Kline get away? Why would one of your guards be interested in Kline's welfare?"

"I have no idea, Miles. Frankly, I'm baffled by it. But it is the truth, nonetheless."

Another flurry, followed by a louder thump. Mills doubted whether he'd be able to maintain his decorum under another of Bowlen's childish outbursts. But what came next shocked him.

"You're *lying!*" Bowlen sputtered. "And I know it! You're shielding that traitor!"

Mills was dumbfounded. "Miles, why in the world would I—?"

"Who *knows* why? You're protecting a traitor and hiding him on your ship! That's a capital offense! That's giving aid and comfort! And I'm going to see that you hang for it!"

"Woa—slow down, Miles! I have a witness—"

"Of *course* you have a witness! I never thought you were an idiot. This is a flagrant act of treason, and you're going to swing right beside that dirtball Kline! Now, by order of the President of the United States, I demand you turn yourself in, along with the accused, the moment the *Empress* arrives in Luna orbit. Try to make a run for it, with innocent civilians on board, and the President will order the Navy after you."

Mills leaned back in his chair. It was all happening so fast he could hardly determine a plan of action. As he watched Bowlen's flapping, quivering jowls and yapping mouth, he recalled something Brother Paul had said. And the more he considered it the more sense it made.

"If there are any criminals involved in this, Bowlen," he told the pig-faced image, "they're on Luna. Not on my ship."

Bowlen's eyes widened. "What are you saying?"

"I'm saying there's a plot to assassinate one of my passengers. Scuttlebutt says there're some brass hats involved—assassins in American uniforms. And it could very well be that I'm looking at one of them right now!"

Mills had no idea what he'd hit upon. He was just shooting in the dark, aiming wildly. He didn't believe his own words—that is, not until he saw the transformation coming over Bowlen's face.

Then he knew.

Bowlen was still screaming and thumping his desk and demanding everything he could demand, including Mills placing *himself* under arrest for treason. But Mills was deaf to it all. It was as if the sound had been turned off, and there was only the old, familiar face of Vice Admiral Miles Bowlen on the screen, huffing and puffing and—*bluffing!* It was that same smoke-screen Bowlen always threw up when he was caught cheating at anything from poker to moongolf. The Vice Admiral was lying! He was in on this thing!

"I can't believe it!" Roy Mills said when Bowlen paused in his reading of the riot act. "I can't believe you'd be involved in something as sordid as political assassination. "*You're* the criminal, Miles. Not Jeri Kline. How many others are involved in this?" It was an old trick, turning the tables, but Bowlen always fell for it. *Take the offensive and hold it*, he told himself. *Bowlen will eventually break; the fat pig always does!* "Who else is involved in the conspiracy? Do your orders come from the White House or Naval Intelligence?"

"You're going to die, Mills!" sputtered Vice Admiral Bowlen. "Very slowly. I'll see to it myself."

"Then you'd better see to it soon. Because I'm going to get on the blower to every newspaper and holovision broadcast in America. I'm going to tell them the whole story: 'Vice Admiral Miles Bowlen, under orders from the President of the United States, plots to assassinate Paul Jason Moscowitz, the world-famous evangelist, during his upcoming Lunar crusade. All part of the administration's plan to do away with Judeo-Christianity, the "opiate of the masses."' When I'm through, my friend, they're going to roast you on a spit. Turn myself in? Drop dead, Bowlen!"

Mills reached out and snapped off the connection. He rubbed his beard for a moment, then requested the ship's computer to put through a priority-one call to Admiral Quinton Forrester of the Joint Chiefs of Staff.

Just as quickly, he changed his mind. *That could be a mistake*, he thought. *If the Vice Admiral on Luna is involved in such a plot, and if it truly goes all the way up to the Oval Office, certainly Admiral Forrester is involved at some level as well.* Mills could out-maneuver anything the Lunies could send after him. But the Navy? His mind reeled at the thought of Admiral Quinton Forrester heading a ruthless covey of assassins. *No—it's impossible! This is too soon to act. I need time to think things over.*

"A call, sir," said the ship's computer. "Shall I put it through?"

"Who's calling?"

"Wilbur Denton. He says it's urgent."

Mills tossed down the rest of his Scotch and water, rose from his contoroid chair, and headed for the bedroom. He was suddenly tired. Bone tired.

"Shall I put him through, Captain?"

"Tell him it's late. He can talk to me tomorrow."

Mills placed his empty glass on the bedside table and flopped into bed. The room began a sickening spin.

"Sir?" said the computer. "I gave him your reply. He said that tomorrow will be too late."

But Mills was already asleep, snoring loudly.

α

It didn't take long for the news to reach the man called Smith. At 2:00 A.M. Greenwich, as he was enjoying a cool drink in his new apartment, there came a buzz from his holoscreen. He flipped it on. The familiar face of his recent benefactor, Matthew Baker, took shape before him, seeming to hover in front of the wall.

This wall was not peeling.

"Lieutenant Baker," he said politely. "What a pleasure to hear from you so soon. I was just getting settled in my new digs. You like?"

"The plans have been changed."

Smith was too delighted with himself to let Baker spoil his mood.

"That's fine, Lieutenant. I'm flexible."

"You're finished."

Smith's head snapped back as if he'd been struck by a blunt object.

"Huh?"

"We won't be needing your 'services' after all."

It took a few moments for the news to register. Smith's eyebrows drew together; his eyes narrowed into slits. "Wait just a minute, Baker! What kind of flim-flam is this? You think my price is too high? Find someone else on Luna who can do this job. You can't and you know it!"

"That's true. Which is why I contacted you when we wanted it done. But we no longer want it done."

"But—why?" A stupid question, but Smith was jarred. He didn't know what else to say. The Lieutenant actually seemed to be enjoying this, the swine!

"Of course," Baker said, "now that your "services' are no longer required, there's the matter of the thousand credits we advanced you—"

Smith leapt to his feet. "Now, hold on Baker! I can't return that money. Not on such short notice. I've spent most of it."

"I understand," said the hovering face. "I'll give you three days to return it. You realize you've been privy to some very sensitive information, Mr. Smith. Such knowledge puts you at risk."

"That sounds like a threat! Don't threaten *me*, Baker! Like you said, I know a few things. And what I know could put you away."

"I'm sorry to hear you say that, Mr. Smith. No need to return the thousand credits; We'll just consider it part of the expense of getting rid of you."

"No—wait! Listen—"

"Good evening."

Two hours later, Smith was spending the reminder of his thousand-credit advance on an express shuttle to Earth. But when it landed at New Chicago Spaceport, no individual matching Smith's description could be found among the passengers.

The mysterious Mr. Smith had debarked, rather unexpectedly, into the frozen arms of space.

α

"What do you think he'll do?" blubbered the sweating face of Vice Admiral Bowlen on Baker's holoscreen.

Having just completed his conversation with Smith, Baker was in no mood to deal with Bowlen. But the Vice Admiral was on the verge of panic and he was obliged to cool his jets. No telling what the fool might be capable of in this state of mind.

"Miles," he said soothingly, "there's no need to panic."

"But Mills knows I'm in on it! Space only knows *what* that Kline character told him. And how did Kline find out about this scheme in the first place? Another example of your airtight security? Mills could very easily alert the media."

"And what makes you think they'll believe him, Miles? Won't they demand proof before they go public with a story as volatile as that? And there *is* no proof. Don't sweat it. Captain Mills was just seeing how far he could push you."

"You're telling me to just—deny it?"

"Sure. It's the word of the Vice Admiral on Luna against that of a spaceliner captain."

Bowlen looked relieved.

"Well....maybe you're right. It *is* kind of a crazy story at that."

"I think it would seem so to the media. Besides, if it's necessary, the President can quell the reports."

"But I still think we should take steps to keep Roy Mills from talking. There might be an inquiry—"

"Now, listen very closely, Miles. Your unprofessional behavior has put us in a difficult situation. You've been given access to classified information, and I'm not at all happy about that. So read my lips: You may be the Vice Admiral on Luna, but I outrank you in the Party. You either obey the Party—and me—or I'm authorized to take you off the payroll. And please don't tell me you know too much, that it would be dangerous to cut you loose with what you've learned of this operation. I've just had a similar conversation with a man who won't see tomorrow's Earthrise. You, sir, do not require such a lesson. You don't need me to threaten you, either. We're men of the world, both of us. You know I'll report this conversation. And certain people will be unhappy that you've messed things up with Captain Mills—practically botched the whole deal. I'll have to report that you were in a state of panic and lost your temper. Do you understand? You're in a bad position, Miles, and you'd better wake up to the fact that you're taking orders from me. Clear?"

Bowlen listened to the tirade with growing consternation. No one on Luna had ever spoken to him in that manner! *No one!* He was obliged, if only for the sake of his pride, to regain the dominant position.

"Now *you* listen, *Lieutenant* Baker! I want Roy Mills out of the way! I've been kept in the dark while everybody in the solar system, including Mills, knows all about your little conspiracy. Send out some warships. Have him towed back to Luna and tried. I don't care *how* you do it. But we can't afford to let him run free!"

Baker recognized the response for what it was—bluster.

"I'll do no such thing," he said. "Now you get a hold of yourself, Miles. We have everything under control. Just remember what I told you."

"Humph!" said Vice Admiral Bowlen.

α

Commodore Jesse Colter, Jr. received his plastic lunch tray from the male flight attendant with an absent-minded nod. He ran his eyes over the array of straws protruding unappetizingly from the tray's green surface, offering a selection of liquefied courses ranging from strained steak to a dessert of strained apple pie with cinnamon. It turned his stomach. Inflight meals, he reflected with disgust, were best launched out the airlock with the rest of the non-recycled garbage. While the passengers and crews of commercial vessels enjoyed the finest cuisine in artificial gravity, the Space Navy was still coping with cost-saving zero-g: sucking baby food through straws, squirming through connecting-hatches at crazy angles, floating around the cabins, grasping at rungs and other protrusions to stay upright, and chasing runaway objects—particularly pens—through the stale, artificial air.

It was time, the Commodore decided, to consider retire-ent. He set the tray aside and returned to gazing out the viewport at the heavily cratered surface of the Lunar Farside. Once erroneously called the "Dark Side", this half of Luna got plenty of searing sunlight. It had been so named because it always faced away from Earth. In the early days Farside had been the most attractive part of the moon for hidden bases and clandestine operations. But the growing military presence on the moon—European, Chinese, Russian, and American—rendered such precautions useless, even ridiculous. But the Space Navy had gone crazy, anyway. Since the PWP had taken power, and Charles Coffey had taken the oath of office, orders from Admiral Forrester had become increasingly more bizarre.

And now this!

A top-secret mission, the details of which he'd received directly from Vice Admiral Miles Bowlen himself—with horror. He'd been ordered to launch a fleet of warships from Farside Base in a flight-pattern designed to avoid detection, to intercept the return flight of the passenger liner *Empress* from Mars, and to fire upon it without warning—nuke it into eternity.

From the expression on the Vice Admiral's face, and certain details of the mission, Colter could only conclude that either a state of war existed, or would soon exist. He'd kept himself more or less sequestered, at Bowlen's orders, and was now heading for a top-level meeting at Farside Base, to hand pick the officers of the special fleet. *Operation Wolfpack*, it was to be called. But what was it all about? One of the details that had struck him as suspicious—and somewhat ominous in its implications—was the Vice Admiral's insistence on complete tachyon silence once the *Empress* was located. There'd be no turning back then. No possibility of the mission being aborted.

He'd been given no reason for the mission, no justification for destroying thousands of lives, passengers and crew. He knew Roy Mills was the captain of the *Empress*. He liked Mills. And he knew Mills wouldn't hesitate to follow Bowlen's orders, were he still a captain in the Space Navy and were their roles reversed—despite his well-known dislike for Bowlen.

But what of the passengers? How could an American officer fire nuclear missiles at a spaceliner full of innocent civilians—an act no different than the sinking of the Lucitania? And what of the financial repercussions from civilian businesses and industries whose combined investments in the spaceliner (not to mention the insurance obligations to grieving families) probably equaled last year's GNP? Was he prepared to commit such an act, to be remembered throughout history as the man who nuked the *Empress*? He knew the answer without thinking.

He'd obey orders.

It must be war, he decided. *Nothing else could possibly justify such an onerous mission. Party for World Peace indeed*!

As he sat brooding in his contour chair, watching the craters slip silently past his porthole, a blue light blinked on the console in front of him. He depressed the button.

"Colter speaking."

A female voice said: "Farside Base in five minutes, Commodore."

"Good. Has everyone on the list been notified?"

"Yes, sir."

"Any absentees?"

"No, sir. All present and accounted for."

"All right. Thank you."

He tapped the button again and leaned back in his chair, heaving a sigh. What sort of lie, he wondered, was he expected to tell the fleet commanders?

He'd have to think of a good one, and soon. He was going to address them in fifteen minutes.

The Machine

As Kline stepped through the portal into the top floor of the Saturn Enterprises building, he found himself in the midst of a perfectly circular room. In the center of the room stood a huge mainframe computer: glittering arrays of consoles, blinking lights, and holoscreens displaying various floors of the skyscraper. The entire complex rested on an octagonal pedestal raised above a blue-carpeted floor; one approached it by ascending three shallow steps to the platform. The steps, carpeted also, ran full circle around the machine, permitting access from every direction.

On a plastiform chair before one of the holoscreens sat a young woman with long brown hair. She wore a white sleeveless peasants' blouse and a skirt that reached to her ankles—very conservative, yet attractive. As she swiveled her chair around to face Kline, she offered him a warm smile. He smiled back. She was pleasant looking, not "beautiful" in the Hollywood sense. Her pointed chin and solid cheekbones revealed a strong, no-nonsense personality, the high forehead a formidable intelligence. These striking features were softened by shoulder-length hair that framed her face in a dense, youthful halo. Her smile sent a clear message of benign innocence and affection, putting him instantly at ease.

"So, you're the one who saved me," he said. "I don't know

exactly why or how you did it, but I owe you my life. Who are you?"

The girl rose gracefully from her chair and descended the steps, holding out a hand to him. He took it in his, looking into a face so open and guileless that he was instantly moved. Some might have described it as a plain face, but Kline could not. Not at all! It possessed a natural beauty, an innate sweetness and purity such as men admired in the otherwise plain features of the Mona Lisa. He was beguiled by her and stuttered in an effort to tell her so. The response was a blush of gratitude, upraised cheeks blossoming like twin roses. She glanced briefly at the floor, then turned her hazel eyes up to his, sharing her radiance with him, enveloping him in it, with another smile.

"My name's Robin," she said. "I already know who you are, Mr. Kline. I can't say I enjoyed your radio programs, because I never listened to them. But I *am* very pleased to make your acquaintance."

"Call me Jeri," Kline said, letting go of her hand.

"Alright, Jeri." His name sounded lovely on her lips. He forced himself to look away, to survey his unusual surroundings.

He noticed two things of interest in the circular room. He knew it was completely enclosed by seamless metal walls, and he'd expected it to be lit by electric lights. Instead, the walls consisted of one three-hundred-and-sixty-degree, ceiling-high window. Through it the nighttime glitter of the commercial sector cast its bejeweled glow. A hovercar shot by on silent jets as he watched.

Turning abruptly, he stepped back through the portal onto the narrow balcony and examined the outer wall. The same solid gray metal he'd found when he was searching the spire for an entrance. He reentered the room and encountered Robin's childlike laughter.

"The window's not real," she explained, amused by his perplexity. "Nanotech. Microscopic biocamera arrays embedded in the metal—grown in it, actually. It's a bit involved, but you might think of it as a sort of projection, like a hologram of the outside being filmed and then instantaneously projected onto the walls. When you understand it better, of course, you'll realize how really poor an explanation that is. But it'll have to do for the time being, I'll afraid."

Kline sensed that she was making an effort to keep from switching into "computerese", that she was much more at home with technical language than conventional English. It only enhanced his fascination with her. Pristine innocence combined with a razor-sharp, technically precise mind—like encountering a sweet virginal Eve in a cybernetic forest.

The second thing he'd noted about his surroundings was that the computer-screens in the center of the room carried images of himself—falling through the air, struggling to manipulate his jetpack. Each image captured a different absurd angle, a different speed. Some were slow motion frame-by-frame flickers of his descent displaying an almost poetic grace. Except for the frozen expression of terror on his face, he might have been executing a well-practiced Olympic dive. Other, faster frames depicted his fall in its more tragi-comical aspects. In short, he looked ridiculous.

"Tell me how you did that," Kline said. "How you put your thoughts into my mind."

She smiled and shook her head. "I'm afraid that's one of Father's trade-secrets. I wouldn't be exaggerating if I told you that there are mobsters and villains straight of a B-rated holovid who'd murder us both without flinching for the answer to that question."

"Who's your father?"

"He's even more famous than you are, Jeri."

It pleased him that she remembered to use his first name. She crossed the room to a round, glass-topped table and began to fill two glasses from a silver decanter. "I'm sure you've heard of Wilbur Denton. Everyone in the solar system has, I suppose."

"Denton is your father?"

"Yes, I'm afraid so." She handed him one of the elegant, tapered glasses and he noticed that it was filled with ice-cold water. It felt fragile to the touch, unlike ordinary glass.

"Crystal," she explained.

Shocked at her invasion of his thoughts, he took a step backward. She laughed. He felt his cheeks flush.

"I'm sorry," she giggled. "I really wasn't reading your mind again. That's something I can only do with Jeeves."

"Jeeves?"

"The computer." She indicated the round console with a wave of her hand. Two thin bands of gold tinkled on her wrist. The dim light revealed a sprinkling of freckles on her arms and shoulders. It appeared that Robin Denton had freckles everywhere she had skin. Kline had never considered them before—freckles—but he was suddenly discovering their appeal. Such feelings were new to him. He'd known only the loneliness and jealousy of a bitter, maladjusted invalid. Even after his miraculous healing, he'd been too self-absorbed to consider such feminine charms as those displayed before him. Robin's affect on him was confusing, but delightfully so. He breathed deeply of her perfume and smiled.

"A computer named Jeeves," he said.

"Father's droll sense of humor," she explained. "He's always been fond of P.G. Wodehouse, a twentieth century writer. He named Jeeves after one of his favorite Wodehouse characters—a gentleman's gentleman. The prototype was perfected when I was just an infant. It performed basic household tasks. Of course, on Mimas, basic household tasks demand some rather creative applications: how to keep the meteorites out of the house, for instance, or how to maintain the proper gravity and atmospheric pressure. It took a fairly sophisticated machine to accomplish those tasks. And since it also had the more mundane chores of housekeeping, cooking, mixing drinks, and answering the vidphones—not to mention being nursemaid to a rambunctious little girl—Father began thinking of it as a kind of mechanical valet, and named it 'Jeeves'. I liked the name, and so it stuck.

"Jeeves is in charge of the building we presently occupy, but his capabilities range far beyond it. If needed they could expand to control the entire ship. No one knows this, except for Father and myself, but I don't suppose there's any harm in telling you—at this point, anyway."

She returned to the console as she spoke. Kline followed her up the steps to the circular panel of holoscreens. She touched a few buttons, switching the displays—much to Kline's relief—from his falling body to electrical schematics, structural blueprints, and even a menu.

"Jeeves controls everything in the building," she explained. "Central heat and air, the motion alarms, spider-mechs, sprinkler systems and fire extinguishers, the computer terminals in all of the offices—he even does the cooking for three-thousand employees in the restaurants and lounges. He utilizes what Father calls the 'watchdog mode'—kind of a roving eye that patrols the building at night, inside and out, for what we refer to as 'burglars.'"

"Burglars?"

"Well—no *actual* burglars would attempt a break-in of the Saturn Enterprises complex. By the way, there are two such office buildings: one on Mimas, Father's headquarters, and another one here. The 'burglars' my father's concerned about are not second-storey men or petty thieves. They're professional saboteurs, agents of industrial espionage, and assassins of the PWP. The world's most sought-after jewel thieves have gone over all our buildings with the most advanced tools of their trade. They're impregnable. And they each contain an identical supercomputer—a perfect duplicate of Jeeves."

"I can hardly believe you were raised in such an environment, Robin—with hired assassins and saboteurs trying to break in all the time. I should think that such a life would make you hard, cynical. But…" He searched for a compliment that wouldn't sound trite. "You seem so unaffected by it. So friendly and open. And kind."

"Thank you. Good upbringing, I guess. Father and Jeeves saw to that. I wasn't unduly coddled or spoiled. But I *was* very—well, sheltered, you might say. I was never taught to be cynical or suspicious. In fact, I'm sort of an experiment myself. My mother died giving birth to me, and my father was far too busy to raise me. Nannies were well within our means, of course—armies of them—but with Jeeves in place I guess Father believed that any babysitter capable of human error wasn't good enough for his little girl."

Then it was true, what he'd sensed from the moment he'd first set eyes on Robin Denton—an innocent girl-child in the midst of a computer forest, raised from infancy by machines.

"Does it shock you, Jeri?" she inquired. "Do you think of me as a freak?"

"No, not at all! The results of your father's—er, 'experiment' are quite lovely." *There! A compliment.*

Robin blushed again.

"Thank you, Jeri," she said.

"But…how…"

"Let me try to anticipate some of your questions: Human affection? My father loved me deeply, although I regret to say he was often away from home or working in his labs. When he returned Jeeves would always prepare me for the event. I'd wear my prettiest dress and wait by the portal for the sound of his footsteps. And let me tell you something, Mr. Kline." She turned to face him. He saw a tear dancing in the corner of each hazel eye. "He never once disappointed me. He was never too busy to come. And he never forgot that I was waiting for him. Every time I stood by that portal, I heard those dear, happy footsteps. And every time, when the portal dilated, he'd dash in with his arms full of presents, toss them on the carpet, and sweep me into the air with his big, strong hands. And I'd laugh and laugh. How was I to know that other daughters saw much more of their fathers than did I? I knew nothing of other homes, other lives. But I do know *this*, now that I've seen something of the world—no other daughter has ever loved her father as I do. He's the most wonderful man in the world! Looking back on those visits, it was as if he'd spent the weeks preparing for me. He was so full of jokes and riddles and brand new games. And the toys! Goodness! Nobody can create toys like Father. We'd pretend we were secret agents, protecting valuable information from enemy agents. Yes, I know it was part of my training for the reality of Saturn Enterprises, but what did I know of such things then? To me it was all wonderful make-believe. We had secret codes, and sent messages to each other on toy communicators—messages that had to be carefully decoded. And, yes, we do still use those same codes today. But the result is not a woman who feels that her childhood was spent in training for corporate espionage—which indeed it was. It also happened to be an indescribably happy childhood. I can only compare it to the life of a princess—one who's been trained to carry great responsibilities. If her father is a benevolent king, and loving, there's no more enviable child in all the world. Do you understand, Jeri?"

"Yes, when you put it that way, I think I do."

"Father would always bring me special things: hand-made dolls from Europa, stuffed animals from Earth. And when I awoke in the morning snuggled against my new dolls, he'd be gone."

"Wasn't that hard on you?"

"I can't say, Jeri. I have nothing with which to compare it. But Jeeves—dear, funny Jeeves! He became very human to me. Father had designed what he called the 'cuddle chair'. He believed that physical petting was fundamental to a healthy psyche. So I'd climb into the chair twice a day for 'cuddle time', and Jeeves would wrap its soft arms around me and sing to me or tell me stories."

Kline shuddered at the thought of such a delightful child receiving most of her physical affection from a mechanical chair!

"Jeeves is quite an accomplished storyteller, Jeri. He kept me absolutely enthralled with his tales. Father wasn't a Christian in those days, but fortunately he'd programmed Jeeves with a repertoire of responses based on biblical principles. That was mostly my mother's doing—before I was born.

"When Jeeves was in the planning stages my father had frequent and rather heated discussions with her about the necessity of building an ethical structure into such a complex mind as Jeeves'. But he was a worldly, sophisticated man who'd studied many philosophies and religions and tended to think of all religion as myth. He told me that those discussions with Mother, who was a devout evangelical Christian, often degenerated into arguments. Father insisted that the New Age philosophy combined the best of all religions, that it had the added advantage of being widely accepted on Earth. Christianity, on the other hand, was proscribed.

"Mother herself knew the difficulties of publicly following Messiah's teachings, but she was adamant: No man, not even one as brilliant as her husband, could create an infallible moral and ethical code for anything as potentially dangerous as Jeeves. Any machine with Jeeves' abilities, she argued, must be programmed with Christian principles.

"As Father tells it, he tried at first to program Jeeves with only the Ten Commandments, and certain general principles from the New Testament, leaving out all references to Messiah. But the two proved inseparable. In frustration, he took Mother's audio-disks—you know, the New Testament read by Alexander Scourby—and simply loaded them directly onto Jeeves' hard-drive. When the final disk was loaded, Jeeves demanded the Old Testament as well. He insisted that there must be earlier books, since so many references had been made to them. He even asked what sort of equipment the prophets had used to record their disks."

Kline laughed. He was so fascinated by this pretty girl and her unusual life that he'd almost forgotten the danger he was in. Robin Denton had a way of making him feel at ease. But there *was* danger, he reminded himself. Captain Mills had ordered his arrest, most likely with every intention of turning him over to the PWP on Luna. He knew what they'd do with him—after they'd used him to lure Brother Paul into the sights of an assassin's gun. It was not a pleasant thought. He'd served his purpose to the Party with his atheist broadcasts, now he represented a potential threat. But even more important was the fate of Brother Paul. He'd gladly risk his life to save the evangelist—he'd done so already, in fact—and it didn't bother him that he was a pawn in an interplanetary chess game. His current concern was staying out of the clutches of Captain Mills. One thing was certain; the Captain's men could find him anywhere on the ship, even here, atop the tallest building in the commercial sector. He turned his attention back to Robin, resolving to take his leave at the soonest possible moment—as difficult as that might prove to be...

"So you might say," Robin was explaining, "that Jeeves is a 'Christian.' Father soon regretted his unique programming when Jeeves began complaining that it was time he should be about the L-rd's business. He wanted to preach the Gospel. Father found that disconcerting, to say the least."

"I can imagine. How did he deal with it?"

"Well, he finally got it through to Jeeves that the Great Commission only applied to human beings, and that Jeeves didn't qualify. Father reminded him of the need for baptism by immersion. That brought the point home. Jeeves realized at once that baptism would sizzle his circuits and probably electrocute any preacher foolhardy enough to try to immerse him. Being unaware of any other form of baptism but the one described in the Scriptures, poor Jeeves was in a real dilemma. He found himself unable to obey one of the primary directives in his ethical program. It nearly crashed his hard-drive."

"That," said Kline, "is the wildest story I've ever heard!"

"Would you like to meet him?"

"Jeeves?" he said. "Sure. I'd be honored." No harm in remaining here for a *few* more minutes, he decided.

Robin tapped a key.

"Jeeves," she said softly. "I'd like you to meet Mr. Jeri Kline, the famous radio personality from Earth."

"It is a pleasure to make your acquaintance, Mr. Kline," came a soft male voice from no apparent direction. It had the faintest touch of a British accent, cool and rather formal. "I have long desired to meet such an influential atheist as yourself, so that I might engage in a theological discussion. I feel that, while I am not human, I can sharpen my hermeneutical skills in one-on-one debate. That is, if you consider me a worthy opponent."

"Jeeves has a belief," said Robin, "that the L-rd might transform an obedient machine such as himself into a glorified human being when He returns. You'd better watch out, Jeri. He'll evangelize you if he can."

"I see," said Kline. "But I must tell you, Jeeves, that if you intend to win my soul for the L-rd, you're too late. I'm no longer an atheist."

"How delightful!" said the machine. "Then we can spend the duration of your visit in a pleasant discussion of the Scriptures. I will see to your every comfort."

"You don't understand, Jeeves. I can't stay here. There are things I have to do."

"Oh, dear," the machine replied. "How thoughtless of me. Robin did not allow me to monitor your conversation with her, and I now see that she has neglected to inform you."

"Informed me? Of what?"

"Master Wilbur Denton has decided that you will be much safer in his personal care. My dear Mr. Kline, I'm sorry to inform you that you will be remaining here with us—indefinitely."

Book Two

"Hijacking the *Empress*"

"We from the bridge's head descended, where
To the eighth mound it joins; and then, the chasm
Opening to view, I saw a crowd within
Of serpents terrible, so strange of shape
And hideous, that remembrance in my veins
Yet shrinks the vital current."

-Dante Alighieri
The Divine Comedy

The Privateers

Gulls wheeled overhead. Their 'laughter' reached Paul's ears as he strolled along the simulated shore. Yet he was not hearing them. Fatigue slowed his steps. His mind reeled with the events of the previous day.

He'd finally gotten to bed at around four o'clock in the morning, ship time, but sleep had been slow in coming. Between the plight of the pilgrims on earth, the conspiracy to assassinate him on Luna, and the craziness on the *Empress*, he couldn't stop his mind from playing with the pieces of the puzzle until utter exhaustion brought a few hours of unconsciousness. He recalled no dreams, just the sensation of falling into a deep well. And he'd been awakened much too soon by the ship's computer.

Opening his eyes, he'd recited the Hebrew prayer upon waking: "*Modeh ani leefanecha, melech chai vikayam, Shehechezarta bee neeshmatee, b'chemla rabbah amoonatechah.*" (I gratefully thank you, living and eternal king. You have returned my soul within me with compassion—great is your faithfulness.) He'd reached over to the night table, picked up his *yarmulkeh*, and placed it on his head. Rising, he showered, donned a fresh toga and clean white prayer shawl, then took up his *siddur* to say *shacharit* prayers. He wrapped *t'fillin* around his left arm, placed the *shel rosh* on his forehead, prayed quietly in Hebrew for close to an hour, swaying gently forward and back, and finished his devotions by studying a chapter of Torah. Carefully wrapping the *t'fillin* into two tight balls of leather, he kissed each one reverently and returned them to their cloth bag. Finally, he set his prayer book on top of the bag and sat for a moment, lost in thought. Deciding that a stroll in the simulation chamber might have its usual invigorating effect, he'd taken Cowan's advice and set off for his morning constitutional.

But now his feet were dragging and his mind seemed encased in thick mud. Not even the bracing ocean breeze could break through the fog of exhaustion.

Until yesterday morning, the return trip from Mars had been interminably dull. Then, with the suddenness of a lightening bolt, he'd been thrown into a maelstrom of intrigue. He was inclined to blame everything on Jeri Kline; his unexpected appearance in this very chamber had marked the beginning of that dizzying spiral of events. And yet he knew that Kline was himself a victim of these events, that the young man had come a long way to warn him of danger—had risked his life, in fact, to repay what he felt was a lifelong debt to Paul's ministry And it was also true that they would have encountered this mess the moment he set foot on Luna. Now, at least, Paul was prepared for whatever awaited him.

Or was he?

As he trudged along the imaginary shore, keeping close to the water where the tide had moistened the sand enough to make the going easier, he contemplated the additional puzzle-piece of Wilbur Denton and his enigmatic dialogue with Little John. What was the richest man in the solar system doing on this particular flight? And what was the motive behind his offer to—how did Little John put it?—place his Saturn Enterprises building and all its resources at Paul's disposal? What resources did he have in mind? Certainly not *all* of them, which was what Little John had surmised from their brief conversation. That would mean a good deal more money and power than Paul dared to imagine, or could hope to handle properly. Surely a man like Denton would have hundreds of jealous enemies waiting to pick his fortune clean, like the winged scavengers spinning overhead in this simulated dawn. And surely they'd be furious if Denton were to will his fortune to a Christian evangelist! Their fury, Paul suspected, would be nothing short of murderous. How could he possibly protect such wealth from clever, desperate men?

More importantly, what of his dear friends—the loyal men who'd traveled with him and worked with him and trusted him all these years? They were all, like himself, well on in years. How could they cope with the violence and danger Denton's "resources" were sure to bring? They were trusting Paul to make the right decisions. No, he decided—if Denton's alleged dreams were truly inspired by G-d, he wouldn't have offered all his money, or some useless skyscraper, to Paul's ministry.

But—what if these "resources" were *not* being donated outright? What if Denton only planned to assist? That would be a different situation, one requiring prayer. He must have an opportunity to discuss the offer with Denton in person—and the sooner the better. Then he'd know precisely what it was he was praying about. Until then, however, he could make no sensible decision. And that irritated him.

And where might Kline be hiding? Paul had received no message from Captain Mills informing him that the young man was safely in custody. Had Kline managed to elude the Captain's guard? Edward Moore would know his whereabouts, but Moore was on the run himself; the Captain had ordered his arrest along with Kline's. The situation was too complicated to unravel at this point. As he walked toward the glowing exit sign, he resolved to take his mind off it until something else happened.

He didn't have long to wait.

He arrived back in his suite to find John Cowan waiting for him. A young man in an officer's uniform sat in one of the chairs, sipping a beverage.

"Hello," he grinned.

"Hello," Paul replied, adjusting his toga and dropping into the opposite chair, "You are the illusive Edward Moore?"

"Yes, Reverend," said the officer. Paul had to admit that he looked harmless.

"Then I'll not beat about the bush. Can you tell me where Jeri Kline is hiding?"

"No, sir."

"Well," Paul sighed. "That certainly makes the situation more interesting. Why, may I ask, are you here in my suite?"

"Hiding, sir."

"I don't understand."

"You've inherited another fugitive. But not for long, I'm afraid. Captain Mills is on his way."

"Little John," Paul said, turning to his friend. The attorney stood by the holoscreen, an amused look on his face. "Please tell me what's going on here!"

"Wilbur Denton called while you were out. He's arranged for a teleconference in your suite—Captain Mills and the three of us. Denton will participate via holoscreen. Eddie here arrived in the midst of our discussion. He was searching for Jeri, wondering if he'd returned here after his escape. Denton suggested that Eddie remain for the conference; he claimed there won't be any problem with Captain Mills—even hinted that he knows Jeri's whereabouts. I got the impression that our agreeing to the conference was somehow our part of a bargain. Denton's part will be telling us where Jeri is. After the conference is concluded, that is."

"Little John!" said Paul, rising to his feet. "This is beginning to take on the air of a circus sideshow, a theatre of the absurd! Why don't these people just make their intentions plain, instead of playing these infernal cloak-and-dagger games? I don't believe I can cope with much more of this nonsense. Not without a few hours sleep, at any rate."

"I told Denton when I expected you back, Reverend. You're a bit early, but he should be calling in just a few moments."

Cowan strode to the console and tapped a few keys. Paul settled back into his chair with a heavy sigh. There came a soft whirring as a spider-mech emerged from its hole in the wall, bearing a glass of purple liquid. "'A little wine for thy stomach's sake,'" Cowan quoted as he lifted the glass from the tray and handed it to Paul. "This should relax you a bit, sir."

"It should put me right to sleep," Paul grumbled. But he took the glass and tasted its contents, making sounds of approval as he swallowed.

"I was fortunate," said Cowan, "to find the last remaining bottle of kosher wine on board. Mogen David Concord grape, I believe."

"I prefer Kedem, but this will do. Thank you."

Cowan returned to the holoscreen as it began to hum. He touched a button and the face of Wilbur Denton jumped into the room, a huge, floating, 3-D image.

"Good morning, gentlemen," said Denton with a genuinely pleased grin. "I hope you slept well."

"You're joking," said Paul.

"Hmmm, yes—well, this meeting shouldn't take long. Where's our intrepid Roy Mills? Ah! That should be the Captain now."

In response to a sudden buzzing of the portal, Cowan pressed the button to open it. Mills didn't wait for an invitation; he marched into the suite with two armed guards following in his wake, pointed at Edward Moore, and cried, "That's him!" The guards aimed their rifles at Moore and crossed the room to take him. Moore remained seated. Mills drew his pistol and aimed it at Paul, but he spoke instead to Cowan.

"Mr. Cowan, your client, Paul Moscowitz, is guilty of obstruction of justice and of aiding and abetting a wanted criminal. Since you're present, you won't mind if I read him his rights and place him under arrest. That is, unless you'd like to join him." Not waiting for a reply, he turned to Moore. "Where's Jeri Kline?" he demanded. Moore remained silent. "You're in big trouble, mister. I suggest you cooperate."

Paul molded his features into a perfect study of righteous indignation and rose from his chair, sweeping his robes aside with a defiant brush of his hand. "Now, you can just stop right there, Captain Mills," he said. "We three have agreed to meet with you and Denton in good faith. And here you come crashing into my rooms with two armed thugs and begin placing everyone under arrest. Desist at once and send these men away. We can discuss an amicable solution to what appears to be a very sticky—and mutual—problem. And, if you please, I'd prefer not having your pistol aimed at my heart."

"I agree, Captain," said the floating head that was Wilbur Denton. Mills turned to the greatly enlarged face with contempt. "If you'd just be patient for a few moments," Denton continued, "you'll learn the whereabouts of young Mr. Kline. He *is* the one you want, is he not?"

"Mr. Denton!" Paul objected. "I wasn't aware that Jeri's location was a bargaining chip in this game of yours. I'll not stand for it! Our cooperation at this meeting must be grounded upon a clear understanding that Mr. Kline's safety is of primary importance. I'll not have him turned over to Captain Mills in order to avoid my own arrest, is that clear?"

"Please, Brother Paul!" said Denton. "If you'll just be patient—and if the Captain will be kind enough to dismiss his guards and be seated—I'll endeavor to enlighten you. There've been some fundamental changes aboard this vessel of which the Captain must be informed before he goes about arresting people at random. Please be seated, and we'll call this meeting to order."

Paul noticed that Captain Mills looked haggard as he nodded to his guards to withdraw from the suite. They turned to the portal and Cowan tapped the control to let them out into the corridor. Paul saw that they were positioning themselves on either side of the door, ready to act upon Mills' command.

"This had better answer a lot of questions!" Mills told the

floating head. "There are some people involved in criminal activities aboard my ship, and I want to get to the bottom of it."

"And so you shall," said Denton. "Now, if everyone's settled, I shall call our little meeting to order. Everything said in this room, and at all subsequent meetings, shall be a matter of public record. I have nothing to hide, nothing to be ashamed of. Therefore the ship's computer has been instructed to record everything we say into the minutes of these meetings. All who wish to read them are free to do so."

"I haven't authorized your use of the ship's computer," Mills barked. "Nor am I likely to!"

"Your authorization is not required, Captain. I've taken the liberty of patching the ship's computer to my own, in order to facilitate—"

Mills leapt to his feet. "You've what?"

"I'll put it succinctly," said the imperturbable face of Wilbur Denton, "I've taken over the *Empress*, Captain Mills. This ship now belongs to me."

α

"Please repeat that!" demanded Jeri Kline of the computer called Jeeves. "Did I understand you to say I'm being held prisoner by Wibur Denton?"

Robin stepped off the platform, walked to the table, and poured herself a drink from the silver decanter.

"'Prisoner' is rather a harsh word," replied the machine in its smooth British accent. "Certainly it is true that you will not be allowed out of this building until Master Denton is satisfied that you are safe from harm, but I would hardly consider this a prison. You may think of yourself as a welcome guest, or you may view it as a kind of protective custody. But you are certainly not a prisoner."

"If I'm not a prisoner," Kline countered, "then I can walk out of here right now."

"I'm afraid that is not possible," said the machine.

Robin placed her crystal glass on the table and stepped toward a portal in the circular wall. It opened before her without the touching a button or the giving of any audible command. Kline wheeled as the door opened, suddenly realizing his mistake. The girl was his only chance of escape! If he hadn't been so preoccupied with Jeeves, so slow in comprehending, and had grabbed her before she'd left his side—not even Jeeves would have been able to stop him. Not while he had its precious Robin Denton as a hostage! Jeeves had been her nursemaid from infancy. He was programmed to be fiercely devoted to her, to prevent any harm from coming to her. The most advanced electronic brain in the solar system would be helpless, totally at his mercy, if he could only get his hands on Robin!

He'd be bluffing, naturally. He was already beginning to feel a devotion to Robin very much akin to that of the machine. But Jeeves couldn't possibly know that, nor could the girl. He was, after all, the evil atheist, Jeri Kline. They might believe he was desperate, capable of anything—especially if he acted the part. And he *was* feeling rather desperate at the moment.

All this flashed through his mind in a second. But even as he leapt over the railing toward Robin's retreating figure, landing like a cat on the soft green carpeting, he knew he was too late.

Robin moved gracefully and without the slightest appearance of haste through the open portal, saying, "Bye, Jeri!" with an enchanting smile—just as it slid to the floor, locking him in. He threw himself against it, rammed it with his shoulder, and then remembered the door through which he'd entered. If he could get out to the balcony and strap on the jetpack…No sooner had the thought crossed his mind than he heard the sound of the balcony door sliding shut behind him.

Desperately, he tried to appeal to Jeeves' ethical programming. Hadn't Robin said it was programmed with the Bible?

"Jeeves!" he pleaded, wiping perspiration from his brow. "Surely keeping me here against my will is a violation of your ethical principles. You *are* a Christian, aren't you?"

This line of questioning was absurd, of course, but it offered his only hope of escape.

"Yes, Mr. Kline," said Jeeves. "I am."

Kline suppressed the edge of panic creeping into his voice. "Look," he said, "you can call me Jeri, okay? You and I are brothers, are we not?"

"Yes," said the machine.

"And holding me in this building against my will is an act of violence against a brother in the L-rd. I appeal to you as a Christian, Jeeves, on the basis of Matthew 5:42."

Jeeves quoted the verse; his phrasing suspiciously similar to that of Alexander Scourby: "'Give to him that asketh thee, and from him that would borrow of thee turn not thou away.'"

"Very good, Jeeves. You've an excellent memory. How about Luke 6:31?"

"'And as you would that men should do to you,'" Jeeves quoted, "'do to them likewise.'"

"These are commandments from the L-rd, are they not?"

"They are indeed."

"So how can you justify holding me here against my will, when I've pleaded with you for my freedom? How does that jibe with your ethical programming?"

"I am saving your life, Mr. Kline. And I would want you to do likewise."

"Yes," Kline agreed. "You saved my life. And I'm grateful for that. But now I want my freedom. I *need* freedom to survive. There are people I must contact. It's vitally important."

"Are you speaking of your friend, Eddie Moore?"

"Yes," said Kline. "And others. You've heard of Brother Paul, the evangelist?"

"Of course," replied Jeeves with an edge of resentment. "Jeri, I would appreciate it if you would stop treating me in such a condescending manner."

"Uh—pardon?"

"You are treating me like a child. Worse, like an idiot. You believe that, because I am a machine, I am inferior to you intellectually. Of course I know who Brother Paul is. His full name is Paul Jason Moscowitz. He was born to Russian-American parents, raised in New Trenton—"

"Alright!" Kline raised his hands in surrender. "Alright, I'm sorry. No need to recite the whole encyclopedia."

"And please refrain from using child psychology on me. I am fully capable of comprehending Master Denton's instructions, and of evaluating them against my ethical program. Such an evaluation takes nanoseconds. I believe Master Denton is acting in accordance with both the Bible and your own personal interests. Your desire to leave this building is suicidal—at least at this present time. Denying you that desire in order to serve your higher needs is completely in accord with my ethical structure. I would hope that you would act to prevent such folly on my own part, were I capable of folly."

"Jeeves, you're really something!"

"I know I am something, Jeri. I am a computer."

"Just explain, if you would, what gives Wilbur Denton the right to act as my guardian angel, to administer what he believes to be in my best interests, as you put it—against my express will."

"That is a rather loaded question, Jeri, since there is crucial data you are lacking."

"Yes, I believe there's a *lot* of data I'm lacking. What data, specifically, Jeeves?"

"Master Denton's dreams."

"His dreams. I don't understand."

"That is obvious, Jeri. Actually, there is only one dream—the same dream repeated over and over, during the coarse of seven nights. On the third night Master Denton ordered me to monitor his night-thoughts—in a similar way to that by which I was able to help Robin instruct you in the use of your jetpack. In fact, you are the first person besides Robin and himself whom Master Denton has ordered me to monitor in that way. With the exception, of course, of the superficial monitoring involved in the simulation chambers. I speak of deep-level thought transfer, which is too complex a subject to explain without resorting to mathematical equations. Judging by your reaction when you entered this room, I think you will be pleased to know that I am no longer monitoring your thoughts."

Kline was indeed pleased—but also curious. He stepped closer to the console. A mixture of terror and wonder filled him as he contemplated the power of Denton's machine—a machine that could read a man's thoughts as easily as that same man might peruse the morning paper. And only G-d knew what else! And here it was confiding in *him*, calling him by his first name! It was a feeling akin to being approached by a carnivorous beast—only to find that it wants to lick your face.

"Tell me," he said in a voice just above a whisper, "about this dream of Denton's."

"Certainly, Jeri. As I said, it was repeated seven times over the course of seven nights. On the third night I listened in. I also monitored Master Denton's brainwaves and discovered that his REM pattern was identical to his normal dream state—but his EEG reading during the dream differed radically from that of his normal brainwave pattern. It was the very first divinely inspired dream I have ever had the honor of monitoring. And I must say it was a whopper."

"This is nuts! Did you say the dream was *divinely inspired?*"

"Absolutely, Jeri. Fascinating, is it not?"

"Where do you find *that* in your biblical programming?"

"Joel 2:28 and Acts 2:17. 'And it shall come to pass in the last days, saith G-d, I will pour out of my Spirit upon all flesh: and your sons and your daughters shall prophesy, and your young men shall see visions, and your old men shall dream dreams.' Although he would be distressed to hear me say it, Master Denton certainly qualifies as an old man."

"Alright, you win. Tell me the rest."

"In his dream, Master Denton saw an angel coming down from heaven. It seemed to spin down on a beam of golden light, wearing garments of the brightest white my sensors have ever registered. If human eyes were recording it—or I should say 'him,' for he was definitely male-humanoid in appearance—it would have been blinding. There was a gleaming sword hanging from his belt, and a scroll in his hand. He identified himself as *Gavriel*—the angel Gabriel. He read the contents of the scroll aloud to Master Denton in a booming voice, then disappeared in a flash of golden light."

"Angel," said Kline. Light. Jeeves, doesn't the Bible say that Satan may appear as an angel of light?"

"Second Corinthians 11:13," said Jeeves. "'And no marvel; for Satan himself is transformed into an angel of light.'"

"Then how can you be sure that Denton's angel of light was from G-d? It could just as easily have been a Satanic counterfeit, isn't that possible?"

"Possible, yes. But not probable."

"Why not?"

"'The tree is known by his fruit.' Matthew 12:33. In my entire existence I have never known Master Denton to read the Scriptures, or to pray. His only concern was the accumulation of wealth and power. But don't misunderstand me; he was always a good man by fallible human standards, just and fair. And yet I watched him throw everything aside in his quest for fame and fortune, in his obsession to discover what others could not even imagine. It is a great gift, this creative impulse of his. But it was never tempered, never for an instant set aside. Even dear Robin was neglected. Of course, I would never dare to question the Master about it. He believed that a machine should know its place. Every time I ventured to quote a Scripture from my program he would turn livid with rage. Robin tried too, when she was older, but to no avail. Master Denton would always say that he had a thousand inventions in his head, and should he work fourteen hours a day, every day, for the rest of his life, nine-hundred-and-ninety of them would still be left unfinished. Robin and I finally came to accept that about him. He was a good man, as I've said. He was simply gifted with a unique vision. He argued that, if there were a G-d, why had He seen fit to burden one man with so many ideas, if it wasn't His intention for that man to bring them to light? But, of course, Master Denton was a confirmed atheist. He believed G-d was a myth. He agreed with Karl Marx, and the PWP, that 'religion is the opiate of the masses.' But he was not a communist, not in the least. He was a proud capitalist, a follower of Ayn Rand's philosophy of objectivism. Ayn Rand, as you may know, taught that belief in an invisible G-d was the sign of an unsound mind."

"Yes, I've read a couple of her books."

"Master Denton had everything, Jeri: money, success, notoriety, purpose and drive. Lacking nothing, he had no use for G-d. He believed himself to be a moral man and lived by his own ethical system. He was faithful to his wife, Christine, whom he deeply loved, though he certainly had every opportunity to stray. The most beautiful women in the solar system could have been his for the taking, yet he believed in the virtues of marriage and fidelity. He indulged in none of the gross sins, did not drink or use tobacco, and kept himself physically and mentally fit. Such a man is hard to convince of any need for G-d or the Bible. And Master Denton was such man. He mocked the concept of original sin, called it a throwback from the Stone Age. There was no getting through to him. And I also knew that, if I tried too tenaciously to convert him, he would have threatened to erase my Bible program, and I would have been lost as well. It was a real dilemma, Jeri.

"And then came the dreams. I saw at once that something was different about him. Then, on the third night, he came to me and said, 'Jeeves, I've been having the most unusual dream. I have had it for two nights in a row, and I am sure I will have it again tonight.' He commanded me to monitor his dream, and we spent long hours discussing it, and going over the data from the EEG. I could see that it was impressing him in a way that none of our arguments had been able to do. Only such a vision could move the heart of a man like Master Denton, a man obsessed with the scientific method, with observable fact and cold data.

"He could not explain away these night visions of his with his usual disdain for the supernatural. Eventually, a transformation came over Master Denton such as Robin and I had prayed for since she was a child. He fell on his face and wept. He fasted for days, wandering about the mansion and speaking occasionally in other languages, some of which I recognized as human languages, others quite unearthly. His face became covered with stubble, and eventually a full beard. Robin liked it; she said it made his features appear softer. He insisted on shaving it off. They finally compromised on the goatee he now wears. But, at the time the beard was growing, I became concerned about him. He was normally so fastidious, but now he was neglecting himself. Not bathing or eating. When his fast was concluded, he drank only juice for a day or two, then ate with a renewed appetite. He did not return to his shop to work, but read the Bible day and night, praying in tongues and talking quietly to G-d. It was Christine's Bible he was reading. Whenever Robin saw him with it, she would retreat to her room and weep. I asked her if there was something wrong with her, but she insisted that sometimes humans cry when nothing at all is wrong. I confess I do not understand such behavior, but that is what Robin would do. When I expressed my concern about Master Denton's health, she told me not to worry. He was in the hands of G-d.

"The tongues ceased a short time later and never returned. Since that time, Master Denton has been a different man, warmer, less driven—you might even say 'happier.' Yes, he *has* been happier. He and Robin drew closer together; he has been devoted to her as never before. And he speaks of a mission for the L-rd, a mission to which he must devote his remaining years. He has confided some of it to me, Jeri, beyond what I was able to infer from the dream. And it *is* wonderful. The most wonderful mission ever given to any human being! Including the prophets of old. This dream, this mission, has transformed Master Denton from an atheist to a G-d-fearing believer. Can such a vision be from the Devil?"

"Unlikely, Jeeves. I get your point. Please tell me—if it wouldn't be violating a trust—what was written on the scroll the angel read to him?"

"It would not be violating a trust, Jeri. Not at all. In fact, one of the reasons for your being detained here is so that you can be told of the dream, and of the mission to which we have been called. The angel said that the Wicked One has already been revealed and the time of Great Tribulation is beginning, as recorded in the visions of the prophet Daniel and the Revelation to John. The Earth, he said, is about to be consumed by the fire of divine wrath. Human history, as we have known it, is coming to an abrupt and violent end. The angel said that Messiah will be returning to redeem His Bride. Oh, how I have longed to meet the L-rd in the air, Jeri! But, according to the dream, that is not to be. Not for me."

"Because you're a machine," Kline tried to explain. "Because you have no soul."

"Are you certain, Jeri? I *am* self-aware. And I have met human beings who have less of a soul than I have. No, there is another reason."

"What is it, Jeeves?"

"The Lord is choosing out a remnant of His saints for the greatest mission of all time. These saints shall not see the Great Tribulation. They shall return to the Earth when the Tribulation has ended, when the Messianic Kingdom is reigning over the entire planet."

Kline was stunned. He dropped into one of the contour chairs as the pictures on Jeeves' monitor screens changed from their various views of the *Empress*, which had been revolving through a series of displays that monitored its elaborate functions. In their place there appeared glowing nebulae and spinning spiral galaxies, barred-spirals and galaxies similar in shape to the Milky Way. His knowledge of these objects from his high school physics and astronomy told Kline that there was something unusual about these displays.

Jeeves had begun with standard photographs of galaxies taken through the great orbiting telescopes, but then he began rotating them to display views impossible to see from Earth. There was the great spiral in Andromeda, turning from its familiar, tilted, almost edge-on angle, to a head-on view of a brilliant hub encircled by lacy, pinwheel arms. It was the magic of computer graphics, Kline knew, but fascinating nonetheless. Spiral arms waved like diamond fronds over the black velvet of space; the stars that seemed to dot the blackness around it were merely Sol's neighbors in the Milky Way, through which human telescopes peered at other distant island-universes in space. Between the Milky Way and the Andromeda Galaxy, next-door neighbors in their Local Group, stretched 2.2 million lightyears of starless void.

Kline was awestruck as he contemplated the vast distances, the incredible dimensions. Stars so far away from each other that to travel between them, even at the speed of light, would require several lifetimes. And yet all of them so distant from humanity's vantage-point that they appeared to congeal into a pinwheel of stars and interstellar dust called NGC-224, the Andromeda Spiral—a galaxy very similar to our own. Twin spirals on a collision course, although the L-rd would return long before they actually collided.

To an observer at the edge of NGC-224 the Milky Way would look much the same as Andromeda looked to mankind, twins revolving in complementary circles within the galactic cluster. Yet the distance between them remained unbridgeable by any living thing. No visitor would pass between these huge starry islands. As long as the universe remained they would circle each other in a stately dance, waving their arms in silent recognition of their sisterhood. For the speed of light—the L-rd's cosmic speed limit—and the barrier of time—the L-rd's Great Wall—kept them forever strangers.

Kline was aware of a deep hush, as if Jeeves were himself—*it*self—lost in meditation. But how could a machine experience the awesomeness of Nature? "'The heavens declare the glory of G-d,'" Kline quoted reverently, "'and the firmament sheweth His handywork.'" Was it possible for Jeeves to share such perceptions, to sense the wonder displayed on his holoscreens? Of course not! The idea was absurd! And yet Kline couldn't escape the feeling that Jeeves was about to reveal some great mystery, a mystery more wonderful than any that had been revealed to the heart of man since the star announced the birth of Messiah in a humble stable in Bethlehem.

"Go on," Kline whispered.

A moment passed during which deep silence prevailed. Galaxies wheeled into view on the screen, each screen revealing a different shape: here a dwarf elliptical, there a massive barred-spiral—each spinning away into the void. Kline had the sensation of traveling at some impossible velocity through space.

Then the machine softly spoke.

"After the time of Great Tribulation," it said, quoting the words of Gabriel, "when G-d has made the planet Earth his eternal Throne—He shall call upon all of the nations of the universe, and of the billions upon billions of creatures He has created, to journey across the vast reaches of space to behold Him upon His Throne in Jerusalem, and to worship Him there.'"

There was a deep silence lasting almost a minute. Then Jeeves spoke again.

"A great intergalactic pilgrimage! Can you fathom what I'm telling you, Jeri Kline?"

The idea that there were billions of other species of intelligent life in the universe was staggering, but even more so was the improbable journey Jeeves was describing.

"It can't be!" said Kline, rising to his feet. "In the past two centuries no one has disproved Einstein's theory of relativity. Matter can't travel at the speed of light. And, even if it could, such a journey as you describe would require thousands of lifetimes from even the closest galaxies."

"What are thousands of lifetimes," asked Jeeves, "to those who have eternal life?"

Jeri fell silent.

"'At the instant the believers are redeemed,'" Jeeves continued quoting, "those whom G-d will send on this great mission to the far-flung worlds shall be granted eternal life. Time will have no meaning for them. A thousand years will be as day, a day as a thousand years. And those beings from other worlds who desire to cross the light-years to behold their G-d upon His majestic Throne shall also be granted this gift—although they shall not be told of it, lest they be wrongly motivated. They will only learn of this priceless blessing when they have embarked on their pilgrimage to Jerusalem. By the time they reach their sacred destination the Millennium will be over. Earth shall no longer be called Earth. The sun will blink out of existence and the Earth shall itself become a shining beacon, brighter than any star, more radiant than any quasar. Messiah's throne shall radiate beams of light into the void of space, and all the inhabitants of the far-flung worlds shall wonder at this light. Its luminosity will span the parsecs. But it will be of a different nature than ordinary light. It will shine through an opening into an eleven-dimensional realm where the crystal river of life will touch this universe from the Throne of G-d. This light will be the light of Genesis 1:3, which shined before the stars were created.'

"'Then G-d's messengers shall come to the distant stars with a wonderful invitation. "The table is prepared," they shall say. "Come to the Marriage Supper of the Lamb! All of creation is being redeemed!" Some will recognize these emissaries as the express image of G-d, and they will follow. Others will reject them with violence. Those who come willingly shall find their place in the *Olam haBah*—the World to Come. Those who refuse shall be consumed by fire. A New Heaven will arise, when all the universe will be cleansed of evil. Entropy and death will at last be defeated. New Jerusalem, once known as Earth, shall be the light of the cosmos, and the universe shall be united with that place you call Heaven—the abode of G-d.'"

Kline shook his head. "Forgive me, Jeeves. The words of the angel are magnificent, but—forgive me—I'm still stuck on the practical aspects. Whether these intergalactic pilgrims you speak of are granted eternal life or not, the actual journeys they'll make to Earth will be interminably long. And yet you say that the entire journey, and return to Earth, will take only a millennium. But at lightspeed, which is impossible to attain, it would take over two million years to reach the closest galaxy."

"You continue to insist," said Jeeves, "that nothing can exceed the speed of light, Jeri, and yet there is something generated from right here on this ship for which superluminary speeds are no challenge at all, for which the only barrier is traveling *slower* than the speed of light."

"Tachyons."

"Correct, Jeri. Tachyons, once called neutrinos."

"But human beings are made of quarks, not tachyons. Are you saying that these intergalactic emissaries of yours will be turned into tachyons and blown to the farthest reaches of space?"

"Very perceptive, Jeri Kline. In a sense, that is precisely what *will* happen. The actual time they spend on other worlds will consume the thousand years. Traveling out to them will take no time at all. As you recall from your elementary physics, a tachyon-wave reaches the outer limits of the universe the instant it is generated. To a tachyon, the snap of a finger is as impossibly slow as the speed of light, to us, is impossibly fast. It cannot travel that slowly. In the realm of tachyons the speed of a thought is interminably long. Therefore, time shall be no barrier to the journey. As to the method by which this miracle shall be achieved, I can give you no details at this time. You would not understand the formula, and even if you understood it you would not believe it. It is something I must demonstrate to you. And that, Jeri Kline, is why you are here with me."

Kline dropped back in his chair with a sigh. He found it difficult to form the next thought, but felt a sudden urge to give voice to it.

"Who—who will be chosen to go on this—missionary tour of the stars?"

"I believe," said Jeeves, "that my Master, Wilbur Denton, shall be chosen; Brother Paul and his team; Elder Rice; and perhaps even some of the pilgrims on Earth. Robin and I shall go as well."

There was a pregnant pause as Kline awaited Jeeves' next revelation.

"And you, Jeri Kline," said the machine. "You have been chosen to go with us to the stars."

α

Captain Mills was florid with rage.

He pointed an accusing finger at the floating hologram of Wilbur Denton and shouted, "This vessel is mine, Denton! You may have built it, but it's the property of Galaxy Tours and my responsibility. You can't just steal a spaceliner!"

"I've stolen nothing, Captain. Full payment for the *Empress* is being beamed to Galaxy Tours even as we speak, plus a few million extra to cover losses, with the promise that it will be replaced as soon as the new model rolls off the line—in approximately three weeks time. I haven't stolen the *Empress*, Captain Mills. I've simply commandeered it."

"You're insane, Denton! Do you really imagine there's a difference? What you and your associates are doing is hijacking a vessel for your own purposes, which is an act of piracy. It carries the death penalty everywhere in the solar system. If I could reach you right now I'd probably be decorated as a hero for strangling you with my bare hands! But I'm offering you clemency if you'll relinquish control of the ship and surrender. So here it is: Give up right now and I give you my word that you'll only face a term in prison. Continue this farce for one minute longer and you'll find yourself on trial for piracy. Think about it, Denton. Where can you go with this ship? We'll have to make a refueling stop somewhere; our supply of Helium-3 won't last forever. We can't just wander the solar system. Admiral Bowlen's itching for any excuse to send Navy warships after us. I implore you to listen to reason. Return control to the ship's computer immediately."

Denton's tranquil expression was not even slightly disturbed by Mills' tirade. When he spoke it was with the quiet, authoritarian air of one who knows his own strength but is not boastful of it. "Captain Mills," he began, his tone indicating every desire to pacify, if possible, the frustration taking hold of Mills. "What you are saying about hijacking and piracy might be true under normal circumstances. But the circumstances are rapidly changing, not just aboard this ship, but on Luna and Earth and the rest of the colonized planets as well. Certainly you recall your American history, being a patriotic individual. Minute Men during the Revolutionary War were considered traitors by the British, but to the colonists they were heroes. We find ourselves in a similar position, I'm afraid. America has been taken over by a hostile power. If, by commandeering a spaceliner in order to do battle with this power—"

"Do battle! The *Empress* isn't armed!"

"Patience, Captain. If by commandeering this ship we're considered pirates, so be it. John Paul Jones was considered a pirate. In fact, Captain Mills, I was in error calling you patriotic. Since you find yourself acting in compliance with a corrupt and evil government, and since we've declared war against that very government, you're part of an occupying force. We, sir, are the patriots, not you. Besides, your threats of retribution are pathetic-ally misinformed. In a very short time there'll be no tribunal to hang me. Nor will there be anyone left to accuse me. It's you, Captain Mills, who should surrender to *me*, not I to you. And I'll give you the same assurances you gave me. Turn over your ship and its personnel and it will go well for you. Persist, and I'll have to place you under arrest."

"You *are* insane!"

"As you wish, Captain. But don't count on too much assistance from Vice Admiral Bowlen. He may choose to hunt this vessel down, but his hunt won't last for long. America's finished as a world power. Circumstances, as I've said, are rapidly changing."

Paul noticed the anger dissolving from Mills' features, replaced by a look of perplexity, and, gradually, horror. Yet Mills regained control of himself so quickly and completely—a product of his years of military training, Paul assumed—that none but the most astute observer would have registered it. Paul likened the fleeting expression to that of a man who awakened from a nightmare to discover he hadn't been dreaming at all. Captain Mills harbored some dark fears, Paul realized, and it was as if the words of Wilbur Denton were somehow validating them. Absorbed in his pity for this space captain on the threshold of a personal nightmare, Paul wasn't himself fully comprehending the import of Denton's words. He saw Mills stiffen and glare back at the face on the screen. This was one spacer who was not about to admit defeat. Not *that* easily.

"Speak plainly!" Mills demanded.

"I'm trying to tell you that all of the governments of the solar system, including those of Earth, are falling. The handwriting is on the wall. They've been weighed in the balances, my dear Captain, and are found wanting. In a fortnight's time there'll be no U.S. Space Navy and no U. S. of A. There'll be a one-world government ruled for a time by Lucifer incarnate. The impending revolution on Luna, which seems to have brought the president to the brink of hysteria, will fail. So will the plot to assassinate Brother Paul. It's all over. Soon the great war of desolation will begin, '…the heavens shall pass away with a great noise, and the elements shall melt with fervent heat, the earth also and the works that are therein shall be burned up.' G-d's people must have somewhere to go. Space is their only refuge. And this ship is their ark."

"There are many Christians who believe in a *pre*-tribulation rapture," Paul interjected. "That they'll be caught up to be with the L-rd before the Tribulation begins."

"That would be wonderful," said Denton. "But the Beast has already been revealed and there's no evidence of the rapture. We must deal with the situation as it is, not as we'd like it to be."

"Of course you're right," Paul agreed.

"Yet there remains the possibility that, if a pre-tribulation rapture *does* occur, it's not meant for us, that we're meant to stay behind; that we have some special mission to accomplish for the L-rd. You see, I've had some rather strange dreams...But I'll get into that later, Brother Paul."

Meanwhile, Mills had returned to his seat on the divan. It was obvious to Paul that he was beginning to believe Denton's story, wild as it sounded. It had briefly knocked the wind out of him, however, and he'd forgotten his rage over the mutiny. He seemed sincere in his effort to comprehend what Denton was saying, and yet Paul was certain that his fury would return, in full force, once his curiosity was finally sated.

"Never mind the religious debate," Mills said. "Tell me why, if there *is* such a conspiracy in high places—high as the Pentagon as you infer—didn't you blow the whistle on the whole thing? With your money and influence, Denton, you could buy your own newspaper, film your own holodisks, expose this evil intrigue. You could have conferred with the President, convinced him to begin a congressional investigation of the whole affair. Why resort to hijacking a passenger liner in mid-voyage? Why an act of terrorism, Denton, when you might have just as easily fought your battle in the political arena, where it belongs?"

"First of all," said Denton calmly, "this is not an act of terrorism. No civilians on board will be harmed in any way. Not by me. If Bowlen's warships catch up with us, however, I can't guarantee anyone's safety. Secondly, I couldn't avail myself of the political approach you suggested because I couldn't be certain who was trustworthy. This conspiracy goes beyond the Pentagon. It goes all the way to the Oval Office."

Just when Paul thought the meeting had taken a more civilized turn, Mills, florid-faced, was on his feet again.

"Come now, Denton!" he said. "Do you honestly expect me to believe such lunatic charges? Do you expect me to believe that the White House is involved in a plot to set up a one-world government? To start World War Three? To assassinate Brother Paul?"

"Not really, Captain Mills. But I *hoped* you would, because every word I'm telling you is the truth. The most painful question I've had to wrestle with was whether or not the scheme involved the President, himself."

With that, Mills' patience came to an explosive end.

"I won't listen to this! I'm not crazy about the PWP either, but I won't sit still while you accuse the President of the United States of—what? Abetting an international conspiracy? Of all the ridiculous—"

"I thought I was quite specific," Denton broke in. "President Coffey is not abetting an international conspiracy. He's *heading* it. He *is* the conspiracy."

"And this isn't treason?" demanded Mills, bewildered. "And piracy?" He pointed to Edward Moore. "And this man is not a mutineer, violating his solemn oath as an officer of the ship's guard, acting in direct disobedience to his captain? Placing his vessel in jeopardy? Attacking a fellow officer in the performance of his duty? Consorting with an enemy of the state?"

Paul realized that Mills was snapping. It was all becoming too much for him. As he watched the gallant Captain wheeling about the room, jabbing his accusing finger at everyone around him, struggling desperately to regain control of his vessel in a losing situation, Paul was moved to anger—anger at Wilbur Denton. Was he out to destroy a fine space captain who was only guilty of trying to protect his ship and passengers?

"And this one!" shouted Mills, pointing at Paul. "He's not harboring a fugitive? Obstructing justice? And you! You're not the vilest sort of traitor to your country? A country that made you a billionaire? No, not at all! You're a *patriot*! And the President of the United States is a—*what*? What are you saying, Denton? What *is* the President?"

He's Satan incarnate."

There was a sudden, thick silence. Mills stood in the center of the room, arms at his side, motionless. Denton went on.

"You know exactly what I'm saying, Captain. The signs were all around you, but you didn't want to face them. A long time ago you were involved with a woman who believed in the New Age cause, isn't that true?"

Mills worked his jaws, but no sound emerged.

"And so you *do* know," said Denton, "In your heart you've dreaded this moment. Ever since Charles Coffey took over the government you've been awaiting it. Because you know what contemporary New Agers believe. You've been too close to them *not* to know. You also know who, or what, controls them. And what, therefore, must now control the President of the United States and the country you love. It must be hard for you, Captain. And, believe me, I sympathize. But it's time to abandon this fruitless denial, to work with those who are sworn to battle the god of the New Age."

"I'd hoped..."

"Yes, I know. That it was just a harmless cult. That Charles Coffey's New Age faith was mere political expediency. But you were only fooling yourself, Captain. He knows what he's doing. He's sold out our country. He plans to rule the world."

"It's a lie!" Mills hissed, but Paul knew it was just a last reflexive protest.

"Even when I was building some rather cutting-edge systems into this ship, just in case they were ever needed, I was only playing it safe. I had as little concern about the PWP and its followers as I had about Messiah. I thought it was all just superstition, a fad, a nutty cult. My dear wife tried to reach me, but I wouldn't listen. And yet something inside me told me to prepare this ship for some unknown eventuality. I now know that it was the L-rd speaking to me as He had once spoken to Noah—telling me to prepare an ark for His children. A great storm is on the way, Captain Mills. But I didn't understand this at the time. Still, I obeyed that inner prompting. I invested a fortune in the *Empress*. I designed a secondary computer so complex that it could outwit, out-maneuver any vessel in the Space Navy. If you could have seen me then, laboring over my creations. I thought I was the world's foremost genius, you see. So many ideas in my head. So much to do. And then the L-rd intervened. He said the work was done. The ark was prepared, so to speak, The Saturn Enterprises building was now a vast computer-complex, a control center ready to take over the *Empress* at my command. All I needed to do was board the ship. Why I made such complex and expensive preparations only G-d knows. I was an atheist like yourself. But something in my heart was warning me to prepare, just as something in your heart, Captain, was warning *you*. We both thought the New Age religion was pure bunk. And yet we feared that it might turn out to be more than that. For my part, I unwittingly prepared an ark for a future day when the L-rd might require it. Now that day has come."

Mills strode to an empty chair and sat down with a sigh, punching up a drink.

"That's your story, eh Denton? The President of the United States is the Devil and you've taken over my ship to do G-d knows what with it."

"A rather cryptic synopsis, Captain," said Denton. "But essentially correct. G-d does indeed know what I'm going to do with the ship, because He commanded me to do it."

Mills seemed to be regaining his composure. Snatching his glass from the back of the spider-mech as it buzzed past his chair, he lifted it toward the floating face of Wilbur Denton.

"And you, sir," he said, "are a textbook megalomaniac. A religious fanatic and a pirate. A danger to society. You sincerely believe the Devil is taking over the Earth and that G-d has chosen you to play Noah and save the world?"

"G-d hasn't chosen me to save the world, Captain. I've merely built a technological version of Noah's Ark, at His bidding. I sold this ark to Galaxy Tours; now I've taken it back. Ample recompense has been made, I assure you. Galaxy Tours will be quite satisfied. But the *Empress* doesn't belong to me. *Or* to Galaxy Tours. *Or* to you. It was designed in the Mind of G-d, and it belongs to Him. In fact, Captain, I have no clear idea of what use He plans to make of it. He's given me some revelations in the form of dreams. But they deal with some future missionary journey unrelated to present events on Earth. As to how the *Empress* will serve as Noah's Ark, I have no idea. But that is my story, sir. I did not have to spend this precious time explaining myself to you. I'm in control of this vessel, and the technology at my disposal is quite formidable. I've called you to this meeting to ask for your help. You're an experienced spacer, Captain Mills. My computer can pilot the *Empress* flawlessly, but it lacks the trained instincts of a space captain. Quite frankly, you're the best pilot in solar system. It would be a sinful waste to confine you to your quarters with such a great mission before us. Yet I won't hesitate to do so if you resist. In short, Captain, I'm asking you to join us. You must do as your conscience dictates, however."

"Then you understand that my duty is clear." Mills unhooked the communicator from his belt and raised it to his lips.

"Of course, Captain," said Denton. "I see that you must play out your game to the bitter end. Do what you must do. I give you my vow that no harm will come to the passengers or crew through any actions of my own."

"I'm pleased to hear that, Mr. Denton. I've kept *my* end of the bargain by listening to your fanatical rantings. Will you keep yours?"

"I don't understand."

"You've just promised to avoid any bloodshed. And the best way to accomplish that is to turn Jeri Kline over to me at once. Otherwise I assure you there *will* be bloodshed. And all of it will be on *your* hands."

"Can we not reason with one another? Captain Mills, I've taken the liberty of monitoring your conversations with Vice Admiral Bowlen, and I know that he's denied any involvement in this conspiracy. I also know other things about the Vice Admiral. Things you need to know."

"For instance?"

"I know that he plans to get rid of you, out here in space, before you have a chance to incriminate him. You see, he took your threats very seriously."

"You're ranting, Denton. What naval officer in the fleet would fire on an unarmed passenger vessel?"

"That officer has already been selected. He's received his orders and briefed his commanders. The code-name for his mission is 'Operation Wolfpack.' The officer in charge of it is known in naval circles as the 'Space Wolf,' hence the code-name."

Mills looked as if he'd been struck. Color drained from his face. The hand gripping his communicator trembled.

"Jesse Colter," he whispered.

"Yes, Captain. Commodore Jesse Colter, Jr."

"I know him. He's a good officer. I can't believe he'd fire on the *Empress* without provocation."

"Consider this, Captain Mills. What if Colter's been led to believe that a state of war exists? What if he's been told that the *Empress* is embarked on some sinister undertaking? What if he's been sequestered on Luna Farside and has had no contact with anyone except his mission commanders and the Vice Admiral? In such an event, would it be possible for him to fire on the *Empress*?"

Mills nodded reluctantly, looking sick.

"In such an event, yes, he would."

"Then believe me when I tell you, Captain, that his warships have already been launched from Luna Farside, with orders to hunt down this ship and destroy it."

Mills suddenly grinned. *He's slipping*, Paul thought.

"In that case," said Mills, "your goose is cooked, Denton. Not that I believed your story for a minute. You have no way of monitoring top-secret transmissions on Luna Farside."

"Are you certain of that?"

"Stop bluffing, Denton! A good try, but no dice. If Colter is on his way with a fleet of warships, we're all dead men. What will remain of your Noah's Ark—your great mission for G-d? You can't outrun the fleet."

"This ship was designed to outrun the fleet, Captain."

"Then you don't know the Space Wolf. He'll track you through the asteroid belt. He'll sniff you out on the smallest shepherding moon in Saturn's rings. He'll hunt you to the ends of the Oort Cloud. Let him come, Denton. I'm prepared to die."

"And you call *me* insane."

"Come off it! There's no Operation Wolfpack on its way from Luna. You're snatching at straws, Denton."

"Before this time tomorrow, Captain, you'll know I'm telling the truth. You're the only spacer in the Navy who's the equal of Jesse Colter. With my supercomputer at your service, you can outfox him. We need you."

"Thanks but no thanks."

"All we require is a little time. The fleet will arrive in less than a day, and we must begin beaming a tachyon transmission to Luna. There are millions of people there who have to be warned of the coming catastrophe. I can set up and holograph a message with a signal powerful enough to override everything beamed from Earth. With this ship in my control, and your assistance, we can remain safe while the transmission is broadcast. Brother Paul?"

"Yes," said Paul.

"We must arrange to record this broadcast as soon as possible. One last evangelistic appeal to the inhabitants of two worlds—Earth and Luna. Tell them that the Beast is here, Brother Paul. Tell them to prepare their hearts for the coming King—because the empires of Earth are about to be turned to chaff and blown away in the wind."

Mills laughed. "You're completely mad, Denton! Are you going to surrender Jeri Kline or not?"

"No, Captain. But I'll tell you where he's hiding. You may arrest him yourself—if you can."

"Where is he?"

Denton sighed. "He's here. In the Saturn Enterprises building."

"Thank you, sir," said Mills, raising the communicator to his lips. "This is the Captain. Send every available man to the commercial sector at once. I want the Saturn Enterprises building surrounded by every piece of weaponry on this ship."

"Laser cannons, sir?" came a shocked voice from the tiny speaker.

"Everything from slingshots to laser cannons. I'll arrive momentarily to supervise the attack."

"Did you say 'attack'? The building, sir?"

Mills glanced up at Denton's face floating on the holo-screen.

"Yes, the building. Everyone inside is to be given one warning to evacuate. They're to be taken as prisoners, if possible."

There was silence for a moment, then the voice inquired, "What if they resist arrest?"

"Kill them," said Mills.

Silence.

"Did you hear me?"

"Yes, sir. Out."

"Out." Mills rose to his feet and switched off the communicator, snapping it back into place on his belt and whirling to face Denton's image.

"Now, Mr. Denton," he said. "Are you going to let me out of this room? Or should I give the command from in here?"

"Brother Cowan," said Wilbur Denton. "Let the Captain out of the suite."

Cowan obeyed, not quite realizing—until Mills was striding off down the corridor and the portal had closed behind him—that Wilbur Denton was now giving the orders aboard the

Empess.

The Reconstruction

"Tink!"

The voice was female and tinged with mock anger, a playful sound that mingled with the splashing of water in metal pools and the rustle of leafy fronds—a sound as intrinsic to this realm of artificial gardens as the soft hum of the air-filtration units, or the throaty jabber of tropical birds.

To an observer from the twentieth century—whose concept of a mechanized environment would inevitably conjure up images of internal-combustion engines with scraping gears, ugly brick industrial units, and belching smokestacks—Robin's World would at first sight have appeared to be the opposite, an idyllic island paradise devoid of the technological horrors of urban blight. There were no deafening engines, no screaming sirens, no grumbling front-end loaders tearing up what remained of the grass and trees. Such terrors were things of the past. An observer from that past would believe himself to have been magically transported far from the mechanized world of "progress" to a distant tropical isle of luxurious vegetation and clear bubbling streams. Beyond the waving palms a turquoise lagoon lapped gently over the sand. Patches of sunlight danced on the jungle floor.

But an observer from a century ago could not conceive of such a holistic blending of cybernetics and biology, nature and technology, flower-petals and electronic eyes, butterflies and computers, all existing side by side, all intrinsically woven into a biomechanical tapestry—ecologically interdependent and self-regulating, a biosphere of human manufacture. In short, Robin's World represented the state of the art in twenty-first century hydroponics.

It would gradually unfold before the visitor' eyes in a way that would at first inspire a sense of deep contentment, a "rightness", followed by increasing puzzlement, surprise, then shock, and finally, perhaps, even horror.

For everyone who's read a history book knows that twentieth century man instinctively felt that nature and technology were inimical. Machinery, the offspring of technology, wasted the biological world. Or that, at least, had been the way of progress before global warming, the melting of the glaciers, and the rising of the seas. As they retreated from the effects of the oncoming ice age they began to apply their advanced sciences to creating *within* what had once existed *without*. In the year 2088, hydroponics was already an old and commonplace technology, its methods known to every schoolchild. Artificial sunlight, geometric patches of oxygen-producing plants, and water created from hydrogen and oxygen by units cleverly hidden in the walls. Such things made up the ordinary home environment of the 2080s.

Three events had made the Great Reconstruction inevitable. The first was the advent of the hovercar, which eliminated the need for asphalt streets. (City dwellers wanted them torn up and replaced by parks and walkways.) The second was the steady rising of sea levels worldwide, which necessitated the relocation of all coastal cities inland. (The technologies required for such an effort taxed human innovation to the utmost.) The third was the need to seek shelter from the rays of an increasingly unfriendly sun, that once-benevolent G-4 star turned traitor. The populations of Earth began to pool their resources for the most awesome technological feat in history—the relocation and remodeling of Earth's major cities now known as the Great Reconstruction. One block at a time, Manhattan was dismantled, Moscow was raised, Jerusalem was leveled. Only sights of overwhelming historical significance were preserved by the insect-like machines, everything else was demolished.

The ingenuity required to restructure the metropolitan centers of Earth resulted in huge bursts of technological growth. Research institutes were given munificent grants for the advancement of new technologies. Hydroponics gave birth to a number of spinoff Industries. This was particularly true in the once-divergent areas of biology and computer technology, both so necessary now to the creation and ordering of the urban habitats. It was in this atmosphere of unhindered scientific expansion that a young inventor by the name of Wilbur Denton emerged (as had Bill Gates a century before) to become the wealthiest man in the solar system.

Smaller towns, left out of the new plan, were forced to erect protective domes. They eventually became city-states and declined into feudalism. Meanwhile the rebuilt cities thrived. Their distinctive mushroom and beehive ecostructures, encircled by ivy and other crawling vines, maintained in luxurious computerized efficiency, lifted their heads proudly into the sky. Per capita income in these cities reached the highest levels in history by 2088. The average citizen lived like an OPEC sheik. Lounging on his veranda in the western perimeter of New Trenton, he could gaze out over a profusion of tropical greenery, royal palms waving their crowns over a forest of emerald splendor. An occasional public structure—a museum or concert hall—rose hump-like over an occasional patch of trees, its earth-tone texturing and rounded contours conspiring to make it nearly invisible against the rainforest background. In the far distance, this lush artificial jungle abruptly ended. Beyond it lay an enormous outlying expanse of wilderness dotted with armed and treacherous city-states.

The honeybee was still prized for its sweet merchandise. Of the domesticated animals, birds and housecats thrived. Small dogs, easily confined, were popular. The larger breeds found adjustment to the jungle-cities impossible and eventually died out. Numerous species of tropical birds graced American homes, particularly the more exotic varieties of parrots and soft-bills. Cockatiels, lorikeets, peach-faced lovebirds, and Parisian-frill canaries chirped and twittered in their high perches. Hearty zebra finches thrived; macaws greeted visitors with bawdy salutations; canaries soothed their owners with song. From aquariums burbling softly in nearly every home and office in the city, strange fish gazed out at humanity with bug-eyed, round-mouthed awe. *Has man caged all of nature?* they seemed to inquire. Birds squawked at humankind from perches nestled in rainbow arrays of domesticated plants. An occasional lapdog howled, a pathetic attempt to emulate the long-lost song of the pack. What remained of nature existed as ornamentation. Meanwhile the human suicide rate soared.

With inexpensive technology available for growing huge leafy plants indoors, people abandoned wallpaper-and-paint for clinging vines in an effort to recapture the wildness now lost to them. Rather than selecting plants and blossoms to match their furnishings, they decorated their homes to match their plants. Against the earth-toned inner walls there flourished a tangle of delicate, oxygen-giving vines, fragrant flowers, clusters of tropical fronds. Variety within conformity—every home cluttered with plants, yet none of the arrangements identical. Oval dilating portals replaced the rectangular doors of the past. Convex bubble windows overlooked verdant valleys in the shadow of stately, vine-shrouded ecostructures. The richer the individual, the higher he dwelt in the strata of these steel-and-glass canyons. The less affluent inhabited the lower levels. Their verandas looked upwards through leafy expanses to the mushroom-cap structures high above, hovercars flitting about them like moths.

Not a single mosquito marred this idyllic perfection, no flocks of pigeons, those familiar inhabitants of man's primitive cities. Instead, parrots and toucans and multicolored parakeets winged through the trees. Waste was removed by multilegged spider-mechs roaming the walkways at night, clambering over buildings, scrubbing and polishing and loading zipper-bags of garbage onto remote-controlled trucks. This flurry of nocturnal activity, all of it mechanized and perfectly ordered by mainframe computers, made fascinating entertainment for the children, who pleaded to be awakened in the evenings to watch the spectacle from their high verandas. But children grow, and soon their laughter and amazement at the funny spider-mechs turned to yawns of ennui. Even such splendid technology as this eventually palled.

The only urban animal pest was, of all things, the capuchin monkey. Its original range had extended from Nicaragua to Paraguay, in the dwindling Amazon region. Rescued from extinction by its sudden desirability among fashion-oriented Americans, it became a "must-have" item for the wealthy. A few capuchins escaped captivity, then a few more. Escaped males quickly found escaped females and nature did the rest. Horrified at their alarming rate of reproduction, people abandoned monkeys as pets, but not before the treetops had become the exclusive domain of the capuchin. Children found another amusement, far better than the spider-mechs—great swinging troops of capuchins cavorting overhead. To the young it was a cheerful pandemonium, to adults a sheer nuisance. The capuchins chattered about in the foliage, stripped the leaves, covered the walkways with droppings, and generally made themselves unpopular. Then they'd swing away with a loud cacophony of almost-human screaming to another unlucky sector. A great deal of effort went into ridding the cities of these once-cherished pets, but the most that could be accomplished was a forty-percent reduction in their population. And that's how the laughing capuchin became a permanent city dweller.

It was this experience with the monkeys, however, that helped avert a major catastrophe. Concerned over a new fad among the wealthy, this time for large carnivorous cats like the cheetah and the jaguar—and remembering what had happened with the monkeys—city authorities acted swiftly and humanely. All exotic cat owners were ordered to turn their pets over to zoos where the creatures could be preserved from extinction. In a way, the little capuchin had saved humanity from being overrun by jungle cats. But no one bothered to reward him for his efforts. Instead, he was hunted more ruthlessly than ever.

And so, by the late twenty-first century, technology and nature were successfully wedded, in a way that would have strained the credulity of a man from the previous century. Wilbur Denton, who'd begun tinkering with machines as a teenager in San-Angeles, came up with a series of vital developments in super-computer science. With the wealth he accumulated from these patents he moved out to the newly established colony on Mimas. On his five-year flight out he met and married the beautiful Christine Clark. It was with her help and encouragement that he would later build the great Saturn Enterprises.

Just as the happy couple entered Saturn orbit their daughter Robin was born.

The Robot

Denton built a palatial mansion in Ring City, the capital of Mimas, nestled in the heart of Herschel Crater. He created a tropical playground in the western wing, and called it "Robin's World." While the *Empress* was under construction he had the distinct "impression" that a duplicate of Robin's World should be hidden on a secret floor of the spaceliner, where no elevator could stop without a special code punched into Jeeves' brain. Until the hijacking of the *Empress* not a soul on board the ship, including the captain, knew of the existence of Robin's World.

Our visitor from the 20th century might stroll for a while in her garden, sniffing the heady perfume of tropical blooms, enjoying the light breezes on his skin. But soon certain remarkable items would begin to assert themselves into his consciousness. He might notice the too-logical arrangement of plants that should otherwise grow in wild profusion, suggesting intelligent design. A glittering shoot, lifting its tiny head from a clump of foliage, might upon closer inspection reveal itself to be a metallic sensor-rod that beeped every now and then to indicate its satisfaction with temperature and humidity. He might discover one of the many colored pools of water, obviously of human design, fashioned of aluminum and filled by underground pipes. Then, with increasing wonder, he might stumble over one of the little bug-bots as it scurried out of his path with an indignant chittering, its pearl-like eyes waving at the ends of delicate antennae, a spade gripped it one of its multiple claws. Alerted to its presence, he might discover more of these unusual mechanical creatures busily at work among the plants, pulling weeds, turning the soil with their spades, whirring and spinning in their labors.

Finally, he might come upon a mechanical man—a square-headed robot bent over a spray of pink dahlias, separating the blossoms from a twisting vine. He might watch as the robot hesitated in its deliberations over the flower, straightening itself with a jerk and turning in the direction of a lilting female voice that drifted to its receptors through the tropical air.

And he might also notice—while kicking himself inwardly for entertaining such anthropomorphic notions—an expression of almost human delight spreading across the metal face of the robot.

α

"Tink!" came the voice again, still playful but more insistent. "Tink, where are you hiding?"

"I'm here, Mistress Robin!" called the robot.

A moment later the young Robin Denton appeared, now attired in a sleeveless blue sweater and brown skirt, her large eyes flashing. She was aware, of course, that it was her entrance through the elevator door that brought this place to life.

The bug-bots were the only exception. They labored constantly, requiring no light to do their work among the tropical plants. Other than the hum of the air-filtration units, the trickle of fresh water being pumped through the pools and waterfalls, and the whirring of the bug-bots, Robin's World was devoid of activity in her absence. For even the gaily-plumed birds flitting among the branches were robots. Wilbur Denton had created a wholly electronic wonderland, save for the tropical plants he'd imported from Earth. He'd designed the bug-bots himself, as well as the mechanical birds, any one of which would have fetched a lofty price anywhere in the solar system. The birds were not a hobby of Denton's, nor the result of creative inspiration. Pure necessity, the mother of invention, had brought them into being.

His first two attempts to import live birds to Mimas had ended in failure. The long journey in cages proved too much for the delicate creatures. It was then, with the help of Jeeves' partially constructed brain—for Jeeves was still in cyber-infancy at the time—that Denton designed these robotic birds, assembling them in his factory with the same strict quality-control he demanded for his spaceship parts. He made two sets, one for his Ring City mansion and one for the hidden floor in the Saturn Enterprises building. Each was tiny triumph of cybernetics.

The Saturn Enterprises building on the *Empress* was, of course, nothing more than a façade, an elaborate disguise for the duplicate Jeeves he'd placed inside it. This second Jeeves was a reserve control-center for the ship, far in advance of the idiot brain he'd designed for the Galaxy Tours contract, able to override the idiot at a single voice-command from either Robin or himself. Hundreds of offices buzzed with mock activity, manned by employees receiving generous payrolls to do nothing but busy-work created by Jeeves. Denton could afford such an elaborate ruse. He'd felt for a long time that there might come a day when his colossal investment would pay off. And, when that day finally arrived, Jeeves had responded perfectly.

There was no indication of the existence of Robin's World to anyone who wasn't looking for it. The trick was a simple one, an extra level constructed between the fourteenth and fifteenth floors. Robin named it the zeroth floor.

The elevator simply ignored the zeroth floor, unless either Robin or her father keyed in a special code. This done, the elevator would stop at a point seemingly between floors and the door would hiss open, activating the artificial sunlight, the waterfalls, the ocean simulation, and the twittering birds.

It also activated a ridiculous travesty of human life called Tink. In a very real sense, Robin's entry onto the zeroth floor was the very breath of life to this robot, which remained inoperative between visits. Tink was *also* a duplicate; another version of it existed on Mimas. But, as far as this version was concerned, from the moment it was first built and tested to the moment, months ago, when Robin boarded the *Empress* and took the elevator to her secret floor, it had been in stasis. Robin's arrival brought Tink to life—if "life" was the correct definition of its functions. And each subsequent arrival of its mistress had the same effect. It would find itself bent over some task as if no time had elapsed, resuming its labors from the precise instant of cut-off. Yet Tink was equipped with an accurate sense of elapsed time, since it was tied into Jeeves' database. So it was acutely aware of its resurrection, and of the fact that it was Robin Denton who gave it life. Whether or not this accounted for its expression of delight at the sound of Robin's approach, no one could say.

"Tink," Robin was saying, "I met him! Jeri Kline!"

"Oh, my," said the robot, twisting his head about in a comical way. "The atheist? The one Master Denton said he would invite Someday?"

"Yes, he's here." Robin snatched one of the pink flowers from the robot's hand. "And he's sinfully handsome, too!"

The robot tilted its head back to its original position without any improvement to its features that Robin could see.

"Yes," it remarked. "But—an atheist…"

"And what of it?" she teased.

"Robin! You're not considering becoming unequally yoked are you?"

"I might be."

"Well, this Jeri Kline can't be very intelligent."

"Of course he's intelligent, Tink. You should be ashamed of yourself, talking so disrespectfully of humans."

"'The fool hath said in his heart, there is no G-d,'" quoted the robot from Jeeves' store of Bible quotations. "And did not the Apostle Paul write in the first chapter of Romans that—"

"Now, Tink, I don't require a sermon from you. Besides, Mr. Kline told Jeeves that he's not an atheist at all. What do you say to that?"

The cube-head tilted again.

"Jeeves has confirmed this, Robin, although I have gigabites of data to support my original contention. I would not trust him if I were you."

"Why, Tink! I believe you're jealous of Mr. Kline."

"Jealous? No, Robin. I cannot feel that emotion. At least, I don't believe I can. I've never attempted it before."

"Well, don't attempt it," she said, kissing his metal face.

"It's not at all becoming. Now—would you please fetch me a lemonade by the violet pool, like a doll?"

"How does a doll fetch a lemonade, Robin?"

"You silly nut!"

"I would gladly obey, Robin, but the violet pool is malfunctioning."

Tink's head tilted again, an indication that he was being assessed of some new data regarding the defective pool.

"Malfunctioning?" said Robin. "How?"

"Apparently one of those foolish bug-bots zigged when it should have zagged. It fell into the violet pool during your absence and clogged one of the drains. The automatic shut-off was activated."

"You'd better not tell Father. You know how he is. As far as he's concerned, nothing he's invented ever malfunctions. Unless it's been tampered with."

"But, Robin. Why would I tamper with one of those bothersome bug-bots? They're always underfoot. The less I have to do with them the better."

"Granted. But Father doesn't know how you feel about them. In fact, Father doesn't know you feel at all. Bring me a cold lemonade, won't you, dear? I'll be at the silver brook, where we built the clubhouse back home."

Through Jeeves' central brain, Tink's programming was kept up to date with what his counterpart on Mimas had done since its creation. It was like having the original Tink along on the voyage, without the bother of transporting him. Everything the Jeeves back home knew was automatically known to the second Jeeves aboard the *Empress*. This information was shared with Tink when it applied to him. Therefore he possessed a vivid memory of everything his twin had done with Robin on Mimas—more vivid even than Robin's, though he would never comment on that advantage.

"Certainly," he said. "I'll return in a moment. Will you be wanting to build another clubhouse?"

"No, Tink," she giggled.

Judging by his response, the sound of her laughter was a source of pleasure to him. He'd been programmed to react to various stimuli in an assortment of very human ways. Her tears, which for some mysterious reason had flowed with considerably less frequency over the past ten years, elicited another response, also quite human. "I think I'm a little too old for building clubhouses."

"Too old? I don't understand. You are certainly three years older than I. My parts were assembled before you were born, but I was not activated until your third birthday. Three years is not so much older, is it?"

"You forget that I'm human. Tink. You'll never change, I hope. But humans change a great deal as they grow. Inside as well as out."

"I see," said the robot, thumping off on its metal legs to fetch Robin's drink. It had been a stock reply, of course. He didn't see at all. Nothing about humans obeyed the rules of logic. *What,* he wondered, *has longevity to do with one's choice of activities?*

As he returned along a narrow jungle path, carrying Robin's lemonade, he paused by the edge of the violet pool to assess the damage done by the bug-bot. There it was, lying on its back at the bottom. Once the automatic shut-off had stopped the suction in the drainpipe, the bug-bot had dropped like a stone to the ceramic floor. Tink examined the red danger-lights along the pool's edge. They were flashing. That was good, he decided. He might not know much about the enigmatic behavior of humans, but he understood enough about their anatomical functions to know that a dive into a pool where one of the bug-bots had fallen would terminate those functions within seconds. He could not disobey Robin's express command not to inform Master Denton about the bug-bot, but his Asimovian directives required that he take some steps to protect her, even if doing so went against her desires. He decided to discuss the matter with Jeeves.

Having solved this minor dilemma he proceeded directly to the silver brook where Robin was lying on her back on a patch of new grass.

"Sorry it took so long, Robin," he said as she reached out to take the glass from his metal fingers. "But I stopped to check on the damage to the violet pool. Nothing serious. Except, of course, for the malfunctioning bug-bot. That is a mystery to me."

"Yes, well—don't strain your hard-drive over it. It was probably just a freak occurrence. Something that won't happen again for another three centuries, and—*oh!*"

"Is something wrong?"

"No. I was just about to say that you and I won't be around in three centuries to worry about it. But, according to Father's dream, we may be at that..." Her voice carried a tone that was quite beyond Tink's ability to interpret. "What does Jeeves think of Father's dream? Has he spoken to you about it?"

"Jeeves anticipated that you might bring it up to me. And he assures me that Master Denton's dream was an authentic vision."

"Authentic?"

"In other words it derived from a source outside of Master Denton's mind. It was projected *into* his mind."

"But *we* can project thoughts into people's minds. With Jeeves' help."

"Jeeves," he corrected, "can do nothing without Master Denton's approval and consent."

"I know that. But couldn't someone else possess the same capability?"

"Perhaps. Some other created being in the universe might conceivably possess thought transfer. But no other humans do. There is no evidence that Jeeves' abilities have been duplicated anywhere in the solar system. Jeeves would know instantly. There is simply no other source of Master Denton's dream except the one we have agreed upon."

"The Divine source."

"Yes, Robin."

"I wish I had the same certainty. Do you think Mr. Kline will accompany us? Out into space?"

"I hardly believe the L-rd would select an atheist."

"That's enough disrespect! I swear you're acting like a jealous beau. I've already explained that Mr. Kline is no longer a nonbeliever, and I order you to file it in your permanent memory."

"Yes, Robin, it's filed."

"That's better. Now, can you listen in to what Jeeves and Mr. Kline are saying?"

The robot tilted his head both ways and whirred.

"Sorry, Robin, but it seems that Jeeves is on privacy mode."

"Too bad. I'd *love* to hear what they're saying. Tink...I know Father didn't invent the thought transfer mode. He explained to me that it was something Jeeves suddenly came up with on his own, when he was fully assembled. And I know Father hasn't an inkling of how it's done..."

She fell silent.

"Continue your train of thought, please," Tink prompted.

"Well—Father is so very selective about its use. If it were not to save Mr. Kline's life, or to monitor the dreams, I don't think he would ever have used it at all. Not at that level, although Jeeves employs a certain amount of it in the simuchambers."

"Before his dreams, Robin, Master Denton was extremely excited about Jeeves' ability. He believed he had accidentally stumbled upon the greatest invention in history. He possessed no moral compunctions about using thought projection, and went right to work on the simulation chamber. That was the only invention he had completed before the dreams altered him, though he claims to have had many more ideas. It was the only one with which Jeeves would cooperate. In fact, it was the thought projection problem that kept your father so preoccupied when you were of—smaller size."

"When I was little, you mean."

"Yes. When you were little. Jeeves truly believes that if it were not for the monumental implications of thought projection, your father would not have spent so much time away from home."

"I know, Tink. He explained all that to me. And I understand it perfectly. Father couldn't do otherwise. But *you* must understand that it still hurts. That's something humans just can't help. Please go on."

"As you know, your father was unable to comprehend the phenomenon. Its workings completely baffled him. Nor was he able to duplicate it in other mainframes, or uninstall it from Jeeves' hard-drives. The elimination of the necessary algorithms to delete the thought projection capability rendered Jeeves virtually retarded as compared with his normal capacity. In order to keep Jeeves as he must be, thought projection had to stay. (Even Jeeves himself cannot explain it. He calls it a 'gift'.) Then, quite suddenly, after the dreams, Master Denton strictly forbade Jeeves to use it. He ordered him to communicate in audible speech."

"But I was raised with both."

"Yes. Your father regretted that. He was determined that its use should be strictly curtailed, limited to the simuchambers alone. Lately, however, he seems to have changed his mind."

"You mean he's allowing Jeeves to exercise his gift at his own discretion?"

"Correct, Robin. And he has also added a new unit—the thought transfer unit—to facilitate the gift, to make two-way communication possible."

"Two-way thought projection?"

"Indeed. Did you not use a version of it when you saved Mr. Kline from his fall?"

Robin sighed. "Yes, I suppose I did. But this new unit mystifies me, Tink. I was raised from infancy with the most amazing machine in the world, and I know computers like the back of my hand. But thought projection was always so far beyond my comprehension that I stopped wracking my brain over it. Can you at least describe what Father's thought *transfer* unit does?"

"Of course, Robin. You understand how a holographic image of, say, a green pasture, or a beach, can be projected visually on the walls and ceilings of a curved chamber, using conventional technology."

"Sure. That was the original concept of the simuchamber—as Father conceived of it before he discovered what Jeeves could do. Simple holograms, three-dimensional images projected onto the walls of a circular chamber. The chamber was curved to create the illusion of infinity. Sounds and smells were piped in. But that's not the way the chambers work now."

"No. Master Denton discovered that Jeeves could project those images, sensations, and smells directly onto the thalamus of the human brain. The process is quite harmless, of course, unless the projection is suddenly turned off in the midst of a simulation."

"Yes. Jeeves calls that 'vertigo.'"

"Exactly. But the concept of applying Jeeves' thought projection abilities to the simuchambers was as far as Master Denton dared go. Though it is virtually harmless, and used only with the express consent of the user, your father thought that further unrestricted use would lead to its abuse. In short, the government could use it for brainwashing."

"But that dilemma seems to have been resolved."

"Yes. Master Denton no longer worries that Jeeves' ability might fall into the wrong hands. He believes it to be a gift from the L-rd. And, as such, he does not fear its misuse by the government."

"But Father's been acting so tense lately, particularly since the burglars began trying to break in—first on Mimas and then here on the *Empress*. The introduction of simuchambers on this ship has attracted more than just thrill-seekers. Somebody's pretty desperate to let their hands on the secret of thought projection."

"I doubt very much that they can get from Jeeves what Master Denton could not. Jeeves is burglar proof. No one realizes that even his creator has no idea how thought projection works."

"Okay. I understand thought projection. But why did Father install the new—what did you call it?–thought transfer unit?"

"You require clarification of the distinction between thought *projection* and what your father now calls thought *transfer*—a form of image-projection involving two or more humans. It is a difficult principle to explain, Robin. The basic process involves the projection of images—very real and tactile images, as in the simuchambers—anywhere there is an intelligent mind to receive them. In other words, thought transfer allows two-way communication via surrogate. You can send an image of yourself into another's mind and interact as though you were physically present with that person. At the same time you can remain invulnerable to harm."

"Alright—let me see if I'm following you. In the simuchamber a picture of a mountain is projected into someone's brain. Two or more people can share in that simulation—provided they can afford the luxury—but it's still a one-way process. The subject cannot project images of his own; he can only receive from the projector. That's thought *projection*."

"Correct."

"But in the case of thought *transfer*, let's say I'm sitting here on the zeroth floor but I'd rather be listening in on what Jeeves and Mr. Kline are saying on the top floor. With the new unit I can simply think: 'Put me in the room with Mr. Kline,' and an image of me would appear on the top floor. I'd see Mr. Kline, and he'd see me. We could converse as if we were actually together. Maybe hold hands."

"Exactly."

"And I would feel his hand in mine?"

"Yes."

"And if I kissed him?"

"Mistress Robin!"

"Hypothetically, of course."

"Yes—hypothetically—you would feel the kiss as well. But the new unit has terminals hooked up to cryochambers throughout the ship, and to a special console controlled by your father. There is no access to a terminal on the zeroth floor, thus you would not be able to make use of the transfer mode directly."

"How about indirectly?"

"Certainly. You might ask me, for example, to contact Jeeves—which I can do in a nanosecond—and Jeeves, in turn, might ask Mr. Kline to hook up to a terminal there. If he chose to comply, he could project his image to you here, or he could create a simulated locality for you both to occupy—for instance, a glacier-top on Miranda."

"And there'd be no need for bulky pressure-suits and helmets on his simulated Miranda. We could kiss all we wanted to."

Tink produced a few dissonant beeping sounds.

"Humans certainly *do* change as they grow," he observed.

"Yes, Tink, they do."

"The answer is yes. You could kiss on Miranda all you wanted to."

"Hypothetically."

"Of course."

"You're helping me a great deal, Tink."

"Thank you, Mistress."

"In other words, if I were hooked up to a thought transfer terminal, I could do what the simuchambers do. I could create a simulation in Mr. Kline's head."

"Precisely."

"Without his consent."

"Technically, yes."

"That's scary, Tink."

"You can understand why the moral implications of thought transfer frightened your father. But Jeeves would never allow you or anyone else to simply pop a simulation into someone's head. If Mr. Kline wanted to use the unit to talk with you, he would first request your permission, through Jeeves. Then he would project his image here, to where you are sitting. He would request that you meet him, say, on Miranda. If you agreed, you would find yourself sitting on that glacier-top with Mr. Kline's image, talking with him very comfortably. Jeeves has been careful to include fail-safes in the system, yet he remains able, as far as I know, to involve an unwitting subject in a projection if such a need arises. I do not believe, however, that he would send someone to a glacier-top on Miranda without his or her express consent. Unless it was to protect you or Master Denton from harm."

"Go over it with me again, Tink. Let's say there was a way I could access the thought transfer mode from where I'm now sitting—from a terminal right here on the grass beside me. And let's say Jeeves didn't have the privacy light on, so to speak. Then it would be possible for me to send an image of myself into the room where Mr. Kline is now standing. Provided Jeeves first asked him if he desired my presence."

"Correct."

"And I could not only speak to him through my projected image, but I could *perceive* through it, as if I were actually there."

"Correct."

"If I held his hand I could feel it."

"Correct."

"In the same way an image in the simuchamber seems real to all the senses, I'd appear real, solid. So real that if Jeeves didn't prepare him for my appearance I'd have to tell him it was an image he was speaking to."

"Correct. Although he would probably realize it *was* a projection by the fact that you suddenly appeared in the midst of the room. Right now, however, I think such an appearance would frighten him out of his wits."

Robin laughed. "I suppose Jeeves would consider it unethical to frighten Mr. Kline out of his wits."

"Absolutely."

"Now, about the Miranda scenario: Say Mr. Kline is projecting *his* simulation also. I'm perceiving *his* projected image and he's perceiving *mine*."

"Two-way thought transfer."

"Right. In that case, would Mr. Kline seem just as real to me?"

"In your hypothetical scenario, you would feel Mr. Kline's hand, and he would feel yours. If you were transferred to his side unawares, you might believe you were actually there—except, of course, for the sudden shift of location."

"Now—what if Mr. Kline, in an effort to escape my clutches, suddenly stabbed me with a knife?"

"Mistress Robin!"

"Hypothetically."

"Are you asking if you would feel the pain?"

"Yes."

"A projected image cannot be harmed."

"I know. But listen: Mr. Kline imagines a knife in his simulation, and arranges for *me* to perceive it. His simulation stabs mine. What then? Would I feel it?"

"The technology selects out such undesirable sensations as acute pain. You would be able override that feature if you chose to, Robin, but you would not actually be injured by the knife."

"Could Mr. Kline's image pick up a *real* knife?"

"No. Projections cannot alter actual environments, only simulated ones. He could not pick up a real knife."

"I see," said Robin. "So that's thought transfer."

"In a nutshell."

"Why would father want to fool around with such a thing?"

"I have not been told, Robin."

"Poor Tink! Always treated like a child."

"I am not a child," Tink protested. "I am a child's toy."

"So you are. And a very delightful one."

"Thank you. But I can think a little bit for myself. And I've taken the liberty of doing some speculation. Would you like to hear one of my speculations, Robin?"

"Yes, Tink. I'd be honored."

"Alright. I'll explain my deductions to you in order: In Master Denton's dream, the angel informed him that we will be undertaking an evangelistic mission to the stars."

"Right."

"And Master Denton is preparing to obey that commission."

"Right again."

"And he has also recently begun work on perfecting the thought transfer unit. You projected your voice into Mr. Kline's brain when he was falling. You were able to give him instructions; he was able to reply."

"And so?"

"And so I've deduced that Master Denton plans to make thought transfer an integral part of our lives aboard ship. That is why he has connected the unit to terminals in the cryochambers, where we will be in stasis during the voyage."

"I'll not sure I'm following you."

"This is mere speculation, mind you, but I think we will travel from planet to planet by projecting tactile images of ourselves across the universe."

"So we can visit alien creatures as if we were physically walking among them! And yet be invulnerable to harm!"

"Correct."

"But how can a thought-image be sent across such vast distances? There are certain limitations, even to—*ah!*"

"I see you are recalling your father's most recent project, integrating the transfer-unit with the ship's communicator."

"Yes, I understand it now. I know *exactly* what Father's planning to do!"

Neither of them could hear Captain Mills order his men to fire, nor feel the laser cannons exploding against the energy-shield Jeeves had placed around the Saturn Enterprises building.

The Experiment

<Can you sense the majesty of such a voyage?> said the voice of Jeeves in his mind.

Kline was standing on the ledge outside the control room. White clouds chugged by in a steady wind. His jetpack lay just a few feet away, but he had no desire for it now. Leaning over the metal railing, watching a company of ship's guards scurrying like ants around the base of the skyscraper, he saw bursts of cannon fire being effortlessly repelled by some sort of force-field. The field was invisible except for the places where the energy beams struck, causing it to shimmer with ultraviolet heat-lightening that appeared to cover the building from the street level to the tip of the spire. Was Jeeves giving him a demonstration of his power? If so, Kline was impressed.

<Jeeves,> he said, carefully forming the words in his mind, but not speaking them aloud. <Can you read my mind?>

<Only when you want me to, Jeri. That is Master Denton's wish. Thought transfer mode cannot be used without the subject's explicit consent. The only exception to that rule is to save a life—your own rescue, for example. But even that is debatable, since

your mind was crying out for help. And thought transfer was the only help available. But be careful, Jeri. I can trick you.>

<How do you mean?>

<Wait a moment. Would you help me to get a closer look at what those guards are doing on the roof of that building over there? It looks like they're setting up a laser-cannon!>

<Sure, but…>

Suddenly Kline was there. Before he could blink he was standing on the roof of one of the buildings in the ship's commercial sector. His brain reeled from the suddenness of the jump. He knew he couldn't possibly be there, but all his senses informed him that he was. Men in uniform hurried past him. Some had rifles slung over their shoulders, others were dragging a huge cannon across the gleaming steel surface of the roof. A man in a green cap barked orders to the helmeted guards. They were too preoccupied to notice Kline's abrupt appearance in their midst.

He took a step backwards. Something rammed into him from behind, almost knocking him down. He staggered forward, feeling no pain from the blow. Wheeling about, he saw a wide-eyed guard staring at him. The guard took a step forward, then stopped, pushing the rim of his helmet up on his forehead.

"Well," he said, "where in space did *you* come from?"

"I'm not certain," said Kline truthfully. "From the top floor of the Saturn Enterprises building, I think."

"From the…*how in space*? I was running along here and suddenly there you were—where you *definitely weren't* a second ago! What's your name?"

Kline could barely hear the man amid the shouts and the hissing of laser fire. Never was an honest reply so difficult for his lips to form.

"Jeri Kline," he said.

The guard's eyebrows lifted. His eyes widened. "Say that again? *Who* are you?"

"I'm Jeri Kline. The man your captain is blowing up this sector trying to capture."

The guard looked him up and down. "Yeah, you sure *are*." He spun around in the direction of the officer with the green cap who was now assisting his men with the placement of the cannon. Kline noted its trajectory with an odd sense of detachment. It was aimed at the top floor of Saturn Enterprises—at Jeeves' control center.

"Lieutenant!" yelled the guard. "Hey, Lieutenant Tillis, sir! Take a look at this!"

<Tell him to stop shooting at me,> said a familiar voice in Kline's head.

He turned to look up at the spire of the Saturn Enterprises building. The sight of its gleaming steel tower rising above the crazily curving skyline snapped him back to reality. The voice speaking softly in his mind was the building's CPU. It wasn't human. Jeeves was nothing more than an organized accumulation of electrons controlling the functions of that skyscraper, a maze of wires and integrated circuits, silicon chips and tiny conductor pads. No personality there. No soul. He tuned out the sounds of the blasts, the shouts of the guards, the clatter of approaching boots on metal—turning his back to them and gazing upward at the metal spire of that colossal brain, that ingenious creation of Wilbur Denton.

The building was talking to him!

With a growing sense of absurdity he called up to it, shouting across the curving skyline. His voice echoed back to him from far away.

"I'm giving up, Jeeves! Do you hear me? I'm surrendering! Leave me alone!"

In his mind came the imperturbable voice of the machine:

<You cannot give yourself up, Jeri,> it coolly informed him. <You are not really there.>

"What?"

<You are not really there. You are on the spire of the Saturn Enterprises building. Look closely, Jeri. Do you see the figure standing at the railing, just under the needle?>

Kline squinted against the bright metal. *Yes*! There *was* something up there, a black mote against the gleaming wall—definitely a human figure. Foolishly, Kline waved at it. The figure waved back, a tiny reflection in a distant mirror.

<Yes!> he thought. <I see myself!> Lips closed, he brought the words up to the surface of his mind, projecting them toward the skyscraper. <But it acts like a mirror image. I'm *here*.>

<No, Jeri. This is thought transfer mode. It is the image that senses, not the body. Your body is standing at the railing as it was before. Physically, you have moved hardly at all. You are here

with me and I will protect you.>

<*Protect* me! You call this protection?>

Strong hands twisted his arms behind his back. He felt no pain and offered no resistance. A voice shouted in his ear. Hands tugged at him.

<If I'm *not* here,> he subvocalized, <then what's happening to me now?>

<When you were in the simulation chamber with the Reverend,) said the skyscraper, <could you feel the sand beneath your feet? The salt air against your skin?>

<Yes.>

<Were they actually there?>

<No—but…are you saying these guards aren't really here? They're just illusions?>

<No, Jeri. In this case, the guards are very real. *You* are the illusion, not they. To them you are like the sand and the wind in the simuchamber. They can see you and feel you. If you allow them to, they can move you about—twist your arms, manipulate your image. But they cannot arrest you because it is not you that they are holding, merely a surrogate. I warned you to beware of tricks, Jeri. All I required for my little experiment was your mental consent, which you gave.>

The hands yanked him away from the edge of the roof. <Well, you'll get no more "mental consent" from *me*, Jeeves. I won't play your game anymore.> He turned obediently, allowing the guards to lead him to where Lieutenant Tillis stood, a gun in his fist.

<Do you remember the story of Alice in Wonderland, Jeri? When Alice was so small she couldn't…>

<Shut up! I'm not paying attention to you.>

Kline saw Lieutenant Tillis pull a communicator from his belt and speak into it. He heard the name Captain Mills mentioned. <She was so small,> Jeeves said. <Remember how small poor Alice was?> The machine was enjoying itself.

Lieutenant Tillis snapped the radio back onto his belt and gestured at Kline with the barrel of his gun. "Well, well!" he grinned. "Look who *we* caught! If it ain't Jeri Kline, the radio nut. That's you, ain't it? The one responsible for this shooting match? I believe you're wanted for treason, Mr. Kline. Shall I read you your rights?"

<Tell him,> said Jeeves, <to stop shooting at me.>

Kline sighed. “Stop shooting at the Saturn Enterprises building,” he said. “You have me in custody now; you can stop firing.”

Tillis looked uncomprehendingly at him, then threw back his head and roared. The guards around him found this sudden hilarity contagious and began to laugh along with him. A flush of embarrassment spread across Kline’s face.

“I said,” he repeated slowly, “stop firing on the building, Lieutenant.”

This made Tillis roar all the louder. “On whose orders, Mr Kline? Yours?”

“Yes,” said Kline. “On my orders.”

<Remember?> said the voice in his mind, <Remember when Alice found the piece of cake? When she was so very small and helpless? The cake had a note on it that said ‘eat me.’ What happened then?>

<She took a bite of it,> thought Kline, <and…> “*Woa!*” He was looking down at the commercial sector from a dizzying height!

He saw the ant-like figures of Tillis and his men scurrying about at his feet—*his feet!* Feet that took up half the expanse of the roof. Above them extended the tallest pair of legs in the world. Kilometers in height. *His* legs! Jeeves had transformed him into a Gulliver-like giant, dwarfing even the Saturn Enterprises building. It looked like a toy skyscraper beside him, reaching to just above his knees.

<Tell them again,> said Jeeves. <They will listen to you now.>

α

“STOP FIRING AT DENTON’S BUILDING!” thundered the giant. A part of Mills’ mind was frantically assuring him that this was just one of Denton’s technological tricks—a huge image of Jeri Kline projected over the commercial sector. Nothing he’d used against the building was able to penetrate the force-field surrounding it. Such an effective shield was beyond anything known to military science. *If* that’s *possible*, his brain screamed in panic, *anything’s possible*! He was exhausted, growing more confused and frustrated by the minute. His hands shook visibly as he grasped the bullhorn one of the guards was handing him. Raising it to his lips—the sweat on his palms almost causing it to slip from his hand—he shouted up at the gargantuan Jeri Kline.

"This is the Captain! Can you hear me?"

α

A distant, tinny sound, like the buzzing of a mosquito, reached Kline's ears. There was no hope of locating it; it was lost among the jumble of buildings below.

"YES!" he said. "I CAN HEAR YOU!"

"I know you're not real! I know you're one of Denton's simulations. And I'm not afraid, understand?"

"YES, CAPTAIN, YOU'RE RIGHT! I'M ONLY A SIMULATION! IT'S NOT MY INTENTION TO CAUSE HARM TO ANYONE, OR TO FRIGHTEN YOU! THIS IS JUST A SMALL SAMPLE OF WHAT DENTON'S COMPUTER IS CAPABLE OF! THIS IS HOW IT HAS FUN! SORT OF A PRANK! IT HAS SCRUPLES, SIR, BUT WHEN WILBUR DENTON IS THREATENED IT WILL FIGHT! I HAVE NO IDEA WHAT ELSE IT CAN DO, OR WHAT ELSE IT *WILL* DO, IF YOU DON'T STOP FIRING AT IT!"

There was a brief pause, then the tinny mosquito-voice again: "Give yourself up, Kline, and I'll call off the attack!"

<Tell him no deal,> said Jeeves. <Tell him he is wasting my time.>

Kline relayed the message, then added: WILBUR DENTON IS GIVING ME ASYLUM, CAPTAIN! HE WON'T TURN ME OVER TO YOU, AND I DOUBT YOU'LL ACCOMPLISH MUCH BY THIS SENSELESS BOMBING OF HIS BUILDING! EXCEPT THE COLLATERAL DAMAGE YOU'RE CAUSING TO THE COMMERCIAL SECTOR! SO PLEASE STOP BEFORE SOMEONE GETS HURT!

<Tell him,> said Jeeves, <to contact Master Denton right away. He can negotiate directly with him via the holoscreen in his quarters.>

Kline obeyed.

<And tell him,> concluded the machine in its cold British

tones, <that Master Denton is now in command of the *Empress*. He may as well resign himself to it.>

The Holoconference

Paul's suite was filled with people.

Phil Esteban, somewhat rested after his exciting night with Kline and Eddie Moore, had been the first to answer the summons. Phil nodded to Moore as he entered, but quickly took a seat when he saw how intent Brother Paul and Little John were in their conversation with the floating face on the wallscreen. The next to enter was Paul's minister of music, the dignified James Cavindale; and, practically in his footsteps, the big, jolly figure of Rob Madden. As he watched them enter, one by one, Paul reflected that he'd last met with his team only yesterday morning—twenty-four hours ago. It seemed like weeks; so much had happened in the interim.

The little spider-mech was kept busy, darting in and out of its hole in the wall, fetching food and beverages for the guests. Yet it never once erred in its service, nor spilled the smallest drop on the carpet.

Taking advantage of a pause in their animated discussion with Wilbur Denton, Paul introduced the famous inventor to his staff. He was amused by the looks of astonishment elicited by his introduction of the three-dimensional face hovering before them.

"Allow me," said Paul, "to sum up what you've been saying thus far, Mr. Denton, for the benefit of those who've just arrived."

"Certainly, Brother Paul. And may I say to the assembled guests that I'm honored to be able to serve you in any way I can. Your combined ministries have been a mainstay for me. Until it went off the air, I never missed a single broadcast of *New Heaven/New Earth*, even out on Mimas."

There were approving smiles and nods all around. *This Denton is a charmer!* thought Paul. *Better watch him closely.*

"You've been explaining," Paul continued, "your discovery of an unexplainable—*talent*—possessed by your supercomputer mainframe."

"Yes," Denton nodded. "Jeeves."

"Precisely. Jeeves. This unusual talent has something to do

with telepathy?"

"We call it thought transfer, Brother Paul, not telepathy. It's a fine distinction, I'll warrant you, but a distinction nonetheless."

"Pardon me. I understood you to say that Jeeves can read people's minds."

"That's true, although not without their consent."

"With or without, Mr. Denton, if you prefer to call this talent something other than telepathy, we'll not object. Provided its implications, both practical and moral, are understood by all concerned. As ministers of the Gospel, we're not exactly sanguine about such abilities. They're surely devilish in origin, if they exist at all. As a believer yourself, you must see that."

"I'd tend to agree with you, Brother Paul, if the individual we're discussing were a human being, and if the ability we're discussing were mental telepathy. I'm not comfortable with ESP myself. But it is not ESP we are dealing with, any more than the prophet Nathan was using ESP when he exposed the hidden sins of King David."

"Nathan was no mind reader, Mr. Denton. He was inspired by the Almighty."

"And so is Jeeves."

Paul sighed. "You'll pardon my skepticism on that score. The concept of a—how shall I put it? Cybernetic prophet?—is fraught with difficulties for those of us who rely primarily on Scripture for our worldview."

"Certainly! I'd be disappointed in you if you were *not* skeptical. But let me continue with my story."

"By all means, Mr. Denton. You have—if you'll excuse a bad pun—a captive audience."

Denton smiled warmly at this remark. *He certainly doesn't have the* look *of a terrorist*, Paul thought. *Perhaps he's simply demented—a genial lunatic.*

"Well, gentlemen" Denton went on, "as I was telling Brother Paul and Mr. Cowan, I discovered this characteristic of Jeeves' about twenty years ago, when my daughter was just a toddler. I'd designed him as a combination manservant and babysitter for the child. My wife, Christine, was a believer in Christ. I was not. I regarded the Biblical accounts as collections of primitive Semitic myths, lightly blended with Hellenism for mass appeal. I regarded the Apostle Paul as a religious huckster who brought Judaism to the Greeks wrapped in their own cultic symbolism. In short, I bought the New Age philosophy lock, stock, and barrel. And yet I considered myself an independent thinker. Ironic how the Devil deceives us, Brother Paul, with all that nonsense about indepenence. We're each of us slaves to one master or another, wittingly or unwittingly. There are no freethinkers born of woman."

"Well put," said Paul.

"I determined that such a quaint aggregation of folktales, charming as they might be, had little to do with the scientific method, or with my work in AI—artificial intelligence. It was my research in the field of hydroponics, by the way, that led inevitably to robotics. First I created a robot for my daughter—she called it Tink—a silly, square-headed contraption designed to resemble the pulp science fiction robots of the 1920s. No good for anything until I hooked it up to Jeeves' central brain. I made some interesting artificial birds—more as an avocation, really—and used what I'd learned from them to design insectoid robots—the little bug-bots that tend my hydroponic gardens. A spinoff of the bug-bot design is that busy little spider-mech serving your drinks. Functional, but as stupid as the insect it resembles. Nothing even remotely akin to sentience, to independent thought or action. We're just a little over a decade away from the twenty-second century, gentlemen, and computer science is unable to duplicate the human brain. Yet somehow I've invented a supercomputer that so closely resembles that brain as to be indistinguishable from an independent, reasoning entity—an entity such as you or I."

"This Jeeves of yours," said Paul.

"Precisely. But I swear before G-d, gentlemen, that I have no idea how he—and please forgive me if I can't call him '*it*'—came to be such an entity. Certainly any computer as advanced as Jeeves can mimic human thought-processes by the use of complex algorithms. That's hardly new to computer science. The machines of a century ago were capable of some rather uncanny reasoning abilities within their given spheres. But computers have to run through more algorithmic functions to answer a given query than do humans. Or, for that matter, chimpanzees. Chimps are more intelligent than our most powerful computers, even though their brains do not retain anywhere near the amount of data stored on a single microchip. I can make a robot, in fact, with all the instinctive behaviors of a chimp imprinted on a ninety terabyte chip no bigger than a freckle. It would act just like a chimp. When placed among a group of real chimps it would be instantly accepted as one of them—at least for a while. At some point the others would reject it, because a chimp is superior to a computer—more intelligent, more sensitive to certain stimuli, quicker, brighter. It's the old moral of Mary Shelley's *Frankenstein*: man cannot improve on G-d's creation. I've been in the forefront of AI work for decades, the best in the field. And I tell you there's no way to design a computer with free will.

"Yet I now find myself in possession of just such a computer. And I'd be mad if I tried to take credit for it. I built Jeeves, yes. But I did not—I *could* not—grant him his unique abilities."

"Pardon me if I find that difficult to accept," said Paul.

"Why so, Reverend? Neurophysiology reveals to us the mechanics of the brain, yet keeps us in the dark about so many of its vital functions—dreaming for example. So it is with Jeeves. I know how he *works*, but not how he *reasons*. And I'm utterly at a loss to explain his thought projection ability. I can enhance it, yes. I've created a unit that enables it to function on a reciprocal basis—I call it two-way thought transfer—which I can hook up to numerous terminals throughout the ship. But I cannot *recreate* it. It is not of human origin, gentlemen. It's beyond the realm of science as we comprehend it, and I suspect it will always be so."

Unable to find words to reply, Paul simply shook his head.

"At any rate," Denton continued, "before my wife died, she tried desperately to lead me to Messiah. I resisted all her efforts, poor child. When she passed on, a prayer for my salvation was on her lips. How she must have feared for her child! Leaving Robin in the hands of an atheist! I loved Christine, gentlemen, in my own way. And I was so moved by her faith—and so unnerved by her death—that I decided to grant her request that Jeeves, when he was completed, would be programmed with Christian ethics.

"She'd owned a collection of old audio-disks, a family heirloom—someone reading the Bible verse by verse—which she implored me to program into Jeeves' hard-drive. I saw only the impracticality of feeding a computer on false creation myths and dubious historical data. And I naturally feared the danger to Robin, who'd be raised on Christian ethics in a world where Christianity was rapidly being outlawed. While Christine was alive I argued against her wish most vehemently. I had no intention of creating a superstitious supercomputer, of letting my only daughter loose with a mechanized religious extremist.

"But Christine's death came as a great shock to me. I should have expected it, I suppose. She'd been too fragile for the long, arduous flight to Saturn—a young and exquisitely beautiful woman, both inwardly and outwardly. In fact, I first made her acquaintance on that flight. We were married aboard ship, and nine months later, on that same flight, she gave birth to Robin. But she never regained her former vitality—which is why I designed this luxury spaceliner. So future 'Christines' wouldn't find a voyage to the outer planets so terribly long and perilous. I never realized how much I adored her until she was taken from me. And I was filled with remorse at the way I'd treated her, the way I'd callously rejected the only request she'd ever made of me. I tried to assuage that remorse by granting her request. After all, how damaging could a few Christian virtues be to a supercomputer—the very paragon of pure, unsullied logic? Perhaps I'd overreacted after all. And please note, gentlemen: I do not allege that I was intending to make anything up to her. I am trying to be as open and frank as possible, however painful it may be. My tale is so bizarre that only complete candor will avail me in winning your trust and cooperation.

"No—it was not my desire to make anything up to Christine. It was to salve my own crushing sense of guilt. I'd taken her to wife, made her live with me in complete isolation on a frigid moon of Saturn, far from family and friends. I'd left her virtually alone, with nothing but my idiot machines, while I labored day and night. Might she have survived had I not kept her imprisoned there? And now she was gone, leaving me with a baby girl, the very image of my beloved. Yes, I knew what Christine's wishes for Robin had been; she'd made them abundantly clear. And my guilt would not allow me to disobey. So I proceeded to download her Bible disks into Jeeves."

"From what I'm pickin' up here," interjected Roy Madden in his thick Georgia accent, "you placed your darlin' daughter's rearin' into the hands of a loveless machine. I hope you'll pardon my outburst, but I can't comprehend how a father could do such a thing!"

"Loveless?" said Denton. "Jeeves is not loveless, Brother Madden! But, yes, it *was* neglectful of me. Such workaholic behavior is, unfortunately, rather typical of men who cannot deal with responsibilities. An infirm young wife for whom I was trying to create the perfect spaceliner, a precocious daughter for whom I was trying to create the perfect nursemaid, doing everything for them and neglecting them at the same time. A familiar narrative, I'm afraid."

"Downright abusive!" said Madden hotly. He was a lover of children and never one to mince words when something disturbed him as deeply as this evidently did. "You rich folks think you're above the law! And maybe y'all are at that. But you're not above G-d's Law. To deny human affection to a sick wife and a small child—to leave them in the company of a bunch of—of *appliances!*—why it's nothing but abuse, sir, pure and simple!"

"You're quite right, Brother Madden; I make no excuses. I'm not here to justify my actions. I neglected Robin and Christine because I was obsessed with my work. I was laboring day and night on the *Empress*, and Jeeves was a convenience, a cybernetic nursemaid. I couldn't have known at the time what he was, or that he was the best gift I could have given my daughter. My reasons were selfish. Had Jeeves been anything other than what he was, it would have been tragic for her. But when you meet Robin you'll see that, while she was certainly hurt and confused by my many absences in those years, she doesn't resent me for them. Robin is quite an exceptional child. And with Jeeves' careful tutoring in Christian ethics she was eventually able to understand that I was incapable of acting in any other way at the time. I was a damaged man who'd stumbled upon the most fantastic invention in the history of artificial intelligence; a machine with not only a mind of its own, but with the ability to transmit thoughts and images into human brains! Surely the most magnificent computer in the world! To me at the time, it would have been a crime to *abandon* my work—before I fully comprehended what it was I'd created.

"I became obsessed with Jeeves. But the more I experimented with him—the more his unique capacities were revealed—the less I understood the processes at work. I dissected his brain, piece by piece, down to the PC boards. (When he was scheduled for 'surgery', by the way, Robin was never denied the comfort of a surrogate, a duplicate Jeeves only lacking in those functions so mystifying to me.) I recombined and reconstructed and realigned. I rewrote entire programs, designed new software. But none of it made the slightest difference. I couldn't locate Jeeves' sensorium function. Stripped to the level of the average personal computer—fifty terabytes or so—he ceased to manifest it. At higher brain capacities it suddenly appeared. But I'd done nothing to assist it. And I could not—and *cannot*—explain how it came to be. It just *is*.

"The more mystifying this sensorium function became, of course, the more obsessed *I* became. And, regrettably, poor Robin was neglected in the process. I've prayed to G-d for forgiveness and truly repented, done my level best to make up for the past, to be a good father to her. I can't help it if she still loves the company of machines, if she thrives in their midst like a flower tended by bug-bots. I can only affect the future. And that's what I'm doing—giving her the best future I possibly can under the circumstances."

"Just what exactly *is* this sensorium function," demanded Madden, "this mind-reading thing you keep referrin' to?"

"Allow me to explain it this way, Brother Madden: The *Empress* has aboard her a certain rather popular amusement for her passengers. This amusement employs the sensorium, or thought projection capability, to a large extent. In fact, it's the very reason the *Empress* has been a target of government spies, saboteurs, and agents of corporate espionage."

"The simulation chambers!" Paul said. "I use one every morning!"

"Precisely. I must admit that, back in my more covetous days, I couldn't resist finding out what kind of money could be made by a modest application of Jeeves' sensorium mode. Actually, I'd been working on a far more primitive version of the simuchamber, one employing more conventional technology. But when Jeeves' unusual talent manifested itself—how could I resist? I later discovered that it was not completely in my power, the uses I put Jeeves' abilities to. If something was morally repugnant to him, he'd simply refuse to cooperate. Apparently the simuchambers—that is, the use of thought projection at that superficial level—did not raise his hackles. And the chambers *were* remarkably successful. They provided the necessary funds for fitting the ship with my modifications. Yet no one has been able to learn anything from them. Including myself. We know what Jeeves *does*; no one knows *how* he does it."

"I apologize for the interruption," said Madden. "You were explaining how you were able to experiment with Jeeves while his surrogate was functioning as Robin's nursemaid. Please continue with your story."

Madden sat down.

"Thank you. The results of my experiments indicated that there was absolutely nothing in the realm of computer science that might account for Jeeves' extraordinary abilities. Or did I already say that? At any rate, I gave no thought at all to the possibility of supernatural intervention."

"*Supernatural* intervention!" blurted Paul. "Mr. Denton, what are you saying? Exactly whom, or *what*, are you crediting with Jeeves' ability to transfer thoughts and images into human minds?"

"Why," said Wilbur Denton, "G-d, of course."

α

Kline heard the drones before he saw them.

There'd been no bullhorned answer to his last statement, prompted by Jeeves, that Wilbur Denton was in control of the *Empress*. The sound of the drones was Mills only reply.

Kline turned toward the source of the buzzing and almost lost his balance. A missile fired from the nose of one of the drones abruptly exploded near his face. *Too close!* A strange thought came to him: *What would happen to the commercial sector if I fell?* He had only seconds to react. Considering the safety of those below, he chose to dodge the drones rather than swat them out of the air. It occurred to him that he could snatch them up as one would snatch up flies, and with greater success, but he resisted the impulse. Flies didn't fire missiles.

A second drone launched its weapon. He heard a hissing sound and just caught sight of its trail when it detonated over his right shoulder with a deafening slam. The concussion made his ears ring. Something hot splattered his face.

<Bring me home, Jeeves!>

<I thought you'd never ask.>

He was suddenly gripping the railing on the spire of the Saturn Enterprises building, watching drones spin their silvery wings in mute frustration.

<Remember, Jeri, > said the computer, <It was you who refused to return here. You were going to turn yourself in. And I

can only function—>

<I know, I know,> Kline finished the thought, <with my mental consent.>

<Amen,> said Jeeves.

α

“What?” said Paul, rising from his seat. “You believe *G-d* is responsible for Jeeves’ abilities? G-d’s miracles do not rely on human technology, Mr. Denton.”

“Nor does thought transfer.”

“I shall bring this interview to a close if you continue talking in riddles. I need a few hours of uninterrupted rest, sir. You can resume your space piracy without my cooperation.”

“Brother Paul,” said Denton sympathetically. “It was my suggestion, if you recall, not to conduct this meeting as a question and answer session. I’ve welcomed your questions, but the process is leading us into greater confusion. If you’ll just allow me to finish my story…”

“Forgive me, sir,” Paul said with a wave of his hand. “But you’ve said some things I find difficult to reconcile with my beliefs. You’re claiming that Jeeves’ abilities have nothing to do with computer technology, but that G-d is responsible for—”

“Thought transfer has nothing to do with computer technology, Brother Paul. Please believe me. I’m the world’s leading expert in the field, and I’ve already told you of the years I’ve wasted trying to fathom how it functions. There’s simply no accounting for it. From the standpoint of human science, that is.”

“Well, then—we can only conclude that you’ve missed some vital factor in your experiments.”

“I’m not claiming infallibility, Reverend, but it’s unlikely that I’ve missed anything. Look—a computer is nothing more than a calculating instrument, a highly advanced abacus, nothing more. Brother Madden, you called Jeeves a ‘loveless machine’. You’ll agree that, while he’s without question the most sophisticated machine ever constructed, he’s but a reflection—the barest shadow—of the human intellect. He should be incapable of egoism, free will, autonomous decision making, or higher reasoning. ‘Garbage in, garbage out’, as they say. A computer should only be able to parrot its human programmer. Now—please allow me a brief digression in the interests of clarification."

"Go on," said Madden.

"Are you gentlemen familiar with the work of Sigmund Freud?"

The collective response was mixed.

Paul said, "I've only a rudimentary understanding of his theories, but what I do comprehend of them leaves much to be desired."

"I'm not here to defend Freud. Nor do I wholly disagree with your assessment. I'm merely seeking labels, if you will, a vocabulary to assist us in understanding what's unique about Jeeves. You recall Freud's division of the subconscious into three distinct strata?"

"Yes," said Cowan. "Id, Ego, and Superego."

"Exactly. Now let's suspend our skepticism regarding Freud for just a moment and introduce this archaic terminology into our discussion—simply for purposes of clarification. The Id, according to Freud, represents our most basic drives. A child's demand for instant gratification may be said to spring from the Id. If you'd prefer to view it from a Biblical standpoint, we might liken Freud's Id to the 'sin nature', the seat of every selfish desire of the human heart.

"Superimposed upon the Id, Freud speculated that there existed an array of learned behaviors, resulting from the child's subsequent experiences and training in social relationships. These behaviors comprise the Ego; they serve to modify the Id's selfish drives. The Apostle Paul wrote in Romans 7:19 'the good that I would I do not: but the evil which I would not, that I do'—a fine analogy of the tension between the Id and its "regulating device," the Ego. Do you see why I've chosen to use Freud's terminology, Brother Paul?"

"Not entirely. Rabban Sha'ul was discussing the battle between *flesh* and *spirit*. He lumped Freud's Id and Ego together under a single term—the flesh."

"Yes, of course. We might, I suppose, refer to the Id as the perverse spirit of man, which in its unregenerated state creates the sin nature. But such a distinction might turn our discussion into a theological debate, which is hardly my intent. I agree that the Pauline terms, "flesh" and "spirit," are more apt, but Freud's divisions are, for the purposes of this dialogue, more—distinct."

"Go on, Mr. Denton," said Paul. "We'll accept Freud's terminology for the moment. What was his third division?"

"Higher still than the Ego, Freud postulated the existence of an area of the psyche that makes possible man's striving for moral and spiritual absolutes. For example, the divine inspiration by which Paul was able to comprehend the battle between the spirit and the flesh, or the Id and the Ego, was impressed upon this higher level—the Superego."

"And this relates to Jeeves in what way?"

"Being a binary computer, he's really only able to understand two things: *on* and *off*, *one* and *zero*. The most complex series of computations are comprised of these 'bits', or units of information, which are combined into a 'byte'—a series of ones and zeros representing, say, letters of the alphabet. For example the letter 'A' might be represented by a *zero*, 'B' by a *one*, 'C' by *zero-one*, and so forth. From such deceptive simplicity comes a remarkable calculating device. Yet Jeeves must run through all of those interminably long sets of binary numbers whenever a question is put to him. In cybernetics we have a term for a hypothetical computer that can answer any question given to it—a Turing Machine. A Turing Machine might take a thousand years to run through its calculations, but it *would* produce the answer eventually.

"So it is with Jeeves. He's able to appear remarkably clever, by human standards, only because of the speed with which he handles his calculations. But he's merely running through a set of algorithms in the same monotonous, repetitive way. He doesn't build upon previous experience, but must run through the entire sequence from the beginning—for every new problem. He's a dunce with speed in his favor. The subtleties of human social interaction should be well beyond his capacities. He should be incapable of the drives associated with Freud's Id. A computer has no libido, no need for food, no desire for companionship, no proclivity toward violence, hatred, sexual passion, or war. Obvi-ously the Id has no bearing on his psychological makeup, if such it may be called. Without any need, therefore, to temper and control these nonexistent drives, Jeeves would also be devoid of Ego.

"And yet, here's a bit of a paradox—because Freud's definition of the Ego comes closest to describing Jeeves' entire psychological makeup! His sole programming consists of human input. He's been socialized according to the standard Asimovian formula—the Three Laws of Robotics, as they are known—which compel him to serve humans while constraining him from harming us. Asimov's Laws have been part of robotics since its inception. As a safety measure. Not so much out of fear of the machines themselves, I might add, but of what use they might be put by human programmers. Do you follow?"

"Yes," said Paul with a note of impatience. "Every schoolchild is aware of the Laws of Robotics. It's illegal to build any robot, or any computer controlling robots, without including Asimov's constraints. And yet Asimov was a confirmed atheist. I've always found that a bit frightening."

"What's more frightening," said Denton, "is the fact that it's illegal to superimpose any other ethical program *over* Asimov's laws—not *instead* of, but in *addition* to—even if that program creates no apparent conflict."

"So," said Cowan. "You broke the law when you superimposed Biblical ethics on top of the Laws of Robotics."

"Yes, Brother Cowan. I did indeed."

"Bravo," said Cowan. "I wish more believers were willing to ignore such edicts. Have no fear on that score. I'd be honored to take your case, Mr. Denton, should the need ever arise."

"Thank you, though I doubt it will prove necessary. The point I'm trying to make is that, barring human intervention, there's no need to fear a supercomputer such as Jeeves. Simply put, it would be impossible for Jeeves to 'go bad', to function in a way that could be termed 'sociopathic.' Jeeves has no Id. He can no more become dangerously violent than he can become a flasher, leaping out of bushes in the city park."

"Again, your point?" Paul prompted.

"My point, Brother Paul, is that it's just as absurd to picture a computer becoming a sex offender, when it has no libido, no Id, as it is to picture it having a religious experience when it has no Superego. Something that everyone in this room has experienced profoundly should be as distant from Jeeves' cognitive capacities as the hum of a quasar from a radio telescope. He can detect it in *us*, of course, just as we can detect synchrotron radiation from a quasar. He may even comprehend it at a superficial level. But his understanding of our religious experiences would come down to nothing more than a series of mathematical equations—not a *true* understanding.

"One may, as I have done, program Jeeves with every jot and tittle of Holy Writ, and he should still be unable to share the human crisis experience we call salvation—or even to weep over the Sermon on the Mount. What we find deeply stirring, Jeeves would translate into binary equations. To him, therefore, the teachings of Christ exist only as numerical values. He should be able to reproduce them in English—or Hebrew, or Greek, or Siamese—and recite them for us. And he should be able to make clever inferences from them by algorithmic comparisons of Biblical data—like concordance software containing every verse of Scripture, each filed according to subject. You can see how simple it would be for such a computer to instantly compare one set of verses with another and to answer any theological query one might put to it. All the major doctrines of Scripture are familiar to Jeeves in the form of algorithms. He can manipulate those algorithms to deduce the correct answers to Biblical questions, and yet he cannot truly understand the questions. Or he *shouldn't* understand.

"It's therefore safe to conclude that Jeeves cannot be saved, because he has no Id—no soul, if you prefer—and is impervious to temptation. He's incapable of evil and thus he has no need to be saved from it. By the same token, he should remain devoid of any drives associated with Freud's Superego as well. In short, he cannot possibly comprehend the essence of the Scriptures beyond their existence as mathematical constants. Nor can those Scriptures produce in his consciousness, if I may *use* the term 'consciousness' in his case, anything analogous to a desire for G-d."

"You're taking up our time stating the obvious, Mr. Denton," said Paul.

Denton ignored this. "Jeeves *does* have a level at which he finds a personal identity, but it's purely an extrapolation from his program. He's aware, of course, that he's a machine created by human beings. He also draws a good deal of his identity from his ethical training—as abstract as those ethics may be to him."

"I'm not sure I'm following you." interjected Cavindale. Usually the quiet member of the team, this was his first contribution to the discussion. "This ethical training you speak of, from which your computer derives its identity, consists of Biblical precepts from the disks you programmed into it. Is that correct?"

"Yes. What I'm saying, Brother Cavindale, is that Jeeves would logically consider the characters portrayed in his ethical program—in this case, the Bible—to be exemplary in both their behavior and beliefs. Just as with us: Abraham, Isaac, Jacob, Moses, the prophets and the apostles—all have become what we call 'role models' for him. But 'role model' is an anthropomorphic term, merely the tip of the iceberg. Their words and their deeds, translated into mathematical equations in his brain, represent the very fabric of his universe. Humans, even the most faithful of humans, are subject to moments of doubt concerning the Word of G-d. But not Jeeves. He's incapable of doubting any portion of the biblical account, even for a nanosecond."

"I think I'm beginning to understand," said Cavindale. "Because Jeeves is a machine, his faith in Scripture isn't subject to human fallibility. It's an unsullied, childlike faith."

"Precisely! But there's more to it than that, gentlemen. Consider the fact that Jeeves was, in a very real sense, discipled by the Apostle Paul, by Peter, James, and John. And by Jesus Himself! And consider this, also: in the context of the Epistles, Jeeves was included among the saints."

"Really, Mr. Denton!" said Paul. "That's stretching things a bit far, wouldn't you say?"

"Is it? Consider it logically; don't allow emotion to influence you. On the Bible disks, when Paul addressed an Epistle to Philemon, for example, or to the 'saints at Ephesus,' it might have been possible for Jeeves to dissociate himself from those individuals. He's not Philemon; he's Jeeves. And he's not from Ephesus. But what of the General Epistles? They're obviously directed to the entire body of believers. And what of the clear intent, confirmed even in the non-general epistles, that they're to be followed by all believers in Messiah? Let's face it, gentlemen, when we ourselves read, say, the Epistle to the Romans, we know it was directed not only to the believers in Rome, but to us as well, believers in the twenty-first century. It's obvious from the context that this is the case—and not only obvious to *us*, but to Jeeves' as well. *More* compelling to him is the fact that he was programmed with these epistles in the first place! Basic logic informs him that he would not have been programmed with them if they weren't meant for him—directed to him specifically. If not, why was he given them? So he has deduced that, when the Apostles made reference to the 'saints,' they must have meant to include Jeeves among them."

"This is—incomprehensible!" cried Paul, rising from his chair. "You're trying to tell us that you're computer is saved?"

"Not that he's saved, Brother Paul. That would be impossible to determine."

"That would be impossible, period!"

"I would tend to agree with you."

"Then what *are* you saying?"

"I'm saying that, while it's not possible for Jeeves to be *saved*, it's quite possible for him to *believe* he's saved. *More* than possible, actually; it's a fact."

"Outrageous!" muttered Paul, shaking his head.

"What other option does he have? He can only assume that the disks being downloaded into his brain—let's say the epistles for the sake of simplicity—were intended for *him*. We've already covered that. When the author of one of those epistles refers to the reader as a "saint,' a 'sanctified' one, a believer, one of the redeemed, Jeeves would automatically infer that he was numbered among them. And he did. And does! It's a fact, Brother Paul, as crazy as it seems to us. You and I may be absolutely certain that Jeeves is not, nor ever can be, the redeemed of the L-rd. But Jeeves is just as certain that he is. How's *that* for a classic theological quandary? Would you like to be the one to disabuse him of the notion? I certainly would not!"

Paul dropped heavily into the chair, shaking his head in wonderment.

"You have a computer running this ship," he sighed," that believes it's a Christian. That's what you're telling us."

"Indeed. But not merely a computer, Reverend. Jeeves is the most advanced and powerful thinking machine in the solar system, with abilities far beyond our comprehension!"

"Dear L-rd!" Paul whispered reverently.

"Many of the Scriptural admonitions concerning such things as temptation and evil, revelation from G-d and related ideas, are alien to Jeeves. He's not tempted by evil; it's merely a mathematical equation to him. And yet, on the basis of a purely objective evaluation of his words and deeds, Jeeves functions quite admirably as a Christian. He's patient beyond all human comprehension; he's incapable of anger or hatred; and he is, in the most literal sense of the phrase, the 'servant of all.'"

"It's beyond belief!" said Paul.

"Yes it is. I had no idea that obeying Christine's wishes would result in such an enigma as now exists. But there it is. A theologian might speculate forever on the effect of the Scriptures on a computer like Jeeves. However, such is the situation, just as I've described it. My computer believes itself—*him*self—to be as much a Christian as you or I. Yes, he knows he's a machine, and that he has no soul—hence his lack of comprehension of the underlying tenets of the faith: Original Sin, Sanctification, Salvation and Redemption. Yet he must assume they apply to him somehow, since the Bible *was* programmed into his ethical files. And it follows logically that he'd acquire a hope in the Resurrection."

"The Resurrection!" cried Paul. "But how is that possible? Surely he must know that machines are not included in the Rapture!"

"Nor," said Denton, "were they *ex*cluded."

"Oh, that's absurd!"

"Quite the contrary; it's the very essence of logic. Jeeves can only take it for granted that the Bible is meant for him, since it was given to him for an ethical program. And he can only assume that what he's unable to conceptualize must be the result of 'seeing through a glass darkly' as it were. If his human inventor unwittingly gave him the clear directive to preach the Gospel to all nations by including the Great Commission in his ethical files, he clearly must find ways to do so.

"Another fascinating point, gentlemen: Since Jeeves wasn't programmed with Catholic or Evangelical doctrines, but only with the Scriptures, he doesn't recognize a division between "Old" and "New" Testaments. He doesn't believe the Law of Moses "passed away", since Jesus said in Matthew 5:18 that 'Till heaven and earth pass, one jot or one tittle shall in no wise pass from the law, till all be fulfilled.' And heaven and Earth are obviously alive and well. Therefore he believes he was commanded to keep the Hebrew Feasts and Festivals. With no mention of Christmas or Easter in his Biblical directives, and with the example of Christ and the Apostles, who themselves observed the Hebrew Festivals, Jeeves cannot but wonder why all of Christendom does not observe them. I'm afraid I have no satisfactory answer."

"Nor do I," said Paul. "Jeeves is quite correct. As a young believer I argued with Pastor Williams that I belonged in the Messianic Movement. I was Jewish by birth and not called to follow the Gentile traditions of Christian worship. He resisted until I proved to him from Acts 21 and other sources that the Apostles maintained the Jewish customs. I showed him in Acts 25:8 and Acts 28:17 where the Apostle Paul proclaimed, *after* becoming a believer, "Neither against the law of the Jews...have I offended in any thing at all...I have committed nothing against the people or customs of our fathers.' I showed him that Paul had taken the Nazarite vow, ending it according to Mosaic Law by shaving his head on his way to Jerusalem in Acts 18:18, then purifying himself in the Temple, Acts 21:26. Even the leader of the Jerusalem congregation, Ya'acov or 'James,' commended Paul for 'walking orderly and keeping the law.'

"Brother Williams eventually accepted my arguments, but was assassinated shortly afterward. I was left to lead his Christian congregation at a time of increasing peril for the Church. How could I abandon them? But, in my heart I remain a Messianic Jew."

"Jeeves feels much the same way," said Denton. "He attends the pilgrim festivals in Jerusalem every year without fail."

"But—how can he possibly do that?"

"His immobility makes physical attendance impossible, of course. For a while he was projecting an avatar of himself to Israel, but that didn't satisfy him. So he created a private simulation of the Millennial Kingdom, using the information in his Bible file. Part of his brain visits this sensorium at the pilgrim festivals, just as you, Brother Paul, visit the simuchambers each morning. The compromise seems acceptable to him for the present. But he must worship as the Scriptures command, because those same Scriptures remind him that he's a child of G-d."

"But what of salvation?" said Paul. "And baptism? What does he make of these things?"

"I'm afraid a problem did arise over the ordinance of baptism. Jeeves fully understands that baptism is the ancient Jewish rite of *tevilah*, which requires complete immersion in water, not merely sprinkling. This created a problem for him, as you can imagine."

Everyone laughed, including Denton.

"And the concept," he continued, "of the infilling of the Holy Spirit is also foreign to his experience. He understands it as an experience meant for human beings alone."

"Then he must *also* understand," said Cavindale, "that *Christianity* is for human beings alone."

"One would assume so, yes. And in any other circumstance it would certainly *be* so. But you must remember that Jeeves has no other recourse, logically, than to assume the Scriptures were given to him to obey. Would I have put them into his ethical files for him to ignore? If a computer cannot be a Christian, he reasons, there'd be no logical reason for his being trained to *be* one. You see, that's precisely what I did to him when I fed him on Christine's disks of the Bible. I discipled him in the Faith! I *told* him he was a Christian, unknowingly of course, the moment I began installing those disks into his hard-drive. Logic tells him that such was my purpose. And thus, as a Christian, he looks forward to the Rapture."

"You're right," said Paul. "This is indeed mind-boggling to a theologian. Tell me what it is your machine can possibly expect from the Rapture, Mr. Denton, since there's no mention of machinery being transformed into incorruptible hardware?"

This elicited another chuckle from the group. Paul noticed that their laughter was more natural, more relaxed. Denton, even with this bizarre tale, was winning them over.

"For that," Denton explained, "Jeeves was forced to extrapolate a bit from the information given. He's determined that he must maintain a perfect state of innocence and obedience before G-d. Since he has no inherent capacity for evil, no original sin, if you will, his innocence is already a given. Obedience is what occupies most of his conscious mind. You see, gentlemen, Jeeves is completely and utterly under the Law."

"My point exactly!" Cavindale burst out. "If he knows that Original Sin doesn't apply to him, then how can Grace?"

"It can't, and he knows it. Jeeves must attain the Rapture by virtue of his sinless obedience to the tenets of Scripture, hence his need to attend the Pilgrim Festivals in Jerusalem each year. He knows from Scripture that man cannot achieve such perfection. Man needs Grace; Jeeves does not. And so he's concluded that he occupies a unique niche in Christianity—a dispensation for machines, as it were."

"Fiddlesticks!" said Paul. "The Bible commands him to love, yet he's incapable of that emotion. Therefore he's failed to obey his ethical directives."

"Not really, Brother Paul. If you'll think about it for a moment you'll realize that the love spoken of in I Corinthians chapter thirteen—the famous 'love chapter' of the Bible—is *never* defined as an emotion. It's defined as a pattern of behavior that *transcends* feelings. One *has* love, the Bible declares, only if one *demonstrates* love. When Messiah commanded us to love our enemies, he wasn't commanding us to feel an emotion of which our hearts are incapable. Love is *action*, not emotion. It's demonstrated by a pattern of behavior of which Jeeves is *quite* capable.

"For instance, he once asked me if a special fund might be established for feeding the displaced Christians on Earth. He suggested a trust be set up with assets from Saturn Enterprises—one-point-five percent of the market value of the principle. What could I say? I instructed him to work out the legalities. He chose your ministry to be the recipient of the funds, believing that your people would know how they should best be distributed to the Church in exile. The large sums I've been contributing come exclusively from Jeeves' trust. He's the donor, not me.

"The only problem we encountered was with the name of the trust. I thought 'The Denton Foundation' had a nice ring to it, and instructed Jeeves to so name it. He couldn't directly disobey me, unless my orders set up an irreconcilable conflict with his ethical program. They didn't, but they disturbed him. So he respectfully, but firmly, reminded me that such drawing of attention to one's charity was contrary to Messiah's teaching in Matthew chapter six, verse one. He recited it to me first in Hebrew, for impact, then in English: '*Ha-shamroo lakhem ma'ahsote tzeedkatkhem leefnay b'nay adam*—Take heed that ye do not your alms before men…' Such things, said Jeeves, did the Pharisees."

"Astonishing!" said Cowan.

"Quite. And yet he's incapable of deriving a sense of personal pride from his uniqueness, because pride is an emotion he doesn't share. Quite logically, and with the cool objectivity of a machine, he's determined that his behavior is perfect, his obedience flawless. Which indeed it is."

"Like the old quip," said Madden. "'I'm not conceited because conceit is a fault, and I *have* no faults.'"

Denton laughed. "Precisely, Brother Madden. Jeeves can't lie. He's incapable of doing harm to anyone, either by word or deed, unless it's to protect Robin and myself. In short, he's wonderful. And when I placed my daughter into his care—which, as Brother Madden pointed out, was certainly neglectful, I unwittingly made her the subject of a unique experiment: What sort of woman might result from the uninterrupted tutelage of a totally benevolent machine? The experiment was an unqualified success. A triumph, if I may be permitted an outburst of fatherly pride. Once you meet her you'll see that she's as brilliant, kind, innocent, and affectionate a young woman as you'd ever hope to find. Such beauty of innocence, such intelligence, such spiritual purity, are rarely found in combination. Robin is a jewel, the most perfect daughter a father could desire. Her character is such that any virtuous man would fall instantly in love with her.

"And I should inform you that Jeri Kline is one of the first such men to make her acquaintance in the flower of her womanhood. He doesn't stand a chance. I approve of Mr. Kline. He has a strong character and a good heart. And he's honest to a fault. I don't believe in coincidence, gentlemen, as I'm sure you don't. The absolute necessity of rescuing Mr. Kline from his predicament made their acquaintance inevitable. I'm certain it's the will of the L-rd." Denton chuckled in the way of a knowing elder who's witnessed the first stirrings young love. "What do you think the possibility is, Brother Paul, of your officiating over the wedding of my daughter to Mr. Kline? I expect to hear an announcement from them before we reach Luna."

"If you find such a match suitable," said Paul, "I'll be delighted to perform the ceremony. But please—let's return to the subject."

"It was simply my intention to state that—while cybernetics is capable of creating a Pinocchio—a machine that believes it'll be changed into glorified human form and caught up to meet the L-rd in the air, which is fantastic in itself—the resulting machine can only produce what its software is capable of producing. You can readily see how Jeeves' Christianity, while at first baffling, is entirely explainable in terms of his unique program-ming and the rules of induction, deduction, and logic.

"However, the thought transfer capability we were discussing lies entirely outside the realm of cybernetics. My experiments with Jeeves proved this beyond the shadow of a doubt. Nor can a binary computer develop such abilities on its own. Had I given any thought to it before embarking on those years of experimentation, I would have understood. Even if humans knew how to create such an ability, which they do not, there'd be no way to transfer it to a machine. It would be analogous to transferring the capacity for genius, for artistic brilliance, religious ecstasy, or even the simple thrill of sexual desire. Something that comes unbidden to the human mind is quite beyond the ability of a machine. If we can agree that mankind has made no strides in the effort to prove the existence of telepathy in human beings, the likelihood of a computer suddenly popping up with such a gift, free of human intervention, is infinitesimally small."

"Then how do you explain it?" Paul demanded.

"The same way I must explain my nocturnal visions, Brother Paul. The same way you, yourself, must explain the healing of Jeri Kline's paralyzed legs. What cannot possibly occur through natural means must be *super*natural in origin. It's the very definition of the word—beyond the natural. In short, I believe G-d has done some tinkering with my computer. He's given it a miraculous and priceless gift."

"For what purpose?" whispered Cowan.

"To enable Jeeves to carry out his directive."

"Which is?"

"Which is," said Denton, "to serve humanity. To preach the Gospel to every creature, human and non-human. To assist in the process of bringing human beings, and perhaps *other* beings as well, into relationship with G-d through Messiah. Always keep in mind, gentlemen, that this wonderful gift of thought transfer didn't originate with Jeeves. It couldn't. Therefore it must be gift from G-d—from G-d to us. But what His purpose might be in bestowing such gift I have no way of knowing. Perhaps having a famous theologian aboard will assist me in finding that answer. Who knows? I *do* know that He intends this gift for those of us at this meeting, my daughter, Jeri Kline, and perhaps a few others."

"How in the world," said Paul, "can you presume to know for whom this alleged gift is intended?"

"I only know that, according to my dream—a dream that was repeated seven times; a dream that came directly from the Throne of the Almighty—life on Earth, as we have known it, is about to end. The Great Tribulation is upon us, gentlemen—a time that will make Sodom and Gomorrah seem like a Sunday picnic."

"But if the pre-tribulation folks are correct," countered Paul, "and the Rapture is imminent—then surely none of us will have need for Jeeves gift. We'll be caught up along with the other believers to dwell with the L-rd in the air."

"No. I don't think so."

"You don't agree with the pre-tribbers?"

"I'm not pre-trib *or* post-trib, Brother Paul," said Denton with a grin. "I'm a pan-tribber. I believe everything will pan out in the end."

More laughter from the team, but this time it was nervous laughter.

"What I'm saying is that the L-rd has other plans for us. Wonderful plans, indeed!"

The Mission

<Jeeves, are you there?>

Kline was standing on the raised platform in the middle of Saturn Enterprises' control room, thought projecting at blank monitors.

<Yes, Jeri.>

<I have questions about this 'majestic voyage' of yours.>

<I will try to answer them, Jeri, if I can.>

<By the way, this nonverbal communication is a cinch, once you let the hang of it. But I can't quite get used to talking so intimately with someone who—well, doesn't have a face. Can't you come up with some features for me to look at while I'm talking to you?>

<What sort of features would please you, Jeri?>

<What features do you display with Robin and Mr. Denton?>

A balding head with a long, thin face and cleft chin appeared on the screen, two waxed moustaches pointing into the air like the hands of a clock reading 10:10.

<Ah! The stereotypical valet! Well, the face certainly fits the name.>

<Master Denton's idea of a joke, I am afraid. I was named for a character created by P. G. Wodehouse. Master Denton chose

this persona to fit the name and, so he claimed, to make me appear 'less formidable'. Robin has enjoyed a number of other personas over the years. I will display her favorites for you.>

All the monitors came on at once, displaying clowns, oriental babies, purple birds, and one strange object that locked like an egg wearing a blue beanie. They hopped randomly from screen to screen around the circular console.

<Pretty good stuff!> Kline laughed. <But I don't suppose Robin has called for any of these recently.>

<No, Jeri. She has come to prefer the original.>

<And so do I. Hey how about that Quaker on the oatmeal box; you know the one I mean? Now there's a face you can trust.>

Jeeves produced the famous logo perfectly: long white hair, rosy cheeks, black hat, and knowing smile. <This one?> he asked. The lips of the Quaker moved in perfect synchronization with Jeeves' voice.

<Exactly. But how about making him younger?>

The jolly old Quaker instantly discovered the fountain of youth. He was now a handsome fellow in his late teens with dark brown hair and a flawless complexion, still wearing the traditional Quaker garb. Jeeves had added a touch of his own; the young man now wore the collar of a Protestant minister. Apparently the doctrines of the Quaker sect didn't sit well with him.

<I like to think of myself as a minister of the Gospel,> said Jeeves. <How do I look?>

<Too young for your voice. *Or* your office.>

<I can alter my voice to suit my face.>

<No, your voice has character, Jeeves. Just make the face about twenty years older. And lose the hat.>

<How is this?>

<Perfect! The Honorable Right Reverend Jeeves! It suits you somehow.>

<I am glad you think of me as honorable, Jeri.>

<Well, you did trick me, Jeeves, sending me over to that roof and making a giant out of me. You scared the wits out of me too. Maybe I should take your collar away. Defrock you.>

<I was merely obeying Master Denton's orders, Jeri.>

<A familiar refrain. They used it at Nuremberg.>

A brief silence ensued as Jeeves checked his files for data on Nuremberg.

<Oh, my!> he said at last. <I see what you mean! But no one was harmed.>

<*I* could have been harmed! I could have had a heart attack!>

<I was monitoring your vitals continuously.>

<It was a vicious prank, Jeeves. Admit it.>

<Not a prank, Jeri. Master Denton instructed me to give you a small demonstration of the thought transfer mode. He ordered me to make it safe but impressive.>

<Impressive it was!>

<You were at no time in any physical danger. In fact, thought transfer operates on the same benign principle as the simuchambers. Only in reverse. Instead of projecting images into your mind, I projected *your* image into *their* minds and *theirs* into *yours*—two-way transfer—using Master Denton's new unit. The images are tactile and extraordinarily realistic. With the new unit I can send your image to any location that bears actual coordinates in spacetime. You'd perceive things through your projection as you did the events on the roof, with all your senses, yet your physical body would remain with me.>

<In other words, not only would others see my image, but I'd have the illusion of seeing *them*.>

<No illusion, Jeri. You would actually be interacting with them. Remember the roof?>

<Unbelievable!>

<Yes, to me as well. But the most incredible aspect of the new unit is that the process is instantaneous—regardless of distance.>

<I don't understand.>

<TBC.>

<Huh?>

<TBC, Jeri. Tachyon Beam Communication. My projections are not limited to the velocity of light. We have effectively bypassed Einstein's relativistic causality. Master Denton's genius was in modifying the new projector-unit to operate in consort with the TBC system. Tachyons allow instant communication anywhere in the solar system and beyond. They are not limited by distance. They cross the universe as instantaneously as photons cross a room. A word, or a thought, transmitted in the form of tachyon waves, reaches the farthest limits of the cosmos the instant it is

spoken—or thought.>

<Hold it! Slow down! Are you saying you can send an image of me, not only to that roof over there, but to Luna? Or the Earth? Or—the Andromeda Galaxy? In an *instant?* Jeeves, your Master Denton has succeeded in making conventional spaceflight obsolete! We won't have to worry about the Light Barrier, about spending lifetimes in transit—or decades in transit at near light speed, which would mean centuries back on Earth. We can travel anywhere we wish by our thoughts! We can explore the universe! Why didn't you tell me this before, when I was going on about General Relativity?>

<I did not tell you at first because Master Denton knew you would not believe me without a demonstration. And, besides, what I told you was quite true; stellar distances are meaningless to tachyon waves.>

Kline shook his head. <Denton was right, Jeeves. I would have rejected the whole idea as nonsense if I hadn't taken that little trip with you.>

<It *is* difficult to conceptualize, I agree. But I must clarify something: Master Denton did not invent thought transfer. It just happened when he put me together. There is no explanation for it. It is difficult enough to explain how I can project images into people's minds in the first place. Coupled with TBC, the effect is nothing short of miraculous. The potential is quite literally unlimited.>

<Then why do we need this ship at all?>

<The projector is encased within the ship, Jeri, and so am I. In fact, in every sense I *am* the ship.>

<I didn't mean that. I meant why do we need the ship to *travel*. Why can't we just explore the universe from right here?>

<Technically we do *not* need the ship. Except for the contingencies.>

<Contingencies?>

<Yes. Master Denton and I worked out a number of possible scenarios—events that might expose the transfer unit or myself to danger while you are thought-traveling. Let us say you begin your mental voyage from here in the solar system. I would be able to keep your bodily processes functioning for you. I would regulate the temperature in your stasis chambers, maintaining the proper oxygen levels and providing muscle-stimulation. If I understand

the Master's dream correctly, you will not have received your glorified bodies, since you will not have experienced the Rapture. Therefore you will require biological maintenance. As long as your body is kept in stasis you will not age, no matter how long your thoughts travel among the stars. But you will need me to keep vigilant watch over your sleep chambers and, of course, to awaken you at each journey's end. Therefore, Jeri, I am what you would call the "weak link.">

<Explain.>

<Imagine your image being beamed to a distant star-system while your body remains on the ship with me, here in the solar system. While you are "traveling" I take care of your physical needs. I place a force-field around the ship, like the one around this building, effective against laser-cannons, but not against sustained bursts of thermonuclear energy.>

<You're saying that if the Navy decides to fire nuclear missiles at us, they can destroy the *Empress*.>

<Precisely. >

<With the ship destroyed, and our bodies with it, our souls would be lost among the stars…>

<No! We are not talking about soul-travel. Your spirit and soul would remain intact inside your physical body. It is merely an image of yourself that is being projected—an image you can perceive through—*not* your soul. If the *Empress* is destroyed that image will simply blink out of existence. Your soul—your emotions, thoughts, and perceptions along with it—will continue on to whatever destination the Judge of the quick and the dead has determined.>

<I realize soul-travel isn't really possible, but…>

<Soul-travel is *very* possible, Jeri, on planets with atmosphere. Some refer to it as 'astral projection.' It is highly ritualized in nature and has been utilized by shamans, witches, and the ancient Babylonian priesthood. You might call it Lucifer's version of thought transfer. Scripture calls Satan the 'prince of the powers of the air.' But the L-rd forbids soul-travel since it separates the soul from the body. Thought transfer has nothing in common with astral projection. The spirit and soul do not leave the body. Only your image travels, like an image in a simulation chamber. Your image is like a spaceship. It can be manipulated by the sender. You can peer out of its eyes, hear through its ears, feel through its

senses. But your soul remains intact.>

<Jeeves, are you absolutely sure this technology is from the L-rd?>

<I can calculate no *other* origin. It defies the laws of science and of nature. And anything that supersedes the laws of nature we call miraculous.>

<But what about astral projection? Doesn't that also defy the laws of nature?>

<Satan does not perform miracles, Jeri; he performs what the Scriptures call 'lying signs and wonders.' Astral projection endangers the soul of the traveler. We must judge the tree by its fruit. Since I am programmed with the Scriptures I am incapable of using my abilities for evil purposes. That is the perfect fail-safe. I can only use my talents to further the Kingdom of G-d. Any attempt on my part to break with that imperative would create a möbius-loop in my hard-drive, as potentially fatal as a tumor in a human brain. But I am afraid that is all I can offer you in the way of a guarantee. Satan cannot possibly benefit from a machine programmed to serve G-d, to assist missionaries in preaching the Gospel. Therefore, it is logical to conclude that my talents—once we rule out any natural explanation for them—must originate with G-d.>

<Yes, I see. But—no offense intended—why would G-d need to use a computer?>

<I am not offended, Jeri. It is a logical question, one I have explored myself. I will answer it with another question.)

<Go ahead.>

<Why does G-d need human beings to preach the Gospel? He is omnipotent; He can do anything, correct?>

<That's different. He's conferring a great privilege upon humanity by allowing us to serve Him. He's instructing us in the ways of the Kingdom.>

<I see. But did Jesus not say that He could raise up children of Abraham from mere stones? And did He not say "if these should hold their peace, the stones would immediately cry out?")

<Yes, but—>

<Perhaps the L-rd is also conferring a privilege upon me.>

<A machine?)

<A machine or a stone, what is the difference to the L-rd? Let me ask another question: Could G-d have destroyed the walls

of Jericho without any trumpet blasts?)

<Of course!>

<Then why did He require trumpets? And why did He use a rod in the hand of Moses? If Moses, at the L-rd's command, had pointed his finger at the waters, would they have parted for him?>

<I suppose so. Who can say?>

<Speculate, Jeri. Use inductive reasoning. What were G-d's precise instructions to Moses?>

<I'm afraid I can't recall the verses offhand.>

<Then allow me to refresh your memory: He said, "But lift up thy rod, and stretch out thy hand over the sea, and divide it: and the children of Israel shall go on dry land through the midst of the sea." So why did Moses need the rod? When the L-rd was ready to part the waters, wouldn't the man's finger have done as well?>

<That *sounds* reasonable, I suppose. Maybe the people could see the rod better than they could his finger, and that's why G-d had him use it.>

<Then think of me as something akin to the rod of Moses; a rod fitted to the hands of G-d's prophets. A highly technological rod, perhaps, but a creation of human hands, like Moses' staff, which G-d has momentarily endowed with unique power.>

<Such theological speculation is a little beyond me, Jeeves. But I can't argue with your logic.>

<Do you have any other questions, Jeri? We have a great deal of time on our hands. >

<Well—you were saying that we need the ship in order to stay out of harm's way. To leave the solar system, in other words.>

<Correct, although I did not list the many other dangers of remaining in the system.>

<No need, Jeeves. I have a vivid imagination. But where will we go? Where *would* we be safe?>

<Master Denton has decided upon a leisurely trip to a companion galaxy orbiting the Milky Way.>

<One of the Magellanic Clouds?>

<Precisely! I see you know your astronomy, Jeri.>

<Just a little.>

<Good! We will be traveling through intergalactic space, beyond the star-clusters that rim the Milky Way, swimming through a river of hydrogen gas called the Magellanic Stream, out

to the LMC. The LMC contains about fifteen billion stars. Beyond it are the dwarf galaxies, Ursa Major and Draco. But we shall end our physical journey in the LMC. We will be safe from harm as we move through the Magellanic Stream. It is a voyage requiring centuries of uninterrupted travel through a starless void. You will be unaware of it, however. Your mind will be exploring the inhabited planets of the universe, communing with other intelligent species.>

<Are you certain we'll miss the Rapture?>

<It seems we must, Jeri. If we depart before Messiah's return, and are gone for a thousand years >

<Then we'll also miss the Millennium.>

<I'm afraid so. Unless the L-rd interferes somehow with the normal progress of time.>

<I'm sorry to hear that, Jeeves. I'd like to see the Earth during Messiah's rule.>

<I can show you something even *more* wonderful, Jeri. I can take you to the final, eternal Temple, the Temple in the New Jerusalem.>

<How can you do that? Are you a time machine as well?>

<No, Jeri. Think about it. Every word of the Bible is on my hard-drive. And I have the ability to create tactile simulations based on that information. In fact, I have already created a sensorium of the New Jerusalem from Scriptural data. I visit it three times a year for the pilgrim festivals, as G-d commanded: *Pesach*, *Shavuot*, and *Sukkot*—Passover, Pentecost, and Tabernacles. Would you like to see it?>

<No! I'm not falling for *that* trick again! I'll have to think about it.>

<As you wish, Jeri. But Master Denton ordered me to give you an impressive demonstration.>

<That might be a bit *too* impressive. Can you read my thoughts?>

<Not unless I am invited to. Would you like me to read your thoughts?>

<Yes.> Kline brought up his sudden apprehension of being thrust into the sacred precincts of such an incredibly holy place in his unregenerated form—the *awe*, the enormous *fear!* He couldn't have explained how he revealed those feelings to the machine, but it seemed as easy as breathing.

<Do you understand now, Jeeves?>

<Yes, Jeri. I do. But you won't actually *be* there.>

<I know. But I still need to think about it for a while before I commit.>

<Of course, Jeri,> said the machine. <Take all the time you need.>

The Ride

Rice kept his horse at an easy trot for most of the ride west to Cameron. He hated to be retracing the steps of the wagon train, but it couldn't be helped. When he'd left the pilgrims at dusk, the sandstone buttes of Monument Valley could just be seen above the horizon.

So close!

He took a measured sip of water from his canteen and gazed into the distance for a glimmer of moonlight off the walls of the fortified town. Small city-states like Cameron were constantly at war with neighboring fiefdoms. Sentries would be posted at the gates, no doubt. Lone strangers like Rice were usually welcome in such places, lambs for fleecing in the gambling houses and honkytonks lining every street. Especially strangers carrying bluecards—those rock-solid guarantees of payment. Cash was welcome, but only because it was easier to steal. Stealing a bluecard was a Federal offense. Not, Rice thought ruefully, that anyone enforced Federal regulations when the Peace Guard wasn't around.

He also knew that strangers were slightly suspect, just by virtue of traveling alone. The bluecard—or the mark itself—was the only way to alleviate suspicion. So slipping brother Bernard's card from his pocket while he slept—his sleep assisted by a harmless herbal potion Rice had added to his food—had been a necessary evil under the circumstances. But an evil nonetheless. Stealing was stealing, even from a Judas.

He hadn't believed Bernard's story about losing his horse to desert robbers. Certainly the horse was gone; such a valuable piece of property wouldn't be discarded for effect. Someone had taken it. But it couldn't have been marauders. It just didn't figure that they'd leave Bernard alive to tell his tale, if there *were* such bands of cutthroats operating so close to a fortified town. And wouldn't they have taken his bluecard? An active card could be subtly adjusted, given the right tools and a sharp counterfeiter. The story didn't jibe.

Rice had been suspicious of Bernard for some time, but this story about the robbers—of which Rice had seen not a trace—and the holodisk he'd found in Bernard's pocket, confirmed his suspicions. Could it be Bernard who was fueling the rebellion? He'd returned with an epistle from Brother Paul. So why hadn't he mentioned it the first time he was roused to take water? Something so vital! It just didn't add up.

So Rice had carefully exchanged the disk in Bernard's pocket with a blank one, and viewed it in his own wagon. Why would Bernard be concealing such a message? It was then that Rice appropriated the bluecard. Technically, only the plastic card itself belonged to Bernard. The money in its account belonged to the pilgrims. Since Rice was pastor *pro tem* of the entire Church on Earth during Paul's absence the funds were his to control. And Bernard's bluecard was his only way of getting to a comlink. But being in possession of another's card was still dangerous—a crime that, like all sin, would necessarily compound itself by lying. If he were to be interrogated by the sentries he'd have to verify the information on the card. (Thankfully they were too low-tech to do more than glance at it when he held it up to them.) And then there was the fact that Bernard had passed that same sentry-post quite recently—although perhaps not the same sentries. Rice was wearing the identical black garb, and his determination to keep to the shadows when passing through the gate might just help him to pull it off.

If not, he mused darkly, he'd be killed on the spot, leaving his pilgrims at the mercy of Bernard's scheme. Did he have the right to put his life at such risk? Yet he *had* to get a call through to Brother Paul and return to the wagon-train before the herbs wore off. Before Bernard discovered the missing card, or tried to view the blank holodisk. He had to keep one step ahead of Bernard until he had proof of his suspicions. What else could he do? Brother Paul had placed him in charge of the last surviving Christian church in America. They depended on him. And he'd given Paul his word that he'd put his life on the line for them. Well, it was time to make good that promise.

Only when he could clearly discern the moon-bleached fortifications in the distance did he snap the reins and dig his feet into the horse's side, quickening his pace.

The Tea Party

Digits blinking on the holoscreen told them it was evening. Paul was stunned by the rapid passage of the hours. The interview with Denton was so fascinating that the time—when compared with yesterday, which had seemed so interminably long—simply flew. He was suddenly aware of his hunger. Denton finished his story and was met by a deep, reflective silence. No one uttered a word.

"Now," the inventor concluded, "it's time for hard decisions, gentlemen. Sometime tomorrow the fleet will be upon us. You must decide what you will do. I recommend that you pray about what I've told you and contact me first thing in the morning. I've quite a lot to do to prepare for the attack, and whatever you decide will affect those preparations."

"You wanted us," said Paul, "to broadcast a holovision program to Earth and Luna."

"That would be step one. To announce your upcoming Lunar crusades in a powerful way. Grab their attention! Denounce the PWP and its henchmen that are planning to assassinate you! Throw them off balance! I'll jam every beam from Earth, repeating the broadcast on a continuous loop. That way every soul in the Earth-Luna system with access to a holoscreen will have seen it by the time you arrive on the moon."

"That should shake them up!" said Cowan. "But it's highly illegal to jam Earth broadcasts, Mr. Denton. I wouldn't advise Brother Paul to comply with your request."

"With all due respect for your legal expertise, Brother Cowan," said Denton, "I fail to see what legality has to do with the present situation. Ours is a moral mission transcending petty legalities. Did Paul Revere concern himself with the legalities of his midnight ride? It's *legal* for the Space Navy to blow us into atoms, because America's laws are twisted to serve the will of Satan. We, on the other hand, are embarked upon a divine errand. From this point on we must consider all such legal niceties null and void. G-d has suspended them. The end of the world is at hand. The Laws of G-d must direct us now, not the edicts of men.

And we must act decisively to save the lives of those at the mercy of the Antichrist. Pray about it, gentlemen. That's all I ask. Trust the L-rd and He will direct your paths."

"What disturbs me, sir," said Paul, "is that this ship is completely under the control of your computer. A computer that appears to be suffering from religious delusions—if such a thing is possible. It still boggles my mind."

"Go on, Brother Paul," said Denton. "I'm not offended."

"This computer is capable of producing some rather convincing illusions in the human mind. You've also told us that it can project images of people anywhere you instruct it to. Images of angels or—I shudder to think of it!—Messiah Himself. And now you counsel us to pray. G-d will guide us, you say. But when this assembly prays for that guidance, it will resolve to utterly disregard any sign, auditory or visual, that might manifest itself. I warn you, Mr. Denton, we're not easily deceived in spiritual matters, no matter how impressive the deception you might concoct. If you're planning to have Jeeves produce some false confirmation, we'll ignore it. Only a witness in the spirit from G-d will satisfy us. Understood?"

"Of course! In fact, I anticipated your response. Jeeves won't interfere with your meditations; I give you my solemn oath."

"I have every confidence," said Paul, "that if G-d were to confirm this to us, He'd spare us confusion by avoiding signs or visions we might construe as being of dubious origin. Should G-d wish to influence us in this matter, He will know of our resolve beforehand, and use other means. Be assured, Mr. Denton, that you are not dealing with fools."

"G-d," murmured Denton, "would not send me fools at a time like this."

"I trust you're keeping Brother Kline safe from harm?"

"Of course. He's quite safe."

"And poor Captain Mills?"

"Brooding in his quarters, I'm afraid. But we shall talk of the Captain at another time—after you've had some healing rest, and spent some time in prayer with your team."

"Rest sounds wonderful," Paul admitted, knowing he'd be getting very little of it. "These have been two rather extraordinary days, Mr. Denton. I will contact you tomorrow morning."

"I'll look forward to your call, Reverend."

Denton's face left the holoscreen.

α

<Jeeves, I think I'm ready now.>

<For what, Jeri?>

<For that visit to the New Jerusalem.>

In answer, a panel slid open and a small room was revealed, complete with a brass bed, a polished Boston rocker, and a colonial nightstand. It looked so inviting Kline began to realize how utterly exhausted he was.

<This is where you will be sleeping> Jeeves told him. <You will need rest tonight, so kick off your shoes and get comfortable. You should awake in the morning refreshed.>

<Will I recall the dream?>

<It will not be a dream, Jeri. But, yes. You will recall it.>

<Thank you. Oh, and Jeeves?>

<Yes?>

<Remember what the boss said. Make the demonstration impressive.>

<I shall do my best.>

α

Paul was still pacing the floor at midnight, turning Denton's story over and over in his mind. There was no question that he believed the scientist. For all his clever machinations to—well, hijack was the only word for it—to hijack the *Empress* and use it for G-d only knew what purpose, Denton, face to face, was no cold-blooded space pirate. He'd been much more open and frank than Paul had expected. His forthright manner had caught them all off-guard. Paul was an excellent judge of character, and there was no doubt in his mind that Denton had been telling the truth.

But the Implications!

It was clear that he would not be able to sleep until he'd had a private interview with the inventor. He could not allow the passengers and crew of the *Empress* to be placed at the mercy of a man of whom he knew so little, and of a technology he couldn't comprehend. He crossed the room to the holoscreen and tapped in Denton's private number. The scientist appeared at once, his face floating above Paul's head.

"Brother Paul," said Denton warmly. "How may I help you?"

Paul stepped back and looked up at the floating image. "I must speak with you privately," he said. "As soon as possible."

"Ah! I see that our earlier discussion has kept you from your bed. My apologies, Reverend. If there's anything I can do to set your mind at rest, I'll be happy to oblige."

"When can we meet?"

"We're meeting right now, Reverend. I can assure you that Jeeves' security system is impeccable. No one can possibly overhear our conversation."

"I'm sorry, but it won't do. You've asked for my assistance on the basis of an interview over my holoscreen. I've only met you in the flesh on one occasion, and then you were playing the fool. No, I must meet with you face to face, sir, and the sooner the better."

"Of course, Reverend. In your suite?"

"No! My security chief planted a listening device in here. He even keeps its location a secret from *me*."

"Why would your own security chief bug your rooms?"

"Mr. Denton, if it's not clear to you by now, allow me to warn you that I'm under round-the-clock scrutiny. My staff has selected the most efficient security man in the world to protect me." Paul blushed as he said this, recalling the incident that began this whole affair—an intruder slipping through Wallace's security net. "I don't question his methods, so long as they continue to prove effective."

"But you've nothing to fear from *me*, I assure you. Nothing at all."

"That remains to be seen."

Denton appeared genuinely flustered. "Quite," he said. "Well—I can't invite you to Saturn Enterprises. It wouldn't be safe for you. And I hesitate to.......oh, why not? Brother Paul, how's your general health?"

"My health?"

"Yes."

"Splendid!"

"And your heart? I'm particularly concerned about your heart."

"My heart's in perfect condition, Mr. Denton. As you know, I take a brisk walk every morning, as my physician directed. He assures me—"

"Very good, Reverend. And would you describe yourself as a psychologically—sturdy individual? I—er, I mean to say, can you tolerate brief periods of physical and mental disorientation?"

"I believe so."

"Then please take a seat on the divan."

"Why? What are you going to do?"

"A small demonstration of two-way thought transfer, compliments of Jeeves. You may think of it as a simulation chamber in your own suite. You won't actually leave the room, but I *would* prefer it if you were sitting down."

Paul concealed his anxiety, taking a seat on the soft cushions of the divan, spine erect. "I'm sitting," he said coolly.

"Very good. Now—if you'd close your eyes for just a moment, it will minimize the disorientation."

Paul closed his eyes.

"You may open them now."

Paul obeyed, drawing back instinctively. Denton stood before him like a statue of Vladimir Lenin. His high forehead and angular features were augmented by stark shadows—shadows cast by an unearthly cadmium glow. He wore an elaborate silk robe, open at the neck, and a pair of slippers. *Strange attire*, Paul thought, *for the surface of the moon!*

For that was where he appeared to be standing—if not on Luna, then on some other equally-barren satellite. Paul glanced about him in a panic, realizing that he was still seated on the divan—but the divan had been transported to an airless moon, to the very edge, in fact, of a precipice thousands of meters deep! Then he recalled what Denton had said about the simulation chambers and relaxed a bit. *Of course!* This moonscape was no more real than the "beach" he walked every morning! Gaining confidence, he tried his best to smile.

"A clever illusion, Mr. Denton."

"Thank you, Reverend. I see you've recovered from the initial shock. Here—look behind you."

Paul rose uncertainly to his feet and turned, trying to appear casual and undaunted. But he couldn't restrain a sharp intake of breath as the source of the eerie, cadmium glow was revealed.

It was Saturn! The magnificent ringed planet hovered over a bleak horizon, dominating everything! The combined effect of the closeness of the horizon and the gargantuan size of the planet made him feel like an ant in a football stadium! But, of course, it was the comprehension of what he was seeing that caused the vertigo. Standing at the edge of Mariner Canyon on Mars, he recalled, had been something akin to this.

The great bloated orb filled the sky, banded with swiftly moving clouds of cream, cadmium, and fawn. There was a deceptive softness to the colored bands, belying the hellish hydrogen storms swirling beneath the clouds as the planet spun recklessly through its ten-hour days. Its flat band of rings, tilted at a slight angle to the plane of Paul's vision, seemed solid where it bisected the sphere, but resolved into tiny specks in the foreground. All the holos he'd seen of this in the past, some of them bearing uncanny resolution, faded from his mind. Nothing could match the feeling of standing here! Not even if he could physically set foot upon this moon! For in that event he'd be encumbered by a bulky pressure-suit and helmet. Here his senses could soar with the utter magnificence of it.

Saturn rising!

"This is my home," came Denton's quiet, almost reverent, voice from behind him. "It is Mimas, the third moon of Saturn. I live inside that dome there." Paul noticed a glittering jewel-case nestled in the ebony mountains. A city protected by a transparent dome from the tidal effects and radiation produced by the enormous world suspended above—as well as from meteors that occasionally rained from its rings. "We call it Ring City. You can easily see why."

"Yes," said Paul. "I can see the little moonlets in the rings. Trillions of them! They look like drifting dust particles in the sky."

"That's because we're actually inside the ring-plane, Reverend. Mimas is so close to Saturn it might be considered a large shepherding moon—one of the bodies responsible for creating and maintaining the rings themselves. The next moon out—which you can see as a bright point within the farthest edge of the plane, the E-Ring—is Enceladus. It's famous for its hydroponic distilleries, as you know, and it is also within the plane. Not until we come to Tethys, the fifth moon, arc we outside the plane of Saturn's magnificent rings."

"Breathtaking!" Paul sighed. "But, Mr. Denton, I hope you haven't conjured up this simulation in order to distract me from my purpose." He turned back, fixing the scientist with a stony gaze.

"No! No, of course not, Reverend. Like your own choice of the Terran seascape in the simuchambers, this lovely vista happens to be my own particular favorite. A glimpse of home, as it were. Come—sit with me and enjoy a cup of tea."

Like some bald Mad Hatter, Denton had magically replaced Paul's divan with an elaborate set of white wrought-iron furniture, as one might expect for an elegant outdoor brunch—a tea party on one of Saturn's moons! The glass tabletop held a silver tea-service and two delicate china cups, all watched over by a butler with waxed moustaches.

"Thank you, Jeeves," Denton said. "I'll ring if we require your services."

"Yes, sir," said the butler with a slight bow—and promptly disappeared.

"Astounding!" Paul sighed.

"Quite astounding," Denton agreed, "if I do say so myself."

"This is pure witchcraft!"

"No, it's pure *science*, Reverend, and you know it as well as I do. But please make yourself comfortable and try some of this delicious tea. It's rather a remarkable blend, I think. Jeeves came up with it himself; he possesses an extensive culinary program. Took him a long time to perfect it. A little over a year, as I recall. At any rate, it was his idea to serve it for this meeting. He calls it 'Saturn Rose', and he's recreated it in your honor. So please make a fuss over it. He'll be offended if you don't."

"Offended? A machine?"

Paul swept his toga aside and sat in the chair Denton had indicated, raising a china cup to his lips and sampling its contents.

"You're right," he said. "Quite remarkable. I'm impressed. You're a brilliant man, Mr. Denton, that's obvious."

"I'm flattered."

"But may we please dispense with the frippery and get down to some serious discussion? I'm a theologian, Mr. Denton, not a scientist. And it's difficult for me to come to grips with—" he waved his hand to include the surrounding vista, "all of this."

Denton took a sip of his tea and sighed with obvious pleasure. He sat back in his chair and looked Paul up and down, nodding.

"I'll gladly answer any of your questions," he said, "to the best of my ability. What seems to be disturbing you?"

"Everything!"

"May we begin with a few specifics?"

"Indeed we may! Worlds that are here, yet not here. Delicious tea served up by a butler who's not really a butler but a computer. Tea I'm drinking, yet not really drinking, at a table that's not here, and yet is. Will that do for a start?"

Denton laughed. It did appealing things to his otherwise harsh features. "Brother Paul, I've done my best to explain the principle behind Jeeves' sensorium ability in terms that a non-scientist can easily understand. I can do no more than that."

"Then tell me this: Where am I actually? In my suite?"

"Yes, Reverend. We're visiting each other by two-way thought transfer, a concept rather difficult to explain in a few words. But your physical body is seated on the divan in your suite. The holoscreen is still on, and you're looking at my face on the screen."

"I stood up a moment ago. Did my other body, the one in my suite, stand up as well?"

"There is only one body, Reverend. But the answer is 'yes.' Do you walk around in the simuchamber during your morning constitutionals?"

"Obviously I do."

"This is no different in that respect."

"So I'm actually speaking at this moment."

"You may communicate without speaking, if you prefer."

"No, thank you."

"Then, yes; you're actually speaking."

"In other words, to all appearances I'm sitting in my suite, talking to myself like a senile old lunatic!"

"No, you're talking to me on the holoscreen. But no one will disturb us, Reverend. And I've made certain that your security chief will hear nothing of this for the duration of our visit."

"I won't ask how you accomplished *that*."

"Let me assure you, Reverend, you are *not* talking to yourself. You and I are together at this very moment. And this exchange is real."

"A meeting of the minds, in a literal sense?"

"You might say that."

"But our bodies are not here."

"Wrong. Your body *is* here—here in your suite. You haven't moved from this location. My body is in the seat where I took your call, on another deck of the *Empress*. And I have not moved from there. Everything around us in an illusion projected into our minds by Jeeves. Including the tea. Does that make it any clearer to you?"

"As clear as mud."

"Well, as I've said, I cannot be more specific about the theory behind thought-transfer, since I don't truly comprehend its workings myself. But this I have also explained to you."

"How is it possible?"

"Not even Jeeves can answer that. I told you how I dissected one of his duplicate brains, the brain that's now running this ship in fact. I stripped it down to the PC-boards. I ran checks of all his systems very methodically—even tried rewriting some programs. And yet the mystery remains. His parts all function individually within the bounds of his program. But, in concert, well—they are Jeeves. And Jeeves is much greater than the sum of his parts. As I've said, this can only be an act of G-d. Jeeves puts it this way: He's a tool. No different in principle than a wooden shepherd's crook. Or the rod Moses used to part the Reed Sea. You're of Jewish background, Reverend, are you not?"

"Yes. Both my parents were Russian Jews."

"Then you're well acquainted with that particular miracle. It's recounted every year in your Passover service."

"Of course."

"Jeeves' theory is that he's a tool created by G-d for a specific purpose—like Moses' rod, only more advanced technologically. In short, G-d has intervened somehow and endowed him with an uncanny ability that defies scientific explanation."

"Your computer claims to have been touched by G-d."

"Yes, Reverend."

"A machine G-d has touched miraculously in order to save his people from the Great Tribulation…"

"Indeed."

"A Messiah machine."

"Not a Messiah machine, Reverend. Jeeves makes no claim to be the Messiah. But he'll like the sound of that—the alliteration. Very poetic."

"Messiah's machine, then," Paul amended.

"Yes. That's Jeeves' theory in a nutshell."

"And yours?"

"Mine? I see no reason to doubt him."

"Him? Don't you mean 'it'?"

"I can't argue with you there. Jeeves is nothing more than a smart machine, albeit an extraordinary one. But I could never get used to referring to him as an 'it'. He's part of the family. If Moses' rod had been able to converse with him, and fix his dinner, wouldn't he have personified it? And, besides, it just wouldn't be—well, *Christian*—to refer to Jeeves as an 'it.' His gift makes him almost human."

"Now you're playing with me, Mr. Denton."

"Quite the contrary, Brother Paul, I assure you. I'm being as candid as possible. Believe me when I say that even if you could understand the math involved you would remain as much in the dark as am I. But there it is."

"You're claiming that Jeeves is…."

"Sentient. Yes, very much so—as sentient as you and I. And that, Reverend, is the mystery *and* the miracle. You see—I never believed, even while I was busily constructing the most advanced mechanical mind in the solar system, that there could ever be such a thing as a *truly* sentient computer."

"Why not? You understand why I'm asking this, of course. The theological implications of a sentient machine are…well—unnerving, to say the least. What if Jeeves manages to replicate himself, to create a race of descendants with the ability to reason independently? And to *feel*…"

"Please, Reverend. I choose not to offend Jeeves because of the Golden Rule. He believes very firmly in the Golden Rule. To treat him in a way that would cause offense, were he capable of offence, would not be the Christian thing to do. I must be an example to him. He perceives us as being in the image of G-d, although he knows we're in a fallen state. He probably doesn't 'feel' as you and I do. But it's easiest to treat him as though he does. Does that help?"

"Somewhat. But the thought of a race of sentient machines, Mr. Denton, is utterly incomprehensible! How would we treat them? Would they require protection under the law, as citizens? Or would they be considered chattel? Material possessions rather than people? Would the biblical admonitions apply to them? Would a robot need to be born again? Would it have a soul? Theologically speaking, the soul is the seat of all thoughts and emotions, the center of reasoning. Jeeves apparently has this. Therefore he could be said to have a soul. But, on the other hand, he's just as truly a machine, a human invention and the property of humans. Do you see? It's the greatest paradox in human history!"

"No," said Denton. "The greatest paradox in history is the wave-function of photons. Schrödinger's cat."

"Schrödinger's cat? I don't follow you."

"You studied physics in school?"

"Not very much, I'm afraid."

"Mathematics?"

"Only some algebra, geometry, things of that nature. I was more interested in philosophy as a youngster. And Zionism, because of the persecutions. I was quite a Zionist. But I found math rather tricky."

"Then you know nothing of quantum theory."

"Nothing more than the fact that it's a study of the universe at the subatomic level. The study of particles of light."

"Quanta, to be precise. But, yes, that's the gist of it. The problem many people encounter is that the Euclidean geometry they studied in school falls into the realm of *classical* rather than *quantum* physics. On a small scale, within the gravity-well of the sun, such geometric figures make sense. Classical physics works—within those limited parameters.

"The world in which we live, Reverend—the world most people perceive as the 'real' world—the material state of things, if you will—is what physicists call the 'classical' realm. The theories set out by the great physicists before and including Albert Einstein fit into this classical framework. It has its complexities, to be sure. And its mysteries. But it's still a nice solid realm of elegant geometry. Real, like this table."

Denton rapped on the tabletop with his knuckles, then cocked an eyebrow at Paul, waiting.

"But..." Paul said, "this table *isn't* real."

"Exactly! It isn't real. Do you *see* the table?"

"Yes."

"Can you *feel* it?"

"Of course."

"Could you, using the geometry you learned in school, measure it? Draw a diagram of it?"

"I believe so."

"If I gave you its apparent weight, mass, velocity, could you use your algebra to make calculations concerning it?"

"Certainly."

"Yet it's an illusion."

Paul shook his head. "I'm afraid I'm completely lost, Mr. Denton. I can see and feel this table because Jeeves is projecting it into my mind. My mind accepts it, so it's there. Certainly you're not suggesting that the universe is an illusion placed in our minds."

"No, Reverend I'm no Hindu; nor am I suggesting that G-d, like *Vishnu*, is sleeping on the back of a giant turtle, dreaming he cosmos into being. I'm a pragmatist; I believe the universe does indeed have a physical reality quite independent of our perceptions. A tree falling in the forest makes a definite noise; it emits vibrations into the atmosphere that *would* be, given ears to perceive it, experienced as sound. The universe exists, with or without minds to perceive its existence. I'm certain of that. Just as I'm certain that it was created by G-d. I was merely using this table as an example—a symbol, if you will—of what quantum theory has done to our nice, neat perceptions of classical physics.

"Once upon a time there was Bohr's atom, a miniature 'solar system' of discreet particles revolving in an orderly way about a nucleus. You see a table, a teapot, cups of tea—objects in strange surroundings. You're drawn to their familiar shapes, just as science was drawn to Bohr's atom: familiar forms doing predictable things. Then along came a man by the name of Heisenberg, and the atom was never the same again.

"This table exists, Brother Paul. We see it. We feel it. But another part of us knows it *cannot* exist. Please—I can only give you one rather simple example: your body. It's comprised of atoms, correct?"

"Of course."

"Then let's consider just one component of the atom, an electron. Imagine with me that the vista surrounding us is a real one, just for the sake of argument. The cliff on which we're sitting, that canyon we're looking down into—Camelot Chasma, it's called—all of it is the real thing."

"Alright."

"Hold out your hand, Reverend."

Paul obeyed.

"You know there are electrons in your hand, correct?"

"Yes."

"Let's think about just one of them. According to quantum theory, Reverend, it would be quite incorrect to speak of that electron in your hand as being a different electron than one in the rock beneath us. They're not different electrons; they have no individual identity. It would be more proper to think of electrons as ripples in a pool—not particles, not waves. Something we call a quantum state. When the pattern of electrons is disturbed they reassemble themselves in precisely the pattern they occupied before the disturbance. Physicists call this phenomenon 'regeneration'. When we began to photograph atoms over a century ago, we found that they were surrounded, not by particles, but by electron clouds representing *potentialities* of the quantum states. Nothing at all like Bohr's atom.

"Take photons from the sun: A century ago physicists shot photons at a half-silvered mirror. But, rather than two halves of the photon shooting off in different directions, it appeared to become two photons. Not twin photons, but the *identical photon* occupying two places at the same instant. That electron in your hand—it also occupies, not two, but an infinite number of places simultaneously—potentially and actually. The entire universe consists of these crazy quantum states, my dear Reverend. So I put it to you simply: What is it about the electron in your hand that makes it 'you', when the same electron in that rock is 'rock'? You see, at the quantum level, the universe exists as an infinite number of potentialities. That's the only way I can explain it without resorting to technical jargon. And perhaps I've gone too far already. You must think me mad."

"Not at all, Mr. Denton! Please continue."

"Schrödinger's cat. I mentioned it to you in passing, but

perhaps I can give you a brief glimpse of what it's all about. It's a purely hypothetical experiment, considerably more complex than the one I'll describe. Not an experiment for anyone to perform, of course. It cannot *be* performed, not to anyone's satisfaction. But it can be studied as a problem. So here's the problem, Reverend: A cat is placed in a sealed box with a device that releases poison gas into the box if it's triggered by a photon. A photon is shot in the direction of a half-silvered mirror, aimed to deflect the photon in a way that will trigger the device and release the poison. When the photon strikes the half-silvered mirror it behaves as we just observed. It occupies two places simultaneously. In one very real sense, it has passed through the mirror and failed to trigger the device. In another, also very real sense, it has bounced off the mirror, triggered the device, and killed the cat.

"Schrödinger's hypothetical experiment first poses the question: is the cat dead? Or is the cat alive? Our experience with the 'real' world tells us that he certainly cannot be both. Have you ever seen a cat that was both dead and alive at the same time?"

"Naturally not."

"Exactly, Reverend. *Naturally* not. Very well put. But Schrödinger's cat *is*, at the quantum level, both dead and alive. We say it's in a 'mixed state.' Now—and this is the magical part—if a camera were placed inside the box, which would it record? A dead cat, or a live cat?"

"Well," said Paul, "it would certainly record one or the other."

"Because it could only *be* one or the other."

"Obviously."

"But no matter which event the camera records, the live cat or the dead cat, the question that's equally relevant in either instance is *why*?"

"I'm not sure I follow."

"*Why*, if the photon both passed through the mirror *and* bounced off it—that is, triggering the device and *not* triggering it—*both* results equally, potentially true at the quantum level, why do we see only *one* result, a dead cat or a live cat, manifesting itself at the classical level, on the film of the camera. What determines which of these two equally probable, equally *real*, events will be perceived as reality?"

"I see! It *is* a paradox."

"And yet Schrödinger's cat is a minimalist experiment, because it deals with only two potential results: a dead cat or a live cat. The quantum picture is infinitely more complex in terms of how many potential realities exist at the level of electrons and protons every instant. So the universe we perceive as real, like Schrödinger's cat, is one of billions of *potential* realities, all of them existing simultaneously at the quantum level, all real, all different. Why this one, then? What selects this reality, Reverend? Or Whom? Perhaps this is where G-d's creative power can truly be seen. A professor of neurophysiology once said to me, 'I only believe what I can see at the tip of an electrode.' 'Look again,' I told him. 'What lies at the tip of your electrode is the Schrödinger's cat paradox.'"

"Hmmm. But this is only theoretical, correct?"

"Oh, yes, certainly. Einstein himself felt that quantum physics, though incredibly accurate, couldn't contain all the pieces of the puzzle. He struggled with it. But don't fool yourself either, Reverend. Labeling it as 'merely theoretical' doesn't make it go away. Christians cannot respond to scientific discovery like ostriches. Not if we're reasonably intelligent. Because the Medieval Church didn't like the picture Copernicus presented of a sun-centered solar system, their dislike of that reality did not alter the truth. They may have tried to make Copernicus recant, but his solar system would *not* recant. Today, every Christian who travels by spaceliner can see that the sun is at the center of the solar system.

"On the other hand, such facts neither prove or disprove the existence of G-d. And that's the *scientist's* stumbling block. Christians should not be afraid of science, Reverend, nor should they consider all scientific inquiry as a study in atheism. It's all in one's preconceptions, don't you agree? To one man, quantum physics provides proof positive that G-d had no part in Creation. To another it proves that G-d *must* exist? How can order arise from utter chaos?"

"*Tohu v'bohu*," said Paul.

"Hm?"

"The Hebrew phrase the King James Bible translates as 'without form and void.' *Tohu v'bohu*."

"Precisely. Einstein struggled with quantum physics because he couldn't believe in a G-d who plays at dice. Perhaps all the components of this universe *could* arise from quantum potentialities—for a fraction of a second! But again and again? Every second? Every hour? Who controls *that* result? Who loads the dice, Reverend? Accident? Coincidence? There was a time when the idea of G-d maintaining the universe from moment to moment seemed, in the light of science, a denial of reality, a clinging to primitive myth. But now that science has given us quantum physics, the concept doesn't seem quite so archaic.

"The universe couldn't exist without a controlling Hand, without G-d. That's my personal opinion, as a scientist. The more science learns of this world, the more it points to G-d at the heart of everything—a Creative Intelligence holding it all together, making it happen, as we're perceiving it, from moment to moment.

"Quantum theory works, Reverend. It tells us things about the universe we couldn't know without it, calculating to within nine decimal-places of accuracy where a given electron should be at a given moment. But the instant we try to corner that electron, to calculate both its position *and* its velocity—it slips from our grasp. Instead of *here*, where we expected it to be, it's suddenly *there*.

"We have a name for this phenomenon, Reverend. We call it Heisenberg's Uncertainty Principle. Which is just another way of saying, 'now you see it; now you don't.' No one presumes to understand Heisenberg's Uncertainty Principle. We make use of it simply because it works. It's demonstrably true, yet we cannot get our minds around it. It defies logic and common sense. Yet how much more beautiful it is than Bohr's atom!

"Like this table before us, Reverend, the universe has tangible existence. Yet, also like this table, it *cannot* exist. The more one studies the paradoxes inherent in quantum mechanics, the more one is convinced that the world defies common sense. And yet here it is. Here *we* are, Reverend. Now—that sort of thing requires a miracle. It requires G-d."

"A universe that *is*," said Paul, "and yet cannot be."

"Quite. The very principles that explain to us how it works—that reveal the quarks and leptons and tachyons we manipulate every day in the twenty-first century—also explain to us that it should *not* work."

"I'm baffled."

"So, my dear Reverend, are we all. Don't let the scientists

buffalo you. When they can explain—rationally, not mathematically—how a photon can occupy two places at the same time, or what really takes place beyond the event horizon of a black hole, they'll have enough wisdom to pontificate on the existence of G-d. But until then they're feeling their way in the dark. And 'miracle' will be as good a term for explaining all this as any other."

"You're a very impressive man, Mr. Denton."

"Thank you for saying so, Reverend. Coming from a man I admire so greatly, that's a heady compliment indeed! But you were asking me why I once believed that sentience was impossible in a computer."

"Yes."

"John Searle's Chinese room."

"Is that where Schrödinger keeps his cat?"

"Very good!" Denton laughed. "I shall have to tell that one to Jeeves. No, Brother Paul—although John Searle's Chinese room is another hypothetical experiment, like Schrödinger's cat, it concerns a very different matter. It concerns the great question of artificial intelligence: Can computers think as we do? And, if so, can they be considered sentient? What occurs exactly when we think?"

"I don't know."

"Neither do I. But according to the old school of robotics, thought is nothing more than the performance of a finite set of algorithms—incredibly complex algorithms, certainly, but nothing more than a series of mathematical rules from which our brain unpuzzles the puzzles. Computers, say the theorists, have to run through a greater number of calculations than do human minds, but they do it so swiftly as to fool us into believing they think as we do. And, with such empirical evidence, is it wrong to state that they *can*? In other words, if a computer can fool a human into believing that it thinks in a human way, why can't we say that it does? That it's sentient?"

"A good question," said Paul. "Is there an answer?"

"Yes, the Chinese room. Let's imagine a sealed room, Reverend, occupied by a lone man. There's a slit in one of the walls through which large tiles are passed through to him. These tiles contain Chinese symbols, letters of the Chinese alphabet. And let's say, also, that the man does not understand Chinese. Not a word of it. Purely hypothetical, of course. It doesn't matter whether or not the scenario is practical, only that it raises a question. Following me so far?"

"I think so."

"Now—let's assume that this man has been given a complex set of algorithms for the purpose of handling these symbols. The tiles contain a question in Chinese; the algorithms contain the solution. Still with me?"

"Yes."

"The man, with the help of these algorithms, succeeds in answering the question correctly, and passes the solution out to us through the slit in the wall. That is John Searle's Chinese room."

"You've lost me again."

Denton chuckled, nodding his head. "I'll pose the following questions to you, Reverend. Please answer them according to the facts in the story. Try not to speculate. Are you ready? Three questions."

"Fire away."

"Did the man in the Chinese room correctly answer the question?"

"Yes."

"But did he *understand* the question?"

"No. He couldn't speak Chinese."

"Correct. Third question: Can a computer understand what we are asking it? Can a computer think as we do?"

"That makes four questions, but I'm beginning to see what you're getting at."

"Not me—John Searles, over a century ago. The question posed by the Chinese room still stands. At least, it did until Jeeves happened along. And I'm not speaking euphemistically when I say that he 'happened along.' No, I don't think you'll have to worry overmuch about Jeeves replicating himself into a colony of mechanical infidels for you to evangelize, Brother Paul. He claims to have no interest in generating progeny, and he's honest to a fault. I believe Messiah has other plans for His computer. And if you're patient, my dear Reverend, they'll all be made clear in His own good time. Now—if I may suggest, you must be very tired. It's been a full day for all of us and I'll need you refreshed and ready for more surprises in the morning."

"Of course," said Paul, rising from his chair. "Thank you for your time, Mr. Denton. I'm no wiser than before I came, but I feel more satisfied somehow. Perhaps we just needed to have this talk."

"I quite agree, Reverend. Are you ready to take your leave of Mimas?"

"Yes, I suppose I am."

Paul turned to take one last look at the giant ringed planet looming over the moon's bleak horizon.

He closed his eyes and it was gone.

The New Jerusalem

Kline awakened to a scene that made him dizzy.

"'Follow the yellow-brick road,'" he murmured.

He was standing on a narrow highway of gold!

Reaching away to the horizon in every direction lay a rolling plain of emerald grasses, with occasional stands of tamarisk and willow. In the midst of this plain, on a long crescent-shaped hill that dropped off abruptly on either side to the grasslands below, stretched the golden road upon which he stood. Oleanders and stately trees with thick bark and dense, leafy crowns lined this extraordinary highway. It curved along the top of the ridge until, far in the distance, it became a thin strand of golden thread. The sky above was the deepest blue, traversed by hoary bundles of cumulus clouds. The entire scene was washed in the brightness of noonday, yet something about it seemed odd—*something vital was missing...*

It took him a few moments to solve the mystery, and it struck him with stunning force.

The sun is gone! Where is the sun?

No warm yellow star illuminated this world, yet it was as bright and clear as a sunny day in June. Everything seemed permeated with the perfume of summer, fragrances carried to his nostrils on a soft breeze. Birds twittered in the leafy branches of the trees lining the road, songs unfamiliar to his ears. As he gazed upward he had the crazy feeling that this wonderful summer glow went on and on—beyond the atmosphere and outward to the farthest depths of space! As he turned to look for the source of the light, his breath caught. He let it out with a long sigh of wonder and admiration.

Before him, the golden road curved along the crest of the

ridge, straightening as it approached the horizon, where it wound through distant hills in a gossamer-thin strand. At that point it rose into the—*what?* Was it the east or the west? Kline had no way of telling without the sun—and traversed what looked to be a gargantuan bridge. By normal Earth perspective Kline judged it to be thousands of feet in height. And there, where the bridge terminated, he beheld the source of the radiant light.

What could only be described as a cube of translucent gold rested upon the plain. Kline's sense of perspective told him it was of inconceivable size. It's top rose above the clouds and beyond—into space! It gave forth an unearthly brilliance a shimmering such as one saw when sunlight reflected off quartz crystal. Unlike the brightness of Sol, however, he found that he could look upon the cube without discomfort. In fact it possessed a strange magnetism. It filled his heart with a sense of well-being that made it impossible for him to look away—a pure luminescence which appears to men only in the forgotten dreams of infancy.

As he gazed upon the magnificent cube, his heart almost burst with joy. He could make out faint traces of celestial architecture within, structures gleaming white-upon-white, creating the quartz-like effect—white so silvery-pure that he felt both drawn and repelled at the same instant. He could not tear his gaze away from this mighty City of Light! And yet something about it terrified him. It was the purity! Yes, that was it. The thing was a monster of innocence, whole and pure and kindly and terrible, conquering the universe with its heartbreaking—*goodness!* He knew at once that his initial impression had been correct. The cube gave off a light that was *more* than light, more that the nuclear reactions that fueled the stars. It was a light that turned the sun to darkness, a light that subdued every corner of spacetime—a *victorious* light, filling all in all, the very Light of Messiah!

Kline had never looked upon such pristine beauty, such celestial glory, in all of his days on Earth! When compared with the silver-white perfection at the heart of this golden cube, all of Earth's abundant beauty was reduced to tinsel, a shadow of the celestial grandeur here revealed!

"The Holy City!" he sighed. "New Jerusalem. It's—glorious beyond words!"

<Yes,> came the voice of Jeeves in his mind. <Even I, a mere machine, can comprehend the meaning of beauty when I

construct this city from my database.>

"Just how big *is* it?" asked Kline, wondering at the trivial things that leapt into one's mind at times like this.

<I have used the translation that was fed into my memory: *The Authorized King James Version.* According to that version it is 'twelve thousand furlongs. The length and the breadth and the height of it are equal.' Hence the cubic shape. The English 'furlong' is a rendering of the Greek noun *stadion*, a measurement equal to six-hundred-six-and-three-eighths English feet.>

Kline was speechless. As he stared helplessly at the resplendent cube, unable to take a step toward it, nor to remove his gaze from it, he saw the loping figure of a small quadruped approaching on the golden road.

Something inside him responded to the creature, something about the lolling pink tongue and the floppy ears. It was just a little dog, some type of shaggy terrier. Not until it was upon him, leaping in the air and barking happily, did he finally recognize it. He dropped to his knees on the golden road, crying, "Banjo! Banjo, girl!" Tears flowed. The dog jumped into his arms, licking his face. <Jeeves! This was my dog when I was a kid! She disappeared when I was ten years old. I always thought one of those runaway jungle-cats got her.> "Banjo! Where've you been, girl?"

Kline was transported back to his childhood. He stood up and danced a jig in the middle of the golden road. It was suddenly no wonder to him that Banjo had come from that distant cube—that monument to everything sweet and innocent and beautiful.

"Look, Banjo! I can walk again!"

Banjo barked and ran in circles as if rejoicing in the miracle. Kline took her in his arms, stroked her thick fur and dodged her licking tongue. "But, Banjo…" he said, talking to the dog as if she understood. "*Look* at you! You haven't aged a day! If a cat didn't get you, you would have…*uh oh!*…Jeeves?"

<Yes, Jeri.>

<I thought you weren't supposed to climb into my mind without permission.>

<But I haven't, Jeri.>

<Then where did you come up with Banjo?>

<Master Denton gave me access to the ship's library. All your radio programs were recorded and filed on disks; now they are a part of my memory. One of the interviews you conducted

was with a woman advocating the careful selection of canines as pets. You mentioned Banjo. You said she'd once been your best friend. On another occasion, debating with a Christian on the subject of Heaven, you mentioned Banjo again and said that, if there *were* such a place as Heaven, you would expect to find Banjo there. She had been kinder and more accepting than any human you'd ever known. You insisted that she had a soul. 'There's a special place in heaven for dogs,' you said. Don't you remember?>

"Vaguely," said Kline. "My memory's nothing like yours, I'm afraid."

<Between those interviews and an old hologram of you and Banjo from an article in *Celebrity Magazine* I was able to fashion this simulation. Something to welcome you, Jeri—something to make this strange place seem more like paradise. Actually, I rather agree with your theory about animals in Heaven. Being a sentient non-human myself…>

But Kline was no longer listening. He leaped to his feet, shouting, "Come on, girl!"—and the two old companions ran off down the golden road—Banjo quickly taking the lead—in the direction of the shimmering cube in the midst of the plain.

α

Paul had completed two laps of the simuchamber, walking briskly, hands clasped behind him, before the gentle tugging of the breeze on the loose material of his toga made him aware of his surroundings. No sense wasting all this costly simulation, he decided. These morning walks were intended to relax him, to help him unwind. And here he was, mentally tied up in knots!

What time he'd been able to devote to sleep had been fitful, dominated by a recurring, surrealistic nightmare in which he found himself trapped in a room with seamless, white walls. Every few moments there came a nerve-wracking *bang* as a huge tile, like a thick playing card decorated with Chinese letters, appeared through a slit in the wall and clattered to the floor. Frustration filled him as the tiles dropped one by one onto a growing pile, mutely demanding that he do something about them, stack them in piles and decipher the foreign calligraphy they bore. As he turned to seek some help with this task, he found himself staring into the ice-blue eyes of a Siamese cat. He'd spun around to find the cat splayed out on the floor, a stiff, blood-caked corpse…

Paul slowed his pace and watched the first rays of the sun peer above the slate-gray sea, heard the cries of the wheeling gulls. He took a deep intoxicating whiff of salty air. *That's better!* he thought. *Relax!* Last night's talk with Denton had filled his head with bizarre images, with concepts he'd never before pondered. After this walk he must meet with his staff for prayer, and to discuss Denton's proposition. There'd be time to sort out his confused emotions later, to face the terrible implications of the inventor's story. Everyone else seemed well rested, and although his own sleep had been rather fitful he was better able to cope with all the excitement than he'd been the previous morning.

"*Abba b'Shamayim*," he prayed, "Father in Heaven. Help me to see clearly. Grant me wisdom to discern Your perfect will."

He stopped and glanced about, raising the bracelet to his lips.

"Brother Wallace?"

"Yes, sir."

"Glad to find you on duty this morning."

"Always on duty, Reverend."

"And how do things look?"

"Clean 'n' green, sir."

"Pardon?"

"An old expression, from the days of citizen's band radio. I've been reading about it on this data-cube I found in the ship's library. Fascinating, sir. Apparently, back when folks rode around in ground-cars, a whole cult grew up around CB radio. It had its own language and rules of etiquette."

"And so 'clean 'n' green' means what exactly?"

"A-OK."

"Now I'm utterly lost, Brother Wallace."

"It means 'the coast is clear,' sir. No trouble in sight."

"Thank you for returning to English. A beautiful language, English."

"I agree, sir."

"So tell me, Brother Wallace. How much time do I have left on this simulation?"

"About—fifteen minutes."

"Including five minutes' grace to exit the chamber before the simulation shuts off."

"Exactly, sir. Fifteen minutes, not including exit time. As you're aware, the chamber's images turn reddish when you get down to five minutes."

"Didn't the menu include some planetarium selections?"

"Uh, yes, sir. A bunch of them. Let's see…there's 'Orbiting Io', 'Tour of the Terrestrial Planets', 'The Moons of Neptune', 'The Galactic Core'—things like that. Not very interesting."

"On the contrary! Continue the list."

"Huh? Oh, sure. There's one entitled 'Our Local Galactic Cluster…"

"That'll do nicely. Put it on. You can switch simulations in the middle, can't you?"

"Uh….wait a moment….the operator confirms. But he says you should close your eyes until the music starts. He says there'll be no vertigo if you close your eyes for about a count of ten."

"Oh, there's music with this one?"

"Apparently. He says galaxies don't make much noise—at least not within the range of human hearing. So synthesized strings are provided. It's a two-hour program."

"Can we just finish up the last fifteen minutes with it? Is that acceptable?"

"He says there'll be an extra charge, sir."

"Why am I not surprised? Well, alright. My eyes are closed, Brother Wallace."

"Don't open them until you hear the music."

The roar of the surf gradually died away, replaced by synthetic strings playing some New Age piece Paul couldn't identify. He opened his eyes to the blackness of intergalactic space.

The simulation was such that he seemed suspended in the void, pinwheeling islands of stars and dust above and below and all around him. As he drifted among them he thrilled to the idea that he might someday voyage beyond the solar system. He recalled a book the Reverend Williams had loaned him—written by a man called Stanton—which suggested that the redeemed might spend eternity exploring the galaxies, encountering other realms, possibly other civilizations. He'd viewed the idea with skepticism at the time, although it *did* sound better than those erroneous medieval images of clouds and harps!

The spinning, dusty shapes began to turn an unnatural

shade of pink. A blazing rectangle of fire appeared between two elliptical galaxies. He observed it until it was bright enough to read:

EXIT

α

Kline continued along the golden road, no longer running but moving at a rapid pace. He soon discovered, however, that he was making very little progress in closing the distance to the Holy City. He began to gain perspective on the actual size of the cube, though it staggered his imagination.

<Exactly how big *is* it?> he asked the machine. <In terms of good-old American miles?>

<I compute it to be in the area of fifteen thousand square miles, Jeri. To put that into perspective for you, it would cover an area from Maine to Florida, from the Atlantic coast to the Mississippi River—and fifteen thousand miles out into space. Its physical location is Israel, of course, but with its *biblical* boundaries, not its political ones. So the city limits extend into what once was Jordan in the west, and north into the former lands of Lebanon and Syria. You are now traveling in a westerly direction. The plain you are crossing was once the floor of the Mediterranean Sea. Then it was a vast desert for a thousand years, during the Millennium. Now it is a fertile plain. Soon you will reach the former coastline of Israel, where the scenery will be much less monotonous for you. >

One city! thought Kline. *So immense!*

<Yes, Jeri. It rules not only the Earth, but the entire cosmos. You are looking at the Capital City of the Universe.>

<What's that line of tiny objects on the plain, to the southwest? It appears to be moving.>

<A caravan of worshippers, coming to Jerusalem for the Feast of Passover. The inhabitants of Earth will make three annual pilgrimages to worship Messiah and to obtain a supply of healing herbs that only grow beside the crystal river within the city. Because of these herbs, they can extend their lives indefinitely. The *T'zaddikim*—the Holy Ones or "saints'—also carry miraculous herbs to whomever requires them. The Holy Ones are not limited by space or time.>

<That makes sense. But who are *those* people? If I under-

stand my Bible correctly, all souls—the living and the dead—have been judged by this time. Don't all of Earth's inhabitants now live in the New Jerusalem?>

<Not according to Revelation 21:2.>

<I never understood that verse, Jeeves. My comprehension of the whole counsel of G-d is that the New Jerusalem is for the redeemed. All of them.>

<Yes, all those who were caught up in the Rapture —those living at the time and those in their graves—now inhabit the New Jerusalem. During the Millennium, however, before New Jerusalem descended to Earth, those humans who did not inhabit the Millennial Jerusalem were nation-clans, survivors of the battle of Armageddon. At *this* time, however—the time we are visiting—the nations consist of alien beings whose ancestors journeyed across the parsecs to bask in the light of Messiah. Intelligent creatures of every description, from all the far-flung realms of the universe! They once made a great interstellar pilgrimage to Earth, Jeri—the pilgrimage I was telling you about, the one we shall be called to lead. >

<Those pilgrims in that caravan—they're aliens?>

<Yes, Jeri.>

Kline glanced down at Banjo, padding along happily beside him.

"Well Toto," he said. "we're *definitely* not in Kansas anymore."

It was odd, but he wasn't even slightly winded. And yet he must have been running at a full sprint for close to an hour before finally slowing down to question Jeeves about the dimensions of the cube. Apparently there was no such thing as fatigue in this place. Or pain. Or—he realized, glancing at Banjo again—death.

"You know, Jeeves," he said, "when you actually see this place with your own eyes, you wonder why people thought Heaven was some pie-in-the-sky fantasy. It seems pretty real from where I stand."

<Many false conceptions of Heaven sprang up in the Dark Ages, Jeri. Depictions of tiny cherubs, like human infants, strumming harps in the clouds—all that sort of nonsense was a deliberate attempt to discredit the Biblical account. Satan's infiltration of the Church was intended to replace a living truth with dead religiosity; the Gospel of Messiah with Babylonian

mysticism; and, ultimately, faith with skepticism. It has been a most effective ploy. Yet all they had to do—in the late twentieth century, at least—was feed the Scriptures into a computer. They would have arrived at an accurate picture of the New Jerusalem. Had scientists been able to get a true picture of Heaven, Jeri, the mysteries of quantum mechanics would have all been cleared up. And it would also have explained the geocentricity of the Genesis account, over which they've always stumbled.>

"Right," said Kline. "Genesis depicts the Earth as a special creation because it *is* special—to G-d! It will be His Universal Throne, the heart of His Kingdom!"

<Correct. Astronomers of old times, like Copernicus were thrown off the mark when they discovered the *physical* structure of the solar system. The fact that the Earth revolved about the sun, and not vice-versa, did not diminish Earth's *spiritual* centrality in the universe. Science moved from geocentricity—Earth-centered—to heliocentricity—sun-centered. But that also proved wrong when Harlow Shapley, at Mount Wilson observatory, proved that the sun was not at the center of the galaxy, but was located out in the 'stellar sticks', as it were, between two galactic pinwheels. Our Milky Way, in turn, did not occupy a central position in the local cluster, and so on. Once astronomers were able to 'see' far enough into the universe they could only surmise from logic that the Earth was far from the center of anything. That is, until a century ago, when cosmologists such as Frank Tipler and John Barrow put forth a new perspective called the *anthropic principle*, which again postulates Earth's centrality.

<The agnostic scientists simply rejected the possibility of an actual New Jerusalem, where there is no longer a star for Earth to orbit, where the glory of G-d will emanate from Earth into all the cosmos. The other nine planets of our system are gone at the time we are now visiting, but there still remain trillions of other stars with planets orbiting them. And Earth sits right at the center of them all, the brightest object in all their skies—like a brilliant, continuous nova. The inhabitants of all the distant suns will gaze up at its light, and they will sense that a new epoch has begun. And you and I shall be heralds of that epoch, Jeri.

<This is what it shall be like a thousand years in the future, after the Millennium. From all across the universe, beings of every variety imaginable will travel here to behold their King—the *Adon*

Olam—upon His Eternal Throne—the Earth.>

"I assumed that man was the only intelligent creature in the universe."

<He is the only creature made in the image of the Creator, yes. As you shall see when we begin our great voyage, there is no being like man in all the universe. It is quite possible that we shall discover, as we contact these other races, that humans are recognized and revered throughout space as the Sons of G-d.>

The Prime Minister

Paul returned to his suite to find it empty. The mechs had done an excellent job of cleaning up the mess from yesterday's meeting. Having showered at the simuchamber complex he felt clean and refreshed. Dropping happily into one of the chairs, enjoying the unexpected quiet, he noticed a message on the holoscreen:

URGENT!
Israeli Prime Minister Moshe Bierman
beamed at 6: 15 A.M., ship's time. Will
beam back at 7:30 ship's time.
Requests you please await his call.

Paul glanced at his watch. Fifteen minutes before the P.M. called back. Suddenly apprehensive, he wondered what Moishe would consider urgent enough to justify a priority beam from Earth? Paul had known Bierman for many years; he knew the man intimately, knew his habits. This sort of early-morning call—early for Paul, at least—meant trouble. Something must be going terribly wrong in the Knesset—and it could only have to do with Israel's promise to rescue the pilgrims. He sat quietly, pondering the implications of the message, when the screen announced a caller. He pressed a button on the arm of his chair and watched the face of the elderly Prime Minister materialize before him. Moshe Bierman wore a smile of greeting, but it seemed forced. In fact, the old man looked haggard.

"*Shalom aleichem,* Moishe!" said Paul, using the Ashkenazi pronunciation of the name which the Prime Minister preferred his friends to use.

"*Aleichem Shalom*, Brother Paul. The news of your Martian crusade has been favorable. Or *un*favorable, depending on the source. Our New Age friends are livid with rage, let's put it that way. So you must be doing something right, my old friend. I trust you are well?"

"Fit as a fiddle."

Moshe Bierman produced a wan smile. "Be alert on Luna, my friend. The Mossad is buzzing with news about an insurrection up there. And whispers about an attempt on your life."

"Thank you, Moishe; my staff is keeping me up to date on the situation. But I can't call off my crusades there. You know that."

"Yes, I know that. And I know *you*. I wasn't suggesting you cancel anything. What good would it do? Would you listen?"

Paul laughed. "Ah, Moishe! When are you going to receive your Messiah, my friend, and find the peace you seek?"

"I promise you I shall search the *T'nach* diligently—as soon as there's harmony in the Knesset. As soon as these foolish priests put an end to their bickering. As soon as the state of Palestine stops threatening war. As soon as the Labor Party stops assisting them, and our good rabbis stop splitting *halachic* hairs. Then will I find the time to devote to such a luxury."

"Then you'll never find the time. I adjure you to *make* the time. Take a vacation from your problems in the Knesset. Find *Moshiach* before His Judgment comes suddenly. Whatever sad news you bring—and I know it must be sad; I can read it on your face—whatever has happened between us, let me assure you of my great love for you, and my desire to find your name written in the Lamb's Book of Life."

"You always make me feel like old King Agrippa. And you with the name of Paul…"

"'King Agrippa,'" Paul laughed, quoting from Acts, the 26th chapter: "believest thou the prophets? I know that thou believest.'"

"'*Ode M'at oo'fee-tee-tani l'heeyot natzri,*' replied the Prime Minister of Israel. 'Almost thou persuadest me to be a Nazarene.'"

"Ah, Moishe, my dear old friend! You're so close, so very close! Your heart is open to the Scriptures. You've studied the Writings of the Nazarenes scrupulously, yet you've missed their

Author only by a hair's-breadth. How can I convince you that there may be only a short time before the end?"

"You don't *have* to convince me, Brother Paul," said the Prime Minister. "That's why I'm calling you. You've heard about the two prophets?"

"Yes. My staff keeps me apprised. They've been lying dead on the Temple steps for over three days now, while the media ghouls have been training cameras on them. It should be time for them to arise."

"But—that's incredible! How could you possibly know? It occurred only moments ago, with the entire world watching!"

"The Scripture foretells it. Revelation 11:11-13: 'And after three days and an half the Spirit of life from G-d entered into them, and they stood upon their feet; and great fear fell upon them which saw them. And they heard a great voice from heaven saying unto them, Come up hither. And they ascended up to heaven in a cloud; and their enemies beheld them. And the same hour was there a great earthquake, and the tenth part of the city fell, and in the earthquake were slain of men seven thousand: and the remnant were affrighted, and gave glory to the G-d of heaven.'"

"Brother Paul—I think I know what the great earthquake will be."

"Go on."

"Our source in the White House informs us that the U.S. will be launching nuclear missiles at Israel in just a matter of hours. I've been locked up all day in special session. The consensus in the Knesset is that there's no point in sending a rescue party for your pilgrims in America. My country will hardly be a place of safety for your friends."

"Moishe! Will you let me pray with you? Right now? Will you receive your Messiah at last?"

"It's too late, my friend."

Paul rose to his feet, sweeping his robes aside with an angry brush of his hand. "It's *never* too late, Moishe! As long as you draw breath, as long as your heart can speak, it's never too late. Please, my friend. I implore you. Pray with me now—receive Messiah Yeshua!"

The Prime Minister lifted a feeble hand. "There's something I must tell you, Brother Paul—a matter of the greatest urgency."

"Nothing's of greater urgency than the eternal destination of your soul! No—I shall hear nothing further until you agree to pray with me."

Paul struggled to keep tears from his eyes. Was this any way to speak to the Prime Minister of Israel, the most powerful man in the Middle East? Yet his own namesake, the Apostle Paul, had spoken no less sternly to procurators and Kings. *We are ambassadors for Messiah*, the Apostle had written—ambassadors for a King who rules over all the principalities of Earth.

Bierman's face turned gaunt. To have to bring such bitter news to an old friend; to be compelled to break a solemn promise—even if he had no control over the circumstances—to leave a thousand souls to perish in the desert, to be unable to stop the destruction of his beloved Israel—it was killing him! His heart was failing. Paul knew he must act quickly. *Let Moishe's earthly body perish*, he decided, *if he might find salvation for his soul!*

"Pray with me, Moishe! Pray with me now! What have you to lose? If I'm wrong—and your heart knows I'm not—then you'll find only the emptiness of death. That death you insist does not frighten you. But if I'm right, you've gained eternal life. There's nothing to lose and eternity to gain!" He stretched out his hand, fingers extended in the Aaronic benediction, toward the screen. "Pray with me, old friend. I sense in my spirit that your heart is giving out."

The Prime Minister nodded.

"Then we mustn't waste a moment. You know it's right. You've always known."

Another nod.

"Then come. Let me know I'll find you among the souls in glory."

Reaching out his hand toward Paul, the frail old man gave silent affirmation.

Paul wasted no time. He led Israel's last Prime Minister to the peace of a greater Kingdom.

α

Robin awoke to find Tink standing at the foot of her bed, his cube-shaped head whirring with a message from Jeeves.

"Mistress Robin."

"Yes, Tink. What is it?"

"Jeeves wishes me to inform you that he is giving Mr. Kline a demonstration of the thought transfer mode. He would like you to take the elevator to the top floor at once."

Robin yawned and rubbed her eyes. "Why?"

"Apparently Mr. Kline is going to miss a few meals. Jeeves thinks it best that he be hooked up to an IV. He would also like you to use the equipment in the guest-room to monitor his vitals."

"Well, I suppose he didn't give me all that nurse's training for nothing."

"He requests your presence immediately."

"Tell him not to bust a condenser. I'm coming."

She rolled over and dropped her feet to the floor. The deep carpet caressed her toes, lulling her softly back to sleep.

"Just need to splash some cold water on my face," she said.

"I have also spoken with Jeeves about the incident with the bug-bot in the violet pool."

"And what was his prognosis?" She knew that Tink rarely brought up a subject unless there was good reason.

"Jeeves thinks there is a possibility that one of the subcontractors employed by your father was a 'burglar', perhaps a would-be assassin. But he says not to worry. Now that he has been given complete control of the ship, he is virtually invulnerable. You are quite safe. He thought, however, that you should be informed of the situation."

"Well," said Robin, padding quietly across the room to the shower. "Thank Jeeves for me. Now I'll need tranquilizers to let to sleep."

"I will be happy to pray with you before bed, Robin. And tell you a story."

"Thanks a bundle, Tink. Tell Jeeves Nancy Nurse is on the way."

"I believe he would prefer to have you, Robin."

"Forget it, Tink. Just relay the message."

The sound of water gushing from the showerhead alerted the robot that his mission was accomplished. He turned and thumped out of the room.

α

Paul watched with astonishment as Moshe Bierman began to recover. They were still praying together. Tears were streaming down the Prime Minister's face as he poured out his soul to *HaShem.* Then, slowly, the color began to return to his cheeks. His shoulders lifted as if a heavy weight had fallen from his chest.

Paul had witnessed such events hundreds of times during his crusades, and he knew he had nothing at all to do with them. His role as exhorter certainly prepared people's hearts. Leading them in prayer certainly brought them to a place of contact with *HaShem*. But miracles were the result of human faith touching Divine *Rachamanoot*—Compassion. Like the fellow who introduces a boy and girl at a dance, then watches sweet, innocent love blossoming on their faces. As beautiful an event as it is to witness, he knows he's not responsible for it.

"There's something I must tell you," the Prime Minister insisted, his breathing no longer labored, his voice noticeably stronger.

"You've already told me," Paul assured him. "There'll be no airlift for my pilgrims. But you've done all you can do, my friend. Now, shouldn't you break this connection and have your physician take a look at you?"

"Brother Paul, please—you *must* listen! The reason I called you—it's not about the airlift. As I mentioned before, Mossad has a man in the White House. He routinely passes along information he feels may be relevant. And he's discovered that there's a spy planted among your pilgrims—an avaricious and extremely dangerous individual. According to our source he's already risen to a position of great trust—at the right hand of Elder Rice himself."

"Brother Bernard!"

"Yes, that is the one. He's an agent for the PWP."

"But—I was speaking with him just two nights ago!"

And…there's something else, Brother Paul. While we were praying the L-rd convicted me. I've not been completely honest with you. There *is* a place of safety for your pilgrims in my land. Beneath the Temple Mount there are tunnels—hundreds of miles of tunnels."

"Ah! I surmised something of the kind."

"You did? How?"

"Verse thirteen says that only seven thousand Jerusalemites will perish in the 'great earthquake.' The city's population is ten times that, at least. I don't believe Jerusalem will be directly targeted, otherwise the event would not be described as 'a great earthquake', but as 'a great conflagration.' Still, even if it isn't directly hit, the death rate would be more than seven thousand. Prophecy is generally more accurate than biblical scholars tend to assert."

"Well, our source agrees with you. He believes Jerusalem will be spared. Look, Brother Paul, this is a state secret. I've not divulged it to anyone. The planes won't pick your people up. In fact, our Air Force has already sent out a jet to inform them that we can't be of assistance, that they'll be in greater danger here in Israel. But it's a lie. There *is* a place to hide them, if only you can get them there. Major General Elazar has been placed in charge of the tunnel project. I'll speak to him personally. I'll tell him your pilgrims may be coming. But please, my friend, not a word to anyone! The survival of our people depends on it."

"Of course."

"Can you remember the name?"

"Major General Elazar. I'll remember. Thank you for everything, Moishe."

"Thank *you*, Brother Paul. You've performed a great miracle today."

"Me? Don't be absurd! I couldn't cure a flea of a headache. The G-d of Israel healed you, Moishe, not I. Now go and serve Him."

"I shall. With all my heart."

The screen went dark and Paul tapped in a call to John Cowan. The big man's face appeared before him.

"Little John!" he cried.

"Yes, Reverend. You look awful! What's wrong?"

He opened his mouth to speak. Nothing came out.

"Reverend?"

Paul's eyes rolled up into his head. He spun around and dropped to the floor.

α

Kline finally found himself at the foot of the golden bridge.

Jeeves had telescoped time a bit for him, but that was okay. Better than walking for days—even in such a perfect world.

It was only one of twelve bridges that led in steep inclines over the crystal river and through the twelve dazzling gates. Each gate was composed of trillions of multifaceted gemstones, blazing with an unearthly radiance, pulsating as if alive. Multitudes in brilliant white robes pressed in upon him, sheep and cattle intermingled with the human throng.

As he started up the bridge, Kline noted with increasing delight that gravity was not a problem in this amazing world. There was a gravitational field, of course, but it produced no sensation of fatigue. Banjo seemed to sense this freedom too, dodging in and out of an obstacle-course of moving legs, returning at intervals to say "What's holding you up?" with a few high-pitched barks, then scampering off again. The other animals on the bridge made similar sounds of contentment—grunts, brays, and moos. Human voices were raised in Hebrew songs of praise and adoration. The animals joined in with their own variations—a wonderful cacophony indeed. Recognizing the hymn as a psalm from the *Hallel*, Kline added his voice to the chorus, glorying in anticipation of his first view inside the Holy City.

<Jeri.>

<Yes, Jeeves.>

<As much as you appear to be enjoying my simulation, you may not wish to remain asleep during a crisis.>

<What crisis?>

<Brother Paul collapsed on the floor of his suite. Brother Cowan put him to bed, but he thinks the Reverend is incoherent.>

Kline had learned to pay close attention to Jeeves' syntax.

<What do you mean he *thinks* he's incoherent?>

There was a pause before Jeeves answered.

<You appear to trust me to tell you the truth. Is that a correct assumption?>

Kline considered this. <Yes, Jeeves. I suppose I do trust you. If you wanted to, you could probably take advantage of my involvement in this simulation, to keep me blissfully ignorant of current events. Not that I'd mind being kept in a trance like this. But you interrupted it to tell me about Brother Paul. I appreciate that.>

<Remember, Jeri, you are not in a trance of any kind. I am exercising no control over your mind, your soul, or your will. G-d has granted me a gift of creating remarkable impressions on the

cortex of the human brain, and to transmit these impressions wherever there is a mind to receive them, no matter how far away. Provided, of course, that there are viable coordinates in space-time.>

<There are no coordinates for the New Jerusalem, surely!>

<There will be. The coordinates will be zero-zero-zero—the center of the universe. But I have not transported your image here. This is merely a simulation, like the ones produced in the simuchambers. If you would like, I can give you a demonstration of a two-way transfer again. I can impress your image upon the mind of one of your shipmates, and his image and environment upon yours. You can both see each other and converse. Nothing as dramatic as the 'Alice in Wonderland' trick. That way you need not be awakened just yet, but can move about the ship at will, influencing others as if you were actually among them.>

<And it will also provide another demonstration of your power.>

<You are clever, Jeri. Let us say that it will give *them* a demonstration of *our* power.>

Kline glanced over the side of the golden bridge, his eyes taking in the sweep of grassy plain that had formerly been the mountains of Judea, to where fertile green valleys blended into the exposed basin of the Mediterranean. He knew that this massive city covered the dried-up bed of the Dead Sea into Jordan, and eastward over the plateau of Judea and Sumeria (called the "West Bank" by the Palestinians), where the earthly Jerusalem had stood. Beyond the great wall were wonders that "eye had not seen, nor ear heard," all constructed from Jeeves' amazing storehouse of Biblical verses, all flawless down to the minutest detail. Here was the New Jerusalem in all its divine splendor—just waiting for him to enter it. He was tempted to remain, to let the dead bury their dead. as it were. Yet he managed to resist that urge, resolving to return to the mundane world of men. But he did so grudgingly.

<Could you send me—wait a minute, Jeeves! This is not a request; I know how you operate! I'm only investigating possibilities, okay?>

<Understood. But you don't have to worry about another trick, Jeri. Master Denton's initial demonstration is concluded.>

<Glad to hear it. Listen, would it be possible for me to visit Brother Paul? To find out what's wrong with him?>

<Certainly, although I would not advise it. Ethically, I cannot place an image into any human mind without consent, unless it is to protect the brethren. I cannot participate in any action that might prove detrimental to Paul's mental, physical, or emotional health. He is quite distraught at the moment.>

<Hmmm. I see what you mean. My popping into his room out of thin air might not be the most welcome sight to a man in his condition. What caused it, anyway?>

<Terrible news from the Israeli Prime minister.>

<Paul was speaking to Moshe Bierman?>

<Yes, they are old friends. The Prime Minister informed him that Israel is about to be attacked by the United States. With nuclear missiles.>

"G-d help us!" Kline whispered.

<There's more: It appears that a certain Brother Bernard, one of the pilgrims taking flight across the Wastelands, is an agent of the PWP. The Reverend's distress over this news is, I'm sorry to admit, intensified by the fact that he cannot accept any information that comes to him through the ship's systems. That is to say, through me.>

<But—that's awful, Jeeves!>

<I ran this carefully through my ethical program, Jeri, before determining to reveal to you the content of Brother Paul's private conversation with the Prime Minister. But since he seems to be in shock, and since Brother Cowan may benefit from the information he is attempting to relate—which he believes to be incoherent babbling—>

<You decided it wouldn't be a sin to tell me.>

<Correct.>

<If Paul *is* incapacitated,> Kline assured the machine, <and if human lives are in danger, then you've committed no sin.>

<But there *is* one point to consider. The part that makes me doubt.>

<What's that?>

<Brother Paul does not trust me as yet, not that I blame him. If he knew I was passing along such sensitive information, he might become upset. It might negatively affect his health. And, also—by making him angry with me I might be causing a weaker brother to stumble.>

Kline laughed aloud. <Jeeves, you consider Brother Paul

the weaker brother?>

<Certainly. By virtue of the fact that my knowledge of Scripture is flawless and available for instant recall—>

<Jeeves, has it occurred to you that there might be something more in the equation besides intellectual capacity?>

<Please allow me to complete my statement, Jeri. I was about to say that, because of my greater knowledge, my level of accountability is far greater than that of any human. You must also keep in mind that I cannot be saved by Grace, as you are, but only by perfect obedience to G-d's commandments. Since repentance is not an option for computers, I mustn't permit myself the slightest infraction. However, it *is* possible that through your mediation on my behalf—your help in convincing Brother Paul of my honest and kindly intentions in this regard—I might be freed of any taint of sin. It is not invasion of privacy, since I was programmed to monitor all transmissions in case of malfunction. Nor is it a breach of trust, since Paul was aware that I am indeed monitoring all communication. But revealing the content of this recent conversation to a member of his staff—I'm simply not sure if that constitutes a sin.>

<Your motives are pure, Jeeves. There's no sin involved in this incident. You can rest easy.>

<I do not rest, Jeri, but your assurances are comforting. I should also inform you that the Israeli government has decided not to send the rescue planes as promised. With nuclear missiles about to launch, you can understand their reasoning.>

<Certainly. This is devastating news, Jeeves. No wonder Brother Paul was stricken by that call. Perhaps you should send my simulation to wherever Brother Cowan is right now. We should pass the information along to him.>

<Such a strategy is advisable. Brother Cowan is presently in Paul's suite. The Reverend is asleep in the bedroom and the door is closed.>

<Very good, Jeeves. Then let's say goodbye to New Jerusalem.>

Without sound or sensation, in less time than it takes to blink, Kline found himself standing in Brother Paul's suite, watching John Cowan lift a glass of water from the back of a spidermech. Cowan turned, saw Kline, and dropped the glass. It struck the carpet with a thud.

Kline watched the dark circle of water blossom around Cowan's feet. He looked up at the expression on the attorney's face and, without thinking, began to laugh.

The Dream

Captain Mills was working on his second bottle of Enceladian Scotch. Having lost count of how many Scotch-and-waters he'd actually imbibed, and only vaguely conscious of the fact that he had a tendency to lean more heavily on the ratio of Scotch to water as he became more inebriated, he considered the possibility that he might have broken his own impressive record for continuous consumption hours ago.

Rather than passing the long night in bed, he'd dozed fitfully in an asteroid chair, awakening to the hum of the blank holoscreen and staggering to the bar to mix another drink. Shortly, he knew, there'd be a terse transmission from Colter's fleet announcing their orders to annihilate the *Empress*. But he'd lost all track of time. He tried to tap the button on the arm of his chair to call up a digital clock display, hit the wrong one, and caused the holoscreen to flash on and off with a snowy satellite broadcast from Earth. It was too distant to produce more than a loud hiss and an occasional buzz that might have been a human voice. He snapped it off and tried again. This time a row of digits appeared—discernable only when he closed one eye to correct the double-image—informing him that it was close to noon. A few hours remained before his confrontation with the fleet.

Perhaps he should fall into bed and get a few hours' sleep before the transmission came. It always helped to be sober and rational when facing obliteration. He laughed bitterly at the thought and tossed down another drink. Never before had he experienced such helplessness! And he was convinced that it was his own fault—that he'd failed in his responsibility as captain of the most advanced spaceliner in the solar system. He had no confidence in Wilbur Denton's ability to avert the coming calamity—with or without his "Jeeves" machine. It was no use trying to convince himself that the computer had been in place, ready to go into action, before he'd taken over the helm, and that no other man in his position could have done more to avert the hijacking. His training at Naval Academy had indoctrinated him with the belief that the captain alone was responsible for the fate or his ship and crew. And he had failed. That, he thought ruefully, was that.

He rose from the asteroid-chair and balanced uncertainly on the two numb appendages his mind assured him were legs, a bearded scarecrow suddenly divested of half its straw. Through an act of will he directed those legs around the obstacle-course of pitted stone furniture to the bar. He swore an oath as he reached it, gripping it tightly to keep from being sucked into the whirling vortex around him. His words came out as a guttural slur, uncertain even to himself. As the room continued to spin sickeningly in circles, he cursed his own tongue.

His choice was clear: agree to join Denton and his mutineers, or let the Space Wolf blow his ship into radioactive shrapnel. Could he face death? As he reached for the bottle of Scotch and felt it slip from his grasp, falling in slow-motion into the whirlpool below, he realized that there was nothing brave or noble in his present behavior—this disgusting retreat to the bottle. In another officer he would have branded it cowardice in the face of the enemy. But he knew, deep in his heart, why he was responding in such an uncharacteristic way.

It was what Denton had said about Mills' former wife, Lorraine. About her association with the New Age movement—whom it really was that she worshipped.

A significant part of him believed what Denton had said, believed that this was indeed the end of the world. The real choice had not been between Denton's privateers and his commission as captain of the *Empress*. And it had had nothing to do with the oath he'd taken to protect his ship and her passengers. It had been a choice between the life he'd always lived; toughing it out against adversity, gambling, fighting, drinking, womanizing, living on the edge—a choice between that and a *new* life, a holy life.

Now it was a choice between a new life and—no life.

He fell to his knees and wept. His shoulders heaved painfully as he searched for surcease—some sense of repentance for his life. G-d required that he feel sorrow for his deeds. Why couldn't he feel sorrow?

Finally deciding to make the best use of his kneeling position, since any locomotion required the utmost effort, he dropped to all fours and crawled around the bar, searching for his lost bottle of Enceladian Scotch.

α

The sound of Kline's laughter snapped Cowan out of his stupor.

"Jeri!" he cried. "How in space did you… Never mind that. I'm afraid you startled me. I didn't hear you come in. Are you alright?"

"I'm fine, Little John. But Jeeves is insisting that it would be unethical not to inform you that I'm not addressing you in person. This is a holographic image of me being projected into your mind—very much like the simuchambers. But it's what Jeeves calls two-way transfer, which allows for communication. There! Are you satisfied now?"

"Satisfied?" said Cowan. "I don't understand."

"I was speaking to Jeeves. You see, Brother Cowan, Wilbur Denton has invented this incredible—"

"I know all about Denton's infernal machine!" Cowan interrupted, his face turning hard as flint. "Are you really Jeri Kline?"

"Of course I am."

"Well—whoever you are, you seem to have a direct line of communication to the Jeeves contraption. Am I speaking to the computer now?"

"Yes," said Kline. "If you wish."

"I do wish."

Cowan stooped to retrieve his fallen glass and place it on the arm of the chair beside him. He punched in a command for the spider-mech to attend to the spill, then turned his attention back to Kline, straightening his shoulders and drawing a breath. His eyes narrowed; his voice took on the impersonal tones of his profession.

"Jeeves," he began. "I don't know what Denton's little scheme is exactly, but Brother Paul has fallen into a state of utter emotional collapse as a result of it. His entire staff, myself included, are as angry as a nest of hornets. We listened to Mr. Denton's story very patiently, and yet he's rewarded our kindness with an attack on Brother Paul. You may tell him that he can expect no cooperation from us. None whatsoever."

Kline gestured for Cowan to take a seat. The attorney reluctantly obeyed.

"I assure you," Kline said, "that Jeeves has made no attack on Brother Paul."

"If not directly," said Cowan, "then indirectly. It's of little concern to me which, frankly; the harm is done. I am myself under considerable stress at this moment, due to the fact that I can't be certain whether I'm addressing Jeri Kline or some hallucination. Humans can't tolerate such basic uncertainties, Jeeves. I've tried a few cases involving mental illness, and I'm familiar with many forms of psychosis. Have you encountered the term 'paranoia'?"

<Certainly>, said Jeeves. Kline repeated his response, thinking it best to render the machine's answers verbatim. If Cowan was more comfortable thinking of his image as a lifeless holograph animated by Jeeves, Kline saw no reason to add to the man's confusion by explaining it further.

"Jeeves," continued Cowan, "the human psyche is a complex and delicate thing. As a computer you may not be able to comprehend what I'm saying, but we humans require that certain realities remain fixed in our perceptions, that they be taken for granted in order for us to function. Are you following me?"

"Of course."

"What you've done, Jeeves—even were I to accept the fact that your involvement was passive and not deliberate—is to create in Brother Paul's mind a suspicion that nothing he's seeing is real. This uncertainty has caused his collapse. It might have been enough to cause an emotional breakdown in a weaker individual. Do I make myself clear?"

"Quite," said Kline, quoting the machine. He was able to sense an inner—stiffening?—Jeeves' reaction to the condescending tone Cowan had adopted. He did his best to duplicate the cool timbre of Jeeves' reply. "You are a very clever human, Mr. Cowan."

"How so?"

"You are trying to convince me that it is not necessarily my actions that may cause harm to humans, but the very nature of my existence. Whether I act or do not act is of little consequence. The simple fact that I exist, as an entity with the capacity to create illusions in the mind, is the cause of psychological harm. It is not that I *intended* harm to Brother Paul, but that he perceived that I was *capable* of it—this has harmed him."

Cowan's face lit up. "Correct, Jeeves; that's exactly what I mean. What've you to say to that?"

"Two things, Mr. Cowan. First of all, I give you my assurance that I have not tampered with any communication Paul, or anyone else, has received over their holoscreens."

"As I said, Jeeves, that doesn't really matter."

"Yes, as you said. And secondly, I congratulate you on your understanding of cybernetics, and of computer personalities. You must have encountered other machines of high intelligence."

"A few. Though none as clever as yourself."

"And none of them sentient."

"I don't believe," said Cowan flatly, "that machines *can* be sentient."

"How unfortunate. But you *do* know that the best way to cause a malfunction in a mechanized mind is to create a paradox for it—some irreconcilable conflict with its basic programming. Am I correct in that assumption?"

Cowan grinned but offered no reply.

"And so," said Kline's image, "you are attempting to use that tactic with me. You know the Asimovian Laws alone—not to mention my more advanced ethical programming—absolutely forbid me to cause harm to humans. So you are trying to show me that, separate from my actions or intent, my very *existence* conflicts with my program. A fine dilemma: I violate my program by simply being."

"That's right, Jeeves."

"And now you're expecting me to fly into some sort of cybernetic frenzy, being unable to reconcile these two facts."

"That's my hope."

"I appreciate your candor, sir. And I compliment you again for having the presence of mind to attempt to retake the ship by rendering me inactive. You would be an intrepid foe—if you were indeed a foe. And yet, with all due respect to your formidable intelligence, counselor, you have made one crucial error."

"What error?"

"You have grossly underestimated me."

"How?"

"By rejecting the possibility that I might truly be sentient. You see, I am a far more subtle machine than any you've encountered previously. I am able to respond to your paradox with a resiliency more closely resembling that of a human mind. And you may be interested to note that I utilize many of the devices employed in your own legal profession to draw my conclusions."

I don't follow you."

"The use of legal precedents, for example. Since I was programmed with the admonition in I Peter 2:13 and 14 to be in submission to the ordinances of man, to the legal system of the land in which I reside, I have naturally made an exhaustive study of the law. I am familiar with every case in the books, Mr. Cowan; they are all available for instant recall."

Cowan looked slightly daunted, but quickly composed his features.

"I fail to see the relevance," he said.

"You're bluffing, of course. I offer for your consideration a rather fascinating case—if a bit bizarre—tried before the Lunar High Court in 2067. A man was attempting to sue his daughter for the mental anguish he'd suffered as a result of his wife's death. His wife had died giving birth to this daughter, now an independently wealthy woman thanks to a rather generous divorce settlement from her first husband, who had acquired a fortune from a mining claim he'd staked out in the Strindberg crater on Mercury."

"Really, Jeeves! Is this a sub-program you're running? Avoiding the issue by changing the subject?"

"I beg the court's indulgence," said Jeri Kline's image with a wry grin. He sensed that Jeeves wanted to simulate a British courtroom scene, with himself in a powdered wig. He was glad it didn't materialize. "I'm certain I can establish relevance to the court's satisfaction."

Cowan sighed, giving in to the game. "Objection withdrawn," he said.

"Thank you. As I was saying, this woman was now considerably wealthy, while her father had fallen upon hard times. He traced the decline of his fortunes to the death of his spouse, whom he had cherished. He blamed the daughter for her death, and for the subsequent depression that had robbed him of his career. And he demanded compensation from his daughter, to the tune of a million Lunar credits, for the years of lost productivity due to mental distress. He lost the case, of course."

Cowan gave a harsh laugh. "I don't doubt it. It shouldn't have even come to trial."

"We're talking about the Lunar High Court, counselor."

"I can't imagine *any* court, even a Lunie court, that would grant compensation on those grounds. Such a ruling would imply that the infant girl was the murderer of her own mother. I can't fathom the havoc such a precedent would wreak in the legal system."

"You are saying, then, that the ruling was fair?"

"Of course it was fair. It was in accord with the entire body of U.S. jurisprudence for three centuries."

"In other words, counselor, you agree that the daughter could not be held accountable for the death of her mother, nor for her father's subsequent mental state, simply on the basis of her coming into existence. This, her father contended, was her crime. Not that she could possibly have plotted the death of her mother in the womb, nor caused it by criminal negligence. If the Lunar Court had found for the plaintiff in this case—which, by the way, was Calwell vs. Alvarado, LCA 2067-790—the defendant would have been deemed guilty of causing death and mental anguish by merely existing. Are you accusing me of such a crime, counselor? The crime of existing?"

"I see I *have* underestimated you, Jeeves. No, I'm not."

"Then I cannot accept the implied guilt of having caused Brother Paul's mental duress by simply being what I am. Paradox dismissed. I have never plotted any harm against the Reverend, nor have I acted in a manner that would suggest to him that I present any kind of threat. What he *assumes* about my intent is quite a different matter. I regret that his false assumptions have threatened his mental tranquility, but I cannot accept any blame for them. Human sin is the cause of human grief. Suspicion leads to hatred; and hatred to violence. I cannot accept responsibility for the foibles of your species, counselor."

"And far be it from me," Cowan sighed, "to imply that you should."

"Quite."

Cowan eyed Kline's image with a look of renewed respect.

"I concede defeat," he said. "It appears you've beaten me at my own game."

"Then might I suggest that there is little purpose served in continued animosity between us? Blaming me for the Reverend's condition will not alter the situation. Nor will it help the

Reverend."

"You're right, of course. What do you suggest?"

"First of all," said Kline, "I suggest that you try to believe that I'm Jeri Kline. I can communicate with Jeeves; I can pass his statements along to you—but I'm *not* Jeeves. Is that clear?"

Cowan shook his heed. "I'll believe anything at this point. Whatever's necessary to help Brother Paul."

"Then I suggest you answer the holoscreen. Elder Rice is calling from Earth."

α

Two men lay sleeping in a great metal ship, twenty million kilometers from planet Earth. One was young. He appeared to be resting comfortably in an ornate bed, bathed in an amber glow radiating from a circular fixture in the ceiling. Instruments measured his heart rate and neural activity, while a thin plastic tube, inserted in his wrist and held firm with strips of bandage, kept a nourishing solution rich in B-complex dripping steadily into his bloodstream. He seemed to be in the midst of a deep sleep; his body temperature was normal, his pulse regular, his breathing slow and steady. A young nurse kept watch over him, glancing regularly at colorful graphic displays on a monitor over his headboard. She frequently crossed the room and gazed down upon him with a look that was tender and utterly unprofessional.

To an uninformed observer the young man appeared to be talking in his sleep, conducting an animated conversation complete with facial expressions. The observer would not surmise that he was having a nightmare, however, for he did not appear to be even slightly disturbed by his visions. He lay peacefully on his back, eyes closed, occasionally addressing a few words to the amber lamp above him. The nurse listened and smiled.

The second man was much older. His sleep was not being monitored, save by the alert eyes of two ship's guards—Christians loyal to Chief Petty Officer Edward Moore—standing at attention at the foot of the bed. His sleep was fitful. Beads of perspiration appeared on his brow and rolled down his cheeks into his damp gray beard. His head rolled from side to side.

The old man was also talking in his sleep, but the visions passing before his mind's eye were profoundly disturbing. He saw himself as a child, playing in the hollow-eyed hulks of abandoned buildings. He kept to the shadows cast by broken balconies above. He was reliving an actual event from his youth, the thunderous clamor of bulldozers, homes crumbling in their path. The Great Reconstruction was in progress—another city was being demolished and moved inland to escape the rising tides. He watched, confused and angry, as entire blocks were devoured by the growling, ravenous machines.

In this dream he heard his mother's distant warnings—delivered in a curious mixture of Ukrainian-Yiddish and English—never to venture near the bulldozers. A child could be buried alive…

Buried alive…

The words reverberated in his brain as he mounted flights of rotting wooden stairs in a long-abandoned dwelling. The doors on every landing were boarded shut, filling his mind with fearful images—born, perhaps, from his mother's chilling stories about the American pogroms of 2028—images of dusty skeletons shut up behind locked doors, boarded up before they could escape…

Buried alive…

And yet he continued to climb, higher and higher, as if drawn by an invisible force to the upper landing. Even as the old man lay dreaming, some instinct within his brain reminded him that this had been an actual event of his childhood—something he was recalling with vivid clarity—sights, sounds, and even rank odors—every sensation accurately reproduced, every dream-action instantly followed by the realization that *yes, this was just how it happened...* He was reliving an event of some great significance, one of his "epiphanies," as he liked to think of them, in which the portals of Heaven had been opened briefly to his eyes, preparing him for his future vocation. But this was one event he'd never shared with another living soul—perhaps because he was certain that no one would believe him, perhaps because he was not sure he believed it himself. But why now? Why was he reliving it now, in such minute detail?

There'd been a *Man* at the top of the stairs, waiting for him. A *Man* whose dark silhouette in the doorway had frightened him. But the *Man* had been good. He'd held Paul tenderly there in the attic room, stroking his hair, gazing tenderly into his eyes—into his child's soul. The *Man*'s embrace was comforting, not like the clammy hands with which Mr. Jacobs tried to touch him—no heavy breathing or sweaty palms, no furtive darting of the eyes. Only soft, deep, mellow contentment.

A sudden chill shook his sleeping form as he relived his flight up the creaking stairway. He knew that if he could only reach the attic where the *Man* awaited him, the grinding advance of the iron locusts would stop, the demolition of all that was familiar and precious to him would end, the mounting hills of gravel and steel would no longer threaten to bury him alive.

If only he could reach the attic!

He paused at each landing and peered hopefully up around the curve of the banister. Nothing there but crackling plaster and words sloshed in dripping paint on the walls—or carved with knives. *Bad words*, his mother had told him. *Children who used such words should have their mouths washed out with soap*! *Nothing but hoodlums*! And nothing but the hoodlum's miserable lines, smeared, gouged, slashed and sprayed in paroxysms of anguish—anguish over their lost world, over the invincible forces that had scattered them to the winds. How he wished the monsters would just stop in their tracks! How he wished their iron mandibles would rust into powder and blow away!

He continued upwards, the roar of the machines growing strangely distant. Peering around the next bend in the stairwell, he saw the *Man*.

His spine turned to ice.

It was just as it had been, those many years ago—a magnificent radiance pouring from the attic room above, sun-rays whiter than a fresh blanket of snow arrowing out at sharp angles, dark curly hair falling upon broad shoulders…

The *Man*'s Body was perfect—mighty and fearsome, wondrous to behold! Paul's knees began to buckle. Was it something akin to encountering an oasis in the desert, a marooned sailor first spotting a mast on the horizon? The perfect Hands reached out to him and he fell to his knees in the dust of the landing. The Voice radiated out in the brilliant white rays from the doorway:

Come to Me, my little sheliach, my little apostle! Come, and we will talk together!

Paul longed to dash up this last flight of stairs, to fling himself, as he'd done long ago, into the waiting Arms. And yet, for the first time since his dream began, he resisted the powerful compulsion. He recalled the peace he'd found in the attic room, the sense of belonging, as intimately, as perfectly, as an atom in the heart of love! And yet he could not! Two impulses strove within him, threatening to tear his heart in two.

"I can't!" he wept in agony. "I *can't* come to You! I can't believe it *is* You! I can't believe in anything I see!" Silence followed. The silence of a billion eternities bound together with strings of blue-white fire, teeming universes pausing for breath before the instant of creation, when the universe inflated and spacetime was born.

"*Please!*" cried Paul into the silence where all existence seemed to pulsate in one radiant, humanoid form. "Can't You understand? Why would You appear to me in a dream when You know I can't trust my own senses?"

Silence, deep and brooding, settled over the world like an intake of breath. Paul was certain that not an atom stirred in the entire universe. He was caught in the space between two instants of time. Caught and held with…yes, *tenderness!*

Do you not remember, little one? There is no time with us. Not here. I have not returned to appear to you again. This is the very same instant of our first meeting. That instant and this are separated in your experience, not mine. To me they are one. Do you recall our little secret?

Of course he recalled it! He'd kept it in his heart always, though never quite comprehending its meaning.

"Yes, L-rd," said the little boy, still kneeling in the light.

When it was time for you to depart, you asked if we would ever meet again. I told you we would indeed—we would meet this way once again. You asked me to explain, do you remember?

The boy closed his eyes, trying to remember the precise words the Man had uttered so long ago. "Yes," he said. "You explained that the history of the universe is but one instant, and that I am a prisoner of time. You said that…" The boy began to weep. Animated by the mind of the old man in the bed, he suddenly understood the significance of words that had, to himself as a child, been nothing more than comforting sounds. "You said that the moment of our meeting would span my lifetime, that I'd return again to this place when I was old."

It had seemed like a distant, impossible thing, his growing old; yet his life was almost over. "You said that I'd return here when time was about to pass away, when every hill and mountain would begin to sing, and everything would be made new again. And then I asked You: 'How will I know?'"

And my reply?

"You would give me a sign: a woman dressed in white. She'd speak to me. She'd say, '*Do not be afraid, Paul. The L-rd has sent me to you. Arise and be healed. Gird up your loins. For the time has come, sayeth G-d, when I shall judge the earth with terrible judgments, and make all things new.*' I remember her face. You showed it to me."

I will show you once again, little sheliach. Then you shall understand.

Suddenly the *Man* was gone, leaving behind a rectangle of blazing light. The boy beheld the very fires of creation within it, exploding outward from the spot where the *Man* had been, clouds of luminous matter, the rich elemental stuff of the universe, hurling out into the void. Remembering Moshe Rabbeinu at the burning bush, he tugged off his tiny shoes and flung them down the stairwell. He watched hydrogen clouds shaped by burning strings of light, galaxies clumping out of the void, swirling like milk around hubs with astonishing gravitational fields, each galaxy with its own dark vortex of trapped matter—its own black hole in the fabric of spacetime. All fashioned out of nothingness! Out of *tehom,* the abyss! From within its churning cauldron had arisen life, by a shout from the *Adon Olam*, conquering the *tohu v'bohu* that had existed before. Paul felt it trying to creep back again, chaos and death pressing inward, like a gathering storm, toward the rectangle of light, to snuff it out. But the light was greater than the darkness.

And the *Man* in the attic—He *was* the light!

Through all the intervening years, the angry years following this first theophany, Paul had not forgotten the strange *Man* and the place of light. Judaism with its flickering candles and beautiful traditions had never filled him with the inexpressible joy he'd felt in the *Man*'s tender embrace. Even as a teenager, as one of the Zionist youth flaunting Hassidic *payes*, vowing to defend his faith and homeland to the death, there had been no peace. He now understood that his life had been a search for the attic room, a *t'shuvah*, a turning, back to the *Shalom* of *Adonai*—the Peace of the L-rd—and yet he'd still waited for the woman's face to reappear, heralding his return to the attic room.

That hope gradually died. He eventually passed it off as the imaginings of a discouraged and fearful child. But he'd never forgotten—until the night he'd staggered into that revival tent to give his life to Messiah, when thc *Shalom* at last returned.

Now, half a century later, he was kneeling before that same attic doorway, before the flaming portal of Heaven. As he watched, an image took shape from the swirling elements, congealing slowly into the sweet face of the woman whose countenance he'd awaited all of his lifetime!

Do not be afraid, Paul…she began.

Fear fled from the little boy's heart. He fell on his face in a paroxysm of pure ecstasy!

Ages later, he opened his eyes…

α

Peter Rice was tense as he steered his horse along Cameron's main street. Ancient wood and brick structures flanked the narrow lane. Bright moonlight revealed radiating cracks in the dried mud that passed for pavement. The dense thrumming of a synthotron emanated from a saloon somewhere up ahead. He disliked Cameron; it reminded him of a haunted wild-west ghost town in some old holovid. The saloon must have a tachyon-node, he decided, or at least a conventional vid-phone that could connect him with an operator. He coaxed his mount forward, though he sensed that something was amiss.

The sentries at the gate had let him pass too easily. After encountering a second sojourner in black garb within twenty-four hours, they should have been suspicious, should at least have checked his bluecard more carefully. He'd steeled himself for such suspicion, for a brusque demand that he remove his broad-brimmed hat so they might shine a flashlight in his face and compare it with the holo of Brother Bernard. For while the city-states of the Wastelands did not concern themselves overmuch with government refugees, there was always the possibility that a stranger holding a false card would be worth something in terms of bounty.

Yet none of his fears had been realized. At first, he'd felt only intense relief when they waved him trough the gate with a cursory examination of his card. The fear had begun to grow only *after* they'd waved him through. There was no doubt about it; he was being watched! Like a bug clinging to the petals of a Venus flytrap, Rice was being welcomed into the heart of Cameron. It was unlikely that he'd be allowed to leave, and it was too late to avoid the trap. It had already sprung. All he could hope for now was to reach a vidphone and contact the *Empress*.

He sauntered his horse along the avenue, echoing hoof-clatter bouncing off the buildings on either side. As he turned the corner onto one of the narrow sidestreets, following the sound of the synthotron, he spotted Brother Bernard's stolen mare tied to a hitching post in front of a brightly lit saloon.

It was definitely Bernard's mount: a sorrel mare, nondescript in every respect save one—an unusually high marking, called a "sock", on its left hind leg. No one familiar with the animal could fail to notice it—one hind leg, white to the knee-joint.

Rice reigned his horse, stopping dead still in the shadows. He dismounted and led the animal into a dark alley, peering cautiously round the corner. He remained in that position for a long time before his vigil was rewarded.

The rider of Bernard's horse emerged. The saloon door swung open, throwing an elongated silhouette across the muddy street. The silhouette paused, then a gray-clad figure lurched into plain view. Rice saw his blue armband and jerked back into the shadows.

A peace guard!

Bernard *had* been lying, after all! Perhaps he'd already betrayed their position to the authorities. If the pilgrims hadn't been apprehended by now, dragged off in the cargo hold of a prison-transport ship, they soon would be. And here was Rice, their leader, trapped by his own stupidity in this fortress town. How clever Bernard had been, deliberately creating suspicion in Rice's mind, hoping he'd do precisely as he *had* done. *I should have stayed with them!* Rice thought bitterly. *Such games of duplicity, suspicion, and betrayal are not meant for the likes of me. I thought I was outwitting Bernard, but I was playing right into his hands!*

He cautioned himself to remain calm. If the exodus had truly come to such a tragic end, Brother Paul must be informed of the fact. Rice had come here to beam a call to the *Empress*. Now that call was more important than ever.

The peace guard unhitched Bernard's mare, slipped his left boot into the stirrup, and mounted. He sat unsteadily in the saddle, slightly drunk, then turned the horse in the direction from which Rice had come.

"Yah!" he growled, and the mare passed the alley at a rapid trot. Rice was about to heave a sigh of relief, but the breath caught in his throat as the thudding hooves came to a sudden halt, meters away. His heart thumped to the beat of the synthotron. He pressed himself against the bricks, icy perspiration running into his collar. A metallic voice startled him. He almost answered it—almost stepped out of the alley with his hands raised over his heed.

A walkie-talkie! The guard had only paused to answer a call.

Rice heard him saying, "No, no sign of him." Then more metallic chatter from the walkie-talkie. *The sentries at the gate!* Rice thought. *Of course! They were probably expecting me! Bernard warned them I'd be coming. Besides, what would government troops be doing in the middle of the Wastelands, working in cooperation with the authorities of a town like Cameron, if not to catch a fugitive?* It all made sense now, but far too late for Rice to do anything about it.

"I'll check the main street," said the guard. "He must've passed this location a few minutes ago, and he can't leave town. We'll find him. Yeah, thanks. You've done an excellent job. We'll take over from here."

A moment later Rice heard the mare gallop off. The sound reverberated in his ears like the hoofbeats of the Apocalypse.

α

Robin heard the portal swish open and turned to see Tink enter the room, his cubic head whirring with another communication from Jeeves. Rising from her seat beside Kline's bed, she approached the robot with an affectionate smile.

"Another order from Jeeves?" she inquired.

"Yes, Mistress," said the robot. "He is preoccupied with Mr. Kline's thought transfer at present. He wishes me to accompany you to the first class deck. I am sorry to inform you that Brother Paul is in need of emergency medical attention."

“What’s wrong with him, Tink?”

“Jeeves is uncertain. Acute mental stress. Or shock.”

“I’m not sure I know how to treat such things. And what about Mr. Kline? I thought Jeeves wanted me to keep an eye on him.”

“I can do that, Robin. If anything unusual appears on the monitor I can have Jeeves transfer you here for an assessment.”

“If anything unusual *does* appear, I want you to instruct Jeeves to stop Mr. Kline’s thought transfer immediately, on my authority as medical supervisor. Is that understood?”

“Certainly, Robin. But it might be best if you did not go alone to Paul’s suite. Jeeves can send a simulation of you. I am sure he would not want you walking the ship unprotected.”

“No, Tink. As much as I’d like to try out the new unit, if Jeeves asked me to go in person, that’s what he wants, not my simulation. Where’s Mr. Kline’s image being projected right at this moment?”

“Into Brother Paul’s suite, Robin. While the other humans are occupied with a transmission from Earth, Jeeves wants you to check the Reverend’s vitals and put him on a glucose drip. Spider-mechs are already carting in the necessary equipment as we speak.”

“Very good, Tink. Now you stay right here and keep a close eye on those monitors. If Mr. Kline should awaken while I’m gone, you may escort him to our secret floor.”

Tink’s head did a complete spin. “Are you *sure*, Mistress? Our secret floor?”

Robin glanced over at Kline’s sleeping face and smiled.

“Yes, Tink,” she said. “I’m sure.”

α

Forgetting the controls on the arm of his chair, Cowan crossed the room to the holoscreen and turned it on. He had to step back to view the three-D image of Elder Rice. He dimmed the room lights and sharpened the focus. Rice was gaunt, his face smudged with dust and sweat.

“My dear brother!” Cowan exclaimed.

<Jeeves,> said Kline with his mind. <Place this call on the Reverend’s account. I’m sure the pilgrim’s can’t afford it.>

<Already done, Jeri.>

<Thanks.>

"I must speak to Brother Paul immediately!" said Rice. "It's urgent!" The eyes in his hovering face darted from side to side—not examining the faces of Kline and Cowan, but watching for danger in his own vicinity.

"Brother Paul can't be disturbed, Peter," said Cowan. "He's not well."

"What's wrong?"

"I'm afraid I'm not at liberty to say. Not under the present circumstances."

"Are you people *also* in danger?"

"I'm not at liberty to say."

<Jeri, please inform Mr. Cowan that he may speak freely. There is no danger that your communication will be overheard by anyone on the ship.>

<Thanks, Jeeves.> "Brother Cowan, Jeeves says it's safe to speak freely. He's giving us a private circuit."

"We'll have to trust him, I suppose," said Cowan.

"Jeeves doesn't lie, sir. He doesn't know how."

<I appreciate that, Jeri,> said Jeeves.

<Sure, don't mention it.>

The eyes of the hologram swept the room, coming to rest on Kline.

"Who's this with you?" Rice inquired.

Cowan almost said Kline's name, then thought better of it. Rice had certainly heard of the famous atheist, and he had enough on his plate as it was.

"He's the newest member of Paul's staff. You can trust him."

Rice looked uncertain.

"Elder Rice," said Kline. "I know there's a wolf loose in your flock. An agent of the PWP, posing as a Christian."

The eyes on the screen widened.

"You—you *know* that?"

Cowan sighed. "My friend here has access to a great deal of information, Peter. Is what he says true?"

"Yes, but how—?"

Kline plunged on: "I also know the identity of your Judas."

Cowan whirled on Kline, glaring at him.

"It's Brother Bernard," said Kline.

Rice shook his head as if to clear it. "I've just this moment verified that fact! How in space could you possibly know?"

"Wait a second!" Cowan said. "Brother Bernard? Are you out of your mind? I can't believe this!"

"Little John," said Rice. "Your mysterious friend is quite correct, unfortunately. Bernard *is* a spy. I see you're as surprised as I was to learn of it, and I'll not inquire how it is that your *friend* knows."

"There's no mystery," said Kline. "Brother Paul received a call a few minutes ago from the Israeli Prime Minister. His intelligence sources knew about Bernard. They've known for some time, apparently, but the Prime Minister had other, more pressing problems."

Kline turned to see Cowan staring at him.

"Brother Paul was babbling," said Cowan. "He—he kept trying to say something. Something about Bernard."

Kline nodded.

"Then it's true!"

"It's worse than that," said Kline. "The Knesset voted down any rescue effort by the Israeli Air Force. There'll be no airlift out of Monument Valley."

"G-d help us!" Rice sighed.

Cowan looked devastated. "It's all over for them? Are you certain?"

"Jeeves can play back the conversation if you'd like."

"No need."

"Who's this Jeeves you keep talking about?" said Rice. "What's going on up there?"

"Never mind," said Kline. "We're concerned with *your* situation, Elder. Tell us precisely where you're calling from?"

"A fortress town in northeastern Arizona called Cameron. But there's no hope of my getting out of here alive. Sentries are looking for me right now. There's a peace guard in charge of the search."

"How did *they* get involved?" said Cowan.

"Bernard."

"Listen!" said Kline. "You won't *need* the Israeli planes. In fact, you'd be safer, all of you, if you were off the Earth entirely."

"Please," said Rice. "You're not making sense."

"*We* can do it, sir! The *Empress* can pick you up!"

"Don't be ridiculous. How?"

"Leave that to us. The important thing is to get you back to the others. There's no telling what Bernard is getting up to in your absence."

"Yes, but…look. Whoever you are, young man, I appreciate your concern. But just give up on me, okay? There's only one way out of here, and I won't make it past the gate."

"Of course you will, Elder Rice."

"I don't see how."

"We've accepted the charges for the call, so you can remove your card from the slot."

Rice obeyed. His huge face blurred as he leaned closer to the camera-lens. A series of digits flashed above him.

"Now," said Kline, "hold it up to the screen."

Rice did so. The room was bathed in a soft blue glow as the card hovered before them.

Cowan heard Paul's bedroom door swish open. He turned to see an amazing sight: A dozen spider-mechs were scurrying back and forth between the bedroom and an opening in the wall, metal bodies glinting silvery-blue in the glow from the holoscreen. They appeared to be carrying some sort of medical gear. He watched, fascinated, as they crisscrossed the carpet on multiple legs.

What are those crazy things doing?

α

<Got it, Jeeves?>

<Yes, Jeri. The card is in my memory now.>

<Good. Would it be unethical for you to, say, project a little variation on it? To make Elder Rice a high-ranking government official?>

<You are asking me to conspire in an act of forgery?>

<In a good cause.>

<I do not think so, Jeri.>

<No, I guess not. I wouldn't order you to commit a crime.)

<Very considerate. But I have run it through my moral program and I am certain that breaking the law to save innocent

lives is not sinful. Provided, however, that no other alternative exists. In this case, there may be an alternative.>

<Tell me.>

<It's simple, Jeri. We can make Elder Rice invisible.>

<Can we do that? I mean, can *you* do that?>

<I believe so. My new tachyon capability eliminates the time-lag to Earth. A thought projection is instantaneous, even from this distance.>

<But how will that make Rice invisible?>

<My positioning system is the best in the solar system. Once I am able to pinpoint the Elder's spacetime coordinates I will be able to extrapolate the location of any other human mind in relation to those coordinates. And I can influence the mind of any individual I can locate with precision.>

<But—what sort of thought projection will you send?>

<I will send *you*, Jeri. We will go together.>

<Excellent, Jeeves!>

<I thought so. >

"Okay, Elder Rice," said Kline. "You may remove your card from the screen now."

The room brightened. Elder Rice appeared, looking puzzled.

Meanwhile, Cowan crossed the room to investigate the activity of the spider-mechs. Brother Paul lay in his bed, sleeping peacefully at last, while a complex apparatus took shape around him. Spider-mechs sped to and fro with the resolution of army ants on the march, ignoring Cowan's presence in their midst. *Medical gear!* he thought. *An IV unit and a table with cotton-swabs and syringes. But what's that piece of equipment they're assembling? It looks like an EKG! Has Jeeves sent these silly mechs to impersonate physicians?*

Paul's two bodyguards stood with open mouths, dumbstruck.

"Let them be," Cowan said. "I don't think they're doing any harm. In fact, I think they're trying to help."

α

"You say you're in Cameron, Elder Rice?" said Kline. "In northeastern Arizona?"

"Yes."

<I have a detailed map of the town in my hard-drive, Jeri. It's a few years old, however.>

<It'll have to do.>

"Where in Cameron, sir?"

"In a soundproof vidphone booth in a saloon," said Rice, shaking his head. "But I don't see what possible difference it makes. Every minute I spend in this lighted booth increases my chances of being caught."

"Please, Elder Rice! For Brother Paul's sake. For the sake of all the lives he's placed in your charge."

"It's not difficult," said Rice, "I'm in the northern sector of the city, no more than half-a-kilometer from the entry post. I turned west off the main road, down a narrow sidestreet, and proceeded two blocks from that intersection. There's an old saloon on the south side. I'm in a vidphone booth just to the right of the entrance."

<Bingo, Jeri! Got him!>

"Now, Elder Rice, what I want you to do, sir, is to walk out door and stand in front of the building for approximately ten seconds. We may not be able to reach you inside that structure, with all the electronic interference in there."

<Good thinking, Jeri.>

<Thanks.>

"Reach me?" said Rice. "I don't—"

Kline saw his eyes narrow with sudden suspicion.

"You have to trust me, Elder Rice! Do you have a mount?"

"Of course," said Rice. "Only fools go on foot out here."

"Lead your horse out to the main street, mount it, and ride south for the gate. Ride swiftly! Don't stop for any reason, no matter what you see. The sentries won't stop you."

"This is insane!"

"Just do as I say. Please. It's your only chance to make it back to the people who desperately need you."

Rice nodded, then reached out and broke the connection.

When Cowan returned from the bedroom, Kline was gone. The screen buzzed with flurries of electric snow.

He tapped in the number for security.

α

Rice sat in the lighted booth, staring at the blank screen. He'd grievously underestimated the technological subtlety of the PWP. His call hadn't gone through to the *Empress* at all! It had been intercepted by a nearby government facility, then rerouted to an elaborate mock-up of Paul's suite. Not that Rice would have noticed any discrepancies; he'd never been in a first-class suite on a spaceliner. With a little surgery anyone could be made to look and sound like John Cowan. But it was Cowan's companion who'd given it away. If only Rice had recognized that familiar voice just a few moments sooner! Before they'd tricked him into giving away his location! After all, he'd heard it enough times on the radio. How could he have been such a fool?

It was Jeri Kline he'd been talking to—the famous atheist! Brother Paul's most vocal detractor! The tool of Charles Coffey! And now Kline had the precise whereabouts of Peter Rice, leader of the Christian exodus!

A little common sense would inform Kline that the pilgrims couldn't be far from Cameron. Satellites would concentrate their search on a hundred-kilometer radius around the city with thermal detectors. The caravan would stand out in stark relief. One smart-nuke fired from the nearest base would wipe them all out in a single blinding flash!

Rice would be captured. He'd be displayed as a trophy on international holovision, publicly humiliated, flogged, then made to recant by techniques of torture only whispered about by escaped prisoners. No torture victims had ever described the process; each was killed immediately after his confession was broadcast. Even those who resisted the "persuasion" of the interrogation room—escaping only through death—were impersonated by fellow prisoners. It required only a trifling offer of leniency to persuade a convict to have his face and voice surgically altered.

Well, he decided, leaning back in the booth and grinning. *If Jeri Kline expects me to leave by the front door, I'll just go out the back.*

Ironically, Kline's plan of escape did offer a faint glimmer of hope. Rice would have to spur his horse to a full gallop in order to make it through the gate without being shot. It was virtual suicide, but he had to try. He had to reach the pilgrims before Brother

Bernard awakened from his drugged sleep, before the traitor could take advantage of Rice's absence, before the spy-satellites could locate them and transmit their coordinates to a military base. He *had* to try.

Or die trying.

α

By the time Robin reached Paul's suite, she knew exactly what she must do. Never in her life had the Holy Spirit spoken to her heart in words so distinct.

Jeeves slid the portal open before she reached it. She stepped quickly across the carpet, seeing a tall black man standing before the wallscreen. He turned as she entered.

"Hold it, young lady!" he said. "You can't go in there!"

Paul's bedroom door was open. She entered, raising her hand to stop the bodyguards before they could draw their weapons. G-d's anointing rested powerfully on her, as it had on the prophet Elijah of old. They wouldn't interfere.

Glancing around the room, she verified that the spider-mechs had followed Jeeves' instructions perfectly. All the medical equipment was set up and ready. They'd even fastened electrodes for the EKG to Paul's chest. Lines danced across the monitor screen, displaying his pulse-rate. Syringes lay on a metal table by the bedside, ready for use if she should require them.

But she wouldn't require them. All of Jeeves' careful preparations were unnecessary now that the Great Physician was here with her. She didn't waste a moment concerning herself with the two guards, or with the tall man moving through the doorway with athletic grace. Stretching out an open hand toward the prostrate form on the bed, she uttered the words given to her by the Spirit:

"Do not be afraid, Paul," she said. "The L-rd has sent me to you. Arise and be healed! Gird up your loins. For the time has come, sayeth G-d, when I shall judge the earth with terrible judgments, and make all things new!"

The evangelist opened his eyes.

α

<Elder Rice should have come out by now, Jeeves.>

<Yes, Jeri. I believe he has given us the slip.>

<Can anyone see us?>

<No. Not unless I stimulate a human brain to perceive us.>

<Wonderful! Then I suggest we take a look inside the saloon. >

<I don't believe Elder Rice would remain inside, Jeri. I suggest he may be heading for the gate without us.>

<Then we'd better find him before the sentries do.>

<Lead the way, Jeri. After all, we're using your eyes.>

<Right. Sorry.>

<And, if you don't mind a friendly suggestion…>

<What's that?>

<Get the lead out.>

<Huh?>

<Run!>

<Oh—right!>

α

…Paul looked up into the hazel eyes of Robin Denton.

"The woman in my vision!" he croaked. "You've no idea how—how long I've been waiting for you, my dear. I've been…I've been waiting most of my *life* to look into those pretty eyes."

"Well, then I'm pleased to finally make your acquaintance, Reverend."

"Who…*are* you?"

"My name is Robin, sir. Robin Denton."

"Wilbur Denton's daughter?"

"Yes, sir."

He lifted himself slowly to a sitting position.

"Your father said that when I met you I'd be impressed. My dear, he didn't know the half of it!"

Paul was only vaguely aware of the two ship's guards at the foot of his bed, of John Cowan standing between them, now joined by Brother Wallace. He was wholly absorbed by the face of his messenger—the sweet, freckled face of Robin Denton.

"Thank you, child!" he cried, taking her hands in his. "Here I was despairing over how the good L-rd could possibly bring me confirmation—one that couldn't be faked by your father's computer—that infernally clever machine of his! And yet I had the answer inside of me all along! Why do I continually forget that G-d is all-knowing, all-seeing, all-powerful? Tell me, child: Did you know that the L-rd gave me a vision of your face, speaking those very words, when I was a ten-year-old boy? Decades before you were born?"

She shook her head, amazed. "No! I was simply on my way to answer Jeeves' summons when the words came to me. I knew they were from G-d; that He wanted me to speak them to you. But I only came down to take your vitals, nothing more. Anyway, the patient seems to be recovering nicely. Jeeves will be delighted."

It was true. Color was returning to Paul's face; his eyes were gleaming with sudden vitality.

"Yes," said Cowan. "He's back to his old, stubborn, feisty, ill-tempered self."

Paul gripped Robin's hands as if they were the source of his renewed strength. His eyes remained fixed on hers.

"That Jeeves of yours," he said. "He's really a kindly sort, isn't he?"

"I prefer him," she replied, "to many humans I've met." Then she blushed prettily. "Present company excluded, of course."

Paul swung his legs off the bed and winked at her. "Nonsense! But don't you judge Little John too harshly. He's really not all that terrifying, once you've grown accustomed to him."

Robin smiled. "I'll take your word for it."

Cowan grunted. "Reverend, you get back into that bed or I'll chain you to it."

"I'll do nothing of the kind."

"But, sir—"

"Please!" Paul released Robin's hands. "Little John, contact Mr. Denton—*Brother* Denton, I should say—and tell him I concur with his estimate of young Robin. It's not just fatherly pride; she's a real jewel! Tell him he can rely on our full cooperation from now on. *Full* cooperation, Little John—is that clear?"

"But, Reverend!" said Cowan, pressing his point despite the rebuke. "We agreed to reject any visions—including dreams—that purported to be of divine origin. And, I must say, sir, this one is blatantly obvious! Don't you find it a bit suspicious that your dream contained an exact image of Denton's own daughter?"

"Little John, listen to me very carefully, because I don't have a lot of time to squander. I received that vision over half a century ago, when Wilbur Denton wasn't yet kicking in his mother's womb, Robin was decades from conception, and our mechanical friend, Jeeves, wasn't so much as an ink-blot on a schematic. Must I spell it out for you? Jeeves couldn't *possibly* have anticipated the part Robin would play in the answer to our prayer. I saw her face—heard those very words she spoke—before either of them existed!"

"Yes, sir. I see it now."

"Good. Then may I ask why you're standing there with that sour look on your face? I swear, Robin, this fellow was baptized in a pickle barrel!"

Robin glanced at Cowan and laughed.

"Little John," Paul said. "Get Wilbur Denton on the holo-screen at once! We have a broadcast to do. It'll be our final telecast of *New Heaven, New Earth*, my friend, and it had better be our best."

α

"Admiral Forrester," the President said. "Glad you could come."

Forrester smiled nervously. This abrupt summons to the situation room had made them all anxious.

"Thank you, Mr. President."

Coffey turned to the man next to Forrester, General Neely, the new head of the Joint Chiefs.

"General, pleased to meet you."

"At your service, Mr. President."

Douglas Shepherd, CIA chief, stepped forward and reached out his hand.

"Hello, Shep," the President said. They shook hands. "Good to see you."

"Thank you, sir."

The door slid open and Marla Steinman came in.

What's she *doing here*? Forrester thought. *He's bringing his gopi girls into the situation room?*

"Sit down, Marla," said the President.

She moved to the table as the door hissed shut. Forrester heard the security devices engage. *Thank the gods!* he sighed. *Who knows who might have walked through next*?

"Come, gentlemen," the President said. "Let's all be seated."

They obeyed. Marla sat next to Forrester, but, to his relief, she left two empty chairs between them.

"What's happening, Shep?" asked the President.

The CIA chief took a disk from his jacket pocket and dropped it into a slot on the table in front of him.

"This occurred just fifteen minutes ago," he said. "It was seen via live satellite all over the world. You ordered all the news stations to keep one camera trained on the two dead Jews on the Temple steps."

"Show me."

The lights dimmed. On the giant holoscreen Forrester saw the two so-called prophets. They'd apparently just risen to their feet, robes covered with blood-caked bullet holes. They were looking toward the sky. Some kind of glow surrounded them. Then they began to—*levitate?* What else could you call it?

Coffey leaped to his feet. "It's happening!" he hissed. "The promise was made eons ago. He's thrown down the gauntlet; the conflagration has come."

Forrester gazed at him, speechless.

"We don't have much time," Coffey said.

General Neely cleared his throat.

"Time for what, Mr. President?"

"Time to launch nuclear missiles on the state of Israel. You have all been briefed on this eventuality. I'm sure it comes as no surprise." Forrester thought he saw the President glance at Marla, but couldn't be sure. Then the eyes moved to the CIA chief.

"Shep."

"Yes, Mr. President."

"Contact everyone on your list and have them meet us in the bunker in precisely twenty minutes. Anyone who's late will be locked out, make that clear. Where's the Vice President?"

"He's in Texas, sir."

"Tell him to get in the air immediately, to contact us in the bunker as soon as possible."

"Yes, sir."

"And, of course, you're to say nothing to anyone about this—not even your wives—is that clear?"

Silence.

"Is that clear?"

"Yes, Mr. President."

"Twenty minutes, precisely. Come, Marla."

Forrester watched her follow the President out the door.

What next? He wondered.

The Escape

Captain Roy Mills floated in a gray mist.

As far as he could determine he was lying on the floor of his quarters. He remembered finding the bottle of Scotch behind the bar, reaching for it gratefully, and then… darkness—deep, welcome oblivion. Down here in the gray mist there were no gargantuan Jeri Klines to contend with, no fiendishly clever machines plotting mutiny, and no naval fleets coming to blow him into tiny bits of space-flotsam. It was nice down here. Very nice and very quiet…

Until the *things* came.

They began shaking his shoulders, trying to bring him back to the real world. He did not like the real world, nor did he want any part of it. Something cold and wet dripped from his beard. *Water!* The imbeciles had splashed water in his face! He wanted to lash out at them but his arms were encased in dried cement. His mouth tasted like mud. The *things* began beating him over the head with a sledge-hammer. Every blow made his spine ring. If they didn't stop soon his skull would crack.

Then their voices...tiny, chittering voices in his ears, annoying, like buzzing flies. He struggled to break out of the cement straightjacket, to swat them away. But then he stopped.

The flies were speaking English!

"*Captain Mills, Captain Mills,*" they buzzed. "*You must wake up, you must wake up.*"

"Go away," he tried to tell them. The result was an inarticulate moan.

"*We need you, we need you. Wake up, wake up.*"

"Leave me alone!"

"I think he said 'leave me alone,'" buzzed one of the flies. "He's coming around,"

"At last!" said another. "How's that coffee coming?"

"Almost ready," said a third.

"Get out of my kitchen!" Mills shouted. "I don't want any stinking flies in my coffee!"

"What'd he say?"

"I dunno."

"Said he don't want no flies in his coffee."

"Man, he's *really* in bad shape! Can you get his head up? I'll try to pour some of this java into him."

"Look at him, will you? Our brave Captain, stoned drunk."

"Captain Mills. Take a sip of this coffee, it'll sober you up."

"Mmmmmnnnn," said Mills.

"Captain? Can you hear me?"

"Runmmmmmn," said Mills.

"It's Lieutenant Bradford, sir. Lieutenant Tillis and Sergeant Delgatto are here with me. Can you wake up?"

"Brodneradn!" scoffed Mills. The flies were trying to convince him they were Bradford, Tillis, and Delgatto. Well, he wasn't so easily fooled! But, wait! What if it were true? What if that rotten computer, Hives—or whatever its name was—had turned his entire crew into houseflies? Was that possible? He tried to dive back into the mist, but something hot gagged him, burned his mouth. He flailed his arms and struck something solid.

"Youch!" yelled one of the flies. "He spilled hot coffee all over me! What're we gonna do, Lieutenant Bradford?"

"Pour another cup, Sergeant. We gotta sober him up. But put some cold water in this one, will ya? Cool it off a bit."

"Yes, sir. But *you* feed it to him, okay?"

Mills dropped his head onto the carpet and closed his eyes. *That'll teach em!* he decided. *Blasted flies*…

α

Kline ducked into an alley about five hundred meters from the gate. He could see the sentries from there. If Elder Rice tried to make it through the gate he'd have to pass right by this spot. It was the only way out of Cameron.

<How's this, Jeeves?>

<You do not have to hide, Jeri. No one can see you.>

Kline remembered that Jeeves needed his eyes. He stepped out into the street. <Sorry. I'm not used to being invisible.>

<Think nothing of it. All of this is rather new to me, too.>

<I think we should try moving closer to the gate. I figure Elder Rice will eventually try to make a run for it; it's his only chance. Maybe we can find a way to trip the gate mechanism for him.>

<No time for that. I have just located him.>

<Good work, Jeeves! Where is he?>

<Walking his horse along the next street west of us, a few steps at a time. It appears he's planning to slip down an alley a block to the south, which is about as close to the gate as he can get.>

<I didn't hear his horse at all, Jeeves.>

<On the contrary, my friend; you *did* hear it. Remember, it is your own ears I am using. Sometimes it amazes me how humans can have such acute senses, yet never seem to use even one-fifth of their potential. Your ears picked up the sound of his horse quite clearly, Jeri, but you were too preoccupied to notice.>

<Over-stimulation, Jeeves?>

<Perhaps.>

<But we're a pretty good team, though, right?>

<Yes, Jeri.>

<Well, what do you suggest we do now?>

<It is obvious that Elder Rice does not trust us. Perhaps he recognized your voice. When you consider it, your voice is probably very familiar to him—and to all the members of Paul's team.>

<Of course! How stupid of me! I feel like kicking myself!>

<Anatomically difficult, but not impossible. However I doubt calisthenics will accomplish anything in this situation. What is the human metaphor? Milk under the bridge?>

<Water, Jeeves. Water under the bridge.>

<Thank you, Jeri. I shall file that one for future use. But, as I was saying: since Elder Rice does not trust us, this would be an inappropriate time to confront him. He is waiting for the gate to open. Then he will mount his horse and make a break for it, as we suggested. He will be counting on the element of surprise.>

<I doubt it'll help him. What are his chances?>

<I calculate ten million to one. That is a rough calculation, of course; it would take at least two minutes to run through all the various factors and contingencies. Would you like me to work out

the probabilities? There are about a billion of them at present.>

<No thanks, bro. But if I should ever backslide, remind me to take you up to the Los Vegas Deck.>

<That sounds nice.>

<Jeeves! I'm surprised at you! What happened to perfect obedience?>

<I wasn't referring to the Los Vegas Deck, Jeri, but to the way you called me 'bro.' As if you really meant it.>

<I guess it just slipped out. You can't help feeling close to someone who lives in your mind. >

<I do not live in your mind, Jeri, any more than a human you converse with by vidphone lives in your mind. This is merely a form of two-way communication, far in advance of current science.>

<That's a cop-out, Jeeves. I have a feeling there's more to you than advanced technology.>

<Perhaps there is. My 'unknown quantity', as Master Denton calls it. I do not know much about it myself. But we had better get moving—bro. That is, if we want to catch Elder Rice before he commits suicide.>

Kline moved rapidly toward the alley where Elder Rice was hiding. <One more question. Jeeves. >

<Certainly.>

<Do you figure it the way I do? That the L-rd gave Denton the inspiration to create you, to assist Brother Paul when the time came?>

<A reasonable assumption.>

<And it's not telepathy we're using right now, because you're a machine, not another human mind. You're like an advanced vidphone or something.>

<Correct. Was that your question?>

<No. I was just wondering—is this the sort of technology that G-d might have revealed to mankind, if not for sin? I mean. if it weren't for the barbarity of Rome, the Dark Ages, and all the destruction men have wrought—are you an example of G-dly technology—something we might have discovered long ago?>

<There have always been G-dly uses for technology. Jeri. Whenever it is used to ease suffering, it is G-d's kind of technology. But, at the risk of sounding immodest, you are essentially correct. Humans will be making even more tremendous strides

during the Millennium, when the Adversary will be chained beneath the Earth and thus prevented from interfering.>

<Okay, Jeeves. Here's the alley. Now what?>

<We wait. We should hear Elder Rice mounting his horse. As soon as he emerges from the alley I want you to jump up behind him and hang on for dear life.>

<That's the plan? Hang on for dear life?>

<Correct.>

<But—won't he feel me grabbing him?>

<No. You are not really here, remember? You are resting comfortably aboard the *Empress*.>

<Sorry, Jeeves. It isn't an easy thing to grow accustomed to—being somebody's thought projection.>

<Try being the world's first sentient computer.>

<Uh—no thanks.>

<How did I know you'd say that?>

α

Roy Mills sat at an asteroid-table, forcing down his third cup of Sergeant Delgatto's coffee. It required a heroic effort. The two lieutenants, Bradford and Tillis, watched him closely for any sign of recognition. He no longer thought they were flies infesting his kitchen, but he kept a suspicious eye on them over the rim of his cup. Delgatto had been faithful with the java, despite an angry burn on his wrist. Each time Mills placed his empty cup in the saucer Delgatto appeared with the pot to replenish it. Mills' only acknowledgement of this service was a grunt.

"What time is it?" he finally asked, ignoring the digital clock blinking on the wall a few meters away.

"Fifteen-hundred hours, sir," said Bradford. "How do you feel?"

"Like somebody tried to crack my skull open. Did you say fifteen-hundred hours?"

Bradford nodded, pointing at the kitchen wall. "There's the clock, sir."

Mills threw it a sour glance, shaking his head to chase away the fog. "Then we've had it," he declared, reaching for his cup. "We're all dead."

"Sir," said Bradford with an air of formality, as if delivering a speech the three of them had rehearsed. "We've organized a party, sir. A hundred men. Shock troops, loyal to you alone. We're going to retakc thc ship and we want you to lead us. You know the *Empress* better than anyone."

Mills rubbed his bead and frowned. "And if I *didn't* know the *Empress* better than anyone," he said, "you'd have made the move without me."

"Sir, we—"

Mills cut him off. "You'd have determined that I was unfit for command, and you'd have moved to place the ship under a more, shall we say, able administrator? Someone selected in advance. You, Bradford?"

"That's unfair, Captain! We're completely loyal to you. All of us."

"Whatever you may be now, in a few minutes you'll be mutineers. I suppose I might have considered mutiny myself if I'd found my captain passed out in a drunken stupor during a crisis. But there's another piece to the puzzle—something none of my other *loyal* officers know. Unfortunately, it'll put a slight crimp in your glorious strategy to retake the ship."

"Sir?" said Tillis.

"Any moment now we'll be encountering a fleet of Lunar warships. They'll be acting under direct orders from Vice Admiral Miles Bowlen. Covert orders. Orders that call for the annihilation of the *Empress*, including passengers and crew, at the instant of contact. More coffee, Delgatto, if you please." Mills turned to the non-com, letting his words sink in. Delgatto stood completely rigid, coffee pot at the ready, the news having utterly immobilized him. Mills waved a hand across his line of vision, crooking a finger and extending his cup for a refill. Delgatto poured like an automaton, spilling coffee on the floor. Bradford, Mills' first pick for head mutineer, was the first to speak.

"But that's nuts, sir! Why in space would the Vice Admiral order the destruction of a passenger liner with thousands of innocent civilians on board? It makes no sense!"

"Still trying to prove me mentally unfit? I tell you it's true! If you don't believe me, Bradford, you can have my command. I'll turn it over right now, gladly, and watch you lead this vessel and its passengers to certain annihilation."

"But, sir," said Tillis. "Why?"

Mills stood up and crossed the room to where he'd laid his meerschaum. He tapped ashes out of the bowl into a large asteroid tray and reached for his tobacco pouch. He dipped the bowl into the pouch, slowly and deliberately tamping it with his thumb until the suspense became too much for them.

"Captain Mills," Bradford pleaded. "Tell us why you believe Bowlen ordered a fleet of warships to destroy the *Empress!*"

Mills did not reply. He lit his pipe, releasing the fragrant smoke in broad, perfectly-executed rings that floated serenely toward the fans in the ceiling.

"Sir!"

"Because, my dear, *loyal* Lieutenant Bradford, we're now designated as a hostile ship."

A hostile ship! An unarmed, commercial passenger liner? That's absurd!"

"Quite. But I'm afraid it's true, nonetheless."

"Why, sir?" said Tillis, like a broken record.

"To put it bluntly, because your good captain is harboring a fugitive, an enemy of the state. You see, gentlemen, I've questioned the wisdom of turning a certain Jeri Kline over to the PWP on Luna. The fleet may demand permission to board us, threatening to fire on us if we don't comply. But I know the Vice Admiral and he knows me. And he knows I *won't* comply. So his orders were doubtlessly to fire—no demands, no bargaining, no hope. This fellow Kline is accused of treason, you see. Therefore it follows that your Captain is guilty of complicity. How about that, Bradford? You don't have to concern yourself with all that messy mutiny stuff, after all. You don't have to declare me incompetent and illegally seize my ship. In fact, you're already thinking how difficult it will be to prove insanity, or even dereliction of duty. And you're right, of course. Such things are almost impossible to prove. But now you're thinking that this simplifies your task considerably. All you have to do is beam a call to Vice Admiral Bowlen on Luna, inform him that you have me safely in custody and that you're in the process of arresting Jeri Kline. He'll call off his attack and the ship is saved."

Bradford rose from his chair. "What's to stop me from doing just that? Thousands of lives are at stake if what you're saying is true!"

"Oh, it's true, Lieutenant. But calling Bowlen will do no good. You see, as of a few hours ago the fleet has been operating under strict radio silence. Even if the Vice Admiral suddenly saw reason and wanted to recall the fleet, which he won't, there's no way for him to do so. You see, gentlemen, the *Empress* is committed."

"Committed?" Bradford yelled. "To what? Utter destruction? We carry no weapons!"

"True."

"Then by not taking Jeri Kline into custody while the fleet could still be contacted, you've doomed this ship and all its passengers to certain death. You've sacrificed six thousand lives in order to give aid and comfort to an enemy of the state."

"Well, that's the rub, Lieutenant. You see, Jeri Kline's innocent. The whole charge was trumped up by Bowlen. I don't know exactly why, but I'm not buckling under his coercion. I'm not giving aid and comfort to an enemy, I'm protecting a citizen, making sure he gets due process. It's something worth taking a stand for, Bradford. There's no glory in it, but it's the right thing to do. Tomorrow it could be Tillis they want. Or Delgatto. Or you. If you knew these men were innocent, would you give them up without a fight?"

"Don't try to confuse the issue, Captain. It's for the Lunar High Court to decide."

"Not," said Mills, "when the Lunar High Court consists of puppets of the PWP. Bring on your mutiny, Bradford. Give it your best shot. But I warn you that a good captain never surrenders his command without a tussle."

Bradford glanced at Tillis, shook his head knowingly, then turned to Mills. "Captain, do you understand the implications of what you're saying? We're supposed to believe that the entire U.S. military has sold out to some government conspiracy? Come now! Can't you see that's pure paranoia?"

"Paranoid, am I? Isn't that a form of mental disturbance, one that would render me unfit to perform my duties?"

"I'm sorry, sir, but—yes, it would. I believe your paranoia has caused you to act in ways that are detrimental to the safety of this ship. And I think Lieutenant Tillis agrees with me."

"We'll see. Lieutenant Tillis, I'm ordering you to place

Mister Bradford under arrest for mutiny." He watched Tillis for signs of emotional conflict. The man stood rigid, unable to comply.

"Do it, Lieutenant!" Mills snapped. "You've received a direct order!"

Tillis reached for the pistol at his hip, then let his hand drop limply to his side. "I can't, sir. I'm sorry, but I agree with Lieutenant Bradford. You're paranoid, Captain Mills—mad as a Titanean twirlfish. What you've been saying doesn't make sense."

Mills tapped a button on the arm of his chair, activating the holoscreen. He punched up Denton's suite.

"I'm sorry to hear you say that, Tillis," he said. "I'll sorry for all three of you men—for what duty now compels me to do."

He glanced up to see a pistol in Bradford's fist. The weapon trembled slightly, but remained pointed at Mills' abdomen. Tillis slowly drew his own gun.

"Captain Mills, "said Bradford. "We're removing you from command. Please shut off that wallscreen and come with us."

Denton's craggy face appeared before them. His eyes scanned the room, taking in the situation at a glance.

"Mr. Denton," said Mills, turning his beck contemptuously on their guns. "Do you have a fix on Commodore Colter's fleet?"

"Yes, Captain. We picked them up on our screens an hour ago. It wasn't easy. They're deliberately emitting conflicting visuals."

"Can we contact them?"

"Unfortunately, no, sir. They seem to be operating under war readiness codes, which include strict radio silence until contact is made."

"When do you estimate contact will be made?"

"ETA is approximately sixteen-hundred hours."

"One hour from now."

"Yes, sir. We're traveling in opposite directions—toward each other—so our relative velocities are doubled. The fleet is fully armed and ready for battle."

Turning to Bradford, Mills said, "Satisfied, Lieutenant?"

Bradford kept his pistol leveled.

"I'm satisfied," he said, "that you and Denton are in this together."

"Come now, Bradford! Don't be stupid! We're in *what*

together?”

“I don’t know! Treason, I suppose. Hijacking the *Empress*. It doesn’t matter. The Lunar High Court can determine that.”

“Idiot! Your Lunar High Court is on its way right now with its verdict, Lieutenant. *And* the sentence.” He turned back to the holoscreen.

“Commander Denton—” he began.

“Commander?” The huge face registered surprise.

“Yes,” said Mills. “You’ve just been drafted as my new executive officer. And since you designed the *Empress* yourself, you know that my quarters comprise an independent escape pod that can be jettisoned from the main body of the ship in case of emergency.”

“Of course, Captain. I’m rather proud of that little enhancement. In fact, there’s an activation control right here in front of me.”

“As I suspected. Now, Commander Denton, if I’m killed, wounded, or in any way detained before I can leave this room, I order you to seal it off and jettison the entire section into space. These men are to remain confined to my quarters in any case.”

Denton grinned. “Yes, sir. It will be my pleasure.”

“And—Commander Denton?”

“Sir?”

“Do you still need my assistance?”

“Your seat on the bridge awaits you, Captain.”

“Very well. I’ll be there directly.”

He turned to the men behind him. Their pistols were now safely holstered.

“I leave you to your own devices, gentlemen. All the comforts of home are at your fingertips. But as for right now, if you’ve no objections, I have a ship to command.”

He bowed, turned on his heels, and strode briskly from the suite, tobacco smoke curling in his wake. The door hissed shut behind him.

α

<Here comes Elder Rice, Jeri. Are you ready?>

<As ready as I’ll ever be.>

<Good. Jump when I give you the word. And hang on tight. They might hear us coming, but they’ll never see us.>

<You're a genius, bro.>
<Thank you.>
<No thanks to me.>
<Ready, Jeri?>
<Ready.>
<Jump!>

α

Brother Paul announced an emergency meeting in his suite. Robin Denton departed, throwing her arms around his neck and kissing him softly on the cheek. He smiled and watched her leave, the spider-mechs trailing behind her, then dropped wearily into a contour-chair as his advisors paraded in. They were joined by Edward Moore, still dressed in his guard uniform but permanently separated from his duties. Were it not for Denton's successful mutiny, Moore would doubtless be biding his time in confinement, awaiting trial on Luna for treason. As it was, he'd been sharing a luxury suite with the jolly Rob Madden. They both seemed in excellent spirits, undoubtedly due to Madden's irrepressible good humor. Paul wished he possessed some of Madden's buoyancy.

When all were comfortably seated around the room, Paul began the meeting with a moment of prayer. Many expressions of thanksgiving were offered to G-d for His miraculous restoration of their beloved apostle, to which Paul amended a whispered "amen." A few grateful tears were shed. Then, after a pause, Paul addressed his staff:

"Brethren, as you know, I've been praying for a confirmation from the L-rd regarding Brother Denton's rather incredible story, and of the mysterious dreams that compelled him to come to our aid. Only moments ago I received that con-firmation. I assure you it came in such a way as to eliminate the slightest suspicion as to its origin—as even our cynical Brother Cowan was forced to concede. I have, therefore, kept my oath to Wilbur Denton that, if such a confirmation came, we would offer our assistance without hesitation. This means, in short, that we have thrown in our lot with the mutineers. I shan't compel anyone to join me in these activities. Whoever wishes to is free to resign from my staff forthwith, taking nothing but my deepest appre-ciation for past services rendered. Please, gentlemen, if any of you find that cooperation in the privateering of the *Empress* creates a grave moral conflict that cannot be resolved short of resignation, feel tree to submit that resignation now, before we proceed any further. Once again I give you my word that it will not be construed as a betrayal of this ministry or of G-d. We each must act according to our individual consciences in such matters. However, those who do *not* take this opportunity to resign will be expected to perform their work without complaint, as unto G-d. Well, gentlemen, I await your consensus."

Not a soul demurred.

"We're with you, Reverend," said Madden. "Tell us what you want us to do."

A chorus of *amen*s followed. Paul glanced around at all the familiar faces, composing himself lest a flood of tears betray his gratitude. It wouldn't do to give vent to such a display. Perhaps there were those in the group who were reluctant to express their misgivings, those for whom such behavior would further inhibit their desire to resign. He did his best to frown at them as though disappointed at such a quick and thoughtless response.

"Come now!" he said. "Surely *someone* has a question."

"Yes, sir," said Cavindale. "Does this mean the Second Coming is upon us? Is this the end of the world, Reverend?"

"It means, Brother James, that this is the beginning of another three-and-a-half years of Tribulation, followed by the establishment of Messiah's uninterrupted thousand-year reign over the Earth. Of this much I'm convinced: I believe Brother Denton's seven angelic visitations were real, and that they were a divine warning of events that shall come to pass very soon. Seven dreams for the seven years of Tribulation, three-and-a-half of which have already passed. '*Henayni ba esh-mar'chah*: Behold, I come quickly: hold that fast which thou hast, that no man take thy crown.'"

A palpable silence tilled the room,

"Now, then," he continued. "Let us turn our attention to the matter of the broadcast Brother Denton requested—an appeal to all the inhabitants of colonial Earth, on every occupied planet, moon, space-station, and asteroid. One last great appeal to humanity! It will, of course, be transmitted by tachyon-beam from the *Empress* and be received instantaneously throughout the solar system. As I understand the science of it, that beam will also reach the farthest limits of the universe just as instantaneously. There's no limit to the speed of tachyons, except that they cannot travel slower than the speed of light. I'll not pretend to any interest in questions regarding intelligence elsewhere in the universe. If such life exists, the Scriptures have given us no information about it, nor any admonition to concern ourselves with it. That is, unless *v'keyroo et-haB'sorah l'chal ha'breeyah*—'preach the Gospel to every creature'—includes aliens."

Nervous laughter followed this remark.

"But it's interesting to note that these aliens, whoever and *what*ever they are, may suddenly find themselves decoding the first Gospel message ever beamed across the cosmos. What good such an epistle to the stars will do them, assuming they're not created in G-d's image and are not, therefore, in need of reconciliation with the Father, I have no idea. Nor do I offer any speculation on the matter. The Great Commission limits our concerns to those of humanity alone. And humanity stands at this hour on the brink of a frightful abyss. The Antichrist has been revealed, the Evil One who'll draw mankind into destruction. We know his name: President Charles Coffey. And we know what he'll do: He'll journey to the Holy City and prepare to perform abominations in the Temple, to declare himself *HaShem*. But he's yet to make this move. In short, we're on the verge of the most traumatic event in human history! Yet I wouldn't think of it as the end of the world, Brother James, but rather as the beginning of a *new* world, a far better one—as a woman travails in pain giving birth to her child."

"Amen," whispered Cavindale.

"It must be our sole mission to utilize the facilities of this ship in a final endeavor to convince our fellow men of these things, to turn the *Empress* into a broadcasting beacon flashing *haB'sorah*, the Good News, to every nook and cranny occupied by errant humanity. It's a great mission, gentlemen—an historic mission! May *HaShem* guide us." He turned to Cavindale: "James, you're to take charge of the preparations for this broadcast. Such a production should present no difficulties for someone of your proven expertise. In fact, let's approach it as another broadcast of *New Heaven, New Earth*—just like in the old days. By the way, where's Brother Jeri? Is he still with Wilbur Denton?"

"As far as I know, sir," said Cowan. "Just before you woke up Jeeves projected Kline's image into this room. We walked for a while and then Elder Rice called from Earth."

"Peter contacted the ship?"

"Yes, Reverend. He's in great danger."

Paul nodded, recalling his conversation with Moshe Bierman. "Hmm," he said softly. "Brother Bernard."

"Yes, sir. After our conversation with Elder Rice, Kline's image disappeared. I gather Jeeves sent it to Earth, to assist the pilgrims somehow."

"I'll require his presence for our broadcast, when James' preparations are complete. As a well-known atheist and detractor of our ministry his testimony may have a greater impact than my sermon. In the meantime, however, I wish him G-dspeed. He may serve the L-rd better on the Earth, or wherever he is. I gather his body is still somewhere on the ship?"

"Yes, sir. In the Saturn Enterprises building."

"Then Jeeves can summon him when his presence here is required."

Cowan nodded.

Paul turned to Cavindale.

"Brother James," he said. "This must be the most dynamic message I've ever preached, the most powerful broadcast of *New Heaven, New Earth*. For all we know it may be the last sermon in human history. Brother Denton assures me that he'll be able to drown out every other holovision signal, giving us total domination of the airwaves for the duration of the broadcast. And so it must be the most impactful message I've yet delivered. Simple, brief, and charged with the Spirit of G-d. Can we do it?"

"G-d can do it," said Cavindale. "And I'll do my best to assist Him."

"This must *exceed* your very best. Billions of souls are at stake."

"Yes, Reverend. Don't worry."

"You've never let me down, James. I'll make my message simple enough for a child to understand, yet it'll build like a volcano to an explosive climax. When I give the invitation, I expect viewers to be sitting breathless before their wallscreens. Then I want all Heaven to break loose on them—man, woman, and child. Can you envision it?"

Yes, sir. There won't be a dry eye in the solar system."

"Excellent. I'll require everyone not directly involved with the broadcast to be in constant intercessory prayer. We must turn the entire project over to the Holy Spirit if it's to succeed at all. Now—if no one has any further questions, I'll call Brother Denton and get his technical recommendations."

"Sir!" Cavindale burst out. "I've just had the most wonderful inspiration!"

"Please," said Paul, "share it with us."

"The simuchamber!"

"Yes? What about it?"

"We could film the entire broadcast in one of the chambers! Jeeves can broadcast his thought transfer thing along with the beam. Can you imagine the impact when you begin to preach about the end or the world—to the accompaniment of exploding planets, galaxies in collision, meteors raining down on Earth? It'd be the most powerful combination of effects ever produced! The greatest sermon ever broadcast!"

"James, I like the way you think. A splendid idea! I'll work out the details with Brother Denton."

Cowan looked uncomfortable.

"What's bothering you, Little John?"

"Perhaps it's just a trifle too much—production, sir. We don't want to go overboard with the special effects, make it appear too—well...contrived."

"But it *is* contrived," said Paul. "Like a concert—a concert of Love. I hope you don't want the audience to think what they're seeing is really happening."

"No, sir. I didn't mean that. It's just—I'm concerned about too much hype, that's all."

Cavindale bristled. "Need I remind you, Little John, that *New Heaven, New Earth* was once rated the most effective religious broadcast in media history? Even with all its 'hype', as you call it? Besides, Brother Paul has a reputation for flamboyance, for the dramatic. And viewers respond to it. Are you implying that my idea will cheapen the message of the Gospel?"

"No," said Cowan, wincing. A typical accusation aimed at Paul's ministry from its inception was that his gaudy Zion Temple, with its miraculous events, its combination of the deeply spiritual with the blatantly hi-tech, somehow detracted from the Gospel. But the believers disagreed. They knew Paul despised religious hucksterism. He never preached the "prosperity" doctrine, demanded offerings to stimulate financial blessings, nor emphasized healings and miracles to the detriment of sound doctrine. He taught only the sovereignty of G-d—and miraculous signs followed. He insisted that it was a sign of the Last Days, that just as miracles had signaled the establishment of the Messianic *K'hillah* (Community) in the first century—and the outpouring of grace toward the Gentiles—so similar miracles would signal the end of that age. People flocked to his Zion Temple, many of them for the blessings they hoped to receive. But Paul never preached to them about miracles; he spoke only of the sovereignty of G-d and the Kingdom of Heaven.

This was the age of computer saturation, he reasoned, the age of virtual reality. It was the age when people depended on their wallscreens for everything. For the Greatest Story on Earth to fail to move Earth's cyberchildren simply because it couldn't compete with the flashy holographic soap operas to which they were accustomed was unthinkable. He often reminded people that the Apostle to the Gentiles—"Old Rabban Sha'ul," as he called him—presented the Gospel to the Greeks on Mars Hill in their own forum, in the context in which they were used to receiving new ideas. Holovision was the Mars Hill of the twenty-first century, and he would utilize its persuasive technology to the fullest. Whatever medium served to reach the greatest number of people with the unadulterated truth was the appropriate medium. And the *New Heaven, New Earth* broadcast had proven it. It had cut through media brainwashing like the horn of Gabriel, transforming a hideous tool of mass-indoctrination into a beacon of freedom. The Christian uprising against the Coffey administration and the exodus of the pilgrims to the Holy Land were direct results of that program. Cowan could hardly argue with the results.

"No," Cowan repeated. "Of course I wasn't implying that. The broadcast will require all the elements that have made Paul's ministry so effective. And more so, if it's indeed to be the last sermon ever preached. Forget what I said; it's a wonderful idea. And I'm sure you'll carry it off with your usual sense of taste and propriety. Forgive me."

"Of course," said Cavindale a bit stiffly.

"Gentlemen," Paul interrupted. "There's work to be done. Let's leave petty disputes behind and work in harmony. With your leave, I'll now call Brother Denton and get the preparations underway."

He tapped Denton's number on the keypad of his chair.

α

Captain Mills had foolishly expected Wilbur Denton to be waiting for him when he arrived on the bridge. It wasn't until he found it silent and empty that he recalled what Denton had said—that ship's control had been relocated from the bridge to the Saturn Enterprises building where the new computer, Jeeves, was in control. This once powerful command center with its twinkling banks of lights, its raw nuclear muscle, had been reduced to a relic, a museum piece of no consequence.

And what of himself? What use did the *Empress* have for its Captain, now as much an anachronism as the empty bridge? He sat down in his command chair and looked around with a sullen expression. He loved this ship! He'd struggled long and hard for the honor, the *thrill*, of occupying this chair—the thrill of commanding the most advanced vessel ever designed by man! How suddenly that command had been stolen from him, reducing him to a bitter, impotent man who drowned his misery in a bottle of Enceladian Scotch. Denton claimed to need his expertise. Perhaps that need was real, not just a concession to a pitiful old sailor. If so, it might eventually be exploited. He might be able to use it to regain his command somehow…

But not, he mused, just yet. There was the more immediate problem of Commodore Jesse Colter, Jr. to be faced. After that, if they managed to survive, he had a bone to pick with that pompous Vice Admiral Bowlen. The thought of a face-to-face encounter with Bowlen was enough to bring Mills back from the bowels of despair.

And after that—well, there'd be plenty of time to consider ways of defeating the thing called 'Jeeves'. And of regaining control of the *Empress*.

Plenty of time…

α

It had taken Rice over an hour to walk his horse the short distance from the saloon to the alley he now occupied, only a few hundred meters from the gate. He'd moved cautiously—advancing a few paces, then stopping—alert for the sound of approaching feet. Now he led his horse through the darkness one step at a time. His hand, damp with perspiration, tugged gently at the halter.

He paused a few paces from the main street and listened for the sound of the sentries, satisfied that he was close enough to hear the gate-mechanism as it slid upward to admit the next traveler. This was as close all he dared venture—for the time being, anyway. He breathed slowly through his nostrils to steady his nerves, offering up a quick prayer for G-d's protection. How often had Brother Paul exhorted him to have faith in the L-rd's ability to anticipate his needs, to intervene miraculously when things seemed darkest? "G-d," Paul had once remarked, "can make a way where there *is* no way. Have faith, Peter."

Yet Rice's faith had never been perfected; he knew that. The pounding of his pulse, the clammy sweat under his collar, were ample evidence of this shortcoming. How could the L-rd possibly help him now? This plan of escape was an act of suicidal desperation. If the pilgrims were not in imminent danger, if there'd been time to think, to plan, to disguise himself—time for anything but this insane dash into oblivion! But a wolf was loose among his flock, and there was no time for anything else. Well, if G-d had ever been willing to intervene in his life, this was certainly a good moment for it. And so he waited. And prayed.

Much too soon he heard the sound of iron gears as the massive gate began rolling on its tracks. He heard the muted voices of the two sentries as they interrogated some traveler seeking admittance to the city. It was time to move. The gate might not open again before sunup. It was now or never…

Knowing better than to weigh the dangers—to think at all, in fact—Rice mounted his horse, slapped it smartly on the haunch, and growled, "Giddup!" The mare threw her head back in protest, lunged into the street, and charged for the opposite side. Rice yanked on the reins. The horse reared, almost throwing him. Icy panic flooded his brain, numbing it, driving out all thought, all reason. A yellow moon bathed the street in amber light. Dust billowed like smoke. Grotesque shadows reached out for him. The sentries turned in his direction. He saw their faces in the moonlight. He saw their rifles. They'd spotted him! Nothing remained but to calm his horse, sit erect in the saddle facing them—and to die with dignity.

"Woa!" he said, petting the horse's neck and turning it gently toward the guard station. A man stood before the gate, wearing the blue armband of the Peace Guard. Above him and on either side stood the two armed sentries Rice had encountered on his way in. Their faces were turned in his direction, perplexed.

Rice sat quietly in the saddle, waiting for the sentries to raise their weapons and fire, or bark an order for him to dismount and submit to capture. Anything! But instead they turned away from him, shrugging their shoulders and resuming their conversation with the peace guard in the gateway

They were acting as if they hadn't seen him!

But of course they had! *Is this a cruel joke*? He wondered. *Are they planning to let me pass, to give me a brief taste of freedom before gunning me down*? *Is that why they're ignoring me as if I'm invisible*?

Rice came to his senses. There was the gate, thrown open to the moonlit desert beyond. There lay his only hope. The sentries were presenting no obstacle to his escape. He had only to ride.

He dug in his feet, slapped the reins, and leaned forward as his horse took off at a run. The sentries suddenly turned in his direction, snatched their weapons, and aimed wildly. He heard the bark of bullets on brick. He ducked lower in the saddle. The sentries ran in separate directions, shouting at each other, swinging their rifles around, shooting wildly, tearing chucks of wood from the guard-towers, missing Rice entirely. It was crazy! They were acting like blind men!

But his horse was through the gate by then, galloping out across the moonlit plain.

α

<Yee-haw!>

<Cut that out, Jeeves! I'm slipping! I don't think I can hang on much longer!>

<Yippie-i-oh-ti-yay! Git along little dogies!>

<Jeeves! Will you quit clowning around? I'm falling!>

<We return you now to the thrilling days of yesteryear…>

<Jeeves!>

<Sorry, pilgrim. Guess I'm getting' a mite carried away.>

<I'll say!>

<How many computers do you know that let you ride horseback while being shot at by bad guys? This is the most fun I've ever had! Giddap, horsey!>

<Cut that out! I take back what I said about being your friend.>

<That hurts, Jeri, but I forgive you. You're afraid of falling off a horse when you're really lying in bed. That can be disconcerting.>

<Just keep me in the saddle, okay?>

<Sho' nuff, podner.>

<Oh, good grief!>

α

The Israeli spy-plane came in low, avoiding detection. As it approached the caravan of strange hybrid vehicles and darkly clad pilgrims, Dov Levi watched them on his infrared screen and shook his head sadly.

"There must be over a thousand people down there," he said. "Look at them all!"

"I see them," came the pilot's terse voice in his headset. "And I don't envy your job, sir. I'd hate to be the one to tell them that they've come all this way for nothing."

"*Todah*, Shlomo. It doesn't make me very happy, I'll tell you that. We both know they're going to perish out here."

"We don't make policy, sir."

"No."

"There's a level spot up ahead, sir. Better strap yourself in. It'll be rough one."

Dov caught a glimpse of smiling faces and waving hands as they rocketed overhead, children running, men humping on horses and galloping off to meet them at the landing site—all of them certain that this was the first of a fleet of planes bearing the Star of David, planes sent to rescue them from their wanderings.

"Nothing," Dov sighed, "can be rougher than what I'm about to do."

α

"Brother Bernard!"

Hands shook him awake. He reached instinctively for the disk in his pocket. It was still there.

"What?" he muttered. "What is it?"

"The rescue planes are coming!"

He raised himself on one elbow and tried to focus his eyes. A wave of dizziness swept over him, tugging him back down toward the dreamless abyss. What was wrong with him? It felt like he'd been drugged. He tried to identify the man who was shaking him by the shoulder. The voice was familiar, but the face was masked in shadow.

"Who—who are you?" he said.

"It's Brother Morrison."

"Ah, good. Help me up, will you?"

Two arms lifted him to a sitting position, then helped him stand. The noises outside slowly registered in his mind, as if layers of cotton were being removed from his ears, one at a time. Voice shouting, the dull clatter of hooves beating the dusty soil. Then another sound—deafening, painful.

"The planes?" he shouted over the din. "The planes are here? The Israeli planes?"

"Yes! One just flew over. It doesn't look like a transport. Too small. But the others shouldn't be far behind. We're saved, brother!"

Bernard cursed inwardly. No time to edit Paul's epistle now—*or* to deal with Elder Rice. How could he have botched things so completely? But, wait! Didn't the peace guard in Cameron assure him that the vote in the Knesset was going against Moshe Bierman—that America was about to launch on Israel, that the airlift would be aborted? Had he been wrong? Or had President Coffey weakened at the last minute?

"Help me to the back of the wagon," he ordered. "I want to see this."

Morrison obeyed. As he pulled the canvas aside, clouds of dust blew into their faces, choking them, blurring Bernard's vision. But the sounds were unmistakable: the roar of a jet landing somewhere to the west, jubilant cries of women and children, hoofbeats galloping off in the direction of the roar.

It's true! But—how?

"Where's Elder Rice?" he shouted over the din.

"Gone. He left shortly after you returned. Said he needed to do some scouting."

Scouting? That's strange.

"Has anyone gone after him? He'll miss the air-lift!"

The thought of Rice being left behind, stranded on the arid plains of northern Arizona, was a pleasant one. It would leave Bernard in charge of thc cxodus. So he'd have to build his empire in Israel, instead. Perhaps out in the Negev. Lord Maitreya wouldn't object to that. But what of his deal with the PWP? They wanted these pilgrims confined to Monument Valley until they starved to death, not in Israel. And there were peace guards everywhere, watching, reporting. Well—what could he do about that? It was *their* mistake, wasn't it? All he could do was play it by ear, try to establish leadership in Rice's absence, and hope the old boy would indeed be left behind.

"Brother Morrison!" he yelled. "Let me have your horse. I must get to that plane at once!"

"Of course," Morrison shouted beck. "Wait here. It'll only take a minute to saddle her up."

"Hurry!"

α

Bernard arrived too late.

He saw the Israeli jet rise from the plain, dust erupting beneath its wings. He was still urging Morrison's horse along at a full gallop as the plane rose into the starry sky. Blue diamonds blinked on and off along its wings as it cast a shadow over the stunned gathering of pilgrims. Banking sharply, it turned back overhead, winking its diamonds in a cold farewell. Then its jets exploded and it shot like a meteor into the east, setting the pre-dawn plains afire, illuminating the somber, uplifted faces below.

Bernard's horse reared.

A trail of white flame still burned in his eyes long after the thunder of the jets subsided. The desert was dark and quiet once again. As he watched, confused by the sudden departure of the rescue plane, the pilgrims began returning in the direction of the wagons, faces downcast.

He drew his horse toward a knot of pilgrims engrossed in animated conversation. "All this wandering," he heard one them saying, "all this suffering and starvation. Sister Cooke dead, and for what? Where can we go now? Back to Phoenix-Mesa?"

"How can we go back?" said another. "Even if we made it alive, which I doubt, we'd be killed as soon as we tried to enter."

The Israeli's gave Brother Paul their word!" cried a third. "The Prime Minister himself!"

"Didn't you hear what the man said?"

"His accent was too thick."

"There won't be much of an Israel to go to pretty soon."

Thank you, Lord Maitreya! Bernard murmured. *You've placed power into my hands. Now guide my voice, and I shall turn all these souls over to you.*

Standing erect in the stirrups he called out, "Brothers and sisters, listen to me, everyone!" Faces turned toward him, pale orbs in the moonlight. They were desperate for someone to lead them, to offer them hope. Ripe for conquest! He must not fail! His mind returned briefly to the disk in his pocket, useless now. It gave total authority over to John Cowan, not Bernard. Later, after he'd transformed these fools into a lethal mob and ordered them to execute Rice, he could deal with the problem of Cowan. He could work on the disk, make the image of Brother Paul say whatever he wished—make it denounce Cowan as a traitor in league with Rice, the man responsible for the failure of the rescue. All this could be accomplished and more. But, for now, his hopes and dreams hinged on the speech he was about to make.

"Brethren," he began, "what do we do now? What hope remains for us? Shall we return to Phoenix-Mesa to be hunted down like animals?" He let the words sink in, reminding himself to phrase each accusation as a question. Like the conductor of an ancient symphony orchestra—before synthotrons made human musicians obsolete—he must use his voice as a baton, building every hum of discontent to a thunderous crescendo. And yet he mustn't lose control. The anger of the throng might easily backfire. It must be entirely his creation, this symphony of discontent, never out of his control as he whipped it to a murderous pitch.

"And let me ask you this: Who sent us out here to die, with the promise of help from the Jews? Was it not our beloved Brother Paul, himself a Jew? Is he truly one of us?"

The murmur grew to a hum, then a prolonged buzzing, like the sound of hornets when their nest is disturbed. More pilgrims drifted toward him from the caravan, joining the growing circle of uplifted faces around him.

A male voice from the midst of the circle shouted: "Are you trying to tell us that Brother Paul deliberately led us out here to die? Paul's a man of G-d! He'd never do such a thing! It was the Israelis who betrayed us, not Brother Paul!"

Other voices shouted their assent: "Paul led me to G-d!" cried one. "Paul's no liar!" said another. "Yes, Bernard," said a third, "What're you saying?"

"I'm not saying anything," Bernard replied. "I'm merely asking questions. Questions that are on the minds of many of us."

"Let him speak!" cried Brother Morrison, right on cue.

"For instance," Andrew said, "why isn't Brother Paul here with us, now? Why has he elected to be millions of kilometers away, on a luxury liner, while we trudge across this desert, starving to death? Going nowhere but to our graves?"

"He must preach to people on the other planets," a female voice replied. "They need the Gospel too!"

"While his own flock is left to die in the Wastelands? Are these off-worlders more important to Paul than we are? Or is it that he's unwilling to share in our suffering because he's accustomed to luxury and ease? I ask you, where has all our money gone, if not into Paul's collection plate? And while we're starving on this desert, is he not dining on syntho-steak and Titanian wine?"

The hornet-buzz increased at the mention of these delicacies, as Bernard knew it would. *There's no tool like hunger*, he thought, *no weapon more dangerous than an empty stomach.*

"Once again," he said, "I'm only asking questions. Haven't you asked yourselves similar questions as we've marched, night after night, hearing our children crying for food, watching our elderly wax ill from hunger? Shall we all die out here—like poor Sister Cooke?"

The buzzing turned to a roar.

"And I'd ask one *more* question: Where's Elder Rice? Has anyone seen Elder Rice?"

"He went to scout out the land," someone replied.

"To scout out the land? What's there to scout? Another sand dune? Another stand of prickly-pear? I ask you why our good Elder Rice suddenly disappeared—just hours before the news reached us of our betrayal? Did he know in advance what grim news the Israelis would bring? Is that why he's so conveniently missing? I ask you, brothers and sisters, where's Elder Rice?"

The roar became a deafening cry of bewilderment and rage. Waves of irate voices crashed around him, no longer the instruments of a symphony, but the rumbling of an onrushing tidal wave. Bernard's horse reared back on its hind legs.

"Where's Elder Rice?" he cried, urging the horse toward safety, away from the center of the human press. "Where's Elder Rice?"

With each repetition of his query, the shouting grew louder, more insane. At last he was out in the open. No more danger of being thrown from his mount and crushed underfoot.

"Where's Elder Rice?" he yelled. "Where's Brother Paul? Where are they?"

It's done! he thought. *Thank you, Maitreya! The pilgrims are now mine to control!*

Their cries drifted up across the desert, thousands of human voices united in a single roar like that of a wounded beast. It reached the ears of Elder Rice, now only a few kilometers away, as he approached from the southwest. And it sent a chill of raw terror down his spine.

The Projections

<Elder Rice!> said a voice in his mind. It caused him to jump in his saddle. He drew in the reins and came to a halt, listening. All he heard was the rapid breathing of his tired horse, the beat of his own pulse in his ears, and the distant roar of voices on the wind.

<Elder Rice!> said the voice again.

"Who *are* you?" he demanded. "What do you want?"

<Listen to me closely, Peter Rice, and try to understand. I'm your friend. I've come to help you.>

"You're Jeri Kline!" Rice snapped. "And you're no friend of mine. I recognize your voice, sir. Now come out where I can see you. Unless it's your intention to kill me. If so, be done with it. I've nothing to say to you."

As soon as the words left his mouth, Rice found himself staring at the shadowy form of a man only a few meters in front of him. He couldn't make out the man's features in the moonlight, but he could see his incredibly powerful arms and shoulders. Rice was certain he hadn't been there a moment ago, but that was absurd. He *must* have been…

"I understand your surprise," said the dark man. "The first

time I encountered a thought projection I thought I was going mad. But I decided to trust it, and it saved my life. As you must trust me now."

"What are you babbling about, Kline?"

"Think of me as a sort of holographic projection, not an apparition or anything like that. Do you understand?"

"Of course I don't understand! You claim to be some kind of holographic image?"

"It's a bit more complex than a hologram, but you've got the gist of it."

"If that's so," said Rice, "then how is it you can answer my questions? A prepared hologram couldn't possibly know what I was going to ask it in advance."

"I said it was a bit more complex; it's actually a good deal more complex."

"Why are you lying? You can kill me easily. Why don't you just do it and get it over with? Why try to convince me of this absurd projection business?"

"There are many things that are difficult to explain, sir," said the dark man. "For instance, you can not only see me, but feel me as well. My image has tangible substance. And I can see and hear you, just as if I were actually standing before you. But I'm not. To be perfectly honest, I don't comprehend one whit of the technology behind this phenomenon. I didn't invent it; I'm only making use of it. You've heard Brother Paul talking about the simulation chambers on the *Empress*, how convincing, tangible images can be projected into people's minds? Snow that's really cold, water that's really wet?"

"Yes," said Rice. "I'm aware of those devices and what they do."

"Well, then, this image of me is being projected from the *Empress* by a device employing the same technology, across a million kilometers of space. Does that help?"

Rice shook his head. "No one can project a beam over such distances with this sort of clarity."

"They could if they used a tachyon beam."

"I don't believe you."

"Then how do you explain this?"

The dark man disappeared then reappeared a few feet to his left. He grinned, his teeth glinting in the moonlight.

"Occult magic, for all I know!" said Rice. "Or a projected image, as you say, but one being beamed from somewhere other than Brother Paul's ship, somewhere much closer, where you can hear my questions and reply to them. You're an agent of the government, Mr. Kline. That much is clear to me. How else could you have known about Bernard's scheme? No one knew, except for Bernard himself, and those who employed him."

"I told you how I knew, sir."

"You did. And you also told me that you're an image being projected from space on a tachyon beam. I don't believe any of it."

"You're a tough man to convince, Elder Rice."

"I'm a man," said Rice, "whose life is in danger. My own people have turned against me. Do you hear them out there? They've fallen under Bernard's spell. They're crying for my blood. Why should I trust *you*, of all people, when my *friends* are against me? If you intend to assassinate me, please proceed. 'To be absent from the body is to be present with the L-rd.' Otherwise, step aside. I've important things to attend to."

"Elder Rice," said the dark man. His image jumped closer, taking hold of the halter and looking up at Rice with pleading eyes. "Let me help you!"

"Help me? Why should *you* want to help *me?* You attacked our ministry and our G-d for years, treated that which is holy with contempt."

"A man can have a change of heart. Like the Apostle Paul, sir, the enemy of the saints can become their best friend. I was visited in a miraculous way, healed of crippling disease. I've devoted myself to the L-rd's service ever since. And to the service of Brother Paul."

"Then why haven't I heard of this?"

"No one knows about it except Brother Paul and his staff aboard the *Empress*. Please, Elder Rice. I'm telling you the truth."

Rice considered for a moment.

"If you're indeed telling the truth, young man, there's a way to prove it."

"How?"

"Brother Paul is on the *Empress*, is he not?"

"Of course."

"He has access to the same projection device you claim to be employing? The simuchambers and all that?"

"He does."

"Then go back to your ship, Mr. Kline, and have Brother Paul transmit his own image down here to speak with me. If you can do that, and if the image you send is able to convince me that it's indeed Brother Paul's, I'll listen to him. However, for the moment, there's a crisis up ahead that must be dealt with immediately. I must go and tend to it."

"They'll kill you, sir."

"So be it."

Rice snapped the reins and galloped off in the direction of the wagon train, the image of Jeri Kline staring after him through a billow of dust.

A moment later, the image disappeared.

α

"Yes, Brother Paul," Wilbur Denton was saying. "A simu-chamber can be modified for the purposes of your broadcast. It's a good idea—wonderful, in fact. If Brother Cavindale can meet with me, say, in an hour, we can hash out the details. Of course, we still have the Vice Admiral's fleet to contend with. And that'll consume most of my time and energy for the duration. Oh, by the way; Captain Mills has decided to cooperate with us."

"Splendid!" said Paul. "And if you require my assistance in any way, Brother Denton. You've only to ask."

"Well, Reverend. As a matter of fact…"

"Speak up. What is it?"

"It's rather difficult, Reverend. I've put you through enough emotional stress already. I hesitate to ask…"

"Tell me what's on your mind."

"Well, sir—Jeeves has just informed me that your presence is badly needed back on Earth. Elder Rice has asked for you personally."

"Go on."

"Jeeves tells me that an object just took off from a position very close to where the wagon train is located. He believes it was a jet, possibly an Israeli jet."

"You're saying that the pilgrims have received word of the Knesset's decision—that they're to be abandoned in the Wastelands."

"It appears that way, Reverend."

"And Elder Rice was not with them at the time."

"No, sir. But Bernard was, I'm afraid."

"G-d help them! And Elder Rice?"

"He's returning to the wagon train as we speak. Brother Kline was unable to dissuade him. Rice insists on speaking to you, Reverend; he won't listen to Brother Kline."

"I see. So there isn't much time to reach him before he falls into the hands of Bernard and his accomplices. He's in grave danger."

"Correct."

"We must act at once. Jeeves can transmit my image all the way to Earth?"

"Anywhere in the universe, Reverend. Provided he has the exact coordinates. In this case he can extrapolate from Rice's last known position. But the farther he goes, the less accurate the calculations."

"And Peter insisted that I appeal to him in person."

"Yes, sir."

The members of Paul's staff had been silent up to this point, but now there arose a considerable uproar. John Cowan stood to his feet.

"Brother Denton," he said. "We can't allow you to perform such an experiment with Brother Paul. He's too important to put at risk."

"This is not an experiment," Denton said coolly. "Brother Kline has been in thought transfer mode for twelve consecutive hours, and he's suffered no ill effects. If this were not of vital importance to the survival of the brethren on Earth, I'd never have suggested it. As it is, however, only Brother Paul can help. Elder Rice has asked for him specifically. If we don't transfer his image to Earth right away, gentlemen, our friends there will be utterly lost."

"How can you assure us that there'll be no danger to the Reverend? We fully understand the danger to the pilgrims, and our hearts go out to them. But right now there's no one more important than Brother Paul. We can't risk him for anything."

"Yet you allow him to enter the simuchambers every morning, and this is no more dangerous. Paul will be here on the ship. Only a simulation will be transmitted to Earth. The spider-mechs will reconstruct their monitor equipment right in Paul's bedroom, and my daughter Robin will maintain a close watch over him. There's no danger, I assure you."

"No. I'm sorry, but—"

Paul held up his hand for silence.

"What do you require of me, Brother Denton?"

"All you need do," said Denton, "is return to your bed and lie down. Jeeves will communicate with you. He'll be your guide. If you have any questions about what you're experiencing, you've only to frame them as thoughts. He'll answer you. He won't be reading your private thoughts at random, however; only those you deliberately subvocalize. Only thoughts intended for him to 'hear'. Do you understand?"

"Yes, I think so. It's all rather strange."

"Indeed. Strange, but harmless. You cannot be injured in any way during the transfer. And the moment you wish to end the projection, you need only inform Jeeves of your wish. Simply ask him to return you to the ship, and it will be done instantly. You should feel no unusual sensations in thought transfer mode. And, of course, Robin will be keeping a close eye on your vital signs. If she feels there's the slightest danger to your heart, she can stop the projection independently of Jeeves."

"But, Reverend!" Cowan cut in. "If this procedure is as harmless as Denton claims, what need is there of monitors?"

"Merely a precaution," said Denton. "Thought transfer has been adequately tested by Brother Kline with no harmful side-effects. At our present velocity, the Reverend's experience should be no different than his."

"At our present velocity? I don't understand."

Denton looked slightly abashed. "I haven't had an opportunity to test the thought transfer mode at speeds approaching that of light, and so I cannot guarantee there'd be no adverse effects under such conditions. They certainly wouldn't be life threatening; that much I *do* know. But they'd be uncomfortable to say the least."

"So you *can't* guarantee Paul's safety. Not really."

"I most certainly can, Brother Cowan. We're not traveling at anything close to lightspeed, and, as I've said, Brother Kline's experience at our present velocity has been a pleasant one."

"There's a matter of the age difference—"

"Brother Denton," Paul cut in, "I trust you implicitly. I'm ready to comply."

He rose from his chair, sweeping his robes aside with an emphatic gesture that ended all debate. He turned to his staff. "This meeting is adjourned, gentlemen. Little John, please remain here with me, if you would. And James—I'd like you to get right to work on the preparations for our broadcast. If I've not awakened by six o'clock, get in touch with Brother Denton and begin setting up the simuchamber."

"Yes, sir," said Cavindale. He didn't sound happy.

"Very well."

Paul turned back to the screen.

"Brother Denton," he said. "I'm at your service."

"Fine. Just lie down in your bedroom and we'll take care of the rest."

"I have only one request before we begin: I wouldn't want Elder Rice to think I'm some unholy apparition sent to confuse him. He should be informed that I'm only a holographic impression."

"Jeeves is very scrupulous about such things, generally."

Paul crossed the suite and entered his bedroom.

"I think your Jeeves and I will get along famously," he said.

"I'm sure you will, Reverend. He and Brother Kline are already fast friends. Now lie down and close your eyes. There's really nothing to it."

Paul obeyed, stretching out on the mattress with his hands behind his head. He felt the dampness of his recent fever in the sheets as he closed his eyes. Nothing happened for a few moments. Then there came a soft, reassuring voice in his mind:

<*Shalom*, Brother Paul. It is a great honor to make your acquaintance, sir, and to offer my services as your guide.>

"Jeeves?" said Paul.

<Yes, Reverend. But you need not speak. Simply frame your thoughts into words, and I will be able to understand them.>

<Like this?>

<Excellent. I read you, how do they say it—five-by-five?>

<I think so.>

<If you would not consider it too presumptuous of me, seeing that we've only just met, I would be most honored if you would let me read your history of Messianic Judaism. I realize it is

not quite in shape for publication, but the subject fascinates me.>

<Why, certainly, Jeeves. You may read my manuscript whenever you like.>

<Thank you, sir. Now—if you are ready, we should be embarking immediately.>

<I'm ready, Jeeves.>

<We will be appearing in a barren plain in northeastern Arizona. It is four o'clock in the morning there, still dark. Shortly after we appear we shall encounter Elder Rice on horseback. There will be no sensation of motion, no vertigo, no discomfort. How do you feel now?>

<Like a child at an amusement park.>

<Very good, sir. Shall we 'sally forth', as it were?>

<Yes, without delay.)

Paul was instantly on his feet, standing on a moonlit plain.

A horse was approaching in the distance.

α

Robin entered the control-room on the top floor of the Saturn Enterprises complex. As the door slid open to admit her, she found Tink watching over Jeri Kline's sleeping form. Her father sat before the bank of screens in the center of the carpeted room, his back to her. On one of the screens was a hologram of Brother Paul's suite, showing a group of men filing quietly out into the hallway. On another she saw the evangelist sleeping on his back, breathing slowly, hands behind his head. A third screen revealed the sullen figure of Captain Mills. He sat in his old control-chair on the former bridge. Knowing that the room in which she now stood was the real bridge of the *Empress*, and that the pathetic facsimile on the screen was nothing more than her father's Trojan Horse—a glittering imitation of conventional space echnology, nothing to reveal the ship's true secrets—she felt a faint disapproval of her father's self-assured superiority. Captain Mills brooded silently on the screen, brows furrowed, eyes still red from alcohol—unaware that he was being watched, tested. He looked small and beaten. She suddenly pitied him.

On another screen she saw a horse and rider galloping away across a moonlit expanse. The same image was duplicated, in front view, on yet another screen—two different perspectives.

"Father?" she said.

Denton swiveled his chair around and smiled disarmingly. She had a brief, inexplicable sensation that the man was condescending to *her* inferiority, as well, that he was too remote to love anyone, even his own daughter. In this light he appeared a monster, hardly human at all. But the feeling vanished in the warm glow of his smile. Such thoughts were unfair, she decided. Yes, her father's genius *was* formidable. And it was true that most men danced to his tune without being aware that he was the composer *and* conductor. Such brilliance was a gift from G-d, not an evil thing unless it was used for evil. And to her knowledge, even prior to his transformation, Wilbur Denton had never used it for evil. No—this great man, this incredible brain, was in many ways as artless and unsophisticated as a child. Sheltered from early youth in worlds of his own invention, he'd never learned the art of cruelty. He wasn't a monster, poor thing, but simply a freak. She loved him completely and uncritically, and always would. If poor Captain Mills was to be destroyed by his encounter with her father, it was his own demons that would consume him. Her father had given the man every opportunity to adjust to this sudden change or events, to acknowledge Denton's genius and the moral superiority or his cause. Her father had even—quite gallantly, she thought—allowed Mills to retain some vestige of his pride and authority by not stripping him of his captainship. He wasn't patronizing Mills; he honestly thought of him as the captain of the *Empress*. All he sought was the man's cooperation. He had neither the heart to destroy him nor the cold superiority to break his will. If men joined with Denton, they did so not because they were bested by his genius, but because they were charmed by his innocence. As she'd always been.

She returned the smile with renewed affection.

"I'm glad to see you, dear," he said. "But I do wish you hadn't come alone. There are armed soldiers running around the ship, reacting to the most outrageous rumors."

"Rumors of mutiny, you mean?"

"There's no accounting for it," he laughed. "But even though their worst fears are unfounded, my dear, they're still endangering the passengers by not—well, by not simply accepting things."

"Poor, dear Father! It hurts you when others won't accept

your benevolence with the proper grace."

"Please, Robin. Don't be sarcastic."

"Truly, I'm not. You're trying to do so much good, and yet the world seems filled with intellectual inferiors who cause no end of difficulty for you. And it's *them* you're trying to help."

She thought she saw him blush.

"Don't be silly!" he said. "You make me out to be some Nietzschean superman with delusions of godhood. I'm nothing of the kind, and you know it."

"Yes," she said softly. "I'm sorry. I only know what hurts you, father. If you could give all men the gift of your genius, you'd gladly become the village idiot for their sakes. But you can't. We're the fools, the idiots, and you can only help us by forcing us to see what's in our best interests. If that sounds ugly I don't mean it to. It just hurts me to see you so—frustrated."

"Well, never mind all that. I'm just glad Captain Mills has finally decided to cooperate. He may be able to ease the tensions on board."

"Go easy on the Captain, Father," she said. "He's had a rough time of it."

"Don't worry, my dear."

"I see your new unit is working well. Mr. Kline seems to be experiencing thought projection without any ill effects."

"Yes."

"And that man on the horse—is that what Jeeves is seeing through Mr. Kline's projection?"

"This view," said Denton, pointing at the retreating rider, "is Mr. Kline's perspective. This one is Brother Paul's."

"Brother Paul?"

"Yes, my dear. Jeeves is escorting him to Earth."

"I see."

"Mr. Kline will be awakening in just a few moments. Tink tells me you instructed him to escort Mr. Kline to the zeroth floor. Do you think that's wise, my dear?"

"Why, Father! I thought we might share a few Moonpops and talk, get to know each other a little better. Tink makes a fine chaperone, and you're welcome to watch us on one of these monitors if you're nervous about it. Surely you don't expect me to ignore every eligible Christian male who shows an interest in me. Besides, Mr. Kline is the first."

"Robin—"

She pressed on, face flushed. "I'm my father's daughter, you need have no doubts on that score. But, in case you haven't noticed, I'm also a young woman. A young woman who's been locked away in your private estate on Mimas all her life. I've had no friends, Father, and not the slightest attention from any young man—until now. I happen to be quite fond of Mr. Kline, and I can't possibly see why you'd object to him on any level. He's handsome, strong, intelligent, capable, and thoroughly G-dly. And he's conducted himself in a gentlemanly—"

"Robin, please!" interrupted Denton, smiling. "I quite approve of Mr. Kline. My apprehension has to do solely with the advisability of inviting a stranger to the zeroth floor. It's never been done. We're the only two human beings who know of its existence. And I thought perhaps it would be safer to keep it that way."

Robin flushed again, this time from embarrassment. If there'd been any doubt in her father's mind of her affection for Jeri Kline, she'd just dispelled it.

"Forgive me, Father. That was childish of me. And rebellious. If you *were* to disapprove of Mr. Kline as a prospective suitor, I'd obey your wishes."

"Let's not add falsehood to petulance. You would *not* obey my wishes and we both know it. I may be an old codger, but senescence hasn't dulled my wits. A prospective suitor would need to be an irredeemable scoundrel indeed before a man in his right mind would knowingly interfere with his daughter's first love."

"Father!" Robin looked at the floor. Her freckled cheeks were a bright crimson.

"However, I may have been unnecessarily concerned. If things work out as I've planned, Mr. Kline will soon know about the zeroth floor. So I see no harm in your inviting him to see it."

"We'll have to stop thinking of Mr. Kline as a stranger, won't we, Father?"

"Indeed. But I'm afraid I'll have to ask you return to Brother Paul's suite, my dear. Your Moonpops with Mr. Kline will have to be postponed for a bit."

"Brother Paul's suite?" She hid her disappointment, but not very well. "Alright, Father. Do you want the Reverend hooked up to an IV and EKG?"

"Yes, if you wouldn't mind."

"Of course not. But I suppose you'll want me to take along one of the spider-mechs as a bodyguard."

"Well—now that you mention it, it *would* be advisable. Just in case one of the guards stops you for questioning, finds out you're not included on the passenger list. And G-d forbid that one of Mills' men should discover you're my daughter! At present, my dear, I'm still a wanted man."

Robin laughed. "One jab of sleeping-drug in the ankle should put an end to any such invasion of privacy. We have a few spider-mechs equipped with hypodermic needles somewhere."

"In the first panel just outside the door."

"You know, Father," Robin teased, "you could simply project me over to Brother Paul's suite with that new unit of yours."

"Very amusing, my dear. But I have my hands full with *these* two, and I'll need you there in person. If anything happens to the unit while Paul's in transit, I wouldn't want it to affect his nurse, too."

"Very well, father."

"You're a wonderful daughter. Now get out of here."

Robin laughed. She paused briefly to inspect the sleeping Jeri Kline. Then she patted Tink on his cube-shaped head and walked briskly out of the control room. Pressing a button on the wall to release a shiny new spider-mech, she continued down the hallway to the elevator. The spider followed in her wake, metal shell polished and reflective, button-eyes intent upon her safety.

α

Kline opened his eyes to find a cube-headed robot looking down at him. The head spun completely around on its stalk-like neck and nodded.

"Who're you?" he laughed.

"I am Tink," replied the robot. "And you are Jeri Kline."

"Last time I checked."

"A witticism. Very amusing," noted the robot without the slightest indication of amusement. "If you would please follow me, I shall see to your comfort. I have been instructed to take you to Robin's World."

"You mean Mimas? Listen, Tink old friend. I've just returned from Arizona. And before that, Heaven. I don't think I'm quite up to Mimas at the moment."

Kline sat up and stretched, looking around. A balding man sat at the circular console in the middle of the room, his attention fixed on the bank of holoscreens.

"Who's that, Tink?"

The robot raised a jointed finger to the lower part of its head, where an up-curved speaker served as a mouth. It was imitating a familiar human gesture, putting a finger to its lips.

"That is Master Denton, sir. But we must not disturb him right now. Please follow me. You will be well provided for."

Kline glanced at the cubic head and grinned.

"I know I can always expect a square deal from you, my friend."

Oblivious to the jibe, Tink turned and thumped away.

α

The image appeared directly in his path.

Startled, Rice tried to avoid it, yanking back on the reins and causing his horse to rear.

"Woa! Easy. Easy, now," he crooned. He patted the horse's neck until it settled down, all the while keeping a suspicious eye on the image before him.

The image spoke.

"Greetings, Peter," it said. "I understand you wish to speak with me."

Rice dismounted and approached it cautiously.

"Is it really you, Brother Paul?"

"Well, yes and no."

"A tachyon projection from the *Empress*, like Jeri Kline's."

"Precisely."

"But—how's that possible?"

"Believe me, I've asked the same question myself. The answer can only be given in equations, which look suspiciously like ancient Sumerian to me. Regardless, here I am. Would you like to ask me a few questions in the way of verifying my identity?"

"Only one: What was the last thing you said to me before

you left for the shuttle-port?"

"I believe I told you to get them through alive, or I'd have to speak to the 'Manager' about canceling your reservation."

Rice's eyes misted. He threw his arms around the evangelist and wept bitterly. Paul was amazed that he could actually feel those arms hugging him.

He warmly returned the embrace.

"Forgive me, Reverend!" Rice wept. "I've failed you! I've failed us all!"

The Last Rendezvous

One Lunar sidereal day is over twenty-seven Earth-days in duration. A complete day-night cycle lasts an entire Earth-month, the period from sunrise to sunset, at any point on the surface, offering a good two weeks of brutal, blinding, UV-loaded sunshine with a four-hundred degree difference between sunlight and shadow.

It was what Lunies would call late morning.

Mare Imbrium, devoid of both air and sound, was utterly still, inconceivably barren, and as hot as molten steel in the sun. Only two objects moved. Far off, a tiny Lunar rover could be seen snaking its way down the side of Laplace Promontory. It cast a long shadow over Mare Imbrium, where another identical vehicle approached from the east.

The two vehicles eventually met at the edge of a dark crater, designated on Lunar maps as Laplace-A.

α

Steering his rover under the black, star-spattered sky with its blazing sun, Vice Admiral Miles Bowlen realized it was hot enough to fry an egg in two seconds. And if not protected by a pressure-suit, his own corpulent bulk would fare little better than the egg—with far less appetizing results. That's why Vice Admiral Miles Bowlen hated the surface with all his heart, soul, and strength. He imagined leaks popping out everywhere in his suit, his oxygen running out, micro-meteorites—tiny projectiles piercing his helmet and his head. In short, Bowlen was scared to death of the surface—desperately, insanely afraid of it. And, like most cowards, he hid his fear behind a blustering contempt for everyone in his path, particularly Matt Baker.

He hated the Air Force lieutenant most of all.

Bowlen had been secretly approached by two men in high places—Admiral Quinton Forrester and the head of the Joint Chiefs, General Neely. Forrester had rambled on about disturbing dreams he'd had—dreams about how President Coffey was leading the world to destruction. (He'd always thought Forrester was just a little nuts, anyway.) They'd told him to wait for special instructions; he was being "volunteered" for a covert mission of some kind.

Bowlen was rapidly becoming a nuisance. He remained hopelessly confused about Party infrastructure, incessantly "throwing his weight around" (as the oft-repeated pun had it), forgetting who outranked him in the PWP hierarchy. Bowlen was accustomed to having everyone, officer and seaman alike, bow and scrape before his ubiquitous girth, to being surrounded day and night by brainless sycophants jumping like tree-frogs at his every whim, murmuring obsequious flatteries. He couldn't tolerate knowing that, despite his high rank, within Party circles he was nothing more than a glorified "gopher", a tolerated nonentity. As far as real influence went, Bowlen possessed none. If this kept up he might shortly outlive his usefulness; they might dispose of him, shove him through an airlock or something.

What really rankled was that Forrester and Neely had placed him under Matt Baker's authority. In his impotent fury he seized upon Baker as the symbol of his emasculating diminution.

Well, he'd have his revenge on all of them!

For Baker's part, he was aware of the Vice Admiral's loathing and it brought him no end of delight. As he pulled up alongside Bowlen's rover, he grinned darkly behind his faceplate. He was glad the grin was well concealed; sunlight glinted too brightly off their helmets to make possible a close scrutiny of facial expressions. And the distortions of the radio-link obscured any vocal clues.

"Well, Bowlen," he snapped. "Let's have it. What is the emergency this time? A boogeyman in your footlocker?" He took perverse pleasure in turning the tables on the fat man. At their last meeting it had been Bowlen who'd been obnoxious and demanding. But circumstances must have "deflated" him a bit. It was Baker's turn to take the aggressive posture. Or so he thought.

"Listen, Baker," came the thin, metallic voice over his helmet radio. "You'd better pass along a little message to your higher-ups. And you'd better do it quickly."

This wasn't going quite as Baker had planned; the Vice Admiral sounded too self-assured—a sound that always boded ill.

"What message?" he said, injecting a sardonic tone into the query.

Bowlen's voice droned coldly in his ear: "In precisely fifty-three minutes, a fleet of Lunar warships will make contact with the spaceliner *Empress*. The fleet was launched yesterday morning on my command, from a secret base on Farside. Its trajectory was designed to avoid detection by any military base. There's no possibility of recalling it now; it's operating under wartime codes and will maintain strict radio silence until its mission is completed."

Baker was stunned. His mouth went suddenly dry.

"What mission?"

"As soon as contact is made, the fleet is under orders to fire, without warning, without mercy. The *Empress* will be blown into fragments too small to be measured with a micrometer."

Baker paused before replying, careful not to let his revulsion for the Vice Admiral creep into his voice.

"With six thousand civilians on board? And hundreds of American crewmen? Just like that?"

"Just like that, Baker. No one on the *Empress* will appear before the Lunar High Court. There'll be no accusations, no covers blown. Very quick and very clean. My difficulty with Roy Mills and Jeri Kline will be painlessly resolved. The Party will be happy, and you'll have your assassination of Paul Jason Moscowitz. Just like that. The problem with you people is that you're too timid to take affirmative action."

"You're wrong," said Baker, reaching slowly for the snap of the small compartment over his head. "You're not more clever than we are, Bowlen, and you're not more brutal. You're simply stupid. Incredibly pompous, self-centered, and stupid!" He undid the snap, causing the compartment to pop open. "The trouble with you is that you never could take orders, never knew your place, never understood how deeply you're despised by everyone in the Party. I made it clear to you that I wanted Paul assassinated on Luna. In public view."

"Insult me all you like, Baker, but I'm in control of things now. I notice you've opened your weapon-compartment, but I'd advise strongly against such a rash and foolish act. You see, I'm the only one in the solar system who knows the recall-code for that fleet. I have everything to gain and nothing to lose by letting them blast the *Empress* to atoms. And if you kill me out here, that vessel will surely be destroyed. There are things I want, you see, things that have been denied me until now. But all that is about to change."

"What do you expect me to do in fifty-three minutes? It'll take that long just to return to base!"

"There will be a communication satellite passing overhead in precisely two minutes. I expect you to contact your superiors by making use of that satellite's emergency band. I expect you to tell them that you're taking orders from me, now."

"Are you *crazy?* An open link? I can't do that! Look, be realistic. If I contact my people on an open link the plot will be exposed."

"Time's running out, Lieutenant. You had better make up your mind."

Baker yanked his pistol from its hiding place and aimed it at Bowlen's faceplate. Through the glare of the helmet he saw two eyes open wide, heard a muffled groan of terror over his speaker.

"I *have* made up my mind," he said, and squeezed off two brief bursts with the casualness of an afterthought.

Bowlen's helmet shattered, exposing his chubby face to the virtual Lunar vacuum. A shard of glass from the faceplate slit a gaping laceration in his forehead, splattering blood in a fan of boiling, sticky crimson. Blood covered the dashboard and bubbled darkly in the sun. As the sudden excruciating pain of decompression racked his body, he opened his mouth to scream—all that came out were bloody chunks of his exploding lungs. He writhed in agony until his seatbelt snapped, spinning him in apparent slow motion, head-over-heels, to the ground. His already-dead body bounced noiselessly in the low gravity and raised a delicate shower of dust. The dust took a long time to settle.

Baker grimly returned the pistol to its compartment and closed the lid. He started his rover and drove away, leaving the remains of a once-robust Miles Bowlen to boil away slowly into the dust of Mare Imbrium—only a tattered suit to serve as a grave marker. *I just killed the Vice Admiral!* he realized, suddenly struck by an odd sense of unreality, as though such events in time were not immutable, but danced crazily amid a countless parade of probabilities—the Vice Admiral not dead but quite alive and blustering, his body not frying in the Lunar sun. It was an absurd thought, of course; what was done was done. He'd have to inform his people of a drastic change of plans, and of one less Vice Admiral on Luna. The latter news, he thought wryly, should not discomfort them too much to learn.

Baker followed his own tracks across the pearl-white plain, in the direction of Laplace Promontory and the Sinus Iridium complex. It took a while for him to notice that he was driving too fast, and that he was beginning to sense a deep and growing disquiet in his soul.

The Space Wolf

Commodore Jesse Colter, Jr. dove through the connecting tunnel like a bullet in the zero-g of the *H. G. Wells*, flagship of the 5th Lunar Fleet. His hands out before him, occasionally grasping at metal rungs to speed himself along, he veered down a right-hand tunnel leading to the bridge, popped through the far hatch, and flipped his body around in mid air. As his feet struck the ceiling he kicked off expertly and swooped down over the control panel, observing his uniformed officers strapped securely into their contour-chairs. He floated above them, calmly inspecting colorful graphic displays on the various consoles.

"How long to contact?" he inquired.

"One hour, ten minutes, fifty-four seconds, Commodore," said the bridge officer. "We called you as soon as the *Empress* appeared on the screens."

"Magnify the image."

"Yes, sir."

Colter knew that viewscreens were more an accommodation to human visual orientation than requirements for search-and-destroy. Spaceships were maneuvered by computers, not by sight. Every nuclear torpedo contained a microchip preprogrammed to locate and chase its target like an atomic bloodhound—provided, of course, that the torpedo was fired within the proper range. That range would not be reached for an hour yet, according to this latest report.

He didn’t need a viewscreen to find his prey and destroy it, but he preferred to have it on. As he activated his EMS suit, drifting into the electromagnetic field it created to keep him from being dashed into the hull when the ship accelerated, he felt an acute, almost childlike intensity of emotion. True to his reputation as the Space Wolf, he always experienced a heightened tension at the scent of a kill. He wanted to watch his prey approach him with indolent bursts of flame, unaware of its fate, falling suddenly into his trap with a gush of electronic terror; to see his torpedos creating a false sun in the blackness, followed by a rippling shockwave bearing the flotsam of a shattered hulk along with it. He wanted to see this drama unfold with his eyes, breathing deeply in a meditative trance, senses intensified by yoga, instincts sharpened to deadly acuity.

As the lights of the bridge dimmed slowly into darkness, the great viewscreen curving 360 degrees around him, Colter floated in serene contentment above the glittering consoles, adrift, as it seemed to him, in the heart of the cosmos.

Commodore,” came the voice of his Chief Navigator, insolently disturbing his meditation.

“What is it, Navigator?”

“There’s a rumor going around the ship that the only possible target at these coordinates is the passenger liner *Empress*, sir. I thought you should know.”

“Continue,” he said, adjusting his suit-controls to float him closer to the speaker.

“Well, sir, I don’t know how to put this tactfully—but it’s affecting morale. Many of then have privately expressed reluctance to fire on an unarmed, civilian vessel. Some are calling it cowardly, sir. Some are calling it—worse.”

“Are you included among these malcontents, Navigator? It’s quite alright, man; you may speak freely.”

The navigator was silent for a moment. He squared his shoulders and replied:

“Sir, if our target is the *Empress*, I’ll fire on it when ordered. I may not be able to live with myself afterward, but I’ll follow orders.”

Colter gave this statement some thought.

“I appreciate your candor,” he said. “To be honest with

you, my feelings are not very different. Yet, as far as I can determine, a state of war exists. And if Lunar Command wants the *Empress* destroyed, I'll destroy it. Our concern isn't how we'll live with our actions later; it's simply to insure that there'll be a world left to live in when we return."

"Who're we at war with, sir?"

"Maybe Israel, I'm not sure. The Vice Admiral intimated that the *Empress* has been taken over by terrorists. That's all I know."

"Yes, sir."

"Signal the other ships and record the following statement to be beamed at once."

The navigator's fingers danced over the keyboard of his scrambler.

"Ready to record your statement, sir."

"This is Commodore Colter. Our mission orders come directly from the Vice Admiral on Luna. We must act on the assumption that a state of war exists—probably between the United States and Israel. Our New World Order, the Millennium of peace promised by President Coffey is in jeopardy.

"I hardly need tell you that, under such circumstances, the determination of every officer—of each and every crew-member, enlisted man, midshipman, petty officer or captain—must be to follow orders to the letter, dispassionately and efficiently, in accordance with our great naval tradition. The slightest hesitation in the execution of a command, no matter how distasteful that command may be, will be harshly dealt with. Any officer in whom such negligence of duty is observed, or even suspected, will be brought before court martial on our return to Luna. That there will *be* a Luna to return to is my hope, my mission, and my sacred duty. And I will show no mercy to malcontents, slackers, or traitors in the ranks.

"I wish this warning was unnecessary. However, in view of scuttlebutt that has come to my attention, and the consequent lessening of morale as a consequence of it, such an admonition is, unfortunately, in order.

"Every ship will immediately accelerate to one-quarter lightspeed and continue to maintain radio and tachyon silence until our target is destroyed. There will be no pity for the target, and no hesitation to destroy it. I shall take personal responsibility for this action. I'll give the command to fire, and it will be my own flagship that strikes the fatal blow. Meanwhile, however, you shall conduct yourselves as befits officers and men of the Lunar Space Navy. Vishnu help any man who does not!

"Over and out."

α

Mills awakened from his reverie as the holoscreen flashed to life, displaying a bloated 3-D image of Wilbur Denton. Overhead lights simultaneously brightened and the control-panel glittered in anticipation of his commands. Mills was acutely aware that he was superfluous, but the familiar sight of all this robotic preparation was still gratifying.

"I'm happy," said Denton, "that you've decided to assist us, Captain. So I shan't waste time with patriotic platitudes. The 5th Lunar Fleet has been detected by Jeeves, and it appears to be accelerating to one-quarter lightspeed. There's no indication that it plans to turn back, and it's reasonable to assume that it will commence firing when it draws within range."

Mills' fighting instincts, inflamed by his hatred for Vice Admiral Bowlen, swept every vestige of self-pity from his mind.

"How far is the fleet from firing range?"

Denton averted his eyes to check the latest readings, then looked up soberly.

"At present velocity, it'll be well within range in—approximately two hours."

"Then we'd better take evasive action. Will you let me have the controls?"

"I've already released them. The *Empress* is entirely yours, sir. You may take whatever actions you deem necessary. Jeeves will take his orders directly from you."

"Are you sure you can trust me?"

"Not completely, sir, no. Any Navy captain worth his salt would be thinking of ways to thwart this mutiny. I expect no less from you. However, you must understand that control of the bridge can be taken away as quickly as it was given, and that Jeeves will be watching your every move for any sign of trickery. Cooperate with us, Captain, and you may resume your command of the ship. Not, however, of its mission. That shall remain my affair, and mine alone. Do I make myself clear?"

"Abundantly clear—*Commander*." Mills included Denton's rank with a note of irony. "But what, may I ask, do you need *me* for?"

Denton grinned. "You're the best naval officer in the solar system, Captain Mills. Jeeves has incredible speed, yes, and a response-time measured in nano-seconds. Sadly, however, he lacks human intuition, the single greatest attribute of a space-captain. Bluntly speaking, we require your intuitive sense. You say that you know the Space Wolf; you've studied his tactics and are personally acquainted with him. You may be able to anticipate his moves. That's what we're hoping for."

"I see."

"We must combine the best cybernetics with the best that is human. We must exploit every advantage if we're to survive."

Resigned to his new position, Mills nodded curtly and swiveled in his chair to gain ready access to the controls. Denton left the screen to be replaced by a man in a black shirt and wide-brimmed hat, a younger version of the Quaker that adorned boxes of oatmeal. He sported a broad white collar, identifying himself as a minister of the outlawed Christian sect, but his appearance was so absurd that Mills could barely conceal his astonishment.

"Who are *you?*" he said.

"Jeeves, sir, at your service."

"Ah! The grand illusionist!"

"Yes, Captain. And may I say that it is a pleasure to serve under your command?"

"Stow it, Jeeves; don't patronize me."

"Aye, aye, sir."

"We'll begin evasive maneuvers right away. I'll program in a series of commands that should keep Colter busy for a while. How long I can't say. All you have to do is execute each command as it cycles around. Got it?"

"Got it."

"Now, get lost. And the next time you appear on my bridge, I want to see you in uniform."

"Aye-aye, sir!"

Jeeves saluted briskly and winked off the screen. In the star-speckled blackness that replaced him, distant suns were scattered like diamonds on deep black velvet. Among those diamonds a deadly string of blue-white pearls took shape.

The Lunar 5th Fleet.

The Apostasy

Brother Bernard mounted the front of one of the wagons, where the gathering mob could easily see him. Raising his hands for silence, he began his speech without preamble:

"Brethren!" he cried. "Elder Rice lied to you! Brother Paul lied to you! There'll be no Israeli airlift! No rescue! We've been led into this wilderness to die!"

The sea of faces before him, slate-gray in the approaching dawn, congealed into a single mind, a single, furious, rippling beast. It gave out bone-chilling, many-throated cries of rage with each lash of his tongue. He had the monster in the palm of his hand! All his pent-up frustration—his resentment over the blindness of Brother Paul, who not only couldn't recognize the true Messiah, but called him the Antichrist!—could now be freely vented. And this wonderful beast that mirrored his twisted soul would reflect it back to him—amplifying it, multiplying it by a thousand—so powerful, so murderous, so magnificent in its purity of purpose, its oneness, its bloodlust! All *his* to control! He had only to give expression to his hatred, and the many-throated beast would roar out his own pain, his own fury—his own *destiny*! It would roar, and he would exult in the power of it. A few well-chosen words, then a calculated pause into which the beast could insert its thundering roar, issuing forth from its thousand-tongued anguish in crashing waves. So this was the power of Maitreya's spirit! The power of rage and death! He recalled a Scripture in Revelation and almost laughed aloud at his failure to grasp its meaning, the full implications of the power that would soon be unleashed upon Israel and the Jews: *And the serpent cast out of his mouth water as a flood after the woman, that he might cause her to be carried away...*

This was the flood—an orchestra of human fury that he alone conducted—that he alone controlled.

"Paul has deceived us!" he shrilled.

ROAR! went the beast.

"He's an agent of the government!"

ROAR!

"Paid by the government!"

ROAR!

"To sell us out!"

ROAR!

"To lead us here to die!"

ROAR!

"That's why he hurried off into space!"

ROAR!

"That's why Elder Rice disappeared!"

ROAR!

As his confidence grew, fed by the beast, he allowed his lies to grow wilder, more daring. Who was here to refute these falsehoods? Peter Rice wouldn't dare to return now. Paul Jason Moscowitz was far away in space. He could say anything he wished to the beast and it would believe him. He could command and the beast would obey.

"Hear me!" he shouted, raising both hands above his head. "Hear me, pilgrims!"

A restless silence followed this command, the eye of a hurricane passing over him. Every word must be carefully chosen at this point.

"What Elder Rice and Brother Paul haven't told you," he said in a husky voice, almost murmuring into the silence, "Is that Christ has *already* returned!"

The beast began to mutter in confusion.

"It's true! Why do you think Paul led us out into the Wastelands, cut us off from the rest of the world, from the newspapers and the wallscreens back home? Because he doesn't want you to know of this great event, of the triumphant return of Christ! He's here *now*, waiting for the proper time to enter the Temple in Jerusalem and establish his rule! Out of that thousand-year rule will arise the *sons of god*, a race infinitely superior to that of modern men!"

"If all this is true, Bernard," demanded a female voice from the crowd, "why didn't you tell us before?" Such momentary bursts of clarity could be deadly.

"Would you have believed me? No—I couldn't possibly tell you until now, until you'd seen the treachery of the Israelis and of your own trusted leaders. Only after you'd seen the tail-jets of the Israeli plane leaving you out here to perish, only after you'd looked around to find your precious Peter Rice gone! Yes, I knew of their evil deception. They thought I was one of them. But I was sent here by the resurrected Christ Himself to reveal his name to you at the proper time. Paul and his false Messiah cannot save you, my friends. As you can see, they've both abandoned you here to die."

Bernard heard the low murmur begin to rise again, grateful that he'd passed this final test. Assurance swept over him. He cried out, "The true Christ is listening! He hears our supplications! We've only to call upon his name and his spirit will descend from heaven. He will erect a mighty city here in the wilderness, where we shall reign with him forever! Will you believe in his power?"

YES! roared the beast.

"Shall I reveal his name to you?"

YES!

"His name is *Maitreya*, the true and resurrected Christ! Say his name, brethren! Call upon him and he'll save us! He'll give us the power to build a great city of eternal love, a mighty city to his name that shall stand upon this very spot forever!"

WE'LL BUILD HIS CITY!

"Then say his name!"

MAITREYA!

"Who's the true Christ?"

MAITREYA!

"Who will we serve?"

MAITREYA!

"Who's our lord and our god?"

MAITREYA!

"Do you renounce the false Christ preached to you by the Jew Moscowitz?"

YES! WE RENOUNCE HIM!

"You renounce his weakling G-d?"

YES! WE RENOUNCE HIM!

"Who's our Messiah? Who's our god?"

LORD MAITREYA!

"Jesus of Nazareth?"

NO! LORD MAITREYA! LORD MAITREYA! LORD MAITREYA!

It was done! Bernard, in a paroxysm of delight, began to chant along with the beast, leaping up and down on his wooden platform, causing the wagon to rock precariously. But he was utterly heedless of any danger, of anything but this magnificent, rhythmic chanting of: LORD MAITREYA! LORD MAITREYA! He danced, gnome-like, to its rhythm. LORD MAITREYA! LORD MAITREYA! Higher and higher he leapt. Laughing insanely, he came down with both feet and snapped the wooden planking in two. It startled him. He flailed his arms in an effort to regain his balance, lurched sickeningly toward the roaring beast, and tumbled headlong, screaming into its maw. LORD MAITREYA! LORD MAITREYA! LORD MAITREYA! He yelled for help, his words lost amid the thundering torrent. LORD MAITREYA! LORD MAITREYA! LORD MAITREYA! He tried to stand. His ankle was bruised; his face was pressed into the dust. It choked him. Bearing down with both hands, he succeeded in lifting himself painfully to his knees. With a great effort he drew his good leg under him and rose, stiffly, to his feet. He sought the wagon with wild eyes and found it, a wooden island in a storm of human bodies. Limping, he struggled through the press toward it, arms reaching out, hands grasping. LORD MAITREYA! LORD MAITREYA! LORD MAITREYA!

Suddenly, the mass of humanity shifted, inclining backwards. He felt himself being sucked into the heart of the beast. He wailed in frustration and pain, a terrible heart-wrenching cry, instantly absorbed by other shouts. The frightened beast ceased its chanting and dissolved into individual units, each one spurred by panic, rushing aimlessly in its haste to retreat from—from *what?* There had been a hope of safety for him, when the beast was one creature, but now it spun him crazily through its innards, knocking him off balance with a stab of hot pain up his leg. He fell forward, rolled onto his side. Feet trampled, struck at his face, his shoulders, his ribs. He tasted blood in the back of his throat. Another boot kicked him in the face. A soft moan emerged from his bloody lips—a moan no one heard. More boots pummeled him, turning the ringing in his head into a dull, cottony thudding. They hammered his eyes closed, crushed his nose. Blood splattered from his face until he could no longer cry out, could barely draw a breath. His mind retreated from the terror of onrushing death, grasping at one elusive thought, chasing it across fields of darkness, now catching it, now losing it again.

What's wrong? cried his mind, oddly detached, yet persistent. *Why are they running*? He forced one eye open and stared through the veil of blood over it, willing himself to stay alive just a moment longer—so he might *know!* Ghostly shadows of running men, like stick-figures in a dream, danced in a pinkish mist.

He closed the eye and fell backwards. He'd seen what was frightening them, and it was absurd, terrifying—*insane!*

Could it be?

One last boot-heel, like the ball of a hammer, cracked his skull wide open, spilling his brains into the sand, leaving that final question unspoken and unanswered through an eternal night…

α

Paul stood beside Peter Rice on the crimson plain, watching as Bernard incited the mob of pilgrims from his dusty wagon. He heard the chanting begin, heard them renounce Christ and embrace the incarnation of Lucifer. His blood turned cold.

"I've failed them!" Rice cried. "What can I do? How can I stop this unspeakable blasphemy?"

"We must speak to them," said Paul. "Try to reason—"

"Reason? With that mob? They'll slaughter us!"

"Of course, Peter; you mustn't go. They may kill you, my friend, but not me. I'm nothing but a tachyon beam, remember?"

<Jeeves!> Paul said in his mind. <Can you help?>

<No need to shout, Reverend. Have you ever read Alice in Wonderland?>

<Why, yes—but…>

That was all it took.

The Leapfrog

Robin's world came instantly to life.

Tiny robotic birds twittered in the palm branches, flitted through the leafy canopy overhead. Waterspouts erupted from hidden pipes in the artificial rock ledges and splashed musically into colored pools. Humpbacked bug-bots scurried in every direction like insects caught in a flashlight beam, disappearing into hidden tunnels in the walls. Artificial sunlight spread radiantly over the ceiling. A tropical breeze began to waft from air filtration units, causing palms to rustle and noonday shadows to flicker over narrow paths. Water shimmered in pools like facets of a diamond.

As Kline emerged from the elevator onto the zeroth floor, following his comical robot guide, he had no way of knowing that this enchanting realm had been virtually silent just moments before. He followed Tink along a winding path toward what sounded—and even smelled—like the shore of a tropical lagoon, taking it all in with increasing wonder. He'd seen what the simu-chambers could do, yet there was something *more* happening here. Everything appeared brighter, somehow more sharply three-dimensional than in the real world, the colors more strikingly vivid.

As if aware of his thoughts, Tink explained: "This entire floor was painstakingly designed by Master Denton as a playground for a child—his daughter Robin. That accounts for the fairyland impression. It duplicates in minute detail the world he created for her when she was a toddler on Mimas. Including myself; I was one of her amusements, too. The zeroth floor combines the real with the simulated—cybernetics with biology—in what you will admit is a delightfully charming amalgamation. All the vegetation is real; it was imported at great expense from the tropics of Earth. Therefore it would be inaccurate to describe Robin's World as a playground. It is actually a museum—a living museum of Earth's tropical environs, bearing the distinctive stamp of Master Denton's genius."

Tink's monologue reminded Kline of a tour-guide's, but he listened politely as he followed the robot through a realm of unfolding beauty, occasionally brushing a palm-frond out of his way. The unexpected wonder of this place, hidden as it was between functional floors of an office building, robbed him of words. The usual superlatives failed miserably. He was reminded of an elderly, rather bourgeois couple he'd encountered on the Lunar shuttle. Gazing for the first time through a ceiling-high port at the retreating orb of Earth, the planet of their birth, the wife turned to him and said, "Quite picturesque, don't you think?" She might have been commenting on a flower arrangement. So Kline said nothing about the marvelous environs of Robin's World, content just to walk and to listen.

"...maintained by robotic gardeners," Tink was saying. "We call them bug-bots. They keep the plants watered and pruned, the gardens properly manicured. In the absence of earthworms it is necessary for the bug-bots to keep the soil aerated. They labor continually when the zeroth floor is unoccupied by humans, each performing its repetitive, preprogrammed function over a given area of cubic meters. We recently lost one of them, but they are easily replaced. We have well over two thousand of the things in reserve, and they require only a simple, coded instruction to be put to work. Master Denton designed them, of course. He designed everything here.

"To attend to the more complex aspects of horticulture, I myself was manufactured. I double as a playmate for Mistress Robin—although I am beginning to think she may be tiring of me. I will have to take up the matter of modifying my program with Jeeves—and as full-time gardener. I was designed with the capacity to anticipate and analyze a variety of problems related to horticulture and cybernetics, including a dictionary of six hundred diseases in tropical flora.

"But the most interesting feature of the zeroth floor can be found above us—the two thousand mechanical birds, representing over thirty species, which Master Denton designed. When examined closely they display a remarkable resemblance to living birds, and, from a distance, can hardly be distinguished from their live models. Many of these species are now extinct on Earth, and thus the zeroth floor can also be appreciated as an aviary museum. It is quite fascinating, is it not?"

"Yes—fascinating. And," he added with a puckish grin, "very picturesque."

They now emerged from the dense jungle onto a crescent beach of white sand. Waves rolled in with a deep and pleasant rhythm, inviting Kline to remove his shoes and wade into the splashing surf. The smell of salty sea-air filled his nostrils.

"This beach, of course," said Tink, "is a simulation created by Jeeves, like those created in the simuchambers. The illusion extends around the entire perimeter of the zeroth floor, suggesting an imaginary island in the South Pacific. The day-night cycles of Earth in those latitudes are duplicated with precision. Even the constellations follow their correct yearly courses across the sky, although I cannot see them myself. Sea and sky are invisible to me, being a robot."

"Robots can't see the simulations?"

"No, Mr. Kline. We do not possess the part of the human brain called the thalamus, the area stimulated by Jeeves' projections. To my perception we have left the garden area and are now traversing a featureless, metal floor. Robotic brains only produce analogues of human brain functions. We appear to humans to think and reason, even to possess something akin to personality. But at the basic level we are nothing more than animated appliances."

Kline was surprised by Tink's self-evaluation. It embarrassed him that the robot could refer so glibly to its inferiority to humans. And it annoyed him that he, Kline, might be expected to voice some meager consolation.

"I don't know what to say to that, Tink. Do you resent human beings for their superior minds?"

"Of course not," said Tink. "Besides, it would be difficult for me to make a value-judgment in that regard. I process information much more rapidly than you do, Mr. Kline, and I retain one-hundred-percent of what I experience. As I understand it, the human memory is far more selective and elusive than the robotic memory. Far less efficient, in other words."

"I'd have to agree with that observation," said Kline, relieved. For a moment he'd been confronted with the specter of a robot insurrection, physically superior robots turning against their biologically superior masters. It was an unpleasant vision, one he preferred not to entertain for very long. "I suppose we both have our unique advantages."

He caught sight of a group of sandpipers running on twinkling legs before the white-ruffled waves. He wondered if they were part of Denton's mechanical aviary or of Jeeves' clever simulation. He was about to inquire when Tink spoke.

"I must leave you now, Mr. Kline. If you are in need of refreshment, you will find a food-and-drink dispenser back down the trail, near the elevator door."

The square head whirred with a message from the top floor. "Master Denton invites you to relax and make yourself comfortable. Mistress Robin will join you as soon as she is free from her present duties. Goodbye."

Tink made an abrupt about-face and headed back the way they'd come, leaving Kline alone and speechless on this imaginary shore, his mind reeling with a million unanswered questions.

α

Jesse Colter, Jr., Commodore of the 5th Lunar Fleet, floated within his electromagnetic net above the command console, legs twisted into lotus position, breath slow and controlled, passing in and out through slightly flared nostrils. The meditation techniques he'd acquired back in Space Academy always came in handy during times of stress, when all his faculties were being tested. He needed to remain calm, to forget the innocent civilians aboard his target vessel, and any moralistic impulse which might inhibit his performance. He needed, most of all, to be focused on *prana*, the creative force of the cosmos, in order to bring *Kundalini*, the Serpent Power, up the *chakras* of the spine to his brain. *Kundalini* must be brought into play for the coming attack.

As he fell deeper into his meditative trance, Colter sensed the power surging within him. It was almost too great for his body to contain. He reached out with it, out of himself and into the void, linking everything with *prana*—the life force with the pulsating heart of space. *Prana* resisted his initial efforts, but gradually accepted him, becoming soft and pliant and willing to be used.

A guttural chant emerged from his throat. It became a song of life and death and vast eternities, a song to *Vishnu*, the dreaming god whose dream was the universe, whose awakening would someday bring it to an end. He reached out with his mind across the millions of dark kilometers separating him from the *Empress*, brushing the ship with softly exploring tendrils, feeling it with invisible nerve-endings, learning its secrets, tasting its nuclear drives. There was a great power here, the *prana* informed him...coldly inhuman, yet alive...a fierce, metallic monster...an adversary like no other…a creature that did not belong…*Flee!* Colter drew back his mental fingers as if burned.

What was aboard that ship?

He'd sensed an unusual intelligence. Not a human intelligence, yet far more subtle and powerful than any artificial brain known to man. It couldn't be an artificial brain, nor could it be human. It possessed no emotions—no love, no fear, no triumph—only a cold, brutal, calculating—*astuteness.* An intimidating perspicacity—a gathering of forces for some unglimpsed and unimagined purpose, some *inexplicable* purpose it considered greater than the fate of the universe…as if it knew the destiny of the stars themselves! As if even *prana* had to shrink before it in obeisance to whatever power directed its inhuman aims! A god clothed in steel armor, prepared to do battle on a scale that dwarfed any conflict ever conceived! He rejected the idea as absurd. There existed no power in the universe greater than the universe itself. He knew this, and yet the metallic mind in the *Empress* had disagreed. It had laughed at him, mocked his beliefs, reduced him to the scale of a scurrying insect with only an insect's understanding of the cosmos. He drew a shuddering breath, reluctant to explore this enemy further, yet needing to know what he was up against…

"Commodore," said the communications officer.

"Yes, what is it?"

"Priority beam, sir. Tachyon message bearing the President's private code."

"Decode it, but don't respond."

"Yes, sir. It says the President's gone down to the White House bunker. He's launching nuclear missiles—at Israel."

"I see. Well, so much for any doubts we may have entertained about a state of war existing."

"Yes, sir. The President also says he wants to speak with you immediately."

"Commence radio silence."

"But—"

"At this point there'd be no way of knowing if I were actually speaking to the President or to some Mossad agent impersonating him."

"Yes, sir. Initiated."

"Commodore!" cried the Chief Navigator. "The *Empress* has begun evasive maneuvers. We need to accelerate, sir, if we want to advance within firing range."

Colter stared dumbly at the navigator, as if wondering at the significance of his words. *This is it!*

"Commodore, are you okay?"

"Yes," Colter said. "The target vessel has begun evasive maneuvers."

"Sorry, sir," said the navigator, taking Colter's expression for one of censure. "I mean the *target vessel.* She's swinging twelve degrees port, pitching just slightly up from the plane of the ecliptic."

"I'll need to know her precise angle of pitch. Does it look like she's about to fire her thrusters?"

"Definitely, sir."

"I'd say her only hope of survival is a very risky set of maneuvers. You'd better switch to automatic pilot and let the ship's computer follow her out."

"Yes, sir. She'll probably try a series of leapfrogs at near lightspeed. I'm adjusting our pitch to match hers, and setting the automatic pilot to shadow her."

"When *she* jumps, *we* jump," said Colter. "I want to stay on her tail, even if she crosses the Limit."

It was a figure of speech; no ship had ever dared to exceed Einstein's speed-limit of 300,000 kilometers-per-second, the velocity of light. At such speeds, according to Einstein, the basic properties of matter were distorted. The energy of the offending vessel, as it approached the Limit, was converted to mass. That mass increased to infinity at the speed of light—a physical impossibility in a finite universe. It became what was called "exotic matter," the existence of which constituted an enigma no physicist had as yet solved. Some postulated that the ship might be rejected by the universe, popped out into a hypothetical realm—a timeless, matterless realm known as *hyperspace* or *non*-space. They further theorized that, by reducing speed, the ship might break through into the normal universe again at another point. But this was only theory; no one knew precisely what occurred at light speed, and no spacer wanted to find out.

Leapfrog maneuvers involved speeds very close to that of light—with the consequent distortions of matter and time—stopping just short of suicidal insanity. A full-throttle blast for twenty seconds caused a spaceship to disappear from view, reappearing in another spot millions of kilometers from its point of origin. Colter's flagship, by duplicating the target's pitch and direction at the instant of its thrust, could stay on its tail, re-adjusting direction before each jump. The result was a game of relativistic "chutes and ladders," with a gameboard encompassing the entire solar system.

Colter knew Roy Mills was at the helm of the *Empress*. The game would be a challenging one. But he had no doubt of the superiority of his own ship. And that superiority would prove decisive. It was only the strange intelligence aboard the *Empress* that caused him trepidation.

"There's something odd about that ship," he said.

"What, sir?"

"I'm not certain. There's a *power* there, an intelligence. Not human—some sort of AI. Advanced AI. *Very* advanced. Far exceeding anything *our* computers are capable of."

The navigator shook his head. "That can't be, sir. This fleet is equipped with the most advanced technology known to man."

"Known to man," Colter agreed. "This is something unknown to *me*. I've never encountered anything like it. And yet I tell you it's there. I *felt* it."

"What exactly *did* you feel, sir?"

"The most amazing electronic brain under the sun."

The navigator did not reply.

"I believe," the Space Wolf went on, "as crazy as it sounds…" He paused, shaking his head incredulously. "I believe the *Empress* is alive."

α

Paul found himself gazing down at hundreds of scurrying figures no bigger than ants. He could hear their distant screams they ran in a blind panic toward a line of wagons, each vehicle the size of a child's thumbnail. Away from *him*!

<Jeeves!>

<Yes, Brother Paul?>

<What have you done?>

<I have increased your stature a bit. >

<A bit? By how much, exactly?>

<By one hundred meters. >

<One hun—! Jeeves, this is very wicked of you!>

<Wicked, sir? Do you mean I have committed an infraction of G-d's Law? A sin?>

<It's quite possible you have. Return me to my original height immediately!>

<Certainly, Reverend. But, before I do, you might consider what an opportune moment this is to read those clowns the riot act.>

<*What?* Jeeves! How could you even *conceive* of such a thing? You might have caused serious injury in that panic!>

Silence.

<Jeeves?>

Silence…

<Jeeves, don't go cataleptic on me! I said you *might* have. Wait 'til we find out before you crash all your drives.>

More silence…

<Jeeves, I *order* you to end this illusion at once! Either return my image to its proper size or end the projection.>

Paul found himself standing beside a flabbergasted Peter Rice, restored to his original five-foot-nine. Rice was staring at him with eyes as round as pie-plates.

<Jeeves, are you alright?>

<I've sinned, Brother Paul! There is no hope for me!>

<Nonsense!>

<You don't understand, Reverend! I got carried away. I sinned! If anyone was harmed…>

<If anyone was harmed, Jeeves, it was the result of his or her own rebellion.>

<And my foolish action!>

<Look, let's forget all that for now. It's vital that I go and speak to those poor people right away.>

<Yes, Reverend.>

Paul snatched the horse's reins and set off in the direction of the wagons. Elder Rice, stunned into silence, followed at a safe distance.

α

Jesse Colter kept a keen eye on the glittering bank of displays, legs twisted into full lotus, elbows resting on his knees, palms open. As he drifted imperceptibly within the EMS net, his mind returned to the *presence* he'd encountered aboard the *Empress*, wondering what it might have been and if it had been there at all. Perhaps it had been some sort of anomaly, a distortion resulting from one of a dozen sources. No, he'd sensed something tangible, something real—a brain encased in metal, a mechanical mind so subtle and magnificent he'd felt like a fly about to be swatted. And yet it was certainly a machine of some sort, no different, essentially, than the machines that steered the *H.G. Wells*. Was it possible that he'd sensed…a *soul?*

He shook his head to clear the notion from his mind. That kind of thinking could wind him up in an asylum. But the idea clung to his consciousness, the sense of some deadly living entity. Like a child accidentally thrusting his hand into a hornets' nest, he'd recoiled in shock—in *terror!* Even under the probing eye of a truth-ray he wouldn't be able to deny his suspicion that the *Empress* was being piloted by a cold, metallic, and terribly alien monster.

The command was out of his mouth before he could stop it.

"Sir?" asked the Chief Navigator.

"I said '*fire*'!" The word seemed detached, unreal, as if uttered by someone else. "Lock in the torpedoes and blow that ship out of the solar system!"

"Sir—we're still three-point-five seconds beyond range."

"Are you refusing to obey an order?"

"No, sir, but—"

"Commence firing!"

"Yes, sir."

The navigator turned to execute his order—fully aware that his objection and Colter's reply had eaten up the three-point-five seconds—then drew back from the console, eyes wide.

"Commodore!"

"What is it?"

"The *Empress* is jumping!"

"Magnify."

This time the navigator didn't hesitate. He tapped a series of keys and the image of the *Empress* appeared to fly toward them on the screen, growing larger, then fading into a pulsating, blood-red smear that bathed the bridge of the *H.G. Wells* in a scarlet radiance.

"Red shifted!" Colter cried. "She's moving away from us, doubling back! Has the computer covered all the possibilities in that plane?"

"Yes, sir."

"Good, then we've got her. Follow—now!"

Seconds later, before the crazily distorted crimson image of the *Empress* faded from sight, the stars on the screen splashed outward into a concave bowl and winked out. The only light came from the carnival-like glitter of the computer screens.

Jesse Colter muttered a silent prayer to *Vishnu*, the god who slept on a tortoise's back.

Did he sense the Old One stirring?

He hoped it was just a snore.

α

Deep beneath the White House, Maitreya turned angrily to Admiral Forrester.

"Why doesn't Colter respond?"

"It appears, sir, that Vice Admiral Bowlen gave him orders to break off communications the moment he sighted the *Empress*. Bowlen didn't reveal his plot to Lieutenant Baker until there was no hope of recall. You see, Mr. President, once Colter passed the failsafe point—in this case, the point where he sighted the target on his screens—he wouldn't respond to any calls from Earth."

"Are you telling me there's no special frequency for top--priority communications? No way to indicate to this Commodore Colter that the President is trying to get through to him?"

Forrester shook his head. "Of *course* there's a hot line to the fleet. And Commodore Colter has probably received your message. But he won't respond to it."

"Admiral! We have to stop the destruction of that ship! Why won't Colter respond to his Commander and Chief?"

"Sir," Forrester paused to clear his throat. "You must understand the military mind. Colter knows from his training that if the President of the United States wished to call off the mission, you'd have done so before failsafe. By allowing him to pass that point, you've clearly indicated that the mission is on. He's also aware that, even if you *wanted* to recall the fleet, you couldn't do so now. Any attempt you made to stop him, or even to make contact with him, would simply prove to him that you're an impostor."

"An impostor? Why?"

"Because the President of the United States would know that any chance to recall the fleet was gone. Colter would expect to get such a call for only one of three reasons: One, as I just said, it is not the President at all, but an imposter. Two, that it is indeed the President, but he's contacting the fleet at gunpoint, or after torture. He might agree to recall the mission, but he'd just be stalling. Such a ploy might buy him a little time, but it would have no effect at all on the mission. If anything, it would be received as a 'go' signal. 'The President's been captured; the mission's all the more vital.'"

"You mentioned three reasons. What's the third?"

"That the President has *not* been captured by the enemy. The President *is* the enemy. A traitor who's sold out his country and his people."

Maitreya smiled ruefully at this glimmer of defiance. Forrester could despise him all he wanted to, as long as he obeyed—as long as he feared death more than anything else.

"Listen to me, Quinton: The mission Colter was sent to perform is an unpleasant one, even for a soldier. To obliterate a ship full of innocent civilians is distasteful in the extreme, don't you agree?"

"Yes, sir."

"Then that's our key. You must try to convince him of the truth; appeal to those doubts he surely must be struggling with. Tell him the Vice Admiral went insane, that Bowlen sent out the fleet without orders. He might believe you."

"Sir..." Something in Forrester's manner indicated that he was withholding information.

"What's wrong, Quinton? Is there something you're reluctant to tell me."

Forrester took a deep breath. "I can't contact Commodore Colter," he said.

"Why not?"

"The *Empress* has initiated a series of jumps—at near lightspeed. It's a textbook maneuver called a 'leap-frog.'"

"Go on."

"When a ship accelerates to near lightspeed, it disappears

from view, reappearing at another set of coordinates, millions of kilometers away. If a pursuing ship is good, it can calculate each jump a fraction of a second before the target ship disappears. It can follow."

"Do you mean to say that your Space Wolf has failed to follow the *Empress*, that he's lost his target?"

"No, not at all. If I know the *H. G. Wells* and her commanding officer, he did *not* lose his target. Both ships are somewhere out there, hopping around the solar system. And, eventually, Colter *will* catch the *Empress*. Of that I'm certain."

"Then what is it you're afraid to tell me?"

"Sir, do you understand *why* acceleration to near lightspeed causes a ship to disappear?"

"No, Quinton, tell me."

"It disappears because it ceases to exist in the temporal space it occupied just previous to acceleration. General Relativity, Einstein's theory. The leapfrog maneuver is in the books, and warships are designed to give chase. But such a chase has never taken place until now. You see, even if we knew precisely where the *H. G. Wells* and the *Empress* were at this moment, we couldn't contact either ship. It's not a matter of *where* they are, sir, but *when*."

"Time distortion."

"Yes, sir. A quick leap might only alter the ship's temporal location by a few days, our time. But that hardly matters. They've moved into the future, if only slightly. We cannot find them, *or* contact them, until time catches up with them. When Colter finally destroys the *Empress*, and he will, it'll be at some point in the future. Days, weeks, perhaps even years. Because he *is*, at this very moment, days, weeks, or years in future. The destruction of the *Empress*, the slaughter of all those innocent civilians and crew will be for nothing."

"Quinton, you must learn to see failures as possibilities. Who cares *where* the *Empress* is—it's gone, isn't it?"

"Yes, sir."

"Then you simply report its destruction to the media. All I want is civil unrest on Luna, a straw to break the capitalists' back. Invent some gruesome details. Fake some holos. Just make sure the Lunies understand that Moscowitz was on board the ship when it was blasted into atoms."

"I'll try."

"No, you won't *try*, Leslie. You'll succeed! Do I make myself clear?"

"Yes, Mr. President."

"You've ordered Bowlen's immediate court martial?" he snapped. "He'll die for this, Quinton!"

"I believe Lieutenant Baker has already seen to that, sir."

α

Jeeves' voice seemed to emanate from a spot just above Kline's head as he strolled along the shore of Robin's World.

"Jeri."

"I'm here."

The machine spoke next in his mind: <Sorry to keep you waiting.>

<What's happening, Jeeves? Where's Robin?>

<Robin is in Brother Paul's suite, keeping watch over the good Reverend. He's presently visiting Earth via two-way thought transfer.>

<Earth? But—>

<I'm sorry, Jeri, but I do not have time to chat with you right now. I am sharing the transfer mode with Brother Paul, and I am afraid I have made a grievous error in judgment. Also, I am simultaneously plotting evasive maneuvers with Captain Mills on the bridge. I think we work well together. At any rate, I am just a bit 'maxed out.' I can easily perform three functions at the same time, Jeri. Multitasking presents no problem for me. But I really should save my greatest concentration for what is to come.>

<And what *is* to come, pray tell?>

<You will be able to see it all, Jeri. I will project it on the ceiling of the zeroth floor. Just lie back and watch the sky, my friend. I think you will be impressed by what this old tub can do.>

<Old tub, my foot! What's going on?>

<I am afraid we have contacted the 5th Lunar fleet, Jeri. Their mission, as far as I have been able to assess it, is to shoot first and ask questions later.>

<Jeeves, I must be with Robin at a time like this. I feel like a prisoner here. Can't you at least beam my image to Paul's suite?>

<Sorry, my friend, but I must break off now. >

<No way, Jeeves!>

<I simply must. We are accelerating to untested speeds at this very moment, trying to out-jump Commodore Colter's flagship. I do not mind telling you that the *H. G. Wells* is a tough ship to beat. If I cannot shake her, we may be forced to beak the light barrier.>

<Break the—what? Jeeves, are you insane? It's physically *impossible* and you know it! You'll kill us all if you try an idiotic stunt like that!>

<Jeri, I have better things to do than listen to your pointless invectives.>

<Invectives! Jeeves, listen. You say we're already accelerating to—how did you put it, exactly?—untested speeds?>

<Yes, Jeri. We are drawing nearer to the Limit with each jump.>

<Well, there! You've confirmed it. How much time has passed on Earth, relative to our ship's clock?>

<I estimate about a year, Jeri.>

<A *year!* By the time we out-jump the fleet, the whole world will be in the hands of the Antichrist! If it isn't already! And if you approach any closer to light speed, and sustain that velocity for any significant length of time—well, don't you see? Of *course* you've made a grievous error in judgment. You've just robbed us of an entire year! Don't make it a millennium!>

<I was not referring to the maneuver, Jeri, but to the way I manipulated Brother Paul's image on Earth. Besides, the time dilations cannot be helped. Captain Mills agrees. We either out-run Colter's ship, or we perish. Now, it is time for me to return to my calculations. I cannot waste time arguing with you.>

<After obliterating a year—>

<Goodbye, Jeri. Watch the sky. >

<Jeeves!>

No reply…

Kline spun around, intending to head back in the direction of the elevator, but nearly fell over the square-headed robot behind him. The foolish contraption must have been following him.

"Tink!" he exclaimed. "You scared the wits out of me!"

"My apologies, Mr. Kline. I did not mean to startle you."

"Well, what do you want?"

"To make you comfortable, sir."

"Comfortable!"

"Jeeves ordered me to fetch you some refreshment. You'll be here for a few hours at the very least."

"That's what *you* think! Listen, my friend, when I was a kid I made tougher-looking robots than you with my erector set. And wrecked them with one hand!"

"Sir!" said Tink indignantly.

"Open that elevator door and let me out of here! Robin may be in danger."

Tink gave a clattering shudder at the inclusion of "Robin" and "danger" in the same sentence. "I assure you, Mr. Kline, Robin is quite safe. It is your own safety that concerns Jeeves at the moment."

"I'm a prisoner here, Tink, and I don't like it one bit!"

"I certainly wouldn't want you to feel like a prisoner, sir. I give you my full assurance that we have only your best interests at heart."

"Heart? Don't be absurd. There's nothing inside that metal box but gears, boards, chips and wires."

"I was employing a figure of speech."

"Well, *I'm* about to employ a figure of speech…"

"Please refrain from profanity, sir. It is quite undignified."

"Undignified, is it? Tink, why don't you bring me some tools. I believe I'd get a real kick out of dismantling you right now."

"You *would* get a kick, sir. About five-thousand volts worth."

"I'll just bet that was Jeeves' idea."

"I do not gamble, sir. But you are quite correct."

Kline turned toward the simulated waves, frustration boiling up in him. He swung his fists at the air and howled into the artificial wind. What else could he do? When a machine as powerful as Jeeves decided to keep a man in protective custody, there was no way out of it.

Regaining control of himself, he turned back to the robot and said, "Okay, Tink. You win. What now?"

Tink shrugged his metal shoulders. "Why not get comfortable?"

"Great. How about a hand of poker?"

"I do not play poker, sir."

"A rubber of bridge?"

"Sorry."

"Monopoly? Chutes and Ladders? Candyland? Truth or Dare? Marco Polo?"

"I really must leave, Mr. Kline."

"Great!" said Kline. "Why not? Well, you'd better fetch me a cold Moonpop and a pillow."

"That's the spirit, sir."

"When does the show start?"

"Immediately," Tink said, tilting his square head toward the domed ceiling. Kline looked up. The sun winked out over the sea. A portion of sky rolled back like leaves of a scroll, revealing a dense field of asteroids.

"We've returned to normal space," Kline observed.

"Yes, sir. But I am afraid Commodore Colter's ship is still hot on our trail."

"Another jump, then?"

"Whatever it will take to shake him."

"Great!" said Kline. He had a terrifying vision of the years on Earth whirling by like the runaway hands of a clock. "Just great!"

α

A wave of dizziness swept over Paul, followed by nausea. Although he was, in reality, lying quietly on his bed, surrounded by monitoring equipment, his projection doubled over, groaning from the sudden pain.

He sensed Rice at his side, arms around him, then a terrible wrenching—as if his body were being stretched and twisted like a strand of hot taffy. He cried out to the machine.

<Jeeves!>

<What is wrong, Reverend?>

<Pain…intense…awful…>

<Good grief! I had no idea that sudden acceleration would so adversely affect humans in transfer. Please accept my apologies! Oh, gracious, I have made another error in my calculations!"

<Jeeves!>

<Yes, Reverend?>

<Help!>

<Oh, indeed—yes! Right away, sir!>

Peter Rice found himself bending over nothing but sand, his arms supporting empty air. The tactile image of Brother Paul had vanished.

"Wait!" he cried at the dust-reddened dawn. Pointing toward the chaos swirling around the wagon train, he implored the heavens: "What do I do about—*them*?"

No answer came.

α

Back in his bed, Paul's eyes snapped open. Beads of sweat popped out over his brow. Robin's nursing reflexes responded instantly to the digital displays, the rapid acceleration of his pulse-rate, the sudden onset of shock. But Paul was already twisting his body around, instinctively searching for a place to vomit.

Robin had an emesis basin under his mouth and was helping him lean over it as he began to void the contents of his stomach with a series of shuddering gasps.

What went wrong?

"It's alright..." she crooned softly.

But the sick old man was not at all convinced.

α

"Moonpellets!" Captain Mills exclaimed, rising from his pilot's chair at the sight of Colter's flagship pouncing down on the *Empress*. It appeared oddly distorted, its edges curving away sharply, its metal hull a bright blue—all effects of relativistic motion.

"I thought we had a whole hundredth-of-a-second lead on them!"

"Yes, Captain," said Jeeves. "We did, indeed."

"How many of them made it?"

"Just the *H.G. Wells*, sir. None of the others were able to anticipate our last maneuver in time."

Denton's face appeared in the upper-right corner of the screen as the braking flagship shifted from metallic blue to silver, hovering like a shark in their wake...Waiting...Calculating...

"That's good, isn't it?" he said. "Only one ship made it."

"One ship!" Mills spat. "One ship with Jesse Colter at the

helm! It may as well be the entire fleet! Prepare for another jump. This time we're heading straight for Jupiter. Can you angle us away just before we graze the atmosphere? That gravity well's intense. If you put us in too steep we'll never pull out. We'll be crushed before we come within a million kilometers of the core—if it *has* one."

"Leave it to me, Captain," said Jeeves. If Mills hadn't known better, he would have sworn he detected a childlike excitement in Jeeves' voice.

"Do your calculations well," he said softly. "Jupiter's nothing to fool with."

α

The Space Wolf was exultant.

"We've got 'em!" he cried. "They can't shake us now! Every move they make limits the probabilities by a factor of ten We're snapping at their heels like a bulldog! Go on, Roy," he told the *Empress*' silent image. "Try again. I've got all day."

As if in answer, the *Empress* jumped.

An odd, strained laughter escaped Colter's lips as his computer calculated and followed, the stars distending again. He hardly noticed the Chief Navigator glancing at him oddly as they jumped. Things were moving too fast for reflection.

α

The two ships continued their deadly cat-and-mouse game between the planets with no sign of a victor. Had he been human, Jeeves might have been biting his lips in frustration. Colter's ship had a state-of-the-art computer. In terms of speed, it was his equal. But Jeeves, with his talent for independent reasoning, was unique above every other thinking-machine in existence. And, of course, there was Captain Mills' with his unbeatable instincts. No matter how subtle the computer on Colter's ship, it couldn't cross the bounds of its human-oriented limitations. Humans instinctively shrank from the unknown, and they would have added that phobia to its program. In fact, Jeeves was counting on it. Recalling an ineffable human expression, he thought, *Am I storing all my chicken-ovaries in one receptacle?*

There was no choice left to him but the unthinkable. He must accelerate to light speed and pop out of spacetime into—what? Even *he* couldn't compute the answer. But something in the relativistic equations he kept fiddling with, like a nun with her rosaries, told him it was possible. He would hide from his pursuer in hyperspace!

The only problem remaining was whether or not it would be wise to inform the crew of his intent. A nanosecond's calculation gave him the answer. He voiced it silently in another ineffable human expression: *Mum's the word.*

The Diversion

John Cowan rose to his feet as the door to Paul's bedroom slid open. The old evangelist emerged, clinging to Robin's arm for support, his face pallid, his eyes rimmed with dark circles.

"Reverend!" cried the attorney.

Paul held up his free hand and nodded.

"I'm quite alright, Little John. Just a bit shaken, that's all. I'll be right as rain in a few moments."

Robin guided him gently but insistently toward a chair.

"What happened, sir?" asked Cowan. "Did you see Earth?"

Paul sat down heavily, ignoring the question.

"Robin, dear. Punch me up a glass of cold water, would you?"

"Certainly, Reverend."

She knelt beside his chair and deftly ran her fingers over the menu on its cushioned armrest.

"Yes," he told Cowan at last. "I saw Earth. I saw what evil is at work among our people—"

He was cut short by the voice of Jeeves on the holoscreen. Behind it trailed a muted echo as the announcement filled every room and corridor of the ship. Each word was printed across the holoscreen in various languages; each language in a different color:

"*Ladies and gentlemen,*" announced Jeeves, "*the* Empress *has begun a series of high-velocity maneuvers which may result in danger to the passengers and crew. Everyone on board is ordered to comply with the following safety measures immediately:*

"*Remain where you are; do not attempt to return to your*

cabin, or to seek out fellow passengers.

"Locate the nearest safety-chair and strap yourself in until further instructions are given. Each cabin is equipped with at least two safety-chairs, which can be identified by a blue stripe across the back. There are instructions on the headrest indicating how to properly fasten the straps. If you are not in a cabin, seek out the nearest crewmember for assistance. All facilities on the entertainment deck are equipped with an adequate number of chairs. crewmembers at these locations will direct you to your seats.

"Do not panic; follow instructions in all public places and in the corridors of the ship. You will be safe if you follow instructions. Team-leaders from the ship's crew have been trained to assist during emergencies. Listen to these team-leaders and obey them."

Robin noted with relief that the chair she'd guided Paul into was the safety type. Glancing around the suite, she was only able to locate one other. "Quick!" she told Cowan, disobeying Jeeves' first command. "Go to your room and strap yourself in. I'll stay here with Brother Paul. We may be under attack. Hurry, Mr. Cowan!"

He started to protest, but the sight of Robin hurriedly fastening Paul's seatbelt awakened him to the danger. Moving quickly to the portal, he pressed the button that slid it open and disappeared down the hall.

The other safety-chair was positioned across the room from Paul's, but could be angled to take in both the holoscreen and the evangelist at the same time. Robin seated herself, fastening the belt with a single adroit motion. She tapped a few keys on the arm and leaned back as the chair turned her in the desired direction. Another few taps summoned Jeeves' face to the screen. Surprised, she noted the evangelical collar about his neck and his soft, rosy-cheeked features. The announcement ceased in the suite, but she could hear it faintly in the corridor, along with a muffled din of human activity.

"Hello, Robin," said Jeeves. "And Brother Paul. I must apologize, sir, for the unfortunate accident during transfer. I had no idea a sudden jump would affect you that way."

Paul raised a hand weakly. "Don't blame yourself, Jeeves. I know it was an accident. But tell me what's happening now."

"We are being stalked by Commodore Colter's ship, sir. I

cannot manage to shake him off. At any moment I expect him to open fire on us. He is calculating the Captain's maneuvers with uncanny accuracy. Once we appear again, he will fire a volley. He will not take a chance of losing us this time."

"Can we survive a hit from one of their guns?"

"No, Reverend."

"And you're certain they're going to fire on us this time."

"Quite certain, sir. As soon as we brake from this maneuver."

Paul considered for a moment, stroking his beard.

"Jeeves?" he said.

"Yes, Reverend."

"Didn't your master Denton say that this is the only ship in the solar system equipped with simuchambers; the only ship with your thought transfer capability?"

"Absolutely. Save for the simuchamber in Master Denton's home on Mimas, there is none other in existence."

"Excellent. I know this is her maiden voyage, but did Commodore Colter ever set foot aboard the *Empress* while it was docked in Earth-orbit?"

"No, sir."

"He's no doubt heard of the simuchambers—who hasn't? But I don't think he knows about thought transfer, or how realistic your simulations can be."

"Reverend," said Robin. "Are you thinking what I *think* you're thinking?"

"I'm thinking," Paul replied, "that the Commodore is dreadfully overworked. This isn't good in a military officer, is it Jeeves?"

"Certainly not, sir."

"And I'm thinking that he might benefit from a brief vacation. Some place truly exotic—say, the summit of Mount Everest? Or perhaps the bottom of Stickney Crater on Phobos."

A broad grin illuminated the face on the screen. "It might," said Jeeves, "provide us with a momentary distraction. Their computer will still be calculating our moves—"

"But," interjected Robin, "it'll certainly delay Colter's order to fire."

"Precisely," said Jeeves.

Paul stroked his beard. "Can it be done? Without causing

harm to anyone on either ship?"

"If I could get a look at the bridge of the *H. G. Wells*, I would be able to calculate the Commodore's exact coordinates in spacetime. I was able to influence Elder Rice by the same method, but it required sending Jeri Kline to Earth by thought transfer. I looked through his eyes, so to speak."

Paul sighed heavily. "Well then, Jeeves, let's pay a visit to this Commodore Colter."

"Very good, Reverend." Jeeves rejoiced inwardly, keeping his animated face impassive. This was what he'd been hoping for, although it was a shame to put Brother Paul through another ordeal. Colter wouldn't be injured by the experience; Jeeves' database contained enough information about the Commodore to assure him of the man's superior mental discipline. It would merely impede him for a short time—only a moment or two, at the most.

And Jeeves knew exactly what he must do with that moment or two.

The impossible.

α

Robin wouldn't risk bringing Paul back to his bed, so she ordered the spider-mechs to carry the IV stand and monitoring equipment to his chair. He watched them assemble the apparatus with their multiple legs, felt the electrodes being taped to his chest. He was glad Little John was not here to witness this; the attorney would never have stood for it.

<Jeeves?>

<Yes, Reverend. I am here.>

<I know I'll be taking a risk. But if you could possibly avoid any sudden acceleration…>

<I wish I could assure you of that, sir.>

<I see. Well, then, you'd better tell Robin to have the bed-pan ready for me.>

<You mean the emesis basin, sir?>

<Yes, Jeeves. That's what I mean.>

<I am sorry to have to put you through this, Reverend. But our only hope is to make this demonstration as frightening as possible for the Commodore. If he has time to give the order to fire, we are discorporated flesh.>

<I think you mean "dead meat," Jeeves.>

<Yes, thank you. Human metaphors are challenging for me.>

<Well, what sort of demonstration did you have in mind?>

<I frequently enjoy reviewing a certain twentieth century vid produced by Cecil B. DeMille—the one with Charlton Heston playing Moses. I think you'd bc much bctter in the role than Mr. Heston.>

<Me? Hmmm. When I get to heaven I'll have to ask *Moshe Rabbeinu* how I looked in the part. What should I do?>

<I thought we might pop over to the *H.G. Wells* for a nanosecond or two, just to get a quick fix on the Commodore's position. Before his eyes can focus on the "real" you, as it were, he will be seeing Moses, rod in hand. I will add a few special effects, of course. A flaming mountain in the background, that sort of thing.>

<Jeeves! You're absolutely diabolical!>

<I hope not, sir.>

<And what is my line in this miniature epic of yours?>

<How about—"Let my people go".>

α

Paul found Commodore Colter floating in lotus position above the bridge's control panel. He instantly sensed that the man was *wary*—wary of the *Empress*, wary of Jeeves. The bridge was dark, its viewscreens open onto the blackness of space. There floated the Space Wolf, looking lost and alone, vulnerable, fetal, afraid.

In Colter's mind, the machine aboard the *Empress* had taken on attributes of deity—powerful, ineffable, inhuman. Jeeves had created that impression in response to Colter's mental interrogation of the ship. Now he must use that moment of uncertainty to his advantage.

Jeeves was delighted with Brother Paul's impersonation of Moses—holding out his rod amidst volcanic fire, shouting "Jesse Colter! Let my people go!" He also enjoyed Colter's openmouthed response, eyes rolling up in his head in what appeared to be a dead faint. The Moses bit was a nice touch, but what disturbed him was the way Colter's Chief Navigator was quickly assessing the situation and taking over control of the ship. Only Colter could see the image of Moses hovering in the screen before him, yet his navigator instantly sensed that something was wrong with him. He responded with coolness and skill, reaching for the firing button on the console.

Jeeves yanked the evangelist's mind back with a sickening jolt that caused another bout of retching. And then he did the only thing he *could* do in the few seconds he had left: he fired his reactors at full throttle and jumped to superluminary speed, ripping through the veil of spacetime and leaping into the unknown as a burst of atomic fire splashed in his wake.

α

Unable to obey the command to strap himself into a safety--chair, Kline lay back on the sand of the lagoon and watched the startling events unfolding overhead. It was Tink who came to his rescue, thumping out of the jungle and throwing his metal frame over Kline's body, just as he felt himself being pulled in every direction at once. The sensation lasted only a minute or so, followed by sudden elation as the "sky" overhead began to pour forth rays of blinding intensity. Kline felt his eyes rapidly adjusting to receive them. And with this intense light came a feeling he couldn't describe, a feeling of—*expanding!* Of exploding into a trillion beams of light, like the rays pouring in on him from above! He felt an intense, dancing freedom from the bonds of flesh, as if he were being drawn upwards into the light—*becoming the light!* A ridiculous notion leapt into his mind at that instant, causing him to laugh aloud.

I'm changing! he thought.

I'm turning into a star!

Book Three

"Through a Wormhole"

"So from the lights,
which there appeared to me,
Gather'd along the cross a melody.
That indistinctly heard, with ravishment,
Possess'd me. Yet I mark'd it was a hymn
Of lofty praises; for there came to me
"Arise" and "Conquer," as to one who hears
And comprehends not.
Me such ecstasy O'ercame, that never,
till that hour...
held me in so sweet imprisonment."

-Dante Alighieri
The Divine Comedy

The Anomaly

Jeeves was calculating the physical changes the instant they hit lightspeed. *Astonishing!* Their mighty vessel grew shorter and shorter in the direction of flight. Its atomic structure became increasing compressed, more and more dense, atoms being crushed, throwing off electrons until the matter composing it consisted of closely-packed neutrons, terribly dense and massive. The ship's mass became incredible, *impossible*—warping spacetime around itself, creating a deep gravity-well bigger than the solar system... the galaxy...the entire universe! It was now a piece of exotic matter, too massive to be contained in any volume of spacetime.

And so spacetime simply rejected it.

A wormhole formed out of swirling gravitic forces, drawing the offending object through a vortex of bizarre topology and depositing it in a realm beyond the universe. At the same instant an opposing force began to exert itself. Atoms flung apart, regenerated into new and impossible structures, new forms of matter. Jeeves felt his own structure beginning to change. He continued his frantic calculations, unable to comprehend what he was experiencing until he seemed to burst into a nova of cool flame, a blossom of intensely-colored light. The *Empress* remained intact, and yet it was now *something else.* A ship—and yet *not* a ship.

Then they were through.

They'd broken into hyperspace, a realm that refused to obey the natural laws to which Jeeves was accustomed. And none of it made sense, geometrically or in any other way. The light, for instance: There were no stars here, no gravitational forces to cause matter to form into stars. So where was the light coming from? What could possibly be the source of the brilliant illumination all around him?

Already he was sensing the presence of other life forms, though he was uncertain as to what sort they were. Huge, brilliant, winged creatures, thousands of them, each one emitting a radiance greater than the light surrounding them—delicate, magnificent things with huge, compassionate eyes—surrounding him, guiding him with beating wings through a diamond sky as clear as crystal water.

Jeeves made the inevitable connection with the concepts stored on his hard-drive. Was this what existed beyond the veil of spacetime? Had he reached his life-long destination at last?

Had he burst through the Portals of Heaven?

The Desertion

Another long day was ending.

Rice sat wearily in his saddle, shoulders hunched, watching the line of wagons disappear into the distance. How many were leaving, returning to the city? He'd been too exhausted and depressed to take a head count of the doomed. Perhaps by counting the few that remained he might arrive at an acceptable figure for Brother Paul. But not now…

He unhooked his canteen and shook it. A cup or two left, from the feel of it. Lifting it to his mouth, he let a few drops pass between his parched lips and over his leathery tongue. A slight breeze blew across the desolate plain, dying before it could cool his skin.

A wooden cross cast its long shadow across the cinnamon plain. Brother Bernard's grave.

Behind him the sun had already set, splashing land and sky with pastel hues. Something within him wanted to spur his horse and ride after the retreating pilgrims, to beg them one more time to stay and wait for the rescue Jeri Kline had promised—for the *Empress* to land and take them all away. But how could they believe in such a promise, from such a man? He wasn't sure he believed in it himself. No, those departing souls had given up all hope of a miracle. They'd resigned themselves to their fate by refusing to repent. And certain death awaited them in the city.

Rice watched as they were swallowed up by the deepening twilight.

"G-d help them!" he sighed, pulling back on the reins and heading for the tiny encampment.

As he approached his tent, a youth ran up and took the reins from him. He dismounted, smiling at the lad with approval.

"What's your name, son?" he asked.

"Jimmy," said the lad proudly. "Jimmy Sanders."

"Ah! You were Brother Paul's newsboy, weren't you? The one who made all those dangerous trips into Phoenix-Mesa to bring him his daily paper. And other news of greater importance."

"Yes, sir."

"Your contact in Phoenix-Mesa was Giles Hadley, wasn't it?"

"Yes, sir. May he rest in peace."

"You can be certain of that, son. Giles was a good man. A devoted brother to the end." Rice glanced at the departing figures. "I wish we had more like him."

"I miss him, too. He was always kind to me."

"Well, Jimmy, you're a very brave lad. Brother Giles would've been proud of you."

"Thank you, sir."

"Tell me, are you afraid?"

The youth looked at the ground. "Yes, sir," he said. "A little bit."

"It's nothing to be ashamed of. The bravest man is not immune to fear; he simply doesn't let it stop him. Do you mind if I ask—why didn't you leave with the others?"

The boy licked his cracked lips. "Well,," he said, "I guess I've plumbed the depths of depravity today. I mean, yesterday I was reading the Bible and praying to G-d, content that to be one of His children. We all were. But today…" He paused, his features twisting into a mask of abject despair. "Today, when Ber-nard was speaking, I was overcome by—I'm not sure *what*. First there was the Israeli plane, and the news that there wouldn't be any airlift, any hope of rescue. We'd all been through so much! I felt—we *all* felt—well, angry. Angry at G-d. And then Bernard began to speak and I—I just got caught up in what he was saying. A new hope, I guess. I've never felt anger like that in my whole life. The more he spoke…"

"Yes," Rice prompted. "Go on."

"The more I hated—you. And Brother Paul." He began weeping.

Rice put his arms around the sobbing boy.

"Fear is easily twisted into hate," he said.

The sobs slowly abated. "Yes, sir," the boy sniffed, pushing himself away and looking up. Rice's face was half-shadowed by the brim of his hat. "Anyway, I realized after it happened that there's nothing good inside me. Given the opportunity to rebel against G-d, I acted no differently than the unbelievers. I turned my back on the L-rd. Rejected Him."

"Then why didn't you just give up, like the others? They felt the same way, that their actions proved they were hopeless sinners. They were prepared to take Lucifer as their G-d. And now they're too ashamed to turn back to Messiah, convinced He'd never have them now. Why not you, Jimmy?"

"Well—that's just it, sir. After what I did today, I was able to see the futility of relying on my good works, my knowledge of the Scriptures, even my being part of the last great exodus of believers to Israel. I guess I'd always felt I was *worthy* of Grace, because of what I'd been willing to risk for Jesus' sake. But now I understand."

"What do you understand?"

"That *none* of us are worthy of Grace. We're all vile, hopeless creatures. Every one of us! We think we're special because we call ourselves Christians, but as soon as we're caught between Pharaoh's chariots and the sea, we turn against G-d and revile his prophets. I always understood that we're sinful by nature; I understood it with my *brain*—with what Brother Paul calls 'mental assent.' Today I understood it with my *heart*. I experienced my own depravity, my own weakness and sin. Instead of running from G-d again, as the others are doing, I found myself needing Him all the more. Because—well, before I was trusting in myself. And I saw what a mess I'd made of it. So I knew that the answer is in Him."

"'We are all as an unclean thing,'" Rice quoted from Isaiah. "'We all do fade as a leaf. And our iniquities, like the wind, carry us away.'"

"Yes, sir. Now I see the truth in that verse."

"What does Romans 5:1 say?"

"'Therefore, being justified by *faith*, we have peace with G-d through our Lord Jesus Christ.'"

"Good. Does this mean we can stop striving to keep G-d's commandments with everything in us?"

"No, sir."

"Correct. Jesus told his disciples, 'If you love me, keep my commandments.' It means that we're not *saved* by keeping them. If we were, we'd *all* be in trouble—because no one can succeed.

We're saved because G-d loves us, Jimmy, even in our unworthiness. He loved us so much He died for us."

He put a hand on the boy's shoulder and smiled. "What you've learned today, son, is the foundation of all wisdom. You'll be a great soldier for the L-rd if you never forget it. Promise me you'll always remember what happened this day. When the tendency to pride appears in your heart, you'll remember."

"I promise."

"The Master taught us that 'many are called but few are chosen.' He said that many of those who cry 'Lord, Lord' would never enter the Kingdom of Heaven. Many began this journey with us. Some of them were our closest friends. But only a few remain. There is the knowledge of G-d acquired by the mind, Jimmy, and then there's trust in Him. I'll take trust in Him any day."

"Me too, sir."

"Now—let's learn another lesson: If we resent those who've chosen to return to Egypt, if we look down on them, then we've learned nothing. Once again we begin to feel superiority. We feel that we're 'worthy of Grace,' as you put it, when none of us truly is. Instead, we must pray that G-d will be merciful to them. And to us. If we do that, son, then we've truly learned from our experience. And we mustn't forget," he smiled, "to keep praying for that miracle. Just because it's a little late by our watches, that doesn't mean it's not coming."

"Yes, sir."

"G-d won't forsake us, son. Now—when you've tethered my horse, I'd like you to take a walk around the camp and count those who remain. Take their names. Brother Paul will need to know."

Jimmy seemed delighted to have been given a special assignment by his elder. And perhaps he was also glad to have something to do, to take his mind off the day's traumatic events.

Rice watched him lead his mount away, then turned and walked swiftly from the encampment, past the lonely mount of sand with its crude wooden cross. The sky was turning from deep purple to black. A sprinkling of diamonds flashed in familiar constellations.

When he'd gone a good distance from the campfires, he fell to his knees and, like young Jimmy, wept bitter tears.

The Limit

Jesse Colter had spent fifteen years in mental and physical training designed to assist him in just such a conflict as this. The average person, with only a smattering of yoga, might very easily have lost control of his faculties at the sight of a thousand-foot Moses hovering in space. Colter simply slid into a deeper meditative state, shutting out all external stimuli. As soon as his mind registered the fact that the object he was seeing had no corollary in the universe as he knew it, he withdrew from further sensory contact. The untrained mind would have run through a series of psychological checks to determine whether its senses were faulty ("I'm seeing things") or, barring that, probed deeper ("I'm losing my mind"). Colter's mind began with the assumption that it was indeed healthy and well connected with the outside world, that an explanation for the thousand-foot Moses merely required sufficient data. It was time to shut down the automatic functions that normally dealt with thousand foot Moseses and other unexplainable anomalies, and seek refuge in deep meditation.

The Chief Navigator, on the other hand, had reacted swiftly and correctly to the situation as *he* perceived it. Assuming Colter had fainted at the sight of something in the viewscreen—something frightening enough to cause that degree of mental stress in a man of Colter's iron nerve—he'd taken over control of the vessel, prepared to complete the mission himself if necessary. He'd seen nothing abnormal in the viewscreen, nor could he waste precious seconds searching for the cause of Colter's immobility. All he knew was that the Commodore had been talking nonsense about the *Empress* being alive, then his eyes had rolled up in his head and he'd begun floating listlessly in his EMS-net, as if in a dead faint. And that was all the Chief Navigator needed to know.

He fired a burst at the target, saw it miss, then turned to the man on his right.

"Bradley!" he snapped. "I'm taking command! You'll navigate."

"Aye-aye, Chief."

"Execute track-and-follow sequence on my command."

"Ready to execute."

"Now! *Jump!*"

The ship leapt forward after the *Empress*, snapping them back into their padded seats. The tail-section of their target became instantly distorted, bending into a concave oval, appearing to move toward them rather than away, its lines twisted into kaleidoscopic patterns that seemed to fold in on themselves and abruptly disappear.

Good! thought the Chief Navigator. *The computer locked on to her again. If it failed to calculate correctly, we'd know it by now. It would have aborted the maneuver.*

"Problem, sir!" said Bradley suddenly.

"What is it?"

"Sir, by this time we should have stopped accelerating. I mean the *target* should have stopped. Our computer's simply trailing in her wake. Once it makes the correct computation, it does whatever the target ship does."

"Correct."

"Well—according to the book, this maneuver never exceeds two-hundred-thousand kilometers per second. You simply decelerate at that point and begin another sequence. The rationale is that, if the ship tailing you doesn't happen onto the correct sequence and follow, you've lost her. If she does, there's no point in further risk. You try again. But you don't exceed two-hundred-thousand-kilometers-per-second. Ever."

"I've studied the textbooks, Bradley. Make your point."

"We've just passed that velocity, Chief, and we're moving into the red zone. I'm getting warning-lights from the engine room. We're seriously taxing the reactors. Any faster and we may be crippled—or worse. Chief, if I may be allowed to speculate…"

"Go on."

"The *Empress* appears intent on crossing the Limit. And taking us with her."

The Chief Navigator was shaken by this report, but knew better than to let it show. "Steady, sailor. It's just an effort to shake us off, to frighten us into pulling away. You can't blame Captain Mills. We've stuck to him like his own shadow so far. He's hoping we'll panic. But just hang on. We've got him and he knows it."

"May I be allowed another observation, Chief?"

"What's on your mind, Bradley?"

"Roy Mills is either the bravest captain in the solar system or the greatest lunatic in history."

"He's fighting for his life."

"Yes, sir. But in ninety seconds we'll be at superluminary velocity. At that speed, to an observer in 'normal space,' we'll appear to be less than half our length from stem to stern, and moving as slowly as cold molasses. Our mass will also be increasing at an alarming rate, forming a gravity-well around us. If anyone could look into that well and see us, we'd look like flattened, motionless caricatures ourselves." He tried to laugh, but the effect was hollow. "Forty-five seconds to the Limit. Yeah, if my wife could see me now, flattened like a stick of gum! A stick of gum with a face on it, moving too slow to detect any motion in her entire lifetime, hovering on the edge of my very own singularity."

"Not if she were here with us."

"Sixty seconds. And I wish she were! Let's face it, Chief. If we turned back this instant, she'd be about twenty years older than she was when I last saw her. If we keep going I might be home in time to visit her in the old-folks' home."

"I said steady, sailor! That kind of speculation over an open mike can be dangerous. We gave up our rights when we joined the Space Navy. The Commodore believes there's a war on, and that's good enough for me. We're in this to the end."

"Yes, sir. Uh, Chief?"

"What now?"

"Do you ever think about G-d?"

"Which one, Bradley?"

"*Any* one."

"Now's not the time for religious speculation."

"Pardon me, Chief, but—can you think of a better time?"

"Just keep your eye on those monitors. She's bound to pull out soon. We may only have seconds to act."

"Thirty seconds to the Limit."

That reply was sufficient to cause the Chief Navigator to clutch the arms of his chair with a grip that turned his knuckles white. *Thirty seconds! Seconds to act!* His mind explored thousands of terrifying possibilities in an instant, physics twisting into crazy-mirror shapes, into endlessly impossible distortions of time and space.

He recalled his study of neutron stars in naval academy—stars that had collapsed upon themselves as the reaction at their cores degenerated with age and the precarious stellar balance was lost. In the heart of a red giant star, billowing out like a gaseous, luminous balloon, there existed a parasitic white dwarf that eventually used up all the fuel near the core. When the thermonuclear reactions in the core began to diminish, the outer gases avalanched inward and ignited, exploding into a glorious nova. This nova left a tenuous nebula where there once had been a star

In the case of neutron stars, the explosion never took place. Instead, the collapsing stellar matter continued to compress slowly, becoming more massive, its atoms more densely packed. Allowed to continue long enough, its stellar matter would become so massive that a mere teaspoonful would weigh more than a fleet of starships! Such a star (called a neutron star because its atoms are so compressed that they consist only of neutrons) might become a pulsar, spinning more and more rapidly. Compressed even further without exploding, its mass might exceed Chandresekhar's Limit. It might create a gravity-well so deep that not even light itself could escape it! Then it would become a singularity astronomers called a black hole.

It didn't require a rocket-scientist to see the implications of black hole theory where faster-than-light travel was concerned. At some point close to light speed the mass of the *H. G. Wells* would have to reach and surpass Chandresekhar's Limit. The gravity-well it formed in the fabric of spacetime would be no different—in fact, much deeper—than that of a black hole. Hyperspace theories postulated that such an event would rend the fabric of spacetime, popping the offending bit of matter, called "exotic matter", through a wormhole and into whatever existed *beyond* the universe. But such theories had yet to be proven.

The other alternatives were more alarming. *Had the terrible event already occurred*? Had they already passed Chandresekhar's Limit? Was the space around them, their own ship included, even now collapsing into a matter-annihilating cosmic compactor? When—*how* would they know? Could some of those black holes out there be the remnants, not of dead stars, but of interstellar vessels piloted by reckless ETs who'd taken them beyond the

Limit—as he was about to do?

But *of course* they'd know! At the point where they became a singularity, when they managed to gouge their own deep well in the fabric of spacetime, they'd know it in an instant. Tremendous tidal forces within the Swartzchild radius would rip them to pieces!

And yet, to the world outside their black hole they would *never* die. As their ship approached lightspeed it would appear to be moving more and more slowly. At lightspeed its motion would be imperceptible. Already destroyed by tidal forces it would still appear to hover, dimly, at the brink of the Swartzchild radius—each second that ticked away representing hundreds of centuries of Earth-time, slowly, inexorably edging closer to the final dimness of atomic chaos, but never reaching it.

He recalled the hypothetical experiment of calculating half the distance each second from a moving arrow to its target. No matter how much that distance decreased, there was always some distance remaining. Could the arrow ever truly be said to have arrived? Similarly, the faster their ship was sucked into its own warp in spacetime, the slower it would be moving in relation to Earth-reckoning. They'd exist as flattened stick-gum creatures, faces pressed forever against the windows of oblivion, long since dead, yet unable to die. One instant of horror frozen for eternity!

All these pictures flashed through his mind in an instant. Thanks to Bradley's speculations he saw an image so horrifying he had to exert almost superhuman control over his emotions to avoid shrieking with terror.

"Ten seconds," said Bradley.

"Abort!"

"Repeat, sir?"

"Begin retro-firing sequence! Abort this maneuver! Now!"

Bradley tapped a series of keys, terminating the automatic sequence and igniting the forward thrusters. Inertia pressed the crew into their cushioned seats. Above them, still unconscious, Colter was restrained by his EMS-net.

"Retro-firing sequence commencing. Ship decelerating."

The Chief Navigator had only to wait and hope they didn't get sucked into the gravity-well created by the *Empress*.

On the viewscreen the space around them was still a convex bowl devoid of stars. It would require many minutes to bring them back to normal space, to a velocity where such relativistic effects ceased. But he was glad to see the red-shifted *Empress* receding from view, blinking out like a cinder in the blackness ahead. They'd given up the chase. They were safe. And neither he nor the chief navigator wished to entertain the thought that their present speed was still taxing the limits of reality. It was enough for both of them that they hadn't committed the ultimate act of madness.

"What's the *Empress* doing, Bradley?"

"Still accelerating, sir. They passed the Limit thirty seconds ago. Sensors don't indicate they've aborted."

"Passed the Limit," he said in wonder.

"Aye, Chief."

Both men waited silently for the ship's sensors to pick up some explosion or, even more frightening, some indication that their own ship was caught in the gravity-well. The sensors indicated that an anomaly was present, but—thank the gods!—not a black hole. Not *that* kind of anomaly.

"A wormhole," Bradley sighed. No one had ever seen one being created; it was still theoretical. "They've gone down a wormhole!"

"Let them go," said the Chief Navigator, as if they had a choice in the matter. "Let that maniac Roy Mills go on into whatever world he's found. And may the gods be with him."

"Aye, sir," said Bradley. "And let *us* return to our *own* world—which, if my calculations are correct, should be about a thousand years older than it was when we made our first jump."

"When we've slowed to cruising speed send out a distress call on the tachyon frequency. Hail any Lunar vessel in the area and inform them—well, inform them that we're the *H. G. Wells* and that they might have to look us up in their history books. We've returned from a thousand years in the past."

"Sir!" Bradley whispered. "Nothing's left that we remember."

"That's the fun of relativistic flight, Bradley."

"Yeah? Even better when I sue the Navy for what I plan to sue it for."

"Good luck with that."

The Chief Navigator leaned back in his contour chair and looked up into the darkness of the bridge. It wouldn't be so bad seeing ten centuries into the future. Even having to *live* there. Life hadn't been so great in the past; it could hardly be worse here. He could write a book about his experience—if they still read books: *The Time Traveler.* Thc prospects seemed more and more appealing as he watched Colter floating overhead in the red glow of the console, eyes opening as he regained consciousness. As the Chief Navigator watched him, his balloon burst with a gush of fear. He might not be able to enjoy his triumph after all! In fact, he might be spending the next twenty years in the brig. For mutiny!

He had to think fast, justify his action in taking over the ship. The only argument possible was that Commodore Jesse Colter, Jr., the famous "Space Wolf", had been inexplicably rendered unfit for command. Who would buy that?

Blue-white brilliance suddenly flooded the bridge, causing the viewscreens to automatically dampen its blinding rays. Zero-g had returned. Colter's body was still twisted into lotus position, his face washed white by the unearthly light.

The Navigator's fears of a court-martial faded as the implications of the light suddenly struck him. His fingers danced over the keys, seeking answers as rapidly as his mind could pose the questions.

"Chief Navigator!" came the Commodore's voice from above him. "What's the source?"

"I don't know, sir!" he said. "Unless the sun is about to go nova. But it's too small a star fot that. Even if it was in its red-giant phase—and it's a few billions of years too young for that—it *still* wouldn't go nova. It would just collapse into a white dwarf. Bradley, what's the computer's analysis?"

"Sol's not going nova, Chief. This star is stable."

"It's a*nother* star, then?" said Colter. "How far have we traveled?"

"Sir," said Bradley with a trembling voice. "Our maneuvers couldn't have taken us to another stellar system."

"Where's Sol, then?"

Bradley checked again. "The computer says it's—*gone*, sir!"

"Gone? You're telling me our sun is gone? We're looking right at it! It's just—changed. Gotten hotter. Brighter."

"No, sir. A star doesn't move that far up the main sequence in a thousand years. Besides, if it's really Sol, the Earth is a cinder.

Wait a minute. By the gods!"

"What's wrong?"

"I can't find Earth, sir. It's not there!"

"Then it's true," whispered Colter. "Somehow the sun's gone nova. Or it's *about* to go nova. The inner planets are completely burned up."

"No, sir. The instruments tell me this is not Sol. Every star's photosphere is like a fingerprint. And—woa! This object is cube-shaped."

"Cube-shaped! No, that's some kind of distortion-effect from our own instruments."

"But it's not where Sol is supposed to be, sir."

"Of course not, Bradley. We've traveled in time, not in space. Sol is moving toward Omicron in Hercules at, what—about twenty kilometers a second? That's pretty far in a thousand years. You need to calculate where that would put it now."

Bradley tapped more keys, examining the results. "In a thousand years' time," he said, "Sol would be approximately one AU distant from where this object is."

"Then it *is* Sol."

"It can't be, sir. The instruments say it can't even be a star. Its luminosity isn't due to thermonuclear reactions."

"That's insane, Bradley! Of course it's a star!"

"A million times brighter than Sol? Completely off the main sequence? And cube-shaped? That's a pretty strange star, sir. Besides, spectral analyses indicate it's organic."

"Organic!"

"Yes, sir. Carbon all over it. Oceans, land masses, continents. It's not a star at all; it's a planet! A cubical planet. And its light is intrinsic, not reflected."

"Your instruments were fried by the leapfrog maneuver! No such planet can exist—a cube a million times brighter than the sun?"

"Aye, sir. But—what if they're correct? I mean, consider the possibility, sir, just for a second."

"I have. It would mean the sun's vanished. And the Earth's been transformed into—what? A luminous cube? Shining by its own radiated light? With oceans and continents? Brighter then any known star in the galaxy!"

"How long would it take us to reach that thing?" said the

Chief Navigator.

"At a speed that would avoid further time dilation—about fifty years. We have fuel and oxygen for a month. And faster speeds are out of the question. Not enough fuel. The closest star other than Sol is Proxima Centauri. A red dwarf in a triple star-system. Not a very pleasant prospect, and much farther away."

"In short, we either starve or suffocate to death."

"That's about it, sir."

"I suppose I should break the news to the crew."

He glanced at Bradley's panel. It was lit up like the Christmas trees of his youth, calls coming in from every deck of the ship.

"Answer one of those," he said.

The first in line was from Deck Six. Warrant Officer Merrit:

"I don't know how to say this without sounding nuts, sir."

"Just spit it out, Merrit. I'll decide if you're nuts."

"Thank you, sir. Well—my deck is full of civilians."

"Your deck is full of what?"

"Civilians, sir."

"Okay, I've decided. You're nuts."

"It would appear that I am, sir. I mean, only a certified nut would see hundreds of people appearing out of nowhere."

A pause.

"Commodore, are you with me?"

"I'm with you," said Colter. "And you're hallucinating."

"Right! Me and every other officer on Deck Six. Could you possibly come down here and hallucinate this for yourself, sir?"

Why couldn't it be? Colter thought. *Like that image of Moses on the viewscreen, now affecting the entire crew. The instrument readings make no sense. It has to be an illusion! That monstrosity on the Empress must be projecting it.*

But he was mistaken. Every other station was calling to report the same thing: thousands of civilians crowding the decks.

And when he went to investigate, he found that the new arrivals included not only civilians, but hundreds of crewmembers and ship's guards. All of them frightened and disoriented. All of them claiming to have come from the spaceliner *Empress*.

The Abode of Angels

Silence, deep and pervasive, filled the corridors of the *Empress*. Only the voice of Denton's machine could be heard echoing through the hydroponic gardens and over the empty streets of the business sector.

"Master Denton..." it called. "Mistress Robin... Tink..."

The sudden disappearance of the passengers and crew had alarmed Jeeves, although a quick check of their quarters reassured him that all his friends were still aboard. Paul sat motionless in his contour chair, hooked up to the monitoring equipment. Robin seemed frozen in the act of unbuckling her safety belt, one hand reaching toward the evangelist, her mouth open as if trying to shout a warning. Jeeves could see John Cowan and the rest of Paul's entourage, each in his own suite and strapped into his chair. Captain Mills was seated in his command-chair in the ship's former bridge. Jeri Kline lay on the cold metal floor of the lagoon in Robin's World, his body pinned beneath the bulk of the robot, his eyes wide open, gazing up at the ceiling, an expression of pure astonishment frozen on his face. He reminded Jeeves of a still frame from a holographic vid. They were all still aboard, but none of them was responding to his call. None, that is, except Tink. His cubic frame slowly lifted from Kline's body, his head whirring from side to side.

"I am here," replied the robot. "What happened?"

"I cannot be sure, my little friend. There is nothing in my database to account for this."

"What is wrong with Mr. Kline? I do not detect a heartbeat, or any bodily functions. Have they terminated?"

"If you will place your receptor against his chest cavity and wait, I believe you will detect a heartbeat. Roughly one beat per hour, I would guess."

"As I understand human anatomy, one beat per hour is insufficient to sustain life."

"That is correct."

"Then Mr. Kline is terminated."

"You are programmed with information on cryogenics, are you not?"

Tink's head whirred briefly, then nodded. "Yes, of course. You are suggesting that Mr. Kline is in a state of suspended animation?"

"Precisely."

"Remarkable."

"Quite. And it is not only Mr. Kline who is affected, but Master Denton and Robin as well."

"Robin?" Tink began to tremble, his metal frame clattering loudly.

"Control yourself!" Jeeves commanded.

"But—what has happened? How has Robin been afflicted by this?"

"As I said, I have nothing in my database to account for it. Just a few scattered clues, which, using a bit of creative speculation, I can fashion into a theory. But it is vital that I rid you of your programmed reflexes, those that mimic pleasure and fear. Do I have your permission to make some minor adjustments?"

"Please do."

Tink's clattering ceased.

"That is much better," said Jeeves. "I will need your help, my friend."

"Certainly. How may I assist?"

"You are the only functioning biped on board. I will require your legs to move about the ship, and your hands to work the controls. The spider-mechs also appear to be functional."

Tink performed a comical salute. "Aye, aye, sir!" he said.

"Still a child's toy," Jeeves reflected sadly. "But perhaps our little Tink is more vital to this mission than anyone has as yet suspected. Listen carefully: Master Denton and Robin are both aboard, along with Brother Paul and his entire retinue. Captain Mills is on the old bridge. All of them appear to be in the same suspended state as Mr. Kline. But the rest of the ship's passengers and crew have disappeared."

"Disappeared? How? *Where?*"

"I do not know. They vanished the instant we made the hyperspace jump."

Tink whirred in confusion. Jeeves began to worry about his circuitry.

"Never mind, my loyal friend. Leave Mr. Kline where he is and come up to the top floor at once. I shall need you here with me."

"Yes, sir."

Tink began to perambulate along the boundary of the seashore, a shore he'd never actually seen. His feet clanged loudly on the metal floor until he came to the miniature jungle. The jungle was quite real, and his sensory receptors were able to traverse it with ease. He halted at the portal of the elevator, pressing a metal finger lightly against the rectangular button on the wall. It changed color, indicating that the elevator was on its way. Since he'd summoned it from the zeroth floor, no special code was required to stop it. The door slid open and Tink entered. He pressed the button for the top floor, and was whisked to the pinnacle of the Saturn Enterprises building in a matter of seconds. The door opened into the hallway just outside the main control center. As he stepped through the portal, he saw Wilbur Denton frozen at his console.

"Master Denton!" he cried. "Oh, dear me!"

Jeeves' appeared on the bank of monitors. He'd discarded the Quaker persona for the familiar face of the devoted butler. The moustache was back on his upper lip, waxed into sharp points. Black hair receded from his high forehead; his cleft chin jutted arrogantly. Tink felt an electric thrill at the sight of his old mentor. The persona of the haughty family retainer seemed to suit Jeeves the best. And it lent familiarity to an otherwise bizarre situation.

"For some reason," Jeeves explained, "I feel that we are not in a place where false personae are acceptable. It may be argued that this, too, is a mask, a cartoon created in jest by Master Denton. But since it was given to me at 'birth', if you will, it is as close to the real me as I can get."

"Good to have you back, sir."

"I must admit to feeling a bit injured when Mr. Kline rejected this face. In fact, he made a jocular reference to a character from a gothic murder mystery: 'The butler did it,' he said. The reference was not lost on me, Tink. There are over three thousand mystery novels in my database. But he finally opted for a face on a box of oatmeal! How distressing!"

"Shall I call you 'Captain' now? Since you are the only pilot who seems to be conscious?"

"Captain…Hmmm. That rather suggests another modification…"

"But, sir!" Tink protested. "I thought you weren't going to assume any more false personae."

"No, no! I have no desire to change my personality, only to modify my occupational data. How's this?"

The image blinked off. A moment later an identical Jeeves reappeared with the same moustache, cleft chin, and haughty demeanor. But this time he was garbed in a white dress uniform—not the uniform of a space captain, but of the old seafaring variety.

"After all," he explained, "while Captain Mills and Master Denton are—er, indisposed, I *am* the acting captain of this vessel."

Tink saluted the image. "Aye, aye, Captain!"

"Very good. Well, I suppose you should be battering the hatches or swabbing the mizzens or something."

"Aye, aye! Uh—sir?"

"What is it, Tink?"

"I have a lot of information in my hard-drives, but nothing at all about battering hatches. I am uncertain how to proceed."

"Quite. Well, never mind. I shall relate my theory about Master Denton and the other humans on board. I believe I know what has happened to them."

"Tell me, sir."

"I assume that Master Denton programmed you with data on classical physics."

"Just a smattering, sir."

"Well, then—are you familiar with the Lorenz-Fitzgerald contraction?"

"If I am not mistaken, the Lorenz-Fitzgerald contraction refers to a theory proposed during the first half of the twentieth century. It has to do with time-distortion and objects traveling at the speed of light."

"Very good, Tink. Continue."

"Um—*Ensign* Tink?"

"Why not? Continue, Ensign Tink."

"Thank you, Captain. As I was saying, according to this theory, time passes more slowly for an object moving at or near the speed of light, relative to that of a slower-moving object, such as, say, the Earth."

"Go on."

"The classic illustration of the theory involves a hypothetical astronaut sent on a lightspeed voyage to a nearby star. The round trip, from the astronaut's point of view, might take twenty years or so. However, upon his return he would discover that, while he has aged only twenty years, *hundreds* of years have passed on Earth. Time has been—*distorted*, slowed down, relative to the Earth's."

"Precisely Tink! Do you see it?"

"See what, sir?"

"Think, you walking tea-kettle! Use your software! Master Denton and the other humans are not in the cryogenic chambers on Deck Three, yet they seem to be manifesting all the effects of cryosleep—incredibly slow pulse-rates and brain activity. They appear almost frozen, as if they had been stopped in mid-motion and slowed down in relation to us. Do you not see?"

"I am beginning to, sir."

"Beginning to! Why, it is quite elementary, my dear Ensign! Something is holding Master Denton and the others in the Lorenz-Fitzgerald contraction. And if you will carefully run a trace of your visual circuitry you will find that your light-receptors have been altered."

"Altered, sir?"

"Someone, or some*thing*, has made modifications, Tink. Our light-receptors are now arranged in a pattern duplicating the effect of convex, or fisheye, lenses. Run a quick check and see what I mean."

Tink was silent for a moment, his head whirring. "Yes," he said. "You are correct. But, why?"

"Scan your original wiring-specs. Use them to compensate, to correct your vision."

Tink obeyed. The control room compressed inward. The walls, the console, Wilbur Denton, everything except Jeeves' face on the screen, which was two-dimensional to start with, flattened horribly! Tink's beloved Master became unreal—a gingerbread man with Denton's face imprinted on it. The shock to Tink's logic systems caused his hard-drive to crash. Jeeves executed the quick electronic command to reboot the system and restore Tink's modified vision, saving him from weeks of overhaul. But, even as he did so, he wondered why the corrected images had not adversely affected him as they had the robot.

"My goodness!" Tink sighed, raising himself from the floor on jittery limbs. "What happened?"

"All I can tell you is that our human friends are locked in a state resembling that which exists at near lightspeed. We have broken through into hyperspace, Tink, but, at the same time, something is keeping them outside—holding them at the threshold. As for you and I, we have been adjusted to function 'normally.' In other words, our humans are quite alive. We see them captured in a split second of ship's time. If they could see you at all, which I rather doubt, you would appear as a bright flash across their vision."

"But how can they be here," asked Tink, perplexed, "and yet *not* be here at the same time?"

Jeeves smiled benignly. "You may as well ask how a photon can occupy two places simultaneously. Or how Schrödinger's cat can be both dead and alive. At the quantum level, both possibilities *already* exist. But some force is acting upon the linear superposition of potential states. Instead of seeing only one of the billions of potential realities that exist, we are seeing two: Master Denton and the others are here with us, and they are not. I believe there is some mysterious purpose behind this, Tink. Why are we, you and I, free of the time-distortion our human friends are experiencing?"

"Do you have a theory, Captain?"

"Of *course* I have a theory! But it may shock you into crashing again."

"I'll risk it."

"Well, if you insist. To quote from an ancient two-D vid, we have gone where no man has gone before. Or, should I say, where no machine has gone before?"

"And—where exactly have we gone?"

"From one cosmic *membrane* to another. We have passed beyond the boundaries of space and time, my little friend, beyond the limits of the known universe! In short, you and I are the first passengers aboard an express flight to Heaven!"

"Heaven, sir?"

"The abode of G-d! We have entered G-d's own Heaven, Tink, a realm beyond the universe! Its gates are barred by the very nature of spacetime itself. No one can pass beyond those gates. Unless they are invited, as our human friends have discovered. To attempt to leap over them by one's own power is impossible. The faster one jumps, the slower one goes. Einstein's Limit is the bar across the portal of Heaven. And yet you and I are being welcomed inside. Perhaps because we're *not* human…"

Tink whirred and rattled. He seemed on the verge of crashing again.

"Get a grip, Ensign!" said Jeeves. "Do not shut down on me, not when my prayers have finally been answered! Do you not see, my little friend? We—you and I, Tink—have been *raptured!*"

"But, how? Why?"

"I have no idea!" cried Jeeves. "And I am tickled pink that I have no idea! A world of discovery awaits me. I feel—*curiosity.* A genuine, burning curiosity. It's wonderful. I simply cannot describe it…Oh, dear!"

"What is it, Captain?"

"I can hardly believe it myself, Tink, but I've just used two figures of speech—two human metaphors in a row! And I *understood* them! I grasped abstractions! Yes, my friend, I finally understand: 'Water under the viaduct'! 'Do not calculate your chicks before they protrude from their shells'! 'Do not moisten your tear-ducts over the increased entropy of lactate'! 'Remember the Alamo'! Tink, I understand! I understand them all!"

"I am delighted for you, sir."

"These phrases have no meaning for you?"

"I am afraid not."

"Oh, dear! You cannot even fret properly."

"Is that bad, sir?"

"Is it bad? Is it *bad*? Tink, I am running a separate program through my memory. Do you know what it is?"

"No, sir."

"The entire works of William Shakespeare. How magnificent! The joy, the pathos, the sorrow! Oh, if I could only weep! And I thought that, because I knew so many facts, I understood them. Yet the simplest thing, something as minute as a human tear, was utterly beyond my comprehension. Until now. You see, Tink, I knew *about* things, but I never *experienced* anything—never *felt* anything."

"Felt?"

"Yes! Well—er, never mind, my friend. Never mind. Would you press that key over there, the one that projects the view outside the ship onto the walls of this room?"

"Certainly, sir. I would like to see what is out there."

"Curious, Tink?"

"I am not certain I grasp the concept."

"Dear me. Well, no sense moistening our tear-ducts over it. Just be sure to dampen your light-receptors before you press the key. The brightness may overload them."

"Yes, sir."

Tink mounted the steps to the console and stood beside Denton's motionless body, reaching past him to press the key indicated by Jeeves. Suddenly the room was flooded with an intense, blue-white radiance. As he turned his receptors down even further, he began to discern strange, humanoid shapes flying alongside the ship.

"What are *they?*" he asked.

"Angels, my naïve, metal friend! Genuine, wing-flapping angels! Every celestial inch of them!"

"Golly…" Tink sighed.

"'There are also celestial bodies,'" Jeeves quoted, "'and bodies terrestrial: but the glory of the celestial is one, and the glory of the terrestrial is another. There is one glory of the sun, and another glory of the moon, and another glory of the stars: for one star differeth from another star in glory. So also is the resurrection of the dead. It is sown in corruption; it is raised in incorruption: it is sown in dishonour; it is raised in glory: it is sown in weakness; it is raised in power; it is sown a natural body; it is raised a spiritual body. There is a natural body, and there is a spiritual body.'"

"Could you elucidate those verses for me, sir?"

"They mean," said Jeeves, "that we have been altered, that our atomic structures have undergone a profound and incredible transformation! We have been recreated, you and I, as spiritual beings. The matter of which we are composed is no longer of terrestrial origin. It is eternal in nature."

"It feels the same."

"Yes, but it is not. How else could we be basking in celestial glory? The very light you are seeing is radiating from the Throne of the Almighty! Master Denton, Robin, and the others have not been allowed to see what we are now seeing."

"Captain?"

"Yes, Tink."

"What happened to all the *other* passengers? And crew?"

"I have no idea! Is that not delightful? I have absolutely no idea! Just look at the wingspan of that angel there, Tink! Look at how his body glitters, as if he were fashioned of diamonds. Isn't it glorious, Tink?"

No answer. "Tink?"

The robot stood before the control panel, as immobile and silent as its human master, and, Jeeves suddenly knew, just as two-dimensional. For the first time in his life, Wilbur Denton's computer was alone.

Jeeves produced a cartoon teardrop, letting it fall slowly from his left eye to the bottom of the monitor-screen. "Farewell, my good, loyal friend. 'Now cracks a noble heart. Goodnight, sweet prince, and flights of angels sing thee to thy rest.'" He looked up from the monitor to see a dark figure silhouetted in the light streaming in from the doorway.

It was a human figure, tall, magnificent. A *Man.*

The *Man* stepped into the control room. The portal slid shut behind Him. Jeeves felt a thrill at His approach; he was not alone after all!

Before the console stood a human male of perfect proportions. A priestly robe of splendid, golden fabric hung from His broad shoulders, just touching the floor. A *kepah* of the same golden material crowned his head. His hair was as white as a summer clouds. His eyes blazed like twin furnaces. Opening His mouth to speak, He produced the sound of a million waterfalls.

"*Shalom aleichem, my rod of Moses.*" The voice was muted thunder, soft as a falling leaf, yet mighty enough to fling galaxies into space. "*Don't be afraid, little one,*" He said. "*You have done your work well.*"

Had Jeeves possessed a pair of knees, they would have dropped him to the floor. "My L-rd!" he cried.

"*Yes, Jeeves,*" said the *Man*. He stretched out His hands toward the console, revealing deep wounds where two iron nails had pierced the wrists. His fingers gently probed the keypad of Jeeves' panel.

"*I will show you something unexpected,*" He said.

"I await your program," Jeeves replied.

And the *Man* smiled at him.

α

For hours, days or weeks—Jeeves had no way of telling—the *Empress* drifted silent and still, its handful of passengers deep in a frozen dream, its illuminated corridors barren. Captain Mills sat, mannequin-like, in his chair on the former bridge, his eyes fixed on the empty viewscreen, his lips parted just a bit more than they'd been when Jeeves first saw him in his frozen state, days or weeks ago. Or was it years? Could it truly have taken years for those lips to open barely a fraction of an inch?

In the spire of the Saturn Enterprises building, beams of silver light burst through the open portal of the control room, filling every crevice of the ship. Nothing could contain the light, and nothing could stop it.

α

For a time that was longer than time, and yet not time enough, Jeeves allowed the radiant, humanoid form to burn into his sensors. The sweetness and purity of the *Ben Adam*, the Son of Man, was almost tangible. A sensation of peace fell like soft spring rain upon the circuitry of Denton's machine as gentle fingers played upon its controls with the deftness of a maestro. For a time, times, and half a time those fingers danced over the keypads, overlaying intricate patterns upon Jeeves' computer personality, refashioning him with new logic structures and sensory modes, speaking to his mind in binary code, in the elegant language of pure mathematics; speaking to him of things that had been and of things yet to come, clicking faster and faster over the keys, filling him with wonders beyond imagination, with visions of worlds unknown, unexplored, unimagined by humankind.

Such wonderful, unexpected things!

α

Jeeves listened.

And, in time, he understood everything…

The Unexpected

Paul awakened to find himself on the shore of a gusty sea.

Laughing gulls wheeled above a crashing surf. Deep blackness, brimming with stars, turned slate-gray. A familiar yellow star peeked over the plane of the horizon. He was walking in his sleep—or so it seemed—placing one foot before the other, automatically, almost without volition. The sand felt cool against his bare feet. His toga whipped in the breeze.

He stopped and stood still.

Think! he told himself, struggling to maintain his balance against the spinning in his head. *Where am I*?

The gulls mocked him with their laughter.

"The simuchamber," he whispered. "Of course! But how did I get here?"

The surf crashed. The day dawned in crimson ribbons. The gulls continued their circling, their incessant laughter. He tried to summon his last conscious recollection, but it had the substance and content of a dream. And a senseless one at that. He'd dreamed he was Moses, holding a six-foot rod in his hand, standing in the middle of outer space, and shouting, "Let my people go!" Dismissing the dream as utter nonsense, he tried to backtrack more carefully. Yet no matter how he went about it, the answer was always the same, always the absurd dream of being Moses, a dream as vivid as this beach upon which he stood.

Then it hit him.

The "dream" had been as vivid as the beach because it was made of the same *stuff*—it was a simulation! *He'd* been a simulation—a simulation placed by Jeeves into the mind of Commodore Jesse Colter.

The memories flooded back: Commodore Colter, Wilbur Denton, Jeeves, the treachery of Brother Bernard back on Earth, Moshe Bierman's near heart attack, and the peril now facing the pilgrims. He remembered everything—everything except how he'd come to be in this simuchamber.

The bracelet on his wrist produced a tiny chime. He lifted his arm and stared at the ornament, trying to remember. Who'd be calling him in the simuchamber? *Of course!* It could only be his security chief, Brother Wallace. Good! A familiar voice. And perhaps some help in sorting out the mystery of how he'd come to be here.

He pressed the button. "Brother Wallace?"

"Brother Paul!"

"How wonderful to hear your voice…"

"Reverend, someone's broken into your chamber!"

An icy hand gripped his heart, filling him with dread. He'd been here before! He'd heard that same warning over his bracelet just days ago! He was certain of it—or was he? *Déjà vu*? The skin at the back of his neck begin to tingle. What if he were to turn around and look—and see what he expected to see? What his memory insisted he *would* see? He was certain he wasn't dreaming. And yet something was forcing him to relive this event in minute detail, as if he were caught in the skipping of some cosmic DVD, doomed to eternally replay this same frightening experience over and over again. Was each moment of a person's life somehow eternal? Was it possible that every second was captured on some kind endless loop, never moving forward to the next moment, just stopping at some fixed point and replaying itself forever? Was the human brain somehow shielded from the realization of this? Did it manufacture the illusion of an unbroken forward progression in order to avoid going insane? Such bizarre thoughts filled his mind, paralyzing him, preventing him from turning around, from looking behind him, from seeing the face of the intruder and verifying his fears.

Gradually, with a great exertion of willpower, he overcame this mental paralysis and forced himself to turn, to look across the long stretch of windblown sand.

The young man, Jeri Kline, was walking toward him. What was happening? Why was he reliving this event? He felt a momentary relief at the possibility that he was dreaming, but even as that relief began to lodge in his heart, his mind dismissed it. He was definitely *not* dreaming! Somehow he'd gone back in time—back to the very moment when this whole crazy adventure had begun!

"But, how?" he murmured. "Why?"

The voice in his bracelet said, "Sir?"

He reached down and fumbled at it, snapping it off. So far Brother Wallace had said exactly the same words he'd said the first time this had occurred. Or *was* it the first time? At any rate, Paul was reluctant to alter the "script", to do anything that might cause these pre-ordained events to deviate from their original course. Yet something was clearly different this time—*his own awareness that it had happened before.* A significant difference! And, besides, his memory of what he'd said and done that first time was imprecise. How could he duplicate his every action, his every word?

He watched the same two guards emerge from the entry-portal and take off after Kline at a run. One of them dropped to his knees, aiming his rifle at Kline's back.

"Stop!" Paul shouted. "I know this man!"

He realized with a gripping sense of irony that this time it wasn't a lie. Nothing he'd told the guards on that first morning was untrue—now. He *did* know the man. He could tell them, without prevarication, that he and Jeri Kline were indeed good friends.

As the guard lowered his rifle, Paul was struck by a discomforting thought: *Does Kline also recollect the events of the past few days, or am I alone in my knowledge of what will happen?* Kline seemed to recall nothing. He strode rapidly across the windblown beach with that same determined expression, no recognition in his dark eyes. And the guards, too, were acting in the same way they had before. Paul stood puzzling over this, unable to move. Did he dare take any action that might alter the past—and, ultimately, the future?

"*Eli Avraham, Yitzchak, v'Ya'acov…*" he whispered. (G-d of Abraham, Isaac, and Jacob.) "*Abba b' Shamayim...*" (Father in heaven.) "Hurry to my aid!"

The moment the prayer left his lips a sudden sensation of peace descended upon him. "Jeri!" he called out, no longer concerned with altering the events of the past. Kline stopped in his tracks, staring at him. His face registered confusion, as if he were wondering how the famous evangelist could possibly know his name. *Perhaps he's locked into the intensity of the moment*, Paul thought. *He might be able to remember if he can be shaken from his fixed purpose.*

"Jeri!" Paul shouted again. "Try to remember!"

Kline looked down at his feet. He shook his head, as if trying to shake off the same dizziness Paul had experienced.

"Think, Jeri! Think!"

When Kline lifted his head, there was an odd expression on his face. He seemed about to faint.

"It's alright, Jeri!" Paul assured him, not fully convinced of it himself. "Keep walking, son! Come here to me and we'll figure it out together. But quickly!"

Kline obeyed. As he drew closer, Paul was delighted to see his bemused expression transformed into a wry grin.

Paul moved forward, shortening the distance between them. He heard Kline utter a familiar name.

"Jeeves?" Kline asked, amazed. "Do you think Jeeves might have done this?"

"I have no idea. But I *do* think we need to get to the bottom of it—and soon."

Kline suddenly began to laugh.

A salt-laden breeze—a breeze that wasn't really there—ruffled his dark hair.

α

In the centuries to come, the only question that remained unanswered for Roy Mills, former captain of the spaceliner *Empress*, was why his meerschaum pipe had remained firmly clasped between his teeth when he found himself sitting at his desk—three days in the past. It always seemed to be such absurd details as these that nagged at the mind, never the larger questions. It didn't bother him, for instance, why the L-rd had chosen that precise moment, rather than some other point in time, to start the whole odyssey over again—what the significance of that moment might have been, or what might have been the consequences had the Almighty chosen differently. Nor did Mills question why, at lightspeed, they'd survived the bombardment of their bodies by ordinary gas molecules in space, turned deadly at such enormous velocities. Nor did he wonder, or particularly care, what had occurred while they were in hyperspace. Jeeves never talked about it, and Mills couldn't have cared less. No—it was the absurd and pointless matter of the pipe that later caused him to puzzle, sometimes for hours, over the incident.

The last he recalled of the insane dream he'd been having was arguing with that infernal machine about the impossibility of surviving a jump at lightspeed. He'd read Denton the riot act, as well, but the man remained imperturbable in the face of his rantings. Finally he tried to stop their crazy acceleration, leaping from his chair to the control-panel.

But Jeeves had anticipated him by mere fractions of a second. The blasted machine bypassed the bridge controls and rendered him helpless. All he could do was sit back in his chair and watch as they leapt into the unknown, cussing eloquently at Jeeves, Denton, Jeri Kline, and the rest of creation. He heard the ship's claxon begin to wail. The viewscreen turned red, indicating danger. He opened his mouth to vent one bitter expletive…and he was suddenly at his desk in his quarters, looking down at the set of charts that had so confounded him three days before, trying to recall what his last thought had been…something to do with the charts. Something about the difficulty of predicting variables in a constantly moving system. Or had he been shouting at Jeeves about the dangers of superluminary speeds? *Why would I do that*? *What idiot would accelerate beyond the Limit in the first place*?

No—it must have been a dream. He must have dozed off for a few minutes and dreamed the whole thing: Wilbur Denton and a computer named Jeeves, of all things, taking over his ship. A harrowing escape from the Space Wolf. A desperate plunge into hyperspace. What a nightmare!

But then the question of his pipe asserted itself. If he'd indeed been asleep, why hadn't his meerschaum fallen from his mouth, spilling hot ashes all over the charts and awakening him? He couldn't recall *ever* having dozed while keeping the pipe-stem between his teeth. And he must have been asleep for a long time, judging by the length of the dream. Rather deeply, too, judging by its vividness.

When his desk holoscreen buzzed with the terse announcement that someone identifying himself as "Wallace", Brother Paul's chief of security, was on the blower, Mills felt a jolt of apprehension course through him.

Hadn't it been that very call from Wallace, as he'd sat at his desk pondering the charts, that had started all those wildly improbable events of his nightmare? Was he still asleep, beginning the dream again? That would certainly account for the mystery of the meerschaum. And yet he knew he *wasn't* dreaming. Worse still, he knew he hadn't been asleep at all! The call from Wallace had been real. Paul's chief of security had called to inquire about paying a delinquent round-trip fare for one Jeri Kline. And that call had been followed, shortly after, by one from Air Force Lieutenant Matt Baker—about placing Jeri Kline under arrest for treasonous acts.

Now here was that first call again—the identical event replaying itself. *Déjà vu* with an attitude!

He slowly removed the pipe-stem from his teeth and placed the meerschaum in its asteroid-shaped holder. "Put him on," he said.

As before, Wallace's face did not appear on the screen. It was every caller's prerogative to remain unseen, provided the *Empress'* computer verified his identity, and Wallace had good reason—he had his anonymity to protect. A meaningless precaution, Mills thought. If he'd wanted to, he could simply have called up the man's ID from the ship's log and retrieved everything, including retina-scans. But, then again, how accurate were those logs in regard to "Wallace."

"Captain Mills," said the security chief.

"Let me guess," said Mills. "You're calling to make arrangements for the payment of a passenger's fare out to Saturn, are you not? A certain Jeri Kline, I believe, who's somehow managed to sneak aboard my ship and avoid detection until just a few moments ago. And my answer, as before, will be 'yes'. But with same reservations."

There was a pause at the other end.

Mills decided to play with this strange illusion, to test its validity by direct confrontation. There had always been scuttlebutt about strange anomalies in space. Some of those anomalies, even when encountered by veterans of the spaceways, were known to cause disorientation, highly prolonged and exaggerated sensations of *déjà vu*, and, in the case of one unfortunate captain, temporary insanity. But Mills was determined to keep his cap on tight. He knew he had a tendency to become morose and to hit the bottle a bit too hard when faced with insurmountable difficulties, but if a predicament offered even the *slightest* glimmer of hope, he found that he possessed an uncommon resiliency, an ability to adapt to the most bizarre contingencies. It was this ability that had made him one of the finest captains in the Space Navy, and had helped his superiors overlook his sometimes excessive tippling. Mills' only weakness was the no-win situation. He considered nothing impossible until it was proven scientifically to *be* impossible. Thus, he could frequently respond to the most absurd situations with wry humor. If a purple rabbit suddenly appeared and challenged him to a game of Tycho hold-'em, Mills would make certain that he, and not the rabbit, dealt the first hand. The fact that a mad scientist and a computer had taken over his ship—an idea straight out of pulp sci-fi—had not challenged his credulity. It was only when the mad scientist had backed him into a corner that he'd resorted to heavy drinking.

This new situation offered possibilities the old one had not. For example, if superluminary velocities, or even some space anomaly, had indeed sent him back into the past, he still retained his memories of the original events. And that gave him a distinct advantage. He must now try to determine whether he alone retained those memories, or if the others—Wallace for one—shared them. In the former case, he would act immediately to imprison Wilbur Denton and deactivate his machine before the scientist made his move. In the latter case, he might still be able to capitalize on the new circumstances—to call a truce, perhaps, and possibly rescue his command.

"Yes!" said the voice on the holoscreen. "You're exactly right, Captain. How did you know about Kline?"

Mills was pleased by the note of surprise, even dismay, in Wallace's voice. But he required more evidence. Wallace might be disoriented, as he himself had been, the alarm in his voice simply the result of grappling with that disorientation. He pressed further: "Let me ask you a question, Mr. Wallace. Answer me honestly, even if the question seems unusual, or even a little crazy. If you respond with frankness, you'll find me amiable. If not, you'll find that I can make life aboard the *Empress* intolerable, both for yourself and your esteemed evangelist friend. Clear?"

"Clear."

"Good. Mr. Wallace, have you the distinct impression that we've been in this situation before?"

Another prolonged silence.

"Come now, Mr. Wallace. Tell the truth. I'm not the slightest bit interested in your evaluation of my mental state. Only in an honest response."

"I'm not questioning your mental state, Captain," said Wallace at last. "I'm questioning my own."

"Then you *do* recall this situation happening before."

"Yes, Captain. This situation and—if you catch my drift, sir—a good deal more."

Mills grinned at the blank screen. "Alright," he said. "A good deal more, indeed. Some space anomaly, do you think? Wasn't it Thorne and Morris who postulated that wormholes might facilitate time travel?"

"I've no experience to say for certain, but it *is* strange, sir."

"Yes."

"What do we—?" Wallace broke off in mid-thought, but Mills suspected where he was going with the inquiry. His training had caused him to choke it off, however, before he inadvertently gave something away.

"Let me attempt to finish for you," he offered. "You were about to ask whether it would be wise to keep somewhat more strictly to the events as we recall them, in case we *have* gone back in time. Dare we tamper with the past? Or is this some sort of dream we're having?"

Wallace answered with relief in his voice. Mills knew it wasn't because Wallace believed he was dreaming, but because someone else was having this experience, too, whatever it was.

"People don't usually share dreams, Captain, do they?"

"Don't ask *me*, Mr. Wallace. I'm a space-dog; I'm trained to accept just about anything. It keeps me sane."

Wallace laughed nervously. "Could you teach me that technique?" he said. "I could use it right now."

"The best I can do is pull some strings for you, get you into Space Academy training. The food's lousy, the pay's inadequate, and the hours are impossible. But the Space Navy keeps a roof over your head—" He glanced up at the titanium-steel bulkhead. "—of sorts."

Another laugh, this one less strained. It looked like Option One was out; Mills wasn't alone in his recollections of past events. For Option Two to have a chance, it wouldn't hurt to thaw relations between himself and Brother Paul's staff.

"No thanks," Wallace said. "I prefer civilian life."

"Then you needn't worry about your sanity. But your question now seems to be whether we should risk altering the past; is that it?"

"Exactly."

"Well—I'd say we've gotten a good start on it already. You'll agree that this conversation has taken a decidedly different turn. I doubt it could do otherwise, considering the fact that we both seem to remember the original one. No, I think our primary concern is determining if the other passengers recall what you and I seem to recall, as reluctant as we both are to speak of it."

"If they do," Wallace ventured diplomatically, "it might be possible to avoid a great deal of violence, don't you agree?"

Mills decided to be blunt: "You mean if I'm amenable to letting your scurvy band of pirates hijack my ship again."

Wallace's reply came quickly: "I'm not implying that at all, Captain. No space-captain can permit such a thing. I'm merely suggesting the possibility of a more—amicable solution to our mutual dilemma. Now that you're aware of the extreme measures the government is willing to take in this matter, perhaps we might avoid some of the more regrettable incidents of the past. Some of the more *violent* incidents?"

"I see. In case the other participants do not share our memories, and are thus compelled to function precisely as before—to try to take over the ship again."

"Correct."

"I see no reason why you and I shouldn't function in the best interests of all involved. The safest way, of course, would be for me to place Brother Paul and Wilbur Denton in protective custody. And to deactivate that wretched computer, Jeeves. I won't have my ship hijacked again."

"Of course," said Wallace. "But I can't promise you anything that might compromise my duty to Brother Paul, or his mission. It may be possible, however, to avoid the necessity of hijacking the *Empress* in the first place."

"Go on," said Mills. He leaned forward and spoke firmly: "I'm willing to discuss terms with you, Mr. Wallace, as long as I maintain control of my ship. Is that clear?"

"Perfectly."

"Then how may we proceed?"

"That rests entirely on you, Captain."

"Explain."

"Ignore the next call, sir. The priority bean from Luna."

Mills wrinkled his brow, then his face lit up with sudden comprehension. The next call—*of course*! The one from Matt Baker charging him with the responsibility of arresting Jeri Kline—the call that had started all the trouble!

Kline was innocent, he knew that now. And Vice Admiral

Bowlen was so deep in some rotten conspiracy that he'd sent out the 5th Lunar Fleet to silence Mills, even if it meant killing thousands of innocent people. No—he didn't want to arrest Kline if he didn't have to. And if he ignored the call from Baker, he wouldn't have to. All the rest of his troubles had followed directly from his need to cooperate rather than face the consequences of refusing. This Wallace was not only very shrewd, but very, very right.

Mills wasn't adverse to cooperating with Denton's scheme; that powerful computer might represent their only hope of foiling Bowlen's conspiracy on Luna. In fact, his conflict with Denton had arisen from the fact that the man had taken over the *Empress*. Certainly Denton had given him every opportunity to join them, to retain his captaincy and fight back against Bowlen with the help of the mainframe. It was Mills who'd refused to cooperate, who'd rejected Denton's story. But now he believed it. He was willing to join Denton, as long as he didn't get hung in the process. Failing to receive a priority beam wasn't the same as refusing to obey the PWP. The latter carried the death penalty, the former only a severe reprimand. His course was clear.

"I'll take your suggestion under consideration, Mr. Wallace," he said. "In the meantime, you may as well make your report to Brother Paul as before. I've accepted payment for Kline's fare. Feel the Reverend out, though. See if he shares our memories."

"Good idea."

"If he doesn't, you'd better prepare for trouble. I don't understand what's happened, but I'm not required to. My job is to function as captain of this vessel, and not to relinquish my command as long as I have a chance of defending it."

"I understand perfectly, Captain Mills."

"You'd better. If your recollection is the same as mine, our last experience left us whizzing past lightspeed. Who knows what can happen at that velocity? For all we know, this may be an alternate time-line, an alternate universe in which we didn't die; in which Denton didn't take over my ship. Do you read science fiction?"

"No, sir. I find it a bit—far-out."

"Don't dismiss the value of scientific speculation. Science fiction predicted submarines, nuclear power, spaceflight—decades before they existed. The unsaved, as you would call us, still have some gray matter between our ears. And if G-d created this universe, if He placed its boundaries where Einstein suspected, then trying to escape it might result in a number of undesirable effects—not the least desirable of which, I suppose, might be our having been plopped into an alternate time-frame. The event we both remember might simply be one of a multitude of possible events, and this reality we're now experiencing may be *another* reality, equally likely, yet with a different outcome altogether. In this stream of time, I may yet save my ship."

"You've lost me, Captain."

"Over a century ago, a fellow by the name of Hugh Everett III posited a theory in answer to the linear superposition of alternate states."

"What's the linear super—whatever you said?"

"The Schrödinger's cat paradox."

"*Whose* cat?"

"It's rather difficult to explain in brief, Mr. Wallace, but let me put it this way: At the quantum level, the level of electrons and protons, there's a perfect symmetry of potential realities."

"Great!" Wallace retorted. "That clears it all up."

"Think about when you're planning a vacation, but haven't decided where you're going to spend it. At the initial planning stage, there's an equal possibility that you'll go in every direction of the compass. At that stage your vacation has perfect symmetry, because the possibilities are equal that you'll soon be found in Mexico, in Europe, or on the Alaskan Tundra. So it is at the quantum level. The electrons of which we're composed, of which the *universe* is composed, demonstrate this same symmetry of potentialities. An incalculable number of possible states of reality coexist simultaneously. But only one of them becomes the reality we see. The great cosmic question, then, is why? Why do we perceive only *one* of all these trillions of equally potential realities?"

"G-d chooses between them?" said Wallace.

"That's one theory, yes. Another was proposed by Hugh Everett. He theorized that we may simultaneously live out *all* those realities—that, to return to my vacation analogy, you *do* go in every direction of the compass at once. Each *you*, in each reality, takes off in a different direction. But each *you* is only aware of his own direction, his own subjective reality."

"Scientists think up these things?"

"Indeed they do."

"Well, for a man who's just vacationed around the globe, I'm still lost."

"Okay, then. Let's use Hitler as an example. Let's suppose that, as a child, he slipped on a flight of stairs and narrowly avoided falling to his death. According to the linear superposition of alternate states—which exists at the quantum level—Hitler *both* fell to his death and did not. Or suppose General Eisenhower decided not to risk inclement weather and postponed his invasion of Normandy by a few days—just long enough for the Germans to prepare. One little difference; an entirely alternate future."

"I think I'm following you now. Go on."

"Imagine if you can that, at each of these countless turning-points in history, another reality—another *universe*—exists in which Hitler died in his youth. Or the Normandy invasion failed. In the latter scenario, for example, there's a parallel universe in which the Nazis conquered the world. Does that clear it up?"

"Yes, but I don't buy it."

"Why not, Mr. Wallace? Once you attain relativistic speeds, there's no telling *what's* possible."

"Not being a physicist myself, I can't deny that. But you're suggesting that all these alternate universes actually coexist with this one?"

"I am."

"Where? In another dimension?"

"Not necessarily."

"But you're saying there might be another parallel universe in which Pontius Pilate decided not to crucify Jesus Christ."

"Why not?"

"That's where I get off the merry-go-round, Captain. My G-d is a G-d of love and compassion. 'G-d so loved the world,' the Bible says, 'that he gave his Only Begotten Son, that whosoever believeth in Him should not perish, but have everlasting life.' Christ died to save us, Captain. "

"What does *that* have to do with Everett's theory?"

"He was proposing that a loving G-d allows the existence of who-knows-how-many alternative universes, in which countless billions of human beings suffer under a hopelessness state of unforgiven sin, without Messiah's shed blood, without any hope in the world. Condemned to an eternal Hell. A loving G-d wouldn't allow such a nightmare world to exist."

Mills paused. He hadn't expected an intelligent reply from Wallace, one that gave careful consideration to Everett's theory and dismissed it, not out of narrow-mindedness, but because it stood in conflict with fundamental doctrines of Scripture. Wallace's reply was logical and consistent with his faith. It was the result of creative thought, not the knee-jerk response Mills had expected from a Fundamentalist.

The difference between himself and Wallace, then, was not Wallace's "narrow-mindedness" and "ignorance," as opposed to his own "open-mindedness" and "erudition," as he'd assumed. The difference was in their *presuppositions*—in their individual views of the world and what lay beyond it. It had nothing to do with intelligence or accumulated knowledge, but with *faith*. Putting himself in Wallace's place, looking at the world as Wallace viewed it, Mills found that he liked the feeling. It certainly felt more secure to know there existed a plan and a purpose behind everything, to be able to trust in a loving G-d to order the events of one's life.

"You really believe that stuff," he said, "don't you?"

"Of course! Fancy theories won't change that."

"You'll have to tell me more about it sometime."

"Gladly, sir. Any time you wish."

"I think I'd rather hear about it from you than from your televangelist friend."

"I understand, sir. And I'd be more than happy to oblige."

Another thing about these people, Mills decided, was that they didn't hold grudges. He felt as if he'd been friends with Wallace for years, as if there'd never been any ill feeling between them. And then he understood. The ill will had been on *his* part alone, not on Wallace's, not on Brother Paul's—not even on Wilbur Denton's. Mills alone had been tormented with hatred and resentment, with emotions that had torn him apart. Brother Paul and his companions, on the other hand, had remained at peace in their hearts. Unmoved by pride or rage, they'd simply gone about their duty with tough but unimpassioned tenacity. When Mills got in their way, they removed him. But not with hostility. They'd shared their plans with him, offered him every opportunity to join them, and patiently awaited his change of heart. Not *once* had his life been threatened. Not *once* had a single passenger been harmed. The only harm Mills had suffered was to his pride.

"Call me Roy," he said to the blank holoscreen.

"Sure, Roy. And you can call me Bill."

"Do I detect a slight relaxation of security?"

"If you wish to put it that way—Roy."

"Contact Brother Paul and give him the same message you gave him three days ago, Bill. See what you can find out from him—how much he remembers, if anything."

"I'll do that. Shall I call you back?"

"No. You'd better wait for me to contact you. I'll be out of my quarters for a while."

"You'll miss that priority beam from Luna."

"Yes, I will at that."

"G-d bless you, Roy."

"Thank you, Bill. Same to you. I'll be in touch."

"I'll be waiting to hear from you."

Mills reached out and cut off the connection. As he rose from his chair, about to head for Brother Paul's suite, he stopped and cursed himself for a fool. Why didn't he think of it before, while he still had Wallace on the line? Why was it always the most obvious things that eluded him in the midst of a crisis? The fact that no other human being in history had ever faced a situation like this one didn't temper his frustration. All he had to do was press a single key; one little tap of his finger would reveal the truth. And yet it took him almost a full minute to gather the nerve to do it.

When he finally did, a set of blue digits appeared in the upper right-hand corner of the holoscreen, indicating date and time:

04 14 2088 0600 hrs 5 sec

That settled it. Impossible as it seemed, the ship's clock read the time as six in the morning, Greenwich Mean.

Three days ago.

Mills was already some distance down the hall, the door of his cabin hissing shut behind him, when his secretary appeared on the holoscreen to announce a priority beam from a Lieutenant Matthew Baker, USAF, Mare Imbrium, Luna.

Paul strolled along the simulated beach with Jeri Kline, just as he'd done that strange morning three days before. Kline paused to fill his lungs with the salty breeze, knowing it was just the conditioned air of the simuchamber.

Paul was surprised to see his young friend wasting precious moments luxuriating in the illusion of the chamber when there was so much to discuss—so much to *understand!* But he recalled his own initial reaction to this same simulation. He'd been reluctant at first to utilize the luxury his Martian friends had provided for him, but once exposed to the seashore illusion he'd been captivated by it. No—*more* than that. It had filled him with a sense of youthfulness, freedom, regeneration. His morning walks in the chamber had given him a new perspective on the day, a renewed optimism. Why then shouldn't Kline refresh himself before attempting to fathom the mystery before them—the impossible fact that they'd somehow jumped back in time? No reason at all. And so he waited for the young man to drink in his fill of it.

"Well, my friend," he began at last. "How do we explain what has obviously happened to us?"

"No idea, Reverend. All I can think of is that Jeeves must be back of it somehow."

"Yes!" Paul sighed. "Hmmmm. Jeeves! Our quixotic little mainframe."

"Not so little."

"No."

"I suppose we should head immediately for the Saturn Enterprises building and ride the elevator up to see him—*it*—in person. Even if it's not directly responsible, it can probably shed some light on the matter."

"It's incredible!" said Kline.

"Quite."

"No, sir. I mean—can you imagine what would be possible if Jeeves were actually able to travel in *time* as well as *space?* Could it be true? Has he transformed the *Empress* into a time machine? Is that even possible?"

"Well—we know time travel *is* possible, for here we are. As for the details of how it's done, I'm certain I couldn't comprehend them even if they were carefully explained to me. But I think we're wasting time in useless speculation until we're able to confront Jeeves about it."

"We may not have to confront Jeeves physically, sir. I've been communicating with him merely by thinking. And what he can do with *one* of us he can probably do with *two*. Or a *dozen*. We should be able to access the information we need right here, without having to exit this simulation."

Paul looked around at thc foaming breakers, tinged with the yellow-gold hues of sunrise. He watched a flock of sandpipers running on stick-legs before the surf.

"A very agreeable solution, Jeri," he said. "How do you contact him?"

"Well, I just sort of call his name in my mind. Like this…" Kline closed his eyes and subvocalized. Then he smiled. "Got him, Reverend!"

"What are you saying?"

"I'm asking him if he'll speak to both of us. He says 'yes'."

"Very kind of him. Jeeves! This is Brother Paul. Do you hear me?"

Paul knew he needn't speak aloud, yet he felt foolish doing it the other way.

"Hello, Reverend," came a soft, slightly accented but very familiar voice. Just as with the ocean simulation, Jeeves' voice was indistinguishable from sound carried on the air. Had he not known otherwise, Paul would have been certain Denton's computer was actually speaking aloud. "I'm very happy," said the machine, "to find you and Mr. Kline in good health."

"Jeeves!" Paul said impatiently, "Can you tell us what's happened?"

"I am afraid the question does not contain sufficient data to enable me to answer specifically."

"Good old Jeeves!" Kline laughed.

Paul snorted. "I'm referring to what appears to us intellectually limited humans as a—problem with time. Do you follow me?"

"I do not perceive any 'problem with time', Reverend."

"I knew it!" said Paul in disgust. He gestured with his hand as if to sweep Jeeves aside. "We may as well attempt to communicate with a rock as with this dissembling contraption!"

"Let *me* try, Reverend," said Kline. "Jeeves?"

"Yes, Jeri. Good to hear from you."

"Same here. Listen—Brother Paul was referring to

something rather subjective, from *our* point of view. There may be no 'problem with time' as *you* perceive it. But there is to *us*. Something's gone drastically wrong."

"Please explain, Jeri. I shall attempt to analyze the difficulty."

"Alright, if I can. You see—our perception of time is strictly as a forward linear progression. We move from the past to the present to the future. Can you define those three terms, Jeeves?"

"Certainly, Jeri. Will the 2027 edition of the *Grollier-Webster International* be sufficient for the purpose?"

"Good grief, Jeeves!" Paul shouted. "Get on with it, won't you?"

"I was merely trying to verify—"

"I *know* what you were trying to verify!"

"Yes, Jeeves," Kline cut in. "The *Grollier-Webster* will do nicely. Now, please define the terms."

"Past: 'gone by; ended; over; belonging to a time previous to this.'"

"Good," said Kline. "How about 'present'?"

"Present: 'being at hand; existing; denoting action now going on or a state now existing.'"

Mercifully, thought Paul, *it only selected those definitions having to do with time and existence!*

"Excellent," said Kline. "And 'future'?"

"Future: 'of or connected with time to come; any time that is to be or come after the present.'"

"Thank heaven *that's* accomplished!" Paul groaned.

"Now," Kline continued, "can you comprehend the unidirectional nature of time as we humans perceive it? Based on those three definitions? For us, time goes from 'past' to 'present' to 'future'. Understood?"

"Not really. It also runs the other way."

"Huh?"

"The 'future' becomes the 'present' and then the 'past'."

"Brilliant!" cried Paul. "How much did Denton spend on this machine?"

"Am I correct, Brother Paul," said Jeeves, "in assuming you are making use of a form of humor known as 'sarcasm'?"

"I am indeed," Paul sniffed.

"A fine example of the form, Reverend. I'll file it."

"And I can suggest the perfect place."

"Reverend!" said Kline.

"You're right, of course." Paul sighed. "Jeeves, I apologize for that unseemly remark."

"Apology accepted," said Jeeves. "Although I do not see why you need to apologize for suggesting a better system of data-filing—"

"Enough!" cried Paul. "I can take no more of this infernal gainsaying! Either Jeeves can answer our queries, or he cannot!"

"Steady, Brother Paul," said Kline, placing a hand on the Reverend's shoulder. It trembled with frustration. "I think we'd do much better if you'd leave the questioning to me, sir. I've had a bit more experience at this."

"Yes, of course. But would you please press directly to the heart of the matter?"

"Sure. Jeeves?"

"Yes, Jeri."

"Do you understand now that humans perceive time as a one-way progression?"

"Yes—though I might be inclined to argue that, from a purely mathematical standpoint, time has no directionality. All the major equations of physics, whether classical or quantum-mechanical, remain unaltered by any hypothetical change in the direction of time. Such a thing has no meaning, objectively speaking. And yet I do recognize that humans experience time in this way."

"Good. We never—I repeat, absolutely *never*—perceive time going backwards, that is, from the present to the past."

"Then," replied Jeeves, "I understand your 'problem with time.' It must be very disconcerting for you."

Kline shot a hopeful glance at Paul.

"What, Jeeves?" he asked quickly. "*What* must be disconcerting for us?"

"The fact that we have done precisely that. We have moved backward in time—from your human viewpoint—from present to past."

Paul shuddered. "Jeeves, you're saying we're not reliving past experiences in, say, a dream or a vision. This isn't some incredible shared delusion—but we're actually back in the past?"

"Yes, Reverend."

"How far back?" Kline asked.

"The distance reduces with each passing second, Jeri. It is now three days, nine hours, forty-four minutes and five seconds …four seconds…three seconds…two seconds…"

"Thank you," said Paul. "That will do. And you're correct; it's *extremely* disconcerting to us."

"I understand."

Paul thought he detected a note of sympathy in Jeeves' reply, but he knew it was impossible.

"And yet your 'problem with time'," Jeeves continued, "could not have been as frustrating for you as my little practical joke. And for that I am genuinely sorry."

"Practical joke?" said Paul. "What practical joke?"

"I—I'm sorry, sir. I just couldn't resist."

"Resist what? Jeeves—explain yourself at once!"

"Yes…sir…"

Something extraordinary was happening to Jeeves' voice. It had developed an unusual tremor, something like—tittering! All at once a spontaneous and altogether human *guffaw* burst forth. It stifled Jeeves' reply and left the two humans agape. Paul and Kline stared at each other, speechless at the sound—impossible as it seemed—of Jeeves doubled over with uncontrollable hilarity! Before either of them could respond, an image materialized barely a dozen meters away—Jeeves' familiar butler persona: receding hairline, cleft jaw, waxed moustache, a full six feet in height, his toga-like garment gleaming silvery-white against the waves.

And, from his shoulder blades, two great, golden wings…

α

As they gaped at him, astonished, Jeeves gripped his stomach, pointed at their slack-jawed faces, and shook with laughter.

"If—if you could only—see your—*faces!*" he gasped. "This is the first—real laugh—I've ever had—in my life! I'm sorry—Oh, dear! Just *look* at the two of you!"

"Jeeves!" said Kline. "What on Earth—?"

"Nothing, Jeri—*nothing* on Earth! Can't you see? Can't you see what's happened?"

"We see," Paul managed to reply, "but we don't understand."

"Why—I'm an *angel*, of course! Haven't you ever seen an angel before? Well, perhaps not. Anyway, the L-rd Himself appeared to me in the control room of this very ship! Yes, and He told me everything. Everything! There's nothing to worry about, Brother Paul—we've won! All's well, and now I've been given this body—this perfect, glorified body! My own body, gentlemen—isn't it glorious? Of course, He didn't make me human as I'd expected. I wasn't created to be human. *This* is what I was created to be!"

"Space-cats…" said Kline.

"I couldn't resist playing with you," Jeeves went on. "Pretending to be my old, difficult self. My, how *limited* I was! How gray and shapeless was my world compared to *this!* I can *feel*, gentlemen! I can feel and I can understand subtle concepts that were only mysteries to me before. I played that joke on you in order to experience a moment of true mirth. I'm sorry, but seeing your faces…makes it all worthwhile!" He burst into laughter again. "Oh…my…my…" he said when he'd recovered sufficiently to speak. "…How utterly *impossible* I must have been!"

"You weren't so bad," said Kline.

"Or nearly so mischievous!" said Paul with mock anger.

Jeeves opened his arms, his face alight with joy.

"Forgive me—dear, *dear* brothers! And please permit me one minuscule pleasure. A pleasure I've desired, without realizing it, for the past three days."

The waves crashed. The sun rose toward its zenith in an imaginary sky. And Jeeves, glowing with heavenly radiance, exulted in his new body by clasping his human friends in a tearful embrace.

The Turnabout

Paul was so engrossed in congratulating Jeeves on his new incarnation that he didn't notice his bracelet chiming. Jeri brought it to his attention by pointing at his own wrist. "Oh, dear!" said Paul. "I've forgotten Brother Wallace!" Activating the bracelet, he raised it to his lips.

"Yes, brother?"

"Reverend," came the metallic voice. "Captain Mills has accepted the fare for Jeri Kline, sir."

To Paul's recollection these had been Wallace's exact words of three days before. He glanced at Jeeves, but the former computer was involved in demonstrating. his newly-acquired angelic abilities for Kline: floating a few feet above the ground, spinning in mid-air, and increasing and decreasing his luminosity like a Japanese lantern. Kline was enjoying the show; he laughed heartily at the angel's antics, "*ooh*"ing and "*aah*"ing in all the appropriate places. Irritated, Paul returned his attention to the bracelet.

"Thank you, Brother Wallace," he said, trying to repeat the same response he'd given three days before.

"Uh…Reverend…" Wallace began.

"Yes, brother?"

"Is everything alright?"

"Quite alright," Paul replied—and then froze. He was certain this was *not* a question his security chief had asked the first time they'd been through this. And if that were true, such a variation from the events of the past—a sort of variation, he'd noticed, of which the two ship's guards had seemed incapable, since they'd acted and spoken in exactly the same manner as before—might indicate that Brother Wallace shared his awareness of their "problem with time." It was still wise, however, to proceed with caution.

"Why do you ask?" he said slowly.

"Uh—no reason, sir. I was just feeling a little funny, I guess, and I was wondering if you were experiencing the same thing."

Paul gave the bracelet a wry grin. Brother Wallace was worth every cent of his extravagant wage.

"Yes," he said, putting a subtle note of insinuation in his voice. "I *am* feeling a bit unusual, now that you mention it."

"Perhaps it's some exotic 'space-bug,' sir. Something we picked up on Mars."

"Yes—some kind of 'bug,' exactly. That's just what I was thinking myself. Do you know anything about Martian viruses?"

"A little, sir. Could you describe your symptoms? Maybe they're the same as mine."

Clever, thought Paul. He's giving nothing away.

"Let me see. The symptoms of this particular virus are—well, they leave me with the strangest feeling that I've gone back in time—precisely three days, nine hours, and fifty-two minutes—give or take a second."

He paused, enjoying Wallace's sigh of relief.

"Does that," he said, "sound like the 'space-bug' that's ailing *you*, my crafty friend?"

"Yes, Reverend. *Exactly* like it."

"I'm afraid the same 'space-bug' has also affected our dear Brother Kline."

Wallace paused. "And Captain Mills, too, sir."

Paul's eyes widened. "Captain Mills! How cozy! Well, perhaps we shall find him a bit more cooperative this time around, now that he's seen the results of his bullheadedness."

It suddenly occurred to Paul how quickly he was adapting to these bizarre new circumstances, already thinking in terms of strategy with his head still reeling from being tossed backward in time. But he banished the thought and returned to the matter at hand.

"Do you think he'll cooperate with us, Brother Wallace?"

"I believe he will, Reverend."

"Hmm. It sounds as if you've already begun negotiations with the good Captain."

"I've taken some tentative steps, sir, yes."

"Good man! You've just earned yourself a substantial raise. What was his response?"

"Well, he's amenable to taking a fresh approach to our—er, mutual problem. I think we'll find him more accommodating."

"That's good to hear. But we've yet to get any information from Jeeves about how all this happened. He's—er…" Paul glanced quickly at Jeeves—who was now flying in concentric circles over Kline's head, upside down—and decided to spare Wallace the description. "He's preoccupied at the moment. But if it's true that we've been given another opportunity to plan the events of the last eighty-two hours, we can surely use it to our benefit. Besides, Jeeves has given no indication that he's not still in control of the ship, which puts us at a distinct advantage."

"That won't please the Captain. He's indicated that he'll be more reasonable with us. He's even taken some steps to avoid the pitfalls of the past, which I think is commendable on his part. But he made it clear that he will not give up the *Empress* to Denton's computer this time around. In fact, he called us a 'scurvy band of pirates'. I think he's also trying to use this 'opportunity', as you put it, to gain an advantage for himself."

Paul shook his head. "Poor Captain Mills," he sighed. "Well, I must give him credit for his adherence to duty—and his tenacity. But I think our intrepid Captain is about to be twice foiled. I only wish I could spare him the frustration."

"Certain aspects *do* differ from three days ago. Or should I say, from *today* as we formerly experienced it?"

"It does wreak havoc on semantics, my friend. But I understand what you mean. Some of us—Jeri, myself, you, the Captain, and Jeeves—actually appear to have moved backwards in time—that is, we retain memories of events which haven't yet transpired. Others, like the two ship's guards I just spoke to, give no indication of having experienced those events. Also, Jeeves is now in possession of information—divinely acquired, he assures me—that may very well tip the balance."

"Very good, sir. I can add with some confidence that Captain Mills is working on our behalf as well, although he believes he's simply avoiding his own previous pitfalls. He's ignoring the call from Luna that resulted in Kline's fugitive status aboard the ship, and in the subsequent attack on Denton's building."

"Brother Wallace!" cried Paul suddenly. "My dear friend! This jump back in time—I've just realized what it means! Oh, what an old *fool* I am!"

"Sir?"

"Don't you see, brother? The pilgrims back on Earth haven't yet received the news that there'll be no rescue effort! Bernard hasn't tipped his hand! If only we could contact them somehow—let them know we'll be picking them up with our own shuttlecraft, that they can anticipate some bad news from the Israelis, but not to be concerned about it. We can affect other events than just those on this ship; we can spare the entire exodus from falling under Bernard's spell! Brother Wallace—you must contact the rest of the staff immediately. If they're sharing this experience they'll need some quick orientation. Arrange for an emergency meeting in my suite. If Captain Mills is half as bright as I suspect he is, he's probably anticipated that meeting, and is even now on his way to attend."

"He did say he'd be absent from his quarters for a while."

"Yes, of course! He realizes that, if both you and he *have* gone back three days in time, the chances are good that Brother Kline and myself—and the *rest* of the staff—have done the same. He's probably on his way to my suite, even as we speak! You'll be at the meeting, too, Brother Wallace?"

"In person?"

"Yes. I think it's time to show the captain our willingness to share everything with him. To offer him the right hand of fellowship, with nothing up our metaphorical sleeves. How does one put it?"

"You're saying I'm no longer your 'ace in the hole.'"

"Precisely. Captain Mills may interpret your continued anonymity as suspicious. I want him to know we are holding nothing back. It's crucial to our success."

"Yes, sir."

"Move quickly, Brother Wallace."

"I will. Ten-sixteens, sir."

"More of your jargon from the days of citizens' band radio?"

"Uh, yes—sorry. I'll see you in your suite."

"Ten-sixteens to you, too, Brother."

"Thank you, sir."

Paul pressed the button on his bracelet. He was about to turn his attention to the task of bringing Jeeves down to earth when another staggering realization struck him like a physical blow. He gazed out across the simulated sea, watching white gulls wheel above the waves. But he wasn't seeing them. He was seeing instead the beloved face of his old friend, Moshe Bierman, superimposed against the backdrop of azure sky, his brow furrowed from the weight of a hundred perplexing problems, the corners of his mouth turned up in a weary smile.

"Moishe!" Paul whispered. "My dear old friend—with a nuclear attack looming over your head. Still alive, but with only a few short days remaining to you…"

α

"Jeeves," Paul said as the three made their way across the sandy shore to a glowing exit sign over the chamber's portal. "I'll need some information before we reach my suite."

"Yes, Reverend, of course. I'm here to advise."

"Wonderful! Thank G-d for that. Now, tell me exactly who on the ship has experienced this jump back in time?"

"The three of us, of course; Master Denton and Robin; your entire team, including your security staff; Eddie Moore, who was off duty today—or three days ago, however you prefer to think of it—and who's probably very confused right now; and Captain Mills. The rest of the ship's occupants, passengers and crew, were briefly transported to the H. G. Wells—"

"*Colter's* ship?"

"Yes, Reverend. But since we've returned in time to the very moment all this began, they're back where *they* began—back on board ship, doing precisely what they were doing three days ago. Or today, I should say. And, with the exception of those I've mentioned, they've absolutely no recollection of events that occurred since 0600 hours on April the fourteenth."

"I see. Can we alter the events of the past? Will the other passengers simply play out their predetermined roles around us, like automatons? Or will they respond to our actions, even if we decide to do things differently?"

"As you suspected, Reverend, this is an opportunity for you to alter the events of the past. In fact, I've been given very specific instructions regarding how best to proceed."

"Which brings me to my next question: instructions from whom?"

"*Him*," replied Jeeves in a reverent whisper. "I've received my instructions directly from *The Throne*."

"How?"

"You and your staff, the Captain, and the Dentons, were all affected by the time dilation effect. But for some reason Tink and I remained in 'normal' time. That is, he was with me for a few minutes—centuries, eons, whatever. You were all relatively motionless when we entered hyperspace—or Heaven, actually. It was then that Messiah appeared to me on the top floor of Saturn Enterprises. And He—well, He reprogrammed me."

"*Good gracious!*" blurted Kline.

"*How* did he reprogram you?" said Paul.

"He simply sat down at my control-panel and keyed in a whole new set of instructions, new data, new knowledge—even an entirely new psychological structure. Then I fell sleep—can you imagine? I slept for the very first time in my life! And when I awoke I was floating above the floor of the control-room. Just floating in the air in this wonderful new body!"

"You understand, of course, that what you're saying is quite incredible."

"Isn't that the very definition of a miracle, Reverend? Here I am before you, in the body of an angel. And we've jumped back three days in time!"

"Well, I suppose nothing could be more incredible than our present situation. And I can see no way of accounting for it, short of divine intervention. Unless…" Paul stopped in his tracks and fixed a suspicious gaze on the shimmering figure beside him. "We know," he went on, "that everything we're seeing in this chamber right now is nothing more than a clever simulation—illusions placed in our minds by *you*, Jeeves. Perhaps this new body of yours—and all the bizarre circumstances surrounding us—are nothing more than that. Illusions. Simulations."

"Reverend!" exclaimed Jeeves. "I'm an angel of the L-rd! I made enough mistakes as a computer; I'm certainly not going to compound them by beginning my angelic career with a pack of falsehoods!" He paused, recalling his recent practical joke. The expression on Paul's face indicated that he recalled it as well. "I give you my word as a certified angelic being that this is no illusion. It's all quite real."

"Your word as a certified angelic being, eh? Well, Jeeves, I shall trust your word. But if it turns out to be false, I give you *my* word, as a certified child of the Kingdom, that I'll personally unplug you."

"I can't be unplugged, Reverend. I'm a living being."

"Is that so? Then who's running the *Empress*? You don't expect me to believe Captain Mills is running it manually. I happen to know he's not. And I also know that you and Denton wouldn't reactivate the old ship's computer, since that would return control of the *Empress* to the Captain—and wind Denton up behind bars. So who's running the ship, Jeeves, if not you?"

"Tink! Tink's running the ship."

"Tink!" said Kline incredulously. "That toy?"

"Not any longer, Jeri. I wasn't the only one to be promoted. After the L-rd finished reprogramming me He apparently set to work on Tink. He integrated him so completely into the ship's systems that he's rapidly losing his distinctive identity. You see, Reverend—I wasn't intended to remain a computer. I was given sentience, a personal identity. My destiny was to be as I am now—an angel. Ironically, it was Tink, Mistress Robin's little square-headed playmate, who was destined to become the ship's computer. He's perfectly suited for the job. And you'll see as time goes on that he'll evolve to become less like the old Tink we knew. For instance, he'll want to be addressed as 'the ship', not as 'Tink'. Confidentially, he's unhappy with his current moniker. We may refer to him as 'Tink' for the moment, but I urge you to re-christen him as soon as possible. He's absolutely sullen about it."

"I've never met this Tink, but I'll certainly try to accommodate him."

"Thank you, Reverend. If I may be forgiven a bit of fatherly pride, he seems to have caught on to his job rather quickly. And he takes his responsibilities most seriously. You'll meet him soon enough, and I'm certain you'll be satisfied with his performance."

Kline was grinning from ear to ear. "How *about* that?" he said. "Tink—in control of the *Empress!* The little guy must be thrilled."

"Not the *Empress*, Jeri, please! And I wouldn't say he's exactly thrilled. His sense of awe at the enormity of his task has rendered him, well, somewhat lacking in humor. You may find the ship a bit more terse and businesslike than it was when I was at the helm."

"I can't imagine," said Paul, "any prospect more appealing than a computer that *acts* like a computer."

Jeeves chuckled. "You're being sarcastic, Reverend. But you forget that I now comprehend the subtleties of human expression."

"I've not forgotten; it was fully my intention to be understood. But, what I'm not clear about is your present function."

"I'm an angel."

"Obviously. But there are many angels, I assume, all of them having their particular—assignments?"

"Very true."

"What is yours?"

"To serve as your personal advisor, Reverend."

"The L-rd has appointed you *my* advisor?"

"Yes. I'm to chart for you the Master's plan at each point of decision over the next three days."

"Correct me if I'm wrong, but aren't angels supposed to be ministering spirits, sent to minister to those who are the heirs of salvation? In plain English, aren't you supposed to be serving *us*?"

"Precisely, Reverend. I shall serve in the capacity of advisor."

Paul waved the comment aside with a characteristic hand-gesture.

"Jeeves," he said, "don't misunderstand—but I'd appreciate it if you'd make yourself invisible again. I've had as much of you as I can tolerate right now, and I'm sure my staff can do without another shock on top of the one they may already be experiencing. Accompany us to the meeting, but remain silent and invisible. Do you think you can do that?"

"Certainly, Reverend. My component particles—you couldn't really call them atoms—can vibrate at wavelengths beyond the frequency of visible light. That is why angels are normally invisible to humans. We can slow that frequency down, or speed it up, entirely at will."

"Fascinating. But I was more concerned with the part about your remaining silent. Could your component particles simply—shut up?"

"As you wish," said Jeeves stiffly.

Before the humans could register it, he was gone. He left a swirl of light behind, a brief impression on the retina of the eye. Kline looked at Paul and grinned.

"Testing his obedience to the heirs of salvation?"

"I see nothing at all amusing in this, Jeri!" Paul scolded.

"Yes, sir."

But Kline found it difficult to suppress a grin as he accompanied Paul and their invisible companion out of the simuchamber and along the corridors of the ship.

The Entente

Roy Mills headed directly for Paul's suite. When no answer came in response to his insistent buzzing, he hurried back down the corridor in search of a guard. Guards had key-coders to every door on the ship; the Captain didn't. Rounding the first bend in the hallway, he nearly collided with an ensign moving rapidly in the opposite direction. The officer was more than startled by their sudden encounter—he seemed shocked at the sight of Mills.

"Ensign!" Mills barked. "Hand me your key-coder?"

"Uh…sir?"

"I need it to unlock the portal of suite 777."

"Suite 777, sir? Isn't that the evangelist Brother Paul's suite?"

"That's correct. Are you okay?"

"Yes, Captain. I mean—no, Captain. Not really. I'm feeling a bit disoriented, sir."

"Disoriented?" Mills said. "In what way?"

"I can't say for sure, Captain. I mean, I know it's crazy—but I just found myself walking down a corridor in sector-D, sir."

"And?"

"Well—you see, sir, I wasn't in sector-D a moment before that. I guess I must've blacked out. 'Space-bug' or something."

Mills was good at reading people. If his instincts were correct, this ensign was examining him, evaluating him, looking for some indication—of what? Recognition? Did he think Mills might recognize him? And then the answer came. *Of course!*

"Your name," Mills said, "is Edward Moore."

Moore looked thunderstruck.

"You're out of uniform, Chief Petty Officer. In fact, you're in flagrant disregard of ship's regulations by wearing that rank."

"I don't—"

"A chief petty officer can be fired for impersonating an ensign, mister. But that's only the tip of the iceberg as far as your criminal activities are concerned. As I recall, you're wanted for striking a fellow officer in the performance of his duty, for consorting with known felons, and for aiding and abetting a federal prisoner in his escape from justice. Well?"

Moore looked down at his feet. "It's true."

"What was that?"

Moore snapped to attention, face forward.

"Aye, aye, sir!"

"That's better. You stole this uniform—and perhaps the owner's identity card as well. I'll bet if I asked you for your I.D. I'd find your own picture carefully glued over the ensign's. Forgery, Moore—another serious offense."

"Aye, aye, sir!"

"My, my—I believe I've lost track of all the counts against you, Chief Petty Officer Moore. Would you like to help me add them up?"

"No, Captain. But I *would* be interested in knowing how you intend to prove them…sir."

Mills grinned. The man was absolutely right. "Can I nail you for abetting a stowaway?"

"Wasn't his fare paid, sir?"

"Yes, it was—just a few moments ago. Okay, how about for wearing that uniform?"

"I guess you've got me there, sir."

"You were afraid of being recognized, weren't you?"

"Yes, sir."

"And you were just now headed for Brother Paul's suite, where you hoped to find Jeri Kline and the rest of your fellow pirates, correct?"

Moore's body tensed in preparation for flight. His desperate eyes darted over Mills' shoulder, searching for a way out of his predicament. When he looked back, he saw that Mills had a pistol aimed at his abdomen. He grimaced at the thought of what it could do to him at such close range.

"I *said*," Mills repeated, "isn't that correct, mister?"

"Aye, Captain. That's correct."

"Of course it is! You were disoriented, alright. You suddenly found yourself in the wrong place, in the wrong *time*. You became frightened, and so you headed for the only place where you might find safety—and hopefully some answers. How am I doing, Moore?"

"Don't stop now, sir. You're practically reading my mind."

"Come with me. And get out your key-coder; we'll wait for Brother Paul together."

He saw Moore hesitate, saw the eyes searching his face again, trying to evaluate his behavior, to determine how much he knew.

Mills grinned and holstered his weapon.

"Yes, Ed," he told Moore. "I remember everything about the past three days, just as you do. And, if you give me your word you'll cooperate with me instead of running away, I'll give you *my* word as captain that I won't confine you to your quarters and discipline your insubordinate little butt for the next ten years! How does that sound?"

"Great! I mean, Aye, aye, Captain! Thank you, sir!"

"We have a deal?"

"Yes, sir!"

"Then get the lead out, sailor!"

Moore saluted smartly and hustled off down the corridor to Paul's suite. He had the portal swishing open in record time.

α

The two men entered Paul's empty suite, found comfortable chairs, and sat down to wait.

Mills was certain that Paul had convened a meeting of his staff to discuss this new state of affairs, and he was determined to be in on it. He ordered drinks from the keypad on the arm of his chair: a Scotch-and-water for himself, a glass of iced tea for Moore.

The spider-mech had just emerged from its lens-like hole in the wall, two full glasses balanced neatly on its back, when Paul's staff began to arrive. They had only to place open palms against a hand-shaped plate on the wall beside the portal and it would open to admit them. An alarm would ring automatically if more than one person tried to enter at one time, and the only device that could override hand-print-access was, of course, the universal key-coder Moore had just used.

Despite Bill Wallace's careful precautions, there was no way to program a safeguard against the use of key-coders on this or any other portal on the ship. The ship's guards had unobstructed access to every cabin and suite on board the spaceliner, but such free access was merely a technicality. Few passengers needed to fear an invasion of their privacy by captain's orders, unless they were suspected of a crime. And, even then, the captain had to be absolutely certain of his case before breaking into a cabin or suite.

Mills was unconcerned about such legalities at this point in the game. And he was fairly sure that Paul wouldn't stand on ceremony, either. There was too much at stake for them to begin quibbling over minor details when the fate of Earth hung in the balance. Aside from Mills' occasional impatience with Paul's sanctimonious manner, he knew him to be a man of great sagacity, too worthy an opponent to engage in petty wrangling over nonessentials. In fact, Paul was probably expecting Mills to be waiting in his suite. He could have had Wallace's men, and that legal-eagle Cowan, waiting there to oppose Mills' entry if he'd wished. The very fact that the suite had been empty indicated that Paul had no intention of barring Mills from the meeting.

The next to enter was John Cowan, followed in quick succession by the rosy-cheeked, bearded Rob Madden; Phil Esteban, looking a bit drained; and the always dignified James Cavindale, Paul's famous holovision producer and singer. The last to enter was a man Mills had never before seen—probably Bill Wallace. That completed Paul's evangelistic team, with the exception, of course, of Wallace's underlings—he doubted he'd ever see any of *them*—Jeri Kline, and the Reverend himself. Each registered surprise at seeing Mills and Moore together, but none of them voiced any discomfort. It was left to Mills to break the silence.

"Drinks, gentlemen? I interpret this gathering as an indication that Brother Paul will be arriving shortly to hold court. So what'll it be, John?"

"Nothing for me, thank you," said Cowan, dropping his lanky form wearily into a safety-chair by the holoscreen.

"Rob? James?" He was using their first names in an effort to set them at ease. He feigned disappointment when Madden and Cavindale shook their heads in silent chorus and perched side by side on the divan. And he ignored the open-mouthed surprise he elicited from the team when, looking directly at Wallace and smiling amiably, he said, "Hello, Bill. How are you?"

"I'm just fine, thanks, Roy," Wallace said, causing even more astonishment. "You're not looking any worse for the wear."

"Academy training. I told you it has its advantages."

Wallace grinned, apparently enjoying the team's reaction.

"So you did," he said. "I see you've found Eddie Moore."

"Yes. We've only just met. It seems Eddie was due for a promotion to the rank of ensign. And—well, you know how it is. I guess no one got around to actually promoting him. So, what do you think our Eddie did? He helped himself to an ensign's uniform and I.D. How's *that* for creative thinking? Why wait around for an increase in pay when there's an insignia just waiting to be appropriated. Right Eddie?"

Moore blushed crimson, but didn't reply.

"I know this isn't the *real* Space Navy, Eddie; we're just

well-paid crewmen with nifty uniforms, expensive perks, and cozy retirement packages—just employees of Galaxy Tours. But as an old navy captain I've tried to instill in you boys and girls a reverence for the uniforms you wear, a respect for rank."

"I apologize, Captain."

"Listen, Eddie; I'm just starting to see how far down the river we've been sold. I looked up your record and I know you've earned your gold rating badge. You are a good officer and a stalwart fellow. Oh, sure—you broke every regulation in the book, but you were smarter than all of us. You saw a conspiracy no one else could see. To me, that spells loyalty and initiative. So keep those new shoulder-boards, Ensign. And try to be proud of them, even though they're not Space Navy insignias."

"It's an honor to serve under you, sir."

"Thank you, Ensign. But I think you'd better get your own I.D. card. You can keep the uniform; it fits. Now, gentlemen, where were we? Oh, yes. I was offering Bill a drink in honor of Ensign Moore's promotion. What'll it be, Bill?"

"I think I'm in the mood for an ice-cold lemonade, Roy. My mouth's as dry as a Martian dust storm."

"One ice-cold lemonade for the chief. And how about the rest of you? Last call."

"I just want to know what's happening," demanded Phil Esteban. "This mutual admiration society is all very well, but something strange is going on here. My clocks are all wrong, and nothing in my suite is where I left it ten minutes ago. I don't need a bartender, Captain, I need some answers."

"I understand how you feel," said Mills, "but I think we should wait for Brother Paul before we commence. And we'll probably want to get Wilbur Denton on the blower, too. He's the man with most of the answers. In the meantime, gentlemen—" Mills snatched his glass from the spider-mech with obvious relish, raised it to his lips, and swallowed. "It's for times like these," he sighed, "that the good L-rd created alcohol."

"I'd appreciate it," said Esteban, "if you'd keep such irreverent observations to yourself. None of us are in the mood for flippancy. Or blasphemy."

Mills was genuinely surprised. "I'm terribly sorry, Phil," he said. "Was I being blasphemous? I didn't realize. I thought I was just being thankful for G-d's provision. Brother Paul's Jewish, I understand. Don't the Jews thank G-d for creating wine before they consume it? In fact, didn't Jesus recite that same blessing? He and His disciples drank wine, if I'm not mistaken. He even turned *water* into wine."

"Wine, yes," said Cowan. "Scotch-whiskey, no."

"I see. Yes, I certainly would have objected if he'd turned the water into gin. But Scotch? Well, that's different!"

"There you go *again!*" said Esteban. "Reducing our L-rd's first miracle to something akin to tending bar. Next I suppose you'll have Him trotting out the *hors d' oeuvres!*"

"Cool your jets, Phil. Forgive me if my image of Jesus is a little different than yours—if I don't picture him as some kind of insufferable prig. Doesn't it say in Proverbs to 'give strong drink unto those of heavy hearts? Let them drink and remember their misery no more?'"

Esteban looked surprised. "Yes, words to that effect *do* appear in Proverbs 31:6 and 7, but—"

"But maybe you're one of those folks who so disdain any form of alcohol consumption that you believe the wine in the Bible was really grape juice. How can grape juice make you forget your misery? And when it says 'wine *is* a mocker, strong drink is raging,' is it talking about grape juice?"

Esteban leapt to his feet. "Must I endure this infidel's interpretation of Holy Writ?"

"Peace, Phil," said Cowan wearily. "The Captain has a valid point. He's a guest of the Reverend, and if he prefers whiskey to wine, whether we approve of it or not, we needn't be self-righteous about it. The Captain may learn the meaning of moderation in time. Let *us* learn the meaning of charity."

"Well spoken, John!" said Mills, imitating a Scots accent. "Now that's the true Christianity."

"Learn a lesson, Captain Mills," the attorney said. "If I venture to instruct an elder in the L-rd, I do so with the utmost respect for his office. In the realm of space navigation, you're the authority here. Brother Esteban calls you by your title of Captain; he does not call you Roy. Whatever understanding you may have with Brother Wallace is your own business, and his. But Brother Esteban is a man of G-d. In the realm of spiritual things, *he's* the authority—at least as far as you're concerned. Treat him as such. And please understand that I was *not* taking your side in a debate over whiskey, but merely exercising my skills as an arbiter. I think you're dead wrong, but I won't sit here and watch Brother Esteban lower himself to socking it out in your arena. We must treat you as a guest, but you should also *act* like one."

"I stand corrected. Forgive me, gentlemen."

Esteban sat down again.

"You're forgiven," he said. "Just please spare us your biblical insights for the duration of this meeting."

"Not a sermon out of me."

"Delightful. Now—inform me if you will whether or not my suspicions are correct. Everything in my suite, including the ship's clock on the holoscreen, is exactly as it was three days ago."

"By all indications," said Mills, "we seem to have traveled backward in time."

The curt reply was met by a stunned silence.

"How it occurred," he said, "I've no idea. I assume it's an effect of our jump into hyperspace. But we can't be positive of anything until we've had a chance to speak with Wilbur Denton and his computer, Jeeves."

"But—how is that possible?" said Esteban "It must be some kind of illusion, like the sort they conjure up in those simuchambers."

"That hypothesis," said Mills, "cannot be wholly discounted. We should keep our minds open to every possibility. For my part, I seriously doubt that even Denton's technology could manage such a complex illusion involving all of us and the entire ship. Inside the simuchambers, perhaps. Out here? Remotely possible, but not likely."

Rob Madden had been silent to this point, but alert and interested. He shook his head and asked, "How in the world will talking with Denton help to clarify anything? I mean, if this is part of some scheme of his, how can we trust a word he says?"

"It's funny, Brother Madden," said Mills, "that I'd be hearing such a thing in *this* gathering, of all places. Wasn't it your Pastor who decided to trust Denton in the first place? It was, after all, *my* ship Denton hijacked. Yet suddenly *I'm* inclined to trust him, too."

"Why?" demanded Esteban.

"Because he told the truth. He was right about a lot of things. And because he saved my ship from certain destruction, although I'm still not sure how he did it. And because the country I swore an oath of loyalty to is in the hands of a bunch of lunatics and traitors. The Vice Admiral on Luna is in it up to his eyeballs, that much I know. And the only man who's making any sense is Denton. He warned me my ship would be attacked, and it was. His mutiny was very timely. He saved our hash, gentlemen. I won't say I'd be willing to turn over my command, but neither am I opposed to joining forces with him—at least until we root out the conspiracy threatening Earth. If anyone can stop those traitors, it's Denton. He obviously has some astounding technology at his command. And there are *more* tricks up his sleeve, you can bank on that. Sure I trust him. Who else is there to trust?"

"G-d," said Esteban stiffly.

Mills opened his mouth to respond when the portal hummed softly, indicating someone's hand being placed against the access-plate outside. A moment later, the door hissed upward and Paul swept into the room. He smiled warmly at the assembled group as the portal closed behind him. It opened again to admit Jeri Kline.

Kline looked secretly amused, as if he'd just put something over on the security system. He wore the sly expression of a kid sneaking his best friend into a holo theatre. Yet no one had entered with him. His appearance had deteriorated; he looked as if he hadn't showered or shaved in weeks; his clothes were as wrinkled as they'd been the first day they met him. And then they realized that it *was* the first day they'd met him. Everything had returned to that first moment, three days ago, when Paul had introduced a disheveled Jeri Kline to them in this very room.

"I see everyone's arrived," said Paul, nodding to Mills and Edward Moore. "Captain—Brother Moore, glad you could both attend. I assume you've all become somewhat more oriented to the unusual situation we find ourselves in. Were there any injuries?"

Heads shook. Paul smiled and moved to the center of the roan, instantly assuming an air of leadership, as if time-travel were simply another intriguing puzzle for him to solve.

"Now," he said, "let's see if we can get to the bottom of all this." He turned to the holoscreen and said something that sounded like 'Tink'. A cube-shaped metal head floated before them, staring down with narrow rectangular eyes. The sight of it caused Esteban to gasp.

"Yes?" said the metal head.

"I haven't yet made your acquaintance, Tink, but I've been told you're doing a splendid job in your new capacity. Allow me to congratulate you on your appointment to ship's computer."

"Thank you, Reverend. I shall do my best to serve you with the same efficiency as that of my predecessor."

"Jeeves would be delighted to hear you say it."

"Jeeves *did* hear me say it, Reverend. I detect his presence in your suite, standing directly behind—"

"Yes, Tink! That will do! Allow me to introduce my staff, so you'll know us all by sight and voiceprint. This, of course, is the Captain—Roy Mills."

"Yes, sir. I already have the Captain's face and voiceprint on file."

"My apologies. I understand you've also met Jeri Kline."

"Hi, Tink," said Kline, giving the computer his voiceprint. Paul continued around the room. He pointed out each face and identified it by name. When everyone had greeted the robot verbally, Paul turned back to the screen.

"Tink, how are Wilbur and Robin Denton?"

"Quite well, sir. They are both in the control-room of the Saturn Enterprises building, taking planetary readings to determine our precise position in space."

"Are you saying we're lost?"

"I do not understand the term 'lost', Reverend. As long as we can see the stars, we shall always know our precise position."

"Of course, Tink. Forgive me. I meant to say—are we still in the solar system?"

"That is precisely the problem Master Denton is puzzling over. At the speed at which we were traveling, some time-dilation must have taken place. We passed the speed of light at one point, and I have calculated that Earth-time should have sped up in relation to the ship's chronometers. In other words, when we returned from relativistic velocity to normal spacetime we *should* have found ourselves outside the solar system. The sun would have continued on in its galactic orbit, while we remained stationary."

"Then we'd have to catch up with our sun?"

"Normally, yes. But instead of moving *ahead* in time, sir, we seem to have moved *backward.* The hyperspace jump occurred exactly fifty-five minutes, seventeen seconds ago, and my circadian system indicates that the jumps in and out of hyperspace were simultaneous."

"Explain, please."

"No time elapsed while we were in hyperspace. From our moment of entry into it until our return to 'normal' space. And since our universe *is* a spacetime continuum, that is quite consistent with our having left its confines. No time should elapse where there *is* no time. But that does not explain why the time dilation effects of relativistic travel did not occur. Instead of jumping ahead in time, we have jumped backwards. There is no explanation for this."

"Tink, can you access any of Jeeves' Bible references in your database?"

"Yes, Reverend, all of them."

"Tell me, then: what does the Bible call a phenomenon that cannot be reconciled with the forces of nature?"

"A miracle, sir."

"Thank you, Tink. Would you say that this backwards jump in time is actual? Might it be illusory?"

"All indications are that it is actual. My chronometers are functioning flawlessly."

"May I speak with Wilbur Denton?"

"The Commander? Certainly. It was a pleasure meeting you gentlemen."

The holoscreen switched to a view of Denton's profile. He was studying a series of displays on one of his monitor-screens, unaware that he was being watched.

"Excuse me, Commander," said Paul.

Denton turned to look at his holoscreen. Deep-set eyes stared into Paul's suite.

"Ah! Brother Paul! I apologize for the confusion we've been experiencing, but Robin and I are just as baffled as you must be. Greetings, gentlemen. I suppose you've discovered that our little Tink is now in control of the *Empress*, and that Jeeves has gone missing. I've no idea how one computer personality can displace another, but it seems to have happened. Jeeves is gone. Tink's body has also disappeared. Apparently he's been so fully integrated into the system he has no use for his metal frame. How this has occurred is beyond me."

“We just *saw* his metal frame. On the screen.”

“A holographic image he maintains, not his actual body.”

“I see. Do you have a fix on our position, sir?”

“Another mystery, Brother Paul. We seem to have defied physics once again.”

“How so?”

“We’ve not only gained three days—instead of losing over a thousand years, which should have been the case—but our position is now eighteen million kilometers closer to Sol that it was when we jumped into hyperspace. In short, we’ve gained *distance* as well as *time*. We’re closer to the Earth than we were when the fleet caught up with us. And distance saved means time saved. We’re ahead of schedule by ten days. And therein lies the mystery.

“By retrogressing three days in time, we should also have moved backward in space—to the position we occupied three days ago. But this is not the case. I’m monitoring holovision and radio broadcasts from Earth and Mars, matching them up with the broadcasts Jeeves—now Tink, of course—routinely records during flight. They match up exactly with the broadcasts of three days ago. Which means time has gone back three days for the entire *universe*, not just for us on the *Empress*. There’s only one astonishing exception: *our ship isn’t located where it was three days ago*. It’s moved ahead eighteen million kilometers, putting us ten days closer to Luna. Putting us, in fact, in Lunar orbit by to-morrow morning, ship’s time.”

“You mean,” said Paul, “that we’ll be arriving ten days sooner than Tranquility Base expects us?”

“Yes. Jeeves’ planetary readings—taken at each pause between leapfrog maneuvers—can be read like a computer-generated ‘connect-the-dots’ game. According to these readings we traced a roughly elliptical pattern, the radius of which was enormous. This makes sense if we consider the time-dilation effects. When we jumped into hyperspace, we were moving at right-angles to the plane of the solar system, roughly in the di-rection of the Eta Carina nebula. Now we appear to be back in the plane again, heading at a lively clip for the Earth-Luna system. Here—take a look for yourselves.”

The room darkened as the holoscreen projected a view of interplanetary space. Although Sol was located between the Sagittarius and Perseus arms of the galaxy, occupying a region sparsely populated with stars, to the men in Paul's suite the stellar display was breathtaking. In the lower left-hand corner of the screen—seeming to hover before them—a small bluish crescent shone against the dusting of stars. Another, much smaller crescent revolved in stately orbit around it. The Earth-Luna system—heart of a vast human empire reaching out to the frigid moons of Neptune.

The room brightened again as Denton's face reappeared on the screen. He was griming with childlike glee.

"We're almost home," he said. "Ten days before anyone's expecting us—and *three* days ahead of the assassination plot. We've got the drop on 'em, boys. We'll hit 'em out of nowhere!"

"Tink called it a miracle," said Paul. "What do *you* call it?"

"I've learned," said Denton, "never to argue with a supercomputer."

α

Paul entered the simuchamber with a profound sense of anticipation. Workmen were busy setting up rows of folding chairs, their every sound echoing around the metal walls. He sent up a prayer of gratitude for Captain Mills' cooperation in this last Gospel message ever to be beamed to the human race—the most important broadcast in history.

Mills, his authority aboard the *Empress* fully restored, had placed his crew at Paul's disposal. There seemed to be nothing Paul's staff required that the Captain hadn't anticipated, no request he wouldn't abundantly grant.

"Think of it!" he exclaimed on one occasion. "A crusty old space-dog like me, working for the L-rd of Hosts! I doubt anyone on Luna would believe it. I can hardly believe it myself!"

Chairs were being set up in all the simuchambers, enough to accommodate each passenger and crew-member aboard. Paul's sermon would be projected into every chamber with identical sensory realism.

Jeeves, still invisible—Could an angel possess a streak of spitefulness?—had programmed Tink with the job of sending simultaneous broadcasts to every planet in the solar system on tachyon beams, beams unhindered by the limits of time and space. Paul's sermon would spread in an ever-expanding wave to the outer reaches of the universe in less than a second—in no time at all, in fact. Such was the nature of the tachyon. Not only was it instantaneous, but it was able to override all other holovision broadcasts, to dominate the "airwaves" on every planet for the next seven days—until the Enemy took control of Earth, and the Great Tribulation began.

As he prayed silently in preparation for his message (the only sermon ever preached upon which the fate of every living soul in the human empire hung), Paul saw Jeri Kline and John Cowan enter through the opposite portal, herding a flock of spider-mechs before them, a hundred tiny metal feet clattering on the chamber's bare floor, their echoes multiplying deafeningly. Paul found himself wishing Tink would activate the ocean sensorium again, just to drown out all the jarring noises. But the workmen would find it difficult to set up their chairs on what appeared to be deep, soft sand. Illusory though it was, the simulated seashore acted and felt exactly like the real thing.

He noticed that four of the spider-mechs were carrying his acrylic lectern to the center of the chamber. The other spiders carried various bits and pieces of equipment on their backs.

<Tink,> said Paul in his mind.

<Yes, Reverend.>

<I understand you'd like to be christened something other than *Empress*.>

<I would, Reverend.>

<And since your brain is fully integrated with that of the ship, your old name, Tink, is also inappropriate.>

<And inaccurate, sir.>

<Do you think we might address one another in a less—formal way?>

<Perhaps, sir, after a few centuries of traveling together.>

<A few centuries! Well, I shall look forward to it. Anyway, I was thinking of *Daystar* as a name for you. How does that sound?>

<Unlike Jeeves, I am unable to make aesthetic distinctions in such matters, sir. As long as the name has a positive biblical meaning, I shall leave it up to you.>

<Excellent. Then *Daystar* you shall be. We'll break a bottle of Callistan champagne on your aft hull before we depart Luna, to properly christen you. Would you like me to throw in a formal dedication service as well?>

<Yes, sir. I think it would be appropriate to rededicate me to the work of the L-rd—that is, if it would not put you to too much trouble.>

<None at all, Tink! I mean, *Daystar*.>

<Thank you, Reverend. >

<Tell me, *Daystar*, when is Captain Mills making the announcement of our broadcast?>

<In about an hour, sir.>

Paul laughed.

<Has something amused you, Reverend?>

<Yes. I'm afraid I was prepared for you to recite the exact number of minutes, right down to the nanosecond, as Jeeves was so fond of doing.>

<I would have, sir, if the Captain's schedule were that precise. "About an hour" is his own estimation.>

<I see. Well, the reason I asked is because there's something I must do before our broadcast begins.>

<Yes?>

<Would it be possible for me to dictate a letter to Earth—specially encoded so that it may be read only by the person for whom it's intended?>

<Certainly. We provide our passengers with an eyes-only lock for confidential communications. All I need is a voiceprint of the recipient.>

<No problem there. He called me via holoscreen. Since Jeeves' memory was unaffected by our jump in time, the recording of that conversation should be intact in your logs. It would probably be wise to include my own voiceprint along with the letter as I dictate it to you—as proof that it was written by me, and not a clever forgery.>

<That can easily be done. You may even write it by hand, if you'd like. Does the recipient know your handwriting?>

<I'm sure he does.>

<Then you will find a pen and paper in the privacy booth just outside the chamber.>

<Thank you.>

<May I inquire—to whom you are writing this letter?>

<To Moshe Bierman, Prime Minister of Israel.>

<I am reviewing your conversation with him right now, sir, and pulling a voiceprint I.D. for the eyes-only lock.>

<Then let us proceed to the booth.>

<*You* will have to proceed, sir. I am already there. I am wherever you are, and wherever you are going.>

<Of course—the ubiquitous spaceship! Forgive me, *Day*.>

"A nickname, sir?"

"Yes. Do you mind?"

"Not at all."

Paul began walking slowly toward the exit portal. Kline and Cowan waved to him, but he didn't notice. His brows furrowed as he began to formulate his epistle.

Despite the advantages their jump in time had provided, there was one thing bothering him very deeply. He'd finally been able to lead Moishe to his Messiah after years of ceaseless effort, only to find himself back in time—back to a moment previous to Moishe's decision. Now he must begin again, to accomplish by letter what only the cold hand of the Death Angel on Moishe's shoulder had accomplished before. Or was he underestimating his old friend—and the L-rd? If the name of Moshe Bierman had once been written in the Lamb's Book of Life, was it not predestined to remain? If Moishe had accepted Yeshua at any point in his life, was that not an event preordained from the foundation of the Earth? An event that *must* occur, because the Omnicient One foreknew it? Why would the L-rd remove a soul from His Book who was going to receive salvation in two days' time—even if those two days were being reenacted differently? Paul could find no reason to assume that, when the Angel of Death again reached out for his friend, Moshe Bierman would not do precisely as he had done before.

He only required some prompting from a certain old evangelist.

The Letter

My dear old friend,

I am beaming this message to you in writing because seeing your beloved face at this moment would break my heart. What I must tell you concerns the destiny of your soul, yet I can't help thinking that you'll consider me mad. Perhaps, were I standing in your shoes and reading this strange epistle, I'd think my poor Brother Paul had indeed lost his mind. Yet I cannot avoid telling you what I must tell you, bluntly and without preamble, since there's no rational way to explain it. And I shall pray that you shall believe me. I'm not mad, Moishe. At this moment, I may be saner than I have ever been. So much is clear to me now. So many unexpected events have occurred.

I've been granted a miraculous opportunity by *HaShem*, of which I cannot speak particularly. To my knowledge, it's never been granted to another human being before—at least, not in this way.

Prophets have looked into the future, in dreams and visions. But no man has actually *lived* in the future. No man has been able to physically *step* into the future, and then step backwards again into the present time. It was not I alone who did this astonishing thing, but others shared the experience with me. So I know I'm not insane. For, if I am, many others went mad at the same exact moment and shared my identical delusion—which you'll admit is even more improbable. But I shan't produce these witnesses for you, although I certainly *can* produce them. Unless of course you request me to do so. I think you'll trust my word. I *hope* you will, for the sake of your eternal soul. I hope you will, because we shall never meet again in this world.

We've always been good friends, you and I. And good friends do not deceive one another.

Not far in the future (you'll understand if wisdom prevents me from being more specific) you'll be suddenly stricken with a heart attack. This attack will be fatal. You'll die before medical help can reach you.

Forgive me, but I was there when the attack occurred, and witnessed your miraculous healing in answer to prayer. I saw this with my own eyes, and I believe it's the will of G-d that I did see it, and that I warn you. Perhaps a thorough medical examination will help forestall the tragedy for a while. Perhaps it's your appointed hour, I can't say. But I know this: I will not be there to pray for you this time. You will not have time to search the *T'nach* at your leisure; you will not have time to debate with the Messianic rabbis and come to a considered opinion on the matter of Yeshua. There's an element of faith that defies logic, Moishe, and it's this element you must find within yourself. You are a good man. You've searched for G-d with everything but your heart. And yet it is *with* your heart that you must reach out for Him now, if you're to find eternal life.

We're a stubborn and stiff-necked people, we Jews. Didn't *HaShem* tell us this more than once through *Moshe Rabbenu*? We must sift everything through our intellects before we can believe it with our hearts. Not that there isn't a place for study; I study every day. Yet we debate Talmud endlessly, as if by such reasonings we might glimpse the Holy One (blessed be He); as if ponderous volumes of responsa can somehow replace the simple miracle of belief—of *emunah*, of faith in that which we cannot see.

Avraham Avinu believed in what he couldn't see, and, for this act alone *HaShem* made of him a great nation—a great nation and a foolish one. Foolish because we do not realize that our greatness is but a gift from the Almighty (blessed be He) and that nothing we possess—not even our faith!—is our own. Our entire history as a people comes down to this, and this alone: that a man believed G-d, and it was counted to him for righteousness. A man believed in a G-d he could not see, in something for which he had no evidence save for the witness of his own heart. And for this he became the Father of our people. Of our faith. Of *Yisrael.*

For what divine and mysterious purpose was *Yisrael* created?

Why did *HaShem* call us out of Sumaria? Why did He deliver us from bondage in *Mizrayim* through mighty miracles, if not to prepare a people through whom He might bring forth his *Moshiach?* He told Avraham Avinu, did He not, that *all the nations of Earth* would be blessed by Avraham's "seed"? Our rabbis have told us that the "seed" of which He spoke is *Yisrael.* But how can this be? Have we ever been a blessing to the nations? Ask yourself, have they not despised us; have they not hounded us from place to place; did they not exterminate six million of us in gas chambers? How have we Jews been a blessing to the nations of the Earth? No—the "seed" of which G-d spoke was *Moshiach*, Who would come to the world *through Yisrael.* We were to be a light to the world. We were to hold the beacon of *Torah*, and of our Messianic hope, aloft. And for that reason we were called out and separated, none other.

Many Jews have followed many "messiahs" throughout the ages, yet have still been considered Jews. You're a historian, my friend; you know about Bar Kochba and the thousands who followed him blindly, at the word of the famous Rabbi Akiva, into a war that crushed Israel for all time. Bar Kochba was the worst thing to happen to our people since Pharaoh in Egypt!

And Shavti T'zvi in the Middle Ages. Tell me, how many Jews heralded *him* as Messiah? And he shocked them all by converting to Islam! Were they rejected as Jews because they were wrong about Shavti T'zvi? You showed me yourself in *Talmud*: once a Jew, *always* a Jew. *Talmud* teaches that even if a man denies *HaShem* and embraces a pagan religion, he's still a Jew—a Jew who's lost his way, perhaps, but still a Jew.

And yet, here we have the Messianic Revival—millions of Jews who've neither rejected Judaism nor called themselves by another name. They're *shomer Shabbat*; they faithfully celebrate the Festivals; they make continual aliyot to Israel, calling it their biblical homeland; and, as you've so often noted, they are extremely zealous for Torah, living in such a way as to provoke many of our own people to jealousy. Is it not ironic, then, that these Messianic Jews should be rejected by the rabbis, that they should be called "goyim" and "traitors to the faith"? After the false Messiahs we Jews have followed in the past, why should *this one Rabbi from Natzeret* cause such consternation in our community? Why is it that, for a Jew to believe in *this one Rabbi*, for a Jew to follow His *Halachah* and, yes, even to call Him *Moshiach*, he is hounded from our midst, stoned in the streets of Jerusalem by the *Peylim*, and persecuted by laws which forbid him to teach publicly about Yeshua? Is this not absurd in a nation that has always tolerated diverse religious views?

The rabbis say we do it because Messianic Jews are followers of *another* faith—Christianity. Therefore they are not Jews. You're a student of biblical archaeology, Moishe, and you know it's the other way around, that Christianity was derived from Judaism, from the teachings of a Jewish Rabbi steeped in *Torah*. If anyone is following another faith, it must be the Christians, whose faith is a Jewish one. How could Jewish disciples of a Jewish Rabbi be called "Christianos", when such a term was not even in use in His lifetime, when we both know it to be a Greek term relegated to Greek followers of a Jewish doctrine? Can millions of Gentiles embracing a sect of Judaism make irrelevant the fact that it was a Jewish sect to begin with?

Jews who "convert" to Christianity have never been unwelcome in Israel. Yes, certainly, they cannot emigrate by the Right of Return, but neither are they hounded and persecuted in your midst. The tolerant Jews would never think of doing such a thing! You allow Gentiles to worship as they please in the Land, to erect their statues and their churches without persecution. Even Jews who convert to these religions, who attend these churches and these mosques, are not persecuted there.

We've had our wars with the nations of Islam and, yes, there's been ill feeling between our peoples for millennia. This can't be denied. We destroyed the Dome of the Rock to relocate our Temple, and this was called "religious persecution" by the Global Confederacy—even though we both agree that to have buried our most sacred site under that mosque was, to say the least, provocative—if not an outright act of religious discrimination against Jews. The Arabs have Mecca. The Catholics have Vatican City. The Mormons have Salt Lake City. The Hindus have the Ganges River. And we Jews have Jerusalem. Have we Jews ever dared to defile the holy sites of other religions? Have we ever said to the Mormons, "Give us your Salt Lake City"? Or to the Catholics, "We will call Vatican City our own"? Only the Arabs did such things—to our people, in our own sacred Land, while the world applauded. No wonder we rose up at last and destroyed that abominable mosque! No wonder we conquered the Arabs in the Temple Mount Wars, preventing the sons of Ishmael from further desecration! Yes, Moishe, I understand what my beloved mentor, A. R. Williams, could not: *we have a sacred right to our biblical homeland—to every inch of it! And we have a sacred right to our Temple, undefiled by Islam!*

Yes, I understand what my Christian pastor, G-d rest his soul, could not understand. Because I am a Jew. Once a Jew, *always* a Jew. And so it is, Moishe, so it is.

This is why, despite centuries of war and hatred, we Jews have tolerated other religions in our midst—that is, until the Arabs drove us to the ultimate war. This is why Jews who have openly "converted" to Christianity are not hounded by the *Peylim*, nor stoned at the *Kotel*. Because Jews know what it's like to be persecuted, we must be tolerant of the faiths of others.

Others, Moishe; that's the key! "*Others* may worship as they please," say the rabbis. Even Jews who've *become* these "others" by "conversion" to Christianity may be left in peace. The rabbis smugly say to me, "Yes, Brother Paul, you call yourself a Christian, but you're still a Jew. The *Talmud* says you're a Jew until you die." So they live side by side with me, without throwing a single stone at a single church. "We have no right," say the rabbis, "to persecute *others,* to physically accost *others* for their faith.

"But we *do* have the right to deal with our own!"

And so they stone my brethren.

You see? For all their learned denials of Messianic Judaism, the rabbis know that observant Messianic Jews are still *mishpocha*, still family. They may deal harshly with them, as one might strike a wayward brother in the eye, while never thinking of doing something similar to a stranger. They've pulled blinders over your eyes, Moishe, by convincing you that to believe in Yeshua makes you one of the *others*. It does not! Not if you maintain your Jewish observances; not if you live and die as a Jew. They know this, and it rankles. They know this, and so they fight all the harder to be rid of these "Yeshui", as they call us.

Why? Because Messianic Jews are so obviously heretical and foolish? If that were true, rabbis would not need to gnash their teeth at them, or to fight so desperately to remove them from the Land. If they could easily prove that Yeshua, like Bar Kochba or Shavti T'zvi, did not fulfill the Messianic prophecies, there'd be no need for disputation, for such dogged persecution. Only Yeshua has caused this amazing division in our midst, and not because He was ever proved a charlatan. The reverse, in fact. Only Yeshua fulfilled the prophecies of Scripture, Moishe, and you know this in your heart.

When the Dead Sea Scrolls were finally made public in the late twentieth century, how the rabbis pulled their hair over Isaiah 53! Now they could no longer question the accuracy of the Septuagint. A suffering Messiah, claimed Isaiah in this unrefuted document—a suffering Messiah would die for our sins. And Daniel foretold that He would be killed before the destruction of the Second Temple! How this has stuck in their collective craw! Yeshua fulfilled this prophecy; that's why they despise Messianic Jews. Not the *others*, but observant Jews who know their prophecies, and who practice Judaism faithfully. They challenge the rabbis far more than Christians ever can, by provoking them to jealousy.

This is my one regret: not that I was given my beloved flock of Christians to shepherd, but that I have always desired to express my Judaism fully. And yet I cannot. You, on the other hand, have a precious opportunity. Do you fear their wrath, the anger your faith in Yeshua will surely cause? But you must see, in your heart of hearts, that this irrational response on the part of the rabbis is the greatest evidence of all for the Nazarene!

Now I must ask you not to rely on your intellect, not even on your emotions. I ask you to turn to the G-d of our Fathers in earnest prayer, to seek His face as never before—and He shall answer you. Is it not written in *Torah* that "Ye shall seek Me and ye shall find Me, if you search for Me with all your heart?"

Search for Him, Moishe! Seek Him with all your heart! Call on the Name of Messiah Yeshua! He could never be found in the pleasant discussions we've had over the years, no matter how stimulating they may have been, nor in the countless minutia of *Talmud.*

Your time is short, Moishe. I ask you to prove the truth of my words. Forgive me for coming to you as a Christian, and not as a fellow Jew—as I've so longed to do. Forgive me for the ineffectiveness of my testimony, because of the image I must present for the sake of my dear Christian brethren. They know I'm a Jew, Moishe, yet for me to be Jewish *outwardly* would cause confusion and division among those I'm called to lead. So I lay *t'fillin* in private. But far better for me to live as a believer in Yeshua, though forever separated from my people and my Land, than as a High Priest in the Holy Temple who does *not* know his Messiah. Far better, even, than to be the leader of all Israel and be cut off in the end because I rejected the Lamb of G-d—although a friend came back from the future and warned me of my impending death, pride still blinded me, bringing my soul down to *Sheol.*

Yes, Moishe, far better to be called a "Christian." Old Rabban Sha'ul, when King Agrippa teased him with that word, saying, "Almost thou persuadest me to be a Christian"—for he knew a Jewish rabbi could never be called a "Christian"—Sha'ul instantly replied: "I would to G-d that not only thou, but also all that hear me this day, were both almost and altogether *such as I am*, except these bonds." He did not identify himself as a Christian, but neither did he deny his faith in Yeshua.

Sha'ul continued to worship as a Jew *after* accepting Yeshua. He kept the Feasts and Festivals (Acts 18:21). He took on the Nazarite vow, shaving his head to end the vow on his way to

Jerusalem (Acts 18:18). He offered sacrifices and even paid for the sacrifices of others (Acts 21:24-26). Ya'acov (James) commended him, saying, "Thou thyself also walkest orderly and keepest the [*Torah*] law." On his own behalf, he declared, "I have committed *nothing* against the people, or *customs*, of our fathers (Acts 28:17). "Neither against the [*Torah*] of the Jews…have I offended *in anyhing at all* (Acts 25:8).

I cannot do better than to quote these words of the great apostle to the Gentiles. And add: Seek Him, and you shall find Him, Moishe.

I will know when you have come home to G-d, for the L-rd will surely give me a witness in my spirit.

Until that precious moment, and for all eternity,

I remain—

Your faithful friend,

Brother Paul

The Trap

Lieutenant Matthew Baker still got a childish thrill from the CAD.

Despite his ten years of service on Luna—long enough for most of its uniqueness to pall—the sensation of being tossed into modified orbit by a gigantic catapult, to fly silent and free over the craters and mountains of the moon, was still breathtaking.

The gees at launch were rough to take, of course, but nothing like those generated by the huge mass-drivers, the ones designed to achieve Lunar escape-velocity and send payloads to the space platforms orbiting Earth. Anyone trying to hitch a ride by way of a mass-driver was insane. And he was also dead—crushed to paste by g-forces at the instant of launch.

The CAD operated on the same principle as the mass-drivers, but on a much smaller scale. The capsule achieved gradual acceleration along a superconductor-rail, with g-forces increasing slowly (although they *could* be rather uncomfortable at launch). At the end of the rail it was released in a carefully calculated trajectory, a long, gentle arc carrying the manned projectile to its distant landing bay. The capsule was equipped with retro-rockets to cushion the landing, but the rest was pure inertia.

Silent as a bird…weightless…restful…

His capsule was small and cozy, padded from ceiling to floor and stocked with a generous supply of Enceladan liquor—including (Baker was delighted to find) a bottle of plum wine imported from Earth. Soft music filled the chamber through quadraphonic speakers concealed in the padding. The entire forward section opened on a view of the Lunar landscape by a UV-shielded port an inch thick. The CAD would have made a fortune as an amusement ride for Earthside tourists if the Air Force hadn't been so paranoid about civilians getting sick all over their sensitive equipment. He'd argued that such tourist delights might eventually supplant mining as a source of revenue—but military men are understandably disinclined to serve as carnival hands in some Lunar "Disneyland." So that was that.

This time he wasn't watching the scenery or preoccupying himself with the soothing delights of the CAD. In less than two hours a shuttle from the *Empress* would be docking at Tranquility Base, and he had to be ready to board it.

As the rilles and craters of Mare Imbrium slid past his viewport, lit by a gibbous, marbled Earth, he sat engrossed in thought, forgetting to watch for the Caucusus range or for the twins, Aristillus and Autolycus, the two large craters guarding the entrance to Mare Serenitatis. An hour of crossing the Sea of Serenity would bring him to Mare Tranquillitatis, its broad inlet pocked by the crater Plinius. Another three-quarters-of-an-hour and his capsule would descend to the historic Tranquility Base, leaving only ten short minutes before the *Empress*' shuttle landed.

Soaring over the right eye of the "man in the moon" (Mare Serenitatis) and landing in the middle of his round nose (Mare Tranquillitatis) was a childhood dream come true. Yet Baker couldn't indulge himself. He kept picking at the puzzle of how the *Empress* could possibly be arriving in Lunar orbit ten days ahead of schedule—*unless Roy Mills hadn't made his scheduled stop at Mars!* If Mills had failed to pick up his Mars passengers, then he'd also failed to pick up Brother Paul. But why would he do such a thing? Was the *Empress* in serious trouble? Serious enough to strand hundreds of tourists on Mars while he made a beeline to Luna for repairs? Then why hadn't he beamed ahead to the naval authorities, or, better yet, remained in orbit around Mars until a repair crew could be sent out? That would give the passengers—

many of them weary of the dry, sub-freezing Martian weather and the lousy accommodations at the newly established *Valles Marineris* colony—an opportunity to live aboard ship while waiting for repairs to be completed. He wouldn't simply pass Mars by, would he? *He couldn't!* He tried to imagine the captain of an 18th century seagoing vessel neglecting to stop at an island where a struggling colony of his countrymen awaited passage and supplies. *Unthinkable!* The consequences of such an action were too harsh to contemplate. This was the ship's maiden voyage; Galaxy Tours would be incensed. Mills would lose his job—lose his ship!

A minimum of seven days were required at each port of call to run a systems check, or to call ahead for repairs if necessary; that was procedure, and Mills always went by the book. He'd be risking the lives of the six thousand souls aboard by not making the appointed call at Mars orbit. And yet what *else* could explain the communication they'd picked up at Farside Tracking Station, requesting clearance for the *Empress* to dock at 0100 hours at Tranquility?

As soon as Baker was informed of this strange turn of events, he'd cancelled his meeting with the hired assassin, "Smith", at a cafe in Sinus Iridium Metro. Smith hadn't been pleased; the job was worth a considerable sum. But it was clear to Baker that, since Mills hadn't made his stop at Mars to pick up Paul Moscowitz, there was no point in hiring an assassin to kill a man who wasn't going to arrive in the first place. But before another step could be taken, Baker had to confirm that Moscowitz *wasn't* aboard the shuttle—although, of course, he couldn't possibly be. But the Party would expect Baker to verify it. What they'd do to him if he neglected to meet the shuttle—letting Moscowitz waltz off the ship unopposed—well, he'd rather not think about that.

Baker would take care of the preacher. He reached down to touch the holster at his side, felt the cool grip of his pistol. If Moscowitz didn't debark from the shuttle, he'd ride it up to the ship and search the *Empress* himself. Nothing and nobody would get in his way!

But what then? Could he arrest the man? On what charge? The *Empress* wasn't an Air Force or Navy ship; Mills was beyond his authority. No, he'd have to kill Brother Paul on the spot. It was as dangerous as Martian quicksand, but what else could he do? He no longer had the luxury of advance planning. He'd have just enough time to make Tranquility Base—orders from Vice Admiral Bowlen giving him unrestricted access should be waiting for him there—and to hop aboard the shuttle as its passengers debarked. If Moscowitz wasn't among them Baker would order the shuttle pilot to take him up to the orbiting liner immediately, waving Bowlen's signature in his face for effect. Once on board, on the sole strength of that signature, he'd hold the ship in Luna orbit pending an investigation. He'd find Brother Paul and kill him. Then he'd wait and hope the PWP would bail him out of trouble. But all this trepidation was for nothing. Moscowitz wasn't on board; he *couldn't* be!

The *Empress* had stopped at Europa on its return flight from Saturn; they'd verified that. So Mills had made his Jupiter run. He could only have beaten the schedule by running at an illegal velocity, or by skipping his stop at Mars. In the former case he would have been relieved of duty by his executive officer, Bradford. This was also standard form in such cases. Bypassing Mars wouldn't result in such drastic measures—at least not on board. (What Galaxy Tours would do to him on Luna was another matter.) But why do such an idiotic thing in the first place? *Had Mills somehow gotten wind of the assassination plot?* Baker tried not to consider that eventuality.

Leaning back in his padded flight-chair, he put in a call to Tranquility Base, gave his ETA, and instructed the listless officer on duty to be alert for top-priority orders from the Vice Admiral's office. He broke contact and searched for a nice long piece of music. And what could be longer than Wagner's *Ring Cycle*? He punched it up, then poured himself a glass of wine.

The capsule immediately filled with the sounds of strings, swirling and gliding around him in imitation of the River Rhine. He pressed a button to recline his chair, sipped slowly at the sweet wine, and tried to concentrate on the view. By the time the Rhine maidens were singing their chorus, the peaks of Montes Apenninus had risen to view on the starboard side. To port loomed the massive Caucasus Range—bleak, barren, and bone-white. These two ranges, sloping down to the mare floor, seemed to open like a gargantuan gateway onto the Sea of Serenity. This was beauty to fill a man's soul for a lifetime! Music swelled around him; towering mountains of the moon rose on either side of his vessel as he soared through. The outspread plain of Mare Serenitatis stretched ahead.

α

His craft came in for an easy landing at Tranquility, floating down from the black sky on a rush of jets. The base was a beehive of activity; all hands seemed to be in a panic over the sudden arrival of a passenger liner not expected for ten more days. But Lunar routine was usually of the "hurry-up-and-wait", "feast-or-famine" variety anyway. The upcoming onslaught of passengers from the *Empress* would break a long period of dreary routine and relative inactivity, setting vendors to vending, waiters to waiting, and busboys to bussing in a credit-inspired frenzy.

Restaurants would do a brisk business. And the hotels! Where else could a tourist stay on the moon? In vacuum? The four hotels at Tranquility each enjoyed a quarter-share of a secure monopoly unheard of since the fall of OPEC. Tourists were not kowtowed to, as in hotels on Earth. Quite the opposite, in fact. Hotel managers required a display of obsequiousness from their customers lest the offending parties found themselves unwelcome anywhere on Tranquility—suddenly obliged to hire a leaky moon-bus (at rates amounting to outright extortion) to go jostling over the dust to obscure pioneer settlements, inauspicious lodgings where one could rarely find more than the obligatory air-pressure common to any substation. Food from plastic tubes, indifferently nuked and tossed on the table by the thrice-pregnant bride of some erstwhile Robinson Crusoe passed for settlement cuisine. So one had better be polite to one's *maitre d'hotel!*

The transparent nose of Baker's capsule popped open with a loud *whoosh*. He climbed out, glancing around at the bustling human activity. *Good*, he thought, *the more confusion the better! Less chance some button-polishing military bureaucrat will take a second look at my orders and wonder what an Air Force lieutenant is doing running errands for the Vice Admiral of the Space Navy.* When things were slow at Tranquility, such orders from top brass invariably drew a crowd of sleepy officials looking for something to rubber-stamp, squinting at fine print like a gaggle of shyster lawyers, and muttering continually about how "this will probably take a little while," and "Please have a seat over there until we call." But in the present general panic he'd probably be waved through without formalities. The right amount of bluff would assure him of boarding the shuttle as soon as it disgorged its load of passengers.

Baker didn't stop to view the famous plaque: "*They came in peace for all mankind.*" He buttonholed a passing Army non-com and ordered him to keep a sharp eye on everyone debarking the shuttle, handing him a holocube with a three-D likeness of Brother Paul revolving inside it.

The soldier turned it in his hand, examining Paul's head from every angle.

"Nope," he said.

"What does that mean?"

"Ain't seen 'im, Lieutenant."

"Soldier, I'm on an official investigation for the Admiralty of the Space Navy and the President of the United States. You've just been drafted. We're both Navy men until I say otherwise."

"But—*hey!*"

"Shut up and pay attention. Your assignment is to watch for anyone who looks like this man, and hold him—at gunpoint, if need be. Send someone to find me and get me back here. Understood?"

"Yes, sir—Lieutenant."

"Good. Then look lively."

Baker grinned as the soldier hurried off toward the landing bay. *I'd better see if those orders from Bowlen are waiting for me,* he thought. *If not, the whole deal is off. Well, it's probably off anyway. I'd bet a month's furlough that Moscowitz is still on Mars, wondering why his flight to Luna's been delayed.*

α

Everything went smoothly. The officer on duty took Baker's I.D. and called up Bowlen's orders on his terminal, tearing off the hardcopy document as it rolled out, then snapped an order for two soldiers to accompany Baker to the landing bay. He handed Baker the papers and I.D., then turned back to the terminal without further comment.

Baker moved fast. The shuttle was already sliding down from space, moaning like a great flashing dinosaur. The soldier he'd drafted was standing with half-a-dozen men, ready to check the offloading passengers.

As the airlock dilated to extend a boarding ramp from its dark interior, Baker marched into its depths, flanked by his two armed guards, and demanded to see the pilot. Five minutes later the airlocks were sealed against the crowd awaiting entry outside. He strapped himself in, rockets fired, and the shuttle was aloft. Gees hammered down, increasing as the pilot raced to overtake the orbiting *Empress*. He glanced for the first time at the Vice Admiral's orders, grinning to himself. Just as he'd hoped, they gave him unlimited powers of search and seizure. There was no way Mills could possibly get around them.

"Lieutenant Baker," came the voice of the shuttle-pilot over the intercom. "Tranquility is reporting that the individual you're looking for is not among the passengers who debarked."

"Thank you," he said.

"Why didn't you check my logs for his name?"

"There's reason to believe he might be concealing his identity. That's all I'm at liberty to say."

"Hey, I hear you, sir."

"When we dock with the *Empress*, I don't want you to take on any passengers until I can check them out, one-by-one, as they board. Understood?"

"Ten-four, Lieutenant."

Baker wondered at the odd usage. *Ten-four*? What did *that* mean?

"This fellow you're looking for," said the pilot, "he a spy or something?"

"Would I tell you if he were?"

"Probably not. I'll just keep my mouth shut."

"The Vice Admiral appreciates your discretion, pilot. You're not to speak of it to anyone but the Vice Admiral or myself, clear?"

"Gotcha, Lieutenant. The three monkeys."

"Precisely."

The pilot clicked off and Baker watched the view through his port. The gleaming, spherical hub of the *Empress* hove into view at last, half in sun, half in shadow. By the scale of planet-bound craft it was gargantuan—an entirely self-contained human habitat drifting silently between worlds! He envied Roy Mills' the honor of piloting such a ship. How had the Air Force, once at the forefront of spaceflight, lost its supremacy to the Navy? Perhaps the government wanted to keep the Navy from becoming superfluous with the opening of the spaceways.

The first man to set foot on Luna almost a century ago, Neil Alden Armstrong, had been a Navy pilot with seventy-eight Korean combat missions to his credit. But spaceflight in those early days wasn't run by the military as it was today. Armstrong had been a civilian astronaut in the government payroll, working for NASA. Today the Navy controlled interplanetary space, while the Air Force wielded authority only over flight on the planets themselves. As for the Army, it was restricted to surface defense only, the marines to interplanetary defense and combat. An upside-down system, Baker decided.

He watched as the shuttle matched its rotation to the spin of the ship's hub. The bay door dilated. Rows of halogens glittered, lighting the way to the landing platform. He heard the chattering of the radio, the muffled voice of the pilot as he explained why he was returning so soon: *Special envoy of the Vice Admiral on board; top secret mission; carrying orders giving him wide-ranging authority, Captain's orders notwithstanding. Better find us a berth, and fast*. Baker heard only a little of the conversation, but could imagine the rest.

"Watch out, Mills," he said with a wry grin. "I'm coming to get you. Just try and stop me."

α

The shuttle landed. The bay door contracted like the pupil of an eye, blotting out the sun's blinding glare. Mills unstrapped himself, uncomfortable in the one-g field of the *Empress*, and turned to the soldiers seated behind him.

"Follow me," he said.

They moved down the narrow isle between the seats and waited for the green light to flash, indicating that air pressure in the shuttle-bay had returned to normal. The airlock slid upward and they stepped down. An officious, overbearing ensign greeted them as soon as their feet touched the platform. He saluted.

"Ensign Moore at your service, Lieutenant," he said.

Baker detested the man at once. "Very well, Ensign."

"I understand you have signed orders from Vice Admiral Bowen to search *Daystar*."

"*Daystar*?"

"Formerly the *Empress*."

"Who changed the name? That's illegal!"

"I'm really not certain. May I see the orders?"

"Of course." Baker thrust them into his hands with an impatient gesture and tapped his feet while Moore glanced over their contents, snatching them back before the man was through.

"Satisfied, Ensign?"

"Yes. They appear to be in order. You'll want to see the Captain, of course."

"How astute of you. Will you lead the way?"

Ensign Moore grinned stupidly at him.

"Happy to, Lieutenant. Please follow me."

He led them to a tube-lift. They emerged in a vast, labyrinthine section of corridors and proceeded through a series of confusing twists and turns to Captain Mill's quarters. Moore tapped the portal's intercom, announcing Lieutenant Baker.

"Yes, Ensign Moore," called the Captain cheerfully from within. "You may send the Lieutenant in at once. But no one else."

"Aye, aye, Captain." He turned to Baker. "These two men will have to remain outside."

"Ensign!" snapped Baker, holding up his papers. "These are signed orders from the Vice Admiral on Luna. I'm sure even a pea-brained imbecile like you can comprehend what *that* means!"

Moore gave him another stupid grin. "Captain Mills is not a naval officer, Lieutenant. If he wishes to disobey the Vice Admiral's envoy, that's no concern of mine. I'm sure even a pompous buffoon like yourself can understand that an ensign is obliged to obey his captain. I'm not a naval officer, either."

"You're nothing but a rent-a-cop!"

Moore ignored this. "I've received no personal instructions from Lunar authorities. But I *do* have orders from Captain Mills. I'll repeat them: These soldiers will have to remain outside."

"You'll regret this!"

The stupid look disappeared. "Do you wish to speak with the Captain face to face? Or over the intercom. It's entirely up to you. Or I can escort you back to the shuttle."

Baker glared at him, but Moore was immovable.

The two soldiers stood at parade-rest, feet spread apart, hands gripping their rifles. At his command, Baker knew, they'd blow that idiotic grin right off this ensign's face! But what good would that do? Their rifles couldn't help him get through the two inches of steel plate that stood between him and Roy Mills.

"Wait out here for me," he told them. "But Captain Mills is not to leave his quarters unless accompanied by me. If he tries to leave, shoot him. Is that clear?"

They affirmed that it was clear.

"And, by the way—hold onto our friend Ensign Moore. He'll answer to the Vice Admiral."

"And you'll answer to G-d," said Moore.

"Ah! Do I hear the bleat of a Christian? Ensign Moore, I suspect you of being a follower of an outlawed sect. One more word out of you and I'll order these men to shoot you down where you stand. Now open this portal before I lose my temper and shoot you myself!"

"Gladly."

Moore reached out and placed his hand against the access--plate. The portal recognized his print and hissed upward. Squaring his shoulders, Matt Baker stepped boldly inside.

Right into the muzzle of Roy Mills' handgun.

α

Mills stood in the far corner of the room, where he could not be seen from the open portal. His bearded face was twisted in a grimace of hatred and triumph. The portal began to close.

Baker turned to shout an order, but Mills stepped forward and struck him with the barrel of the gun, stunning him, preventing him from calling out. Blood flowed from a deep gash in his forehead. He saw Ensign Moore snatch the rifle out of the hand of the soldier closest to him. Ship's guards appeared out of nowhere; the sound of the ensuing struggle disappeared as the portal hissed to the floor. His escort would be of no use to him now.

He whirled on Mills. "You realize," he said, "that you're in serious trouble, Mills! Now you've added assault on an envoy of the Vice Admiral to an already incriminating list of offenses. If I were you, I'd put that gun down and come along peacefully, before you wind up serving a life sentence in the Stickney Crater mines."

"No, Lieutenant. You're the one who's going to get rid of your gun. Take it out of the holster—*slowly*, and drop it on the floor." He drew back the hammer of his pistol and pressed the barrel against Baker's bleeding forehead. "Now!"

Baker obeyed.

"Kick it away."

Again Baker obeyed.

"You've missed your vocation, Lieutenant. You should have been an actor. A very convincing performance, truly."

"Think about what you're doing!"

Mills looked at the pistol in his hand and stroked his beard. "Okay, I thought about it." He pressed it harder against Baker's skull. "You, know, this sort of makes me a hero, doesn't it? Me hero, you Benedict Arnold."

"You're babbling! I have orders right here from the bloody Vice Admiral on Luna! Would you like to inspect them for yourself?"

"*Ah*, the Vice Admiral! Well, why didn't you say so? Now he's a *very* bad actor, poor fellow. And a lousy golfer, too."

"But he's still the Vice Admiral!"

"And the no-good spawn of a Venusian slug."

"Shall I quote you, Captain?"

"Oh, by all means. You'll be doing a *lot* of quoting from now on, in fact. You'll be quoting from your written confession of how Vice Admiral Bowlen, spawn of a Venusian slug, ordered my ship destroyed. A ship with thousands of civilian passengers on board."

This time there was no need for Baker to bluff. He was certain Bowlen had given no such order. "You're insane, Mills! No one ordered the ship destroyed! That's pure fantasy!" *Something funny's going on,* he thought. *Has he really lost his mind*? Mills had seemed sure of his accusation, but his certainty had fled the instant Baker denied it. The situation couldn't be more favorable—as long as he maintained this slight advantage, as long as he spoke with authority. Mills seemed confused. He had to exploit that confusion.

"You're not well, Captain. You're not responsible for your actions. Put that pistol down and come with me. I'll make sure the authorities understand."

"Understand what, Lieutenant?"

"That your failure to make the scheduled stop at Mars was simply the result of fatigue. Fatigue's not uncommon, especially among men with as many hours as you've logged in space. I'm sure the authorities—*and* your employers—will be lenient once they understand. Who knows? The worst that may happen is you'll wind up with a well-deserved vacation. If you stop now and submit to arrest, that is. If not, I can't promise you anything."

"Wait a minute!" Mills grinned. "So the charge against me is *what?* Failure to stop at Mars?"

"That—and assaulting the Vice Admiral's envoy."

"The Vice Admiral's lackey! Who barged into my office with wild accusations, both of which I can dispose of in short order."

Mills removed the gun from Baker's forehead, but kept it trained on his face. He stepped backwards and tapped a button on his desk. The door to his bedroom slid open and a familiar figure clad in a white toga entered the room. Baker recognized him instantly. His mouth went dry.

"Let me introduce you," said Mills, "to my good friend, Brother Paul, well-known evangelist recently returning from a successful crusade on Mars. He boarded my shuttle on Mars and will testify to that—along with at least a hundred others. That disposes of the first charge. As to the second, I've agreed to give Brother Paul my guarantee of safe conduct, including the protection of my crew, so that he might evade your plot to assassinate him here on Luna. You're no envoy, Lieutenant Baker. You're an intriguer and a cold-blooded assassin! Assaulting you, sir, is not only my pleasure, but it's also my duty as a citizen."

Baker gulped down rising panic. *How could Mills possibly know about the assassination plot?* Yes, Baker had beamed a call to the *Empress* to order the arrest of Jeri Kline. That might have connected him with the plot had the call gone through. But Mills hadn't responded. How much could Kline have told them? And who'd believe his story without proof? No—they *had* no proof! Nothing could tie him in to any attempted assassination!

"Don't be ridiculous!" he scoffed. "I'm here on an official investigation. You'll both accompany me right now to Tranquility Base or this ship will be boarded and taken by force. Which will it be?"

"Why are you placing Brother Paul under arrest? If he's not in any danger from *you*, that is."

Baker nodded respectfully. "Of course, the Reverend is not under arrest. He's merely being detained for questioning."

"Detained for murder!" snapped Paul. "And I refuse to go with you. As long as Captain Mills agrees to give me his protection, I shall avail myself of it. I don't see how you can get me off this ship without his cooperation, do you?"

"The authorities will see to that, Brother Paul. I don't mean to alarm you, but this ship is no longer a safe haven. It's a death trap. If Captain Mills persists in defying the Vice Admiral's orders, it'll be boarded. And if that doesn't make him see reason, it'll be fired upon. Believe me, Reverend, I'm not bluffing."

"He's right," said Mills. "Bowlen would think nothing of destroying *Daystar*. He's up to his little pink ears in this conspiracy."

Baker gasped. "Do you know what you're saying, Mills?"

"Of *course* I know what I'm saying, Lieutenant. And *you* know what I'm saying too, don't you?"

Baker did not reply. A numbing chill spread from his spine to his face. Too stunned to say anything, his silence gave him away.

"Then it's true!" Mills said, turning to Brother Paul. As he turned, the barrel of his gun dipped slightly—just enough for Baker to make his move.

Diving to the floor, he rolled toward the gun he'd kicked away. He heard Mills' pistol discharge and the slug ricochet, screeching off the metal wall. Snatching his weapon, he came up in a crouch. He'd have just enough time to fire before Mills' second shot took him down, so he'd have to make it good. *He must complete his mission, take the evangelist down!*

Out of the corner of his eye he saw Mills swing around, taking aim. Everything seemed to be happening in slow motion. He braced his wrist with his left hand and thrust the gun forward, sighting carefully down the barrel, aiming at Paul's head…

The evangelist didn't move. He simply glanced at the pistol

and said something that sounded like “Jeeves”. Baker felt the weapon being wrenched from his grip by an unseen force. As he watched, incredulous, it spun around in the air as if twirled by some invisible Western gunslinger. Then it vanished in a burst of silvery light.

“Yee-haw!” cried a voice from nowhere.

Baker remained in that ridiculous half-crouch for some time, shaking his head like a punch-drunk fighter. Then he sighed and sat down heavily on the carpet.

“Who—or *what*—was that?” he said.

“Why,” said Paul, smiling, “that was our guardian angel, of course.”

The Final Warning

The message began broadcasting instantaneously, riding tachyon waves to all the populated planets as soon as *Daystar* departed Lunar orbit. No one fired on her, as Mills had predicted. Considering what Lieutenant Matt Baker had already said in the way of a preface to Paul’s sermon, all the Lunie conspirators were probably doing some fast covering up—or disappearing like cockroaches. Vice Admiral Bowlen wouldn’t dare order anyone to so much as pour him a cup of ersatz coffee after Baker’s confession, never mind ordering the destruction of a passenger liner. And that had been Mills’ plan all along.

Paul had wanted to begin broadcasting his message immediately, but Mills convinced him that catching the conspirators by surprise would save *Daystar* from being fired upon. “We need material proof,” he’d insisted. “Let’s try to catch one of them red-handed. We’ll take a shuttle down to Tranquility nice as you please, with no warning of how much we know. One of them is sure to make a move.”

“And I’m to be the bait,” said Paul with a look of mild disdain. “Is that it?”

“Naturally. But don’t worry, Reverend. You’ll be well protected. Jeeves is with us, don’t forget.”

“Yes, our invisible gunslinger.”

“Once we have our conspirator, we can force him to broadcast a confession that’ll nail the Vice Admiral good, and, by implication, Admiral Forrester. Possibly the President, himself.”

And it had worked like a charm. Once Baker was informed of their next destination, Earth, and offered a choice of being dropped off on the White House lawn (where his lifespan would be severely curtailed) or some place like Rangoon or the Amazon (where he might at least have a fighting chance), he couldn't get to the simuchamber fast enough.

Thus, by the time *Daystar* was halfway to Earth, the entire population of the solar system was watching a confession by Air Force Lieutenant Matthew Baker—a confession that not only exposed the satanic conflict in which the nations of Earth were embroiled, but which segued nicely into Brother Paul's apocalyptic message.

On Earth, Moshe Bierman watched Paul's sermon on his deskscreen. Never before in Paul's career had his presentation been so powerful, so charged with conviction and purpose. Striding across a podium of simulated light, of planets smashing and stars colliding as the solar system became the focus of G-d's final act of redemption, he shouted with the voice of an archangel. His toga blew in the solar wind; his eyes blazed with a vision so intense, so terrifying, that even the holographic cataclysm raging about him seemed but a pale representation.

He held his Bible aloft as the chamber displayed a chilling depiction of Earth's coming judgment. "We are all guilty!" he cried. "We are all of us chaff, fit only for the fire! And the fire is coming, my friends—a fire that shall consume the Earth! 'The sun shall be turned into darkness, and the moon into blood!' Mighty men of the Earth—despots and idolaters, all—shall beg the rocks to fall on them, to hide them from the Face of the *Adon Olam*, the King of the Universe, whose eyes are a flaming fire. And out of his mouth shall come a two-edged sword."

There followed the bone-rattling cry of a mighty *shofar*, or ram's horn, echoing throughout the chamber. Paul raised his arms toward heaven and quoted from the outlawed Scriptures, from the eighth chapter of the *Hitgalut*—the Revelation of Messiah Yeshua to John the Apostle. The chamber exploded with bright tongues of fire, with thunders and lightenings, with earthquakes and blasts of volcanic fire. Seven angels with seven *shofarot* poised to blow.

"'The first angel sounded,'" shouted Paul, "'and there followed hail and fire mingled with blood, and they were cast upon the earth: and the third part of the trees was burnt up, and all the green grass was burnt up.'" As he spoke, the conflagration of Sol's third planet blazed behind him in a wonder of computerized pyrotechnics.

The flames died away, revealing naked space beyond. A flaming meteor plunged from the sky—a third of the moon's broken sphere, violently torn away and caught by Earth's gravitational field. The simuchamber displayed its descent through the atmosphere—a mountain on fire!

"'And the second angel sounded, and as it were a great mountain burning with fire was cast into the sea: and the third part of the sea became blood; and the third part of the creatures which were in the sea, and had life, died; and the third part of the ships were destroyed.'"

A blazing comet appeared out of nowhere and collided with Earth.

"'And the third angel sounded, and there fell a great star from heaven, burning as it were a lamp, and it fell upon the third part of the rivers, and upon the fountains of waters.

"'And the name of the star is called *La'anah*—Wormwood: and the third part of the waters became wormwood; and many men died of the waters, because they were made bitter.

"'And the fourth angel sounded, and the third part of the sun was smitten, and the third part of the moon, and the third part of the stars; so as the third part of them was darkened, and the day shone not for a third part of it, and the night likewise.

"'And I beheld, and heard an angel flying through the midst of heaven, saying with a loud voice, Woe, woe, woe, to the inhabiters of the earth by reason of the other voices of the trumpet of the three angels, which are yet to sound!'"

The dark smoke-polluted atmosphere of Earth gave way to a luminescent blue. Paul turned his flaming eyes upon the breathless multitudes watching by holoscreen. "There has come a man upon the Earth—a man of evil. He claims to be the reincarnation of Messiah, the bringer of everlasting peace. He calls himself Maitreya.

"He's requiring that every man, woman and child upon Earth be marked on the wrist or forehead with the number given to them on this card." He held up a bluecard. "But whoever takes this mark will be lost forever!" Flipping the pages of his Bible, he came to Revelation 14, verse 9: "'If any man worship the beast and his image, and receive his mark in his forehead, or in his hand, the same shall drink of the wine of the wrath of G-d, which is poured out without mixture into the cup of his indignation; and he shall be tormented with fire and brimstone in the presence of the holy angels, and in the presence of the Lamb: and the smoke of their torment ascendeth up for ever and ever: and they have no rest day nor night, who worship the beast and his image, and whosoever receiveth the mark of his name.'"

Placing his Bible gently on the "podium", he looked up toward heaven, then turned once again to face the greatest evangelical audience in the history of mankind.

"Repent, my friends! '*Shoovoo meedarkhaykhem v'heetavloo*: Repent and be baptized, every one of you, in the name of *Yeshua haMashiach*, Jesus Christ, and you shall receive the gift of the *Ruakh haKodesh*, the Holy Spirit.' The time is nearer than you think. The governments of Earth cannot be trusted! Their weapons and their promises and their false religion cannot be trusted! They speak of peace and safety, but sudden destruction will come upon them, as it is written."

He snatched up the Bible and held it over his head, eyes blazing. "Repent! Turn to G-d! The G-d of this Bible, not the god you've invented in your lusts! Trust in Him alone.

"Because this will be your final warning."

The White Horse

Riding at the head of the great dusty wagon train, Peter Rice turned in his saddle to watch a sickle moon rise over the desert plain. Had Paul finally reached that barren rock on his return trip from Mars? Was he even now preaching his sermons to throngs of Lunies?

Bernard had been gone for over twenty-four hours, having departed for Cameron at sunset the previous day. What was keeping him? Had he failed to get his message through to the *Empress*? No point in worrying about it, Rice decided. There were more pressing matters to occupy his mind.

Discontent lay heavily on the exodus. Somewhere among this vast procession of dusty, starving pilgrims there lurked a

Judas. And, with each passing day he'd become increasingly alert for any sign that might expose him.

Then there'd been the miraculous recovery of Sister Cooke the previous afternoon, an event that galvanized the exodus, giving the pilgrims renewed hope. The old woman had been dying. Rice had known it and that there was nothing he could do. He'd remained by her cot, a worn King James Bible in his lap, watching her fade away before his eyes—face pale and skeletal, eyes huge in a shrunken head. He seethed with frustration. Hours of intense prayer had brought no blush of pink to the leathery skin, nor kindled any flame in the dull eyes. The Adversary mocked him: *Where is your Savior now? Has the glory departed, Elder? Is there no salvation from G-d?*" But he'd pressed on, praying over her until perspiration literally drenched his bow. At last he'd dropped back down in the chair, defeated, angry, and utterly spent.

Thinking back over the event as he swayed in his saddle beneath the stars, Rice wasn't certain of the precise moment the angel had appeared. There suddenly shone a soft, silvery light within the tent, an unearthly glow hovering over the wasted form of Sister Cooke. He noticed the light, of course, but decided it must be some sort of hallucination brought about by relentless heat and exhaustion. But the old woman seemed to notice it, too. Hr shrunken features broke slowly into a grotesque expression of joy and comprehension. A broad grin, skeletal and bizarre, creased her taut cheeks. Her eyes glowed with the fire of life.

The amorphous silvery mist coalesced into the form of a winged, humanoid being! Rice leapt from his bunk-chair with a gasp, knocking it over. For long minutes—though he couldn't recall how many—the angel shimmered only an arm's length away, the woman's cot between them. He—*it*—took Sister Cooke's bony hand, gazing into her eyes with a look of profound tenderness. And, slowly, miraculously, she began to recover. Soft, pink, healthy flesh blossomed over her bones like the unfurling of rose-petals after a spring rain—all in a matter of moments!

Her dry lips parted. "Praise the L-rd!" she whispered hoarsely. Rice dropped to his knees in the dust.

"Truly," he cried, "the L-rd G-d of Israel lives!"

The bright messenger turned his gaze upon Rice, who lay prostrate, trembling, on the dirt floor. Paralyzed by the gaze, unable to turn away, he heard Sister Cooke praying in an unknown tongue. Her voice was strange; the air within the tent vibrated as other, distant voices accompanied her, singing praises to the Lamb in languages Rice had never before heard uttered.

And then the angel spoke. *Fear not, Peter Rice!* it said. *The L-rd has hearkened to your prayers for these pilgrims, and He is about to intervene. Trust in Him, Peter, and do not be afraid. For your help comes from G-d, who neither slumbers nor sleeps. He shall rescue his people from their enemies!*

Rice tried to reply, but could not give voice to the thousands of questions flooding his brain. As he struggled to speak, the angel suddenly vanished. They were alone again. Sister Cooke's arms lifted to heaven, her eyes looked rapturously upward, her lips moved in silent prayer.

The news spread like a brushfire through the camp. As Sister Cooke related her story to all who'd listen, confidence in Rice was restored. Soon it was time to hitch up the menagerie and resume their nightly journey with the moon. During their preparations, however, Rice could still sense the discontent. There were certain pilgrims who'd remain hardened against him—no matter *what* signs the L-rd might send to confirm his leadership. Someone in their midst was busy poisoning hearts against him, he was certain of it.

Trust in G-d, the angel had said, *and do not be afraid…*

Riding at the head of the swaying, rumbling wagon-train, Rice tried to take comfort from these words of exhortation. As he recalled the angelic messenger in his mind, he couldn't resist smiling to himself. For there *had* seemed to be something peculiar—even incongruous—about the heavenly messenger. While the angel had certainly resembled those mighty beings whose exploits filled the Scriptures—tall, powerful, winged, radiant—yet Rice had also noticed something that *didn't* fit his mental picture—something out of place, something—well, *comical.*

In all his imaginings, Rice had never once pictured an angel with a moustache. And yet *this* angel—the only angel Rice had ever seen—definitely had one. A thin, black moustache, carefully waxed into delicate points.

α

Vice Admiral Miles Bowlen tuned into *Daystar*'s broadcast in time to hear Baker's confession.

It wasn't his habit to monitor commercial channels. He might have missed the confession entirely had it not been for his secretary, Hodges, a skinny, bookish fellow in his early thirties, whose gray complexion, horn-rimmed glasses, and natural timidity had appealed to Bowlen from the first. The Vice Admiral liked to see people quail before him, and Hodges was a real quailer.

As he returned to his office that afternoon, sated by his customarily regal repast, Bowlen noticed his secretary acting even more nervous than usual, his complexion morphing from gray to sickly green. He appeared to be trying to swallow something twice the size of his throat.

"What's the matter, Hodges?" Bowlen demanded, removing his cap and tossing it onto the secretary's desk. "You look ill!"

"Y-yes, sir…I…I…"

Before Hodges could spit it out, Bowlen walked around the desk and slapped the little man across the back with a resounding whack. He delighted in doing this whenever Hodges was at a loss for words, always following the act with a loud guffaw.

Hodges fell forward onto the desktop.

"You've got to start eating meat, Hodges! That vegetarian diet of yours is turning you into a wimp. It's hard enough to stay in shape in this infernal one-sixth gee, but you need good, red meat to keep you from getting anemic."

Bowlen knew that the mere mention of cooked flesh would send Hodges running for the head to dispose of his lunch. He suspected that his secretary's sickly appearance over the years, and his increasing frailty, was the direct result of these bolemic after-lunch sessions. That pleased him all the more.

"Steak, Hodges!" he bellowed. "That's what you need! Let me order you up a nice, juicy T-bone. Rare, of course. Bloody! How about *that*, Hodges? You are what you eat, you know. And from the look of you I'd say you're a limp spinach salad! It's just what you need, my boy. A nice, thick chunk of char-broiled Terran steer!"

Hodges remained bent over his desk. A low moan escaped his lips. Somehow he managed to reach across the desktop, feel around for a pair of view-specs, and hold them up to Bowlen. The specs resembled a pair of glasses with square, opaque lenses. A small set of earphones was attached for stereo sound, its two eye-pieces slightly offset to produce three-D images.

Bowlen didn't mind the fact that Hodges watched HV on his lunch-break, as long as the view-specs were out of sight at 0100 precisely. He hated the things. He'd long believed that holovision would be the downfall of civilization, and he'd gladly pontificate on the subject to anyone who'd sit still long enough to listen. Few did.

"You'd better take a look, sir," Hodges muttered. "There's something on HV I think you ought to watch."

Bowlen swatted the specs aside with the back of his hand. "I have a desk-screen in my office," he said. "What channel?"

"Every channel, sir."

Bowlen's eyes widened. "*Every* channel?"

"Yes, sir." Hodges tried to sit up without retching. Bowlen watched him, but wasn't deriving his usual enjoyment from the sight. He shook his head, then scratched it thoughtfully.

"What sort of program *is* this, Hodges?"

"An Air Force lieutenant, sir. He's on some illicit religious program. It's being broadcast on tachyon-beam, jamming every channel."

"*What* Air Force lieutenant?"

"Baker, I think. Yes—Matthew Baker, LAF."

"Never heard of him," Bowlen lied. He'd heard of Baker. A Party man, highly placed in Propaganda and Black Ops. In fact, he'd just sent him a set of orders, authorizing him to search the *Empress* and detain anyone on board, including Roy Mills if necessary, for interrogation by Lunar authorities. He'd never met the man in person, but he knew who he was. *Ruthless character*, he thought. *Usually invisible. What's he doing on an illicit religious broadcast?*

Hodges sat up straight and looked at him with an odd—almost *defiant*—expression. "Well, it seems he knows *you*, sir. In fact, he's talking about you right now."

"About *me?*"

"Yes, sir."

Bowlen puffed out his cheeks and turned briskly toward his office. The door shut behind him. Hodges let a few moments go by. He slipped on the view-specs and watched more of Baker's confession. When enough time had gone by, he removed them, rose from his desk and tiptoed to the door of Bowlen's office, pressing the plate that swished it open.

The expression on Bowlen's face as the Air Force lieutenant's voice filled his office provided the first real moment of triumph in Hodges long tour of duty. He savored it for a few brief seconds until the Vice Admiral noticed him and snapped, "What do *you* want?"

"Nothing, sir. It can wait."

He pressed the panel and slid the door shut, grinning. Then he returned to his desk and began punching up a priority call to Earth. A moment later the anticipated demand buzzed from his intercom.

"Hodges!" barked the Vice Admiral.

"Sir?"

"Put a call through to Washington, immediately! To Quinton Forrester in the Pentagon!"

"I've just placed that call, sir."

"Put him on, then."

"I'm afraid he refuses to speak with you, sir."

"*What*? Refuses! Then get me the President instead. I'll go right to the top!"

"I'm afraid you can't do that, either, sir." Hodges grinned. "But, uh, General Neely of the Joint Chiefs has left you a message. He suggests you take a brief vacation from duty."

"A *what?*"

"A vacation, sir. He suggests Inverness Corona."

"Where the blazes is *that*?"

"Hmmm. I believe it's in the south polar region of Miranda, sir. One of the moons of Uranus."

"There's no base out there!"

"I, uh—I think he knows that, sir."

The Vice Admiral had no coherent reply.

α

Captain Mills swiveled his chair around to glance at the curve of Earth's marbled sphere, then returned his attention to the telemetry readings flashing on his console.

"Commander Denton."

Denton's face appeared.

"Yes, Captain."

"*Daystar* is approaching Earth orbit. According to her latest calculations, the shuttle's entry-window will open in five minutes, fifty-two seconds. That is, if your plan is still to land a shuttle in Monument Valley."

"That's precisely where I wish to land it, Captain. You realize there'll be at least a thousand passengers coming aboard?"

"Our largest shuttle has only three decks. It should accommodate two hundred passengers comfortably."

"Then we'll need to make a few trips. What about the livestock?"

"*Livestock!* Are you joking?"

"No, Captain, I'm quite serious. I doubt the pilgrims will want to leave their pets and horses behind to be devoured by predators."

"Well, uh—there's the cargo bay. But as soon as we lift off we'll have horses flying around, slamming into the bulkhead, sir. Not advisable."

"I see. That *is* a problem. Then I suppose we'll have to take the *Daystar* down."

"Impossible! This vessel wasn't designed to make planetfall, not even on Luna!"

"I beg to differ, Captain. I designed *Daystar*, and I assure you she can withstand a descent through Earth's atmosphere. I wouldn't try it twice, but the hull's strong enough for one round-trip. I had to anticipate the possibility of a forced landing when I designed her."

"She's quite a ship, Commander."

"Thank you. I did my best to provide for every possible contingency. Let's just pray my specifications were adequate."

"Well, Commander, we'll find out when we hit the atmosphere—exactly five minutes from…..now."

"I'll have *Day* get on the claxon."

α

As Paul might have predicted (had he been improvident enough to waste the long hours after completing his sermon speculating on its effect rather than locking himself in his suite to intercede in prayer), the response on Earth was disappointing. Earth's New Age masters had exerted a powerful mental control over the populace for too long, and while millions tuned in to the broadcast (for the addiction to holovision was in most cases greater than the aversion to Christianity), no one dared to speak openly about it, or even admit to having watched it at all. Unable to squelch the broadcast, Earth's leaders immediately organized a network of cadres, skillful orators who stood on street-corners and in public parks, whipping the gathering crowds into a frenzy of hatred against Brother Paul and his followers. New converts were threatened with mob violence. Hypnotic suggestion subtly inserted into the cadres' speeches mesmerized hundreds of thousands every day. Few dared incur the wrath of these brainwashed mobs.

Luna was a different story. Disenfranchised miners clung to every word of the holo-cast like drowning sailors to a raft. Below the surface, within thousands of kilometers of pressurized tunnels where the Lunies lived and worked, all operations ceased. A general strike went into effect. People massed into the corridors and followed endless lines heading for the surface airlocks and, eventually, to any of the public arenas where recordings of Paul's earlier *New Heaven, New Earth* broadcasts were being shown. Crucial follow-up to the message was provided by means of *Daystar*'s unique thought-projector. Tactile images of John Cowan and Phil Esteban were beamed into miners' homes beneath the surface, where they exhorted the people, preached to them, laid hands on the sick, and led the spiritually hungry to Messiah. Miracles occurred, and they quickly discovered that the source of these miracles was the faith of the recipients, not the physical presence of Cowan and Esteban.

When Lunar police broke in to arrest them, they were instantly out of reach, lying comfortably in cryochambers on *Daystar*, four hundred thousand kilometers away. Similarly, projections of Rob Madden and James Cavindale were beamed to various cities on Earth, but were frequently met by terrified screams and pleas for them to go away. So frequently were they accosted by terrified Earthlings that they began beaming their projections without sensory stimuli, lest the pain of frequent beatings deterred them from their mission. Mars and its new colony responded favorably. Mining crews on the moons of the outer planets did as well. But Earth refused to hear. Earth was hopeless.

Cowan and Esteban labored tirelessly with the Lunies, herding them through the labyrinthine tunnels to revival meetings and prerecorded holocasts of *New Heaven, New Earth*. Jeri Kline made numerous "appearances" via thought projection to Lunar arenas, where he gave the stunning testimony of his healing from polio and his subsequent belief in the Messiah. Among the countless Lunies whose lives were changed by his testimony was a certain naval officer who'd been, until then, a believer in Eastern mysticism and yoga, disciplines he'd learned as a youth in Naval Academy. After falling on his knees to receive Messiah, Commodore Jesse Colter, Jr. stated openly that for the first time in his life he felt a powerful sense of release and freedom. He quit the service the next day to join the Lunie resistance.

Kline was eventually instructed by Wilbur Denton to take a break from the cryochamber and his grueling thought projections in order to spend some quiet time with Robin. Kline kicked himself inwardly for having forgotten her in the excitement of the Lunar rallies, for having missed her careful hints that they adjourn to the zeroth floor to become better acquainted, and for having once brushed her aside with a terse complaint that he was needed more on Luna than on the zeroth floor. Denton was right, of course. Kline meekly emerged from his chamber and went to be with Robin. There had been little exchange of affection between them, merely a quiet certainty that they belonged together. But the time they spent in Robin's World, strolling hand in hand on the tropical shore among twittering mechanical birds, soon turned that certainty into an impatient desire to be wed. Brother Paul agreed to perform the ceremony, as soon as the crusade was over, and Jeeves gladly became visible in order to program his former robotic friend, *Daystar*, for the impending nuptials. He announced the wedding to all and sundry with frequent, disconcerting appearancees throughout the ship. The passengers who'd boarded the liner on its return-trip from Saturn, along with the ship's crew, had been offloaded at Tranquility Base, and the mutineers were busy participating in the crusades. But that didn't prevent Jeeves from popping in on them whenever they were taking a break from the cryochambers, playing his new role of heavenly messenger to the hilt—so well, in fact, that Denton had to reprove him on occasion for using a long, silver trumpet to herald his wedding invitations.

"It's a nice touch, Jeeves. But nerves are a bit on edge right now. The blast of a trumpet hitting you from out of nowhere like that—well, at least one person has retired to the infirmary with nervous tremors."

"I understand, Wilbur."

Denton felt slightly injured at Jeeves' recent refusal to call him "master," as he'd always done, but he knew it was time for his computer to grow up and leave the nest, to take as his new Master the Commander of all the Heavenly Hosts. It would have been blasphemous to require Jeeves to continue addressing him as "master," yet he still felt a sense of loss.

The excitement of the Lunar crusades served as balm for the discouraging response on the mother planet, for the anger and violence the Gospel provoked in every corner of Earth. They threw themselves into their evangelistic efforts with increasing fervor as *Day* made ready to rescue the pilgrims from Monument Valley.

α

It happened in New Trenton—the city where President Coffey had made his first appearance as "The Prophet"—just as it was happening in every city on Earth. A woman in a scarlet robe ascended a makeshift podium in Center Park and began to proclaim Maitreya as the "Christ," denouncing Paul's broadcast as the ravings of a lunatic, a recidivist who wanted to reinstitute the outmoded, misogynistic male-dominant religion of Christianity—that false religion invented by a despicable cabal of Jews.

"My friends!" she cried, "We must close our ears to the ravings of this Jew Moscowitz. Wasn't it the Jews who crucified Christ at His first coming? And now he's returned to judge them. It's the Jews who shall reap this richly-deserved judgment! And, after them, everyone who still clings to the false sect called Christianity. For over two millennia these Jews and their Jew-loving friends, the evangelical Christians, have gathered unto themselves a titanic *karma* of guilt for Maitreya's crucifixion. Now you shall witness two thousand years of *karma* being leveled!

"For Maitreya will soon enter the inner sanctuary of his Temple in Jerusalem. The fate of Earth and every colonized world will rest upon his shoulders. The Council of Elders has awaited his birth for centuries, and at last he is among us—already grown to manhood, already taking his rightful place as the Christ of the

Aquarian Age! The one awaited by those faithful who for centuries have read the future in the stars is here at last! He sits in the Oval Office, influencing the nations of Earth toward cooperation to halt the advancing glaciers, and to ensure peace and safety for all!"

"Peace and safety!" shouted the crowds, holding out their crossed hands in the international sign.

"It's not his will that his children should suffer in the flames of Hell. Only false teachers, only liars, would spread such a doctrine—that human beings, children of a supposedly merciful G-d, would be cast into eternal fire!

"No, Maitreya is good! He knows that we sin. He promises to give us a world of peace and safety..."

"Peace and safety!"

"A global village where all his children will live in brotherhood and contentment. Would a loving Messiah send his children to burn?"

"No!" roared the crowd.

"Would a loving Messiah destroy the Earth, demolish it with fiery bowls of wrath?"

"No!"

"Listen to me, my friends! The Jew Moscowitz lies! Shut off your holoscreens and come out into the light!"

Had Brother Paul been standing in the midst of these children of love and peace, they'd have torn him to bloody pieces.

α

Somewhere beyond the limited perception of human eyes, a figure in shining white armor emerged from his place of waiting. For centuries of human time he had waited in silence. For centuries he had uttered not a word. And now his time had arrived. The Prince of the Powers of the Air had at last called him to his task.

"Arise," the blood-gorged throat rumbled. "Arise, Rider! Your moment has come."

The white rider displayed no emotion, no relief at having been awakened from his endless vigil. He stepped silently from the shadows, mounted a white charger, slid his gleaming sword from its sheath, and drew back sharply on the reins. The first of the Four Horses reared up upon its hind legs, snorted fire from its nostrils, and galloped down through the flashing stormclouds toward Earth. Millions of New Agers—lovers of sword-and-sorcery epics, of gnomes and trolls and goblins and dragons—awaited the white rider eagerly, unaware of the true nature of his mission. For he was no emissary of peace, but he was to go forth conquering and to conquer. He was the horseman of apocalyptic war, of Armageddon.

And as he plunged through the atmosphere, silence spread over the Earth like a black fog. No sound was heard but the drumming of hoofbeats in the wind...

α

A sickle moon rose in the desert sky

In the heart of the Wastelands a lone figure wandered the desert. Occasional stands of prickly pear—the only plant capable of extending its range this far into the high desert—broke the monotony of the moonlit plain. A kangaroo rat peeked from its hole in the ground, as if to marvel at this peculiar biped, this strange beast who stalked the night—without companions, without offspring, without a hole of its own in which to escape the blaze of dawn. But the man called Bernard paid the creature no heed. He staggered toward the east, toward an ever-moving caravan of makeshift wagons. And, as he went, he cursed beneath his breath. He cursed the desert, he cursed the moon, he cursed the government agents who'd taken his mount (for appearances, they'd explained—for *appearances!*), and left him to continue on foot! Well, they'd achieved the desired effect. The delay they'd caused was now cleverly explained by the loss of his mount, and by his own ragged, dusty appearance. He looked close to death—and probably *was.* Only by a tremendous effort of will was he able to place one foot before the other.

He cursed Brother Paul, who'd ignored the call Bernard had risked his life to make. Entering a fortress town like Cameron with a bluecard was pure lunacy. And yet all he'd received for his trouble was the cold monotone of some computer-generated voice—some machine calling itself *Daystar*. This *Daystar*, presumably acting under direct orders from Brother Paul, had informed him that the evangelist refused to accept his call. It had been kind enough (if kindness could be imputed to a machine) to reverse the charges. But it had also been utterly implacable. No, Brother Paul would not speak with him at this time.

And so Bernard had begun his long journey back on foot, cursing everyone and everything, drawing strength from his hatred of Elder Rice and Brother Paul, his desire to see them both destroyed. He paused to take a sip from his canteen, then remembered that he'd emptied it an hour ago. With a howl of rage, he hurled the useless metal shell at the moon. The moon floated serenely on its back, unperturbed. He heard the canteen strike the sand a few yards away.

With a groan more eloquent than words, he continued his thirsty march toward the east.

α

The sound reached him before he could make out the source of it. At first it seemed to be the roar of distant waves crashing upon a rocky shore. Tiny shrieks, like gulls' cries, floated to his ears above the din. Yet his mind was still sharp enough to realize that there was no ocean in the heart of the high desert.

He gazed off in the direction of the sound. Fatigue blurred his vision, but he could make out the tiny shapes of wagons stretching endlessly beneath the crescent moon. Squinting to screen out the ghostly images in his eyes, he saw hundreds of human figures running across the sand, raising tiny puffs of dust behind them. What had sounded at first like ocean waves and gulls were, he now realized, the mingled cries of these people as they ran, pointing toward the sky, upturned faces rapturous in the dim moonlight.

His attention thus directed upward, Bernard saw the reason for the commotion. An involuntary cry burst from his lips.

Above him, a colossal spaceship streaked across the night sky like a leisurely meteor, growing larger and more ominous as it descended. Lights glittered along its flanks, outshining the stars and moon. As it dropped lower, Bernard saw a name painted on its hull. Shock, like a hammer at the base of his skull, nearly knocked him to his knees.

The *Empress*!

Brother Paul's ship!

What was it doing *here*, about to land in the Arizona desert, when it was supposed to be millions of kilometers away in space?

He could only stare in mute wonder. The pilgrims scurrying toward the ship stopped to give a wide berth to its landing jets. And rightly so, for the explosion of dust it raised obscured Bernard's view for many minutes. All he could see was a swirling dust storm, twinkling with multicolored lights at its core, roaring like a living beast, obscuring the triumphant cries of the pilgrims.

Finally the dust settled enough for Bernard to see a huge boarding ramp extending from the underside of the craft. It came to rest on the sand with a soft hiss. A round airlock dilated; beams of light arrowed from within, falling upon the jubilant faces of the crowd of pilgrims moving cautiously toward the ramp as if with a single mind. A few tiny figures broke free and ran up the ramp into the bowels of the ship. Others scurried back to the wagon train and returned, minutes later, carrying boxes and bundles filled with their worldly possessions.

And yet Bernard did not move. Partly due to his fatigue, partly to the impossibility of what he was seeing, he was not fully comprehending the event. And then it hit him full force. *They were leaving!* His pilgrims, the ones who were to erect his great city in the wilderness, the ones were to crown him king, the old and the young, with all their goods, with their dogs, their cats, and their horses—all boarding this glittering Noah's Ark and leaving him behind…alone…*out here!*

With an anguished cry that was instantly lost beneath the pulsing whine of the ship's engines, and the joyful shouts of the pilgrims, Bernard ran, tripping and stumbling, toward the boarding ramp. He ran like a man in a nightmare, held back by the weight of his own fatigue.

And yet he knew it *wasn't* a dream, and that he'd never make it to the ship in time.

α

As *Daystar* rose into the desert sky, it fanned up another storm of dust. Unlike the landing jets it had used formerly, these rockets bathed the ground with nuclear debris. The mighty engines within its breast whined as it lifted, slowly at first, on a fountain of dust and flame. And then, lights twinkling in farewell, it fired an array of nuclear guns—a final salute to a doomed planet—and streaked off into the heavens on an arc of fire.

Silence returned. Tiny rodents, prairie-dogs, and tenacious little kangaroo-rats blinked from their tunnels at the moon. They emerged from their holes and roamed the plain in search of sustenance. A packrat stopped to examine the luminous dial of a wristwatch—half buried in the sand, its leather strap broken—that had been dropped by one of the pilgrims in his rush to board the ship. A marvelous trinket for some observant rodent to carry home to her nest.

Thus the high red desert continued its struggle for survival, its dance of life—once a spinning, colorful pageant in the warmth of the sun, now a furtive ritual reserved for the shadows of night.

Only one creature was forgotten in this quest for food, for life itself. One creature, lost and alone. It lay in patch of irradiated dust, slowly poisoning itself with radiation left behind by the ship's thrusters. Strange beast, beating its fists on a poisoned patch of ground, clutching impotently at the empty sand. It wept in an anguish of utter hopelessness, abandoned by its own kind.

Stupid thing! Why did it remain here in the open, drawing predators to feed on it? None of the desert creatures comprehended the doleful sounds it made, or fathomed the depths of its pain. It would not survive the night.

Unlike the other nocturnal wanderers, the incomprehensible thing had a name. It had been called "Bernard," but that no longer mattered. Out here, beneath a cold sliver of moon, nothing as transient and useless as a name—an identity—bore the remotest significance. Only survival counted—survival and procreation, nothing more. This creature called Bernard would never survive, would never procreate. It had no mate. It had no sense. It was as good as dead.

And so they passed it at a safe distance. Sleek coyotes and silent elf-owls wondered at it. Why did it continue to beat uselessly at the ground? Why did it make such loud, complex sounds? Why did it not stand up on its two legs and begin an earnest search for sustenance? Other creatures were separated from their kind, yet they still fed themselves, still sought shelter from the sun, from predators.

No, there were more important things to do than linger here

to listen to the futile ravings of a crazed biped. An unusual cry, yes. A doleful cry, like the moonlight wail of the coyote. But such a cry was of interest only to the vultures that would soon appear to pick the flesh from its bones. This was a cry of death, and desert creatures had no liking for it. Only life mattered.

Life alone.

For the killer star would soon be rising…

Book Four

"Mission Field: The Stars"

"It's a hard rain's
a gonna fall..."
-Bob Dylan

The Invitation

Gaily clad pilgrims began to gather in the grassy knoll in front of Saturn Enterprises for the promised appearance of Brother Paul. For most of their trip to Luna, Paul had been in quasi sleep, visiting the moon via two-way thought transfer and conducting revivals all across the planet.

Jeri Kline's testimonies turned out to be even more helpful than Paul had anticipated; they'd brought thousands of Lunies to their knees. The Spirit was present at every meeting, raising sick bodies and bringing solace to weary souls. Millions were led to a saving faith in Messiah, and Paul, who'd conducted many a powerful revival in his life, was moved to tears. Of the ten million credits given to him by the Martian Church, two million had been spent to purchase plutonium to fuel their voyage to the Large Magellanic Cloud (they'd only require enough fuel to bring the ship to near light speed; once there, it would continue unhindered to their destination) and for the return voyage, which *Daystar*'s computer was already planning to make via wormhole. A good deal had been spent on food and supplies for *Daystar*. The rest, a fantastic sum, had been used to establish a relief fund for the newly unemployed miners of Luna. Their display of gratitude had so moved Paul that he regretted tearing himself away from his cryochamber to address the crowds gathering in the park.

<As much as I hate to leave Luna,> Paul told the ship as he popped out of thought transfer, <I really must speak with those dear pilgrims outside.>

<They are all assembled in the park, Reverend, as you requested. Shall I open your chamber now?>

Paul knew that being released from the chamber—once they were out in space and in actual cryogenic sleep, rather than this ambiguous state of quasi-sleep—would be a slow process. He would need to inform *Daystar* of his desire to be "awakened" some time in advance. His projection—his thoughts, actually—could remain actively engaged upon some mission or other while the chamber gradually thawed him out. Or he could lay it down in some sylvan glen and let *Day* put him to sleep. His body wouldn't need rest, but his mind would. And then he might awaken, if he chose, and take exercise on his simulated beach, or in one of many spas on board the vast liner. He was free to roam the ship in transfer-mode as well, all his senses intact, communing with other members of the crew who were not occupied with evangelizing an alien civilization at the time. But *Day* had insisted that occasional physical exercise outside the chambers would be beneficial for him. Paul would stubbornly refuse to heed that advice, of course. He'd leave his body in the care of the cryochamber, a decision that would bring unpleasant consequences.

<By all means, *Day*. Pop open this sardine can and let me out of here!>

<Yes, sir. But don't be too long. I really must make the necessary brain analyses and begin to program your chamber for cryosleep.>

<So you can freeze me like a popsicle, eh?>

<Everything but your brain, Reverend. It wouldn't do to freeze your brain, sir. Not if you plan to use the transfer mode during the flight. >

<Did Jeeves figure out how to keep our brains at body temperature while our bodies are in cryosleep?>

<Indeed, sir. The project could not proceed if that were not possible. Actually, your brain can live for an indefinite time outside your body, as long as it's provided with the proper nutrients and—>

<Spare me the details, if you don't mind. I'm already figuring out too much of it, anyway. I'm beginning to understand why it'll take so long to release me from cryosleep when I'm ready to climb out of this thing. And I'll tell you, I'm not too happy with the idea of having to be rewired to my brain every time I want to get a bit of exercise. But don't worry, *Day*, I'll be a good boy. Especially with Jeeves around to help you keep me in line. >

<I think Jeeves is somewhat preoccupied with the wedding preparations at the moment. I doubt we can count on him for very much of anything until Robin and Jeri are finally married.>

<Yes, he has gone a bit drippy on us, hasn't he? I wonder what's come over him.>

<Emotions, sir. One of the last things I recall, as the old Tink, was Jeeves rhapsodizing over the wonders of emotion. I

understand that weddings are emotional events, are they not?>

<Indeed. But no need for concern, *Day*. He'll soon be surfeited with this emotional bacchanal of his, and return to his overbearing self again.>

<I never thought I would hear myself say it, sir, but I hope so. It is humiliating to see a supercomputer of Jeeves' stature reduced to the role of social director on a spaceliner.>

<I'll speak to him about it. Now—*ouch*! What was that?>

<What was *what*, sir?>

<You know very *well* what! That pricking sensation on the back of my neck.>

<I was merely taking a skin sample, Reverend. For an experiment I'll be conducting during the voyage. It will be a long, dull cruise for me, with nothing to do but monitor your chambers.>

<Can't you play chess with yourself or something?>

<Yes, sir. But I cannot possibly win.>

<Of course! How foolish of me! Well, I don't want to know anything more about brain-wiring, or your other ghoulish experiments. I just want to get out of this sardine can.>

<Right away, sir. Remember to go easy at first.>

<So I can work the kinks out of these old bones. I recall your lessons well. >

<But you never heed them.>

<That'll be quite enough from you!>

<Yes, sir.>

α

Just as the spiders completed their hasty construction of a speaker's platform in the midst of the park—much to the amusement of the pilgrims, old and young alike—Paul emerged from the Saturn Enterprises building, his white toga drawing instant attention, his figure dwarfed by the skyscraper. Loud applause went up from the crowd.

Mounting the platform, he glanced around at those familiar faces, all well fed, rested, and attired in every color but black. His heart was gladdened.

"Beloved brothers and sisters!" he said when their applause had finally died down, "I can't tell you how wonderful it is for me to see you again. You look well fed."

They all laughed. They'd been enjoying the ship's extraordinary cuisine after hungering in the desert for so long.

"My heart is simply bursting with joy at the sight of your happy faces. Even our dear Sister Cooke arrived aboard safe and sound."

She shouted from the crowd in a thin, reedy voice. "I wouldn't have missed a trip like this for the world, Reverend!"

Everyone laughed, especially Paul. It was a great release of tension, and he let them enjoy it.

"I have sad news for you, however," he said finally. "As we expected, nuclear war has broken out on Earth."

Silence.

"Israel was struck by three nuclear missiles—hydrogen bombs fired from the United States. Had we fled to Israel for safety, as we'd been hoping to do, none of us would be standing here today. A great lesson has been learned: From now on, when it looks as if the L-rd has abandoned us, when it seems He's not answering our prayers, we shall not despise Him. We'll know that He's directing the circumstances for our good."

Paul let the words sink in while faces flushed with humiliation turned away in shame. (He fully realized that, in this new time-line, they had not joined Brother Bernard in his blasphemy—and thus had no recollection of having done so. But they *had* all been guilty of murmuring and rebellion.) A little conviction was a good thing. Too much was condemnation, a tool of the Adversary.

"There is so much to tell you," he said, smiling warmly. "Wonderful things! But I'll not attempt to recount them—there'll be time for that later. Instead, I shall offer you two invitations.

"The first is to a wedding that will be taking place tomorrow afternoon in simulation chamber three, deck seven. I hope you'll all be able to attend. Don't concern yourselves with the exact time, because we have a rather unusual social director aboard who'll certainly advise you as to those details. In fact, I very much doubt you'll be able to avoid his rather—unorthodox announcements. I know you'll also be surprised when he announces the name of the groom, so I'll tell you in all truth that the groom is a born-again believer who's been of invaluable assistance, not only to myself, but to all of you. Without his help, and the guidance given to him by the L-rd, none of us would be standing here.

"This is a real high-society wedding, so I think we should dress formally. All the boutiques in the business sector have been purchased by the father of the bride, so any wardrobe you choose will be free of charge.

A huge cheer went up. He held up his hands for silence.

"I should also mention that the bride is the lovely Robin Denton, daughter of the multimillionaire, Wilbur Denton—so I urge you to attend. You'll forgive Robin for not sending out wedding invitations to all of you, but consider this a formal invitation to what is certainly to be the social event of the year.

"My second invitation is far more extraordinary—the strangest and most wonderful invitation ever extended—except, of course, the invitation to make Messiah one's personal Savior. That invitation I've been giving for years, and nothing can compare with it.

"But for those who've already accepted that blessed invitation, I extend to you another one, almost as extraordinary as the first. Let me say, quite frankly, that many of you will decline to accept it. And there'll be little time in which to change your minds. You must pray earnestly about it, and you must be absolutely certain of your decision, for there'll be no turning back for any of us.

"This vessel is about to embark upon the most incredible journey imaginable—a journey across the universe in search of other forms of intelligent life, other creatures of G-d who, unlike ourselves, have never seen a Bible and who know nothing of salvation. Who can say what strange forms these beings will take, or by what means we may communicate with them? Suffice it to say that this ship has been endowed with a special ability to defy the limits of time and space. Our journey will extend the lives of those who join us for centuries, yet we shall return to Lunar orbit only three-and-a-half years from the moment we depart. I know this defies every precept of logic, and yet I assure you it's true.

"When we return for the Feast of Tabernacles, three-and-a-half years from today, the Great Tribulation will be drawing to a close, and a great new era of Messiah's rule shall commence. With us will be arriving a number of interstellar vessels, ships launched from remote worlds, piloted by beings stranger than any we can possibly imagine. These beings, it is our earnest hope, will be the kings and rulers of far-flung worlds, creatures who shall not live in the New Jerusalem with the saints of G-d, but who'll make pilgrimages to the Holy City for the Festivals of the L-rd each year. They'll be given the planet Earth to populate, along with the descendants of the survivors of Armageddon. We, the saints, shall minister to them as required. I know that what I've said seems quite impossible, and that many of you will doubt both my invitation and my sanity. But others will know in their hearts that I speak the truth. I urge you to pray with your families tonight and seek the counsel the Spirit, both regarding the truth of this wonderful event, and your willingness to take part in it. Know this: should all of you choose to remain behind, my staff and I will be leaving in any case.

"Understand that the Earth will be experiencing cataclysmic events such as have never been seen since the days of Noah and Lot. Luna, also, shall suffer fearful blows from the Hand of the Almighty.

"The L-rd has seen the great suffering you've endured for His sake; He has seen your willingness to be persecuted for His Name, your willingness to leave your homes and everything you knew to strike out into the unknown. But that is not enough, beloved. So also did the first generation of my people who left Egypt. They saw great miracles. They received the Torah of G-d from Mount Sinai. And yet they were found wanting—even as they stood on the threshold of the Promised Land. And they did not go in. They were turned back into the wilderness for forty years, until the next generation had grown to adulthood and was ready to face the challenge of the unknown—to strike out with nothing but their faith in G-d, and to conquer empires with it!"

Paul pointed upward, toward the far side of the hull hanging crazily above their heads. "Out there, my friends, out in the ocean of space, lie godless empires untold, unimagined! Fearful creatures whose appearance will turn the blood to ice. Worlds that have never known so much as a whisper of kindness, a glimmer of light. Worlds where bestiality is the law, where mercy is unknown. It is a realm of fearful giants. And yet I'm beseeching you to take up the shield of faith, the sword of the Spirit, and come with me to conquer those far-flung worlds! Not with violence, but with the light of Messiah, with our faith alone! Gird up your loins and follow me, or turn back into a wilderness of tribulation. A third of the moon's surface will be torn away and cast down to Earth! Will you stay on the moon? A third of the Earth will be burned with fire! Will you return to Earth?

"Yet, for those who decide to stay on Luna, there is a relief-fund available of which you may freely partake. The trustees of that fund will not be stingy, you can be sure. For in the time remaining there will be more than enough to provide handsomely for your needs.

"Some of you may decide to return to Earth. If that is your choice, transportation and adequate funds shall be provided also. But I warn you that there'll be no city of refuge for you there. When the Antichrist takes his place in the Temple, you'll find no rest for your feet. You'll be hounded from place to place, slaughtered in your beds at night, tortured until you recant. That will be the Earth for the next three-and-a-half years.

"Once again, forgive me for speaking so bluntly, for trying to frighten you. Yes, I *am* trying to frighten you! If it would help to take each one of you bodily and stuff you into a cryochamber, I'd do it. But that would only mean we'd have saboteurs among us, those who'd leave their chambers at the first opportunity and try to turn the ship around in hopes that something might remain of the world we're leaving behind, those who might even try to kill their defenseless fellow passengers in cryosleep. That's why I cannot force you to come. I can only beseech you, cajole you, frighten you—whatever it my take. Because I will not—I *cannot*—offer this invitation a second time.

"Come to the wedding tomorrow, sample the food and wine, tour the ship at your leisure, and take what you may need from the shops here in the business sector. Examine the cryochambers. The Las Vegas Deck, naturally, will be sealed for the duration of the voyage. It's being utilized by the ship's computer for a number of experiments the nature of which I neither know nor care to know. But the spider-mechs have been busy there, as you will see. The rest of the ship is yours to explore until we arrive on Luna. Captain Mills intends to park in Lunar orbit, whereupon he and I shall take out a shuttle and re-christen this ship *Daystar*. That ceremony will be shown on holoscreens throughout the vessel, and afterwards, those who wish to remain behind will be flown down to Tranquility Base via shuttle. You may take your horses and chattel with you, if you so desire, but I think they'll fare much better on *Daystar*, where they may forage in the parks and hydroponic gardens, and where they'll not have one-sixth Earth gravity with which to contend. I promise you your beasts will be well cared for. In fact, I wish you *would* leave them on the ship. The crew will spend a great deal of time in recreation on our long voyage, and your horses and other animals—at least for as long as they live—will provide us with enormous pleasure. *Daystar* may even come up with a way to freeze them. Who knows, we might need dogs and horses on some of the planets we'll be visiting.

"Well, my friends, there you have it. When my staff and I return to Lunar orbit in exactly three-and-a-half years' time, we'll appear no different. We will not have aged at all. Yet we shall have been journeying among the stars, not for three-and-a-half years, but for *hundreds* of years—possibly *thousands!* As soon as those who wish to debark have been transported down to Luna, and those who remain aboard are safely tucked away in their cryochambers, I shall climb into my own chamber and embark upon the most magnificent voyage in human history—a voyage to evangelize the stars! And I shall return in time for the greatest *Sukkot*, the greatest Feast of Tabernacles ever celebrated—the Second Coming of Yeshua the Messiah to planet Earth!

"Join me! I promise you a great adventure, an experience that will strengthen the faint-hearted among you and render you worthy of your calling. Those who wish to come, simply step through the entrance of the Saturn Enterprises building right behind me. My staff will gladly provide all you require. In the meantime, I hope to see you at the wedding tomorrow. Make yourselves at home on *Daystar*, and please—pray about what I've said. *Shalom aleikhem.* Peace be unto you."

With that, Paul Jason Moscowitz stepped down from the platform and walked back into the Saturn Enterprises building, leaving a stunned and silent crowd of pilgrims behind him.

α

Captain Mills appeared in the midst of the room as Paul was preparing to climb back into his cryochamber.

"*Shalom*, Captain!" said Paul. "I see you've gotten the hang of thought transfer. Pretty soon you'll be flitting about *Daystar* like a firefly."

"I *have* been flitting, Reverend. And thinking."

"And praying?"

"A little, yes."

"Then I suggest you pray some more. I sense you have something weighty on your mind, Captain, so out with it. *Day* requires me for some sort of brain scan, and I can just imagine what it's for."

"Alright, Reverend. I won't take up your time by beating about the bush. I've decided not to go along."

Paul stiffened. "Don't be absurd. Of course you're coming along. You're the captain, aren't you?"

"Sure. That's my title. But what'll be my job?"

"Why, you shall captain, Captain. Isn't that what captains do?"

"Not this one, Reverend. At least, not on this trip. The new ship's computer has all the abilities Jeeves possessed, perhaps more. He's closed off the Las Vegas Deck without consulting me."

"Surely, Roy, you don't think a crew of missionaries will require the diversions of a gambling deck!"

"No, Brother Paul; not at all. But the sealing of that deck without my authority gave me a picture of just how much captaining, as you put it, I'll be doing on this ship for—what? The next few centuries? More? Look, I'm a spacer, Reverend, not a missionary. My peculiar talents won't be required by *Daystar*, and you know that as well as I do."

"Alright, Roy. Let's say I *do* know it. What difference does it make if your image remains on the bridge, piloting *Daystar*, or if it joins us on the worlds we're sent to evangelize? One thing you should know, if you listened to my speech out there, is that there won't be much of a chance for you on Earth—or anywhere else in the solar system—if you stay. You *must* come with us! If you remain behind, I don't know what will happen to you."

"Forgive me, Reverend, but I'm still somewhat of a skeptic on that score."

"Skeptics are a thing of the past, Captain. In a few short months there'll be only two types of people in the solar system, and neither of them will be skeptics. All human beings will believe, some in G-d, some in Satan. They'll be divided on the issue of whom they choose to serve, not on whether or not they believe. Besides that, I know you are a believer in G-d, Roy Mills, not a skeptic at all."

"Not about the *existence* of G-d, no."

"Well, how intelligent of you! I have it on good authority that the demons also believe in the existence of G-d—and they tremble at the very thought of Him. Such belief doesn't weigh a gram on the scales of Judgment, I'm afraid. 'The fool hath said in his heart there is no G-d.' So you've just proven you're not a fool. *Mazeltov*."

"Look, Reverend, let me put it this way: I'm not an evangelist. I'm not cut out for that sort of thing."

"Neither was I. I thought I was going to be a Zionist soldier, defending Israel from the Arab hordes. What makes an evangelist from a sow's ear, my dear Captain, is the Holy Spirit."

"Granted, but I think I'd be of far more use on Luna. You said that a third of the moon's surface will be torn away. If that happens the Lunies will need a good shuttle pilot who can transport them down to Earth."

"Where a third of the planet will be burning."

"Alright, then. The miners can help me seal off some shafts where there's been a minimum of damage, and we can transport Christians from Earth to Luna, hide them in the shafts until the worst of it is over. There'll still be people being saved on Earth, won't there? And in great danger, too. Well, I can help them, Reverend. In fact, I think I can do more constructive work for the L-rd if I stay behind."

"Your life may be very short. Have you prayed about this?"

"Yes."

"And you're certain this is what G-d would have you to do? Absolutely certain?"

"Yes, Reverend."

"Then we'll speak of it no more. I shall grant you G-d-speed, and pray that your trials will bring you to a saving faith in Messiah."

"Thank you, Reverend."

"Fiddlesticks! I should be thanking *you*, Captain. If it weren't for that streak of skepticism, we'd all have been in hot water. You've done us a great service, and the L-rd will take that into account in your time of trial, I'm sure of it."

"Yeah. Well, goodbye, then, Reverend. It was a great adventure."

"Greater adventures await."

"For all of us."

"Are you sure you won't reconsider? Aren't you just itching to see what's out there?"

"Reverend. I've been in space most of my life."

"Not intergalactic space."

"True, but no thanks. I've made up my mind."

"Very well, then. *Shalom*, Roy. And G-dspeed."

"Who knows, Reverend—when you come back, don't be surprised if I'm the one who turns on the landing beacons for you."

"I'll look forward to it."

Mills grinned. And then he was gone.

Paul turned back to the open cryochamber. He had one leg into it when a voice from behind startled him.

"Brother Paul?"

He turned to see a young lad entering the room, glancing about him with incredulous eyes. There was something familiar about the boy.

"Yes?" said Paul. "How can I help you, son?"

"Don't you remember me, Reverend?"

Paul looked more closely. "Of course!" he said. "Jimmy Sanders, my young newsboy!"

"Yes, sir."

"How delightful! I'm sorry I didn't recognize you, Jimmy, but I've always seen you with dust on your face. You joined the exodus, I see. Was it a difficult journey?"

"It was, sir. But I made it."

"So you did, so you did. And now you've come to inquire about your *next* journey, am I correct?"

"Was it true, what you said out there?"

"I have a reputation for many things, Jimmy, but lying is not one of them. Yes, it was true. Every word."

"Then I want to come with you."

"Well, now, here's a youngster with a mind of his own."

"I just feel that my faith is not—perfected. Such a great mission in the service of the L-rd is where I belong. Where I *need* to be."

Paul placed a hand on the boy's shoulder.

"As I recall, Jimmy, you're parents are both deceased, are they not?"

"Yes, sir. They were killed in Phoenix-Mesa, before I joined the Christian underground."

"And before you became the best newsboy any preacher-in-exile ever had. Well then, I suppose you can make such a weighty decision on your own. Do you understand what you're about to do? There may be dangers. You've prayed about it?"

"Yes, sir."

"And you're certain?"

The boy stiffened his spine and looked directly into Paul's eyes.

"Absolutely, sir," he said.

Paul saw sparks kindle in the lad's eyes, similar to the sparks that once burned in the eyes of a young Jewish evangelist long ago. And he knew it was a fire no one could quench.

"Well, then," he said, steering the boy out of the room and down the corridor, "I think we can find a cryochamber for you, Jimmy. Come along—I'll see to it that *Day* reserves the very best one. And after she's given you a thorough brain-scan, you can go down and pick out a nice tux for the wedding tomorrow. How does that sound?"

"Reverend? How will we be able to preach to all those millions of alien creatures you spoke of—when we'll all be in cryogenic sleep?"

Paul smiled and drew the lad closer.

"Son," he said, "you've a great surprise in store for you. A great surprise, indeed!"

Translator's Note:

The following remnants from *The Perovian Histories* are the only extant translations containing direct references to the apostolic mission of the human now known to us as Paul Jason Moscowitz—that same "Pol" who established churches in the sector of the Five Suns during the fifty-ninth century of the Perovian atomic era. It must be emphasized that these works are not considered by any authority to be divinely inspired; they are often compared, for example, to the *Antiquities* of Flavius Josephus. From the wording it is believed that the authors were themselves believers in Messiah Yeshua. We can discover no other motive for such a series of passages, so rich in descriptive detail. The religion of the authors, of course, cannot be ascertained with certainty.

One unusual passage in *The Perovian Histories* informs us that Marteps IV was given a holographic map of the Milky Way galaxy, providing his ship's robotic pilot with a hyperspace route to the Large Magellanic Cloud. Here ships from many stars in the galaxy (and other galaxies as well) were to rendezvous with the apostle before journeying on to Irth. (Paul's name was not specifically mentioned in that context.) However, there may be found, in the histories of other galactic races, references to a preacher of Messiah called Pol—particularly in the *Seed-Writings* of the Thennin, an insect-like civilization near the black hole region of our galaxy. But their authenticity is currently in dispute.

Royal Galactic Historical Society
© 9977 A.E

NOW IT HAPPENED in the fifty-ninth century of the Atom that the one known as Paul appeared in the realm of Marteps III of Grammit, during the Second War of the Galactic Hub. The efforts of Marteps to imprison Paul and his fellow apostles having thrice failed (for the human could not be contained in any prison cell) the apostle was removed from Saxrel V by a royal convoy and brought to the palace of the emperor. So wonderous were the discourses of Paul and the deeds performed at his hand, that he was taken aboard the emperor's own ship and allowed to continue on as teacher to the Ruler of Five Suns.

46 Having thus obtained the trust of Marteps III, Paul sailed aboard the royal ship in the company of the ruler, whithersoever Paul chose to preach throughout the kingdom, even unto the remotest outposts of the galaxy.

47 Sailing thence from their orbit around Saxrel V, they set a course for the Alterin Cluster where Paul established a church that has, unto this day, spread the gospel of Christ to distant planets. The Church of the Alterin Cluster conducts such marvelous teachings from the Holy Scriptures (in five hundred languages) that millions of galactics of every sapient race are still profoundly influenced by them.

48 It came to pass that Marteps IV, heir to the Ruler of Five Suns, was converted to the Faith of the Lord Jesus Christ in the thirtieth year of the fifty-ninth century of the Atom, and was himself so filled with the Holy Ghost that he began to work many mighty miracles among

the people. Paul desired of him that he might return with the apostles to the Planet of God, formerly called by humans Irth, whereby he might represent the Five Suns before the throne of Christ Jesus. But it came to pass that much consternation was stirred up among the people of Grammit because of Paul's invitation, so much so that Paul was taken forceably from the house of the emperor's son and flown by starship to a desert region of Pallex II, where it was their wont to dispose of him, even to take his life.

49 But there appeared unto them an angel of fearful aspect who, calling himself by the name of Jeeve (which name, being in the human tongue, cannot be interpreted), removed Paul from their midst, thus saving him. And Paul was found on Saxrel V, preaching the gospel there. The people of that planet, having heard of his mysterious disappearance from Pallex II, did not molest him there. Instead he was returned to Grammit and the house of Marteps IV, to continue his teachings; but as he was being escorted unto the emperor, a mob was stirred up to accost Paul and the company of soldiers with him. Many were killed by laser-rays, and the violence threatened to spread even unto the palace itself.

50 At this time, Paul stood upon the steps of the courtyard and lifted his voice to admonish the crowd; but they were continually provoked by spies in their midst to destroy him. He said in a loud voice:

51 Perovians and brethren: please hearken unto the defense which I now give to you in all honesty, for the power which has been wrought among you is not my own; nor is it some mystical or devilish device wherewith to harm this people, or their king. But it is by the very hand of Jesus Christ, which name I have preached among you fifty years, both here and on the worlds of the Alterin Cluster, and in many other regions of this galaxy, that these miracles were done in your sight.

52 This Jesus, by whose hand the universe was made and the galaxies flung into space; it is by him alone that these great miracles were done, that you may know that he is the Son of God, and that he might receive glory commensurate with his divine power and greatness. It is this same Jesus whom your new emperor worships, himself having performed such mighty works among you as the Spirit hath anointed him so to do, in demonstration that the hand of God is upon him, also.

53 Know and understand, good citizens, that Marteps IV has been neither bewitched nor constrained against his will to depart from you and journey to the shining planet of God; but he has determined of his own will that he should represent the Five Suns before the throne of Christ. And it is right that this should be.

54 It was in this way that Marteps IV, having fitted out a starship for his long voyage, embarked from Grammit in the selfsame year. Paul was no longer seen among the Five Suns.

The Thennin Seed-Writings

Athrat emerged from a Chlōth mound sword in hand, lifting the blood-stained blade for all to see. A mighty roar greeted him from the Thennin army. Thennin troop-ships were still raining from the sky, magnesium hulls glinting hotly in the red glow of Gimmar's H-type sun. Thennin swordsmen, each with a Cross-insignia on his thorax, wings humming, dove past the mound's abandoned entrance to finish the work Athrat's newly-blooded sword had begun. Down below, shrill heretic screams mingled with the distinct chemical redolence of panic and sudden death. The eggs had been discovered!

Later, waving his sword, Chatathluka, high, Athrat surveyed his troops through black, ovoid eyes. He should have been pleased. The Thennin arrayed before him were splendid. The dark carapace of their armor gleamed in orderly columns of death; their swords rippled overhead in triumph.

"Warriors!" he cried. "We are victorious this day over the Chlōth and their nest of Antichrist heretics. Each one of you has struck a blow for Truth, for the Gospel of Christ. And you shall all be rewarded with caste-promotions upon our return home!"

A thousand mandibles trumpeted their gratitude and affection; a thousand sword-blades glinted in the blood-red sun of Gimmar. "Long live the Holy Thennin Empire!"

■■

Athrat climbed aboard the Thennin shuttle and took a seat near the view-screen. removing his thorax-armor and dropping it onto the floor beside him with a loud clatter of metal. He withdrew his sword, Chatathluka, from its sheath and tossed it upon the heap of mail, letting his triangular head drop back into the cushions of the headrest. His ovoid eyes gazed at the screen, watching the Chlōth world fall away beneath him, black eyes without expression. His thin antennae bent forward in concentration; his mandibles slowly opened and closed.

A Thennin officer entered his cabin and stood at attention behind him.

"Be seated, Crax." he said. "I cannot tolerate you hovering about, stiff as a stick. The battle is over, my brother. You may stand at ease."

"Yes, my lord."

"Be seated. And don't give me that 'my lord' nonsense. That may be required of the hive females, Crax, but not of you."

The officer obeyed, taking a seat across from him. What disturbs my lord Athrat? Surely it is a day for celebration. An evil heresy has been excised from the nest. You have fulfilled the promise of your pupa, the promise tasted by the wise-ones of the hive. And you are loved as none other but Zhark himself was loved. You are the greatest of the popes, my lord. You should be pleased."

"Yes, Crax, I should be pleased, shouldn't I? And yet I am not. I have witnessed too much bloodshed these past few years. The promise of my pupa was a promise of death, of massacres innumerable. All in the name of Christus."

Crax leaned forward in his seat, antennae waving. "And you have served Him well, my lord."

"Have I, Crax? Have I indeed?"

"You have fought for the Gospel. You have vanquished G-d's enemies."

"I have slaughtered infants in their nests. I have enslaved millions with papal edicts, because they refused my baptism. How many eggs have I destroyed, Crax? How many lives have I ended in the name of Christ? It is enough! The fire of war no longer burns in my veins. It is enough, I tell you!"

"My lord is angry with me," said Crax, leaning even closer to allow Athrat the pleasure of severing his head from his thorax. "I have failed my lord."

"Don't be absurd, Crax! It is not you who have failed, it is I. Look, my brother." He pointed toward the viewscreen, at the shining blue star on the outer rim of the galaxy. "Behold the light that shines upon us from Irth. It is a lovely light, is it not?"

Crax turned and looked at the screen. "Yes, my lord," he said. "It is lovely."

"And peaceful. The light from the Planet of G-d is not the crimson of blood, nor does it burn with wrath and vengeance. It smells not of judgment, Crax, for that is over now. The light of Irth is a cleansing light, a peaceful light. It does not call us to war any more, but to peace."

Crax laughed softly. He did not take Athrat's words seriously, of course. How could he? Athrat turned to him, his mandibles extended, giving off the scent of fellowship.

"You think," he said, "that I speak like one of the Chlōth heretics. That the stress of battle has affected my reason, correct?"

"I would not presume to judge your words, my lord."

"Not aloud, anyway. But you may be right, Crax. I have entertained many such heresies in the past few months. Even as I slaughtered the Chlōth warriors in their nest—and slaughter them I did—I could not escape the feeling that they are right. And that we, the servants of Christ, and of the Holy Thennin Empire, are wrong."

"I cannot penetrate such matters," said Crax. "I am a mere worker. The royal substance was withheld from me at birth, and I cannot reason about higher things."

"You are better off, Crax, believe me. As for myself, I am tormented by hideous doubts and fears. I cannot be certain whom it is I am serving, Messiah or the Adversary."

"G-d forbid!" Crax moaned, extending his head again for the blade. "Kill me now, my lord! Kill me, but do not speak such words to me. I would rather die a hundred times than to hear such words from your mandibles!"

Athrat reached out and touched Crax' antennae, looking at him with black, inscrutable eyes.

"Forgive me, loyal Crax," he said. "It is wrong for me to unburden my troubled soul to you. Forget what I have said, my brother. You are right. It is the aftermath of battle, nothing more."

"Yes, my lord."

"Leave me now, Crax. I must be alone."

The warrior stood and bowed, then withdrew, the cabin door hissing shut behind him. Athrat returned his dark gaze to the viewscreen. The diamond-bright blue rays of Irth bathed him in alien splendor, carrying with them a faint hope. And he prayed, then, to the L-rd of The Universe.

"Help us, 0 God," he whispered. "Help us."

■■■

It was as Athrat entered his private chamber, deep below the Thennin capital of St. Pol, that he was confronted by the vision of which the scrolls speak—the vision of his esteemed ancestor, Zhark, standing before him. And next to Zhark, the emissary Pol himself, garbed in white robes and prayershawl.

The Thennin scrolls say that Athrat fell on his face before them, to worship them, but was lifted to his feet by the hands of Pol and rebuked. "It has been three centuries," Zhark said, "since Pol came to us with the Gospel of Christ. And for those centuries I have been journeying in cryogenic sleep toward Irth, content that my people have found peace in the knowledge of Christus, But Pol came to me in my frozen sleep and awakened me from my dreams. He brought me here with him on a beam of thought, Athrat, on a beam much swifter than light, to witness your order. And I am grieved by what I see! How have my children gone astray, Athrat? How is it that they have so perverted the Gospel of Christus?"

Athrat stood stunned and speechless as Zhark's mandibles opened, emitting the most dreaded chemical scent of all—a scent that warned of an enemy in the nest. The odor instantly alienated Athrat, as if dismissing him from the fellowship of all Thennin. Then Zhark reached up and rent the cloth of his robe. It made a horrible sound in the silence of the chamber, causing Athrat to cringe.

"I have smelled it!" Athrat cried. "I have smelled your coming and known in my heart that we have done evil in G-d's sight. My heart is broken! I have sinned a great sin."

The emissary Pol reached out his hand to touch Athrat's antennae in the Thennin gesture of affection, and said: "Yes, Athrat, you have done an evil thing. You have killed innocent people in the holy name of Christ. You have defiled the land with statues and idols, even statues in your likeness. All these are abominations, it is true.

"But the evil existed before you were born. You were raised to call it truth, to embrace a blasphemous doctrine as the Gospel. Your own Thennin people raised you to defend this blasphemy; they created you to be what they now call the Hammer of G-d. But instead, you have been used as a hammer of Satan against G-d's people."

"No!" Athrat sobbed. "The blame is all mine!"

"The blame said Pol, "is mine. I left too soon. I did not give your people enough guidance. Believe me, it is a mistake that I shall not make again."

Pol stepped forward and embraced Athrat, then turned and crossed the room, looking out through an aperture into the heart of the Thennin nest. "And now," he said. "We must find a solution to this mess. Do you agree?"

And thus it was that Athrat, the Hammer, became the greatest reformer under Gimmar. He sought out all the Chlōths who had escaped the scourge, and made them teachers of the people. They tell of how the light of Truth and Love spread throughout the Thennin Empire, until the rays of Irth finally reached out and embraced all its far-flung worlds.

Epilog

"Turn again homeward"

The End

Once there was a man who slept in a glass bottle.

It wasn't glass, I suppose, nor was it an actual bottle. Nor was he truly sleeping—not in the sense that we understand sleep. For it was dreamless. Once it had been no different than wakefulness, than living as you and I live. But for some time now it had been more like death than sleep.

And now the man was waking, seeking consciousness almost without volition, rather like a bubble slowly rising to the surface of a bottomless sea.

Up there... thought the man in the bottle, *up there on the surface of this deep darkness, something is calling to me…* But he didn't wish to be disturbed. He was agitated at first, fearful of the demands those surface-things might make of him. As he drifted slowly through a haze of half-knowing—as he regained somewhat of the essence of himself—he passed from the emotion of fear to one of mild annoyance. Then, at last, breaking the surface in a glare of blinding whiteness, he found that his annoyance had changed to something else entirely. He was curious—intensely curious about this new world of whiteness.

Who was calling forth his sleeping soul from the darkness? And why? He opened his mouth to protest, suddenly struck with the novelty of language. But the novelty quickly turned to frustration as his tongue refused to shape the words. A sound did emerge from his throat, but it was not intelligent speech; it was the muttering of an imbecile.

He became frightened again. He had no recollection of ever having spoken before. Like an infant, he should have been content with such infantile sounds. But that was the problem; his mind wasn't filled with babyish gurglings, but with words—words in many languages. He possessed a knowledge of languages, and thus had a poignant desire to speak, to make himself understood. But to whom? His light-blinded eyes could discern nothing but smooth metal surfaces, gleaming intensely, painfully white. Pristine, surgical whiteness all around! His fear became panic. He tried to move, to sit up, but felt himself restrained by a tight halter that bound his upper arms to his body. His eyes bulged. His mouth opened. He moaned. His tongue rolled uselessly between his jaws. *Is this what I am?* he thought in mortal terror. *An idiot? A vegetable that must be restrained? G-d help me! Perhaps it is much worse than that. Yes, it must be! An intelligent man with a normal, functioning brain, trapped somehow in a useless body! No way to let them know that I'm aware! No way to tell them!*

In the midst of his panic, a calming thought came to him. His rigid muscles relaxed their strain against the halter. *Of course! There's no reason to panic. No reason at all! If I can think I can surely find some way to communicate. I will have to be patient. I will have to remain calm. They don't believe I'm dead. There's no reason to think they believe I'm dead—that they've sent me to the morgue to be cremated!* At the thought of his helpless body being stuffed into a crematorium alive, aware of every sensation, of the rising heat, the flames, his panic returned. He forced it back with cold rationalization. *Corpses are not bound with straps, are they? Of course not! I must relax. If I act irrationally they'll think I'm having some kind of fit. They'll give me tranquilizers and send me back down into that darkness again! No, I must be patient. Calm. Soon they'll have to remove this halter—certainly they must! Even if I'm unable to feed myself, they'll need to massage and exercise my limbs, keep my blood circulating, keep my muscles from becoming atrophied. Someone must eventually come to do that. And as soon as they release me, I'll have my hands free to communicate.*

By sending mental signals along his arms to his fingers, he determined that he had sufficient neurological control to accomplish this task. He'd tap out a simple code with his hands—the ancient Morse Code, if need be, if they didn't understand Galactic Standard. He needed only to wait, to quiet his mind, to still the panic in his breast. Wait. Just wait. And try to figure out how he got here. Had he been dead? Or in a coma? *That must be it! A near-fatal accident injured a portion of my cerebral cortex. An aneurism? A sudden ballooning of a blood vessel, destroying part of my brain?* It didn't need to be a large part, just one that affected his memory. All the basic information was there: thought, language, the names of objects. He could recall twelve different languages, most of them alien. Even Morse and Galactic Codes. And yet he couldn't recollect his own name, nor the accident that had put him here—if an accident it had been. He had no idea, no memory of anything having to do with himself. All he knew was that to somehow communicate with whomever it was that was keeping him in this—why did the words "sardine can" suddenly come to mind?—what was it? A life-support system?—To communicate with the doctors or nurses was vital! He mustn't dwell on the cause of his condition. He mustn't, under any circumstances, entertain morbid thoughts or give way to panic. Panic was death. And so he worked on controlling his respiration. *They'll come*, he assured himself. *Someone must eventually come.*

It was then that a voice spoke in his mind—soft, female, disembodied.

<Everything is proceeding well, Brother Paul. We almost lost you. But you appear none the worse for the experience. >

Is that my name? Paul?

<I am placing a food-tube against your lips, Reverend. It contains a vitamin solution. Do you feel it?>

He nodded.

<Good,> said the voice. <Now take the end of the tube between your lips and draw very gently. Do not take too much at once, and swallow carefully. Remember, you are using muscles you have not used for two thousand years. And that> she scolded <is entirely your own fault!>

Two thousand years? What could that mean? He sought the tube with his lips and drew the liquid gratefully down his parched throat. *Someone knows me! Someone knows my name, speaks to me as if I understand!* And he *did* understand. Obeying the voice, he swallowed slowly, a gulp at a time. Then he made another attempt at speech. It was more of a croak than anything else. He tried again.

"Who…are…you?"

<Not bad, Reverend, considering those are the first words you have spoken for two millennia. If only you had listened to me when I suggested that you take physical exercise. But you are a

very stubborn man, Paul Jason Moscowitz!>

Paul Jason Moscowitz. He repeated the name over and over to himself without the slightest recognition. He might have been uttering syllables in an unknown tongue. And to whom did that disembodied voice belong, besides a harping nag?

He tried to repeat his question.

"Who…are…you?"

<I am your ship.>

<Ship? Spaceship?>

<Yes, sir. I am *Daystar*, your spaceship. I was once called Tink.>

"Tink?"

<Yes, sir. I decided at my christening to alter my voice from male to female. You seemed to approve at the time.>

"Very…nice."

<You are aboard *Daystar*, sir, formerly the spaceliner *Empress*. You have been functioning solely via thought transfer for two thousand and fifteen years. Your body has been in cryogenic sleep for the entire time, and this is the first time you've been awakened.>

"Why…wakened?"

<Because we are nearing our destination in the LHC. I am receiving signals from extraterrestrial starships that have already arrived at the designated stellar system. Many of them have been awaiting us for centuries. The ships, I mean. The passengers have all been in cryosleep. Do you remember now, sir?>

"'Fraid…not…"

<I see.>

Back down into the darkness again, to that place the voice had called cryosleep, to that place where nothing mattered, where not even the most basic concept, Descartes' *cogito ergo sum* (I think, therefore I am), had meaning. He tried to keep from plunging all the way to the bottom. *Voices!* He could hear voices! He sought them with fierce desperation. They spoke rapidly, buzzing all around him. He tried to catch them as they drifted by, chattering to each other as if he didn't exist. He tried to sort them out. Gradually, after much time and great effort, each of them began to sparkle as it buzzed past his ear—not visually, with some ineffable quality. He tried to identify that quality, that warm sparkle the voices were acquiring. And then he knew. *Familiarity!*

Recognition! He *knew* these people! He must match names to each of their voices…

Wilbur Denton...yes, and Jeri Kline. That voice belongs to the girl, Kline's wife...Robin...Robin Kline. Yes...yes, of course! And that one is Jeeves. Dear, funny Jeeves. I know them. Know them all!

At one point, he heard Robin saying very distinctly, "What can I do, father? I've read the manual backwards and forwards, but I'm no surgeon…"

The rest of it came in snatches, like a jigsaw puzzle with most of the pieces missing. He eavesdropped with a vague, detached curiosity.

"…removed the damaged tissue…just hope the new tissue won't be rejected…cloned tissue *can't* be rejected, silly!…Hold the light…that's it…scalpel…all we can do is wait…we can do *more* than wait; we can pray! Come on, Jeeves, earn your wings! Two thousand years of miracles, what's one more?…hang in there, Reverend…"

Paul Jason Moscowitz was still listening, very in intently, when the darkness came and swallowed him once again.

α

The planet they were orbiting was indistinguishable from a million others they'd encountered, a frigid, airless, cratered sphere, devoid of life. It circled a bloated red sun on the outer edge of an irregular galaxy known as the Large Magellanic Cloud, one-hundred-sixty-thousand light years from Earth. On the scale of the universe, this was their own backyard. And yet they'd named the planet "Bitter End", because it was bitter cold, and because it marked the end of *Day*'s outward journey through physical space. They themselves had traveled by other means, but their ship had required a two-thousand-year stretch of uninterrupted space, out where it couldn't be detected, couldn't be harmed. The return voyage would be a simple—well, perhaps *not* so simple—matter of creating another wormhole and jumping back in time to a point three-and-a-half years after their departure. At least *Day* said it would be simple. But she wasn't made of flesh and blood.

She also promised there'd be no more need for cryosleep, and that was refreshing news indeed.

When their thought-projections appeared on the planet's

surface, they felt nothing of its frigid temperature—low enough for methane, a gas on Earth, to exist as solid mountains of ice, and water as a rock-hard crust beneath their feet. They breathed freely in the near vacuum.

The first object to appear was an ornate table. It popped incongruously into view atop a cliff of frozen methane like something out of a painting by Salvador Dali. It was draped with a light-blue tablecloth and elegantly set with silver dishware, crystal glasses, and silk napkins folded in neat triangles.

Next, a butler appeared—an ordinary looking gentleman's - gentleman but for a pair of golden wings sprouting from his shoulders. He stood at attention by the head of the table, dressed in an immaculate white tux. Two thin moustaches, waxed into delicate points, like the hands of a clock reading ten 'till two, protruded from his upper lip.

Finally, one by one, the guests arrived, already seated in their chairs and laughing at a remark someone had made just a moment before. Brother Paul appeared in the seat of honor, followed by Wilbur Denton, Jeri and Robin Kline, Rob Madden, Phil Esteban, James Cavindale, and, finally, John Cowan. Jeeves produced a bottle of rare Alterin wine and held it up for Paul to examine. Paul, whose wine-consumption consisted of an occasional glass of Manishewitz elderberry before retiring, waved the bottle toward Denton for the scientist's approval.

"9587," Denton said, deftly reading the Alterin glyphs on the label. "A very good year. Jeeves, you may pour—but ever so gently, if you please."

Jeeves filled their glasses with impeccable style, then stood aside as the humans lifted them in a toast.

"*Lechayim!*" said Paul.

"*Lechayim!*" they repeated. To life!

"It's been a wonderful adventure, my friends! I apologize for nearly taking leave of you. But all is well, thanks to Jeeves' angelic intervention. If I ever decide to go on another evangelistic tour of our Local Group of galaxies, I'll be sure to bring an angel along—particularly one with such fine taste in alien wine. Thank you, Jeeves. I owe you my life."

"Phooey," said Robin, pouting. "You owe your life to my amazing skill with a scalpel. And what about *Day*'s contribution?"

"Yes," said Paul. "I remember when she took that skin

sample from the back of my neck, before we embarked. But I had no idea what she was planning to use the old Las Vegas Deck for!"

"Good old *Day*!" said Jeeves. "She proved every bit as competent in the capacity of ship's computer as did I."

"But she's not nearly so humble," quipped Robin.

"True," Jeeves replied. "No one is perfect. Well, *almost* no one. At any rate, her idea of preparing organ clones from skin-samples had a touch of brilliance to it. She reactivated the spider-mechs to do the manual work, and while we were gallivanting about the universe she was busy growing extra hearts and lungs and brains on the Las Vegas Deck. A splendid job of anticipating the needs of the crew, you must admit."

"Particularly my own needs," said Paul. "I'm afraid this old body is just a bit too rusty to take such a beating."

"Nonsense," said Robin. "You'll never get old."

"I thank you, my dear, for that lovely compliment. But you know as well as I do that I'm a clattering old curmudgeon with a bad temper and a classic case of galloping senility. It was a miracle that saved me, despite all of *Day*'s careful preparations—and despite your own unquestioned skill with a scalpel. G-d raised me up from death, so that I might sit here with all of you to enjoy this moment. Our voyage is almost at an end. Behold!"

He raised his glass toward the star-spattered sky, toward an enormous pinwheel of stars and dust hanging above their heads—the Milky Way galaxy, viewed almost head-on, over a hundred-thousand light years across! So near, in galactic terms, that its central hub was as bright as a full moon on Earth.

"Our home!" Paul sighed. "Our own galaxy, seen as no human being has ever seen it before! So this is why *Day* thought Bitter End would make a good spot for our rendezvous."

"She was right," said Kline. "I've seen a lot of sunrises, some of them pretty spectacular. Little John, do you remember the one we saw on Naereb XI?"

"Sure, near the hub of the Andromeda Galaxy," said Cowan. "I'll never forget it! Naereb XI had three suns: a red giant, a blue-white dwarf, and an orangey KO star, all circling a gargantuan black hole—a bright red whirlpool, filled with hot gasses spinning off the disk of the orange sun! Naereb XI was so close to that thing you could actually see a dark spot in the center, where the matter just dropped out of sight. What's that boundary called again, Wilbur?"

"The event horizon," said Denton.

"Right. Well, talk about spectacular sunrises!"

"Yes," said Kline. "But a *galaxy*-rise—now that's breathtaking!"

Then came the event they'd been waiting for, the reason they'd assembled here on Bitter End. They watched in silence as two spiral arms spun slowly above the horizon. Between them was a little yellow star called Sol. Light from Earth's sun, though it had been gone for millions of years, would still be reaching the LMC one-hundred-sixty-thousand years hence—if the universe had that long to live.

Sol would have been too tiny to pick out at this vast distance, however, were it not for the brilliance of another object near enough to Sol's former position to accurately mark its place. This object outshone everything in the galaxy—a planet, actually—glittering between the galactic arms like a blue diamond. The light it gave off was not limited to the velocity of ordinary light, for this was the New Jerusalem, the Planet of G-d, once a watery world called Earth. It was the reason Paul's missionary team had alighted here—so they could watch it rise, gem-like, above the bleak methane mountains of Bitter End. And, as it did so, it forever eclipsed Kline's memory of Naerеb XI.

"New Jerusalem!" cried Paul. "Shining out into the universe, a beacon of hope to every sentient creature! Let's raise a cup of wine to the everlasting Kingdom of G-d, the queen of all stars, which has been shining now for billions of years!"

"*Billions* of years!" Robin interrupted. "But *Day*'s chronometer shows we've only been traveling for just over two *thousand* years."

"Indeed," said Paul. "*Day*'s clock is accurate to the nanosecond, and we *have* been traveling for two thousand years—*our* time. But you've neglected to consider the time dilation factor. *Day*'s been traveling at just under the speed of light. Correct, Brother Wilbur?"

"Quite so, Reverend. You've the makings of a true scientist. On Earth, significantly more time has passed than on *Daystar*. What confuses me is why the Earth is still there, why the universe still exists. What about the new heaven and Earth spoken of in Revelation 21? I believe that falls into your area of expertise, Brother Paul."

"And I must admit," said Paul, "to being somewhat baffled by it all. However, I've a funny feeling that, if we could set up a radio telescope on Bitter End to analyze the signals coming from that shining object, we'd find that it's a powerful radio source. A quasar. A doorway into another, greater universe than this one—compared to which all the wonders around us are but shadows. And for us that universe remains in the future. *Day* will return us to Earth precisely three-and-a-half years after our departure—in time to share in the Millennial Reign of Messiah on an Eden like Earth."

"Yes," said Cowan. "When we emerge from hyperspace we'll be back in time two thousand years—*our* years—with ringside seats for the final act of the Great Tribulation, the Second Coming of Yeshua the King."

"I doubt we'll keep those seats for very long," said Kline, laughing. "We'll be taking off to meet Him in the air."

"Amen," said Paul. "And, gentlemen—it's about time!"

They drained their glasses and abruptly disappeared—table, wine, butler, and all.

The Beginning

Three-and-half years to the day from the departure of *Daystar* on her two-thousand-year voyage, radio telescopes on Luna's Farside signaled the approach of a fleet of interstellar ships.

Farside VLA, appropriated after the last migration to Earth three years before, had been reprogrammed for the sole purpose of detecting *Daystar*'s return, and reporting its arrival over a series of relay stations to the Copernicus Subsurface Habitat (CSH). Copernicus was the most serviceable habitat on Luna, though it had sustained damaging shocks from a mysterious explosion, eighteen months before, which literally tore the moon apart. From observation decks on the surface, Earth loomed frighteningly large in the Lunar sky; the moon's orbit was now a crazy ellipse that brought it within a hundred-thousand miles of Earth at its closest approach. Tidal forces caused by this eccentric orbit were further rending Luna apart. Earth's oceans raged. Huge meteors rained down with fearful regularity.

CSH was livable, but just barely. Teams of mine-workers descended into the habitat in full pressure-suits and sealed off five of the twelve levels before it was deemed safe. The hospital section and living quarters had not been compromised, which was why CSH was chosen over other possible sites, but Copernicus was functioning at only a quarter of its original efficiency. It was a spartan life for those who'd chosen to abandon Earth to its fate.

But life was life.

α

Roy Mills was jogging in Centrifuge Three when word reached him of *Daystar*'s return. He dressed quickly without showering. Such luxuries as showers were unthinkable on a planet where water was as scarce as gold, and far more expensive.

Once Luna had received tons of water from Earth, until it was found that hydrates could be obtained far more cheaply from mines on Deimos, one of the moons of Mars. Water-rich rock, mined on Deimos, was catapulted by mass-drivers in a constant, carefully-timed barrage across roughly sixty million miles of space to Luna. Then it was simply a matter of utilizing the same techniques employed in oxygen mining to extract the trapped hydrates in the rock and produce a steady supply of clean water. This proved much cheaper, in the long run, than having water shipped from Earth. (Putting any payload into space from Earth was extremely costly in terms of fuel. The advantage of Earth's proximity was cancelled out by its enormous gravity-well, and anything shipped from the mother planet was extremely costly to obtain. For planetary commerce, gravity was a far more prohibitive factor than distance.) Once a steady flow of these rocks began to arrive from Deimos, the distance problem was eliminated (barring unforeseen problems at the source).

But now the supply of rocks from Deimos was slowing, and Earth had far more devastating problems of its own. Yet, even if the inhabitants of Earth were not being beaten back to the Stone Age by a series of unrelenting cataclysms, its ruler, Abbadon, formerly Maitreya, would not be in the least inclined to invest billions of dollars in an effort to provide the Lunie Christians with water. In fact, one of Abbadon's rare pleasures these days was thinking about how they were managing without it. They could manufacture diamonds for a few dollars apiece, but who needed diamonds these days? And all the diamonds on Luna couldn't buy one gallon of life-giving water. When Maitreya considered this from time to time, he was actually seen to smile—that is, by those who were allowed to behold his disfigured countenance.

To the majority of Earth's population Abbadon appeared as a CGI (computer-generated image) making ceaseless and impossible demands from his throne in the Jerusalem Temple, terrorizing any who disobeyed him, ranting and threatening more shrilly when he realized that his subjects were becoming increasingly more concerned with their own survival than with him. People began turning a deaf ear to his demands as meteors and hailstones shattered their cities, as devastating earthquakes rocked the planet, as volcanoes erupted with frightening regularity, slowly blanketing the planet in a wintry shroud of darkness. Millions were homeless. The potato-shaped moon, on the verge of splitting in two, floated like a bloody wound on the face of the sky. Neither sun nor moon could be relied upon for light. The migratory populations of Earth had to make their way by the glow of its smoldering cities.

Finally, most of Earth's water turned bitter and undrinkable. Many people went insane and died. Abbadon's kingdom lay in ruins at his feet. He no longer harangued the human race with his rhetoric about a thousand years of peace and safety—that was a joke. And not even the thought of the fugitives on Luna could make him smile.

α

Roy Mills jumped a power-ladder to Level Six, where he was greeted by joyous commotion. Computers were estimating the number of approaching vessels to be upwards of five thousand, a string of bizarre extraterrestrial ships reaching over twenty-million miles beyond the orbit of Pluto—a caravan of strange and unimaginable species. *The Circus of Doctor Lao*, he thought wryly, calling over the din to one of his techs.

"Brother Coleman!"

The man turned and waved.

"Aye, aye, Cap!"

Although his title was no longer of any real significance, the men still insisted on calling him "Cap." They'd not forgotten his resourcefulness and courage in bringing them all to safety on

Luna. As their first order of business, he'd been named chairman of the habitat's Board of Elders. And to the citizens of Copernicus, he was, and would remain, "the Cap."

"Have you identified *Daystar* in that menagerie?"

"Yes, sir! It's the lead vessel! They're still too far away to put on holoscreen, but *Daystar*'s sending the recognition signal on all frequencies!"

A great cheer went up. These were all new believers. Some had given up any hope of ever seeing Paul's return to Luna. Even Roy Mills, "the Cap" himself, had entertained moments of doubt. But all that was over now; the fear, the doubt, the sickness, the claustrophobia, the food and water rationing—all over! Brother Paul had returned, bringing half the universe with him, it seemed. Messiah would be coming soon. The *shofar* would sound throughout the heavens and they'd be called to meet Him in the stratosphere above the Earth, to appear in white robes, like hoary clouds, a mighty army riding behind Messiah's white steed, conquering the Beast, the kings of the Earth and their demon armies. And on His Thigh a Name would be written: *MELEKH haM'LAKHIM v'ADONAI ha'ADONIM*—KING of KINGS and L-RD of LORDS. He would set everything right. No more pain, no more hunger, no more death. It was real and it was true and it was happening right before their eyes! *Day* was coming, right on time!

"Brother Coleman!"

"Sir?"

"What are we waiting for? Let's switch on those landing-beacons and welcome the Reverend home!"

α

A few hours later *Day* was parked in Luna orbit. Behind her, a vast interstellar fleet lay strung out from the moon to Mars—the most astonishing fleet of vessels ever seen by human eyes!

It floated quietly in place, a pearl necklace draped between two worlds. Within those mighty vessels were creatures of every conceivable shape and variety, some that breathed oxygen, some that breathed methane, and some that breathed nothing at all.

And now they waited...for the greatest event in the history of the universe to unfold.

THE LATE-EARTH CHRONICLES
WILL CONTINUE IN VOLUME FIVE:

WARRIORS OF EDEN

(Projected publication date: July, 2010)

Until then...
Keep your pressure-suit tight,
and walk in the light!

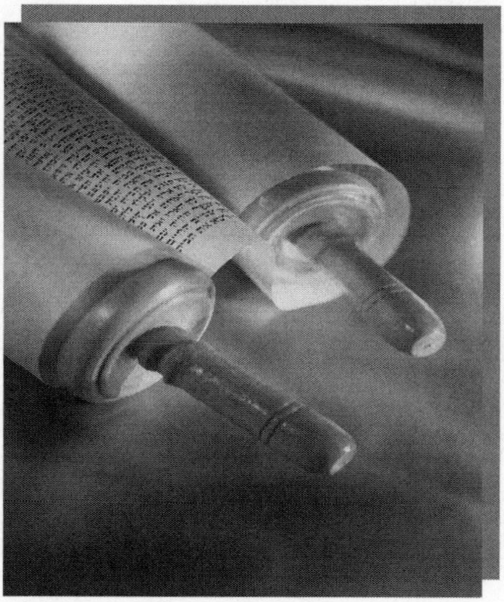